# ANTHROPOLOGY OF T

# ANTHROPOLOGY OF THE ARTS

## A READER

*Edited by Gretchen Bakke and Marina Peterson*

Bloomsbury Academic
An imprint of Bloomsbury Publishing Plc
BLOOMSBURY
LONDON • OXFORD • NEW YORK • NEW DELHI • SYDNEY

**Bloomsbury Academic**
An imprint of Bloomsbury Publishing Plc

50 Bedford Square
London
WC1B 3DP
UK

1385 Broadway
New York
NY 10018
USA

**www.bloomsbury.com**

**BLOOMSBURY and the Diana logo are trademarks of Bloomsbury Publishing Plc**

First published 2017



**British Library Cataloguing-in-Publication Data**
A catalogue record for this book is available from the British Library.

ISBN: HB: 978-1-4725-8593-6
PB: 978-1-4725-8592-9

**Library of Congress Cataloging-in-Publication Data**
A catalog record for this book is available from the Library of Congress.

Cover image © Alessandro Coco and Shidio Tomás Saraceno

Typeset by Fakenham Prepress Solutions, Fakenham, Norfolk NR21 8NN
Printed and bound in India

*For Guillaume and Cassius*

# CONTENTS

# LIST OF ILLUSTRATIONS

# ACKNOWLEDGMENTS

We wish to thank Jennifer Schmidt, our editor, for overseeing the details of the publication process with equanimity and support. Louise Butler and Molly Beck shepherded it through earlier stages. Throughout the development of the Reader we relied on the input of numerous colleagues, some of whose work is included herein but some, due to the inherent difficulties of publishing such a volume, we were ultimately unable to include. Our interlocutors—and fellow anthropologists of arts—whose ideas have most shaped this volume are: Vicki Brennan, Ben Chappell, Margaret Dorsey, Shane Greene, Byron Hamann, Keith Murphy, Jesse Shipley, Bruce Tharp, Matthew Wolf-Meyer, and Marko Živković. Anonymous reviewers gave invaluable suggestions for shaping the content of the Reader and our introductory chapters. In the long labor of editing, writing, and seeking permissions we are most grateful to Anne-Elise Keen, research assistant extraordinaire, who held with us despite also being in the throes of her own dissertation writing. We are also indebted to doctoral students Letha Victor (Anthropology) and David Mitchell (Art History) for editorial support and to undergraduate Nathaniel Lamont for his keen eye on the proofs. We also thank all of the students over the years who helped us learn what material is good for teaching with. Ohio University provided publication subvention support.

The Reader is as much for fellow anthropologists who may or may not be working on the arts as it is for those teaching outside of anthropology who bring the arts into conversation with the world. We are delighted to offer it to a broader readership of both students and scholars.

# INTRODUCTION

*Gretchen Bakke and Marina Peterson*

> O body swayed to music, O brightening glance, How can we know the dancer from the dance?
>
> W. B. Yeats, "Among School Children"

The arts are everywhere. We turn on the radio in the car, look at photos in magazines, dance with friends at a party, do origami, whistle, and go to the opera. Equally, considerations of the arts as multifaceted, often ordinary social processes, have long stood at the center of the anthropological project. What, after all, is religion without ritualized sound, movement, and curated smells (Kapchan)?* What is magic without poetry and incantation (Malinowski)? What is gender without the learned artful practices of the body (Mauss; Goffman 1959; Butler 2011)? What is the law without the rules that govern text and trial? What are cooking, eating, and brewing without craft (Adapon 2008; Paxson; Roosth 2013)? And what is value without cultural transformation (Munn 1992; Levi-Strauss; Bourdieu)?

Though it is not unusual to see the history of the Anthropology of Art written as a history of collecting, most especially that of objects in museums (Morphy and Perkins 2006; Stocking 1985), this Reader approaches the arts as multifaceted social processes that have long been treated by anthropologists as inseparable from other aspects of culture and society. Through readings and case studies spanning geographic areas, urban and rural locations, fine and popular arts, crafts and new media, the Reader addresses what it means to study the arts anthropologically, and how such an approach might be applied in formal and informal settings ranging from museums to everyday soundscapes. In particular, it brings to the fore anthropological tools for examining the making, doing, meaning-making, and context-making integral to the arts, in both practical and semiotic ways.

From the early days of the discipline, anthropologists have taken an expansive view of the social and cultural significance of aesthetic forms. Moreover, whether defining such material in terms of "primitive art" (Boas) or simply accounting for it as an element of socio-economic life (Malinowski), anthropologists have long analyzed visual and plastic forms alongside dance and performance. Grounded in longstanding concerns of the field, the Reader draws together classic anthropological work with an ensuing body of work being done by anthropologists on arts around the world and across mediums. While engaged with the specificities of making art, looking at paintings, listening to music, interacting with institutions that present arts, and following artworks as they circulate though art worlds or around the globe, anthropological work on the arts tends to be less concerned with individual works of art than with an analysis of the artfully made world—be this textual, sonic, kinesthetic, olfactory, or material.

The selections included are for the most part ethnographically grounded engagements with specific conceptual concerns. They attend to how social, political, and historical processes are essential to understanding the arts in the present. At the same time, they direct readers toward

* References with only author's name refer to works included in this volume.

the aesthetics, affordances, and situatedness of art works—toward considerations of art's materiality, social effects (whether phenomenological or political), and the processes entailed in making and engaging with art. Across the excerpts, theory is understood as emergent in and through ethnographic engagement with the arts, in their specificity. While each section includes pieces that present diverse approaches, objects, aims, and theoretical concerns, there are important commonalities within each section and across the Reader as a whole.

The Reader presents an anthropology of the arts that emphasizes the poetics and pragmatics of aesthetic form, in such a way that practice, form, and social relations are always already understood to be inseparable. This approach is encapsulated in Christopher Small's notion of "musicking": "*To music is to take part, in any capacity, in a musical performance, whether by performing, by listening, by rehearsing or practicing, by providing material for performance (what is called composing), or by dancing*" (1998: 9). For Yeats (in the epigraph) this is articulated as the coextensiveness of the dancer and the dance. While for Mary Douglas, this is the exemplary way in which objects are not "signifiers" of relationships, they *are* relationships.

Staying close to the materiality of things and intimate processes of social relationships allows anthropologists to also engage meta-pragmatic meanings. These meanings can take the form of ideological frames or of imaginaries. How, for example, are the arts caught up in social categories? How are social categories made to correspond to—and diverge from—sounds or images (Born; Greene; Peterson)? And how are such connections drawn? How, that is, is signification achieved? These thorny questions are investigated by anthropologists as part and parcel of practice (Bauman). For instance, in his work on how Swedish design is made to embody and represent particular qualities of "Swedishness," Keith Murphy develops the notion of "cultural geometry" to account for ways in which form and ideas are drawn together "through different kinds of semiotic and practical labor," a multifaceted process through which "the forms themselves are rendered almost interchangeable with the meanings that closely adhere to them" (2013: 119). Moreover, by attending to the movement of experience into and through art (Dewey) as well as art's movement through space and across media (Larkin; Marcus; Myers), the Reader underscores how art is a social force, claiming that art works upon—not only within—the cultural contexts in which it is made, engaged, and made meaningful (Gell).

Art is a slippery category, and, rather than making ontological claims about its status that include one thing while excluding another (Danto 1964, 1981; Dickie 1974), anthropologists seek to understand art's geographically and historically contingent meanings. Art's unstable status becomes especially apparent when something moves, changes categorization, or resists the defining parameters of "art" (Myers; Pinney). In its unceasing interrogation of context-making, anthropology differs crucially from other disciplines that make arts their object of study. Art (as category) is not separate from society, but rather, is inherently and intrinsically social. To this end, the structures that shape and define art's meanings must be examined, not assumed (Becker, Bourdieu, Larkin, Marcus). Equally, the longstanding concern over whether or not all cultures have art (Coote; Gell 1995) is examined here in discussions of how the very category of art—along with the "aesthetic"—is defined discursively and in practice.

The Reader is arranged thematically rather than by artistic genre, geographic area, or disciplinary history. Each of the chosen themes, outlined below, provides an analysis of how sounds, movements, or objects are taken up, circulated, and made eloquent. Each also emphasizes intellectual lineages that have been sustained—and debated—across geography, time, and medium. The sections are grounded in classic pieces, followed by more contemporary, influential works, and conclude with a very recent, notable essay that draws upon, explicitly or implicitly, the longer intellectual tradition typified in the section. Hence the Reader aims to reinscribe the actually existing history of anthropological engagements with the artfully made world in order to better address the ways in which the arts are practiced, researched, and written about at the present moment within and beyond the discipline of anthropology.

This orientation toward how anthropologists in fact approach the arts frees the Reader from two biases that are reproduced to varying degrees in most other publications on the Anthropology of Art. First, most existing readers have structured the sub-discipline around visually perceived, material arts—painting, sculptures, masks, pots, and even preserved dead sharks (if displayed in a gallery)—thereby positing a categorization that no longer holds (if it ever did) when considering the vast complexity and fluidity of the arts as they are practiced. By including work by anthropologists addressing a wide range of mediums, the Reader aims to undo silos—or "bubbles" (Latour 2011; Sloterdijk 2011)—that have developed around the study of particular art forms, whether music, visual arts, dance, design, or literature. Identifying common conceptual concerns across a diversity of media, it insists on the importance of approaches developed for the study of divergent art forms, whether that means approaching sculpture with the tools developed for the study of sound, or proposing emendations to long-standing norms of fieldwork methods drawn from the study of theater or dance.

Second, existing texts tend to posit a divide between "primitive" and "civilized" (more recently glossed as "non-Western" and "Western," "indigenous" and "modern," or "colonized" and "colonizer"). As this Reader shows, neither of these organizational strategies reflects the actual history of anthropological work on the arts, which has long taken up a range of mediums and investigated the "West" as much as "the rest" (Mead and Métraux 2000; Pinney 1994; Powdermaker). Seepage across geography and medium reflects the richly porous quality of the arts. Even as popular culture has afforded new possibilities for the conceptualization of mediation and value, work on indigenous culture and craft has been, and continues to be, significant to the study of the arts and aesthetics within the discipline, whether ritual performances or elite institutions. Relatedly, the Reader aims to dispel any claim that a singular concern or approach might ground the anthropology of the arts, whether circulation, colonialism, markets, tourism, mass media, museum studies, or ethnographic fieldwork.

These concerns, among others, put the Reader into explicit conversation with the twentieth-century artistic and musical avant-garde. Gernot Böhme writes, "It is said of modern art in general that it is self-reflexive, that it makes art, art's social position, art's anthropological significance, art's very existence, into art's subject matter" (2000: 17). This reflexive turn takes shape in projects that investigate the status of the work of art in relation to its institutions and forms, "event" scores and "happenings" that test institutional frames by blurring the boundaries of "art" and "life", and compositions, like John Cage's *4'33"*, that experiment with sonic material and its absence to ask "what is music?" Along with such reflexive moves, contemporary art practices push at the relationality of aesthetics, level institutional critiques, incorporate popular culture, force audience participation, and rely heavily upon multidisciplinarity.

Anthropologists take up similar questions and concerns. For instance, Georgina Born insists on the importance of addressing the multiple mediations of music—an inherently nonrepresentational medium—as a means of analyzing how, on the one hand, modern music is constituted as autonomous and, on the other, the ways in which extra-musical signification is projected onto alogogenic sound (166). Or as Jesse Shipley and Marina Peterson suggest, "Anthropological analysis offers a way to examine the processes through which autonomy is produced and naturalized and, in the process, how the social contexts of aesthetic distancing are themselves made" (2012: 402). While there are rich and productive methodological overlaps with both social histories of art (Baxandall 1988) and approaches to visual culture that analyze still and moving images as socially embedded (Mirzoeff 2012; Schwartz 2009), anthropology uniquely provides tools for actually engaging social actors—for putting people at the center of analysis—in ways that afford consideration of both nonrepresentational engagements with the arts and with multiple modalities of meaning-making.

In drawing out commonalities with contemporary art, the Reader is especially concerned with making the arts ordinary and showing how they are part of everyday life, even when removed from daily practice. Many of the readings explicitly thematize slippage and movement across everyday life and aesthetic forms, from Dunham's use of Haitian ritual dance to create a black dance form for Broadway to the sale of images of Aboriginal dreamings on the world art market (Myers). At the same time, the Reader affirms that we are all already experts in and on the arts; we are all expert listeners, viewers, movers, and makers. And while expertise may be generally unacknowledged, casting an ethnographic eye to activities like walking or watching TV demonstrates their significance in themselves as practices as well as their relevance for understanding art in general (Abu Lughod; Dewey; Ingold; Mauss).

## A note on anthropological writing

The relationship between anthropology and creative writing is a much closer one than that between anthropology and other sorts of artistic endeavors. Though some anthropologists dance or make music and others paint, draw, sculpt, take photographs, or make movies, all anthropologists write. And while issues of representation have always held some purchase within the discipline, the issue of how one ought, or ought not, to write has become especially salient since the publication of *Writing Culture,* a missive for anthropologists *as* writers, in the mid-1980s (Clifford and Marcus 1986). "The critiques of the 1980s," says Kirin Narayan, speaking of *Writing Culture* and the many experimental as well as prescriptive or pedagogical texts in the decades since,

> have left the lasting legacy of more room to write in, more references as armor to justify an innovative style. Thanks especially to feminist anthropology, we also have had the chance to recover the fuller range of experimental forms than our anthropological ancestors worked with, forms that were earlier not recognized as a bona fide part of our legacy. There has been a greater acceptance of more openly embracing collaborations—writing *with* rather than writing *about*—and to write with the urgency of ethical and political engagement for wider audiences.[1]

To this, Kathleen Stewart, a fierce advocate in word and deed of using writing as a performative medium—a medium that does the work it advocates (Austin 1962)—adds a similar, more immediate take on the same subject:

> Writing matters, if objects of analysis are to be understood as emergent forms with qualities, intensities and trajectories that can be described or evoked. Writing is not epiphenomenal to thought but its medium. As it sidles up to worlds, disparate and incommensurate things throw themselves together. As it attunes, spatial and temporal dimensions come into play; writing skids over surfaces, pauses on a detail, grows capacious or pinched. (Stewart 2012)

For Stewart, as for many anthropologists writing today, form is always interpolated into and critical to content. Thus, though the question of anthropological writing as an artful genre is not an explicit focus within this Reader, an abiding care for how words come together undergirds much of the work contained herein. We wish thus also to draw the reader's attention to the art, or perhaps craft, by means of which anthropological stories are told, theories constructed, data represented, and implications construed.

## How to use this book

*Anthropology of the Arts: A Reader* is directed first to courses within the discipline such as Anthropology of Art, Anthropology of Design, Anthropology of Performance, Anthropology of Media, and Anthropology of Music. Second, it is meant to serve large introductory courses on the arts in society.

There is a burgeoning interest in "Interdisciplinary Arts" and "Arts in Society," especially in general education undergraduate courses at large public universities in the U.S. and Canada. Though these courses are often concerned with understanding the arts *in social life* they lack a text that facilitates this approach. This situation is especially difficult for those charged with teaching these courses who might not themselves have been trained in methods of social analysis. The Reader provides requisite methodological and theoretical grounding in a clear and directed way, through the selection of texts and accompanying introductory and pedagogical material. As laid out here, anthropology offers tools for studying a range of dimensions of art as a social process, including specificity of form and materials, art making, art in relation to a social order, semiotics, embodiment, identity, and transnational circulation. Moreover, through conversations with colleagues teaching these and similar courses, we have learned that across the board, professors are incorporating multiple art forms into courses labeled as singular (whether Anthropology of Music or Anthropology of Design). Though we have drawn largely from the work of practicing anthropologists in selecting the texts for this volume, we have done so with an eye toward the needs and interests of our colleagues in Performance Studies, Cultural Studies, Cinema and Media Studies, Gender Studies, Sociology, and Art History.

To aid with using this book, a brief overview is provided below outlining the guiding principles of each section. Longer introductory texts open each section. These are designed to immerse students within the thematic landscape, orienting them to the configuration of texts and conceptual concerns therein. Each section closes with ethnographic exercises intended to help students operationalize what they have read and discussed in class. As these incorporate a range of ethnographic techniques, from participant-observation to interviewing, the Reader can also be used to teach ethnographic methods with an emphasis on the arts.

I. **Art as Social Process** offers six selections that argue for an understanding of art as a category of action and as a series of material affordances rather than a set of collectable objects. The readings gathered here underscore the fact that "art" cannot be reduced to visual productions or museum mounted pieces, but encompasses a wide array of practices and objects that are not readily defined and delimited, but which nevertheless are constituted as "art" in context.

II. **Making Art** emphasizes practice over object. In so doing it brings to the fore an emphasis long present in the anthropological treatment of the arts on human presence and practice rather than a study of an art "object." In addressing how forms and meanings emerge through the physicality of bodily engagement with vines, milk, and sound, the pieces included herein demonstrate an approach that puts people, materials, and technologies at the center of a study of the arts.

III. **Form and Aesthetics** addresses the immediacy of experience and media, for example, the entanglement of sound and listening or the physicality of images of deities whose mirrored surfaces reflect the visage of their viewer. As the excerpts in this section demonstrate, an anthropological approach to aesthetics relies upon ethnographic investigation to understand how and what form means in its context, both in terms of perception and apperception. At the same time, form matters, and attention to the particularity of material is critical for understanding not only what people see (or hear, or taste, or feel) but *how* they see, hear, taste, or feel differently.

IV. **Modes of Embodiment** puts the focus squarely on the multifaceted ways of being and knowing, making and performing that cohere in and emerge from bodies. Decorated, manipulated, cut into, altered, reconfigured, and beautified, bodies dance, move, speak, feel, play music, and leave traces. At the same time, they afford analysis of immediacy and signification, of experience, of physicality and its limits. As such, bodies are critical sites through which the multidimensionality of an anthropological approach to the arts is instantiated, and for examining the continuities and ruptures between art and everyday life.

V. **Matters of Engagement** sustains an interest in approaching audiences as *engaged*. By drawing together diverse modes of engagement and media, this section challenges assumptions about the nature of engagement, affording an investigation of how a silent, attentive audience performs a culturally- and historically-specific mode of engagement or how viewers of popular soap operas rework state ideologies of family, education, and female emancipation though their own experiences. All of these trouble the divide between audience and artist (Groys 1999), as well as assumptions of how audiences ought to behave. Yet, as these authors insist, social agreements about convention and genre underpin how audiences respond to performers, whether in terms of appropriate comportment, recognition of virtuosity, or of humor.

VI. **Infrastructures of Art** tackles the institutions and settings that help make art what it is—what we see, hear, and experience, and, crucially, also what is cut off from vision, audition, and involvement. Anthropology of Art's longest standing, and most oft commented upon, infrastructural relationship is with the ethnographic museum. While the Reader does not foreground the status of the ethnographic museum, it recognizes its significance in the history of anthropology. With infrastructure currently a major theme in anthropology (Lockrem and

Lugo 2012; Bakke 2016), this section in particular reflects the inseparability of anthropology of the arts from the discipline as a whole, with the former as much informed by studies of water, energy, transportation, citizenship, expertise, law, and education as those are by the poetics of form and aesthetics.

VII. **Anthropology and The Arts—Intersections and Collisions** grounds the current efflorescence of projects that draw anthropology and art together in a longer history of relationships between anthropologists and artists. Moreover, rather than assuming seamlessness across fields and practices, it draws out the friction that often characterizes the meeting of anthropology and art. Discontinuities and disagreements reveal much about foundational assumptions within fields, as well as how each understands the other. Moreover, deep entanglements between the two afford possibilities for inchoate, nonsensical, and surreal work on the part of both anthropologists and artists.

The aim across all sections of the Reader has been to create an approachable and flexible course tool that is both ethnographically and theoretically robust. The Reader may be used on its own or paired with other work. Its bibliographies include not only cited works, but related books, films, and audio recordings that can be taught alongside this text. Moreover, while we have developed an organizational framework that can be taught as such, whether in whole or in part, other ways of organizing the excerpts are equally possible. Many of the excerpts speak across sections, allowing diverse groupings to be made within this structure. A breakdown of the Reader's contents by artistic genre and geographic region is provided below, along with alternative theoretical strands that run through the text.

## Excepts organized by "medium":

| | |
|---|---|
| Architecture and Sculpture: | Comaroff and Comaroff, Douglas, Meintjes |
| Craft: | Boas, Ingold, Malinowski, Paxson, Sansi |
| Dance: | Coote, Dunham, Kapchan, Morphy, Pierre |
| Film, Photography, Television and Video: | Abu-Lughod, Bateson and Mead, Larkin, Powdermaker, Salen and Zimmerman |
| Literature and Language Arts: | Bauman, Clifford, Le Guin, Pesmen |
| Museums: | Bourdieu, Marcus, Price, Sansi |
| Music and Sound: | Born, Coote, Greene, Feld, Helmreich, Meintjes, Peterson |
| Painting and Drawing: | Fowles and Alberti, Myers, Pinney, Taussig, Winegar |
| Performance and Theater: | Bakke, Barber, Bauman, Geertz, Kapchan, Mauss, Morphy, Peterson, Sansi, Yurchak, Živković |

## Excepts organized by geographic region:

| | |
|---|---|
| Africa: | Barber, Comaroff and Comaroff, Coote, Larkin, Meintjes |
| Asia: | Bateson and Mead, Geertz, Pinney |
| Europe: | Bakke, Born, Bourdieu, Clifford, Ingold, Mauss, Pesmen, Price, Sansi, Yurchak |
| Latin America and Caribbean: | Dunham, Pierre, Taussig |
| Middle East and North Africa: | Abu-Lughod, Kapchan, Winegar |
| North America: | Boas, Fowles and Alberti, Greene, Helmreich, Marcus, Paxson, Peterson, Powdermaker, Živković |
| Oceania: | Feld, Malinowski, Morphy, Myers |

## Alternate thematic routes through the reader:

| | |
|---|---|
| Artists: | Becker, Boas, Bourdieu, Dewey, Pierre, Powdermaker |
| Capital, circulation and value: | Larkin, Malinowski, Marcus, Myers, Powdermaker |
| Creativity: | Bateson and Mead, Boas, Dunham, Pierre, Ingold, Le Guin |
| Cultural collisions and change: | Barber, Comaroff and Comaroff, Dunham, Greene, Le Guin |
| Frames: | Bauman, Becker, Clifford, Živković |
| Globalization/transnationalism: | Marcus, Myers, Price, Winegar |
| Human/non-human: | Coote, Feld, Geertz, Morphy |
| Materiality: | Ingold, Fowles and Alberti, Lévi-Strauss, Myers, Pinney |
| Politics and the state: | Abu-Lughod, Bakke, Sansi, Taussig, Winegar, Yurchak |
| Semiotics and signification: | Bauman, Born, Douglas, Mauss, Pesmen, Peterson |
| Senses: | Feld, Helmreich, Kapchan, Paxson |
| Technology: | Bakke, Helmreich, Larkin, Meintjes, Paxson, Salen and Zimmerman |

Theoretical Pieces

Some of the excerpts are primarily theoretical, drawing on a range of published ethnographic work rather than the author's own. The following lay out key conceptual approaches and can be fruitfully read together, or paired with pieces that work through concepts in relation to specific ethnographic cases: Barber, Bateson and Mead, Becker, Bourdieu, Born, Dewey, Douglas, Gell, Lévi-Strauss, Mauss, Salen and Zimmerman.

Methodological Pieces

Likewise, many of the excerpts can be read for their demonstration of ethnographic engagements with the arts, especially through participation and immersion in making or otherwise engaging arts and artists. A few reflect explicitly on ethnographic methodologies, and on working across art and ethnography. The following excerpts can be read as demonstrating or thematizing ethnographic approaches for the study of the arts: Abu-Lughod, Bakke, Bateson and Mead, Dunham, Feld, Fowles and Alberti, Geertz, Helmreich, Ingold, Kapchan, Larkin, Meintjes, Morphy, Myers, Paxson, Pesmen, Peterson, Pierre, Pinney, Taussig, Živković

## Note

1. Narayan 2012. Elsewhere Narayan says that anthropologists "face the challenge of what Ursula Le Guin (the science fiction writer and daughter of our anthropological ancestors Alfred and Theodora Kroeber) terms expository lumps, that is, explanatory and descriptive materials that occur in passages where information is 'poured out as a lecture, barely concealed by some stupid device—"oh Captain, do tell me how the anti-matter dissimulator works!" and then he does, endlessly.' Le Guin emphasizes that the trick to good writing is to 'break up the information, grind it fine, and make it into bricks to build the story with' (1998: 119). This is just what Geertz does in his opening vignette, constantly slipping in asides about anthropologists, Balinese people, and cockfights so readers may better understand the action" (Narayan 2007: 139–40).

## Further reading

Adapon, Joy (2008), "Cooking as Artistic Practice," in *Culinary Art and Anthropology*, 29–48, Oxford: Berg.

Austin, John Langshaw (1962), *How to Do Things with Words*, J. O. Urmson and Marina Sbisà (eds), Oxford: Clarendon Press.

Baxandall, Michael (1988), *Painting and Experience in Fifteenth Century Italy: A Primer in the Social History of Pictorial Style*, Oxford: Oxford University Press.

Böhme, Gernot (2000), "Acoustic Atmospheres: A Contribution to the Study of Ecological Aesthetics." *Soundscape: The Journal of Acoustic Ecology* 1 (1): 14–18.

Butler, Judith (2011 [1993]), *Bodies That Matter: On the Discursive Limits of Sex*, New York: Routledge.

Clifford, James and George E. Marcus (eds) (1986), *Writing Culture: The Poetics and Politics of Ethnography*, Berkeley: University of California Press.

Danto, Arthur (1964), "The Artworld," *The Journal of Philosophy* 61 (19): 571–84.

Danto, Arthur (1981), *The Transformation of the Commonplace*, Cambridge, MA: Harvard University Press.

Dickie, George (1964), *Art and the Aesthetic: An Institutional Analysis*, Ithaca: Cornell University Press.

Gell, Alfred (1995), "On Coote's 'Marvels of Everyday Vision,'" *Social Analysis: The International Journal of Social and Cultural Practice* 38 (September 1995): 18–31.

Gell, Alfred (2006 [1999]), "The Technology of Enchantment and the Enchantment of Technology," in E. Hirsch (ed.), *The Art of Anthropology: Essays and Diagrams*, 159–86, Oxford: Berg.

Goffman, Erving (1959), *The Presentation of Self in Everyday Life*, New York: Doubleday.

Geertz, Clifford (2000 [1983]), "Art as a Cultural System," in *Local Knowledge: Further Essays in Interpretive Anthropology*, 94–123, New York: Basic Books.

Groys, Boris (1999), "The Artist as an Exemplary Art Consumer." *Filozofski Vestnik-Acta Philosophica* 20 (2): 87–100.

Latour, Bruno (2011), "Some Experiments in Art and Politics," *E-Flux*. Available online: http://www.e-flux.com/journal/some-experiments-in-art-and-politics/.

Le Guin, Ursula K. (1998), *Steering the Craft: Exercises and Discussions on Story Writing for the Lone Navigator or the Mutinous Crew*, New York: Houghton Mifflin Harcourt Publishing.

Lockrem, Jessica and Adonia Lugo (2012), "Editorial Introduction: Infrastructure," *Curated Collections, Cultural Anthropology Online*. Available online: http://www.culanth.org/curated_collections11-infrastructure.

Marcus, George E. (2012), "The Legacies of Writing Culture and the Near Future of the Ethnographic Form: A Sketch," *Cultural Anthropology* 27 (3): 427–45.

Mazzarella, William (2013), "Performative Dispensations: The Elementary Forms of Mass Publicity," in *Censorium: Cinema and the Open Edge of Mass Publicity*, Durham, NC: Duke University Press.

McLuhan, Marshall (1994 [1964]), *Understanding Media: The Extensions of Man*, Cambridge, MA: MIT Press.

Mead, Margaret, and Rhoda Méteraux (eds) (1953), *The Study of Culture at a Distance*, Chicago: University of Chicago Press.

Mirzoeff, Nicholas (2012), *The Visual Culture Reader*, 3rd edn, New York: Routledge.

Morphy, Howard and Morgan Perkins (2006), *The Anthropology of Art: A Reader*, Oxford: Blackwell.

Munn, Nancy D. (1992), *The Fame of Gawa: A Symbolic Study of Value Transformation in a Massim (Papua New Guinea) Society*, Durham, NC: Duke University Press.

Murphy, Keith M. (2013), "A Cultural Geometry: Designing Political Things in Sweden," *American Ethnologist* 40 (1): 118–31.

Narayan, Kirin (2007), "Tools to Shape Texts: What Creative Nonfiction Can Offer Ethnography," *Anthropology and Humanism* 32 (2): 130–44.

Narayan, Kirin (2012), *Alive in the Writing: Crafting Ethnography in the Company of Chekhov*, Chicago: University of Chicago Press.

Pinney, Christopher (1994), "The Parallel Histories of Anthropology and Photography," in E. Edwards (ed.), *Anthropology and Photography 1860–1920*, 74–95, New Haven, CT: Yale University Press.

Schwartz, Louis-Georges (2009), *Mechanical Witness: A History of Motion Picture Evidence in U.S. Courts*, Oxford: Oxford University Press.

Shipley, Jesse Weaver, and Marina Peterson (2012), "Introduction: Audio Work: Labor, Value, and the Making of Musical Aesthetics," *Journal of Popular Music Studies* 24 (4): 399–410.

Sloterdijk, Peter (2012), *Bubbles: Spheres Volume 1: Microspherology*, Cambridge, MA: Semiotext(e).

Small, Christopher (1998), *Musicking: The Meanings of Performing and Listening*, Middletown, CT: Wesleyan University Press.

Stewart, Kathleen (2012), "Precarity's Forms," *Cultural Anthropology* 27 (3): 518–25.

Stocking, George (ed.) (1985), *Objects and Others: Essays on Museums and Material Culture*, Madison: University of Wisconsin Press.

Turner, Victor W. (1969), "Liminality and Communitas: Form and Attributes of Rites of Passage," in *The Ritual Process: Structure and Anti-Structure*, 94–130, Chicago: Aldine Publishing Company.

Waterston, Alisse, and Maria D. Vesperi (eds) (2011), *Anthropology Off the Shelf: Anthropologists on Writing*, Chichester: Wiley-Blackwell.

# PART I
# ART AS SOCIAL PROCESS

## Preface

There is always a warp and weft to culture. One cannot simply take a thing, or a way of moving or of wrapping the body in cloth, remove it from its context and expect it to remain analyzable, or even recognizable, to the same degree. "Texts," by which anthropologists mean modestly bounded phenomena like a gait, the cut of a pair of pants, a fresh caught fish (Douglas), a notion like the soul (Pesmen), carving a needlecase (Boas), or the practice of building a canoe (Malinowski), as well as stories, guns, dances, modes of hearing, sharing, or shuffling, always exist within a "context" (see esp. Silverstein 2004: 622–3). The two—text *with* context—are constantly and mutually informing one another. Some anthropologists emphasize the cultural aspects of this context—an artful walk (Mauss), the shape of a chair (Murphy 2015). Other anthropologists might focus on the social or institutional aspects of context (Douglas). One might ask how the particularities of a local rebellion (text) shape the particularities of a local police force (context). Or, how those of international finance (context) influence those of archaeology (text) (Miéville 2010).

Of necessity, most anthropologists pay a certain amount of attention to both the intimate social and cultural worlds that characterize the context, the text, and the constitutive interrelations between the two; there is no particular reason for art to be treated differently in this regard. And yet, as the contributions of both John Dewey and Alfred Gell to this section make clear, when speaking of art one often has to make the argument for its consideration as just as culturally embedded and institutionally supported a "text" as are policing, or praying, or digging. Dewey and Gell outline two likely reasons that art tends to slip from the analytic clutches of anthropologists (and interested others) before urging anyone actually interested in art to retreat from a bias of decontextualization and return to a careful consideration of the contexts that make art possible to begin with (and vice versa).

First, Gell (2006) offers, there is a tendency for the cultures and social classes that produce anthropologists to also be cultures and social classes that believe in art's capacity to enchant the mind and win over the soul (159). One ought to be moved emotionally and intellectually by means of art, most especially when it is encountered in isolation, set aside from the myriad contexts and institutions that produce it and make it available for disinterested contemplation. Surrounded by gallery white (or black), left in a place of whispers, carefully conditioned air, and intentional lighting, art is made to appear *as if* it stands alone, outside of and beyond the systems of education, infrastructures of electricity, networks of shipping lines and airplanes, and factories producing standardized tubes of paint—though all of these systems are in fact essential to art's being there "alone" in the first place (see Part VI). One result of this, as Gell writes polemically, is that: "Social anthropology is essentially, constitutionally, anti-art." This is not, he is careful to specify, because anthropologists hate art or favor "knocking down the National Gallery and turning it into a car park," but rather the opposite: anthropologists actually believe in art. In his words, anthropologists tend to "attribute value to a culturally recognized category of art objects" and it is "this willingness to put ourselves under the spell of all manner of works of art, though it contributes very much to the richness of cultural experience [that] is paradoxically the major stumbling block in the path of the anthropology of art, the ultimate aim of which must be the disillusion of art in the same way that the disillusion of religion, politics, economics, kinship and all other forms under which human experience is presented to the socialized mind must be the ultimate aim of anthropology in general" (2006:159–60).

In the chapter excerpted here, "The Problem Defined," Gell continues this line of argument even more suggestively by outlining how exactly an anthropologist of art might disenchant art by means of a radical recontextualization of anything called or treated as "art." In so doing, he argues against a host of august anthropologists who have approached the anthropology of art as primarily a project of tracing out culturally particular aesthetic systems. Though it may be the case that such systems are worth understanding in their own right, Gell argues that "the elucidation of *non-western aesthetic systems*" does not in the least constitute an anthropology of art (32). He continues, "It may be interesting to know why, for example, Yoruba evaluate one carving as aesthetically superior to another but that does not tell us much about why the Yoruba carve to begin with" (32). Rather than producing evaluations of particular works of art (which he calls the "the function of the critic"), an *anthropology* of art ought to take as its focus "the social context of art production, circulation, and reception" (32). One must, in other words, resituate the artwork in its social as well as cultural context not as a product of these circumstances (the "function of the critic") but rather as a social force that works upon—not only within—the contexts of its production, display, appreciation, etc. (Gell 1998).

Most of the remaining excerpts in this section suggest (Dewey, Douglas) or demonstrate (Malinowski, Pesmen) ways that one might go about this task of thinking and analyzing art *as a social force*, ever embedded in the particular circumstances of its production and endlessly affecting these in its transits across spaces, through social worlds, between generations, and in time. John Dewey, writing seventy years before Gell, on a different continent, and for a different discipline, suggests that "in order to understand the meaning of artistic products, we have to forget them for a time, to turn aside from them and have recourse to the ordinary forces and conditions of experience that we do not usually regard as esthetic" (37). With this request, not simply to integrate context into our consideration of art works, but to actually ignore art works in favor of a thoroughgoing understanding *of* contexts, or in his terms "the interactions of soil, air, water and sunlight" (37) that condition the transformation ("growth") of everyday experiences into works of art, Dewey foreshadows an anthropological bias "that all knowledge begins in experience" (Feld, 151). For Dewey this is already as true of art as of the law, or "economics, gender, religion and the like … ." (Gell, 33).

Mary Douglas sets all of this contemplation into motion (see also Latour 1983). "Suppose we stop looking at individual objects," she suggests, and "see them instead as participating in a long stream of events that unfold through time; chart their flow; then consider persons only as the points where flows of objects originate, congregate and from which they disperse. This long view takes both producers, distributors and recipient-users into account at once" (48). In tracing out the practices that allow objects to flow through social worlds, to puddle in certain places or around certain sorts of people, Douglas enjoins us to consider objects not as denotational but rather as exemplary. If we move, as Douglas does, from a consideration of how things in motion make social worlds to a consideration of how art works as particular kinds of texts-in-motion are constitutive of certain kinds of contexts-in-motion, we see that that any division of objects from contexts colors our understandings of and approaches to both. It is as useful, thus, to ask how the arts make particular social worlds (contexts) as it is to ask how particular social worlds make artworks (texts).

Bronisław Malinowski, in his classic ethnography of the Trobriand Islands, shows one way in which this might be done. As he recounts the process of making a viable canoe—a process that includes poetry, ritual, dance, skilled craftwork, painting, and feasting—he makes abundantly evident the integrated place of the arts within everyday acts of construction (or gardening, or trading). A canoe, necessary for great sea voyages (in turn necessary for the perpetuation of a trading circle called the Kula, between islanders all around) is a thing made of many arts, wound with many vines, and watertight because of the work of many people. It is the wrong way around to think of it solely as a product—a thing in the world—though it is also this. Malinowski rather shows us that is a thing *of* the world, a process, an enabler, an object built as much of song as human labor, a holder of pride as much as people.

Franz Boas, like Malinowski, is concerned with the reading of an object-in-context, though he is not there when the Alaskan needlecases, whose decorative elements he carefully traces in this essay, were made. Boas is working from a museum collection, and yet despite this he posits two far-reaching conclusions about the liveliness of the worker. After considering the applicability of existing anthropological theories that might account for why a non-useful part of a needlecase was carefully decorated, and perhaps even carved into the shape of an animal, he concludes that the motivation—and history—of such design work resided in the "pleasure felt by the maker," akin, Boas writes, to that of the virtuoso (28). And second, he enjoins those considering objects (or works of art) pulled from their contexts not to assume that similar forms arise from similar histories or similar contexts. The shape of a thing can tell myriad stories or be the final from of cultural processes unimaginable to the student of that thing; it is a mistake to attribute—or seek—a single trajectory that might have caused it to come sensibly into being.

There is another strong trend in this Reader, touched upon here by both John Dewey and Dale Pesmen. These authors, insomuch as they care about art also, perhaps necessarily, care about things that come together poorly, or don't resolve themselves well, thoroughly, or sensibly. For Dewey, most of life is comprised of what he calls the inchoate. Mainly we muddle about. "There is distraction and dispersions [...] We put our hands to the plow and turn back; we start and then we stop, not because the experience has reached the end for the sake of which it was initiated but because of extraneous interruptions or of inner lethargy" (40). These days we might use the Internet or our phones to the same effect. For Dewey, everyday experiences, partial and flimsy as they are, rarely resolve themselves into "*an* experience" (40) which he feels is the starting point—the seed taking root—of art.

Pesmen, herself a painter, begs to differ. Art for her is not the result of a human overcoming of "extraneous interruptions" or base-level "lethargy," it is rather a means by which it is possible to capture and signify the inchoate without necessarily making it more legible. In her painting (also included here) and her work as an anthropologist, Pesmen is interested in the possibilities afforded by incoherence, in the sea legs one does not have for treading through a world of mixed metaphors, in how a static art work can nevertheless exemplify intransience. In this she shares something with Boas' desire to impugn *less* meaning to form.

### Ethnographic exercise

#### *A day of music*

Keep a journal of *all* the music you hear in a day (or a portion of the day).

Note down all the music you hear (try to be as comprehensive as possible—you will have many more than five examples). For all, note the time and location.

For at least five examples, include the following:

- What is this music? Be as specific and thorough as possible, including as much as you know of the following:
  - Name of song/title of work (if you know it)?
  - What does it sound like?
  - What kind/s of instruments?
  - Is it live or recorded?
  - Genre?

Discussion questions:

- Was the music you heard primarily recorded or live?
- What does this tell you about how we hear music?
- What have you learned about art in everyday life?

## Further reading

Bakke, Gretchen (2008), "Reframing History," *Slovene Studies Journal* 30 (2): 185–217.

Boas, Franz (1995), *Primitive Art*, Mineola, NY: Dover Publications.

Bohannan, Laura (1966), "Shakespeare in the Bush," *Natural History* 75 (7): 28–33.

Gell, Alfred (1998), "Concentric Idols and Fractal Personhood," in *Art and Agency: An Anthropological Theory*, 137–42, Oxford: Oxford University Press.

Gell, Alfred (2006 [1999]), "Vogel's Net: Traps as Artworks and Artworks as Traps," in E. Hirsch (ed.), *The Art of Anthropology: Essays and Diagrams*, 187–214, Oxford: Berg.

Hurston, Zora Neale (2009 [1935]), *Mules and Men*, New York: HarperCollins.

Latour, Bruno (1983), "Visualisation and Cognition: Drawing Things Together," in Henrika Kuklick (ed.), *Knowledge and Society Studies in the Sociology of Culture Past and Present*, in Jai Press, vol. 6, 1–40.

Marcus, G. E. and F. R. Myers (eds) (1995), *The Traffic in Culture: Refiguring Art and Anthropology,* California: University of California Press.

Miéville, China (2010), *The City & The City*, New York: Del Rey.

Murphy, Keith M. (2015), *Swedish Design: An Ethnography*, Ithaca, NY: Cornell University Press.

Osborn, R. and J. Tanner (eds) (2007), *Art's Agency and Arts' History,* Oxford: Blackwell.

Silverstein, Michael (2004), "'Cultural' Concepts and the Language-Culture Nexus," *Current Anthropology* 45 (5): 621–52.

Turino, Thomas (2008), *Music as Social Life*, Chicago: University of Chicago Press.

# CHAPTER 1
# CANOES AND SAILING/THE CEREMONIAL BUILDING OF A WAGA

*Bronisław Malinowski*

## Canoes and Sailing

A canoe is an item of material culture, and as such it can be described, photographed and even bodily transported into a museum. But—and this is a truth too often overlooked—the ethnographic reality of the canoe would not be brought much nearer to a student at home, even by placing a perfect specimen right before him.

The canoe is made for a certain use, and with a definite purpose; it is a means to an end, and we, who study native life, must not reverse this relation, and make a fetish of the object itself. In the study of the economic purposes for which a canoe is made, of the various uses to which it is submitted, we find the first approach to a deeper ethnographic treatment. Further sociological data, referring to its ownership, accounts of who sails in it, and how it is done: information regarding the ceremonies and customs of its construction, a sort of typical life history of a native craft—all that brings us nearer still to the understanding of what his canoe truly means to the native.

Even this, however, does not touch the most vital reality of a native canoe. For a craft, whether of bark or wood, iron or steel, lives in the life of its sailors, and it is more to a sailor than a mere bit of shaped matter. To the native, not less than to the white seaman, a craft is surrounded by an atmosphere of romance, built up of tradition and of personal experience. It is an object of cult and admiration, a living thing, possessing its own individuality.

There is no mistaking the natives' great admiration of a good canoe; of their quickness in appreciating differences in speed, buoyancy and stability, and of their emotional reaction to such difference. When, on a calm day, suddenly a fresh breeze rises, the sail is set, and fills, and the canoe lifts its *lamina* (outrigger float) out of the water, and races along, flinging the spray to right and left—there is no mistaking the keen enjoyment of the natives. All rush to their posts and keenly watch the movements of the boat; some break out into song, and the younger men lean over and play with the water. They are never tired of discussing the good points of their canoes, and analysing the various craft. In the coastal villages of the Lagoon, boys and young men will often sail out in small canoes on mere pleasure cruises, when they race each other, explore less familiar nooks of the Lagoon, and in general undoubtedly enjoy the outing, in just the same manner as we would do.

Seen from outside, after you have grasped its construction and appreciated through personal experience its fitness for its purpose, the canoe is no less attractive and full of character than from within. When, on a trading expedition or as a visiting party, a fleet of native canoes appears in the offing, with their triangular sails like butterfly wings scattered over the water, with the harmonious calls of conch shells blown in unison, the effect is unforgettable. When the canoes then approach, and you see them rocking in the blue water in all the splendour of their fresh white, red, and black paint, with their finely designed prowboards, and clanking array of large, white cowrie shells—you understand well the admiring love which results in all this care bestowed by the native on the decoration of his canoe.

## The Ceremonial Building of a Waga

### I

To the native, the construction of the canoe is the first link in the chain of the Kula performance. From the moment that the tree is felled till the return of the oversea party, there is one continuous flow of events, following in regular succession. Not only that: as we shall see, the technicalities of construction are interrupted and punctuated by magical rites. Some of these refer to the canoe, others belong to the Kula. Thus, canoe-building and the first stage of Kula dovetail into one another. Again, the launching of the canoe, and especially the *kabigidoya* (the formal presentation visit) are in one respect the final acts of canoe-building, and in another they belong to the Kula. In giving the account of canoe-building, therefore, we start on the long sequence of events which form a Kula expedition. No account of the Kula could be considered complete in which canoe-building had been omitted.

The construction of the canoe is done in two main stages, differing from one another in the character of the work, in the accompanying magic, and in the general sociological setting. In the first stage, the component parts of the canoe are prepared. A big tree is cut, trimmed into a log, then hollowed out and made into the basic dug-out; the planks, boards, poles, and sticks are prepared. This is achieved by slow, leisurely work, and it is done by the canoe-builder with the assistance of a few helpers, usually his relatives or friends or else those of the *toliwaga*. This stage generally takes a long time, some two to six months, and is done in fits and starts, as other occupations allow, or the mood comes. The spells and rites which accompany it belong to the *tokway* magic, and to that of the flying canoe cycle. To this first stage also belongs the carving of the decorative prow-boards. This is done sometimes by the builder, sometimes by another expert, if the builder cannot carve.

The second stage is done by means of intense communal labour. As a rule this stage is spread over a short time, only perhaps a week or two—including the pauses between work. The actual labour, in which the whole community is energetically engaged, takes up only some three to five days. The work consists of the piecing together of the planks and prow-boards, and, in case these do not fit well, of trimming them appropriately, and then of the lashing them together. Next comes the piecing and lashing of the outrigger, caulking and painting of the canoe. Sail-making is also done at this time, and belongs to this stage. As a rule, the main body of the canoe is constructed at one sitting, lasting about a day; that is, the prow-boards are put in, the ribs and planks fitted together, trimmed and lashed. Another day is devoted to the attaching of the float and binding of the outrigger frame and the platform. Caulking and painting are done at another sitting, or perhaps at two more, while the sail is made on yet another day. These times are only approximate, since the size of the canoe, as well as the number of people participating in communal labour, greatly varies. The second stage of canoe-building is accompanied by Kula magic, and by a series of exorcisms on the canoe, and the magic is performed by the owner of the canoe, and not by the builder or expert. This latter, however, directs the technicalities of the proceedings, in which he is assisted and advised by builders from other villages ; by sailing experts, and by the *toliwaga* and other notables. The lashing of the canoe with a specially strong creeper, called *wayugo,* is accompanied by perhaps the most important of the rites and spells belonging to the flying canoe magic.

## II

After the decision to build a *waga* has been taken, a tree suitable for the main log has to be chosen. This, in the Trobriands, is not a very easy task. As the whole plain is taken up by garden land, only the small patches of fertile soil in the coral ridge which runs all round the island, remain covered with jungle. There the tree must be found, there felled, and thence transported to the village.

Once the tree is chosen, the *toliwaga,* the builder and a few helpers repair to the spot, and a preliminary rite must be performed, before they begin to cut it down. A small incision is made into the trunk, so that a particle of food, or a bit of areca-nut can be put into it. Giving this as an offering to the *tokway* (wood sprite), the magician utters an incantation:

### *Vabusi Tokway spell*

> "Come down, O wood sprites, O *Tokway,* dwellers in branches, come down! Come down, dwellers in branch forks, in branch shoots! Come down, come, eat! Go to your coral outcrop over there: crowd there, swarm there, be noisy there, scream there!
>
> "Step down from our tree, old men! This is a canoe ill spoken of; this is a canoe out of which you have been shamed; this is a canoe out of which you have been expelled! At sunrise and morning, you help us in felling the canoe; this our tree, old men, let it go and fall down!"

This spell, given in free translation, which, however, follows the original very closely, word for word, is far clearer than the average sample of Trobriand magic. In the first part, the *tokway* is invoked under various names, and invited to leave his abode, and to move to some other place, and there to be at his ease. In the second part, the canoe is mentioned with several epithets, all of which denote an act of discourtesy or ill-omen. This is obviously done to compel the *tokway* to leave the tree. In Boyowa, the *yoba,* the chasing away, is under circumstances a great insult, and at times it commands immediate compliance. This is always the case when the chaser belongs to the local sub-clan of a village, and the person expelled does not. But the *yoba is* always an act of considerable consequence, never used lightly, and in this spell, it carries these sociological associations with it. In the usual anticipatory way, characteristic of native speech, the tree is called in the spell "canoe" (*waga*).

The object of this spell is written very plainly in every word of it, and the natives also confirm it by saying that it is absolutely necessary to get rid of the *tokway.* What would happen, however, if the *tokway* were not expelled, is not so unequivocally laid down by tradition, and it cannot be read out of the spell or the rite. Some informants say that the canoe would be heavy; others that the wood would be full of knots, and that there would be holes in the canoe, or that it would quickly rot.

After the rite has been performed, the tree is felled. In olden days, when stone implements were used, this must have been a laborious process, in which a number of men were engaged in wielding the axe, and others in re-sharpening the blunted or broken blades. The old technique was more like nibbling away the wood in small chips, and it must have taken a long time to cut out a sufficiently deep incision to fell the tree. After the tree is on the ground, the preliminary trimming is done on the spot. The branches are lopped off, and the log of appropriate length is made out of the tree. This log is cut into the rough shape of a canoe, so as to make it as light as possible, for now it has to be pulled to the village or to the beach.

The transporting of the log is not an easy task, as it has to be taken out of the uneven, rocky *raybwag,* and then pulled along very bad roads. Pieces of wood are put on the ground every few metres, to serve as slips on which the log can more easily glide than on the rocks and uneven soil. In spite of that, and in spite of the fact that many men are summoned to assist, the work of pulling the log is very heavy. The men receive food in payment for it. Pig flesh is cooked and distributed with baked yams; at intervals during the work they refresh themselves with green coconut drinks and with sucking sugar cane. Gifts of such food, given during work in payment of communal labour, are called *puwaya.* To describe how heavy the work sometimes is, the native will say, in a characteristically figurative manner:

"The pig, the coco drinks, the yams are finished, and yet we pull—very heavy!"

In such cases the natives resort to a magical rite which makes the canoe lighter. A piece of dry banana leaf is put on top of the log. The owner or builder beats the log with a bunch of dry lalang grass and utters the following spell:

### *Kaymomwa'u spell*

> "Come down, come down, defilement by contact with excrement! Come down, defilement by contact with refuse! Come down, heaviness! Come down, rot! Come down fungus! ..." and so on, invoking a number of deteriorations to leave the log, and then a number of defilements and broken taboos. In other words, the heaviness and slowness, due to all these magical causes, are thrown out of the log.

This bunch of grass is then ritually thrown away. It is called *momwa'u,* or the "heavy bunch." Another handful of the long lalang grass, seared and dry, is taken, and this is the *gagabile,* the "light bunch," and with this the canoe is again beaten. The meaning of the rite is quite plain: the first bunch takes into it the heaviness of the log, and the second imparts lightness to it. Both spells also express this meaning in plain terms. The second spell, recited with the *gagabile* bunch, runs thus:

### *Kaygagabile spell*

> "He fails to outrun me" (repeated many times). "The canoe trembles with speed" (many times). A few untranslatable words are uttered; then a long chain of ancestral names is invoked. "I lash you, O tree; the tree flies; the tree becomes like a breath of wind; the tree becomes like a butterfly; the tree becomes like a cotton seed fluff. One sun" (i.e., time) "for my companions, midday sun, setting sun; another sun for me"—(here the reciter's name is uttered)—"the rising sun, the rays of the (rising) sun, (the time of)

opening the huts, (the time of the) rising of the morning star!" The last part means: "My companions arrive at sunset, while I arrive with the rising sun"—(indicating how far my canoe exceeds them in speed.)*

These formulae are used both to make the log lighter for the present purpose of pulling it into the village, and in order to give it greater speed in general, when it is made up into a *waga*.

After this, the canoe-builder proceeds to scoop out the log. This is a long task, and a heavy one, and one which requires a good deal of skill, especially towards the end, when the walls of the dug-out have to be made sufficiently thin, and when the wood has to be taken off evenly over the whole surface. Thus, although at the beginning the canoe carpenter is usually helped by a few men—his sons or brothers or nephews who in assisting him also learn the trade—towards the end he has to do the work single-handed. It, therefore, always happens that this stage takes a very long time. Often the canoe will lie for weeks, untouched, covered with palm leaves against the sun, and filled with some water to prevent drying and cracking. Then the carpenter will set to work for a few days, and pause again. In almost all villages, the canoe is put up in the central place, or before the builder's hut. In some of the Eastern villages, the scooping out is done on the sea beach, to avoid pulling the heavy log to and from the village.

Parallel with the process of hollowing out, the other parts of the canoe are made ready to be pieced together. Four broad and long planks form the gunwale; L-shaped pieces of wood are cut into ribs; long poles are prepared for longitudinal support of the ribs, and for platform rafters; short poles are made ready as transversals of the platform and main supports of the outrigging; small sticks to connect the float with the transversals; finally, the float itself, a long, bulky log. These are the main, constituent parts of a canoe, to be made by the builder. The four carved boards are also made by him if he knows how to carve, otherwise another expert has to do this part of the work.

When all the parts are ready, another magical rite has to be performed. It is called "*kapitunela nanola waga*"; "the cutting off of the canoe's mind," an expression which denotes *a change of mind*, a *final determination.* In this case, the canoe makes up its mind to run quickly. The formula is short, contains at the beginning a few obscure words, and then a few geographical references to some places in the d'Entrecasteaux Archipelago. It is recited over a few drops of coconut oil, which is then wrapped up in a small bundle. The same spell is then again spoken over the *ligogu* blade, round which a piece of dry banana has been wrapped in the manner described above. The canoe is turned bottom up, the bundle with coconut oil placed on it and struck with the adze. With this the canoe is ready to be pieced together, and the first stage of its construction is over.

## III

As has been said above, the two stages differ from one another in the nature of work done and in their sociological and ceremonial setting. So far, we have seen only a few men engaged in cutting the tree and scooping it out and then preparing the various parts of the canoe. Industriously, but slowly and deliberately, with many pauses, they toil over their work, sitting on the brown, trodden soil of the village in front of the huts, or scooping the canoe in the central place. The first part of the task, the felling of the tree, took us to the tall jungle and intricate undergrowth, climbing and festooned around the fantastic shapes of coral rocks.

Now, with the second stage, the scene shifts to the clean, snow-white sand of a coral beach, where hundreds of natives in festive array crowd around the freshly scraped body of the canoe. The carved boards, painted in black, white and red, the green fringe of palms and jungle trees, the blue of the sea—all lend colour to the vivid and lively scene. Thus I saw the building of a canoe done on the East shore of the Trobriands, and in this setting I remember it. In Sinaketa, instead of the blue, open sea, breaking in a belt of white foam outside on the fringing reef and coming in limpid waves to the beach, there are the dull, muddy browns and greens of the Lagoon, playing into pure emerald tints where the clean sandy bottom begins.

Into one of these two scenes, we must now imagine the dug-out transported from the village, after all is ready, and after the summons of the chief or headman has gone round the neighbouring villages. In the case of a big chief, several hundreds of natives will assemble to help, or to gaze on the performance. When a small community with a second-rate headman construct their canoe, only a few dozen people will come, the relatives-in-law of the headman and of other notables, and their close friends.

After the body of the canoe and all the accessories have been placed in readiness, the proceedings are opened by a magical rite, called *Kaluliliva tabuyo.* This rite belongs to the Kula magic, for which the natives have a special expression; they call it *mwasila.* It is connected with the inserting of the ornamental prow-boards into their grooves at both ends of the canoe. These ornamental parts of the canoe are put in first of all, and this is done ceremonially. A few sprigs of the mint plant are inserted under the boards, as they are put in, and the *toliwaga* (owner of the canoe) hammers the boards in by means of a special stone imported from Dobu, and ritually repeats a formula of the *mwasila* magic. The mint plant (*sulumwoya*) plays an important part in the *mwasila* (Kula magic) as well as in love spells, and in the magic of beauty. Whenever a substance is to be medicated for the purpose of charming, seducing, or persuading, as a rule *sulumwoya* is used.

The body of the canoe, now bright with the three-coloured boards, is pushed into the water. A handful of leaves, of a shrub called *bobi'u,* is charmed by the owner or by the builder, and the body of the canoe is washed in sea water with the leaves. All the men participate in the washing, and this rite is intended to make the canoe fast, by removing the traces of any evil influence, which might still have remained, in spite of the previous magic, performed on the *waga.* After the *waga* has been rubbed and washed, it is pulled ashore again and placed on the skid logs.

Now the natives proceed to the main and most important constructive part of their work; this consists of the erection of the gunwale planks at the sides of the dug-out log, so as to form the deep and wide well of the built-up canoe. They are kept in position by an internal framework of some twelve to twenty pairs of ribs, and all of this is lashed together with a special creeper called *wayugo,* and the holes and interstices are caulked with a resinous substance.

I cannot enter here into details of building, though from the technological point of view, this is the most interesting phase, showing us the native at grips with real problems of construction. He has a whole array of component parts, and he must make them fit together with a considerable degree of precision, and that without having any exact means of measurement. By a rough appreciation based on long experience and great skill, he estimates the relative shapes and sizes of the planks, the angles and dimensions of the ribs, and the lengths of the various poles.

After the *wayugo* has been ritually brought in, the lashing of the canoe begins. First of all the ribs are lashed into position then the planks, and with this the body of the canoe is ready. This takes a varying time, according to the number of people at work, and to the amount of tallying and adjusting to be done at the final fitting. Sometimes one whole day's work is spent on this stage, and the next piece of work, the construction of the outrigger, has to be postponed to another day. This is the next stage, and there is no magic to punctuate the course of technical activities. The big, solid log is put alongside the canoe, and a number of short, pointed sticks are driven into it. The sticks are put in crossways on the top of the float *(lamina).* Then the tops of these sticks are again attached to a number of horizontal poles, which have to be thrust through one side of the canoe-body, and attached to the other. All this naturally requires again adjusting and fitting. When these sticks and poles are bound together, there results a strong yet elastic frame, in which the canoe and the float are held together in parallel positions, and across them transversely there run the several horizontal poles which keep them together. Next, these poles are bridged over by many longitudinal sticks lashed together, and thus a platform is made between the edge of the canoe and the tops of the float sticks.

When that is done, the whole frame of the canoe is ready, and there remains only to caulk the holes and interstices. The caulking substance is prepared in the hut of the *toliwaga,* and a spell is recited over it on the evening before the work is begun. Then again, the whole community turn out and do the work in one day's sitting.

The canoe is now ready for the sea, except for the painting, which is only for ornamentation. Three more magical rites have to be performed, however, before it is painted and then launched. All three refer directly to the canoe, and aim at giving it speed. At the same time all three are exorcisms against evil influences, resulting from various defilements or broken taboos, which possibly might have desecrated the *waga.* The first is called *Vakasulu,* which means something like "ritual cooking" of the canoe. The *toliwaga* has to prepare a real witches' cauldron of all sorts of things, which afterwards are burnt under the bottom of the canoe, and the smoke is supposed to exercise a speed-giving and cleansing influence. The ingredients are: the wings of a bat, the nest of a very small bird called *posisiku*, some dried bracken leaves, a bit of cotton fluff, and some lalang grass. All the substances are associated with flying and lightness. The wood used for kindling the fire is that of the light-timbered mimosa tree (*liga*). The twigs have to be obtained by throwing at the tree a piece of wood (never a stone), and when the broken-off twig falls, it must be caught in the hand, and not allowed to touch the ground.

The second rite, called *Vaguri,* is an exorcism only, and it consists of charming a stick, and then knocking the body of the canoe all over with it. This expels the evil witchery (*bulubwalata*), which it is only wise to suspect has been cast by some envious rivals, or persons jealous of the *toliwaga.*

Finally, the third of these rites, the *Kaylapena waga,* consists in medicating a torch of coco-leaf with the appropriate spell, and fumigating with it the inside of the canoe. This gives speed and once more cleanses the canoe.

After another sitting of a few days, the whole outside of the canoe is painted in three colours. Over each of them a special spell is chanted again, the most important one over the black colour. This is never omitted, while the red and white spells are optional. In the rite of the black colour, again, a whole mixture of substances is used—a dry bracken leaf, grass, and a *posisiku* nest—all this is charred with some coco-nut husk, and the first strokes of the black paint are made with the mixture. The rest is painted with a watery mixture of charred coco-nut. For red colour, a sort of ochre, imported from the d'Entrecasteaux Islands, is used: the white one is made of a chalky earth, found in certain parts of the sea shore.

In the first stage of canoe-building, the rites are performed by the magician himself, with only a few helpers in attendance. The general village public do not feel sufficiently interested and attracted to assist, nor are they bound by custom to do so. The general character of these rites is more like the performance of a technicality of work than of a ceremony. The preparing of herbs for the *ligogu* magic, for instance, and the charming it over, is carried out in a matter-of-fact, business-like manner, and nothing in the behaviour of the magician and those casually grouped around him would indicate that anything specially interesting in the routine work is happening.

The rites of the second stage are *ipso facto* attended by all those who help in piecing together and lashing, but on the whole those present have no special task assigned to them in the performance of these rites. As to the attention and behaviour during the performance of the magic, much depends of course on whether the magician officiating is a chief of great importance or someone of low rank. A certain decorum and even silence would be observed in any case. But many of those present would turn aside and go away, if they wanted to do so. The magician does not produce the impression of an officiating high priest performing a solemn ceremony, but rather of a specialised workman doing a particularly important piece of work. It must be remembered that all the rites are simple, and the chanting of the spells in public is done in a low voice, and quickly, without any specially effective vocal production. Again, the caulking and the *wayugo* rites are, in some types of magic at least, performed in the magician's hut, without any attendance whatever, and so is that of the black paint.

One more point must be mentioned here. As we have seen, the first magical rite, of the second stage of construction, is performed over the prow-boards. The question obtrudes itself as to whether the designs on these boards have any magical meaning. It must be clearly understood that any guesswork or speculations about origins must be rigidly excluded from ethnographic field work like this. For a sociologically empirical answer, the Ethnographer must look to two classes of facts. First of all, he may directly question the natives as to whether the prow-boards themselves or any of the motives upon them are done for magical purposes. Whether he questions the average man, or even the specialist in canoe magic and carving, to this he will always receive in Kiriwina a negative answer. He can then enquire whether in the magical ritual for formula there are no references to the prow-boards, or to any of the decorative motives on them. Here also, the evidence on the whole is negative. In one spell perhaps, and that belonging not to canoe but to the Kula magic, there can be found an allusion to the prow-boards, but only to the term describing them in general, and not to any special decorative motive. Thus the only association between canoe decoration and canoe magic consists in the fact that two magical rites are performed over them.

# CHAPTER 2

# DECORATIVE DESIGNS OF ALASKAN NEEDLECASES: A STUDY IN THE HISTORY OF CONVENTIONAL DESIGNS, BASED ON THE MATERIALS IN THE U.S. NATIONAL MUSEUM

*Franz Boas*

We have at the present time three distinct theories regarding the development of decorative design: first, the theory of the realistic origin of conventional motives; second, that of the technical origin of conventional motives; and, third, the theory that the explanations of conventional motives are essentially secondary in character, and due to a later association of the existing decorative forms with realistic forms.

I shall discuss in the following pages the decorative designs of Alaskan needlecases, largely from the region between the mouth of the Yukon River and the western part of Norton Sound, which seem to throw considerable light upon the history of decorative design, and illustrate the applicability of these various theories.

Among the carvings of Alaskan Eskimo we find a very large number of needlecases of peculiar form. They are of the characteristic tubular type of the Eskimo needlecase, in which the needle is inserted in a strip of skin pulled into a tube, which protects the needle against breakage. The peculiar type to which I here refer has, on the whole, a tube slightly bulging in the middle, and expanding into two wings or flanges at the upper end. It is characteristic of almost all these specimens that at a short distance below the flanges there are two small knobs on opposite sides of the tube. In some cases these are well marked, while in others they are so diminutive that they cannot be seen at all, although they can be felt when moving the finger gently over the surface of the tube. They are a characteristic feature of this type, which is so well defined, and whose distribution is so restricted that there cannot be the slightest doubt as to the unity of its origin.

These needlecases have also a characteristic decoration. On the whole there is a tendency to set off a slightly concave surface, which extends along the faces of the tube, between the flanges and farther down. The flanges and the upper border of the tube are generally decorated by a design consisting of a number of parallel lines, which is repeated near the lower end of the flanges, where the parallel lines almost always slope slightly downward towards the tube. Similar line designs are also found on the concave face of the tube. In many cases these lines meet the lower lines on the flanges at an angle, being incised so that they slope downward from the middle line of the tube outward. In other cases they continue in the same direction as the lines on the flanges. Many of the needlecases are so much polished and rubbed off by use that the design lines cannot be recognized distinctly. In other cases broken ends have been cut off, with the result that some of the characteristic decorative traits have become obscure. It would seem, however, that in all the better specimens of this simple type the central concave face of the needlecase is set off by two parallel incised lines, which extend downward to about the middle of the tubing, and which end at this place in two or three small spurs. The border designs on the flanges do not extend beyond these lines inward, so that they form the limits of the flanges. The parallel lines near the lower border of the flanges also generally end at the vertical lines.

Another characteristic decorative design of these needlecases is a narrow band extending around the lower end. This consists always, wherever it can be distinctly recognized, of two parallel lines with short alternating spurs directed toward the space between the two lines. Whenever these spurs are given a greater width this design assumes more or less the form of a zigzag band. A study of a considerable number shows clearly that the primary idea is not the zigzag band, but rather the two lines with alternating spurs.

The features here enumerated comprise those of the most generalized type of these needlecases. They may be briefly summed up as (1) a tube slightly bulging in the middle, (2) flanges at the upper end, (3) small knobs under the flanges, (4) long concave faces on opposite sides at the upper end of the tube, (5) long parallel lines with small forks at their lower ends setting off the concave faces, (6) border designs consisting of lines at the upper and lower ends of the flanges and on the concave face, and (7) an alternate-spur band at the lower end of the tube.

In order to understand the significance of this peculiar type of needlecase, we must bear in mind that the two design elements which are most characteristic of these specimens—namely, the line design with short branches and the alternate-spur design—are characteristic Eskimo motives over the greater part of the Arctic coast.

In view of their wide distribution over the whole Eskimo area, it seems justifiable to consider them as a very old possession of the Eskimo, and to assume that originally they bore no relation to the needlecases on which they are found with such great regularity.

It might perhaps also be argued that the knobs serve for firmly attaching the needlecase to a skin strap, but there is no evidence whatever that the needlecases were thus suspended. They seem to have been carried like all other Eskimo needlecases, by an attachment to the strip of skin into which the needles are inserted.

It seems certain, therefore, that the diminutive knob of the Alaskan needlecase serves no practical end whatever, and that it is a purely conventional feature in the form of the utensil. It is true that the large wings and flanges of the Eastern needlecases also serve no practical end; but it seems well to bear in mind the close resemblance of the two types.

It is interesting to compare the simple types heretofore described with a number of more complex needlecases which clearly belong to the same type.

It would seem that, first of all, the strong inclination of the Alaskan Eskimo to decorate carved objects by means of incised designs has led to further developments of the patterns heretofore described. Examples of this kind may be observed in many specimens.

The specimens collected in Fig. 2.1 show with perfect distinctness the bulging tube, the flange with its decoration, the knobs, and the concave face of the tube. Here part of the specimen seems to be conceived of as an animal. The bulging tube is the body of the animal, whose head has been added at the lower end. Although the transformation of the lower end of the needlecase into an animal has been perfected; it does not seem likely that the whole object was conceived as an animal form. If this were the case, the flanges, when transformed into the tail of a sea mammal, would probably have been modified, and the position of the head would be so changed as to be in proper relation to the tail.

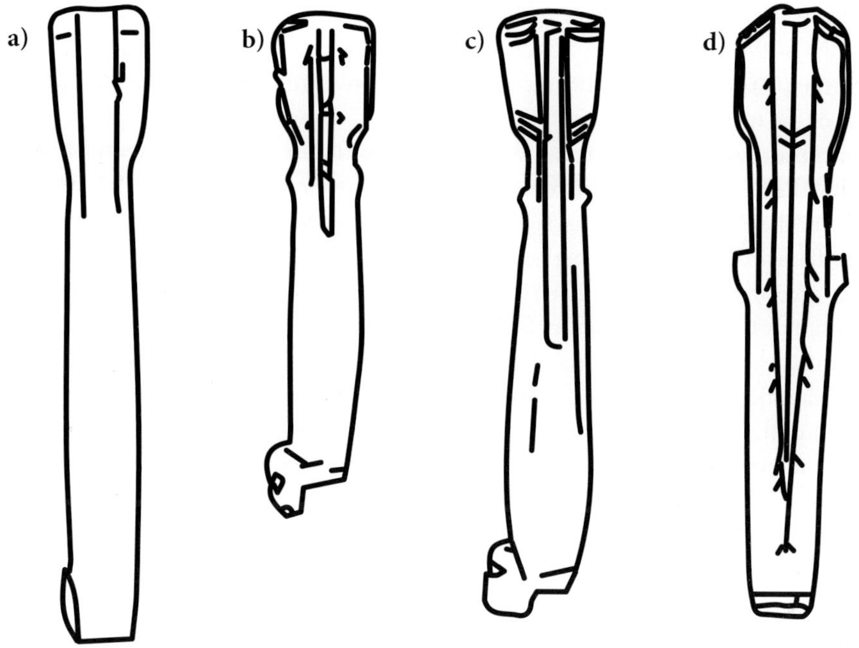


**Figure 2.1** Alaskan needlecases.

It seems entirely artificial to assume that in this case the animal form as such could possibly have preceded the typical needlecase, but that we are dealing here evidently with a secondary interpretation of the design, which finds expression in the addition of the animal head and in other later additions to the whole form. In Figs b) and c), the entire old design may be recognized in all its details; even the alternate-spur band remains, although it interferes with the form of the seal's head which has been added. In Fig. c) the head of the animal has been turned, so that the lower part of the needlecase looks like a sea animal swimming on its back. In Fig. a) we find what may be a still further development of the original design here described. The seal's head has disappeared again, and in its place we find a simple knob. There are three parallel lines near the lower ends of this knob, which makes the whole area, seen from the top, look a little like a small crustacean. The knobs in this specimen are very small. I consider it quite possible that here we may have a case where, under the stress of older forms of the needlecases, a partial reversion to the original type has taken place.

The strong tendency of the Eskimo to utilize animal motives has found expression in another manner in the specimen represented in Fig. d). Here the small lateral knobs have been considerably enlarged and have been given the form of seals' heads. I believe that here also there can be no doubt in regard to the question whether the seal's head or the knobs are older. If the knob had to be considered as a degenerate form of the seal's head, it would hardly be intelligible why only one or two specimens out of a great number should retain the heads in this place, while in practically all other cases the reduction to a simple knob, sometimes so small that it can hardly be felt, should have occurred. It seems quite evident that in this case the imagination of the artist was stimulated by the traditional knob, and that it has been developed, owing to a desire to further decorate the utensil, into a seal's head.

The modification of the central concave face of this specimen is quite in accord with other modifications of the same surface, which have been described before. On the reverse of this needlecase the pairs of oblique spurs attached to the converging lines are directed toward the upper part of the needlecase.

The conclusion which I draw from a comparison of the types of needlecases here represented is that the flanged needlecase represents an old conventional style, which is ever present in the mind of the Eskimo artist who sets about to carve a needlecase. The various parts of the flanged needlecase excite his imagination; and a geometrical element here or there is developed by him, in accordance with the general tendencies of Eskimo art, into the representation of whole animals or of parts of animals. In this manner, the small knobs or the flanges are developed into heads of animals. After this modification has once set in, the animal figures may be repeated on other parts of the implement. Besides this, associations between animal forms and the form of the whole needlecase seem to have taken place, which have to a certain extent modified the manner of representing animal forms which were adapted to use as needlecases; so that the old form and style of the needlecase determined the treatment of the animal form.

If we were to apply to the present series the theory of the origin of conventional form from realistic motives, it would be exceedingly difficult to account for the general uniformity of the fundamental type. It seems to me that, on the basis of this theory, we could not account for the diversity of realistic forms and the uniformity of general type. Neither does it seem possible to account for the series of types by assumption of any influence of technique; and my impression is that the only satisfactory explanation lies in the theory that the multifarious forms are due to the play of the imagination with a fixed conventional form, the origin of which remains entirely obscure. This I freely acknowledge. If, however, we are to form an acceptable theory of the origin of decorative designs, it seems a safer method to form our judgment based on examples the history of which can be traced with a fair degree of certainty, rather than on speculations in regard to the origin of remote forms for the development of which no data are available.

I believe a considerable amount of other evidence can be brought forward sustaining the point of view that I have tried to develop, namely, that decorative forms may be largely explained as results of the play of the imagination under the restricting influence of a fixed conventional style. Looking at this matter from a purely theoretical point of view, it is quite obvious that in any series in which we have at one end a realistic figure and at the other end a conventional figure, the arrangement is due entirely to our judgment regarding similarities. If, without further proof, we interpret such a series as a genetic series, we simply substitute for the classificatory principle which has guided us in the arrangement of the series a new principle which has nothing to do with the principle of our classification. No proof whatever can be given that the series selected according to similarities really represents an historical sequence. It is just as conceivable that the same series may begin at the conventional end and that realistic forms have been read into it, and we might interpret the series, therefore, as an historical series beginning at the opposite end. Since both of these tendencies are active in the human mind at the present time, it seems much more likely that both processes have been at work constantly, and that neither the one nor the other theory really represents the historical development of decorative design.

The assumption of a development from realistic design to conventional design also omits the consideration of one exceedingly important element, namely, the style of convention that prevails in the types of art of different areas. If geometrical designs developed from realistic motives the world over, it still would remain to be proved why a certain style of conventionalism belongs to one art and another style to another art; and in order to explain in a satisfactory way the different styles of art, we should have to accept these as given at a very early stage during the process of conventionalization of realistic designs.

The attempt to explain the processes of conventionalization by the theory of the influence of technical motives does not seem to offer an entirely adequate solution of this problem. It is true that certain very simple designs seem to be due almost entirely to the influence of technique upon simple decorative tendencies. This influence, however, does not reach so far as to determine in detail the character of design in the same kind of material or in the same technique. As examples of such differences may be mentioned, for instance, the designs in woven checkered mattings from West Africa, where peculiar realistic figures alternate with geometrical band designs; the designs of cedar-bark mattings of the Ojibwa and of those of the North Pacific coast, and of designs made in the same technique by the South American Indians. In all these cases the technical conditions are practically the same, but the styles differ vastly. It seems necessary, therefore, to assume in the development of design the existence of tendencies which are due to causes different from the technique, and unrelated to the realistic motives which may be current or may have been current.

I have no theory to offer in regard to the origin of these types of convention, which presumably was connected with a whole series of activities determining the perception and reproduction of forms; but it seems desirable to illustrate by a number of instances the fixity of these conventional forms and the deep influence that they have had even in apparently realistic forms. I have pointed out in the discussion of the designs of the blankets of the Chilkat Indians that a great many of the older forms can be reduced to two fundamental types, and that, no matter what animal may be represented in the art of the weaver, it is almost always reduced to one of these two forms.[1] In the same place I have shown that the treatment of the animal figure on carved boxes of the Tlingit has other fixed conventional forms, which, although closely related to the blanket design, are quite permanent and applied only in the manufacture of boxes.[2]

In a quite different region, among the Tungus tribes of the Amur River, Dr. Berthold Laufer has shown that one of the essential types determining the whole arrangement of decorative designs, which consist of realistic figures as well as of curved lines, is based on the type of "cocks combatant."[3]

It is also important to note that figures conforming to such fundamental types may be interpreted in a great variety of ways by the people who use them. I have pointed out such a similarity of type and fundamental difference of interpretation in explanations given by the Huichol Indians.[4] Here we find practically the same figures once interpreted as the freshwater crab, and then as oak leaves and stems. Other more extended series of such ambiguous interpretations may be found in the art of the Plains Indians as well as in those of other parts of the world.[5]

I have suggested before that in many cases these forms seem to compel us to assume that the interpretations of many simple forms are entirely secondary; that often the forms have been borrowed; and that later on, according to their use in the life of the people, they have been given a fitting interpretation.

I think evidence can be brought forward also to show that the tendency to play, and the play of the imagination with existing forms, have deeply influenced the decorative art of primitive tribes as we find it at the present time.

The first of these traits appears with particular clearness in the tendency to use rhythmic repetitions of varying forms. Bead necklaces are one of the most striking examples of the pleasure that man receives through the use of rhythmic repetition of colors and forms. Among primitive tribes the rhythmic and symmetrical order of such arrangements are often exceedingly complex—so complex, in fact, that they can be recognized by us only by a close study of the arrangement. A case of this kind occurs in the fringe on a pair of leggings collected among the Thompson Indians, which I have described.[6] In this specimen we have a fringe which hangs down in a very disorderly fashion, so that the constituent elements cannot be seen distinctly. Nevertheless a most painstaking arrangement of the component elements is adhered to, the rhythmic unit consisting of five elements—one string having one glass bead and two bone beads in alternating order, one undecorated string, one having alternating glass and bone beads, one undecorated, and one having one glass bead and two bone beads in alternating order. I have found still more complex rhythmic repetitions and symmetrical arrangements on the embroidered borders of coats of the Koryak. These contained sometimes ten and more elements in one group.[7] Still another case of similar kind, from Peru, has been described by Mr. Mead.[8] Here a rhythmic repetition of six units seems to be very common.

I consider it particularly important to observe that in the first of these specimens the rhythmic repetition cannot be seen when the leggings are in use, because this suggests strongly that the reason for the application of the rhythmic repetition is not the aesthetic pleasure in the effect which it produces, but the pleasure felt by the maker. If this is true, then we do not need to assume that in the other cases a much more highly developed appreciation of complex rhythm is found among primitive people than the one we possess. Corroborative evidence in regard to this point is offered by the basketry of the Thompson and Lillooet Indians. I have noticed that here, where in a fine imbricated technique color bands are produced, the basket weavers tend to use with great regularity certain groupings of the number of stitches belonging to each color, although, owing to the irregularity of the size of the stitches, these modifications can hardly be observed.[9] If these facts have a wider application, it would seem that on the whole the pleasure given by much of the decorative work of primitive people must not be looked for in the beauty of the finished product, but rather in the enjoyment which the maker feels at his own cleverness in playing with the technical elements that he is using. In other words, one of the most important sources in the development of primitive decorative art is analogous to the pleasure that is given by the achievements of the virtuoso.

Examples may also be given illustrating the effect of the play of imagination upon the development of design. One of the best examples of this kind is offered by the decorated bag of the Thompson Indians illustrated by Professor Farrand.[10] The analogy of this soft rectangular bag, which is decorated with rows of large diamonds, to other similar bags shows quite clearly that the rows of diamonds have the same origin as the rows of diamonds which are painted on parfleches of the Plains Indians. In this case the diamonds suggested the idea of ponds; and, in order to emphasize this idea, which came to the mind of the woman who used the bag, she added a number of birds flying toward these ponds. Other examples of this kind have been mentioned by Doctor Koch-Grünberg in his observations on the drawings of South American Indians. The development of the triangles in the designs of the Plains Indians to tent designs or cloud designs brings out similar points.

Thus it would seem that the development of decorative designs cannot be simply interpreted by the assumption of a general tendency toward conventionalism or by the theory of an evolution of technical motives into realistic motives by a process of reading in, but that a considerable number of other psychic processes must be taken into consideration if we desire to obtain a clear insight into the history of art.

## Notes

1. G. T. Emmons, "The Chilkat Blanket," *Memoirs of the American Museum of Natural History*, vol. 3 (1907), 355.
2. Ibid., 357 *et seq.*
3. *Publications of the Jesup North Pacific Expedition*, vol. 4 (1902), 22 *et seq.*
4. Carl Lumholtz, "Decorative Art of the Huichol Indians," *Memoirs of the American Museum of Natural History*, vol. 3 (1900), 287, figs. 451 and 465.
5. A. L. Kroeber, "The Arapaho," *Bulletin of the American Museum of Natural History*, vol. 18 (1902); *Clark Wissler*, "Decorative Art of the Sioux Indians," ibid., vol. 18, part 3 (1904).
6. *Publications of the Jesup North Pacific Expedition*, vol. 1 (1906), 384, fig. 313
7. *Publications of the Jesup North Pacific Expedition*, vol. 6, part 2 (1908), 689 *et seq.*
8. *Boas Anniversary Volume* (1906), 193 *et seq.*
9. *Publications of the Jesup North Pacific Expedition*, vol. 2 (1906), 206.
10. Ibid., vol. 1, Plate xxxiii, fig. 1.

# CHAPTER 3
# THE PROBLEM DEFINED: THE NEED FOR AN ANTHROPOLOGY OF ART

*Alfred Gell*

## Can there be an anthropological theory of visual art?

An 'anthropological theory of visual art' probably suggests a theory dealing with the art production in the colonial and post-colonial societies anthropologists typically study, plus the so-called 'Primitive' art—now usually called 'ethnographic' art—in museum collections. The 'anthropological theory of art' equals the 'theory of art' applied to 'anthropological' art. But this is not what I have in mind. The art of the colonial and post-colonial margins, inasmuch as it is 'art', can be approached via any, or all, of the existing 'theories of art', in so far as these approaches are useful ones. Critics, philosophers, and aestheticians have been busy for a long time; 'theories of art' constitute a vast and well-established field. Those whose profession it is to describe and understand the art of Picasso and Brancusi can write about masks from Africa as 'art', and indeed need to do so because of the very salient art-historical relationships between the art of Africa and twentieth-century Western art. There is no sense in developing one 'theory of art' for our own art, and another, distinctively different theory, for the art of those cultures who happened, once upon a time, to fall under the sway of colonialism. If Western (aesthetic) theories of art apply to 'our' art, then they apply to everybody's art, and should be so applied.

Sally Price (1989) has rightly complained about the essentialization and concomitant ghettoization of so-called 'Primitive' art. She argues that this art deserves to be evaluated by Western spectators according to the same critical standards we apply to our own art. Art from non-Western cultures is not essentially different from our own, in that it is produced by individual, talented, imaginative artists, who ought to be accorded the same degree of recognition as Western artists, rather than being viewed either as 'instinctive' children of nature, spontaneously expressing their primitive urges, or, alternatively, as slavish exponents of some rigid 'tribal' style. Like other contemporary writers on the subject of ethnographic arts (Coote 1992, 1996; Morphy 1994, 1996), Price believes that each culture has a culture-specific aesthetic, and the task of the anthropology of art is to define the characteristics of each culture's inherent aesthetic, so that the aesthetic contributions of particular non-Western artists can be evaluated correctly, that is, in relation to their culturally specific aesthetic intentions. Here is her credo:

> The crux of the problem, as I understand it, is that the appreciation of Primitive Art has nearly always been phrased in terms of a fallacious choice: one option is to let the aesthetically discriminating eye be our guide on the basis of some undefined concept of universal beauty. The other is to bury ourselves in 'tribal lore' to discover the utilitarian or ritual function of the objects in question. These two routes are generally viewed as

> competitive and incompatible ... I would propose the possibility of a third conceptualization that sits somewhere between the two extremes ... It requires the acceptance of two tenets that do not as yet enjoy widespread acceptance among educated members of Western societies.
>
> - One tenet is that the 'eye' of even the most naturally gifted connoisseur is not naked, but views art through the lense of a Western cultural education.
> - The second is that many Primitives (including both artists and critics) are also endowed with a discriminating 'eye'—similarly fitted with an optical device that reflects their own cultural education.
>
> In the framework of these two tenets, anthropological contextualization represents, not a tedious elaboration of exotic customs that competes with true 'aesthetic experience,' but rather a means to expand the aesthetic experience beyond our own narrowly culture-bound line of vision. Having accepted works of Primitive Art as worthy of representation alongside the works of our own societies' most distinguished artists ... our next task is to acknowledge the existence and legitimacy of the aesthetic frameworks within which they were produced. (Price 1989: 92–3)

This view is perfectly consistent with the close relationship between art history and the theory of art in the West. There is an obvious analogy between 'culture-specific aesthetics' and 'period-specific aesthetics'. Art theorists such as Baxandall (1972) have shown that the reception of the art of particular periods in the history of Western art was dependent on how the art was 'seen' at the time, and that 'ways of seeing' change over time. To appreciate the art of a particular period we should try to recapture the 'way of seeing' which artists of the period implicitly assumed their public would bring to their work. One of the art historian's tasks is to assist in this process by adducing the historical context. The anthropology of art, one might quite reasonably conclude, has an approximately similar objective, except that it is the 'way of seeing' or a cultural system, rather than a historical period, which has to be elucidated.

I have no objection to Price's suggestions so far as increasing the recognition afforded to non-Western art and artists is concerned. Indeed what well-intentioned person could object to such a programme, except possibly the 'connoisseurs', who derive a reactionary satisfaction from imagining that the producers of the 'primitive art' they like to collect are primeval savages, barely descended from the trees. These idiots can be dismissed out of hand.

All the same, I do not think that the elucidation of *non-Western aesthetic systems* constitutes an 'anthropology' of art. Firstly, such a programme is exclusively cultural, rather than social. Anthropology, from my point of view, is a social science discipline, not a humanity. The distinction is, I admit, elusive, but it does imply that the 'anthropology of art' focuses on the social context of art production, circulation, and reception, rather than the evaluation of particular works of art, which, to my mind, is the function of a critic. It may be interesting to know why, for example, the Yoruba evaluate one carving as aesthetically superior to another (Thompson 1973), but that does not tell us much about why the Yoruba carve to begin with. The presence of large numbers of carvings, carvers, and critics of carvings in Yorubaland at a certain period in time is a social fact whose explanation does not lie in the domain of indigenous aesthetics. Similarly, our aesthetic preferences cannot by themselves account for the existence of the objects which we assemble in museums and regard aesthetically. Aesthetic judgements are only interior mental acts; art objects, on the other hand, are produced and circulated in the external physical and social world. This production and circulation has to be sustained by certain social processes of an objective kind, which are connected to other social processes (exchange, politics, religion, kinship, etc.). Unless, for instance, there were secret societies such as Poro and Sande in West Africa, there would be no Poro and Sande masks. Poro and Sande masks can be regarded and evaluated aesthetically, by ourselves, or by the indigenous art public, only because of the presence of certain social institutions in that region. Even if one were to concede that something akin to 'aesthetics' exists as a feature of the ideational system of every culture, one would be far from possessing a theory which could account for the production and circulation of particular works of art in particular social milieux. In fact, as I have argued elsewhere (Gell 1995), I am far from convinced that every 'culture' has a component of its ideational system which is comparable to our own 'aesthetics'. I think that the desire to see the art of other cultures aesthetically tells us more about our own ideology and its quasi-religious veneration of art objects as aesthetic talismans, than it does about these other cultures. The project of 'indigenous aesthetics' is essentially geared to refining and expanding the aesthetic sensitivities of the Western art public by providing a cultural context within which non-Western art objects can be assimilated to the categories of Western aesthetic art-appreciation. This is not a bad thing in itself, but it still falls far short of being an anthropological theory of art production and circulation.

I say this for reasons that are unaffected by the correctness or otherwise of my views about the impossibility of using 'aesthetics' as a universal parameter of cultural description and comparison. Even if, as Price, Coote, Morphy, and others suppose, all cultures have an 'aesthetic', descriptive accounts of other cultures' aesthetics would not add up to an anthropological theory. Distinctively 'anthropological' theories have certain defining characteristics, which these accounts of evaluative schemes would lack. Evaluative schemes, of whatever kind, are only of anthropological interest in so far as they play a part within social processes of interaction, through which they are generated and sustained.

The anthropology of law, for instance, is not the study of legal-ethical principles—other peoples' ideas of right and wrong—but of disputes and their resolution, in the course of which disputants do often appeal to such principles. Similarly, the anthropology of art cannot be the study of the aesthetic principles of this or that culture, but of the mobilization of aesthetic principles (or something like them) in the course of social interaction. The aesthetic theory of art just does not resemble, in any salient respect, any existing anthropological theory about social processes. What it resembles is existing Western art theory—which of course it is, applied no longer to 'Western' art, but to exotic or popular art. To develop a distinctively anthropological theory of art it is insufficient to 'borrow' existing art theory and apply it to a new object; one must develop a new variant of *existing anthropological theory,* and apply it to art. 'Existing anthropological theories' are not about art; they are about topics like kinship, subsistence economics, gender, religion, and the like. The objective, therefore, is to create a theory about art which is anthropological because it resembles these other theories that one can confidently describe as anthropological.

What constitutes the defining characteristic of 'anthropological theories', as a class, and what grounds have I for asserting that codifying aesthetic-evaluative schemes would not fall under such a rubric? My view is that in so far as anthropology has a specific subject-matter at all, that subject-matter is 'social relationships'—relationships between participants in social systems of various kinds.

In so far as there can be an anthropological theory of 'aesthetics', such a theory would try to explain why social agents, in particular settings, produce the responses that they do to particular works of art. I think that this can be distinguished from the laudable, but essentially non-anthropological task of providing a 'context' for non-Western art such that this art can become accessible to a Western art-public.

A purely cultural, aesthetic, 'appreciative' approach to art objects is an anthropological dead end. Instead, the question which interests me is the possibility of formulating a 'theory of art' which fits naturally into the context of anthropology, given the premiss that anthropological theories are 'recognizable' initially, as theories about social relationships, and not anything else. The simplest way to imagine this is to suppose that there could be a species of anthropological theory in which *persons* or 'social agents' are, in certain contexts, substituted for by *art objects*.

We talk about objects, using signs, but art objects are not, except in special cases, signs themselves, with 'meanings'; and if they do have meanings, then they are *part of language* (i.e. graphic signs), not a separate 'visual' language. This refusal to discuss art in terms of symbols and meanings may occasion some surprise, since the domain of 'art' and the symbolic are held by many to be more or less coextensive. In place of symbolic communication I place all the emphasis on *agency*, *intention*, *causation*, *result*, and *transformation*. I view art as a system of action, intended to change the world rather than encode symbolic propositions about it. The 'action'-centred approach to art is inherently more anthropological than the alternative semiotic approach because it is preoccupied with the practical mediatory role of art objects in the social process, rather than with the interpretation of objects 'as if' they were texts.

I am, of course, still left with the unsolved problem of proposing a criterion for art object status. Fortunately, however, the anthropological theory of art does not need to provide a criterion for art object status which is independent of the theory itself. The anthropologist is not obliged to define the art object, in advance, in a way satisfactory to aestheticians, or philosophers, or art historians, or anybody else. The definition of the art object I make use of is not institutional, nor is it aesthetic or semiotic; the definition is *theoretical*. The art object is whatever is inserted into the 'slot' provided for art objects in the system of terms and relations envisaged in the theory (to be outlined later). Nothing is decidable in advance about the nature of this object, because the theory is premised on the idea that the nature of the art object is a function of the social-relational matrix in which it is embedded. It has no 'intrinsic' nature, independent of the relational context.

In fact anything whatsoever could, conceivably, be an art object from the anthropological point of view, including living persons, because the anthropological theory of art merges seamlessly with the social anthropology of persons and their bodies. Thus, from the point of view of the anthropology of art, an idol in a temple believed to be the body of the divinity, and a spirit- medium, who likewise provides the divinity with a temporary body, are treated as theoretically on a par, despite the fact that the former is an artefact and the latter is a human being.

To suggest that art objects, to figure in an 'anthropological' theory of art, have to be considered as 'persons', seems a bizarre notion. But only if one fails to bear in mind that the entire historical tendency of anthropology has been towards a radical defamiliarization and relativization of the notion of 'persons'. Since the outset of the discipline, anthropology has been signally preoccupied with a series of problems to do with ostensibly peculiar relations between persons and 'things' which somehow 'appear as', or do duty as, persons. This basic theme was initially announced by Tylor in *Primitive Culture* (1875), where, it will be recalled, he discusses 'animism' (i.e. the attribution of life and sensibility to inanimate things, plants, animals, etc.) as the defining attribute of 'primitive' culture, if not culture in general. Frazer returns to precisely the same theme in his voluminous studies of sympathetic and contagious magic. Identical preoccupations surface, in a different way, in the work of Malinowski and Mauss, this time in relation to 'exchange' as well as the classical anthropological theme of magic, about which each also wrote extensively.

The point I am making is that an anthropological theory of any given topic is only 'anthropological' to the extent that it resembles, in key respects, *other* anthropological theories, otherwise the designation 'anthropological' has no meaning.

### *The silhouette of an anthropological theory*

The position I have reached is that an anthropological theory of art is one which 'looks like' an anthropological theory, in which certain of the *relata,* whose relations are described in the theory, are works of art. But what do 'anthropological' theories look like? Can one really give an identificatory silhouette of an anthropological theory as opposed to any other kind of theory? Let us consider what anthropologists do best from the viewpoint of neighbouring disciplines. Anthropology is, to put it bluntly, considered good at providing close-grained analyses of *apparently irrational* behaviour, performances, utterances, etc. (The 'my brother is a green parrot' problem: Sperber 1985; Hollis 1970.) Since almost all behaviour is, from somebody's point of view, 'apparently irrational' anthropology has, possibly, a secure future. How do anthropologists solve problems about the apparent irrationality of human behaviour? They do so by locating, or contextualizing behaviour not so much in 'culture' (which is an abstraction) as in the dynamics of social interaction, which may indeed be conditioned by 'culture' but which is better seen as a real process, or dialectic, unfolding in time.

Correspondingly, the objective of the anthropological theory of art is to account for the production and circulation of art objects as a function of this relational context.

## Bibliography

Baxandall, L. (ed.) (1972), *Radical Perspectives in the Arts*, Harmondsworth: Pelican.

Coote, J. (1992), 'Marvels of Everyday Vision: The Anthropology of Aesthetics and the Cattle Keeping Nilotes', in J. Coote and A. Shelton (eds), *Anthropology, Art and Aesthetics*, 245–75, Oxford: Clarendon Press.

Coote, J. (1996), 'Aesthetics is a Cross-Cultural Category: For the Motion (2)', in T. Ingold (ed.), *Key Debates in Anthropology*, 266–70, London and New York: Routledge.

Frazer, J. (1980), *The Golden Bough: A Study in Magic and Religion*, London: Macmillan.

Gell, A. (1995), 'On Coote's "Marvels of Everyday Vision"', in J. F. Weiner (ed.), *Too Many Meanings: A Critique of the Anthropology of Aesthetics*, Special Issue, *Social Analysis* 38: 18–31.

Hollis, M. (1970), 'Reason and Ritual', in B. R. Wilson (ed.), *Rationality*, 221–39, London: Basil Blackwell.

Malinowski, Bronisław (1922), *Argonauts of the Western Pacific: An Account of Native Enterprise and Adventure in the Archipelagos of Melanesian New Guinea*, London: Routledge.
Malinowski, Bronisław (1935), *Coral Gardens and their Magic: A Study of the Methods of Tilling the Soil and of Agricultural Rites in the Trobriand Islands*, 2 vols, London: Allen & Unwin.
Mauss, M. (1954), *The Gift*, London: Cohen & West.
Mauss, M. (1972 [1902]), *A General Theory of Magic,* trans. R. Brain, New York: Norton.
Morphy, H. (1994), 'The Anthropology of Art', in T. Ingold (ed.), *Companion Encyclopedia of Anthropology*, 648–85, London and New York: Routledge.
Morphy, H. (1996), 'Aesthetics is a Cross-Cultural Category: For the Motion (1)', in T. Ingold (ed.), *Key Debates in Anthropology*, 255–9, London and New York: Routledge.
Price, S. (1989), *Primitive Art in Civilized Places*, Chicago: Chicago University Press.
Sperber, D. (1985), 'Anthropology and Psychology: Towards an Epidemiology of Representations'. *Man* 20: 73–98.
Thompson, R. F. (1973), 'Yoruba Artistic Criticism', in W. L. d'Azevedo (ed.), *The Traditional Artist in African Societies*, 19–61, Bloomington: Indiana University Press.
Tylor, J. (1875), *Primitive Culture*, London: Murray.

# CHAPTER 4
# ART AS EXPERIENCE
*John Dewey*

## The live creature

By one of the ironic perversities that often attend the course of affairs, the existence of the works of art upon which formation of an esthetic theory depends has become an obstruction to theory about them. For one reason, these works are products that exist externally and physically. In common conception the work of art is often identified with the building, book, painting, or statue in its existence apart from human experience. Since the actual work of art is what the product does with and in experience, the result is not favorable to understanding. In addition, the very perfection of some of these products, the prestige they possess because of a long history of unquestioned admiration, creates conventions that get in the way of fresh insight. When an art product once attains classic status, it somehow becomes isolated from the human conditions under which it was brought into being and from the human consequences it engenders in actual life-experience.

When artistic objects are separated from both conditions of origin and operation in experience, a wall is built around them that renders almost opaque their general significance, with which esthetic theory deals. Art is remitted to a separate realm, where it is cut off from that association with the materials and aims of every other form of human effort, undergoing, and achievement. A primary task is thus imposed upon one who undertakes to write upon the philosophy of the fine arts. This task is to restore continuity between the refined and intensified forms of experience that are works of art and the everyday events, doings, and sufferings that are universally recognized to constitute experience. Mountain peaks do not float unsupported; they do not even just rest upon the earth. They *are* the earth in one of its manifest operations. It is the business of those who are concerned with the theory of the earth, geographers and geologists, to make this fact evident in its various implications. The theorist who would deal philosophically with fine art has a like task to accomplish.

If one is willing to grant this position, even if only by way of temporary experiment, he will see that there follows a conclusion at first sight surprising. In order to understand the meaning of artistic products we have to forget them for a time, to turn aside from them and have recourse to the ordinary forces and conditions of experience that we do not usually regard as esthetic. We must arrive at the theory of art by means of a detour. For theory is concerned with understanding, insight, not without exclamations of admiration, and stimulation of that emotional outburst often called appreciation. It is quite possible to enjoy flowers in their colored form and delicate fragrance without knowing anything about plants theoretically. But if one sets out to *understand* the flowering of plants, he is committed to finding out something about the interactions of soil, air, water and sunlight that condition the growth of plants.

In order to *understand* the esthetic in its ultimate and approved forms, one must begin with it in the raw; in the events and scenes that hold the attentive eye and ear of man, arousing his interest and affording him enjoyment as he looks and listens: the sights that hold the crowd—the fire-engine rushing by; the machines excavating enormous holes in the earth; the human-fly climbing the steeple-side; the men perched high in air on girders, throwing and catching red-hot bolts. The sources of art in human experience will be learned by him who sees how the tense grace of the ball-player infects the onlooking crowd; who notes the delight of the housewife in tending her plants, and the intent interest of her good man in tending the patch of green in front of the house; the zest of the spectator in poking the wood burning on the hearth and in watching the darting flames and crumbling coals. These people, if questioned as to the reason for their actions, would doubtless return reasonable answers. The man who poked the sticks of burning wood would say he did it to make the fire burn better; but he is none the less fascinated by the colorful drama of change enacted before his eyes and imaginatively partakes in it. He does not remain a cold spectator. What Coleridge said of the reader of poetry is true in its way of all who are happily absorbed in their activities of mind and body: "The reader should be carried forward, not merely or chiefly by the mechanical impulse of curiosity, not by a restless desire to arrive at the final solution, but by the pleasurable activity of the journey itself."

The intelligent mechanic engaged in his job, interested in doing well and finding satisfaction in his handiwork, caring for his materials and tools with genuine affection, is artistically engaged. The difference between such a worker and the inept and careless bungler is as great in the shop as it is in the studio. Oftentimes the product may not appeal to the esthetic sense of those who use the product. The fault, however, is oftentimes not so much with the worker as with the conditions of the market for which his product is designed. Were conditions and opportunities different, things as significant to the eye as those produced by earlier craftsmen would be made.

So extensive and subtly pervasive are the ideas that set Art upon a remote pedestal, that many a person would be repelled rather than pleased if told that he enjoyed his casual recreations, in part at least, because of their esthetic quality. The arts which today have most vitality for the average person are things he does not take to be arts: for instance, the movie, jazzed music, the comic strip, and, too frequently, newspaper accounts of love-nests, murders, and exploits of bandits. For, when what he knows as art is relegated to the museum and gallery, the unconquerable impulse towards experiences enjoyable in themselves finds such outlet as the daily environment provides. Many a person who protests against the museum conception of art, still shares the fallacy from which that conception springs. For the popular notion comes from a separation of art from the objects and scenes of ordinary experience that many theorists and critics pride themselves upon holding and even elaborating. The times when select and distinguished objects are closely connected with the products of usual vocations are the times when appreciation of the former is most rife and most keen.

The conditions that create the gulf which exists generally between producer and consumer in modern society operate to create also a chasm between ordinary and esthetic experience. Finally we have, as the record of this chasm, accepted as if it were normal, the philosophies of art that locate it in a region inhabited by no other creature, and that emphasize beyond all reason the merely contemplative character of the esthetic. Confusion of values enters in to accentuate the separation. Adventitious matters, like the pleasure of collecting, of exhibiting, of ownership and display, simulate esthetic values. Criticism is affected. There is much applause for the wonders of appreciation and the glories of the transcendent beauty of art indulged in without much regard to capacity for esthetic perception in the concrete.

My purpose, however, is not to engage in an economic interpretation of the history of the arts, much less to argue that economic conditions are either invariably or directly relevant to perception and enjoyment, or even to interpretation of individual works of art. It is to indicate that *theories* which isolate art and its appreciation by placing them in a realm of their own, disconnected from other modes of experiencing, are not inherent in the subject-matter but arise because of specifiable extraneous conditions. Embedded as they are in institutions and in habits of life, these conditions operate effectively because they work so unconsciously. Then the theorist assumes they are embedded in the nature of things. Nevertheless, the influence of these conditions is not confined to theory. As I have already indicated, it deeply affects the practice of living, driving away esthetic perceptions that are necessary ingredients of happiness, or reducing them to the level of compensating transient pleasurable excitations.

Even to readers who are adversely inclined to what has been said, the implications of the statements that have been made may be useful in defining the nature of the problem: that of recovering the continuity of esthetic experience with normal processes of living. The understanding of art and of its role in civilization is not furthered by setting out with eulogies of it nor by occupying ourselves exclusively at the outset with great works of art recognized as such. The comprehension which theory essays will be arrived at by a detour; by going back to experience of the common or mill run of things to discover the esthetic quality such experience possesses. Theory can start with and from acknowledged works of art only when the esthetic is already compartmentalized, or only when works of art are set in a niche apart instead of being celebrations, recognized as such, of the things of ordinary experience. Even a crude experience, if authentically an experience, is more fit to give a clue to the intrinsic nature of esthetic experience than is an object already set apart from any other mode of experience. Following this clue we can discover how the work of art develops and accentuates what is characteristically valuable in things of everyday enjoyment. The art product will then be seen to issue from the latter, when the full meaning of ordinary experience is expressed, as dyes come out of coal tar products when they receive special treatment.

Flowers can be enjoyed without knowing about the interactions of soil, air, moisture, and seeds of which they are the result. But they cannot be *understood* without taking just these interactions into account—and theory is a matter of understanding. Theory is concerned with discovering the nature of the production of works of art and of their enjoyment in perception. How is it that the everyday making of things grows into that form of making which is genuinely artistic? How is it that our everyday enjoyment of scenes and situations develops into the peculiar satisfaction that attends the experience which is emphatically esthetic? These are the questions theory must answer. The answers cannot be found, unless we are willing to find the germs and roots in matters of experience that we do not currently regard as esthetic. Having discovered these active seeds, we may follow the course of their growth into the highest forms of finished and refined art.

It is a commonplace that we cannot direct, save accidentally, the growth and flowering of plants, however lovely and enjoyed, without understanding their causal conditions. It should be just a commonplace that esthetic understanding—as distinct from sheer personal enjoyment—must start with the soil, air, and light out of which things esthetically admirable arise. And these conditions are the conditions and factors that make an ordinary experience complete. The more we recognize this fact, the more we shall find ourselves faced with a problem rather than with a final solution. *If* artistic and esthetic quality is implicit in every normal experience, how shall we explain how and why it so generally fails to become explicit? Why is it that to multitudes art seems to be an importation into experience from a foreign country and the esthetic to be a synonym for something artificial?

## Having an experience

Experience occurs continuously, because the interaction of live creature and environing conditions is involved in the very process of living. Under conditions of resistance and conflict, aspects and elements of the self and the world that are implicated in this interaction qualify experience with emotions and ideas so that conscious intent emerges. Oftentimes, however, the experience had is inchoate. Things are experienced but not in such a way that they are composed into *an* experience. There is distraction and dispersion; what we observe and what we think, what we desire and what we get, are at odds with each other. We put our hands to the plow and turn back; we start and then we stop, not because the experience has reached the end for the sake of which it was initiated but because of extraneous interruptions or of inner lethargy.

In contrast with such experience, we have *an* experience when the material experienced runs its course to fulfillment. Then and then only is it integrated within and demarcated in the general stream of experience from other experiences. A piece of work is finished in a way that is satisfactory; a problem receives its solution; a game is played through; a situation, whether that of eating a meal, playing a game of chess, carrying on a conversation, writing a book, or taking part in a political campaign, is so rounded out that its close is a consummation and not a cessation. Such an experience is a whole and carries with it its own individualizing quality and self-sufficiency. It is *an* experience.

Philosophers, even empirical philosophers, have spoken for the most part of experience at large. Idiomatic speech, however, refers to experiences each of which is singular, having its own beginning and end. For life is no uniform uninterrupted march or flow. It is a thing of histories, each with its own plot, its own inception and movement toward its close, each having its own particular rhythmic movement; each with its own unrepeated quality pervading it throughout. A flight of stairs, mechanical as it is, proceeds by individualized steps, not by undifferentiated progression, and an inclined plane is at least marked off from other things by abrupt discreteness.

Experience in this vital sense is defined by those situations and episodes that we spontaneously refer to as being "real experiences"; those things of which we say in recalling them, "that *was* an experience." It may have been something of tremendous importance—a quarrel with one who was once an intimate, a catastrophe finally averted by a hair's breadth. Or it may have been something that in comparison was slight—and which perhaps because of its very slightness illustrates all the better what is to be an experience. There is that meal in a Paris restaurant of which one says "that *was* an experience." It stands out as an enduring memorial of what food may be. Then there is that storm one went through in crossing the Atlantic—the storm that seemed in its fury, as it was experienced, to sum up in itself all that a storm can be, complete in itself, standing out because marked out from what went before and what came after.

In such experiences, every successive part flows freely, without scam and without unfilled blanks, into what ensues. At the same time there is no sacrifice of the self-identity of the parts.

A river, as distinct from a pond, flows. But its flow gives a definiteness and interest to its successive portions greater than exist in the homogenous portions of a pond. In an experience, flow is from something to something. As one part leads into another and as one part carries on what went before, each gains distinctness in itself. The enduring whole is diversified by successive phases that are emphases of its varied colors.

Because of continuous merging, there are no holes, mechanical junctions, and dead centers when we have *an* experience. There are pauses, places of rest, but they punctuate and define the quality of movement. They sum up what has been undergone and prevent its dissipation and idle evaporation. Continued acceleration is breathless and prevents parts from gaining distinction. In a work of art, different acts, episodes, occurrences melt and fuse into unity, and yet do not disappear and lose their own character as they do so—just as in a genial conversation there is a continuous interchange and blending, and yet each speaker not only retains his own character but manifests it more clearly than is his wont.

An experience has a unity that gives it its name, *that* meal, that storm, that rupture of friendship. The existence of this unity is constituted by a single *quality* that pervades the entire experience in spite of the variation of its constituent parts. This unity is neither emotional, practical, nor intellectual, for these terms name distinctions that reflection can make within it. In discourse *about* an experience, we must make use of these adjectives of interpretation. In going over an experience in mind *after* its occurrence, we may find that one property rather than another was sufficiently dominant so that it characterizes the experience as a whole. There are absorbing inquiries and speculations which a scientific man and philosopher will recall as "experiences" in the emphatic sense. In final import they are intellectual. But in their actual occurrence they were emotional as well; they were purposive and volitional.

Two men meet; one is the applicant for a position, while the other has the disposition of the matter in his hands. The interview may be mechanical, consisting of set questions, the replies to which perfunctorily settle the matter. There is no experience in which the two men meet, nothing that is not a repetition, by way of acceptance or dismissal, of something which has happened a score of times. The situation is disposed of as if it were an exercise in bookkeeping. But an interplay may take place in which a new experience develops. Where should we look for an account of such an experience? Not to ledger-entries nor yet to a treatise on economics or sociology or personnel-psychology, but to drama or fiction. Its nature and import can be expressed only by art, because there is a unity of experience that can be expressed only as an experience. The *experience* is of material fraught with suspense and moving toward its own consummation through a connected series of varied incidents. The primary emotions on the part of the applicant may be at the beginning hope or despair, and elation or disappointment at the close. These emotions qualify the experience as a unity. But as the interview proceeds, secondary emotions are evolved as variations of the primary underlying one. It is even possible for each attitude and gesture, each sentence, almost every word, to produce more than a fluctuation in the intensity of the basic emotion; to produce, that is, a change of shade and tint in its quality. The employer sees by means of his own emotional reactions the character of the one applying. He projects him imaginatively into the work to be done and judges his fitness by the way in which the elements of the scene assemble and either clash or fit together. The presence and behavior of the applicant either harmonize with his own attitudes and desires or they conflict and jar. Such factors as these, inherently esthetic in quality, are the forces that carry the varied elements of the interview to a decisive issue. They enter into the settlement of every situation, whatever its dominant nature, in which there are uncertainty and suspense.

## The act of expression

The primitive and raw material of experience needs to be reworked in order to secure artistic expression. Oftentimes, this need is greater in cases of "inspiration" than in other cases. In this process the emotion called out by the original material is modified as it comes to be attached to the new material. This fact gives us the clue to the nature of esthetic emotion.

With respect to the physical materials that enter into the formation of a work of art, every one knows that they must undergo change. Marble must be chipped; pigments must be laid on canvas; words must be put together. It is not so generally recognized that a similar transformation takes place on the side of "inner" materials, images, observations, memories and emotions. They are also progressively re-formed; they, too, must be administered.

This modification is the building up of a truly expressive act. The impulsion that seethes as a commotion demanding utterance must undergo as much and as careful management in order to receive eloquent manifestation as marble or pigment, as colors and sounds. Nor are there in fact two operations, one performed upon the outer material and the other upon the inner and mental stuff.

The work is artistic in the degree in which the two functions of transformation are effected by a single operation. As the painter places pigment upon the canvas, or imagines it placed there, his ideas and feeling are also ordered. As the writer composes in his medium of words what he wants to say, his idea takes on for himself perceptible form.

The sculptor conceives his statue, not just in mental terms but in those of clay, marble, or bronze. Whether a musician, painter, or architect works out his original emotional idea in terms of auditory or visual imagery or in the actual medium as he works is of relatively minor importance. For the imagery is of the objective medium undergoing development. The physical media may be ordered in imagination or in concrete material. In any case, the physical process develops imagination, while imagination is conceived in terms of concrete material. Only by progressive organization of "inner" and "outer" material in organic connection with each other can anything be produced that is not a learned document or an illustration of something familiar.

Suddenness of emergence belongs to appearance of material above the threshold of consciousness, not to the process of its generation. Could we trace any such manifestation to its roots and follow it through its history, we should find at the beginning an emotion comparatively gross and undefined. We should find that it assumed definite shape only as it worked itself through a series of changes in imagined material. What most of us lack in order to be artists is not the inceptive emotion, nor yet merely technical skill in execution. It is capacity to work a vague idea and emotion over into terms of some definite medium. Were expression but a kind of decalcomania, or a conjuring of a rabbit out of the place where it lies hid, artistic expression would be a comparatively simple matter. But between conception and bringing to birth there lies a long period of gestation. During this period the inner material of emotion and idea is as much transformed through acting and being acted upon by objective material as the latter undergoes modification when it becomes a medium of expression.

It is precisely this transformation that changes the character of the original emotion, altering its quality so that it becomes distinctively esthetic in nature. In formal definition, emotion is esthetic when it adheres to an object formed by an expressive act, in the sense in which the act of expression has been defined.

In its beginning an emotion flies straight to its object. Love tends to cherish the loved object as hate tends to destroy the thing hated. Either emotion may be turned aside from its direct end. The emotion of love may seek and find material that is other than the directly loved one, but that is congenial and cognate through the emotion that draws things into affinity. This other material may be anything as long as it feeds the emotion. Consult the poets, and we find that love finds its expression in rushing torrents, still pools, in the suspense that awaits a storm, a bird poised in flight, a remote star, or the fickle moon. Nor is this material metaphorical in character, if by "metaphor" is understood the result of any act of conscious comparison. Deliberate metaphor in poetry is the recourse of mind when emotion does not saturate material. Verbal expression may take the form of metaphor, but behind the words lies an act of emotional identification, not an intellectual comparison.

In all such cases, some object emotionally akin to the direct object of emotion takes the place of the latter. It acts in place of a direct caress, of hesitating approach, of trying to carry by storm. If the emotion of love between the sexes had not been celebrated by means of diversion into material emotionally cognate but practically irrelevant to its direct object and end, there is every reason to suppose it would still remain on the animal plane. The impulse arrested in its direct movement toward its physiologically normal end is not, in the case of poetry, arrested in an absolute sense. It is turned into indirect channels where it finds other material than that which is "naturally" appropriate to it, and as it fuses with this material it takes on new color and has new consequences.

Expression is the clarification of turbid emotion; our appetites know themselves when they are reflected in the mirror of art, and as they know themselves they are transfigured. Emotion that is distinctively esthetic then occurs. It is not a form of sentiment that exists independently from the outset. It is an emotion induced by material that is expressive, and because it is evoked by and attached to this material it consists of natural emotions that have been transformed. Natural objects, landscapes, for example, induce it. But they do so only because when they are matter of an experience they, too, have undergone a change similar to that which the painter or poet effects in converting the immediate scene into the matter of an act that expresses the value of what is seen.

An irritated person is moved to do something. He cannot suppress his irritation by any direct act of will; at most he can only drive it by this attempt into a subterranean channel where it will work the more insidiously and destructively. He must act to get rid of it. But he can act in different ways, one direct, the other indirect, in manifestations of his state. He cannot suppress it any more than he can destroy the action of electricity by a fiat of will. But he can harness one or the other to the accomplishment of new ends that will do away with the destructive force of the natural agency. The irritable person does not have to take it out on neighbors or members of his family to get relief. He may remember that a certain amount of regulated physical activity is good medicine. He sets to work tidying his room, straightening pictures that are askew, sorting papers, clearing out drawers, putting things in order generally. He *uses* his emotion, switching it into indirect channels prepared by prior occupations and interests. But since there is something in the utilization of these channels that is emotionally akin to the means by which his irritation would find direct discharge, as he puts objects in order his emotion is ordered.

This transformation is of the very essence of the change that takes place in any and every natural or original emotional impulsion when it takes the indirect road of expression instead of the direct road of discharge. Irritation may be let go like an arrow directed at a target and produce some change in the outer world. But having an outer effect is something very different from ordered use of objective conditions in order to give objective fulfillment to the emotion. The latter alone is expression and the emotion that attaches itself to, or is interpenetrated by, the resulting object is esthetic. If the person in question puts his room to rights as a matter of routine he is anesthetic. But if his original emotion of impatient irritation has been ordered and tranquillized by what he has done, the orderly room reflects back to him the change that has taken place in himself. He feels not that he has accomplished a needed chore but has done something emotionally fulfilling. His emotion as thus "objectified" is esthetic.

In other words, art is not nature, but is nature transformed by entering into new relationships where it evokes a new emotional response. Many actors remain outside the particular emotion they portray. This fact is known as Diderot's paradox since he first developed the theme. In fact, it is paradox only from the standpoint implied in the quotation from Samuel Johnson. More recent inquiries have shown, indeed, that there are two types of actors. There are those who report that they are at their best when they "lose" themselves emotionally in their roles. Yet this fact is no exception to the principle that has been stated. For, after all, it is a role, a "part" with which actors identify themselves. As a part, it is conceived and treated as part of a whole; if there is art in acting, the role is subordinated so as to occupy the position of a part in the whole. It is thereby qualified by esthetic form. Even those who feel most poignantly the emotions of the character represented do not lose consciousness that they are on a stage where there are other actors taking part; that they are before an audience, and that they must, therefore, cooperate with other players in creating a certain effect. These facts demand and signify a definite transformation of the primitive emotion. Portrayal of intoxication is a common device of the comic stage. But a man actually drunken would have to use art to conceal his condition if he is not to disgust his audience, or at least to excite a laughter that differs radically from that excited by intoxication when acted. The difference between the two types of actors is not a difference between expression of an emotion controlled by the relations of the situation into which it enters and a manifestation of raw emotion. It is a difference in methods of bringing about the desired effect, a difference doubtless connected with personal temperament.

Finally, what has been said locates, even if it does not solve, the vexed problem of the relation of esthetic or fine art to other modes of production also called art. The difference that exists in fact cannot be leveled, as we have already seen, by defining both in terms of technique and skill. But neither can it be erected into a barrier that is insuperable by referring the creation of fine art to an impulse that is unique, separated from impulsions which work in modes of expression not usually brought under the caption of fine art. Conduct can be sublime and manners gracious. If impulsion toward organization of material so as to present the latter in a form directly fulfilling in experience had no existence outside the arts of painting, poetry, music, and sculpture, it would not exist anywhere; there would be no fine art.

The problem of conferring esthetic quality upon all modes of production is a serious problem. But it is a human problem for human solution; not a problem incapable of solution because it is set by some unpassable gulf in human nature or in the nature of things. In an imperfect society—and no society will ever be perfect—fine art will be to some extent an escape from, or an adventitious decoration of, the main activities of living. But in a better-ordered society than that in which we live, an infinitely greater happiness than is now the case would attend all modes of production. We live in a world in which there is an immense amount of organization, but it is an external organization, not one of the ordering of a growing experience, one that involves, moreover, the whole of the live creature, toward a fulfilling conclusion. Works of art that are not remote from common life, that are widely enjoyed in a community, are signs of a unified collective life. But they are also marvelous aids in the creation of such a life. The remaking of the material of experience in the act of expression is not an isolated event confined to the artist and to a person here and there who happens to enjoy the work. In the degree in which art exercises its office, it is also a remaking of the experience of the community in the direction of greater order and unity.

# CHAPTER 5
# THE GENUINE ARTICLE
*Mary Douglas*

How are we to know what is object and what is context? For example, does the teapot provide the context of a teapot lid? Should we treat the set of silver teapot and milk jug as one object? If so, are the tray and the sugar bowl context or object? How does one define an automobile? Is it a wheeled vehicle? In which case, are the wheels an intrinsic part of the object? Or are they four parts related by complementarity in use to the chassis? The antiques auctioneer would say that a teapot and its lid are one object, since he cannot sell one without the other. But a friend of mine who lives in a dangerous district of London used to park his car in the road outside his house. Naturally the car was insured against theft. One day, to his consternation, he came out and found the car there, but all four wheels removed. He checked his insurance which covered theft of the car but not accessories and, since there is no way that the wheels can be thought of as accessories on a par with the radio and cigarette lighter, he put in his claim. It was rejected. The reply from the insurance company directed his attention to the small print which said that accessories are movable parts, and since his wheels had been moved, there was no arguing with them. So on this accounting the wheels are one kind of object, and the car has to be the context of the wheels. I cannot help wondering what the insurance company would have said if the wheels had been left in the road, and the car removed. The moral is that the idea of context is adapted to the needs of the inquiry and we will need to make our own technical decisions about how we use the idea of context for the semiotics of objects.

Nelson Goodman uses the word "autographic" for production whose value depends on historical continuity. The idea of possible forgery applies to autographic objects such as paintings and sculptures, because the idea of authenticity is somehow central to their value. Goodman uses "allographic" for the object whose value does not depend on its historic uniqueness.

Some art is produced for reproduction, as music, which makes notation systems important. Other art not being produced for replication can display the subtle and complex symptoms of the aesthetic which defy notationality. Sometimes the method of production of the object is susceptible to notationality (in which case it is more apt for allographic production); sometimes it is not (in which case there is a presumption in favor of autographic recognition if only because a dispute about the authenticity cannot be settled by reference to something like a score or other notation system). Beyond recognizing an aptness for notationality, the anthropologist would be doubtful that there is anything intrinsic in the nature of painting or music that swings it to one or other of the two kinds. We can think of contrary instances, such as peoples among whom the unique history of a painting is not treated in the same way as among ourselves, or among whom the option of identifying a piece of music by the score is not available, or where no one but the composer has a right to utter his own composition and could be expected to challenge a player who used it to a duel. Though we can recognize the two categories of object, something more like a collective decision about the kind of prestige and the amount of originality allowed to the various stages of production assigns art forms in these cases to the class of allographic or of autographic objects.

Allographic production can be anonymous, or at least the credit can go to a group of people, not to one person and the actual assigning of origins may not be important in evaluating it. Whether there is a score or not, something about the organization of our music world and the arrangements for paying royalties to the composer and fees to the musicians make it more important to know who composed the music than who performed it at all stages of its history. This is even more true for the organization of the world of painting and sculpture. The makers of canvas stretchers and the paint manufacturers and the other industries which service the painters get hardly any recognition beyond the discriminating choice of professionals who buy their products. On the other hand, Stradivarius is a great name in the making of violins: the violin itself is very much an autographic object. Are we to assume that because of the nature of painting there is nothing equivalent to a violin signed by a master instrument maker in the world of painting? Is the autographic possibility determined by the art form, or by the intentions of the artists and their public to elevate some parts of the process to a special distinction? We can go further by noting that the authentic signature on the violin carries authority. The readiness of the public to confer authority has to be considered. In short, we can recognize two different classes of objects, and also recognize that their difference rests on decision taking in the community of users about the distribution of prestige and reward. Sometimes the community wants authenticity, sometimes it wants inspiration.

The contrast between allographic and autographic does not quite coincide with the well-known line between market commodities and other kinds of objects. That in itself makes it interesting. Objects which are not produced for sale are not necessarily allographic nor does being autographic mean that the object is not for sale. The guaranteed authentic painting can certainly be sold. But the distinction between gift and commodity comes under the same umbrella. The direction to which this distinction leads us is not to different kinds of objects, but to different kinds of relations between persons.

Suppose we stop looking at individual objects. See them instead as participating in a long stream of events that unfold through time; chart their flow; then consider persons only as the points where flows of objects originate, congregate and from which they disperse. This long view takes both producers, distributors and recipient-users into account at once. Now think of a society in which all the objects produced are autographic, every one. A good example is David McKnight's (1973) description of the kinship system of the Wik-Mungkan tribe in Australia. Any kinship role is defined by obligations to give to various relations, and even more strictly defined by obligatory gifts are the relations of alliance by marriage. A father-in-law is a person who received from his son-in-law certain big fishes, so if the catch includes one, the man knows at once that it belongs to his father-in-law. The latter is a collection point, a resting place for the flow of these fishes through the community. All the other fishes in the catch are earmarked for specific relatives. The same for the hunter who kills a wallaby or cockatoo. All his products are destined to mark out the lines of his relationships. Ideally there are no free-floating objects in this system, which incidentally implies that here there is no such thing as a free gift in that system either.

The Wik-Mungkan system of distribution puts every object into the category of public goods which cannot be distrained for private or market purposes. It is not quite the socialist ideal of measuring out to everyone according to his needs, but it gives to all according to their role. In its practical effect the system provides a strong buffer of structure to protect against the jealousy which is apt to tear small groups apart. And these reflections would serve to remind sociologists that small communities that seem to run entirely on public spirited solidarity usually survive by implementing a lot of structure: contrary to the view of German and Chicago sociologists, *Gemeinschaft* is not just a warm, cosy feeling. Furthermore, the comparison on these lines would draw our attention to the person in the gift system who is not an assembly point for gift objects. For example, streams of flowers and hothouse grapes flow toward persons in the sick role; but not all sick persons draw these streams to themselves. The flow of gift objects is a marker for tracing marginality and centrality. Anthropologists routinely make this tracing in their studies, with important results, but the method also has much to tell us about our use of objects in modern industrial society.

In extending Goodman's idea to things perhaps very remote from his original concerns we notice that autographic in his sense only means being able to go back to the point of origin. It is a backward link of the object to its maker. A gift also has forward linkage, tracing the object to its point of destination. I have found it very illuminating to think about objects in this way, as streams issuing forth from known points, and arriving at expected points of assembly.

When anthropologists study a system of objects flowing to various collection points, we learn to read off from the movements of the objects who is who and what day it is and other information. We can rightly say that the flows of objects signify the pattern of roles. But seeing objects as representing or standing for something else has an obscuring effect. The objects do end up denoting relationships, but it is instructive to notice how they first exemplify relationships. To be a father-in-law or grandfather or aunt in the Wik-Mungkan system of prescribed transfers is to *be* a recipient of the fishes and cockatoos, etc. Giving the objects *makes* the role; receiving the objects and redistributing them *is* to perform in the role; to fail to give them is likely to *end* the role. The streams of objects exemplify what it is to be that sort of person. They do not first signify the role, they are examples of what the role is. They are also functional for the role, since father-in-law and grandfather and aunt will also be roles defined by required redistributing of what has arrived at their doorstep. To be given a meal does not signify hospitality, it is actually, truly a sample of the hospitality (Douglas 1984).

It is useful for us at this stage to try to remember that objects constitute social systems and would have no recognizability if they did not. We may often be on the wrong track trying to decide what they signify, since that question does not necessarily lead directly to the part the objects play in human transactions.

## References

Douglas, Mary (ed.) (1984), *Food in the Social Order*, New York: Russell Sage Foundation/Basic Books.
Goodman, Nelson (1976), *Languages of Art*, Indianapolis, IN: Hackett.
Goodman, Nelson (1978), *Ways of Worldmaking*, Indianapolis, IN: Hackett.
McKnight, David (1973), "Sexual Symbolism of Food among the Wik-Mungkan." *Man* 8 (2): 194–209.

# CHAPTER 6

## "A BOGGY, SOGGY, SQUITCHY PICTURE, TRULY": NOTES ON IMAGE MAKING IN ANTHROPOLOGY AND ELSEWHERE

*Dale Pesmen*

Near the beginning of *Moby Dick*, Herman Melville has us enter The Spouter Inn, where his narrator shares a bed with Queequeg and from which they ship on the Pequod. "You found yourself in a wide, low, straggling entry," Ishmael tells us: "On one side hung a very large oil-painting so thoroughly besmoked, and every way defaced, that in the unequal cross-lights by which you viewed it, it was only by diligent study and a series of systematic visits to it, and careful inquiry of the neighbors, that you could any way arrive at an understanding of its purpose." This painting is not just blackened, it is *thoroughly* besmoked. It is defaced in every way. What remains is unevenly lit. Exaggeration. Overkill. Diligent study and a series of systematic visits? *Careful inquiry of the neighbors?* Isn't this patently ridiculous? What's being done? What sort of cards are these on the table? Reading literature can be very much like beginning ethnography. Critical encounters with art can be a fairly precise training for ethnography: noticing what elements and images appear in the work and then carefully following their play in different contexts.

The speaker implies that one might make some sense of the painting, and that he has made some sense of it, sense he is about to reveal. But instead he backtracks into describing how dark the picture really is, and into a series of references to incomprehensibility, unaccountability, assorted obscurities, and multiply compounded disorders that foil efforts at interpretation: "Such unaccountable masses of shades and shadows, that at first you almost thought some ambitious young artist in the time of the New England hags, had endeavored to delineate chaos bewitched." One might begin to wonder whether we are even *trying* to understand anything, but "at first you almost thought" implies that there has been error, and that that error will soon be righted "by dint of much and earnest contemplation, and oft repeated ponderings" (just, by the way, as patently ridiculous as was pestering the neighbors for exegeses). Finally, after all the mystification and contemplation, the most "especially" useful interpretive tool turns out to be "throwing open the little window towards the back of the entry." Melville is, while speaking in the voice of a rabidly contemplative narrator, howling with laughter at him.

Using light to see, we "at last come to the conclusion" that what at first we had "*almost* thought"—that the artist had tried to portray chaos bewitched—"might not be altogether unwarranted." Double-crossed. A prank, logical sleight of hand. Not only is our hypothesis that the picture portrays chaos confirmed, we have not moved a step past where we began: we're up inchoate creek, failing absurdly to make sense. What *most* puzzles and confounds us now is "a long, limber, portentous black mass of something hovering in the center of the picture over three blue, dim, perpendicular lines floating in a nameless yeast." "A sort of indefinite, half-attained, unimaginable sublimity" "fairly freezes you to" the picture as more, extra,

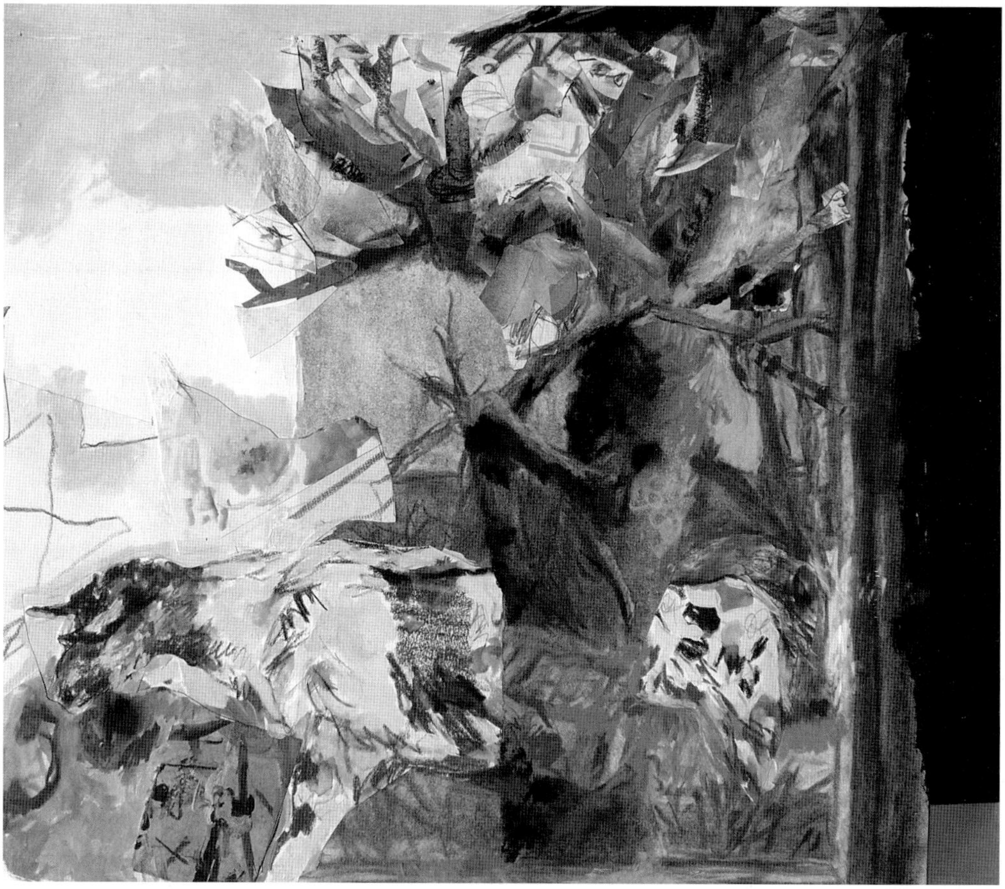

**Figure 6.1** Cow, Trees: A modestly-horned cow, self-involved tree, neutral background. A fine-scale fragmentation of the tree and beast into different directions, mark qualities and styles. There is also a shameless change in the animal as our eyes cross the tree blocking it, such that it's hardly – or isn't? – the same body. This invites the observer to focus many times, differently; a temporal sequence of textural and structural engagements rather than one whole. The fairly empty "background" patch both gives the viewer an opportunity to rest and gestures at traditional figurative composition, confirming that, yes, this is on purpose; one of any number of possible questions about traditions of coherence – in imagery and experience. Drawing/Collage by Dale Pesmen

bonus, additional devices for establishing mystery, including negation, partiality, and implications of transcendence, are piled on and iambically summed up: "A boggy, soggy, squitchy picture truly, enough to drive a nervous man distracted." At this point "you involuntarily took an oath with yourself to find out" what "that marvelous painting" means, *again* dragged back to the initial impulse to chase down some meaning.

As we have supposedly been doing nothing *but* this, the sudden oath seems less dramatic than something repeatedly uttered by a wind-up toy enthusiastically continuing to walk while butted up against a chair leg: "Ever and anon a bright, but, alas, deceptive idea would dart you through.—It's the Black Sea in a midnight gale.—It's the unnatural combat of the four primal elements.—It's a blasted heath.—It's a Hyperborean winter scene.—It's the breaking-up of the ice-bound stream of Time." This repeated display of inability to correctly formulate or grasp

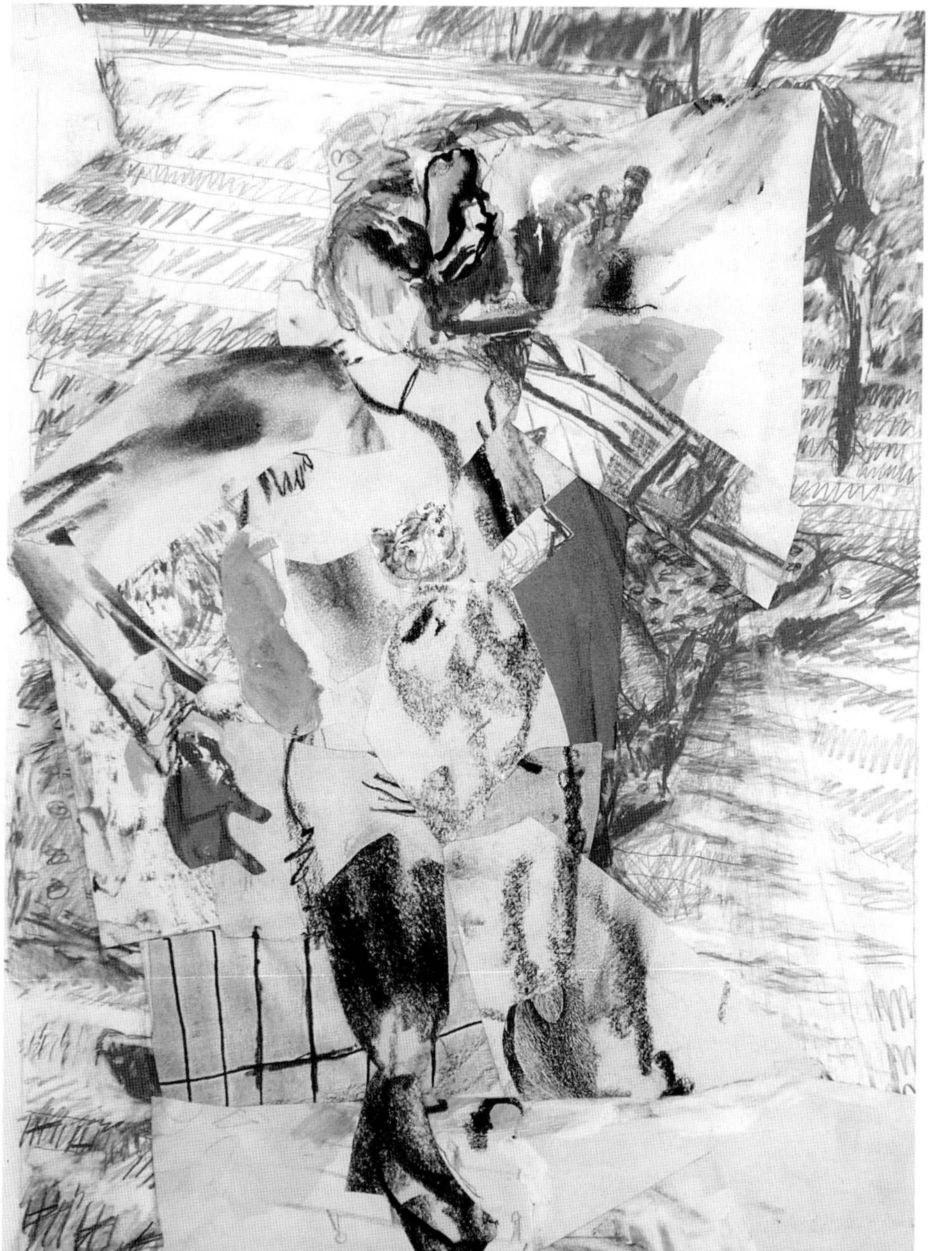

**Figure 6.2** Figure in Room: Sometimes I try to push differences in style, medium and coherence of figure and ground areas as far as I can – exploring and testing the range of styles that I can combine in one picture without reducing it to a stylistic gesture or one-liner. To the degree that that reduction to shtick doesn't occur, the consumer of the image is offered, as in Figure 1, an invitation to a specific process in time, of engaging and re-engaging, not towards any passionate or transcendent unity or understanding, but, instead, in a playful exercise for our faculties of experiencing and interpreting in different contexts and frameworks and, in a sense, as different people. Drawing/Collage by Dale Pesmen

also manages to imply that the picture is *all* of these things at the same time, cumulative to the point of overloading the image:[1] "But at last all these fancies yielded to that one portentous something in the picture's midst," an unclear "something" of a nevertheless authoritative center. And when the narrator finally exclaims, "Stop; does it not bear a faint resemblance to a gigantic fish? even the great leviathan himself?" it feels unlike the sudden illumination it pretends to be. It seems voluntaristic, jerry-built.

Melville's Spouter Inn, one of the book's first rhetorical, ritual, tropic makings and remakings of the whale into everything and vice versa, draws on the power of mentioning utter completeness, enigma, paradox, unaccountability, incomprehension, unformedness and chaos, namelessness, unimaginability, primordial combat, deception, primal elements, breaking up of Time, and vagueness. It claims to be trying to feed all these powers to a *fish*. Poor fish.

* * *

I wrote my first paper about what I have been labeling coherence in the late 1980s for James Fernandez's metaphor class. I suggested that the prohibition against mixing metaphors relates to ways we judge people's sanity and morality, the virtue of structures and systems, and the

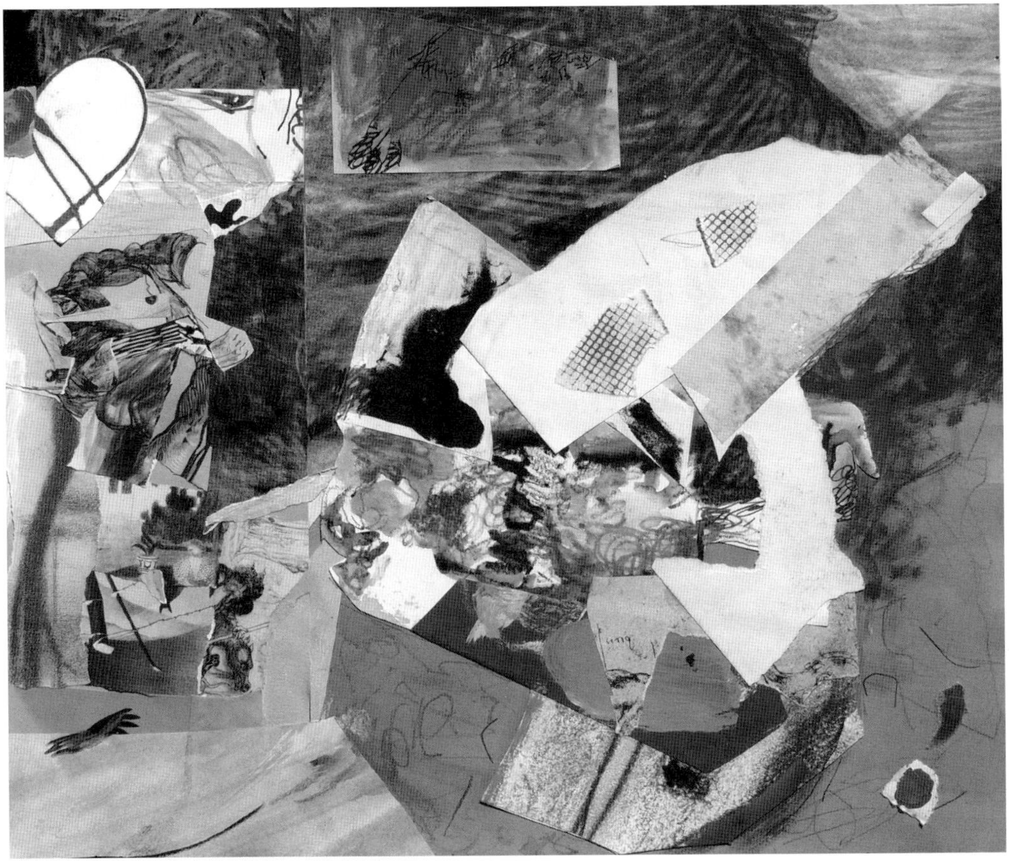

**Figure 6.3** Still Life With Apple. Drawing / Painting / Collage by Dale Pesmen

realism of pictures. Then I showed how these discourses are often conflated. Our descriptions are often shaped by normative expectations of the visual and the static.

Metaphors bring together not only two terms, but the worlds or domains the terms imply: specifically, I found, *visualizable* worlds, ones we can picture. By examining prohibitions against mixed metaphor and eclecticism, I was able to describe some of our habits and habitual ideals. Once a metaphor has been predicated, engaging in another image union seems to adulterate the first world, diminishing its realism, that is, its ability to persuade us. After several such leaps, critics of mixed metaphor move from moral censure to motion sickness, alleging nauseating ontological and rhetorical shiftiness.

We satisfy our passion for a meaningful world, Nelson Goodman (1978) writes, variously at different times. As Jim Fernandez has noted (1987), we constantly shift tropes. One's not enough.

What's more, we do not tend to include this opportunistic flexibility of ours in our picture of reality and meaning. Foucault (1970: xv) says that the juxtaposed points of view of Borges's "Chinese encyclopedia" make us aware of *our* thought's limitations. Mixed metaphor's images similarly defy us to understand "where we stand"—as Foucault calls it, *the site* on which the propinquity of these things would be possible. But maybe we're never standing like that anyway. Maybe where we're standing, legs aren't enough.

* * *

During my fieldwork in Siberia and in the book that grew out of that experience (Pesmen 2000), I examined, among other things, various notions and practices of "coherence." I looked carefully at cultural imagery that indexed and was involved in the production and reproduction of a wide range of coherences and incoherences. This included imagery and practices of what were alleged to be Russian shortages in the domain of reality, nature, validity, form, and civilization. It included images and practices of Russian enigma, hybridity, paradox, unclarity, monstrousness, and chaos. In that book I demonstrate how widespread predications and practices that imply great depth and scale rely on the classification and treatment of phenomena:

- As invisible or hidden by something opaque, as unclearly or as incompletely perceived or perceptible, or unattainable, often because they are allegedly either deeply, centrally "inside" something or very distant.
- Hyperbolically: things are construed as complex, inexhaustible, vast, intense (especially emotionally), or otherwise infinite.
- As inexplicable: things defy clear understanding by virtue of being construed as internally contradictory, irrational, antirational, "not-of-this-world," carnivalized, or dual.

These are all devices and elements, by the way, that Melville uses in The Spouter Inn and throughout *Moby Dick*. Sometimes, as I imply above, I am pretty sure that Melville was, perhaps, at the same time as hopelessly pursuing this sort of transcendent mystery, laughing at or questioning its construction.

In 1990s Russia, when people discussed post-Soviet disorder, they often summed it up by saying: "Now *that's* Russian soul." If an "integrated," "unbroken" individual is a Western ideal of a “person” with a grasp of “reality” (Barrett 1987), descriptions of Russian character and life invoke ill-formedness, schism, formlessness, insanity, disorientation. Eighteenth- and 19th-century Russian nationalists formulated an inexpressible, unmannered, unpredictable, unmeasurable soul, one with no skeleton or not enough skeleton, in opposition to supposed European rational articulation, precision, and predictability (see Greenfeld 1992; Williams 1970). In the 1990s, defects of Russian space, time, and logic were still being set up as flaws and then coopted as valuable assets.

Aspects of what Turner (1969) called liminality are, both in Russia and in, for example, the United States (Pesmen 2000), regularly coopted as *soulful*. Soul is in part a range of rhetorical and practical means by which “depth” is indexed. A “deep place” where contraries are felt to struggle is made, a place that seems what is called “alive” only as long as it is unresolved or unclearly perceived. Internal conflict and sublime scale are felt to imply wholes that cannot be trivialized by what Bakhtin (1984) calls monologic explanation.

Flawed Russian national coherence was proudly auto-exoticized as interesting, uncivilized, Eastern, wild-Western; as metaphorically African, Chukchi, Papuan, or simian. “Uncivilized” could imply jerry-building new things out of bits of old ones. It could also refer to a perceived absence of division of labor, a truly structural flaw. People *both* craved “normal,” “civilized” order and redefined “normal” as against “civilization’s” alleged insincere, naive banality. If a troubled, varied career was offered as evidence of the scale of *one* person’s soul, Russian country and character were, like the Eurasian landscape, understood as too *vast* to be virtuous, neat, refined, or stable. When someone termed Russia or part of it the “theater of the absurd” or a “circus,” or displayed appreciation of the aesthetic that Bakhtin (1984) said erases barriers between genres, systems, and styles, it was implied that the voice that valued coherence was refuted.

In Russia I noticed a genre of succinct one-word indications of “something very big”: *system*, for example, and *Russia*, and *soul*. It has long been claimed that, though Russian “soul” stands for great, meaningful essences, no one anywhere understands them. But without *understanding*, by referring or correctly responding to disorder, people agree that there is some “deep down” meaning. One mission of “soul,” if I may play on Fernandez’s (1986: 11) mission of metaphor, is to reify, form, and idealize the inchoate, making it possible to value, visualize, and represent. The extra twist being that the form “soul” gives is the form of exactly the inchoate, unformed, and transcendent. Soul’s “depth” and the scope of Russia’s “chaos” are simultaneously critical and complicit. They seem to defy reckoning by exploiting and co-opting ways in which people and groups fail to be wholes. The deep and incomprehensibly messed-up are sanctioned, authoritative inchoates that mold references to multiplicity into clear imagery of unclarity, which neatly points at a mess. This valuable irrationality and incoherence is often, of course, pretty much a mirror of rationality and coherence.

In his brilliant 1982 ethnography, which would be as innovative and inspiring if it came out today, James Fernandez describes in wonderful detail how Bwiti knowledgeable ones mix metaphors, cross-referencing domains into spaces where, by condensation, extension, expansion, and performance of metaphoric predications, aspects of what is felt to be a broken cultural life seem to be reconciled (Fernandez 1982). Russian time and space also felt fragmented in the 1990s, and I found similar movements toward weaving coherences there. In the face of this, individuals wove images of failure, incompletion, and communitas into identity, a fabric made dense by conflation of different definitions and contexts into the condensed unity of *soul, system, Russia.*

This portrays pictures of wholes at their best, integrations that in some way help people feel better and help some things work better. But both Russian woven-together depictions and a lot of what those of us living in the United States, for example, can *see* and *see* as acceptable have an element of kitsch, as Karsten Harries (1968) defines it. By offering persuasive, *simplified* images of individual and group coherence, these pictures are in somewhat bad faith. Melville's wicked sense of humor as he grossly overloads the romantic symbol makes me suspect that he, too, at least at times, questioned that kind of meaning.

Standards of reality, community, validity, morality, truth, and beauty, in the name of which pictures of individual souls and groups of people tend to be made, are tied to traditions that portray them as entities defined by *centers*, extremely vast or complex or simple or whatever. I doubt both the *morality* of the representations of group, national, *and individual* souls and the morality of agreeing to believe in their truth or existence.

We can certainly get something like a vast, inexhaustible, overcondensed whale of a whole or soul to exist, but it may not make us better observers, creators, or citizens. The creation of soul is continuous with how ethnicities and classes and so-called blood ties are constructed, politicized, set up against others, and even sometimes taken to the extreme of all that and made violent. Identities created by exaggeration, conflation, and generalization and felt to be authoritatively real are literally *made* to be manipulated.

* * *

I've also thought about coherence by painting. Painting helps me think about it because it helps question the possible value of one act of focusing on something. Although both writing anthropology and painting involve producing images, for me personally the task of realizing something using oil paint, in which one must interact with visual images, leaves less leeway for self-indulgence than does writing academic prose, which can be so ossified with cliché and jargon that all sorts of assumptions are automatically reproduced. By painting, I've been trying to think about what sorts of differences can acceptably share one picture space without being conflated into some version of a traditionally coherent whole. I have also been exploring how pictures can include differences that result in a viewer of the picture getting something of value *other* than "a powerful image."

This is because highly unified compositions can be boring in a certain way. If one is drawing from observation, for example, one looks, makes a mark, then looks again and makes another mark. Habits of integration and resonance and coherence may lead one to, at one or another point in the process, suppress differences between these visions, or fail to appreciate and develop more unaccustomed, specific relations between figures or between figures and background that might be suggested as a result of consecutive moments, glances, and gestures. One afternoon I took a battered-up old picture, cut it up, and masking-taped a piece of it onto a painting I was working on, paying no attention to how its colors, forms, or style "fit" with what I had already done. It would have looked awful had I approached it as a finished picture, but I could suspend that judgement because this crude collage offered something *other* than beauty; what was fantastic was how it was simply *impossible to see.* I looked and I couldn't really *see* it. My definition of "something that can be seen (as something)" had run up against its culturally influenced limitations. This offered me an opportunity to try to unpack and formulate what I habitually mean by "seeing." For one thing, I could absolutely not *take this picture in* all at once. This tiny canvas was, to use an inferior metaphor of scale, "bigger" than any viewing moment.

Trying to make a more and more good, comprehensive, rich one thing ultimately just *reduces more things*. Even a *really good* explanation, model, or trope can only pertain well to so much. On the other hand, there's *always* a next moment. As many as you want.

Maybe each understanding or image or theory has its limit. This would challenge us to expand our tolerance for different kinds of interrelations between successive observations, impulses, pictures.

* * *

Some of the "size" of the human "soul" that makes it seem to defy reckoning, I argue (Pesmen 2000), exploits the fact that people and groups of people are fleeting moments, impulses, tropes, identities, approaches, and practices. The image of the "whole" gets much of its "vastness" by often violent and mistaken acts of rhetorical conflation of human multiplicity *over time*.

In this sense, soul is what human flexibility and incoherence look like or become in interaction with a hegemonic model of the center, of depth. Soul reifies and idealizes unformed phenomena, making them possible to visualize and represent, giving them a clear form. The form it gives, however, is the form of the unclear, unformed, and transcendent. In critique and complicity, soul searches for coherences and rebels against them, timeless Platonic wholes, complete with the futile project of capturing them.

I've been trying to take the collage experiment that I described further. One technique is to cover all of a painting I'm working on with white paper except for a small area that I work on, only sometimes uncovering the rest of the picture, being shocked at the juxtaposition, and allowing respectful but limited negotiation between the parts. This feels *kind*. The masking of most of the biggest "whole" gives my overanxious structuring faculties free reign, but with "wholes" of minor relative size. Of course I *know* that the little structure I'm working on is part of a bigger picture, but there's no rush to bring them together and beat sense into the whole. I wish I knew how to bring this spirit to ethnographic observation and depiction.

It does reinforce my sense of how wrongheaded the critical spirit in scholarship often is. It's no big deal for a smart person to find a flaw in one part of someone else's theory. It's no great coup either. The critic just sets her or himself up in an impoverished, negative world in which one feels obliged to produce increasingly flaw-free texts. How much better to find what's good and appreciate it. Works of theory or ethnography presented as argued or organic wholes are collaged from an anthropologist's creative, analytical, and observational episodes. One passage's value is only undermined by another's defect if we demand that the whole display logical validity. But if, when we smell a rat, see it floating in the breeze, and hear it rustling in the wind, we automatically try to nip it in the bud, when we come to balance the account we'll find we've been fishing in troubled waters and building on a sandy foundation. Neither logical formulas nor romantic, organic, or spatial unities are great tropes for pictures we can make with the material we're fortunate enough to have.

## Note

1. The *Moby Dick* chapter on the whale's whiteness is based on this device. One might argue that in "The Whiteness of the Whale" the snowballing tropic assimilation of everything to the whale is in dead earnest, but even there I would disagree.

## References

Bakhtin, Mikhail (1984), *Problems of Dostoevsky's Poetics*, Minneapolis: University of Minnesota Press.
Barrett, Robert (1987), *Schizophrenia and Personhood* (unpublished manuscript).
Fernandez, James W. (1982), *Bwiti: An Ethnography of the Religious Imagination in Africa*, Princeton: Princeton University Press.
Fernandez, James W. (1986), *Persuasions and Performances*, Bloomington: Indiana University Press.
Fernandez, James W. (1987), Lecture. Department of Anthropology, University of Chicago.
Foucault, Michel (1970), *The Order of Things: An Archeology of the Human Sciences*, New York: Random House.
Goodman, Nelson (1978), *Ways of Worldmaking*, Indianapolis: Hackett Publishing Co.
Greenfeld, Liah (1992), *Nationalism: Five Roads to Modernity*, Cambridge, MA: Harvard University Press.
Harries, Karsten (1968), *The Meaning of Modern Art*, Evanston, IL: Northwestern University Press.
Pesmen, Dale (2000), *Russia and Soul: An Exploration*, Ithaca: Cornell University Press.
Turner, Victor (1969), *The Ritual Process: Structure and Anti-Structure*, Ithaca: Cornell University Press.
Williams, Robert C. (1970), "The Russian Soul: A Study in European Thought and Non-European Nationalism." *Journal of the History of Ideas* 31 (4): 573–88.

# PART II
# MAKING ART

## Preface

This section focuses on practices of making, with pieces that examine technologies of artisanship as well as the crafting or making of aesthetic forms and ideas. It opens with Claude Levi-Strauss' seminal discussion of bricolage, which offers a poignant tool for the consideration of creative production though an examination of the logics of immediacy and abstraction, of cobbling (*bricolage*) versus systems design (*dispositif*), both of which precipitate socially legible aesthetic forms. Art, Levi-Strauss argues, mediates between science and "bricolage," insofar as it is concerned with both representation and material properties. "The painter is always mid-way between design and anecdote, and his genius consists in uniting internal and external knowledge, a 'being' and a 'becoming'" (Levi-Strauss, 68). Many of the excerpts in this section sustain an exploration with the relationship between thought and craft, between ideas and the physicality of production. While Tim Ingold emphasizes meaning as principally emergent in and through the physical process of weaving, Louise Meintjes explores the interrelationships between imagined outcomes and studio practice through the "superior aural competence" of studio music-makers, who "can imagine composite sonic wholes, new sound worlds, and set about creating them with the technical expertise of their sound engineer" (80). As Meintjes demonstrates, these imagined sound worlds are *made* through tactile engagement with mixing boards and computer keyboards.

Like Levi-Strauss, the authors included here aim to validate the skillful artistry of forms of making that may, for whatever reason, have been treated as being of lesser status. For many, this also entails troubling an implicit division between science and technology on the one hand and handwork on the other. Hence Meintjes insists on the creative genius and virtuosity of the studio music-maker while Ingold describes the skill of the weaver, the blacksmith, the carpenter, and the potter, and Heather Paxson affirms the artisanship of the cheesemaker, that is at once haptic and techno-scientific. Many of the excerpts are in conversation with a burgeoning literature on craft, which offers an emphasis on physicality and practice not generally emphasized in the study of the arts (Adamson 2010; Sennett 2008). As demonstrated across the section, when close attention is paid to ethnographic settings, the cultural and historical grounds of assumptions related to the relative status of art and craft become apparent. While technical skill is often a basis for evaluating an artist's competency (and defining the "artist" in relation to her "reputation"—see Becker; Bauman; and also Part V), the forms virtuosity takes differ across mediums and place. Strains of contemporary art have long critiqued virtuosity as a basis of a meaning of "art." As avant-garde dancer Yvonne Rainer's 1965 "No Manifesto" begins, "No to spectacle. / No to virtuosity." The range of practices and forms presented here suggests the applicability of the discussion for a wider array of artistic practices not directly taken up in this section, but addressed elsewhere in the Reader; hence dance, theater, design, and more might also be productively engaged through a focus on making, when conceived of as an engagement of technical practice and matter.

By attending to making, one attends to modalities by which meaning—semiotic or otherwise—is also made, to techniques that connect embodied practice with worldmaking (Brennan 2012; Stewart 2007). In Peterson's essay, we learn how cellists copying the sound of a drum machine destabilize assumptions about classical music and hip-hop and about the ways in which diversity of musical style represents a diverse city. Through an ethnographic account of playing in a hip hop orchestra in Los Angeles, she demonstrates how this work is achieved through the physicality of playing cello. Drawing together the material of the instrument, the bow, the arm, and the fingers through embodied practices learned through years of apprenticeship, the cellists work hard to emulate technological sounds that are counter to what is valued in classical training.

Whether machine or hand, the materials or tools engaged are crucial for an understanding of "making." As drawn out in Heidegger's (2008 [1962]) discussion of the hammer, which, in being picked up and used, becomes "ready-to-hand," a phenomenological merging of arm and tool experienced in and through their doing, as entanglements of human and nonhuman matter and form, practices of making art are always confronted with and shaped by the dense malleability of clay, the steel-wound cello string, the thickness of curdling milk. And tools of art making are also made. This is nicely conveyed by de Duve's (1986) "The Readymade and the Tube of Paint," which focuses on the making of paint as the painterly skill (rather than the making of paintings), bringing anthropological sensibilities about cultural and technological change over time to art history's preferred topic: western European painting.

Human/nonhuman entanglements also take shape as a deep resistance of matter to human making and meaning. Severin Fowles and Ben Alberti describe the effects of atmospheric conditions on rock art; transforming surfaces patterned by human hands thousands of years ago, such conditions remake that which is seen today, casting changing qualities into any understanding of the past. Discussing what they call "a close intertwining of epistemology and ecology," they insist on the significance of atmospheric conditions for considerations of social and symbolic uses and meanings—of rituals that took place in caves with high levels of $CO_2$, for instance, and for ways in which the very possibility of seeing forms etched on rocks is bound up with the density of clouds. A similar emphasis on the ways in which bio-chemical conditions shape matter in ways that challenge and inspire social and cultural categories is found in McLean's (2007) work on anthropology and imagination, in which he takes an ethnographic eye to a sculpture symposium where bogs push against possibilities of human agency, suggesting how imagination is confronted with and shaped by the material world.

And yet, form fails and is resisted. Though there is little anthropological investigation of conceptual art per se or of contemporary art that lacks an "object," the anthropology of time-based arts provides models for engaging with arts that do not take object form. Moreover, as the Reader as a whole conveys, an anthropological approach addresses not only the "object" proper, but social spaces and frames, treating events and activities with and around the arts—"the current of activity to which it properly and originally belongs" (Ingold, 90)—as meaningful and constitutive of meaning (see especially Part VI).

Attending to making art presents methodological opportunities for the anthropology of the arts. "Making with" is already a common strategy for the ethnographic study of music and performance, as well as for visual anthropologists involved in participatory filmmaking. Such a methodological approach might also be productively deployed in the context of plastic arts. A mode of "sensory ethnography" (Pink 2015), drawing, or sculpting, or making a basket with one's informants provides opportunities for experiential, non-discursive understanding, for awareness of arts pedagogy, or, as Ingold and Vergunst (2008) experienced with walking, for congenial conversation and convivial sociability. For, as the Reader's final part (VII: Anthropology and Art—Intersections and Collisions) conveys, anthropology is also a mode of making.

### Ethnographic exercise

#### *Your personal craft*

Take a case in which you make something or participate in an activity that requires a particular craft or skill: cooking, playing music, painting, dance, sport, fishing, carpentry, computer programming, or even walking (this list is not exhaustive—you can choose your own case).

Describe, in detail, how and what you do. Pay particular attention to what your body does: how your hands move, what you smell or hear, how your torso moves, and so on. Be sure to discuss other objects or materials used. Write roughly one page and aim for as much detail as possible.

## Further reading

Adamson, Glenn (2010), *The Craft Reader*, London: Bloomsbury.

Bottoms, Greg (2007), *The Colorful Apocalypse: Journeys in Outsider Art*, Chicago: University of Chicago Press.

Brennan, Vicki (2012), "Take Control: The Labor of Immediacy in Yoruba Christian Music." *Journal of Popular Music Studies* 24 (4): 411–29.

Bunn, Stephanie (2014), "Making Plants and Growing Baskets," in Elizabeth Hallam and Tim Ingold (eds), *Making and Growing: Anthropological Studies of Organisms and Artefacts*, 163–80, Farnham: Ashgate Publishing, Ltd.

Duve, Thierry de (1986), "The Readymade and the Tube of Paint." *Artforum* 24 (9): 110–21.

Heidegger, Martin (2008 [1962]), *Being and Time*, New York: Harper & Rowe.

Hernandez-Reguant, Ariana (2004), "Copyrighting Che: Art and Authorship under Cuban Late Socialism." *Public Culture* 16 (1): 1–29.

Ingold, Tim and Jo Lee Vergunst (2008), *Ways of Walking: Ethnography and Practice on Foot*, Burlington, VT: Ashgate.

McLean, Stuart and Steve Coleman (eds) (2007), "Engaging Imagination: Anthropological Explorations in Creativity." *Irish Journal of Anthropology* 10 (2): 1–69.

Pink, Sarah (2015), *Doing Sensory Ethnography*, 2nd edn, London: Sage.

Rainer, Yvonne (1965), "Some Retrospective Notes on a Dance for 10 People and 12 Mattresses Called *Parts of Some Sextets*, Performed at the Wadsworth Atheneum, Hartford, Connecticut, and Judson Memorial Church, New York, in March, 1965." *Tulane Drama Review* 10 (2): 168–78.

Reynolds, Alastair (2006), "Zima Blue," in *Zima Blue and Other Stories,* San Francisco: Night Shade Books.

Rubio, Fernando Domínguez (2012), "The Material Production of the Spiral Jetty: A Study of Culture in the Making." *Cultural Sociology* 6 (2): 143–61.

Sennett, Richard (2008), *The Craftsman*, New Haven: Yale University Press.

Stewart, Kathleen (2007), *Ordinary Affects*, Durham, NC: Duke University Press.

Yaneva, Albena (2009), *Made by the Office for Metropolitan Architecture: An Ethnography of Design*, Rotterdam: 010 Publishers.

# CHAPTER 7
# THE SCIENCE OF THE CONCRETE
*Claude Lévi-Strauss*

There are two distinct modes of scientific thought. These are certainly not a function of different stages of development of the human mind but rather of two strategic levels at which nature is accessible to scientific enquiry: one roughly adapted to that of perception and the imagination: the other at a remove from it.

The characteristic feature of mythical thought is that it expresses itself by means of a heterogeneous repertoire which, even if extensive, is nevertheless limited. It has to use this repertoire, however, whatever the task in hand because it has nothing else at its disposal. Mythical thought is therefore a kind of intellectual 'bricolage.'

The 'bricoleur' is adept at performing a large number of diverse tasks; but, unlike the engineer, he does not sub-ordinate each of them to the availability of raw materials and tools conceived and procured for the purpose of the project. His universe of instruments is closed and the rules of his game are always to make do with 'whatever is at hand', that is to say with a set of tools and materials which is always finite and is also heterogeneous because what it contains bears no relation to the current project, or indeed to any particular project, but is the contingent result of all the occasions there have been to renew or enrich the stock or to maintain it with the remains of previous constructions or destructions. The set of the 'bricoleur's' means cannot therefore be defined in terms of a project (which would presuppose besides, that, as in the case of the engineer, there were, at least in theory, as many sets of tools and materials or 'instrumental sets', as there are different kinds of projects). It is to be defined only by its potential use or, putting this another way and in the language of the 'bricoleur' himself, because the elements are collected or retained on the principle that 'they may always come in handy'. Such elements are specialized up to a point, sufficiently for the 'bricoleur' not to need the equipment and knowledge of all trades and professions, but not enough for each of them to have only one definite and determinate use. They each represent a set of actual and possible relations; they are 'operators' but they can be used for any operations of the same type.

The elements of mythical thought similarly lie half-way between percepts and concepts. It would be impossible to separate percepts from the concrete situations in which they appeared, while recourse to concepts would require that thought could, at least provisionally, put its projects (to use Husserl's expression) 'in brackets'.

Consider [the 'bricoleur'] at work and excited by his project. His first practical step is retrospective. He has to turn back to an already existent set made up of tools and materials, to consider or reconsider what it contains and, finally and above all, to engage in a sort of dialogue with it and, before choosing between them, to index the possible answers which the whole set can offer to his problem. He interrogates all the heterogeneous objects of which his treasury is composed to discover what each of them could 'signify'. A particular cube of oak could be a wedge to make up for the inadequate length of a plank of pine or it could be a pedestal – which would allow the grain and polish of the old wood to show to advantage.

In one case it will serve as extension, in the other as material. But the possibilities always remain limited by the particular history of each piece and by those of its features which are already determined by the use for which it was originally intended or the modifications it has undergone for other purposes. The elements which the 'bricoleur' collects and uses are 'pre-constrained' like the constitutive units of myth, the possible combinations of which are restricted by the fact that they are drawn from the language where they already possess a sense which sets a limit on their freedom of manoeuvre (Lévi-Strauss 1960: 35). And the decision as to what to put in each place also depends on the possibility of putting a different element there instead, so that each choice which is made will involve a complete reorganization of the structure, which will never be the same as one vaguely imagined nor as some other which might have been preferred to it.

The engineer no doubt also cross-examines his resources. The existence of an 'interlocutor' is in his case due to the fact that his means, power and knowledge are never unlimited and that in this negative form he meets resistance with which he has to come to terms. It might be said that the engineer questions the universe, while the 'bricoleur' addresses himself to a collection of oddments left over from human endeavours, that is, only a sub-set of the culture. Again, Information Theory shows that it is possible, and often useful, to reduce the physicists' approaches to a sort of dialogue with nature. This would make the distinction we are trying to draw less clearcut. There remains however a difference even if one takes into account the fact that the scientist never carries on a dialogue with nature pure and simple but rather with a particular relationship between nature and culture definable in terms of his particular period and civilization and the material means at his disposal. He is no more able than the 'bricoleur' to do whatever he wishes when he is presented with a given task. He too has to begin by making a catalogue of a previously determined set consisting of theoretical and practical knowledge, of technical means, which restrict the possible solutions.

The difference is therefore less absolute than it might appear. It remains a real one, however, in that the engineer is always trying to make his way out of and go beyond the constraints imposed by a particular state of civilization while the 'bricoleur' by inclination or necessity always remains within them. This is another way of saying that the engineer works by means of concepts and the 'bricoleur' by means of signs. The sets which each employs are at different distances from the poles on the axis of opposition between nature and culture. One way indeed in which signs can be opposed to concepts is that whereas concepts aim to be wholly transparent with respect to reality, signs allow and even require the interposing and incorporation of a certain amount of human culture into reality. Signs, in Peirce's vigorous phrase, 'address somebody'.

Mythical thought, that 'bricoleur', builds up structures by fitting together events, or rather the remains of events,[1] while science, 'in operation' simply by virtue of coming into being, creates its means and results in the form of events, thanks to the structures which it is constantly elaborating and which are its hypotheses and theories. But it is important not to make the mistake of thinking that these are two stages or phases in the evolution of knowledge. Both approaches are equally valid.

It is worth showing briefly how, from this point of view, art lies half-way between scientific knowledge and mythical or magical thought. It is common knowledge that the artist is both something of a scientist and of a 'bricoleur'. By his craftsmanship he constructs a material object which is also an object of knowledge. We have already distinguished the scientist and the 'bricoleur' by the inverse functions which they assign to events and structures as ends and means, the scientist creating events (changing the world) by means of structures and the 'bricoleur' creating structures by means of events. This is imprecise in this crude form but our analysis makes it possible for us to refine it. Let us now look at this portrait of a woman by Clouet and consider the reason for the very profound aesthetic emotion which is, apparently inexplicably, aroused by the highly realistic, thread by thread, reproduction of a lace collar.

The choice of this example is not accidental. Clouet is known to have liked to paint at less than life-size. His paintings are therefore, like Japanese gardens, miniature vehicles and ships in bottles, what in the 'bricoleur's' language are called 'small-scale models' or 'miniatures'. Now, the question arises whether the small-scale model or miniature, which is also the 'masterpiece' of the journeyman may not in fact be the universal type of the work of art. All miniatures seem to have intrinsic aesthetic quality – and from what should they draw this constant virtue if not from the dimensions themselves? – and conversely the vast majority of works of art are small scale. It might be thought that this characteristic is principally a matter of economy in materials and means, and one might appeal in support of this theory to works which are incontestably artistic but also on a grand scale. We have to be clear about definitions. The paintings of the Sistine Chapel are a small-scale model in spite of their imposing dimensions, since the theme which they depict is the End of Time.

Even 'natural size' implies a reduction of scale since graphic or plastic transposition always involves giving up certain dimensions of the object: volume in painting, colour, smell, tactile impressions in sculpture and the temporal dimension in both cases since the whole work represented is apprehended at a single moment in time.

What is the virtue of reduction either of scale or in the number of properties? It seems to result from a sort of reversal in the process of understanding. To understand a real object in its totality we always tend to work from its parts. The resistance it offers us is overcome by dividing it. Reduction in scale reverses this situation. Being smaller, the object as a whole seems less formidable. By being quantitatively diminished, it seems to us qualitatively simplified. More exactly, this quantitative transposition extends and diversifies our power over a homologue of the thing, and by means of it the latter can be grasped, assessed and apprehended at a glance. A child's doll is no longer an enemy, a rival or even an interlocutor. In it and through it a person is made into a subject. In the case of miniatures, in contrast to what happens when we try to understand an object or living creature of real dimensions, knowledge of the whole precedes knowledge of the parts. And even if this is an illusion, the point of the procedure is to create or sustain the illusion, which gratifies the intelligence and gives rise to a sense of pleasure which can already be called aesthetic on these grounds alone.

I have so far only considered matters of scale which, as we have just seen, imply a dialectical relation between size (i.e. quantity) and quality. But miniatures have a further feature. They are 'man made' and, what is more, made by hand. They are therefore not just projections or passive homologues of the object: they constitute a real experiment with it. Now the model being an artefact, it is possible to understand how it is made and this understanding of the method of construction adds a supplementary dimension. As we have already seen in the case of 'bricolage', and the example of 'styles' of painters shows that the same is true in art, there are several solutions to the same problem. The choice of one solution involves a modification of the result to which another solution would have led, and the observer is in effect presented with the general picture of these permutations at the same time as the particular solution offered. He is thereby transformed into an active participant without even being aware of it. Merely by contemplating it he is, as it were, put in possession of other possible forms of the same work; and in a confused way, he feels himself to be their creator with more right than the creator himself because the latter abandoned them in excluding them from his creation. And these forms are so many further perspectives opening out on to the work which has been realized. In other words, the intrinsic value of a small-scale model is that it compensates for the renunciation of sensible dimensions by the acquisition of intelligible dimensions.

Let us now return to the lace collar in Clouet's picture. Everything that has been said applies in this case, for the procedure necessary to represent it as a projection, in a particular space, of properties whose sensible dimensions are fewer and smaller than that of the object is exactly the reverse of that which science would have employed had it proposed, in accordance with its function, to produce (instead of reproducing) not only a new, instead of an already known, piece of lace but also real lace instead of a picture of lace. Science would have worked on the real scale but by means of inventing a loom, while art works on a diminished scale to produce an image homologous with the object. The former approach is of a metonymical order, it replaces one thing by another thing, an effect by its cause, while the latter is of a metaphorical order.

This is not all. For if it is true that the relation of priority between structure and event is exactly the opposite in science and 'bricolage', then it is clear that art has an intermediate position from this point of view as well. Even if, as we have shown, the depiction of a lace collar in miniature demands an intimate knowledge of its morphology and technique of manufacture (and had it been a question of the representation of people or animals we should have said: of anatomy and physical attitudes), it is not just a diagram or blueprint. It manages to synthesize these intrinsic properties with properties which depend on a spatial and temporal context. The final product is the lace collar exactly as it is but so that at the same time its appearance is affected by the particular perspective. This accentuates some parts and conceals others, whose existence however still influences the rest through the contrast between its whiteness and the colour of the other clothes, the reflection of the pearly neck it encircles and that of the sky on a particular day and at a particular time of day. The appearance of the lace collar is also affected by whether it indicates casual or formal dress, is worn, either new or previously used, either freshly ironed or creased, by an ordinary woman or a queen, whose physiognomy confirms, contradicts or qualifies her status in a particular social class, society, part of the world and period of history … The painter is always mid-way between design and anecdote, and his genius consists in uniting internal and external knowledge, a 'being' and a 'becoming', in producing with his brush an object which does not exist as such and which he is nevertheless able to create on his canvas. This is a nicely balanced synthesis of one or more artificial and natural structures and one or more natural and social events. The aesthetic emotion is the result of this union between the structural order and the order of events, which is brought about within a thing created by man and so also in effect by the observer who discovers the possibility of such a union through the work of art.

Several points are suggested by this analysis. In the first place, the analysis helps us to see why we are inclined to think of myths both as systems of abstract relations and as objects of aesthetic contemplation. The creative act which gives rise to myths is in fact exactly the reverse of that which gives rise to works of art. In the case of works of art, the starting point is a set of one or more objects and one or more events which aesthetic creation unifies by revealing a common structure. Myths travel the same road but start from the other end. They use a structure to produce what is itself an object consisting of a set of events (for all myths tell a story). Art thus proceeds from a set (object + event) to the *discovery* of its structure. Myth starts from a structure by means of which it *constructs* a set (object + event).

The first point tempts one to generalize the theory. The second might seem to lead to a restriction of it. For we may ask whether it is in fact the case that works of art are always an integration of structure and event. This does not on the face of it seem to be true for instance of the cedarwood Tlingit club, used to kill fish, which I have in front of me on my bookshelf. The artist who carved it in the form of a sea monster intended the body of the implement to be fused with the body of the animal and the handle with its tail, and that the anatomical proportions, taken from a fabulous creature, should be such that the object could *be* the cruel animal slaying helpless victims, at the same time as an easily handled, balanced and efficient fishing utensil. Everything about this implement – which is also a superb work of art – seems to be a matter of structure: its mythical symbolism as well as its practical function. More accurately, the object, its function and its symbolism seem to be inextricably bound up with each other and to form a closed system in which there is no place for events. The monster's position, appearance and expression owe nothing to the historical circumstances in which the artist saw it, in the flesh or in a dream, or conceived the idea of it. It is rather as if its immutable being were finally fixed in the wood whose fine grain allows the reproduction of all its aspects and in the use for which its empirical form seems to pre-determine it. And all this applies equally to the other products of primitive art: an African statue or a Melanesian mask … So it looks as if we have defined only one local and historical form of aesthetic creation and not its fundamental properties or those by means of which its intelligible relations with other forms of creation can be described.

We have only to widen our explanation to overcome this difficulty.

Depending on the style, place and period the contingent plays a part in three different ways or at three distinct points in artistic creation (or in all of them). It may play a part in the occasion for the work or in the execution of the work or in the purpose for which it is intended. It is only in the first case that it takes the form of an event properly speaking, that is, of contingency exterior and prior to the creative act. The artist perceives it from without as an attitude, an expression, a light effect or a situation, whose sensible and intellectual relations to the structure of the object affected by these modalities he grasps and incorporates in his work. But the contingent can also play an intrinsic part in the course of execution itself, in the size or shape of the piece of wood the sculptor lays hands on, in the direction and quality of its grain, in the imperfections of his tools, in the resistance which his materials or project offer to the work in the course of its accomplishment, in the unforeseeable incidents arising during work. Finally, the contingent can be extrinsic as in the first case but posterior, instead of anterior, to the act of creation. This is the case whenever the work is destined for a specific end, since the artist will construct it with a view to its potential condition and successive uses in the future and so will put himself, consciously or unconsciously, in the place of the person for whose use it is intended.

The process of artistic creation therefore consists in trying to communicate (within the immutable framework of a mutual confrontation of structure and accident) either with the *model* or with the *materials* or with the future *user* as the case may be, according to which of these the artist particularly looks to for his directions while he is at work. Each case roughly corresponds to a readily identifiable form of art: the first to the plastic arts of the West, the second to so-called primitive or early art and the third to the applied arts. But it would be an oversimplification to take these identifications very strictly. All forms of art allow all three aspects and they are only distinguished from one another by the relative proportion of each. Even the most academic of painters comes up against problems of execution, for example. All the so-called primitive arts can be called applied in a double sense: first, because many of their productions are technical objects and, secondly, because even those which seem most divorced from practical preoccupations have a definite purpose. Finally, as we know, implements lend themselves to disinterested contemplation even among ourselves.

With these reservations, it is easy to show that the three aspects are functionally related and that the predominance of any one of them leaves less or no place for the others. So-called professional painting is, or believes itself to be, quite free so far as both execution and purpose are concerned. Its best examples display a complete mastery of technical difficulties; the problems which painters have set themselves amount to little more than a game of technical refinement. In the extreme case it is as though, given his canvas, paints and brushes, the painter were able to do exactly what he pleased. On the other hand, he also tries to make his work into an object independent of anything contingent, of value in itself and for itself. This is indeed what the formula of the 'easel picture' implies. Freed from the contingent both with regard to execution and purpose professional painting can, then, bring it to bear upon the occasion of the work, and indeed if this account is correct it is bound to do so. Professional painting can therefore be defined as 'genre' painting if the sense of this expression is considerably widened. For, from the very general viewpoint we are taking, the attempt of a portrait painter – even of a Rembrandt – to recapture on his canvas his model's most revealing expression or secret thoughts belongs to the same genre as that of a painter like Detaille, whose compositions reproduce the hour and order of battle and the number and disposition of the buttons distinguishing the uniforms of each Arm.

The relative proportions of the three aspects are reversed in the applied arts. In these, first place is given to purpose and execution, contingent factors playing an approximately equal part in each, in the examples we consider the most 'pure', at the same time the occasion of the work plays no part. This can be seen from the fact that a wine cup or goblet, a piece of basket work or a fabric seems to us perfect when its practical value manifestly transcends time and corresponds wholly to its functions for men of different periods and civilizations. If the difficulties of execution are entirely mastered, as is the case when it is entrusted to machines, the purpose can become more and more precise and specific and applied art is transformed into industrial art. We call it peasant or folk art if the reverse is the case. Finally, primitive art is the opposite of professional or academic art. Professional or academic art internalizes execution (which it has, or believes itself to have, mastered) and purpose ('art for art's sake' being an end in itself). As a result, it is impelled to externalize the occasion (which it requires the model to provide) and the latter thus becomes a part of the signified. Primitive art, on the other hand, internalizes the occasion (since the supernatural beings which it delights in representing have a reality which is timeless and independent of circumstances) and it externalizes execution and purpose which thus become a part of the signifying.

No form of art is, however, worthy of the name if it allows itself to come entirely under the sway of extraneous contingencies, whether of occasion or purpose. If it did so it would rate as an icon (supplementary to the model) or as an implement (complementary with the material worked). Even the most professional art succeeds in moving us only if it arrests in time this dissipation of the contingent in favour of the pretext and incorporates it in the work, thereby investing it with the dignity of being an object in its own right. In so far as early art, primitive art and the 'primitive' periods of professional painting are the only ones which do not date, they owe it to this dedication of the accidental to the service of execution and so to the use, which they try to make complete, of the raw datum as the empirical material of something meaningful.

It is necessary to add that the balance between structure and event, necessity and contingency, the internal and external is a precarious one. It is constantly threatened by forces which act in one direction or the other according to fluctuations in fashion, style or general social conditions. From this point of view, it would seem that impressionism and cubism are not so much two successive stages in the development of painting as partners in the same enterprise, which, although not exact contemporaries, nevertheless collaborated by complementary distortions to prolong a mode of expression whose very existence, as we are better able to appreciate today, was seriously threatened. The intermittent fashion for 'collages', originating when craftsmanship was dying, could not for its part be anything but the transposition of 'bricolage' into the realms of contemplation. Finally, the stress on the event can also break away at certain times through greater emphasis either on transient social phenomena (as in the case of socialist realism) or on transient natural, or even meteorological, phenomena (impressionism) at the expense of structure.

We have seen that there are analogies between mythical thought on the theoretical, and 'bricolage' on the practical plane and that artistic creation lies mid-way between science and these two forms of activity.

## Note

1. 'Bricolage' also works with 'secondary' qualities, i.e. 'second hand'.

## Bibliography

Lévi-Strauss, C. (1960), 'La Structure et la forme, réflexions sur un ouvrage de Vladimir Propp', *Cahiers de L'Institut de Science économique appliquée* (Recherches et dialogues philosophiques et économiques, 7), 99, Paris: I.S.E.A.

Peirce, Ch. S. (1956), 'Logic as Semiotic: The Theory of Signs', in J. Buchler (ed.), *The Philosophy of Peirce: Selected Writings*, 3rd edn, London: Routledge.

Saussure, F. de (1960), *Course in General Linguistics*, trans. W. Baskin, London: Peter Owen Ltd.

# CHAPTER 8
# REPUTATION AS PROCESS
*Howard S. Becker*

Art worlds, in a variety of interwoven activities, routinely make and unmake reputations—of works, artists, schools, genres, and media. They single out from the mass of more or less similar work done by more or less interchangeable people a few works and a few makers of works of special worth. They reward that special worth with esteem and, frequently but not necessarily, in more material ways too. They use reputations, once made, to organize other activities, treating things and people with distinguished reputations differently from others.

## *The theory of reputation*

It makes sense to spend time and energy assessing and communicating reputations if you believe in a particular, intensely individualistic theory of art and how it is made, but not otherwise. The theory goes like this. (1) Specially gifted people (2) create works of exceptional beauty and depth which (3) express profound human emotions and cultural values. (4) The work's special qualities testify to its maker's special gifts, and the already known gifts of the maker testify to the special qualities of the work. (5) Since the works reveal the maker's essential qualities and worth, all the works that person makes, but no others, should be included in the corpus on which his reputation is based.

Note the historically and culturally contingent character of this theory. Many societies have never had such a theory (and as a result we know nothing about their artists):

> In the Middle Ages the individual artist remains invisible behind the corporate facades of church and guild. Greco-Roman and Chinese histories alone report in any detail the conditions of individual artists' lives. A few names and lines of text are all we have about Egyptian dynastic artists. The records of the other civilizations of antiquity in America, Africa, and India tell nothing of artists' lives, Yet the archeological record repeatedly shows the presence of connected series of rapidly changing manufactures in the cities, and slower ones in the provinces and in the countryside, all manifesting the presence of persons whom we can call artists. (Kubler, 1962: 92)

We presumably would have known about these artists, had we been there, because our theory of art makes it important to know who they are. But Western societies have not always made those distinctions either:

> The contested, but dominant, definition that our society gives to art and the artist is the fruit of a process of differentiation of human activities whose origin can be situated in the Renaissance. Beginning in Italy, at the end of the 15th Century, the activities of the painter, sculptor and architect, considered as radically different from the manual trades,

> achieved the dignity of "liberal" arts. The artist is no longer an artisan, but a creator, a sort of *alter dens* free from ordinary norms; the charismatic representation of the artist merges with an aristocratic image of the work of art, unique and irreplaceable. We are at the point of departure for the modern idea of the creator and the created object.
>
> The second stage coincides with the first industrial revolution, that of the 18th Century. Beginning with that revolution, the artistic product tended to be defined in opposition to the industrial product. The machine is opposed to the hand of man, divided work to undivided, the production of a series of identical objects to the singularity of the unique object. The industrial reality which is translated, in humanistic moral philosophy, into the alienation of the assembly line results, in the economic order, in the negation of uniqueness, the essence of rarety. To show the specificity of their product in relation to the products of the artisan and of industry, artists tried to remove from their own practice the factor common to the other two, the awareness of thc utilitarian plan: the philosophical theory of art as the finality without any purpose justified their survival. By attributing to themselves the monopoly of production of sublime purposelessness and of the essential difference (in opposition to the similarity of objects in an industrial series or the small difference which allows one to distinguish among objects from the same artisanal series) the artists of the 19th Century protected the rarity and, through it, the possibility of giving social and economic value to the symbolic goods they produced (Moulin, 1978: 241–42, my translation).

In short the theory of art which makes it possible and worthwhile to create reputations is not timeless; it arises in societies which subscribe to more general theories emphasizing the individual over the collective, and under particular social conditions. Having arisen, it can then be exported to and adopted by societies which formerly did not bother about such things.

The first premise of the theory of reputation holds that artists have special gifts that are quite rare. Recall the definition Stoppard put into the mouth of Henry Carr in *Travesties:* "An artist is someone who is gifted in some way that enables him to do something more or less well which can only be done badly or not at all by someone who is not thus gifted" (Stoppard, 1975, p. 38). The definition emphasizes traits of the maker of fine works; it asserts that such works do not get made accidentally, that making great works is not something anyone could do on a good day, that the works get their value from being made by unusual people, of whom there are not many. If these unusual people do important work, then we need to know who they are so that we can help them do it, provide them with appropriate circumstances, and not interfere with them. Moulin (1978) and many others suggest that contemporary visual art, following the lead of Marcel Duchamp, has increasingly emphasized the artist over the work, insisting in effect that anything an artist does thereby becomes art.

Most adherents of the theory, however, do not think that everything an artist does is art. On the contrary, they think that artists create works—objects or events—which are especially beautiful or profound, works which stand out from the mass of superficially similar works. The theory recognizes that many people may, by following the rules which govern the making of art works, produce creditable musical performances, readable novels, and not entirely uninteresting paintings. By following the conventions, such workers will produce work others will recognize as competent. One might thus write a tragedy, using Aristotle's *Poetics* as a guide. Of course, that would not necessarily (or even likely) result in an important work. The theory holds, however, that people with special gifts can manipulate the available conventions, perhaps change them or invent new ones, and so produce works which are not just so-so or ho-hum but, rather, are extraordinary. Those works will stand out from the mass the way Dickens' novels stand out from the thousands of roughly similar works produced in nineteenth-century England, the way the recordings of Louis Armstrong stand out from thousands of similar performances by early jazz trumpet players. They have more, a lot more, of whatever characterizes beautiful or profound works than does most work.

Adherents of the theory do not agree on what these special works have. This question—the "what" that characterizes art works and especially great art works—divides aestheticians, audiences, and other art world participants. In one common conflict, some look to art works to be faithful to the world, to interpret and show it to us in a recognizable and yet new way, to explain and make us feel the strength of important philosophical concerns about the meaning of life and how people should live. Realistic fiction and painting, drama, and film which explore ethical, emotional, or social problems (documentary photography, for instance) satisfy that demand. Others look to art works to exhibit an internal order of superior interest, to deal with problems invented within a medium's tradition in a new, unexpected, or exciting way. Paintings devoted to the problems of how to depict light or volume on a two-dimensional canvas, photographs which deal with the paradoxes of visual representation, novels which rely on formal symmetries for their effect, and especially music which manipulates limited sound materials according to accepted rules in a way which leads us to admire the inevitability of the work's construction, all satisfy this second demand.

Many, if not most, aficionados of an art can find virtues of both kinds in work they admire. They enjoy Renaissance portraits both for the exploration of timeless human types and for experimentation with problems of light and geometry. They admire Dickens for his social analysis, his moral indignation, his ability to create unforgettable characters, and his skill in formal construction all at once. Some, more rigorous in their beliefs, attend only to one or the other set of virtues. The "what" of artistic excellence clearly varies from time to time and place to place. We might, in general, say that we expect the special works produced by specially gifted artists to express and to create in their audiences profound human emotions, and to do that (this may be less axiomatic) by their connection to fundamental (perhaps universal) human values and emotions.

Works and makers stand in reciprocal relation to one another. How do we know that artists have special gifts? By their works, which produce special emotional experiences and reveal their exceptional skills.

Since we infer artists' underlying but unobservable talent from the observable work they produce, and since the ability to make that inference is a crucial skill for any art world participant, we need to make it carefully. We want, especially, to base our inference on adequate evidence. The quest for adequate evidence takes several forms. We want to establish the complete and authentic canon of the artist's works, so that we can take into account everything that might help us make our judgment. We want to uncover cases of plagiarism, so that we do not credit an artist with someone else's work. Problems of attribution and authenticity also arise here.

Since artists know that other art world participants make reputational inferences from their work, they try to control the work that becomes available for making such inferences. They destroy work they don't want considered, or label it "unfinished"; if they are lucky, a court may (as French courts can) prevent the circulation of work they don't want publicly attributed to them. They distinguish categories of work, as contemporary photographers sometimes distinguish their "commercial" work (not to be considered in assessing them as artists) from their "personal" work (to be so used), according to the seriousness of their intentions in making it. They revise their work when they can, as Stravinsky and Henry James did.

The five premises, taken together, furnish the basis for making, maintaining, and unmaking reputations as characteristic art world activities.

## Bibliography

Kubler, George (1962), *The Shape of Time: Remarks on the History of Things*, New Haven: Yale University Press.

Moulin, Raymonde (1978), "La Genèse de la rareté artistique." *Revue d'ethnologie Française* 8: 241–58.

Stoppard, Tom (1975), *Travesties*, London: Faber and Faber.

# CHAPTER 9
# THE RECORDING STUDIO AS FETISH

*Louise Meintjes*

## Johannesburg, 1991

I'd come whizzing into the city center on my bicycle. Past the taxi rank where vendors sell oranges, Lux soap, cassettes, and haircuts; past the dilapidated Georgeson Mansions where Isigqi Sesimanje's Joana overlooks the noisy taxi rank from her sixth-floor flat; past record bars blasting the latest house-music out into the sunshine; past the previous Gallo building and the isicathamiya hall above the parking garage opposite it; past musician-dancers Muhle and Mdlolo's room on the corner of Kerk and Bree, just a block west from where musicians Siyazi, Msawetshitshi, and Nogabisela live and a block east from Gallo's 1940s to 1960s headquarters, where records are sculpted like cherubs high up on its concrete walls. I hurtle past Shandel Music, down past Soul Brothers Music. Musicians cruise in and out up to the Soul Brothers' rehearsal rooms. David Masondo, one of the famous Brothers, parks his gold Mercedes. At the next intersection, the corner-shop barber greets me from his spot in the sun (his is not a frenetic business).

It is a dingy part of town here. The roaring overpass loops the city center nearby, while minivan taxis and sealed suburban cars race up thoroughfares to the heart of the city. Messengers on motorbikes weave through the traffic and around pedestrians who move slowly through the district. Along the sidewalks, corrugated warehouse doors alternate with battered burglar-proofing that protects budget stores. Tired business banners peel or flap; luminous posters scream out from cluttered store windows advertising P.A.Y.E., pay as you earn. Take-away cafes serve up slap chips [French fries], *ipapa nenyama* [porridge and meat], and bunny chow [bread and curry]. Outside the fabric store with bright blankets and frocks hanging from the eaves, the old Indian owner smokes his stubby cigar. On the corner a woman sells oranges and tomatoes stacked in pyramids on blue plastic plates. A limping man hobbles by with a stick. Snot splotches the pavement, and sometimes last night's dark, sticky blood.

Downtown Studios stands out from its surroundings on this side of the town, near the bottom of Fox Street, half a block from the barber. A mauve-and-purple awning juts out over the entrance like a winking eyelid from its freshly painted face. I stop on the sidewalk.

When the sun is warm and toasty, musicians and their groupies will be hanging out in its brightness. If it's blazing, they'll be in the shade across the road talking about how hot it is, making arrangements for a rehearsal or a gig, or waiting for loosely promised arrivals. Bra Steve, building supervisor and receptionist, might be sweeping a dawdler off the front steps. 'Regulation,' he says. Gallo wants a clean, always penetrable professional entrance. Cars honk at the side entrance to the garage. *Clatter clatter,* up scrolls the security door, and tightly down again. Engineer Lee has arrived in his zooty BMW or Neil in his brown job or a client or someone from the Gallo headquarters in ritzy Rosebank. I catch a glimpse of Hamilton's minivan—his nickname, Vala Nzimande, stenciled in an area across its tail—as he slips into the garage.

In front of the building, parking is a mess. Incessant traffic officers sporting clipboards and paunches dutifully return on every shift. A truck is backed into the loading entrance, packing equipment in or out. Perhaps building-cleaner David is polishing a car. A personalized minivan or two are sure to be parked—Lucky Dube's, the Dalom Kid's, Peta Teanet's, or Splash's with its peacock logo—people packed in, or people piling out, waiting to go to a gig, returning from a shoot. Sipho arrives with his keyboard slung over his shoulder, Harare with his slim sling bag of drumsticks. "Irene," "irene," "irene," they greet everyone, knocking clenched fists top to bottom, bottom to top, knuckles to knuckles, thumb to thumb with a twist. West's minivan blocks the road, idling. "Here Comes Your Partner In Music" is painted on its front, "There Goes Your Partner In Music"' on the back. West gesticulates, laughs, shouts, organizes from the driver's seat. A late musician leaps down the hallowed entrance stairs, squeezes into the front seat, slams the door. An outsider motorist honks from behind. West finishes his conversation first, drives off quipping to Dumi on the corner. I spot Joana and Janet idling a block away, en route to the studios. Nhlanhla is quietly leaning against the wall, waiting for them, and for the others. Fakes, decked out in his shades, is bumming a cigarette and chatting up Ebony's backing female vocalists. A dude with a briefcase and a rocker's haircut passes into the building. Engineer Peter follows with his candy bar and his cigarettes. Mandla wants to borrow my "Porsche" to cycle all the way to Soweto, but instead he carries it inside and into the elevator, and we cruise up to Downtown Studios on the second floor.

Of the multitude of recording studios in contemporary Johannesburg, Downtown Studios is unmatched in terms of its historical lineage. Its heritage is partly mapped onto the city as landmarks. It is also scattered through the city and through rehearsal rooms and studios in the stories of veteran musicians and producers. "Gallos," they call the company. (The studios are subsidiary to Gallo Africa.) "When old Gallos … ." This lineage, memorialized in bits and pieces, lends to the studios a significance that no other studios in the city can equal.

### *Take 3 studio sound fetishized*

Open the door to the left of Florence and Liza's reception desk. Head down the tunnel-like passage. The carpet creeping up the walls muffles your footsteps. You can hear music stopping and starting, stopping and starting behind those double acoustic doors at the end of the passage. Enter the music box that is Studio 3. It is a space of sonic control, clarity, and separation, a space in which you notice yourself hearing and you miss the everyday reverb on your voice.

The acoustics mark the studio as a space out of the ordinary. But its distinction is not only derived from its focus around a sense other than the eye, the sense privileged in the metalanguage of the everyday (Stoller 1989; Minh-Ha 1991; Taussig 1993; Feld 1996). The studio also draws enchantment from the very quality of the sense it privileges. For "sound is a very special modality. We cannot handle it. We cannot push it away. We cannot turn our backs to it. We can close our eyes, hold our noses, withdraw from touch, refuse to taste. We cannot close our ears though we can partly muffle them. Sound is the least controllable of all sense modalities" (Jaynes 1976, quoted in Alten 1986). In their notion of musical groove, Keil and Feld extend this idea of sound as an uncontrollable modality to one of an infusing, embodied social sensibility (Schutz 1967; Keil and Feld 1994). Because sound as groove is participatory, feelingful, and experiential, its power is essentially unpredictable, unprogrammatic, in a sense, uncontrollable. Both the purely physiological uncontrollability of sound that Jayne recognizes and its social and sensual unboundedness, which Keil and Feld discuss, imbue sound with a particular—and heightened—quality.

The studio both houses and (re)produces sound's physiological, social, and sensual dimensions. The material structure of the studio seals the space acoustically; studio technology can open up and shut down the sounds within it. Engineers control and manipulate the science of sound in order to release and play with that social/sensual uncontrollability. Their function is to harness and fix sounds momentarily in new combinations in order to create new grooves and thereby, eventually, to prompt new social and sensual experiences for those who listen (see Bendix 2000).

Studios regulate and optimize the physical and physiological conditions of listening in multiple ways. They are designed to isolate the internal sonic environment from the noise of the outside world.[1] The hubbub of the vicinity is dampened or extinguished. The world out there sounds far away.

> I'm dropping this in … .
>
> The telephone shrieks like a panic-stricken cricket noticing it's crouched near the console. "Hello?" Peter flicks down the master fader to hear the faint telephone voice. His takeout chicken-and-cheese has arrived at reception.

Inside the studio, the facility is insulated as tightly as possible from the noise of its own operation, for both recording and monitoring purposes. Clean sound separation is an ideal in studio design, from the overall structure of the rooms down to the minute electronic circuitry. Ambient sound from such sources as the ventilation is minimized through design and specialized insulating materials. Soundproofing in the booths and control room blocks out as much external sound as possible and absorbs unwanted internal frequencies. Specialized double-paned acoustic windows visually connect booths and the control room, while blocking the sound. Additionally, in a booth large enough to record more than one source at a time, movable, acoustically insulated baffles partition the area to limit leak-through from the sound source of one microphone into another.[2] To further minimize the effects of ambient sounds and leak-through, gating circuits are installed on microphone lines. These amplifier circuits cut out all signals below a selected threshold, thereby cutting out low-level noise. They are controlled from the outboard effects rack behind the engineer.

In addition to isolation and insulation procedures, other structural and technological features reproduce and monitor sound with minimal sonic disturbance. Music studios are designed to be acoustically dry.[3] An ideal control room is one that is itself acoustically neutral and uniform, so that there is as small a discrepancy as possible between a sound as it is laid onto tape and as it is heard through the monitors. Acoustic uniformity ensures that the quality of the sound is not affected by the spatial positioning of the listener or the live sound source. Sounds produced within this acoustic space can be isolated and listened to for and in themselves with minimal intervention, interruption, contamination, or transformation. Individual high-end headphones can further isolate external noise. The sound piped into each set can be individually mixed to accommodate a single listener's aural balance and volume needs.

Within this fantastically regulated sonic environment, by means of more technology, the infinitely "secret life" of sounds inside space, space inside sounds, and sounds inside sounds can be revealed. The studio becomes a space of sonic virtuosity, of movement, of experimentation, of creative expression let loose through the seemingly mad science of electronics. That is to say, by means of electronic processes that seem as impenetrable as sound itself, one voice is turned into many or into Mickey Mouse; dry sounds echo like a cavern; real becomes more than real; matter is transformed into something more than matter, into symbol, feeling, and aesthetic form.

> "You can just take voices," West says. "You can make them sound like Mickey Mouse—you can make them sound anyhow you want them to. That is a producer's job."

Composite or single sounds seemingly fixed on tape or captured in computers can be minutely manipulated. Peter can control every sound parameter by means of the electronic technology available in the studio. He can manipulate the sound as a whole, or he can dissect and change it track by track or motive by motive. He can erase, shift, add, or precisely repeat any musical feature within the backing. In the mixing process, he can position each track acoustically in any given relation to the other tracks by cutting or boosting their relative volumes, channeling them to the left and/or right farther or nearer from the center for a stereo playback, and adding effects to and shaping the individual complex waveforms of their component tones in order to give a particular sense of dimension, color, and form to the overall sound.

"I like space in music," he tells me. "When I produce I try to create as much space as I can, in the tracks, because I find that you get a lot of relief from a track that is enormous and then just breaks down into absolutely nothing—there's all this space there, and it just gives you a chance to feel what is happening in the track." Peter can manipulate the wave components of a tone in multiple ways. He can play with its shape in time to effect textural features such as the attack and decay of tones. He can alter its fundamental frequency and hence its pitch. He can play with the composite frequency profile in order to shape timbre. He does so by extracting particular frequencies or frequency bands from within the composite signal or by increasing or diminishing their prominence. He can add effects to a tone or series of tones. He has at his electronic fingertips multiple versions of multiple effects programmed in the outboard gear—the signal processing devices—and linked through the MIDI systems into the programmed and recorded tracks.

With this facility, the life within a single sound can be revealed to an extent impossible outside in the everyday. With the studio's scientific precision, the technical skills of its engineers and the aural sophistication of its artists (including the engineers), sounds can be teased out of their surrounding sounds. From the macro to the micro, they are separated out for analysis, reworked, then reinserted in a transformed whole.

Studio music-makers with their superior aural competence can imagine composite sonic wholes, new sound worlds, and set about creating them with the technical expertise of their sound engineer. They can hear the details of complex sounds and set about reshaping them.[4] They can manipulate waveforms in order to give the impression of weight, density, movement, and space. That is to say, they can manipulate scientific technological processes and sound for metaphysical effect. I like space in music. Space here, inside the tracks, is at once a material band on a magnetic tape, a metaphor of that tape band extended to describe digital "space" in a computer, and an illusion and feeling of space.

By its function and the quality of its form, the studio marks sound as privileged, fantastic, enchanted, and enchanting.

### *Take 4 studio artistry fetishized*

Like the patchbay to the board, the studio is the nerve center of the creative process, the mad scientist, the head of the industry, which 'you'll never be able to figure out by observing.'

Sometimes I irritated engineer Neil, just staring at what he was doing, this face always there, in front of him, behind him, over his shoulder, squeezed into an unused space. Not that I was in the way, he reassured me. 'But I reckoned that however much you watched you'd never know what's *really* going on. You could never know what's in my head when I make adjustments on the desk.' I would never be able to detail the creative thought of an artist scientifically analyzing the sound components of what he hears on the monitors, choosing from multiple options for how to improve it, and registering the changes through microelectronic analog or digital adjustments on the equipment in front of him. What does he hear? How does he translate it into science? Why does he boost the upper mids on the DI (direct input) bass line, change the vocal-plate settings on the solo voice, at this moment, in this combination, to these degrees?[5]

I cannot know his head. It is another unknowable, illimitable interior present in the studio and essential to music production. It is a significant phenomenological studio space, similar to the physical and metaphysical realms I have described. His head is a Cuna woman, to whom he grants me, as ethnographer, some alluring access until it appears I might claim to know and describe his creative self.

While I can account for and measure some of the adjustments he makes on the sound gear and console, I cannot necessarily anticipate or explain his choices. Neil is so deeply immersed in a set of engineering practices that his hands can race intuitively across the outboard gear. Much of his manipulation of the controls is felt, learned but not or no longer rationalized. He plays, improvises, and experiments with the technical options his instrument offers, much as performers do with their skills and sonic materials.

Though I cannot know his head, nor systematize his musical-technological body knowledge, I can link him as agent and voice into the creative process and trace the pathways of composition through him as through the other studio realms I have characterized. The sound passes through his artistic sensibility into the technology of the mixing console; transformed into magnetic flux, it passes onto studio tape, then off it, out again through the monitors mounted on the wall, and back into the body. I like spaces in music. There's all this space there, and it just gives you a chance to feel what is happening in the track. While each space is of a different order since each resides in a different kind of material body, they are all similarly imagined in terms of their formal qualities and spatial dimensions. The musical shape of the sound is transformed in the course of flowing.

The merging of these sites for moments and the flows between them are present in the conversation of music-makers, in their perceptions of what it is they do, and their presentations of how they do it.

Fast-forward again.

It is the seventh and last day of Isigqi Sesimanje's recording, 1 April 1992. West and Peter are mixing.

Peter reaches for the logging chart to set up the board for "South Africa is on Fire."

"Heyi! It's very difficult, this one. It's not easy!" comments West as he anticipates the work ahead.

Peter agrees. They have already programmed and overdubbed the song extensively. Janet's original song, titled "Omhlaba wonke," has been translated in part into English, retitled, and transformed lyrically, rhythmically, and in its arrangement during the recording process.

"I've changed the drums, everything, you know. I've changed a lot of things," West begins to explain. *His mind is in the song.* "Now we must start putting them back together. The problem is I did not have the whole cassette for these things, to work out lines."[6] *The song is on the demo cassette, in its tracks.* "So I had to work out lines every night, you know, by thinking, you know, imagining the whole thing." *The song is in West's mind. It exists in his creative sensibility as an ephemeral entity.*

He chuckles a little. Peter is still transferring information from the logging chart onto the console controls. He's not really listening to West's patient rambling.

"So, I'm not sure where we're going!" West muses on. "But I'll pick it up .... And then also this one we need to pick a spot [vacant recording track] again."

"What? To clear?" asks Peter, suddenly alerted.

"Ja, to clear."

"Okay," replies Peter, "maybe we use the computer, let's see."

*The song also exists in the recording tracks and in the computer. They will empty out some of its sonic clutter to make way for new signals, for new ideas. Increasingly, the computer is becoming the mind of the studio; it controls the sound-shaping tools and stores and manipulates creative ideas. However much you observed, you'd never really be able to figure out what's going on.*

While Peter leaves the studio for a moment, West turns to talk to me.

"This one is very difficult!" he says again.

"'South Africa on Fire'?" I ask.

Then in Zulu he repeats the same story to Jane, Michael, Joana, and Janet.

*Reshaped each night by the thoughtful inspiration of an artist churning over forms and ideas, the song eludes him in the daylight of everydayness, returning to him only in the interior presence of the studio with its technical facility to realize the nuance of his ideas in sound.*

"Yes, it's difficult! The problem is I never had a cassette to set it up, you see," he explains to the musicians.

Hansford who is hanging around in the studio backs his friend up with intermittent sounds of agreement as West continues.

"Now I was building it up every night. When I get home, I try it, I work on it. Now some things I forget, and [then] remember when I'm here. Eyi! But to put them together—I've laid them down—but to put them together, it's difficult, I'm telling you! This thing is very difficult! It's not easy! Because now I have to open it up [in order to change the patterns again]. And I don't know which spot I'm going to find."

Jane is thirsty. She diverts the conversation and goes to get a cup of tea.

West presents his own creativity as interiorized, elusive, as unending, as part of his artistic personhood, and as an essential part of the production process. As Howard Becker writes, those activities that are regarded as gifted, as requiring an artistic sensibility to conduct them with excellence, are the "core activities" that are taken to distinguish an artwork from industrial product or natural object within the ideology of capital. This distinction is accompanied by certain status and privileges awarded to the artist (Becker 1982, 16). The charisma of the gifted persona, when present in the studio, lends its quality also to the space(s) of artistic production.

West's story notices distinct spaces occupied in the process of creating and producing expression—his head or imagination, the tape, the form of the song itself, which must be opened up again, the interior of the technology. There are tensions that at times fracture these spaces: "it is very difficult" to hold them together and to negotiate the moves between them. For example, West says it would be easier to rework the song in conjunction with hearing the cassette, albeit a demo of poor recording quality. He has to work with Peter "to find a spot," using the computer. This pull between the self-sufficient interiorized personhood of the artist and factors external to him or her that need to be negotiated is always present in the production process.[7]

*Stand by, I'm dropping this in ... .*

*I want to listen in in the studio one day. West hesitates. 'Because we are composing,' he says. As if by witnessing his compositional process I would intrude too far into his creative interior; as if I then might expose and disseminate his artistic secrets and thereby publicly deconstruct his aura, lay him open to imitation, and diminish his uniqueness.*[8] *He defers to the others sitting around the canteen table. 'Why of course she can come in,' answers Hansford. 'She's part of the family!' 'Do you like* ipapa nembuzi*?'*

It is in the momentary merging of these spaces—the mind roving into the song, the song into the mind or into the figurative and literal spaces in the machine and on the tape—as well as in the fracturing of these spaces and in the movement between them that creativity resides.

## Notes

1. For description of the structural details of soundproofing, see Munro 1994; Burd 1994; Huber and Runstein 1995; and Nardantonio 1990.
2. See again Munro 1994; Burd 1994; Huber and Runstein 1995; and Nardantonio 1990 for technical specification. The amount of leak-through is also affected by the choice of microphone and the settings selected on it, which determine the shape and dimensions of its pick-up pattern.
3. There are, of course, variations in the ideal specifications of the acoustic environment of recording booths versus the control room in terms of ambient noise, sound isolation, absorbency, and acoustic character. Additionally, those specifications are also in part determined by the type of recording project for which the studio is principally constructed. However, preference for a dry environment holds as a general principle, especially for productions and musics that are aesthetically engaged with the technological manipulation of sound.
4. Here my generalization glosses over the differences in aural skill of different kinds of music-makers. Sound engineers' ears, for example, are trained and developed in a particular way, notably to listen analytically to the minutiae of timbre and separation, whereas musicians often do not pick up these differences per se. Tensions over discrepancies in aurality do arise during studio sessions. They are often expressed as judgments of another's musicality. Tom Porcello's recounting of a troubled wind quintet session in a studio in San Marcos, Texas, illustrates the communicative

complexities and value judgments that arise from discrepancies in aural points of reference (Porcello 1996, 191–228).

5. In most mbaqanga and trad sessions I witnessed, two bass lines were recorded simultaneously: a DI line inserted directly into the console and a mike line set up at the bass amp. The two were either combined in the mix or the miked track was discarded. The mike line could be used as a backup while it acted as a means of reassuring bass players, used to recording their music via their amps, that the sound engineer knew what was appropriate to the music.
6. He is referring to a demo cassette. Isigqi had given him a copy of a tape I recorded during rehearsal. Few groups have the opportunity or budget to produce professional demo tapes of their songs.
7. The tension is further troubled by the difficulties of rendering matters of musical hearing and sound into speech.
8. Composition of his own work is qualitatively different from production, in terms of his desire for protection and privacy. West was altogether more hesitant about my taping in the control room than other producers I asked. He deferred to Isigqi's executive producer, Ali Mpofu, when I requested permission to tape Isigqi's production—the only studio production I taped with West, although I was present at many of his other sessions.

## Bibliography


Alten, Stanley R. (1986), *Audio in Media*, 2nd edn, Belmont: Wadsworth Publishing.

Becker, Howard (1982), *Art Worlds*, Berkeley: University of California Press.

Bendix, Regina (2000), "The Pleasures of the Ear: Toward an Ethnography of Listening." *Cultural Analysis* 1. Available online at: http://socrates.berkeley.edu/~caforum/.

Burd, Alex (1994), "Studio Acoustics," in J. Borwick (ed.) *Sound Recording Practice*, 4th edn, Oxford: Oxford University Press.

Feld, Steve (1996), "Waterfalls of Song: An Acoustemology of Place Resounding in Bosavi, Papua New Guinea," in S. Feld and K. H. Basso (eds), *Senses of Place*, 91–135, Santa Fe, NM: School of American Research.

Huber, David Miles and Robert E. Runstein (1995), *Modern Recording Techniques*, 4th edn, Indianpolis: Howard W. Sams.

Keil, Charles and Steve Feld (1994), *Music Grooves*, Chicago: University of Chicago Press.

Minh-Ha, Trinh T. (1991), *When the Moon Waxes Red: Representation, Gender, and Cultural Politics*, New York: Routledge.

Munro, Andy (1994), "Studio Planning and Installation," in J. Borwich (ed.), *Sound Recording Practice*, 4th edn, Oxford: Oxford University Press.

Nardantonio, Dennis (1990), *Sound Studio Production Techniques*. 1st edn, Blue Ridge Summit, PA: TAB Books.

Porcello, Thomas (1996), "Sonic Artistry: Music Discourse, and Technology in the Sound Recording Studio". Ph.D. diss., University of Texas at Austin.

Schutz, Alfred (1967), *The Phenomenology of the Social World*, Chicago: Northwestern University Press.

Stoller, Paul (1989), *The Taste of Ethnographic Things: The Senses in Anthropology*, Philadelphia: University of Pennsylvania Press.

Taussig, Michael (1993), *Mimesis and Alterity: A Particular History of the Senses*, New York: Routledge.

# CHAPTER 10
# ON WEAVING A BASKET
*Tim Ingold*

Artefacts are made, organisms grow: at first glance the distinction seems obvious enough. But behind the distinction, as I aim to show in this chapter, lie a series of highly problematic assumptions concerning mind and nature, interiority and exteriority, and the genesis of form. We have only to consider the artefactual status of such an everyday object as a basket to realise that the difference between making and growing is by no means as obvious as we might have thought. I shall begin this chapter by showing that the reasons why the basket confounds our expectations of the nature of the artefact stem from the fact that it is woven. If the basket is an artefact, and if artefacts are made, then weaving must be a modality of making. I want to suggest, to the contrary, that we should understand making as a modality of weaving. This switch of emphasis, I believe, could open up a new perspective not just on basketry in particular, but on all kinds of skilled, form-generating practices. But it would also have the effect of softening the distinction between artefacts and living things which, as it turns out, are not so very different after all.

## Making and growing

What is implied about artefacts by their characterisation as things that are made rather than things that grow? First of all, a division is assumed between form and substance, that is between the design specifications of the object and the raw materials of which it is composed. In the case of living things, it is supposed that the information specifying the design of an organism is carried in the materials of heredity, the genes, and thus that every new life-cycle is inaugurated with the injection of this specification into a physical medium. But with artefacts, this relation between form and substance is inverted. Form is said to be applied from without, rather than unveiled from within. The very distinction between a within and a without of things, however, implies the existence of a *surface*, where solid substance meets the space of action of those forces that impinge upon it. Thus the world of substance – of brute matter – must present itself to the maker of artefacts as a surface to be transformed.

In commonsense, practical terms, this is not hard to imagine. Many of our most familiar artefacts are (or were, before the days of synthetic materials) made of more or less solid stuff such as stone, metal, wood or clay. The very usefulness of these objects depends on their being relatively resistant to deformation. We ourselves, however, inhabit a gaseous medium – air – which, offering no such resistance, not only allows complete freedom of movement, but also transmits both light and sound. Quite apart from the obvious fact that we need air to breathe, and thus simply to stay alive, the possibilities of movement and perception (visual and aural) that air affords are crucial for any artefact-producing activity. There is, then, a pretty clear distinction between the gaseous medium that surrounds us and the solid objects that clutter our environment; moreover the patterns of reflected light off the surfaces of these objects enable us to see them for what they are (Gibson 1979: 16–22).

These practical considerations, however, all too easily become confused in our thinking with speculations of a more metaphysical kind. To show why this is so, consider the case of the beehive. Is this an artefact or not? Surely, hives don't grow. Insofar as it results from the application of exterior force to raw material, the hive would appear to be as much 'bee-made' as the human house is 'man-made'. Or is it? Musing on this question, Karl Marx famously came to the conclusion that 'what from the very first distinguishes the most incompetent architect from the best of bees, is that the architect has built a cell in his head before he constructs it in wax'. In other words, the criterion by which the house is truly artificial – and by comparison the beehive only figuratively so – is that it issues from a representation or 'mental model' which has been fashioned in the imagination of the practitioner prior to its execution in the material. We may assume that bees, by contrast, lack the powers of imagination, and have no more conception of their hives than they do of their own bodies, both of which are formed under genetic control (Ingold 1983, cf. Marx 1930: 169–70).

Here, the exteriority of the forces that shape artefacts is understood in quite another sense, in terms not of the physical separation of gaseous medium and solid substance but of the *meta*physical separation of mind and nature. Unlike the forms of animals and plants, established through the evolutionary mechanism of natural selection and installed genetically at the heart of the organisms themselves (in the nucleus of every cell), the forms of artefacts are supposed to have their source within the human mind, as preconceived, intellectual solutions to particular design problems. And whereas organic growth is envisaged as a process that goes on *within* nature, and that serves to reveal its inbuilt architecture, in the making of artefacts the mind is understood to place its ideal forms *upon* nature. If making thus means the imposition of conceptual form on inert matter, then the surface of the artefact comes to represent much more than an interface between solid substance and gaseous medium; rather it becomes the very surface of the material world of nature as it confronts the creative human mind.

This is precisely the kind of view that lies at the back of the minds of anthropologists and archaeologists when they speak of artefacts as items of so-called 'material culture'. The last thing they mean to suggest, in resorting to this phrase, is that in the manufactured object the domains of culture and materiality somehow overlap or intermingle. For nothing about their substantive composition *per se* qualifies artefacts for inclusion within culture. The materials from which they are made – wood, stone, clay or whatever – are in any case generally available in nature. Even with objects manufactured from synthetic materials for which no naturally occurring counterparts exist, their status as items of material culture is in no way conditional upon their 'unnatural' composition. A child's toy made of plastic is no more cultural, on that account, than its wooden equivalent. It is the form of the artefact, not its substance, that is attributed to culture. This is why, in the extensive archaeological and anthropological literature on material culture, so little attention is paid to actual materials and their properties. The emphasis is almost entirely on issues of meaning and form – that is, on culture *as opposed* to materiality. Understood as a realm of discourse, meaning and value inhabiting the collective consciousness, culture is conceived to hover over the material world but not to permeate it. In this view, in short, culture and materials do not mix; rather, culture wraps itself around the universe of material things, shaping and transforming their outward surfaces without ever penetrating their interiority. Thus the particular surface of every artefact participates in the impenetrable surface of materiality itself as it is enveloped by the cultural imagination.

## Surface, force and the generation of form

Let us consider the most ordinary of everyday objects, one that crops up in a surprising range and variety of cultural settings around the world: a coiled basket. Has the basket been created through working on the surface of some raw material? Have the forces impacting on this surface been applied from without? Did they serve to impress onto the material a pre-existent, conceptual design? In every case, as I show below, the answer is 'Not exactly'. Thus the basket is not 'made' in the sense in which we normally understand the term. Nor, evidently, has it grown of its own accord. Thus neither of the available alternatives seem to work for the basket. It does not fit our stereotype of the artefact, and it is not a life-form. Let us start instead from the simple observation that constructing a basket is a process of weaving. In what follows, I shall consider what weaving entails, respectively, with regard to the topology of *surface*, the application of *force* and the generation of *form*.

We have seen that making, in what for convenience I shall henceforth call the 'standard view', implies the prior presence of a surface to be transformed. Thus the flint knapper chips away at the surface of stone, the carpenter carves and chisels the surface of wood, the blacksmith hammers on the surface of molten metal, and the potter applies manual pressure to the surface of clay. But once it has been cut and prepared for weaving, the basket-maker does nothing to the surface of her fibrous material. In the process of weaving, the surface of the basket is not so much transformed as built up. Moreover, there is no simple or straightforward correspondence between the surface of the basket and the surfaces of its constituent fibres. For example, the two outer surfaces of the transverse wrapping fibres that stitch successive loops of the coil are alternately 'outside' and 'inside' so far as the surface of the basket is concerned. Indeed it is in the nature of weaving, as a technique, that it produces a peculiar kind of surface that does not, strictly speaking, have an inside and an outside at all.

Basketry, involves the bending and interweaving of fibres that may exert a considerable resistance of their own. Indeed the basket holds together, and assumes a rigid form, precisely because of its tensile structure.[1] In short, the form of the basket is the result of a play of forces, both internal and external to the material that makes it up. One could say that the form unfolds within a kind of force field, in which the weaver is caught up in a reciprocal and quite muscular dialogue with the material.

This point leads me to the final question concerning the generation of form. According to the standard view, the form pre-exists in the maker's mind, and is simply impressed upon the material. Now I do not deny that the basket-maker may begin work with a pretty clear idea of the form she wishes to create. The actual, concrete form of the basket, however, does not issue from the idea. It rather comes into being through the gradual unfolding of that field of forces set up through the active and sensuous engagement of practitioner and material. This field is neither internal to the material nor internal to the practitioner (hence external to the material); rather, it cuts across the emergent interface between them. Effectively, the form of the basket emerges through a pattern of *skilled movement*, and it is the rhythmic repetition of that movement that gives rise to the regularity of form. This point was made long ago by Franz Boas, in his classic work on *Primitive Art*.

> The basketmaker who manufactures a coiled basket, handles the fibres composing the coil in such a way that the greatest evenness of coil diameter results ... In making her stitches the automatic control of the left hand that lays down the coil, and of the right that pulls the binding stitches over the coil brings it about that the distances between the stitches and the strength of the pull are absolutely even so that the surface will be smooth and evenly rounded and that the stitches show a perfectly regular pattern. (Boas 1955 [1927]: 20)

## Spirals in nature and art

Boas illustrates the point with a drawing, which I reproduce here (Figure 10.1a). Opposite, I have placed another drawing, this time taken from the work of the great biologist D'Arcy Wentworth Thompson, *On Growth and Form* (Figure 10.1b). It depicts the shell of a certain kind of gastropod. Although both the coiled basket and the shell have a characteristic spiral form, they are spirals of different kinds: the first is an equable spiral, the second logarithmic (that is, the radius of each successive whorl increases arithmetically in the one instance, and geometrically in the other). The equable spiral, as Thompson explains, is characteristic of artificial forms that have been produced by mechanically bending, coiling or rolling up a given length of material, whereas the logarithmic spiral is commonly produced in nature as a result of growth by deposition, where the material is cumulatively laid down at one end whilst maintaining an overall constancy of proportion (Thompson 1961 [1917]: 179–9). Either way, however, the form appears to emerge with a certain logical inevitability from the process itself, of rolling up in the former case and laying down in the latter.

Just as organic form is generated in the unfolding of the morphogenetic field, so the form of the artefact evolves within what I have called a field of forces. Both kinds of field cut across the developing interface between the object (organism or artefact) and an environment which, in the case of the artefact, critically includes its 'maker'. Where the organism engages its environment in the process of ontogenetic development, the artefact engages its maker in a pattern of skilled activity. These are truly creative engagements, in the sense that they actually *give rise* to the real-world artefactual and organic forms that we encounter, rather than serving – as the standard view would claim – to transcribe pre-existent form onto raw material. It is therefore no longer possible to sustain the distinction between form and substance that, as we have seen, is so central to the standard view of making things. Finally, the templates, measures and rules of thumb of the artisan or craftsman no more add up to a design for the artefacts he produces than do genes constitute a blueprint for the organism. Like genes, they set the parameters of the process but do not prefigure the form.[2]

All these points apply to the making of a coiled basket. Thus the equable form of the spiral base of the basket does not follow the dictates of any design; it is not imposed upon the material but arises through the work itself. Indeed the developing form acts as its own template, since each turn of the spiral is made by laying the longitudinal fibres along the edge formed by the preceding one. Now D'Arcy Thompson was of course right to point out

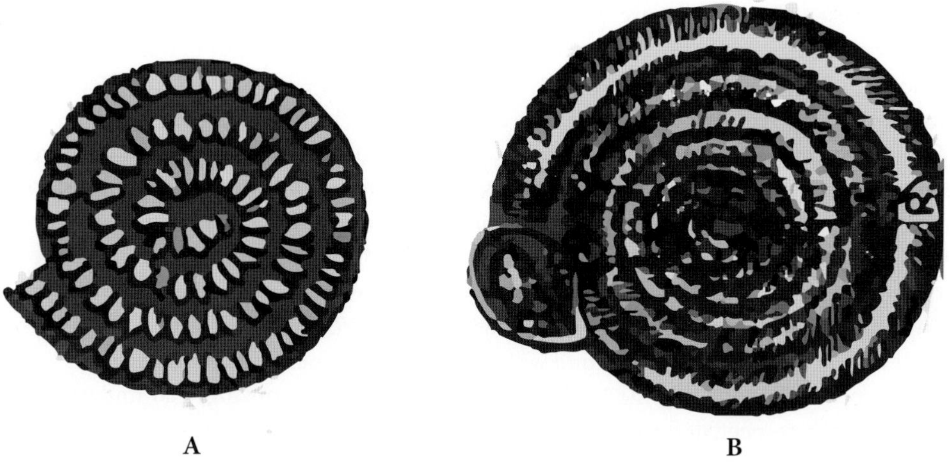

Figure 10.1 Artefactual and natural spirals. (a) Coiled basketry. From F. Boas, *Primitive Art*, published by Dover Publications, 1955 [1927], 20. (b) Gastropod shell. The angle α is known as the 'spiral angle', which in this case is large. From D. W. Thompson, *On Growth and Form*, published by Cambridge University Press, 1961 [1917], 192.

that there is a difference between *bending* material into shape, as in basketry, and an organism's *growing* into it, as with the shell of the gastropod, and that this can lead to forms with contrasting mathematical properties. Nevertheless, if the unfolding of the morphogenetic field is described as a process of growth, would it not be fair to suggest that there is a sense in which artefacts, whose forms likewise evolve within a field of forces, 'grow' too – albeit according to different principles?

We could describe that growth as a process of *autopoiesis*, that is, the self-transformation over time of the system of relations within which an organism or artefact comes into being. Since the artisan is involved in the same system as the material with which he works, so his activity does not transform that system but is – like the growth of plants and animals – part and parcel of the system's transformation of itself. Through this autopoietic process, the temporal rhythms of life are gradually built into the structural properties of things – or as Boas put it, with regard to artefacts:

> The rhythm of time appears here translated into space. In the flaking, adzing, hammering, in the regular turning and pressing required in the making of coiled pottery, in weaving, regularity of form and rhythmic repetition of the same movement are necessarily connected. (Boas 1955 [1927]: 40)

The artefact, in short, is the crystallisation of activity within a relational field, its regularities of form embodying the regularities of movement that gave rise to it.

I would like to conclude this comparison of the coiled basket and the gastropod shell by commenting on the reasons for the remarkable durability of their respective forms. According to the standard view, since form emanates from design, the persistence of form can only be explained in terms of the stability of the underlying design specifications. In the case of the organism these specifications are genetic, in the case of the artefact they are cultural. The constancy of form is thus a function of the fidelity with which genetic or cultural information is copied from one generation to the next, combined with the effects of natural selection – or its analogue in the realm of cultural ideas – in weeding out less well-adapted variants.

The argument I have proposed here, however, is just the opposite. If forms are the outcomes of dynamic, morphogenetic processes, then their stability can be understood in terms of the generative principles embedded in the material conditions of their production. For the shell the principle is one of invariant proportion; for the basket it is the principle that every increment of longitudinal extension is coupled to what has gone before by transverse attachment. Whereas the first principle, through simple iteration, will always and everywhere generate a logarithmic spiral, the second will just as reliably generate an equable one. It is these generative principles, and not the fidelity of genetic or cultural copying, that underwrite the constancy of the respective forms, and explain their persistence over immense spans of both historical and evolutionary time.

## Making as a way of weaving

I now return to my earlier suggestion, that we reverse our normal order of priorities and regard making as a modality of weaving, rather than the other way around.

The notion of making, of course, defines an activity purely in terms of its capacity to yield a certain object, whereas weaving focuses on the character of the process by which that object comes into existence. To emphasise making is to regard the object as the expression of an idea; to emphasise weaving is to regard it as the embodiment of a rhythmic movement. Therefore to invert making and weaving is also to invert idea and movement, to see the movement as truly generative of the object rather than merely revelatory of an object that is already present, in an ideal, conceptual or virtual form, in advance of the process that discloses it. The more that objects are removed from the contexts of life-activity in which they are produced and used – the more they appear as static objects of disinterested contemplation (as in museums and galleries) – the more, too, the process disappears or is hidden behind the product, the finished object. Thus we are inclined to look for the meaning of the object in the idea it expresses rather than in the current of activity to which it properly and originally belongs. It is precisely this contemplative attitude that leads to the redesignation of the ordinary objects of the quotidian environment as items of 'material culture' whose significance lies not so much in their incorporation into a habitual pattern of use as in their symbolic function. In suggesting that the relation between making and weaving be overturned, my purpose is to bring these products of human activity back to life, to restore them to the processes in which they, along with their users, are absorbed.[3]

In what way, then, does weaving epitomise human technical activity? What sense does it make to say that the blacksmith in his forge, or the carpenter at his bench, in transforming the surfaces of metal and wood respectively, is actually weaving? Of course, to adopt this idiom is to interpret the notion of weaving more broadly than is customary. It does however help to draw attention to three points about skill which are exemplified in basketry but which are nevertheless common to the practice of any craft. First, the practitioner operates within a field of forces set up through his or her engagement with the material; secondly, the work does not merely involve the mechanical application of external force but calls for care, judgement and dexterity; and thirdly, the action has a narrative quality, in the sense that every movement, like every line in a story, grows rhythmically out of the one before and lays the groundwork for the next.

The forms of objects are not imposed from above but grow from the mutual involvement of people and materials in an environment. The surface of nature is thus an illusion: the blacksmith, carpenter or potter – just as much as the basket-maker – works from within the world, not upon it. There are surfaces of course, but these divide states of matter, not matter from mind. And they emerge within the form-generating process, rather than pre-existing as a condition for it.

The philosopher Martin Heidegger expressed the very same point through an exploration of the notions of building and dwelling. Opposing the modernist convention that dwelling is an activity that goes on within, and is structured by, an environment that is already built, Heidegger argued that we cannot engage in any kind of building activity unless we already dwell within our surroundings. 'Only if we are capable of dwelling', he declared, 'only then can we build' (1971: 160). Now dwelling is to building, in Heidegger's terms, as weaving is to making in mine. Where making (like building) comes to an end with the completion of a work in its final form, weaving (like dwelling) continues for as long as life goes on – punctuated but not terminated by the appearance of the pieces that it successively brings into being.[4] Dwelling in the world, in short, is tantamount to the ongoing, temporal interweaving of our lives with one another and with the manifold constituents of our environment.

The world of our experience is, indeed, continually and endlessly coming into being around us as we weave. If it has a surface, it is like the surface of the basket: it has no 'inside' or 'outside'. Mind is not above, nor nature below; rather, if we ask where mind is, it is in the weave of the surface itself. And it is within this weave that our projects of making, whatever they may be, are formulated and come to fruition. Only if we are capable of weaving, only then can we make.

## Notes

1. To adopt an architectural term, the coherence of the basket is based upon the principle of *tensegrity*, according to which a system can stabilise itself mechanically by distributing and balancing counteracting forces of compression and tension throughout the structure. Significantly, tensegrity structures are common to both artefacts and living organisms, and are encountered in the latter at every level from the cytoskeletal architecture of the cell to the bones, muscles, tendons and ligaments of the whole body (Ingber 1998).
2. In a wonderful article on the building of the great cathedral of Chartres, in the thirteenth century, David Turnbull (1993) shows that this most magnificent of human artefacts was preceded by no plan whatsoever. The building took shape gradually, over a considerable period of time, through the labour of many groups of workers with diverse skills, whose activities were loosely co-ordinated by the use of templates, string and constructive geometry.
3. I do not intend by this to reinstate the time-worn opposition between practical utility and symbolic meaning. The notion of utility implied by this opposition is an impoverished one that sets up a radical division between the acting subject and the object used, and reduces skilled practice to purely mechanical relations of cause and effect. In speaking of the *absorption* of artefacts into the life-activity of their users my aim is to emphasise, to the contrary, the

inseparability of persons and objects in real-life contexts of accustomed (that is, usual) practice. The usefulness of an object, then, lies not in its possession of utility but in its partaking of the *habituality* of everyday life (Gosden 1994: 11).

4. Among the Bunu, a Yoruba-speaking people of central Nigeria, this idea is expressed in their weaving of lengths of white cloth:

> Cloths are often removed [from the loom] without cutting, accentuating the endless quality of these pieces. When eventually the unwoven warp is cut in order to use the cloth, the fringes are left, again suggesting continuity rather than the finiteness of cut and hemmed edges. (Renne 1991: 715)

## References

Boas, F. (1955 [1927]), *Primitive Art*, New York: Dover Publications.
Gibson, J. J. (1979), *The Ecological Approach to Visual Perception*, Boston: Houghton Mifflin.
Gosden, C. (1994), *Social Being and Time*. Oxford: Blackwell.
Heidegger, M. (1971), *Poetry, Language, Thought*, trans. A. Hofstadter, New York: Harper and Row.
Ingber, D. E. (1998), 'The Architecture of Life'. *Scientific American* 278 (1): 30–9.
Ingold, T. (1983), 'The Architect and the Bee: Reflections on the Work of Animals and Men'. *Man* (N.S.) 18: 1–20.
Marx, K. (1930 [1867]), *Capital*, vol. I, trans. E. and C. Paul from 4th German edn of *Das Kapital* (1890), London: Dent.
Renne, E. P. (1991), 'Water, Spirits and Plain White Cloth'. *Man* 26: 709–22.
Thompson, D. W. (1961 [1917]), *On Growth and Form*, abridged edn, ed. J. T. Bonner, Cambridge: Cambridge University Press.
Turnbull, D. (1993), 'The Ad Hoc Collective Work of Building Gothic Cathedrals with Templates, String and Geometry'. *Science, Technology and Human Values* 18: 315–40.

# CHAPTER 11
## PERFORMING L.A.
*Marina Peterson*

"Code of the Streets," the fourth song in *Gang Starr Remix,* starts with the strings. The violins play sustained half-note chords that descend by half-steps. The cellos play a part that is a combination of the drum beat and the bass line of the original. The physicality of playing an acoustic instrument and the musical technology remain intertwined through processes of learning and performing the parts. The drummer, who also started at the top, brings the bass drum in at the fifth bar. A DJ scratches a record, making a high sound that comes in every few bars. In the cello part, two bars repeat, but the fourth time the pattern changes and there is a rest where the first time the note was held.

We practiced the part in rehearsals. Double G played the loop of the original recording for us. He emphasized the rest, telling us how the note should have as clear an end as a beginning. We were supposed to match the sound of the MPC. The Akai MPC 2000 has been one of the most desirable sampler/sequencers for hip-hop producers. It was a coveted item among the aspiring L.A. hip-hop artists interviewed by Shaw in *Westside* (2002). Schloss (2004) describes how the emergence of samplers allowed hip-hop artists to do what they had been doing with records and turntables in a more controlled and extended manner. Now breaks and other material could be sampled and sequenced, reworked and combined with other material to create beats and hip-hop tracks. The MPC has a specific sound and, like other samplers, repeats the same material identically every time. As Double G explained, the MPC sampler "just generates a sample, so no matter how hard you hit the pad it's the same exact attack every time. By the same token, it has the exact same release because it's the duration of the sound. You're basically trying to play the exact same thing every time." This repetition and a particular sound he characterized as "hka, hka, hka" are integral to hip-hop tracks. Translating this sound to live performance takes discipline, he said. But "it's a different kind of discipline. It's not a discipline of technical virtuosity or anything like that. It's almost a more tai chi approach to music. You have to have the same exact attack every single time." Playing the sound of the drum machine on acoustic instruments requires a particular frame of mind and an understanding of what he is aiming for: "It's real, if you're not into it with that mind-set, it's real fucking boring, 'cause it's the same shit over and over again, but once people understand what I'm trying to do, people are like, oh, that's what he's trying to do."

We repeated the part over and over, trying to match the sound of the MPC we heard on the recording. This meant using no vibrato and working with our bow arm to articulate the beginning, middle, and end of the notes in a uniform way. There should be no audible attack at the beginning, no decay through the note, and a clear cutoff of sound at the end. Our right arms had to stay active and engaged, held more rigidly than usual. We were trying to do what Schloss argues is impossible, "for those who have been educated in this aesthetic, a beat created with live instrumentation alone can lack a sense of purpose, urgency, and direction; it has no center. At the same time, it also lacks boundaries" (2004: 69). Working on the sound production alone was not enough to create the correct sound. Double G was unhappy with the fact that our instruments rang during the rest. "Damp the sound," he said. So we put our hands over the string we were playing, which were the G and C strings, respectively, for the first and second cello parts. They still rang. It was our D strings, which, open, resonated with the D from whichever string we were playing it on. So we covered all the strings with our fingers together, making a paw of our left hand. This worked, and we moved on. Later, in rehearsals and performances, when Double G wanted to remind us to play like an MPC, he would jab his finger at an imaginary waist-high drum machine, each jab indicating an identical, rhythmic impact to the one before and after.

Through the process of learning to make a cello sound like a drum machine we were engaging in and producing musical meaning. As classically trained cellists attempting to replicate the sound of a sampler, we were embodying another musical world with a distinct aesthetics, politics, and history. Music is always embodied: the phrase that tears at your heart is created by a physical gesture or a pause in a vocalization. In learning "technique" musicians are also embodying a musical history with particular aesthetics of phrasing and articulation. When there is an apparent seamlessness between the instrument and the genre the phrasing appears "natural," somehow unworked or unplanned. In "crossing over" and playing a genre with an instrument from another tradition, the work of musicality can become apparent in that disjuncture. As string players playing drum beats, we helped situate daKAH as a hip-hop orchestra in which both aspects were present, with hip-hop found in the beat and orchestra in the instrument.

Instruments have residues of social histories that contribute to their perceived associations (Qureshi 2000). Yet as with musical genre, instruments can mean different things in different contexts. In the case of daKAH, sedimented meanings associated with the physicality of the European classical instrument and the sound of those instruments carry across genre, giving a sociomusical status to the ensemble that does not depend on the musical material played on those instruments. Audience responses to daKAH indicate how musical genres are made through both aural and visual recognition. Seeing and hearing strings, bassoon, and pedal harp help legitimize the ensemble for those who might be turned off by a group playing only electronic instruments or turntables. For daKAH, this is the means by which Grand Performances' desired older—or classical—audience is drawn to the performance, helping mitigate criticisms of hip-hop that focus on the lack of traditional instruments: "Those who are critical of hip-hop have never been shy about equating the lack of live instrumentation with a lack of musical quality … . Such critics seem to operate from a sense that the use of live instrumentation is self-evidently superior to the use of samples" (Schloss 2004: 76).

Having European classical orchestral instruments onstage invokes associations of taste, musical legitimacy, and, in particular, virtuosity, which has become a defining feature of live performance and an evaluatory measure in the context of electronic technology. An audience member articulated a heightened version of this perspective, saying, "There's something about seeing people do physical things that other people marvel at, and they'll pay to watch people do physical things. It's a wonder to watch a great musician play, to physically execute their skill, to move their fingers across the keyboard, to move the bow across the strings of a violin or finger a clarinet." Seeing hip-hop played on European classical instruments reinforces the effect of virtuosity that has taken on particular significance for evaluating music from the Romantic era onward, with musicians and composers increasing speed and technical difficulty. Now, in order to play the repertoire at the level of the standards that have emerged in part from a century of recorded music, people begin playing orchestral instruments when they are very young and spend many hours practicing to be able to play well. This labor is seemingly conveyed by the sound of the instruments, frequently described as beautiful and expressive.

With daKAH, the visual recognition of the instruments invokes this meaning. Aurally, the expected sound of the instrument is undone in its unexpected parts. In daKAH, strings, winds, and horns most often play a repeated part that follows the aesthetic of the drum machine and the loop: play the same thing exactly the same way each time. The DJs and MCs are the ones directed in the score to display virtuosic skills, the DJs on their turntables and the MCs with words, in the form of good rhymes, a good beat, and sometimes, if they choose to do so, speed. Neither of these displays of virtuosity is visible to audience members. There are no fingers moving fast, no bows blurred by violent string crossings. Instead, the turntables are placed flat on the table, and the only visible movement is of the DJ pressing his head to one side of the headphones; his virtuosity—like that of the MCs—is aural. This musical crossover disrupts a simple mapping of social group and genre, complicating the Bourdieuian taste categories on which generational musical-social correlations depend.

## Bibliography


Qureshi, Regula (2000), “How Does Music Mean? Embodied Memories and the Politics of Affect in the Indian *Sarangi*.” *American Ethnologist* 27 (4): 805–38.

Schloss, Joseph G. (2004), *Making Beats: The Art of Sample-Based Hip-Hop*, Middletown, CT: Wesleyan University Press.

Shaw, William (2002), *Westside: The Coast-to-Coast Explosion of Hip Hop in L.A.*, New York: Cooper Square Press.

# CHAPTER 12
## THE 'ART' AND 'SCIENCE' OF HANDCRAFTING CHEESE IN THE UNITED STATES
*Heather Paxson*

Here is a deceptively basic recipe for making cheese: heat milk; sour it by adding bacterial cultures that convert milk sugar (lactose) to lactic acid; add an enzyme (such as rennet) to coagulate the fermenting milk. Once the milk has set into a gel-like substance, use long blades to cut the curd into pieces, separating out the watery whey. Mold and salt the curds. Endless variations on this theme – from choice of goat's, sheep's, or cow's milk, to selection of added bacterial cultures, to timing the steps of the cheesemaking process, to consuming a cheese while fresh or after having aged for months or even years – result in hundreds of varieties of cheese. But what distinguishes an *artisanal* cheese from its industrial counterpart?

Artisan cheesemaking is flourishing in the United States, with the number of artisan producers more than doubling, to near 450, since 2000. According to the American Cheese Society, a non-profit organization of small-scale manufacturers, academic consultants, retailers, and tyrophiles:

> The word 'artisan' or 'artisanal' implies that a cheese is produced primarily by hand, in small batches, with particular attention paid to the tradition of the cheesemaker's art, and thus using as little mechanization as possible in the production of the cheese.[1]

In this formulation, attention to a tradition of cheesemaking art is said to obviate reliance on mechanization. At the same time, open-ended qualifiers – *primarily* (not exclusively) by hand, in *small* (how small?) batches – acknowledge that artisan cheeesmaking is not strictly artistic. As anthropologists Deborah Heath and Anne Meneley argue, contemporary artisan foods rely solidly on technoscience, a modern arena of practice that 'transcends the conventional association of science with knowledge and technology with manual production'.[2] Very few cheesemakers today eschew the enhanced predictability of seeding milk with freeze-dried, laboratory-isolated strains of known bacterial cultures. At the same time, microbiological assessment of pathogenic risk guides scrupulous hygienic practice in milking parlors and cheese rooms.

Here, I draw from participant-observation in cheesemaking workshops and from ethnographic interviews with American artisan and farmstead producers to explore how cheesemakers perceive and seek to enact a balance of art and science in producing safe, recognizable, yet distinctively artisanal cheese. Between 2004 and 2008 I interviewed forty-four cheesemakers, representing roughly one-tenth of artisan operations in the US, during site-visits to cheesemaking dairy farms and creameries in California, Wisconsin, and New England.[3] What it means to negotiate art and science provides much of the vocabulary through which cheesemakers struggle to articulate the tacit elements of their craft. This calls attention to the hybrid constitution and ambivalent status of artisanship in an industrial era, an ambivalence that is most clearly defined in the marketplace. While keen to open niche markets exploring new tastes, the U.S. cheese market comes with high expectations for product consistency and decidedly low tolerance for risk of food-borne illness. Although cheesemakers often speak of their own and their colleagues' inclinations towards either the art or the science end of things as a matter of personal inclination, artisan subjects are inescapably constituted within regulatory and market formations.

## Between art and science: Developing a feel for the curd

Inescapably, artisanal cheese is defined against the industrial: according to the American Cheese Society (quoted above) it is made more by hand than by machine, in small batches compared to industrial scales of production, using recipes and techniques developed through the practical knowledge of previous artisans rather than the technical knowledge of dairy scientists and industrial engineers. Designer David Pye's distinction between craftsmanship and ordinary (i.e. industrial) manufacture adds analytic legibility to this opposition. Whereas industrial manufacture ensures a certain, standardized outcome, in craftsmanship, according to Pye, 'the quality of the result is not predetermined, but depends on the judgment, dexterity, and care which the maker exercises as he works'.[4] Craftsmanship entails a 'workmanship of risk' in which product quality is 'continually at risk' throughout the manufacturing process. Such risk can be introduced from human error or from flaws occurring in the raw materials used. Industrial manufacturing seeks to obviate both sets of errors by deskilling production and by standardizing materials.

Industrial cheesemaking today refers to a fully automated process of computer-aided manufacturing. Recipes are programmed into computers and cheesemaking proceeds uninterrupted, according to a pre-scripted plan, in closed vats that restrict milk and curd from view (let alone smell, feel, or taste). Factory workers attend the transformation of milk into cheese at a hygienic remove while cheesemaking knowledge and skill materialize away from the factory floor, in research and design and in quality control. To begin, industrial processing filters out organic variables by denaturing milk: pasteurizing it to kill off microorganisms, standardizing butterfat content, and homogenizing the size of fat globules – and, before that, breeding animals year-round to blend early/late lactation milk.[5] Industrial cheese looks, feels, and tastes the same from one batch to the next in large part because so much work goes into standardizing the milk used from one batch to the next – and because quality control imposes uniformity on the finished product. Inconsistent batches are melted down to be reconstituted as processed products.

Making cheese 'by hand' is a tricky, uncertain business. The 'tradition of the cheesemaker's art' to which the American Cheese Society contrasts industrial automation reaches back to the pre-industrial practice of farm women who transformed their cows' perishable milk into cheese as a matter of routine domestic labor, whether or not they enjoyed proficiency in the art of their highly particular, idiosyncratic craft. Then, as now, handmade cheese is of varying quality. The apparent arbitrariness of farm-women's cheesemaking success was precisely what the nineteenth-century advent of centralized cheese factories meant to overcome, while the efficacy of tacit knowledge in the hands of an especially skilled cheesemaker is what twenty-first-century reformers, like their nineteenth-century counterparts, strive to capture through objective means.[6]

Artisan cheese begins with minimally treated milk. It may be and often is made from pasteurized (heat-treated) milk, but otherwise milk is rarely homogenized or standardized and is often produced by animals bred seasonally. I have visited farmstead operations where warm milk flows from udders directly into the cheese vat. Milk composition is affected by animal fodder and health, as well as by climatic and weather conditions.[7] 'Seasonality' in cheese may be expressed through shifts in biochemical composition between early and late lactation milk, as well as through beta-carotein and butterfat levels influenced by the fresh hay, pasture grasses, and browse eaten by cows, sheep, or goats. Cheesemakers respond to and work with milk as a dynamic substance. As milk changes, artisan cheesemaking changes. Echoing Pye, a seasoned Wisconsin cheesemaker said this about his work: 'It's something that you got to keep the constant watch on to make a consistent product. There's more room for error because you're doing it yourself instead of being mechanized. That, to me, I think is one of the biggest factors of being artisanal'.

Inherent to artisan cheesemaking is a tension between allowing natural variation to flourish and maintaining sufficient control over fermentation and ripening such that the end result is a recognizable, safe, and tasty food. Dairy scientist Paul Kindstedt puts it this way: 'The challenge for the farmstead cheesemaker is to strike the right balance between art and science. The goal should be to achieve the appropriate level of control to ensure safety and consistently high quality while at the same time giving nature enough free rein to encourage the diversity and uniqueness of character that make artisanal cheeses special'.[8] On this view, artisan production entails calibrating one's intervention in fermentation and coagulation at a delicate mid-point between total domination – Pye's 'workmanship of certainty' – and letting bacteria run wild, risking a possible biohazard and/or unpalatable and unmarketable cheese.

To strike this balance artisans learn how to work *with*, rather than against, such 'natural' variations as may be introduced by seasonality, ambient temperature and humidity, herd health, and inconsistency in human practice. The trick, as a Wisconsin cheesemaker said to me, is to: 'observe what happened today and predict it may happen tomorrow, and from those predictions you may make adjustments'. Objective assessment of carefully observed environmental and material conditions – temperature, humidity, milk acidity, curd pH, etc. – and meticulous record keeping (e.g., how much time the curd took to set before being ready to drain from the whey) are crucial because the idea is that one can and will return to these notes to compare observed phenomena from one day to the next, one season to the next, in order to trouble-shoot a failed batch or to reverse-engineer a successful one.[9] In view of practitioners, this objectivism is a key aspect of the 'science' of cheesemaking. Here, artisan and industrial cheesemaking differ more in degree than in kind, with the variables to track more numerous and given more play in artisan manufacture.

Practitioners widely view the complex observational and interpretive process of reading present conditions in light of past experience as ineffable; eventually, moving from observation through evaluation to practice comes to be a matter of tacit knowledge. Consider, by way of analogy, Michael Polanyi's classic example of tacit knowledge: riding a bicycle.[10] A person can successfully ride a bicycle without being able to articulate precisely how or why. Tacit knowledge for Polanyi is an aspect of *techne*, the practical knowledge of how to make or do something, that Aristotle, in *Nichamachean Ethics*, distinguished from *episteme*, or disinterested theoretical knowledge about what something is.

If bike riding is fully embedded in a social milieu, cheesemaking is fully embedded in an entire ecology of activity that scales from the microbial to the human. Myron Olson, a Wisconsin cheesemaker with some thirty years experience, said to me:

> Over the years, [the] milk has changed. The feed that farmers are feeding has changed. During the year, the milk changes. So you've always got to be aware that there are changes that occur. So you look at pHs, you look at the acidities, you look at the make-up of your milk. So you've got to – you can't just have a formula and figure that's going to last you for ten years or until you're ready to retire. If you do, you're not going to be making good cheese. So it is a constant watching, a constant looking.

In order to problem-solve or reverse-engineer a batch of cheese, the artisan engages all his or her senses to interpret and evaluate seemingly objective data.

I call this *synaesthetic reason*, bringing together cross-sensory apprehension with reasoned analysis. From Vermont to California, cheesemakers described the ability to move from observation through interpretation and evaluation to contingent practice as developing 'a feel' for the milk and curd: 'part of the artisan feel of it is knowing your milk, knowing what cultures complement your milk, what rennet compliments your milk, how to manipulate that'. This is knowledge by personal acquaintance, a more particular way of knowing than abstract epistemic knowledge that something is so.[11] Patty Karlin, a small-scale cheesemaker in California, said to me:

> Cheesemaking is a funny thing because any person who is a good cook [can make cheese] – one time… So what goes wrong? The weather changes, the humidity changes. You have to be able to smell, taste, and feel the cheese. Every batch of cheese, I put it into my hands, I squeeze it, and I know [i.e., recognize] by the imprint of my fingers if that's going to be an aged cheese, or a fresh cheese, or a soft cheese … The *curd* for those different cheeses is different. So having that *feeling* is something that is hard to teach.

That feel is metonymic for knowledge generated through nearly all of the senses – sight, smell, touch, taste. Subjective, sensory knowledge is required to make objective knowledge work in craft practice, which is why excellence in artisan skill is described in terms of virtuosity rather than expertise.[12]

Artisan cheesemakers describe the tacit ability to gather and interpret sensory data and apply it practically as the *art* of making cheese. Their embodied practice moves between what is sensed (apprehension through sensory input and subjective evaluation) and what is being sensed (the empirical conditions and materialities that are manipulated through tweaking a recipe but also through prior orchestration of the ecologies of milk production). Art and science represent the subjective and objective angles from which cheesemakers triangulate on the moving target of a particular vat of milk's transformation into cheese on a particular day.

At the heart of what makes artisan cheese artisanal is reflexive, anticipatory practice guided by synaesthetic evaluation of how the materials (milk, curd, cheese) are behaving and developing in a particular instance, as understood in light of past experience.[13] After years of practice, cheesemakers who 'go by feel' may no longer be able to articulate what it is that gives them the feel that it is time to cut the curd or drain the whey.[14] As proficiency is gained, watching and seeing become habituated – not by virtue of repetition, but by acquiring a reflexive feel for strategic action under contingent circumstances. Tacit knowledge cannot be conveyed through brief workshops and consultancies; instead, fledgling cheesemakers acquire objective tools (thermometers, pH meters, spreadsheets) and a weighty appreciation for the interpretive art of making use of such tools – not once, but dynamically over the course of a season or a career.

## Hands and other tools

Artisan cheese is 'hands-on'. But making cheese by hand does not mean working with nothing but one's hands. Tools are required: vats or kettles in which to heat milk and cook curd; paddles or ladles for stirring; knives or other devices with which to cut curd; implements for removing curds from whey; forms or molds for shaping wheels of cheese; weights or presses for expelling whey. Understanding the centrality of synaesthetic reason to artisan cheesemaking helps to adjudicate a contentious question among producers: how much technology might a cheesemaker adopt and still be considered to be working 'by hand'. Does it matter whether a pneumatic press or lengths of PVC tube filled with food-grade salt are used to express whey from curd? Matter to what? To the resulting taste and texture of the cheese? (probably not). To the operation's start-up costs? (decidedly). To the self-identity of the cheesemaker as an artisan? (likely).

Consider the mechanical stirring device. For those who have adopted the labor-saving technology there is no turning back. Commenting on the 16-A battery that powers a stirring arm affixed to his vat, a Vermont cheesemaker told me, 'I'm not going to be out here stirring curd for 45 min. That's my chance to open mail'. Keeping one eye on the thermometer, he can turn his attention to cheese orders, bills, and payments. After years of manual labor the technological promise of alleviating bodily strain gains increasing appeal. Mary Keehn, former back-to-the-lander and founder of Cypress Grove Chevre in Arcata, California, has introduced a number of automated technologies out of concern for her employees' physical well-being as well as a business' owner's imperative to cut costs (including workmen's compensation); as her business expanded her priorities shifted. Today she is less concerned with whether her cheesemaking process still counts as 'artisanal' than in how her business contributes to the community through little-league sponsorship and food donations, and in how it sustains the families of goat dairy famers on the outskirts of town as well as of the Central American employees who pack curd and package wheels of Humboldt Fog. Considering artisanship as a mode of production – a business enterprise entailing many tasks beyond the making of cheese – sheds broader light on artisan practice.

Jon, a Vermont cheesemaker, was looking to upgrade to a mechanized agitator, explaining that hand-stirring curd in his 4000-pound (465 gallon) capacity vat ties up an hour-and-a-half of labor each day – 'While you're stirring, you're thinking about all the things that need to get done' but that you cannot get to being tied to the vat. Yet, 'one thing I really like about [hand-stirring] is that I can really watch the curd, can adjust the rate of stirring'. Diana Murphy, a goat dairy farmer and cheesemaker in Wisconsin, said to me:

> When I make my Feta or my aged cheeses, I have to be at the vat ..., and I have to get up on a stool to get in there, and I have to stir it [using a hand-held paddle] sometimes for

> hours. And I set the stirrer down, and I go get a cup of coffee sometimes, and then you come back and the curd is kinda stuck together. So I would *like* to have a [mechanized] stirrer. But on the other hand, I see part of the beauty of what I'm doing is – everything is by hand. I don't need all this special equipment to do it. And I can still come out with a good cheese.

Jon appreciate[s] stirring with a hand-held paddle because it offers constant, direct engagement with the material being transformed, affording opportunity for reflexive adjustment of speed, vigor, and depth. Karen Weinberg, who raises sheep and makes cheese in eastern New York (and whose family is not as dependent on farm-generated income), enjoys a sensual engagement with curd:

> My single favorite part of the cheese-making process is stirring curd. I love to do that. I put on a tank top, so I can go up to here [tapping her upper arm]. I just love it. Sheep's milk makes really dense, soapy curd, and it's like folding in egg whites: you have to be really gentle in the beginning, and you really get a sense how the curd changes as the temperature rises and as the whey gets expelled from it. It's just a great learning experience, to get to do that. But you can't be doing anything else while you're doing that, so for the twenty minutes or forty minutes, that's it. I find it sort of therapeutic. You know, I can't answer the phone.

Karen enjoys the sensuous feel of the warm, foamy curd on her arms, a tactile experience augmented by the rich, custardy smell of sheep's milk. The rhythmic motion and focused attention of stirring can generate a therapeutic absorption, or 'flow'.[15] But Karen also regards hand-stirring as a learning experience. When artisan hands touch and feel the curd this is as empirical as it is manipulative – something that the veteran Wisconsinites articulated to me most clearly.

When 'hands are in the vat, feeling the curd' – one cheesemaker's streamlined definition of artisanal manufacture – they are not merely accomplishing the manipulation that industrial manufacture effects with robotic machines. Hands are evaluating the curd through touch, feel – grasping in the metaphorical sense of apprehension as well as the tactile sense of holding in one's hand. In determining artisanship, it is less important *what* a cheesemaker uses to stir the curd – a bare arm or plastic paddle or mechanical device – than *how* a cheesemaker determines *when* to begin cutting the curd and when to stop stirring it. Does one go strictly by the clock, according to a fixed recipe? Or does one plunge hands into vat to feel, and evaluate, the 'grip' of the curd?

The enskillment of artisan producers includes learning to use tools in a way that extends the mind/body into the environment.[16] Such tools include not only cheese knives or harps for cutting curd and various implements to aid in stirring, but also devices to enhance one's understanding of the contingent materiality of milk, curd, and cheese: thermometers, acidity titrators, pH meters, and computerized spreadsheets for data collection. Arms, hands, and noses are other such tools that must be trained, enskilled. One cheesemaker told me admiringly of an Italian colleague who could feel when the milk was ready for starter cultures to be added, saying, 'His hands are accurate as a thermometer'.

Taking me on a tour of the Wisconsin factory he recently retrofitted to make big-wheel Emmenthaler, Bruce Workman pointed out the control panel of a computerized system that regulates milk flow and the addition of bacterial cultures. He has programmed the computer to alert him when sufficient time may have passed for milk to curdle or for the curd to 'cook' sufficiently – and then to pause. Nothing further happens until Bruce gets his hands in the vat and feels, smells, evaluates the curd. Once he has determined that it is time for the next step, he pushes a button and things proceed. The way Bruce uses automated machinery disrupts its 'mechanical objectivity', to borrow a term from historians Lorraine Daston and Peter Galison, referring to 'the insistent drive to repress the willful intervention' of the knower in ascertaining the objective truth of objects of nature.[17] As if to head off potential complaints that his computer system might cross a line beyond artisan fabrication into industrial, Bruce stressed that he purchased the equipment, used, from a school in Switzerland. Indeed, those two or three cheesemakers I visited who use computer-programmed equipment legitimated it by explaining, 'this is what everyone in Europe uses', implicitly claiming that being European itself confers artisan authenticity to a method of manufacture. Such domestic producers (as Cypress Grove) are among those most widely recognized as making artisan cheese – the production volume that warrants and enables imported equipment purchases is also what gets cheese into restaurants and specialty supermarkets nationwide.

Using a patchwork of used and new equipment, American cheesemakers are *bricoleurs*, cobbling together pieces of pre-industrial and cutting edge technologies in often surprising ways. John Putnam uses a mechanical stirrer and powerful pneumatic press, but labors to maintain a 'mother' culture (similar to a sourdough starter) in lieu of buying laboratory-isolated commercial cultures and pre-prepared rennet. Peter Dixon uses a mechanized stirrer but a jerry-rigged weighted lever-arm (beam) press weighted by a plastic bottle filled with water. Contemporary artisanship is not a throwback to the past; it is a modern pastiche.

## Science as a folk theory of magic

Knowing the science behind the craft or, more ambitiously, learning to use science in the service of craft appeals to cheesemakers' sense of wonder about the natural world. *Magic* is a word they evoke frequently to describe the transubstantiation of milk into cheese. Heat some milk, add a little of this, a pinch of that, stir … 'and the magic happens'. Scientific tools and knowledge promise to offer artisans a window onto that magic, giving them a deeper appreciation for the natural processes of which they are but a part. Science for many artisan cheesemakers turns out to be less an instrument to deploy to exert control than a source of humility. The epistemic virtue of scientific knowledge contributes to the making of a thoroughly contemporary artisan habitus. It enhances cheesemakers' sense of wonder about the natural world in an era that has moved from the counterculture of back-to-the-land to the cyber-culture of tracking data using computerized spreadsheets to get back-to-nature.

In contemporary American cheese culture, techne is not the devalued other, the constitutive outside, of either episteme or technoscience. Early twentieth-century anthropologists Bronisław Malinowski and E. E. Evans-Pritchard described magic as a folk theory of science, with both magic and science seeking to explicate the unknown as well as to provide people with means of intervening in the natural world to further human ends.[18] Twenty-first-century artisans speak rather of science as a folk theory of magic, enhancing their sense of wonder and reminding them of the limits of human agency. Mutually defining, art and science in the crafting of cheese are far from mutually exclusive.

## Notes

1. http://www,cheesesociety.org/displaycommon.cfm?an=l&subarticlenbr=51 (accessed 27 August 2010). The definition was developed by committee in the late-1990s.
2. Deborah Heath and Anne Meneley (2007), "Techne, Technoscience, and the Circulation of Comestible Commodities: An Introduction". *American Anthropologist* 109 (4): 593–602, 594.
3. Research was supported by the Wenner-Gren Foundation for Anthropological Research and by the Massachusetts Institute of Technology.
4. David Pye, *The Nature and Art of Workmanship.* London: Studio Vista, 1968, 7.
5. Peter Dixon, "The Art of Cheesemaking," in *American Farmstead Cheese: The Complete Guide to Making and Selling Artisan Cheeses,* Paul Kindsteadt (ed.), White River Junction, VT: Chelsea Green, 2005, 198–9.
6. Sally McMurry, *Transforming Rural Life: Dairying Families, and Agricultural Change, 1820–1885.* Baltimore: Johns Hopkins University Press, 1995.
7. Paul Kindstedt, *American Farmstead Cheese; The Compute Guide to Making and Selling Artisan Cheeses,* White River Junction, VT: Chelsea Green, 2005.
8. Kindstedt, *American Farmstead Cheese*, 37–8.
9. This recalls what James Scott describes as *metis:* "the ability and experience necessary to influence the outcome – to improve the odds – in a particular instance." James C. Scott, *Seeing Like a State: How Certain Schemes to Improve the Human Condition Have Failed.* New Haven: Yale University Press, 1998, p. 318.
10. Michael Polanyi, *Personal Knowledge: Towards a Post-Critical Philosophy,* Chicago: University of Chicago Press, 1958.
11. J. H. Lesher draws a relevant, distinction in Plato's *Theaetetus between gnosis* ("knowledge by acquaintance") and episteme ("knowledge that something is the case"). This sense of gnosis well captures the artisan's knowledge of materials – in the case of cheesemaking, knowing one's milk and curd and how it behaves under given conditions. See J. H. Lesher (1969), "ΓΝΩΣΙΣ and ΕΣΤΗΜΗ in Socrates' Dream in the Theaetetus". *The Journal of Hellenic Studies* 89: 72–8.
12. "As in any craft," writes Tim Ingold, "the skilled maker who has a feel for what she is doing is one whose movement is continually and subtly responsive to the modulations of her relation with the material." Ingold, *The Perception of the Environment: Essays in Livelihood, Dwelling and skill.* London: Routledge, 2000, 357.
13. Erin O'Connor writes similarly of a different craft, "Proficient glassblowers have often said that glassblowing is not about blowing the perfect piece of glass, but coming up with effective solutions to all the problems that consistently present themselves in the process of glassblowing. They nudge towards the idea that non-reflective anticipation is the force of proficiency." O'Connor (2007), "Embodied Knowledge in Glassblowing: The Experience of Meaning and the Struggle Towards Proficiency". *The Sociological Review* 55: 126–41, 137.
14. Polanyi, *Personal Knowledge.*
15. On the psychological state of "flow" see Mihaly Csikszentmihalyi, *Beyond Boredom and Anxiety: Experiencing Flow in Work and Play*. San Francisco: Jossey-Bass, 1975.
16. Ingold, *Perception of the Environment.*
17. Lorraine Daston and Peter Galison, *Objectivity* New York: Zone Books, 2007, 212.

18. Bronisław Malinowski. *Magic, Science and Religion, and Other Essays*, Glencoe, IL: The Free Press, 1948. E. E. Evans-Prichard. *Witchcraft, Oracles and Magic among the Azande*, Oxford: Oxford University Press, 1976.

# CHAPTER 13

## SURFACE REVELATIONS: ECOLOGIES AND EPISTEMOLOGIES OF ROCK ART

*Severin Fowles and Benjamin Alberti*

For archaeologists, it is difficult to have a conversation about art without feeling the Paleolithic tug at us from somewhere deep in our subconscious. We may be having a perfectly nice time strolling around the Guggenheim with our partner, but our minds will never be entirely present. Somewhere, off in a private corner of our thoughts, we will be saying to ourselves, "Yes, but what about all those lions and rhinoceroses in Chauvet Cave?" or "Could it really be that the red hand prints in El Castillo Cave were made by Neanderthals?" It is a distinctively archaeological neurosis, this nagging worry over the ancient origins of things.

Obsession with origins can be a problem. Here, of course, is where we typically locate the ontological anchors that naturalize particular understandings of the world, though this is may be less of a problem for archaeologists than for those who contemplate the past without ever undertaking an actual material study of it. Heidegger (1971 [1935]: 17) might write: "Origin ... means that from and by which something is what it is and as it is ... The origin of something is the source of its nature." But archaeologists rarely say such things. In part, this is because the origins that traditionally consume us are, strictly speaking, more ancient than ontological. But it is also because our studies of ancient worlds regularly rely on an appreciation of the inherent *mutability* of the nature of things.

For instance, it is only by virtue of the breakdown of a uranium isotope into thorium—of the transformation of uranium's nature, in other words—that researchers were recently able to date the calcite flowstones that have formed overtop a series of red hand stencils and other markings at various Paleolithic cave sites in northwestern Spain (Pike et al. 2012). In a few cases, the researchers determined that this calcite began forming roughly 40,000 years ago; hence, the underlying images painted in red must be at least that old. For archaeologists, then, this is "the origins of the work of art," and it is reckoned, significantly, through the origins of the work of water—or rather, through the origins of calcium carbonate deposits left behind by the flow of water, which, in turn, gain chronological significance through the radioactive transformation of the uranium within those deposits.

Concern with very old things often leads archaeologists to dwell on the fact that it is only through particular environmental qualities that traces of the past become legible to us at all. The acidity of the soil, the aridity of the air, exposure to sunlight—these are all standard concerns that immediately arise in the interpretation of any site. But more than this, archaeologists are also keenly aware that the traces of the past under study are always unstable and evolving traces that aren't just legible due to certain environmental conditions but are, in fact, *constituted* by processes of decay, fragmentation, chemical transformation, and dispersal throughout a geological matrix. Hence, there is a large literature focused on what archaeologists call "formation processes" (Schiffer 1987) in which artifacts, architectural features, and the like come to be viewed as arrows and flow charts, ever in a process of formation and re-formation. Decay, in other words, often becomes the very source of meaning for the archaeologist rather than an epistemological obstacle that must be controlled for in the course of interpretation.

Rock art panels like those in the wonderful Paleolithic caves of Western Europe are particularly good to consider if we are to understand this intersection of ecology and epistemology. Upon encountering an image that has been pecked, scratched, or painted onto a cave wall, we are usually propelled by an initial desire to read the surface as one would a text. To be sure, there is a strong tendency to essentialize, to account for rock art by identifying (1) a chronological moment of creation when, for instance, the outline of a cave bear was painted in red hematite (perhaps 30,000 years ago), as well as (2) an immediately prior moment of true origin when "bear" arose as an idea in the mind of the artist, who then proceeded to project this idea materially onto the rock face. In this way, a complex material surface is reduced to the idealized form that has been imposed upon it.

But again, one can only indulge in this sort of reductionism—this old Aristotelian privileging of form over matter—to a limited extent, for rock surfaces have their own ecologies, and the archaeological study of rock art always bumps up against these surface ecologies before too long. Sometimes this happens as one becomes aware of all the other nonhuman agencies that have left patterned traces as well. Many of the earliest human-made images of Paleolithic France and Spain, for instance, were scratched onto the walls of caves that had previously been scratched by bears (Ajoulat and Gély 2001) (Fig. 13.1). And this has raised the fascinating possibility that some of the earliest human art originated as a kind of ursine mimicry. (The origins of the work of art thus become the work of bears.) Be that as it may, it can sometimes be very difficult to distinguish traces made by humans from those made by animals.

Other nonhuman agencies act upon rock faces in ways that are ecologically more complex. Water dripping down a surface leaves behind mineralizations in shapes that can also, at times, be mistaken for intentional human markings. Algae and fungi stake claims on rock faces, producing lichen colonies that expand in patterned formations. These organisms can be beautiful and iconographic in their own right, but they slowly eat away rock surfaces and so are typically regarded by archaeologists as a threat. The most publicized example of this threat is currently playing out at Lascaux, which was regarded as the birthplace of art for many decades after the cave's discovery in 1940. Thousands of tourists were consequently drawn to the cave, and their collective sighs of wonder and amazement seem to have significantly altered internal temperature and $CO_2$ levels; by the late 1950s, panels that had been relatively stable for 17,000 years began to have swarms of new microorganisms growing on them (see Geneste and Mauriac 2014; Martin-Sanchez et al. 2015; Saiz-Jimcnez et al. 2012). Algae colloquially known as "green disease" and fungus known as "black stains" were special problems but various other genera of bacteria, fungi, algae, protozoans, rotifers, and nematodes were also found. This led curators to restrict access and build a complicated air conditioning system. By the late 1990s, microbes were again found to be on the increase, prompting the installation of a new air circulation system in the cave. But the workmen in charge of the installation allegedly introduced additional molds and fungi that began to spread over Lascaux's rock art panels. Subsequent efforts to spray biocides and to actually cut out areas colonized by fungus fusarium have backfired, it seems, encouraging the appearance of different fungal growths.

Another striking Pleistocene example comes from the hauntingly elongate human pictographs in what is known as the Bradshaw rock art tradition of Australia. Here, however,

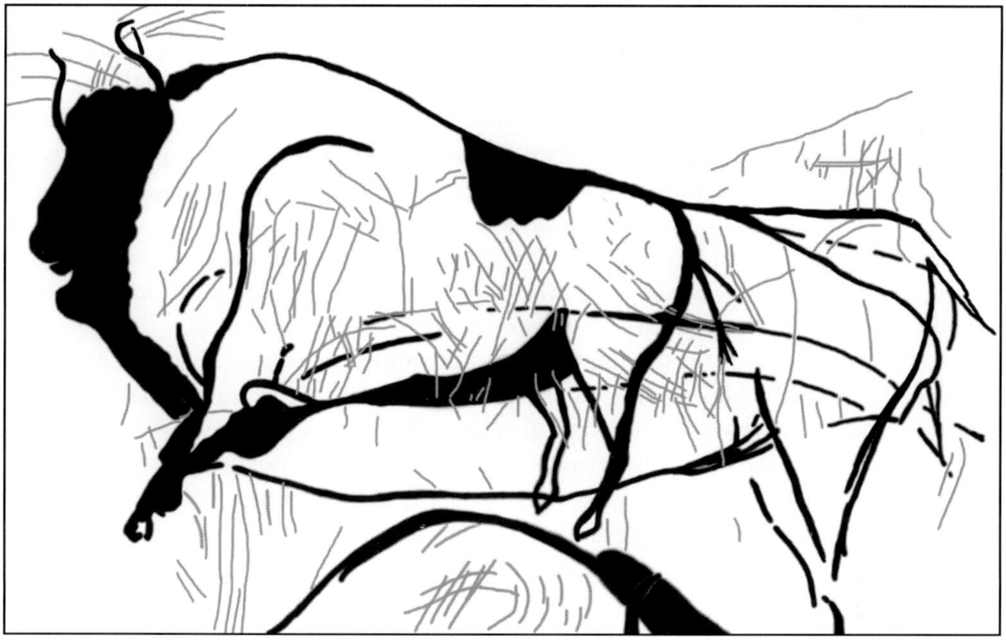

**Figure 13.1** Bison panel from Chauvet Cave. Black = human artists. Gray = ursine artists © Fowles and Alberti

bacteria and fungi are not the enemies but rather the very reason this imagery has persisted across what may be tens of thousands of years. Studies of the curiously vibrant pigment have encountered cases "where the original paint is no longer present … but has been replaced by a biofilm of living, pigmented micro-organisms whose natural replenishment may account for the longevity and vividness of these ancient paintings" (Pettigrew et al. 2010). Glyphs of a "mulberry" color turn out to be predominantly composed of black fungus with microscopic yellow fruit; those of a "cherry" color are predominantly composed of a reddish organism, tentatively identified as cyanobacteria. In each case, the microorganisms appear to have colonized and fed off the nutrients in the paint initially applied by humans, preserving the form over the millennia. It is, then, truly a "living pigment," conclude the researchers who now find themselves in the unprecedented position of needing to study the rock art's genetic history.

Suffice it to say that archaeology's epistemology is profoundly entangled with surface and atmospheric ecologies of various sorts. Indeed, it is often only by virtue of the lively and transformative flux of materials that we are able to demonstrate that certain phenomena actually are traces of the deep past and therefore of special significance. But at the same time, this flux continues to transform archaeological traces, threatening to destroy or, in rare cases, promising to preserve them, but also shifting their meanings. Moreover, efforts to study these processes often have their own ecological impacts.

As students of rock art, however, here is what we find most compelling about this situation: the modern relationship between epistemology and ecology, which is today so strongly evident in the archaeological analysis of cave art, may very well find a close parallel the way rock artists of the past approached their creative undertakings. How, we find ourselves asking, did non-modern peoples think about and derive meaning from their own participation in surface ecologies? Certainly there is now little question—in the case of some cave sites at least—that humans, long ago, read the patterned marks previously made by bears and purposefully added to them. (Bears, it must be acknowledged, made their own annotations on human marks as well; in a few cases there is a complex back-and-forth sequence between these two artistic species.) A number of researchers have also come to examine how various processes of mineralization, staining, encrustation, microbial development, erosion, and the like resulted in shapes and forms that appear to have been engaged semiotically, prompting Paleolithic artists to bring certain phenomena to mind that they subsequently projected back onto the cave wall (Hodgson 2008).

Others have proposed that the strange aesthetics within cave spaces may have promoted not just new forms of image production but altogether new social regimes. David Lewis-Williams (2004) has argued, for instance, that ancient shamans used caves as architectural technologies both to accentuate experiences of altered states and to spatially restrict access to those states. Cave aesthetics, he suggests, would have materially buttressed shamanic quests. The darkness, the play of torchlight and shadow, the glittering speleothems, the rippled and dripping surfaces frozen in motion—all these characteristics would have duplicated and amplified the entopic imagery produced by the brain as it enters into alternative forms of consciousness. Lewis-Williams also draws our attention to the way heightened $CO_2$ levels must be viewed as an atmospheric resource that enhanced image production in the mind and, subsequently, image projection on cave walls. Chauvet's atmosphere is characterized by a 3 percent $CO_2$ concentration, seventy-five times higher than the normal atmosphere at the earth's surface. Breathing and associated cognitive processes are especially affected in the deepest, darkest cave recesses; and the argument is that it was in these narrow and restricted spaces, far from the cave openings, where a select few would have inhaled a rarified air, granting them insight and visions that resided both outside the mundane world and outside the reach of non-initiates.[1] Access to these caves is assiduously guarded today due, in large part, to atmospheric concerns. Only a small number of specialists from among the world's scientific elite are permitted to enter the cave in search of whatever scholarly revelations about the past they may be pursuing. The implication of Lewis-Williams's argument, however, is that a similar sort of distinction—equally premised on questions of access and ecology—existed among communities of the ancient past.

A close intertwining of epistemology and ecology, then, could be said to characterize modern archaeology and Paleolithic artistry—scientists and shamans—alike. It is by entering into ecological relations with an object of study that one gains insight. This, surely, is a timeless truth, despite the traditional appeals to intellectual detachment and objective distance within the Western intellectual tradition.

To explore this point further, let us shift from the Old World to the New, and to the somewhat more recent archaeological record of the American Southwest that has been the focus of our own rock art studies. In this region, Native American communities have pecked, incised, abraded, scratched, and painted images onto rocks for at least the past 10,000 years, sometimes in cave settings but more often in the open air. These images are born of somewhat different ecological entanglements than those just discussed. Along the northern extent of the Rio Grande in New Mexico, for instance, images decorate vast landscapes of basalt boulders that are in the open air, exposed to the elements. Wind deposits clay particles in the

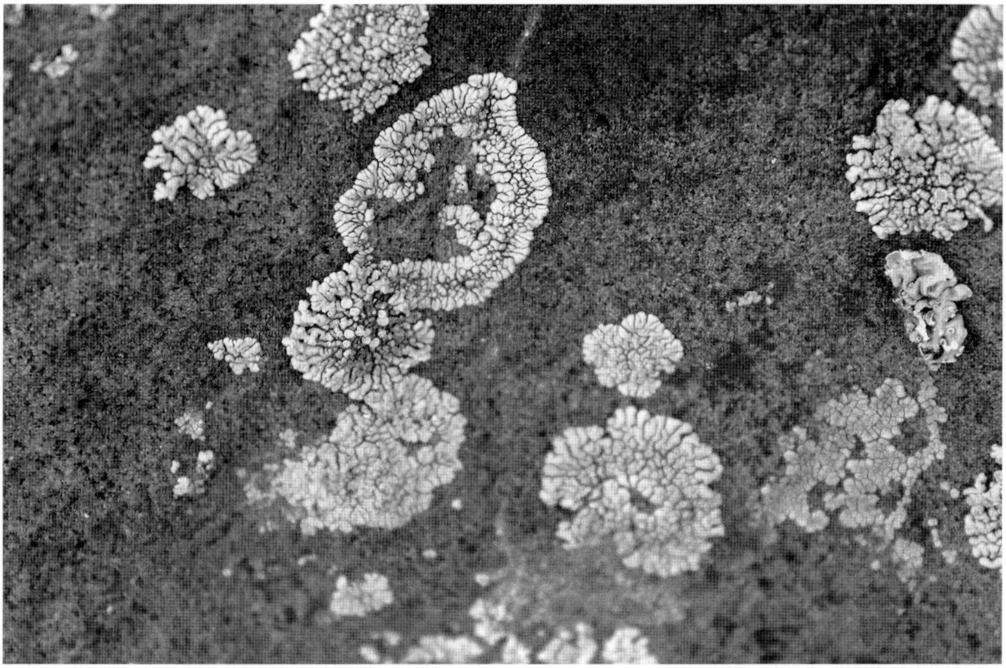

**Figure 13.2** Lichen colonies on basalt boulders along the Rio Grande, New Mexico © Fowles and Alberti

rock pores; the sun then heats up the surface, prompting microbes to fuse the clay particles with iron and manganese, which are already present in the rock. This process results in the development of a dark desert patina, which ancient artists pecked through to create graphic contrasts, and which archaeologists now use to reckon the relative age of images as the patina slowly reforms over the pecked marks.

Lichen is common as well (Fig. 13.2); in fact, lichen growth is often specially attracted to rock art in the area. This is partly due to the fact that when past people pecked into rock surfaces, their alterations created new surficial microclimates, tiny areas of slightly increased moisture, shadow, and particle accumulation that lichens have been able to colonize. As a result, lichen can sometimes seem to annotate a pecked image and add meaning to it.

Figure 13.3, for instance, depicts a faint human form with arms raised and enlarged hands outstretched, the sort of figure frequently regarded as "shamanic" by rock art researchers. It was probably pecked onto this rock surface between one and three thousand years ago, given the extent of patina development overtop the peck marks that constitute the glyph. Since its creation, lichen colonies appear to have come and gone; most inhabited the cracks and shadowy undersides of the boulder, but some have taken hold on the pecked glyph itself. The hand on the left side of the figure, for instance, is now largely indiscernible, and the scars on the surface of the rock in this area indicate that we are looking at the destructive effects of past lichen growth. Today, there is only one main lichen colony living on the shaman's body: a dense growth that almost entirely covers the head, producing the distinct visual effect of being a 'lichen mask' of sorts.

We will never know what face the lichen mask hides. What we do know, however, is that this new hybrid image—collectively authored by human, fungus, and algae—has an iconicity that connects it to very specific sorts of meanings held by native peoples in the region today. This rock art panel is situated in the midst of the Pueblo world, where local Tanoan groups have developed elaborate ceremonial systems involving masked spirits known as *katsina*. Before colonization—particularly before the missionary crackdown on 'idolatrous' behavior—the *katsina* were regularly presenced through the creation of rock art images of masks and masked figures. The *katsina* also appeared—and in many cases, continue to appear—in Pueblo communities during dances in which community members don elaborately painted masks that have the power to veritably transform the wearer into a *katsina*. Appeals to the *katsina* during dances or in other ceremonies are fundamentally ecological; the *katsina* are rain-bringers—"cloud boys" in the local vernacular—and, as such, they are centrally involved in the circulation of water and the growth of organisms.

Given this cultural background, how might past indigenous communities have read a rock art panel like our 'shaman with the lichen mask'? Very little ethnographic work with descendant Pueblo communities has focused on the interpretation of rock art and the

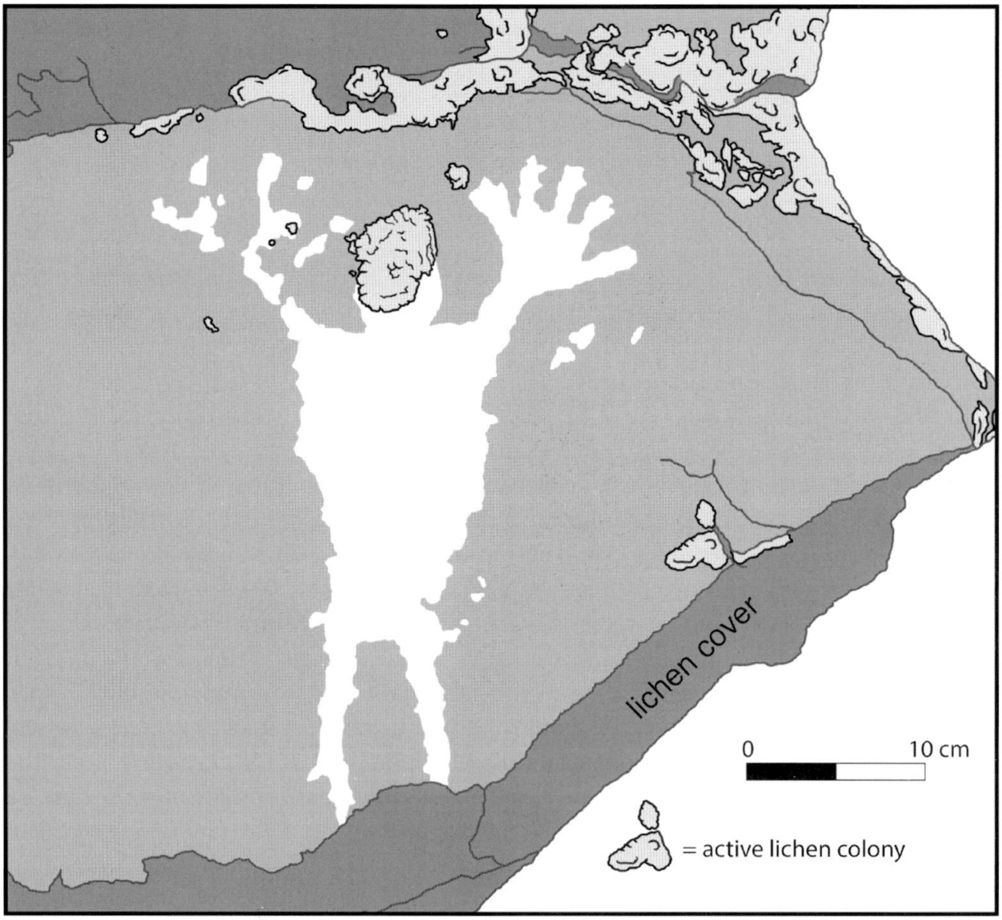


**Figure 13.3** Archaic rock art from the Rio Grande Gorge, New Mexico. A pecked shamanic figure with outstretched hands (in white) is masked by a lichen colony (outlined in black). © Fowles and Alberti

epistemological issues therein (for a rare example, see Young 1988); yet it seems safe to assume that native interpreters would not have divided this panel into meaningful pecks and meaningless lichen, as if the former were a signal and the latter mere noise. Rather, we suspect that there would have been a willingness to regard the lichen colony that has grown over the figure's face as part of the image itself, if not also as a vital sign that has revealed a truth about the nature of the image.

In this respect, we have found it very informative to walk through landscapes filled with rock art in the company of native consultants who are less preoccupied by the chronological placement of images or indeed by the distinction between human and nonhuman markings. On one such occasion in our own research, as we began to point out certain pecked icons on a large boulder overlooking the Rio Grande, a Pueblo colleague redirected our attention to the remarkable lichen patterns nearby, proposing that some of the pecked glyphs may have been less the projection of a preconceived idea than an effort to mimic and, as it were, learn from the local lichen patterns.

During the same outing, we inquired into the significance of a group of small, ground out cupules on the top of a boulder. Such cupules frequently occur at rock art sites along the Rio Grande and are known to serve as important shrine features among certain pueblo groups (see Duwe in press). In some reports, the act of pounding and grinding cupules is discussed as a female ritual practice undertaken as a means of addressing the rising sun, of praying for fertility, and/or of producing pulverized fragments of rock ('stone flour') to be ingested as a medicine or source of power. Examining very old examples of cupules with our pueblo consultant, however, a new set of meanings emerged. To him, the human marks that comprised the cupules weren't particularly interesting, in and of themselves; much more significant was the fact that droplets of water pooled up in these small circular cavities after a rain. Such rainwater was sacred, we were told, and in former times was collected for ceremonial purposes. Indeed, this was similar to many of the discussions we had that day: the human marks were often less clearly meaningful than the traces of natural processes that swirled around them.

Since then, we have been thinking much more about the semiotics of 'natural' features on rock surfaces, and this has led to the discovery of new sorts of patterns that bridge the apparent gap between human and nonhuman agencies. For instance, we have been struck by the fact that the anthropogenic cupules found in association with rock art are paralleled by natural cupules that regularly appear on boulders at the river edge. Figure 13.4 provides a nice example of a boulder covered with circular cavities—roughly ten centimeters in diameter—that have been ground out by the action of rushing water during floods. Looking closely, one can see the various stones and small gravels still filling the cupule just to the left of the center of the image. This is the abrasive material that swirling water employs to grind into the rock. The manner in which rivers sculpt the rocks along their banks is clearly evident to anyone who has spent time traversing the landscape along the Rio Grande. Natural cupules, in this sense, index the power of abundant water. And we suspect that part of what made cupule-production a meaningful practice for ancestral Pueblo people is the way their own grinding of stone mimetically referenced such riverine action. Creating the ecological effects of water may have been regarded as a form of prayer insofar as it expressed the hope that the cause of those effects—namely, rainfall—would come about.

Attending to the growth of lichens or the flow of water across a surface may seem worlds away from the stereotypical methods of knowing a rock art landscape employed by Western

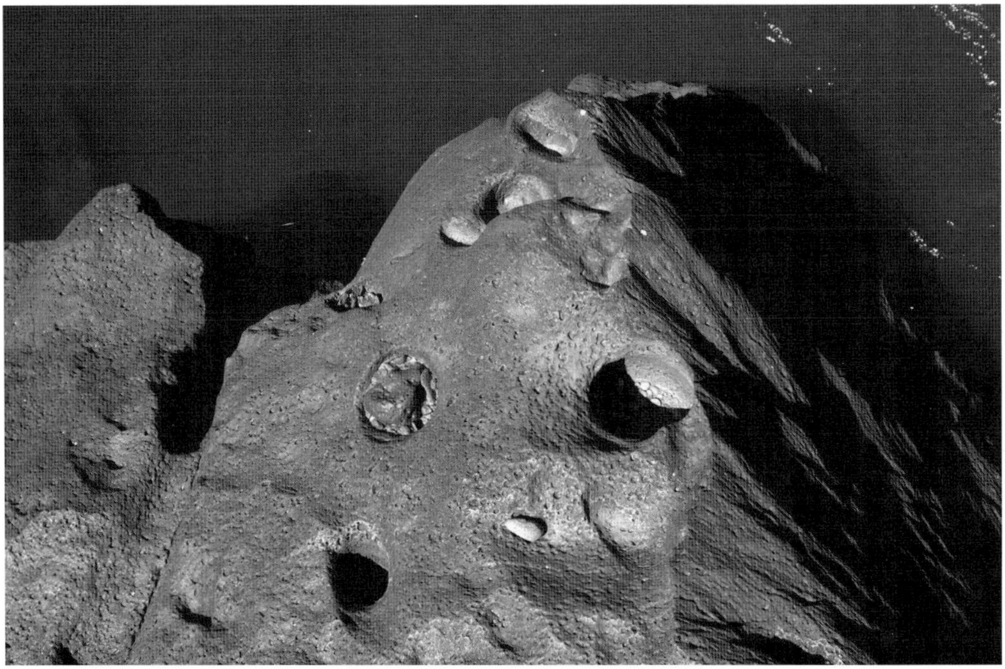

**Figure 13.4** Natural cupules ground out by water, sand, and gravel on the banks of the Rio Grande, New Mexico © Fowles and Alberti

archaeologists, methods that typically involve extracting "cultural" glyphs from the "natural" background noise and reproducing these glyphs as interpreted signs on clean white pages in the form of figures and maps. But such figures and maps are hardly the discipline's epistemological mainstay, even if they are the most visible way a certain kind of archaeological knowledge circulates.

Consider one final example. Out amongst the basalt of New Mexico, it can be very difficult to see rock art in bright sunlight. The desert patina on the rocks tends to be reflective; and when it develops over ancient pecked surfaces, the imagery can be lost in the glare. Until, that is, a cloud passes in front of the sun, shading the landscape with a muted even light, and revealing, all at once, images that up to that point had been entirely invisible. Many times, we have stood amidst a field of boulders, staring at the sky, awaiting the arrival of a cloud that we knew would transform the rock surfaces and substantially improve our chances of seeing whatever ancient imagery was around us. Clouds, in this sense, are revelatory; when they are present, the landscape comes to be filled with legible pictures.

Such experiences bring us a bit closer, we think, to the perceptions of early Pueblo travelers through this same rocky terrain. For them, however, the clouds may have been revelatory in a double sense. In the Pueblo tradition, clouds are avatars of the *katsina*, those masked spirits, discussed above, that bring rain and all the other good things that are necessary for life in the New Mexican desert. "The Cloud boys are coming," say the elders in the Pueblos as the clouds roll in to distribute their blessings (see Parsons 1936). "Soon we'll be able to see what this rock art panel really is," say the archaeologists out in the field, as they wait for the very same clouds to change the play of light across a boulder's surface. In each case, we confront a question of revelation, a question of entering into the surface ecologies that constitute our surroundings and, by virtue of this, make the world knowable.

## Note

1 For a historical example of the use of psychotropic atmospheres in caves to prompt the hallucinations in high-status prophets, see the ancient Greek oracular cults discussed in Ustinova (2009).

## References

Ajoulat, Norbert and Bernard Gély (2001), "La Sallle Hillaire, Autour du Grand Effrondrement," in Jean Clottes (ed.), *La Grotte Chauvet: L'art des Origines*, 88–95, Paris: Seuil.

Delannoy, Jean-Jacques, Bruno David, Jean-Michel Geneste, Margaret Katherine, Bryce Barker, Ray L. Wheat, and Robert G. Gunn (2013), "The Social Construction of Caves and Rockshelters: Chauvet Cave (France) and Nawarla Gabarnmang (Australia)." *Antiquity* 87: 12–29.

Duwe, Samuel (In press), "Cupules and the Creation of the Tewa World." *Journal of Lithic Studies*.

Geneste, Jean-Michel and Muriel Mauriac (2014), "The Conservation of Lascaux Cave, France," in Cesareo Saiz-Jimenez (ed.), *The Conservation of Subterranean Cultural Heritage*, 165–72, Boca Raton: CRC Press.

Heidegger, Martin (1971 [1935]), "The Origin of the Work of Art," in *Poetry, Language, Thought*, trans. A. Hofstadter, New York: Harper and Row.

Hodgson, Derek (2008), "The Visual Dynamics of Upper Paleolithic Cave Art." *Cambridge Archaeological Journal* 18 (3): 341–53.

Lewis-Williams, David (2004), *The Mind in the Cave: Consciousness and the Origins of Art*, London: Thames and Hudson.

Martin-Sanchez, Pedro M., Ana Z. Miller, and Cesareo Saiz-Jimenez (2015), "Lascaux Cave: An Example of Fragile Ecological Balance in Subterranean Environments," in Annette Summers Engel (ed.), *Microbial Life of Cave Systems*, 279–302, Berlin: De Gruyter.

Parsons, Elsie Clews (1936), *Taos Pueblo*, Wisconsin: George Banta Publishing.

Pettigrew, Jack, Cloe Callistemon, Astrid Weiler, Anna Gorbushina, Wolfgang Krumbein, and Reto Weiler (2010), "Living Pigments in Australian Bradshaw Rock Art." *Antiquity*, Project Gallery Issue 326. Available online: http://antiquity.ac.uk/projgall/pettigrew326/ (accessed 10 December 2015).

Saiz-Jimenez, Cesareo, Ana Z. Miller, Pedro M. Martin-Sanchez, and Mariona Hernandez-Marine (2012), "Uncovering the Origin of the Black Stains in Lascaux Cave in France." *Environmental Microbiology* 14 (2): 3220–31.

Schiffer, Michael B. (1987), *Formation Processes of the Archaeological Record*, Albuquerque: University of New Mexico Press.

Ustinova, Yulia (2009), "Cave Experiences and Ancient Greek Oracles." *Time and Mind* 2 (3): 265–86.

Young, M. Jane (1988), *Signs from the Ancestors: Zuni Cultural Symbolism and Perceptions of Rock Art*, Albuquerque: University of New Mexico.

# PART III
# FORM AND AESTHETICS

## Preface

The pieces in this section trace the aesthetic across registers of experience and expression. As Georgina Born succinctly insists, "the social is … in the aesthetic" (125). Jeremy Coote, for instance, describes the multiple arenas into which cattle—especially the pattern of their hides—are taken up, from dance moves, to songs extolling the sheen of hides, to the colors chosen to paint the poles around cattle pens. Yet, as Alfred Gell (1995) aptly points out, Coote, in claiming that the Dinka disaggregate aesthetics and art, relies on European assumptions that art subsists only in collectable objects. As Gell elaborates, though the Dinka may not have "produced much that has attracted the attention of public or private collectors" (21), their songs and dances clearly demonstrate an enmeshing of aesthetics and expressive culture. Hence, Gell writes, "Aesthetics can be discussed in the absences of any attempt being made to manufacture objects according to the aesthetic preferences of a culture" insofar as it "has to do with the perception of aesthetic quality, not the manufacture of objects possessing this quality" (20). While the analytical move Coote makes of separating the categories of *art* and *aesthetics* is useful for relieving the evaluation of formal qualities from discrete categories of things, Gell's critique is a reminder to continue to interrogate concepts and categories, whether those of the anthropologist or the anthropological subject.

Even as anthropologists challenge a notion of aesthetics as grounded in Enlightenment philosophy, Immanuel Kant's aesthetic texts provide foundational points of reference for discussions of sensory knowledge, experience, and taste. Emphasizing the perceptual, sensory, and embodied aspects of aesthetic experience, Steven Feld and Christopher Pinney draw on even as they depart from Kant, whose theory of aesthetics, while grounded in perceptions of nature, nevertheless maintains a distance between the perceiver and that which is perceived. Hence, while classic theories of aesthetics are fundamentally about human encounters, they do not account for the range and extent of engagements that people might have with objects, sounds, or movement, or of the ways in which aesthetic determinations extend across matter and mediums.

Feld's seminal notion of "acoustemology" provides a way of addressing acoustic ways of knowing and being in the world, which he understands as fundamentally and primarily sensory and embodied. His project engages the perception of environmental and musical sound in the Bosavi rainforest, an acoustic field in which human and nonhuman sounds interweave, one or the other coming into relief through an aesthetic of "lift-up-over sounding," in which "One sound stands out momentarily, then just as quickly fades into a distance, overlapped or echoed by a new or repeated emergence in the mosaic" (154). Feld identifies this pattern in the perception of forest sounds, in local "vocal and instrumental" (154) forms, as well as in Bosavi political and social life. For Feld, as for Fowles and Alberti (see Part II), ecology becomes operative as a domain in which aesthetics provides coordinates for human/nonhuman relations. Fowles and Alberti draw out the importance of paying attention to atmospheric qualities as affecting aesthetic perceptions and of transforming objects over time. This is equally applicable to the Bosavi rainforest or a modern art museum as it is to the Caves of Lescaux.

Though aesthetics may be understood as broadly based in experience, as many of the pieces in this section insist, this is grounded in and defined by modes of perception that are coextensive with wider cultural formations and social uses of art forms. Christopher Pinney and Pierre Bourdieu highlight the prescriptive and limited nature of how that experience has been described, which can serve to constitute a proper subject, modality of engagement, and object. To address this, Pinney shifts from "aesthetics" to what he calls "corpothetics," "as one way of comprehending the praxis through which enchantment manifests itself" (1984: 143). This is evident in villagers' interaction with chromolithographs: images of deities that are integrated into religious life, belief, and comportment as they travel between temples, festivals, and homes. In this case, both the content of the image and the object itself are equally important. Continuous with a notion that the proper relationship between gods and people is to see and be seen, the deities are depicted looking directly at the viewer and images are made as mirrors, with shiny surfaces that reflect the image of the viewer. In drawing out the importance of theorizing bodily praxis in order to understand the reception of Hindu chromolithographs, Pinney's essay begs the question whether this is true for "disinterestedness" as well. Is not aesthetics always "corpothetics," even if not articulated as such?

Bourdieu provides analytic and methodological tools for an historical understanding of a modernist aesthetic. Arguing against the notion that formalism—or art's retreat from and refusal of "the social"—is a problem for sociology (or anthropology), Bourdieu asserts a need to address "the historical process through which the social conditions of freedom from 'external determinations' get established; that is, the process of establishing the relatively autonomous field of production and with it the realm of pure aesthetics or pure thought whose existence it makes possible" (1984: 124, see also Benjamin 2008). A mutually constitutive relationship between the "artistic field" and a "cultured habitus" affords a person the possibility to approach an art work with the requisite aesthetic disposition. In other words, the "pure gaze" is cultivated—by formal and informal modes of education, by family background, by modes of display, and more. The "pure gaze" is thus soundly corporeal, even as it appears not to be. Moreover, as Bourdieu elaborates in *Distinction* (1984), a disposition that affords the aesthetic engagement demanded of the autonomous art object is coextensive across registers of social life (see Meintjes in Part II). Structured by "habitus," this disposition is at once embodied, cultivated, and distinguishing.

Aesthetics differentiate, providing the basis for hierarchical social relationships. In the context of European colonialism, differentiation between the architecture brought—and desired—by missionaries and African vernacular styles underscored the formers' measure of civilization. More than representational, a dwelling "congealed a civilized, Christian act of construction" (Comaroff and Comaroff, 160). Locks, doors, and glass windows were understood by missionaries to be symbolic of and themselves embody morals and spiritual potential, for individuals and families. Yet aesthetics—and with them attitudes—are not fixed. Ultimately, as Jean and John Comaroff point out, while African homes incorporated some European attributes, colonial buildings also took on African ones, from a dousing in dung to roundness.

### Ethnographic exercise

### *Soundwalk* (adapted from Ultra-red)

Do a soundwalk in your research site.
"What does [...] sound like?"

Select a site where you are now.
Walking to the site (5 min.):

1. Walking to a place and walking back from it can help understand the place itself. No place exists in isolation. As you walk from the school to the site, be aware. Pay attention to the different sounds and the different visual elements of the journey. Write these observations in your notebooks.

At the site:

1. Stand still and quietly for two minutes. Write down what you hear.
2. Walk around the site you have chosen for 10 minutes. Write down what you hear. Try to describe the sounds themselves, not just their sources.

Your entry should include what you wrote as you walked and listened. Then answer the following questions:

- What do you now know about the place?
- What else would you like to know about the place?
- Are there specific parts of this site to investigate more closely that may help you learn what it is you would like to learn?

## Further reading


Anderson, Richard L. (2004), *Calliope's Sisters: A Comparative Study of Philosophies of Art*, 2nd edn, Upper Saddle River, NJ: Prentice Hall.

Bate, Bernard (2009), *Tamil Oratory and the Dravidian Aesthetic: Democratic Practice in South India*, New York: Columbia University Press.

Bateson, Gregory (2000 [1972]), "Style, Grace, and Information in Primitive Art," in *Steps to an Ecology of Mind: Collected Essays in Anthropology, Psychiatry, Evolution, and Epistemology*, 128–52, Chicago: University of Chicago Press.

Benjamin, Walter (2008), "The Work of Art in the Age of Its Technological Reproducibility: Second Version," in *The Work of Art in the Age of Its Technological Reproducibility, and Other Writings on Media*, 19–55, Cambridge, MA: Harvard University Press.

Bourdieu, Pierre (1984), *Distinction: A Social Critique of the Judgement of Taste*, trans. Richard Nice, Cambridge, MA: Harvard University Press.

Coote, J. and A. Shelton (eds) (1994), *Anthropology, Art, and Aesthetics*, Oxford: Oxford University Press.

Gell, Alfred (1995), "On Coote's 'Marvels of Everyday Vision.'" 'Too Many Meanings': A Critique of the Anthropology of Aesthetics, A Special Issue of *Social Analysis: The International Journal of Social and Cultural Practice*, No. 38: 18–31.

Gow, Peter (1999), "Piro Designs: Painting as Meaningful Action in an Amazonian Lived World." *Journal of the Royal Anthropological Institute* 5: 229–46.

Hamann, Byron Ellsworth (2012), "Drawing Glyphs Together," in Joanne Pillsbury (ed.), *Past Presented: Archaeological Illustration and the Ancient Americas*, 231–81, Washington, DC: Dumbarton Oaks Research Library and Collection.
Ingold, Tim (2007), *Lines: A Brief History*, London: Routledge.
Munn, Nancy (1986), *Walbiri Iconography: Graphic Representation and Cultural Symbolism in a Central Australian Society*, Chicago: University of Chicago Press.
Rancière, Jacques (2013 [2004]), *The Politics of Aesthetics*, London: Bloomsbury Academic.
Taussig, Michael T. (1992), *Mimesis and Alterity: A Particular History of the Senses*, New York: Routledge.
Turner, Terrence S. (2012), "The Social Skin." *HAU: Journal of Ethnographic Theory* 2 (2): 486–504

# CHAPTER 14
# THE HISTORICAL GENESIS OF A PURE AESTHETIC

*Pierre Bourdieu*

The experience of the work of art as being immediately endowed with meaning and value is a result of the accord between the two mutually founded aspects of the same historical institution: the cultured habitus and the artistic field. Given that the work of art exists as such (i.e. as a symbolic object endowed with meaning and value) only if it is apprehended by spectators possessing the disposition and the aesthetic competence which are tacitly required, one could say that it is the aesthete's eye which constitutes the work of art as a work of art. But one must also remember immediately that this is possible only to the extent that aesthetes themselves are the product of a long exposure to artworks.[1] This circle, which is one of belief and of the sacred, is shared by every institution which can function only if it is instituted simultaneously within the objectivity of a social game and within the dispositions which induce interest and participation in the game. Museums could bear the inscription: Entry for art lovers only. But there clearly is no need for such a sign, it all goes without saying. The game makes the *illusio*, sustaining itself through the informed player's investment in the game. The player, mindful of the game's meaning and having been created for the game because he was created by it, plays the game and by playing it assures its existence. The artistic field, by its very functioning, creates the aesthetic disposition without which it could not function.

## The genesis of the artistic field and the invention of the pure gaze

What makes the work of art a work of art and not a mundane thing or a simple utensil? What makes an artist an artist and not a craftsman or a Sunday painter? What makes a urinal or a wine rack that is exhibited in a museum a work of art? Is it the fact that they are signed by Duchamp, a recognized artist (recognized first and foremost as an artist) and not by a wine merchant or a plumber? If the answer is yes, then isn't this simply a matter of replacing the work-of-art-as-fetish with the 'fetish of the name of the master'? Who, in other words, created the 'creator' as a recognized and known producer of fetishes? And what confers its magical or, if one prefers, its ontological effectiveness upon his name, a name whose very celebrity is the measure of his claim to exist as an artist and which, like the signature of the fashion designer, increases the value of the object upon which it is affixed? That is, what constitutes the stakes in quarrels of attribution and the authority of the expert? Where is one to locate the ultimate principle of the effect of labelling, or of naming, or of theory? (Theory is a particularly apt word because we are dealing with seeing – *theorein* – and of making others see.) Where does this ultimate principle, which produces the sacred by introducing difference, division and separation, reside?

Such questions are quite similar in type to those raised by Mauss when, in his *Theory of Magic*, he pondered the principle of magic's effectiveness, and found that he had to move back from the instruments used by the sorcerer to the sorcerer himself, and from there to the belief held by his followers. He discovered, little by little, that he had to confront the entire social universe in whose midst magic evolves and is practised. Likewise, in the infinite regress in search of the primary cause and ultimate foundation of the art-work's value, one must make a similar move. And in order to explain this sort of miracle of transubstantiation (which is at the very source of the art-work's existence and which, although commonly forgotten, is brutally recalled through strokes of genius *á la* Duchamp), one must replace the ontological question with the historical question of the genesis of the universe, that is, the artistic field, within which, through a veritable continuous creation, the value of the work of art is endlessly produced and reproduced.

It is not only a matter of exorcising what Benjamin called the 'fetish of the name of the master' in a simple sacrilegious and slightly childish inversion – and whether one wishes it or not, the name of the master is indeed a fetish. It is a question of describing the gradual emergence of the entire set of social conditions which make possible the character of the artist as a producer of the fetish which is the work of art. In other words, it is a matter of constituting the artistic field (which includes art analysts, beginning with art historians, even the most critical among them) as the locus where the belief in the value of art and in the artist's power of valuable creation is continually produced and reproduced. This would yield not only an inventory of the artist's indices of autonomy (such as those revealed through the analysis of contracts, the presence of a signature, or affirmations of the artist's specific competence, or the recourse in case of a dispute to the arbitration by peers, etc.), but also an inventory of the signs of the autonomy of the field itself, such as the emergence of the entire set of the specific institutions which are a necessary condition for the functioning of the economy of cultural goods. These include: places of exhibit (galleries, museums, etc.), institutions of consecration or sanction (academies, salons, etc.), instances of reproduction of producers and consumers (art schools, etc.), and specialized agents (dealers, critics, art historians, collectors, etc.), all of whom are endowed with the dispositions objectively required by the field and the specific categories of perception and appreciation, which are irreducible to those in common use and which are capable of imposing a specific measure of the value of the artist and of her products. As long as painting is measured by surface units and duration of production, by the quantity and price of the materials used (gold or ultramarine), the artist-painter is not radically different from a house painter. That is why, among all the inventions which accompany the emergence of the field of production, one of the most significant is probably the elaboration of an artistic language. This involves first establishing a way of naming painters, of speaking about them and about the nature of their work as well as of the mode of remuneration for their work, through which is established an autonomous definition of properly artistic value irreducible to the strictly economic value and also a way of speaking about painting itself, of pictorial techniques, using appropriate words (often pairs of adjectives) which enable one to speak of pictorial art, the *manifattura,* that is, the individual style of the painter whose existence it socially constitutes by naming it. By the same logic, the discourse of celebration, notably the biography, also plays a determining role. This is probably due less to what it says about painters and their work than to the fact that the biography establishes the artist as a memorable character, worthy of historical account, much like statesmen and poets. (It is known that ennobling comparisons – *ut pictura poesis* – contribute to the affirmation of the irreducibility of pictorial art, at least for a time and until they become a hindrance.) A genetic sociology should also include in its model the action of the producers themselves and their claim to the right to be the sole judges of pictorial production, to produce, themselves, the criteria of perception and appreciation for their products. Such a sociology should also take into account the effect – on themselves and the image they have of their production, and thus on their production itself – of the image of themselves and their production that comes back to them through the eyes of the agents engaged in the field—other artists, but also critics, clients, collectors. (One can assume, for example, that the interest in sketches and cartoons shown by certain collectors since the *quattrocento* has only helped to contribute to the artists' exalted view of their own worth.)

Thus, as the field is constituted as such, it becomes clear that the 'subject' of the production of the art-work – of its value but also of its meaning – is not the producer who actually creates the object in its materiality, but rather the entire set of agents engaged in the field. Among these are the producers of works classified as artistic (great or minor, famous or unknown), critics of all persuasions (who themselves are established within the field), collectors, middlemen, curators, etc., in short, all who have ties with art, who live for art and, to varying degrees, from it, and who confront each other in struggles where the imposition of not only a world view but also a vision of the artworld is at stake, and who, through these struggles, participate in the production of the value of the artist and of art.

The invention of the pure gaze is realized in the very movement of the field towards autonomy. In fact, without recalling here the entire argument, one could maintain that the affirmation of the autonomy of the principles of production and evaluation of the art-work is inseparable from the affirmation of the autonomy of the producer, that is, the field of production. Like pure painting, which, as Zola wrote *à propos* Manet, is meant to be beheld in itself and for itself as a painting – as a play of forms, values and colours – and not as a discourse, in other words, independently from all references to transcendent meanings, the pure gaze (a necessary correlate of pure painting) is a result of a process of purification, a true analysis of essence carried out by history, in the course of successive revolutions which, as in the religious field, always lead the new avant-garde to challenge orthodoxy – in the name of a return to the rigour of beginnings – with a purer definition of the genre.

What happens in the field is more and more linked to the field's specific history and to it alone. It is therefore more and more difficult to deduce it from the state of the general social world at any given time (as a certain 'sociology', unaware of the specific logic of the field, claims to do). Adequate perception of works – which, like Warhol's *Brillo Boxes* or Klein's monochromatic paintings, owe their formal properties and their value only to the structure of the field and thus to its history – is a differential, diacritical perception: in other words, it is attentive to deviations from other works, both contemporary and past. The result is that, like production, the consumption of works which are a product of a long history of breaks of history, with tradition, tends to become historical through and through, and yet more and more totally dehistoricized. In fact, the history that deciphering and appreciation put into play is gradually reduced to a pure history of forms, completely eclipsing the social history of the struggles for forms which is the life and movement of the artistic field.

This also resolves the apparently insoluble problem that formalist aesthetics (which wishes to consider only form in the reception as well as the production of art) presents as a true challenge to sociological analysis. In effect, the works that stem from a pure concern for form seem destined to establish the exclusive validity of internal reading which heeds only formal properties, and to frustrate or discredit all attempts at reducing them to a social context, against which they were set up. And yet, to reverse the situation it suffices to note that the formalist ambition's objection to all types of historicization rests on the unawareness of its own social conditions of possibility. What is forgotten is the historical process through which the social conditions of freedom from 'external determinations' get established; that is, the process of establishing the relatively autonomous field of production and with it the realm of pure aesthetics or pure thought whose existence it makes possible.

## Note

1 Sociological analysis allows one to escape the dichotomous choice between subjectivism and objectivism, and to reject the subjectivism of theories of aesthetic consciousness *(ästhetisches Bewusstsein).* Such theories reduce the aesthetic quality of a natural thing or of a human work to a simple correlate of a deliberate attitude of consciousness, an attitude which, as it confronts the thing, is actually neither theoretical nor practical but rather purely contemplative. Sociological analysis rejects these theories without falling, as does the Gadamer of *Truth and Method,* into an ontology of the work of art.

# CHAPTER 15
## MUSIC, MODERNISM AND SIGNIFICATION
*Georgina Born*

In this paper I will suggest that in order to understand how music produces meaning, it is necessary to develop a framework that engages with it as culture in the widest sense. The analysis of how meaning is produced by music-as-culture poses a broader problematic than that posed by the apparently narrowly textual arts, visual or literary. But rather than being irrelevant to their analysis, this problematic may, in turn, feed back insights into those other arts.

As a preliminary, it seems to me that the development of an aesthetic theory, in the present context of questions around postmodernism, must first depend upon a greater understanding of what has gone before historically; an understanding that encompasses culture in all its fractured forms. It must be able to give insight into musical modernism, but it must also register the character and complexity of 'the other' – that is, popular musics. At the risk of polemic, I think that such an approach will prove more fruitful than a return to the mode of traditional criticism, and the closure involved in focusing too narrowly on specific texts or specific authors – unless one reads out from these to history, as it were.

It seems to me extraordinary if, in a century that has witnessed and heard the debates around Dada, Brecht's epic theatre, Situationism, conceptual and performance art, we can return to or retain a notion of aesthetic experience as centred on the discreet artwork as single object or text; and of the aim of aesthetic speculation as, primarily, to assess values in order to judge – an aim deeply embedded in the dominant institutional forms of modern culture. The social and political dimensions of the movements cited, highlighting and involving critiques of and ironic comments on both the performative and the institutional aspects of art, direct us towards an exploded and constellatory definition of artistic meaning. Any assessment of value must first depend upon expanding our understanding of the multitextuality of this kind of art – and in fact of all media. I want to propose that especially in regard to music, but also the other arts, since meaning inheres in its social, discursive and technological mediations as well as in 'the music as sound', as well as in the notated or visual text, we should consider the aesthetic as subsuming these mediations. The social is, then, in the aesthetic, just as the discursive constructs and yet is distinct from the artwork itself. The terms and the boundaries of art have been redefined. We could go so far as to say that since these movements, art that disdains to be conscious of, or concerned with, its discursive and its social forms – performative and/or institutional – must be seen as negating or refusing that possibility, or as adopting an 'unconsciousness' of it.

### Meanings around the sound: Mediation and multitextuality

It is noticeable that most orthodox aesthetics of music take as their object music-as-sound, or music-as-notated-text, or music-and-lyric.[1] Yet despite this limited conceptualisation, confusions abound. Thus it is common to fail to distinguish between music-as-notated – the ideal, unrealised work, which foregrounds its systemic and structural character, and which is, in fact, music mediated in visual form – and music-as-sound – its aural realisation. Yet especially in the modernist era, some notated musics have resisted aural realisation, have received only inaccurate and approximate performances, and existed (and gained notoriety) primarily as visual or graphic texts; while many electronic and popular musics are non-notated and exist only in aural form, mediated by performance and by electronic technologies.

We have to develop a theory of musical meaning that can account for these distinctive forms, without which, for example, it would be impossible to grasp the specific importance of the visual and notational and conceptual in the modernist aesthetic, or of the aural and electronic in popular music. Just as, in terms of aural realisation, we have to distinguish between live performance – the immediate social realisation of music – and the various forms of technologically-mediated reception, by record, radio, television, film and so on.

The point is not to debate the relative priorities of music as aural or visual text, as live collective event or isolated experience; but to move beyond the currently impoverished and essentialist notions of how music conveys meaning by developing an analysis of the multiple, specific forms in which it is experienced. As a basis for aesthetic understanding, we need to tease out the particular character of the many mediations through which it is experienced: to assess both their distinctiveness, and the effects of their simultaneity and relatedness. A first principle, then, is the *multitextuality* of music-as-culture; and the need to analyse its particular forms – aural, visual, technological, social, discursive – as an ensemble.

Why might this be important? For four reasons.

First, in order to clarify confusion concerning technological mediation. Grasping the inevitable mediation of music allows us to move aesthetically beyond the nostalgia for a pre- or non-electronically mediated music, or for a return to an idealised ambient soundscape: both forms of yearning for the 'authentic' in music. Rather, the mediations can be perceived as inherently part of the aesthetic, and embraced as such. For example, it is still common in the classical music world for musicians and sound engineers, when recording or amplifying instruments, to talk of aiming to reproduce faithfully the instruments' acoustic sound. But this is an impossibility, since recorded or amplified instruments are *inevitably transformed* by that process and cannot be experienced either acoustically or physically as 'the same as before'. It is the same nostalgia (technology as redemptive of an 'original' musical experience) at a second order that feeds the fallacy of the compact disc, the marketing of which claims that it comes closer to 'real' or 'live' sound than previous forms of reproduction. Whereas it is simply *another* form of electronic transformation, perhaps cleaner, less noisy, more acoustically heightened and colourful than the LP. Radio, cassette, LP, CD, video disc: all are aesthetically distinct forms of musical reproduction, all equally 'artificial' or 'authentic', all attesting to the absence of a 'natural' or original sound.

This aesthetic principle has best been grasped, as a practical logic, by the popular music industry, as shown by the common practice when preparing an album of mixing the same tracks differently – or adjusting the aesthetic – for different technological outlets: car radio, cassette, LP, CD. The final mix of pop chart material is tried out, in the midst of high fidelity technologies in the studio, on tiny car radio speakers so as to assess how the sound comes across on that format – so that the voice, rhythm section, treble and bass can be made to reach out musically over the throb of the engine and the street sounds outside. It would be even more appropriate if those 'extraneous' sounds were also reproduced as part of the total soundscape or listening context in the studio.

A second reason for attention to multitextuality is because, as in the movements cited earlier, certain musics have attempted to innovate and to critique previous forms not primarily or only in terms of the aural or the notated, but also in terms of the social relations of music production. Good and related examples are the attempts at a new performance division of labour characteristic of both experimental and improvised musics in the 1960s and '70s, in which the lines between composer, performer and audience were blurred; or the collective musical composition of free jazz and improvised music in the same period. All of these aimed to deconstruct and demystify the role of the composer-author. To look at these musics as aural or notated texts is to miss a major dimension of meaning. Yet it would equally be a mistake to ignore the visual text: while some of these musics had none (free jazz, improvised music), the simplistic scores of post-Cageian experimental music were central to that music's Dada-esque and pointedly 'un-serious' critique of the extreme complexity and abstraction of the scores of the dominant post-serialist avant garde, and of the mystified and directive role of the 'serious' composer.

A third reason why attention to multitextuality is important is because only with such an analysis of *simultaneous levels* in the production of meaning can one uncover either cumulative and reinforcing effects or, more interestingly, *contradictions and tensions* operating between the levels of the ensemble.

In terms of reception, if pleasure can be derived from the various levels of musical experience, so can displeasure; and the meaning of one level may be in tension with the meaning of another, just as one level may create pleasure while another produces displeasure or invites hostility. This gives us a way of understanding why an audience may be unable to tolerate the experience of a music – for example classical music, or heavy metal rock—not due to the music-as-sound, but due to the associated forms of discourse (respectively, the elitist theories of genius associated with classical music, or the sexist iconography of heavy metal); or the modes and places of performance (inhibited concert hall ritual, or violent and omnipotent mob-behaviour in vast sports stadia) through which particular musics are experienced. On the other hand, it may also be that people are drawn to a music not because of the sound, but because of its social forms or its politicised discourse – which may override an uninterest in the sound. (I've often wondered, for example, if this is not the case for devotees of so-called 'women's music', or for those of the more stolid and worthy folk musics.) This sensitivity to contradictory levels of experience in reception gives us a way of understanding *ambivalence* towards the musical object, and points towards a more complex account of aesthetic experience than hitherto.

Several recent studies provide this kind of reading of musical meaning and pleasure, focusing notably on popular and non-western musical cultures. As yet, orthodox musicology dealing with serious music has evaded these issues, just as it has the social and broader cultural dimensions of music.[2] The studies include those by Barbara Bradby on the Buddy Holly song 'Peggy Sue',[3] and Phillip Tagg's on the Kojak television theme tune and the ABBA song 'Fernando'.[4] Both of these writers focus on the music or music-and-lyric alone, and despite very different approaches, they innovate in two similar ways. First, in focusing on implicit and 'unconscious' factors; and second, in drawing out implicit *contradictions* between levels of the whole – between the musical figures and words, the non-verbal and verbal. Tagg's method also provides an analysis of specifically musical and broader ideological connotations radiating from the aural-musical level alone: a form of intertextuality that he suggests is especially present in the dominant popular musics that he studies.

More interesting are studies by Dave Laing on punk rock[5] and Marina Roseman on the musical culture of the Temiar people of peninsular Malaysia[6] which move beyond the music-and-lyric to embrace the musical culture as a whole, including the discursive, the social and performative.

Laing's study of punk traces every level of meaning – from organisational forms and production practices, to the naming and philosophies of bands, fanzines and record companies, to performance and musical styles (vocal, physical, instrumental), to audience rituals and the punk 'look'. He analyses the way that each level of the whole creates meaning through difference; so that, for example, the organisational and technological forms of punk were not only socio-economic strategies, but also stylised symbolic interventions in, and rejections of, the forms of the mainstream rock industry. Thus punk's experiments in collective and independent (non-)organisation were comments on the entrepreneurial, hierarchical and profit-directed rock business. While at the level of musical style, punk vocalisation – murmured indistinctly or shouted hysterically, usually way off-key or hovering in between pitches – aimed above all to avoid the expressive musicality, the pitch-centredness, the smooth, relaxed and assured communication of most pop and rock vocals. It becomes clear that the movement worked symbolically through the systematic negation of every aspect of mainstream rock. And Laing suggests that the meaning of punk can only be grasped by analysing the simultaneous juxtaposition of these many levels in the bricolage, and by exploring how they work either cumulatively or, more often, against each other in wilful, stylised contradiction.

The kind of contradiction raised by Roseman in her study of a non-western musical culture is equally fascinating. She finds that the beliefs and ritual practices around Temiar musical performance, rather than reflecting the gender differentiation found in Temiar social life at large, systematically invert and negate it. The social character of musical performance exists as a kind of implicit critical commentary on, and questioning of, the dominant social order. Through the myths and feelings associated with their singing, women enjoy a kind of empowerment in fantasy, a utopian premonition. Roseman says, 'Musical and ritual performances do not simply replicate everyday social relations … Symbolic inversions … [furnish] a framework within which to comment upon or question the accepted order of things.'[7] She thus problematises the relationship between musical culture and social order, indicating that the two may not be continuous but opposed, in tension – and that music may provide an arena for social and symbolic struggle.

A fourth, and final, reason for attention to multitextuality is that this allows an awareness of the distance between the music itself, whether as sound or as visual text, and its theorisation – which can then be seen as but one form of a universal tendency to produce discourse around music, as I discuss shortly. This is to question and dislocate any taken-for-granted synonymy between 'the music' and both those discourses that rationalise and interpret it *post hoc* and, more crucially, those that claim to construct and prescribe it. Rather, we can focus on and interrogate the character of the discourse itself. Such an approach is enhanced by returning at this point to the core of a general analysis of musical signification.

## Sounds filled with projection: Metaphor, discourse, intertextuality

The core of music-as-culture is its existence as organised and meaningful sound, which is already encultured, and which is perceived as 'music' only by virtue of its difference from 'noise' or 'sound-in-general'. The character of musical sound can best be grasped by contrast with other media and their forms of signification. Musical sound in itself is alogogenic, completely unrelated to language, non-artefact, having no physical existence, and non-representational, referring in the first place to nothing other than the specific musical system or genre to which it is related. That is, musical sound is a self-referential, aural abstraction. This bare core must be the start of any socio-cultural understanding of music, since only then can one build up an analysis of the many mediations around it. And it is this non-representational core of musical sound that makes it especially resistant to decoding as ideology.

We can clarify by extending aspects of Barthes' analysis to music. In terms of denotation, musical sound contrasts with representational media since it denotes nothing other than its musical expressivity as part of a specific musical system. It calls to mind only its difference from other possible musical expressions within the same genre. This peculiar degree of self-referentiality is why music may be considered a relatively empty sign; and at this level, music may be considered pure expressive form, akin to the formal level of other media.

It is at the second, connotative order of signification that music becomes particularly subject to extra-musical meanings through its extraordinary evocative power. The signifieds that music connotes at this level can be of many kinds: visual, sensual, emotional, intellectual – such as theories, domains of knowledge, compositional systems. All are essentially *metaphorical* in relation to musical sound. And they can remain singular metaphors, experienced simultaneously, or they can combine, cohere and extend into fields of discourse – theory, 'knowledge' – surrounding music. But the point is that the relation of these extra-musical connotations to music-as-signifier is cultural, historical, established by convention and in social practice. Yet they are experienced as 'inherent in' or 'immanent to' the music by a process of *projection* of the connotations *into* the musical sound object. It is this process of projection that achieves the 'naturalising' effect: the connotations appear to be natural and universal where they are cultural and historical. It is the forms of talk, text and theory around music – the metaphors and rhetoric explaining and constructing it – that may be liable to analysis as ideological.

Barthes sees denotation as providing an explicit, value-free, 'blameless' alibi for the deeper, implicit levels of ideological connotation. Paradoxically, in music, the lack of a denotative alibi does not have the effect of undermining naturalisation, but rather the opposite effect: the intertextual connotations become even more transparently, 'naturally' and firmly attached to the music. This can be illustrated by two phenomena. First, music is particularly susceptible to a kind of theoretical pre-determination, as shown by W. D. Allen's survey of music historiography[8] and early sociology of music. Thus, it is striking that historical and sociological analyses of music tend to find in it the quintessence of their conceptual approach, while neglecting to attend to the specificity of the music. Second, throughout history there have been two recurring kinds of universalising theory of musical meaning: that music represents the emotions, and that music is, as Dahlhaus puts it, 'sounding mathematics'.[9] In both cases, these properties are read as immanent to music. We can now understand better why, because of music's transparency as a form of signification, it offers little resistance to discursive invasion.

The stress on intertextual connotation accords with recent ethno-musicology which places metaphors around music at the centre of the analysis of both how musical expressivity is translated into verbal and communicable form, and also who controls knowledge of music, and so how power is distributed in musical cultures.[10]

This analysis, then, indicates the omnipresence of metaphor and discourse as mediations of music-as-sound, and the need for attention to their arbitrary and specific cultural character, their intertextual connections with other, non-musical realms of discourse, other areas of knowledge and practice. It also raises their role in the construction of musical authority and legitimation; since having questioned the self-evidence of all discourses around music, it is possible to deconstruct their rhetoric and become sensitive to their legitimising strategies.

## Notes

1. This can be illustrated by a recent issue of *The Contemporary Music Review* (Vol. 5, 1989) entitled 'Music and Text'. This journal, which began in the early 1980s, sees itself as a radical departure in post-modern music criticism and analysis. Despite the promising title, which might appear to announce a broad consideration of musical meaning, the issue focuses only on the relation between musical 'setting' and words or literary texts.
2. It is significant that the musicologist Joseph Kerman, in a highly influential summary of the field (*Musicology*, Fontana, 1985), calls for musicology to address the social and cultural, while he yet retains a basic analytic split between music and the social. This is shown by his reservations about studies that in his view focus too much on social 'context' at the expense of the 'music as music' (p. 180).
3. Barbara Bradby, 'Pity Peggy Sue', in *Popular Music* 4, Cambridge: Cambridge University Press, 1984; see also her 'Do-talk and Don't-talk: The Division of the Subject in Girl-group Music', in S. Frith and A. Goodwin (eds), *On Record: Rock, Pop and the Written Word*, London: Routledge, 1990.
4. Philip Tagg, *Kojak—50 Seconds of Television Music,* PhD, Gothenburg University, 1979; and 'Analysing popular music: theory, method and practice', in *Popular Music* 2, Cambridge: Cambridge University Press, 1982.
5. Dave Laing, *One Chord Wonders: Power and Meaning in Punk Rock*, Milton Keynes: Open University Press, 1985.
6. Marina Roseman, 'The Social Structuring of Sound: The Temiar of Peninsular Malaysia', *Ethnomusicology* XXVIII, 3, 1984.
7. Roseman, *op. cit.,* 432.
8. W. D. Allen, *Philosophies of Music History: A Study of General Histories of Music,* New York: Dover, 1962.
9. Carl Dahlhaus, *Esthetics of Music*, Cambridge: Cambridge University Press, 1982: 'The idea that music's goal was to represent and arouse affections is a commonplace, rooted as deeply in history as the opposing thesis that music is sounding mathematics' (p. 17).
10. See for example Steven Feld, 'Sound Structure as Social Structure'. M. Roseman, *op. cit.* Roseman explains that 'indigenous musical theories are often articulated using terms drawn from "extra-musical" domains' (note 2, p. 438); and she argues that understanding music as culture involves grasping 'primarily the cultural logics informing (the sound) structures … We need to elicit … the symbolic classifications and metaphors whereby the terms of one domain are layered with meanings drawn from another domain' (pp. 411–12).

# CHAPTER 16
# 'MARVELS OF EVERYDAY VISION': THE ANTHROPOLOGY OF AESTHETICS AND THE CATTLE-KEEPING NILOTES

*Jeremy Coote*

> The current idea that we look lazily into the world only as far as our practical needs demand it while the artist removes this veil of habits scarcely does justice to the marvels of everyday vision.
>
> E. H. Gombrich, *Art and Illusion*

## The anthropology of aesthetics

While it is generally recognized that aesthetics concerns more than art and that art is about more than aesthetics, anthropologists, along with philosophers and aestheticians in general, have tended to work on the assumption, made nicely explicit in the 'Aesthetics' entry in the *New Encyclopaedia Britannica* (Pepper 1974: 150), that 'it is the explanation that can be given for deeply prized works of art that stabilizes an aesthetic theory'. In their accounts of the aesthetics of other cultures, anthropologists have concentrated on materials that fit Western notions of 'works of art', at times compounding the problem by making the focus of their studies those objects which are 'deeply prized' by the Western anthropologist, rather than those most valued by the people themselves. Moreover, what has passed for the anthropology of aesthetics has often been little more than talk about such 'art'; for many years, anthropologists' or art critics' talk, more recently, indigenous talk as systematized by the anthropologist.

While one doubts that works of art are ever deeply prized for their aesthetic qualities alone, it is probably true that in Western societies, and in others with highly developed art traditions, aesthetic notions are most perfectly manifested in works of art, and are given their most refined expression in that type of discourse known as the philosophy of art. But the aesthetic notions so manifested and refined are those of members of the art world, not necessarily those of the general population. For most of us—or, perhaps more accurately, all of us most of the time—our aesthetic notions have more to do with home decorating, gardening, sport, advertising, and other areas of so-called 'popular' culture. The presence of art having become almost a defining feature of Western notions of the civilized, anthropologists have been loath to say of any other society that it has no art. There is, it is true, probably no society that has no art-form at all, but there are certainly societies with no visual art traditions. A Western preoccupation with the visual has led to both the undervaluation of the poetic, choreological, and other arts, and to the widening of the definition of visual art so as to embrace all those objects or activities which have 'artistic' or 'aesthetic' qualities. So, for example, body decoration has been reclassified as art in recent years. While I have no fundamental objection to 'art' being defined in such broad terms, I find it more satisfactory to talk rather of the aesthetic aspect of a society's activities and products.

All human activity has an aesthetic aspect. We are always, though at varying levels of awareness, concerned with the aesthetic qualities of our aural, haptic, kinetic, and visual sensations. If art were to be defined so broadly as to encompass any human activity or product with an aesthetic aspect, then none could be denied the status of art. This seems to me unwarranted; the possible insight seemingly captured by such an argument is adequately caught by saying that all human activity has an aesthetic aspect.

I am encouraged in arguing for such a view by a trend that seems to characterize some recent anthropological and philosophical literature, a trend towards recognizing that aesthetics may be usefully defined independently of art. The anthropologist Jacques Maquet, for example, has argued repeatedly (e.g. 1979: 45; 1986: 33) that art and aesthetics are best treated as independent. Among philosophers, Nick Zangwill (1986: 261) has argued that 'one could do aesthetics without mentioning works of art! Sometimes I think it would be safer to do so.' And T. J. Diffey (1986: 6) has remarked how it is not just philosophers of art who require a notion of aesthetics; philosophers of religion require one too, and 'a notion of it as that which has no especial connection with art, but which, rather, is closer to perception'. Diffey regards 'aesthetic experience' as an as yet 'inadequately understood expression', as a term 'that extends thought, stretches the mind and leads us into new and uncharted territory' (ibid. 11). The task of philosophy, as he sees it, is to clarify and explicate what ordinary language has already 'inchoately discovered'. It is my view that rather than waiting for the clarifications and explications of philosophy, the anthropology of aesthetics should follow such ordinary language usage, disconnect itself from art, and get closer to perception.

The anthropology of aesthetics as I see it, then, consists in the comparative study of valued perceptual experience in different societies. While our common human physiology no doubt results in our having universal, generalized responses to certain stimuli, perception is an active and cognitive process in which cultural factors play a dominant role. Perceptions are cultural phenomena. Forge touched on this some twenty years ago when he wrote (1970: 282) concerning the visual art of the Abelam of New Guinea:

> What do the Abelam see? Quite obviously there can be no absolute answer to this question: it is impossible literally to see through the eyes of another man, let alone perceive with his brain. Yet if we are to consider the place of art in any society … we must beware of assuming that they see what we see and vice versa.

I should argue that, more than just being wary of making assumptions, we must in fact make the attempt to understand how they see. The study of a society's visual aesthetic, for example, should be devoted to the identification of the particular qualities of form—shape, colour, sheen, pattern, proportion, and so on—recognized within that society, as evidenced in language, poetry, dance, body decoration, material culture, sculpture, painting, etc. A society's visual aesthetic is, in its widest sense, the way in which people in that society see. Adapting from Michael Baxandall's studies of Western art traditions (1972: 29ff.; 1980: 143 ff.) the phrase 'the period eye', anthropologists might usefully employ the notion of 'the cultural eye'. It is a society's way of seeing, its repertoire of visual skills, which I take to be its visual aesthetic, and it is with this that I believe the anthropological study of visual aesthetics should be concerned. Such an anthropology of aesthetics will be a necessary complement to any anthropology of art, for it surely must be essential to any anthropological consideration of art, however conceived, that an attempt is made to see the art as its original makers and viewers see it.

## The cattle-keeping Nilotes / Nilotic aesthetics

The cattle-keeping Nilotes need little introduction here. This essay focuses on the Nuer, Dinka, Atuot, and Mandari of the Southern Sudan, concerning each of whom there is a substantial and easily accessible literature, while making passing reference to the closely related Anuak of the Southern Sudan and the more distantly related Pokot and Maasai of East Africa. The Nuer and Dinka in particular are well known to all students of anthropology.[1]

For Nilotic-speaking cattle-keepers, cattle are the most highly valued possessions. This analysis of Nilotic aesthetics is, therefore, centred on cattle. The importance of cattle for the Nilotes is well known, and I do not propose to summarize the literature here. I wish to concentrate on the perceptual qualities of cattle as they are apprehended by their owners. These concern the colour configuration and sheen of the hide, the shape of the horns, and the bigness and fatness of the body including particularly the hump. These are discussed first, and then their ramifications into other areas of Nilotic life are traced.

Of primary importance for this discussion are the cattle-colour terminologies which are so characteristic of the cattle-keeping peoples of East Africa.[2] Nilotic languages in general have many terms to describe the colour configurations of cattle. Even people who no longer keep cattle or depend upon them materially may maintain cattle-colour terminologies. The Anuak, for example, who, according to Evans-Pritchard (1940b: 20), can only have been a pastoral people 'a very long time ago', still based their metaphorical praise-names upon cattle colour configurations when Lienhardt studied them in the 1950s (Lienhardt 1961: 13n.). Cattle colour terms rarely refer to pure colours or shades of colours, but rather to configurations of colours or, in a loose sense of the term, patterns.

For the Western Dinka, Nebel (1948: 51) recorded twenty-seven terms, while for the Ngok Dinka, Evans-Pritchard (1934) recorded thirty. For the Nuer, Evans-Pritchard (1940a: 41–4) showed that there are 'several hundred colour permutations' based on ten principal colour terms multiplied by at least twenty-seven combination terms. In his 1934 article on Ngok Dinka terms, he promised that he would publish a full account of Nuer terms, a promise repeated in *The Nuer* (1940a: 44). The fact that the promised lengthy analysis, of what he noted in 1940 was a 'neglected' subject (ibid. 41n.), has never appeared suggests how difficult such an analysis would be. Indeed, the application of the abstract terminology to real animals is not always straightforward for Nilotes themselves. According to Deng (1973: 96), 'the colour-patterns are so intricate among the Dinka that frequent litigation centres on their determination'. And Ryle has described (1982: 92)—in interesting terms, given the subject of this essay—how

> When discussing the colour pattern of an animal—as they do for hours—the Dinka sound more like art critics than stockbreeders. For instance, when does *mathiang*—dark brown—become *malual*—reddish brown? If the animal has brown patches, are they large enough to make it *mading* or are they the smaller mottling that identifies *malek*?

Such discussions are a matter of both appreciation and classification, perhaps more akin to the discussions of antique-dealers or wine connoisseurs than to those of art critics.

It is not necessary to analyse these terminologies at length here. It is sufficient to identify briefly the principles underlying the perceived configurations. For Mandari, the colours red, white, and black have much symbolic importance (Buxton 1973). With cattle, however, they are not so interested in pure colours; what is important is that an ox should be piebald or variegated. When a piebald is born, its owner is delighted and the beast is set aside as a display ox (ibid. 6). Similarly, Ryle has described (1982: 93–6) the 'hopeful expectation' that attends the birth of a new calf amongst the Agar Dinka. He relates how in one instance Mayen, the cow's owner, 'was ecstatic, beaming with pleasure and singing snatches of song, because the calf was a much desired *marial*'. It is the destiny of such well-marked male calves to become 'song', or 'display' oxen, being castrated when they are eight or nine months old. Animals with the most highly valued configurations are thus excluded from breeding. Ryle was told that one cannot anyway predict the occurrence of such colour patterns, 'and therefore there is no point in trying to breed from them' (ibid.: 93; cf. Howell et al. 1988: 282). For the Western Dinka Lienhardt (1961: 15) records how, when a male calf of a highly valued configuration is born, 'it is said that … the friends of its owner may tear off his beads and scatter them, for his happiness is such that he must show indifference to these more trivial forms of display'. If the dam that has produced the well-marked calf is a good milch cow, Dinka may find it hard to choose whether to keep the calf for stud purposes, knowing that is likely to produce further good milch cows, or castrate it for display. They may hope that the dam will produce another, not so well-marked, male calf later, and castrate the one it has already produced. Mandari also choose their stud bulls from the progeny of good milch cows. All other things being equal, they will choose well-coloured ones; but, significantly, not the piebald or variegated but the plain black or red calves, trusting that these will produce offspring which are well-marked (Buxton 1973: 6).

In fact, most cattle are not well-marked. Buxton noted that the majority of Mandari cattle are a nondescript white (ibid.), and my own experience would support this. That they are relatively rare helps to explain why well-marked beasts are valued to such an extent that the Agar Dinka, for example, 'will trade two or three oxen of unexceptional colourings for one particularly desirable beast, if the owner is willing to part with it' (Ryle 1982: 92).

The sheen of the hides is also appreciated and valued. Though sheen is not a factor in cattle-colour terminologies, its appreciation can be amply illustrated by the amount of time and effort expended in the grooming of cattle, and by frequent reference to it in poetry and song. An Atuot song, for example, includes the words: 'the back of my ox is as white as the grazing in the new grass'—the image, as Burton explains (1982: 274), being 'of morning dew glittering in the sunlight'. A song by Stephen Ciec Lam, a Nuer, refers to 'my sister's big ox / whose glossy hide shines against the compound' (Svoboda 1985: 32). Another by Daniel Cuor Lul Wur, also a Nuer, refers to an ox whose hide 'is like the sun itself: he is the ox of moonlight' (ibid. 19). And yet another by Rec Puk relates how 'Jiok's hide is as bright as moonlight, / bright as the sun's tongue. / My Jiok shines like gold, / like a man's ivory bracelet' (ibid.: 11). In this last example, specific comparison is made between the white-on-black cattle hide and the whiteness of the ivory bracelet shining against the black Nuer skin.

The training of ox-horns is practised by cattle-keeping peoples all over the world. Nilotes cut the horns of young display oxen so that they grow into shapes which their owners find particularly pleasing. To describe such horn shapes the Nuer have six common terms, as well as 'several fancy names' (Evans-Pritchard 1940a: 45). In combination with the cattle colour configuration terms, these considerably increase the number of possible permutations to specify individual beasts—logically, to well over a thousand. The horns may also be adorned with buffalo-tail hair tassels to accentuate the effect. When Burton (1982: 279) was carrying out his field-work among the Atuot, such tassels were exchanged at the rate of one tassel for six cow-calves. Cutting also thickens the horns, and large and heavy horns are especially characteristic of display oxen among the Mandari (Buxton 1973: 7).

Appreciation of horns is expressed in song. A Dinka song, for example, tells of an 'ox with diverging horns, / The horns are reaching the ground; / The horns are overflowing like a boiling pot' (Deng 1972: 84). The range of imagery is vast: Cummins (1904: 162) quotes a Dinka song in which an ox's horns are said to be 'like the masts of ships'—presumably referring to the masts of sailing ships which once plied the Nile and its tributaries. Horns are also sometimes decorated with ash, when oxen are exchanged in bridewealth, for example, the effect being to make them stand out more against the dull background of sky and landscape.

In his discussion of the Nuer attitude to their cattle, Evans-Pritchard (1940a: 22) referred to 'those aesthetic qualities which please him [a Nuer] in an ox, especially fatness, colour and shape of horns'. And, according to him (ibid.: 27), it is fatness which is most important, for 'colour and shape of horns are significant, but the essential qualities are bigness and fatness, it being considered especially important that the haunch bones should not be apparent'. He goes on (ibid.): 'Nuer admire a large hump which wobbles when the animal walks, and to exaggerate this character they often manipulate the hump shortly after birth.' This admiration of humps is shared by the Dinka and Atuot. A Dinka song (Deng 1972: 81) has the lines: 'My ox is showing his narrow-waisted hump. / The hump is twisting like a goitered neck, / Staggering like a man who has gorged himself with liquor; / When he walks, the hump goes on twisting / Like a man traveling on a camel.' Another Dinka song, quoted by Cummins (1904: 162), refers to an ox whose hump is 'so high that it towers above the high grass'.

The qualities of bigness and fatness are also referred to in songs. An Atuot song recorded by Burton (1982: 272) refers to an ox which is the subject of the song as 'the mahogany tree', thereby likening the size of the ox to the tree. Another Atuot song (Burton 1981: 107) tells of an ox which is said to be 'so large like an elephant'. A Dinka song recorded by Cummins (1904: 162) tells of an ox which is 'so big that men can sit and rest in his shadow'. It should be stressed that bigness and fatness are not appreciated because they will lead to a better price at market, or to a larger meal on the death or sacrifice of the animal: cattle are primarily a feast for the eyes, and only secondarily a feast for the stomach.

Before going on to trace some of the ramifications of these elements of Nilotic 'bovine' aesthetics into the Nilotes' appreciation of, and action in, the world, it is worth making the attempt to understand why the particular perceptual qualities identified are so appreciated.

The appreciation of a large hump and of bigness and fatness are presumably at least partly explicable as indicators of healthy and well-fed beasts. And the same can presumably be said for the appreciation of sheen—it indicates a sleek and healthy hide; though it should be noted that sheen is perceptually exciting in and of itself, so its appreciation can be understood as a particular manifestation of the universal appreciation of brightness.

The appeal of horn shapes is not difficult to understand in the field. One quickly learns to appreciate the variety of trained and untrained shapes in a forest of horns in the cattle camp.

Both the symmetrical and the asymmetrical curving shapes of Nilotic cattle horns have great visual appeal, especially when they are seen moving through space as the cattle move their heads, and when the arcs the horns make in the air are exaggerated by the swinging movements of the tassels. Fagg (e.g. 1973) has drawn attention to the frequent use of exponential curves in African art: the Nilotic appreciation of the curving shapes of cattle horns can be seen as yet another instance of this theme in African aesthetics.

As with horns, the appeal of particular cattle-colour configurations cannot be explained by reference to the healthiness or well-being of well-marked beasts. The majority of such beasts, though, are likely to have larger body proportions than other beasts, as the majority of well-marked beasts are castrated, and neutering encourages body growth. They also spend no energy in sexual activity and much less than uncastrated cattle in fighting; so their body growth is further encouraged and they remain physically unblemished. In general, more care is lavished on them by their owners, and one can expect this to have a beneficial effect on their health and well-being. Well-marked beasts are thus also likely to be big and fat, and vice versa. It would, however, be a strange argument which explained the appeal of well-marked beasts by the fact that they are healthier, when their being healthier depends upon their being well-marked.

As aestheticians stabilize their theories by explaining why highly prized works of art are so valued, the explanation for the Nilotes' appreciation of well-marked cattle might be sought in what they value most highly. For the peoples who are the focus of this essay, it is bold pied markings. For the Western Dinka at least, it is in particular the black-and-white configurations *majok* and *marial* (Lienhardt 1961: 15). The former is most simply described as a black animal with a white chest, the latter as a black animal with a white flash on its flank. Black-and-white configurations provide strong contrasts. Buxton offered an explanation of the appeal of such contrasts, noting (1973: 7) that 'marking and patterning are very highly estimated in the Mandari visual aesthetic; and the strong contrast markings of black on white, red on white, or a combination of all three, stand out so strikingly in a landscape devoid of strong colour that the importance given to it can be readily understood'.

The visual stimulation offered by both black and red markings amongst a herd of greyish cattle is not to be doubted. It might be expected, then, that it should be the pure black or red beasts which are most highly valued. This is not the case, for while the appreciation of well-marked beasts should be understood in the context of a dull and pale landscape and herds preponderantly off-white in colour, it is the contrast of black and white or red and white in the single beast which provides the greatest aesthetic satisfaction. The individual beast, then, provides the locus for stimulating visual experience.

## Aesthetics in the wider world

Having introduced some elements of Nilotic aesthetics, it is possible to trace their ramifications in the Nilotes' appreciation of, and action in, the world in which they live.

The cattle-colour terms are associated with a wide range of phenomena apart from cattle. At its most simple, this involves the recognition of connections between, for example, the ox *makuac*—that is, an ox of the *kuac* configuration—and the leopard, *kuac*. In their poetic imagery, however, the Nilotes go beyond these relatively straightforward linguistic connections to more complex associations. Evans-Pritchard recorded (1940a: 45) some 'fanciful elaborations of nomenclature' among the Nuer where, for example, 'a black ox may be called *rual mim*, charcoal-burning or *won car*, dark clouds'. And amongst the Western Dinka, according to Lienhardt (1961: 13), a man with a black display ox may be known only as *macar* 'black ox', but also as, for example, '*tim atiep*, "the shade of a tree"; or *kor acom*, "seeks for snails", after the black ibis which seeks for snails'.

It is not just that Nilotes make metaphorical connections between cattle-colour configurations and other phenomena; it is not just poetic play. In a real sense they see the world through a sort of grid or matrix of cattle-colours:

> The Dinkas' very perception of colour, light, and shade in the world around them is ... inextricably connected with their recognition of colour-configurations in their cattle. If their cattle-colour vocabulary were taken away, they would have scarcely any way of describing visual experience in terms of colour, light, and darkness. (Lienhardt 1961: 12–13)

This is not, of course, to say that they could not perceive the black ibis or the shade of a tree if it were not for the existence of black oxen, but it is to say that their visual experience and appreciation of the ibis and the shade is inseparable from their appreciation of the *macar* colour configuration in cattle.

Those cattle-colour terms, such as *makuac*, which are clearly related linguistically to natural phenomena, are no doubt derived from the term for the phenomenon and not vice versa. Presumably the Dinka called the leopard *kuac* before they called the spotted ox *makuac*. However, the *kuac* configuration in cattle is not called after the leopard because of some significance of the leopard as such, but because it is like the pattern to be found on *kuac*. Children will learn the names of cattle-markings, and then apply them to natural and cultural phenomena, before they ever see the source of the name in markings. A Dinka child will know what *kuac* means as a marking pattern, and will be applying it to cattle and to spotted cloth, for example, well before he or she ever—if ever—sees a leopard. The visual experience of young Dinka is focused on cattle and their markings, and the cattle-colour terminology is learned through listening to daily discussions about cattle. As Lienhardt (ibid.: 12) writes, 'a Dinka may thus recognize the configuration in nature by reference to what he first knows of it in the cattle on which his attention, from childhood, is concentrated'. This fact is of greater significance than the possible historical origins of the terms.[3] That the Nilotes' visual perception of their natural and cultural world is thus shaped by their interest in, and experience of, the colour configurations of their cattle is amply attested, both by their complex cattle-colour terminologies and by the rich poetic and metaphorical elaborations of these terminologies by which associations are made between the most diverse visual experiences and cattle-colours. These associations are not by any means always obvious; part of the pleasure of composing and singing songs is in making creative connections which one's audience has to work at to comprehend.

That these associations are not made only in poetic contexts, however, is shown by Lienhardt's remark (1961: 19) that Dinka 'frequently pointed out to me those things in nature which had the *marial* colour-configuration upon which my own metaphorical ox-name was based'. One might expect a man to become particularly attuned to the colour-configuration of his own name or song ox, but as Lienhardt's anecdote makes clear, this attuning is not exclusive; Dinka recognize and appreciate a wide range of colour-configurations. Agar Dinka friends called me Makur, explicitly referring to the dark rings around my eyes like the black patches round the eyes of the ox *makur.* Other Agar to whom I was introduced immediately grasped why I had been so called.

## Aesthetics and society

So far I have discussed some of the qualities of perceptual experience recognized and appreciated by Nilotes. Little reference has been made to 'art', 'beauty', or 'the good', which are so often taken to be defining terms of the aesthetic. Nor has reference been made to those traditional concerns of anthropology, such as social organization and social structure, to which analysts have attempted to link aesthetics. The discussion of elements of visual appreciation in a given culture is an end in itself, contributing to an understanding of what it is to be a member of that culture. Nevertheless, I shall try to address, albeit briefly, some of the wider concerns often discussed in what has been taken elsewhere to be the anthropology of aesthetics. My concern is to bring out what I take to be the implications for the anthropology of aesthetics of the material presented above.

As for 'art', I have referred to body decoration, mural drawing, and clay modelling, all of which might well have been discussed under a heading of 'art'. I indicated my response to such an approach in the introduction to this essay. Such activities as body decoration and clay modelling have an aesthetic aspect, as all human activity does, and it is the aesthetic aspect of these activities which has been of concern in this essay. No good purpose would be served for the anthropology of aesthetics, as I understand it, in separating such activities as 'art', or in restricting any discussion of aesthetics to them.

As for 'beauty', it is hoped that the terminology adopted in this essay avoids the problems that beset attempts to use such vague terms in accounts of other cultures. An understanding of the aesthetic qualities which we have identified is, of course, relevant for any understanding of Nilotic ideas approximating Western notions of beauty. For example, Lienhardt (1963: 87) quotes a Dinka song in which the singer compares his own 'dazzling array'—glossed by Lienhardt as 'shining beauty'—with that of the ugliness of 'a big coward' to whom a girl in whom the singer is interested has been promised by her father: 'This dazzling array is a poor man's truculence, ee / [That her father] gives her to that big ugly coward to play with, ee / This dazzling array is just truculence'. The words for 'dazzling array' and 'ugly' are, in fact, the cattle-colour terms *marial* and *malou*. As noted above, *marial* is one of the most highly valued black-and-white configurations signifying a black ox with a white splash on its flank. *Malou* is a grey ox, the implication in this context being dullness—*lou* is the Dinka name for a large bustard, probably the visually uninteresting kori bustard (*Ardeotis kori*) (Nebel 1979: 52, 56). That *rial* combined with *nyin*, 'eye', is the Dinka term for 'to dazzle' gives some indication of the Dinka conceptualization of the visual stimulation of the *rial* black-and-white configuration (ibid.: 76). In some contexts, 'pied' and 'beautiful' might be virtually interchangeable: Deng (1972: 63) quotes a song in which some young girls are said to wear 'pied and beautiful beads'.

But what is aesthetically pleasing and what is beautiful are not necessarily the same thing. A better appreciation of Nilotic ideas concerning beauty can be achieved through a discussion of indigenous concepts, such as the Dinka notion *dheeng*, Deng (1972: 14) glosses the term as follows:

> *dheeng* ... is a word of multiple meanings—all positive. As a noun, it means nobility, beauty, handsomeness, elegance, charm, grace, gentleness, hospitality, generosity, good manners, discretion, and kindness. The adjective form of all these is *adheng*. Except in prayer or on certain religious occasions, singing and dancing are *dheeng*. Personal decoration, initiation ceremonies, celebration of marriages, the display of 'personality oxen' indeed any demonstration of an aesthetic value, is considered *dheeng*. The social background of a man, his physical appearance, the way he walks, talks, eats, or dresses, and the way he behaves towards his fellowmen are all factors in determining his *dheeng*.

In the context of this essay it is the perceptual qualities contributing to *dheeng* which are of significance, and some of these, as they relate particularly to cattle, have been identified. But it is clear from Deng's discussion that for the Dinka there is more to 'beauty' than meets the eye.

It is also in the notion of *dheeng* that aesthetics and morality are linked. What is morally good is expected to display valued aesthetic qualities, and what displays valued aesthetic qualities is expected to be morally good. It is recognized, however, that this is far from always being the case. A Dinka man is *adheng* if he has social status, whether ascribed or achieved, if he is virtuous in his relations with others, or if he is physically attractive. Ideally, these three aspects should go together, but Dinka recognize that they do not always do so.

Some of the recent literature in the anthropology of aesthetics attempts to relate aesthetics to social organization or social structure. As presented here, Nilotic aesthetics seems rather to be a contingent product of these cattle-keepers' experience of the world which they inhabit, and to have little to do with any social facts. In his account of the aesthetics of the Fang of Gabon, Fernandez (1971: 373) claims to identify basic principles of opposition and vitality at work in Fang society and culture: 'in both aesthetics and the social structure the aim of the Fang is not to resolve opposition and create identity but to preserve a balanced opposition'. This is achieved in the social structure, he argues, through complementary filiation, and in their ancestor statues through skilful aesthetic composition. Should it not be possible to make such a profound summation concerning the material presented in this essay?

To some extent, one's answer to such a question depends upon one's intellectual temper. No doubt many would find it intellectually satisfying to relate the high value of piedness to the segmentation of Nilotic political structure and to the divided world of Nilotic cosmology. The combination of black and white, or red and white, in the pied ox, the argument might run, is valued because it fits with the principles of the social organization and religious thought. It is probably the case that an intellectually diverting picture of the anthropological material concerning Nilotic aesthetics could be constructed along such lines. But what would it mean? That social structure and cosmology are products of social structure, or that they are all products of underlying principles? For anyone wishing, despite these ontological puzzles, to make links of this sort, there are some suggestive facts in the ethnography to which one might point. They do not, however, stand up to closer inspection.

There is, most famously, the Nuer leopard-skin priest, amongst whose duties it is to resolve conflicts between disputing factions, and to act as an intermediary between man and God. Is it not, therefore, most suitable that he is the *leopard-skin* priest? The leopard-skin is pied, and combines within itself the opposites of black and white. However, the priest is not usually known by this title by the Nuer themselves. The more usual title can be translated as 'earth (or soil) priest'; as Evans-Pritchard (1956: 291) points out, 'the leopard-skin title is taken only from his badge (of office) whereas the earth title is derived from a symbolic association with the earth of deeper significance'. He is, therefore, not in fact a leopard-skin priest, but a priest of the soil who wears a leopard-skin as a badge of office. There is no hint that the Nuer regard a pied skin as suitable, *qua* its piedness, for a priest who is in an intermediate position and whose duty it is to resolve disputes. There is no reason to suppose any more profound reasons for the wearing of the leopard-skin than the symbolic associations of the leopard itself, which are beside the point here, and that it is a visually attractive and bold material symbol.

While Nilotes do not, in general picture God to themselves,[4] Lienhardt relates (1961: 46) how some Western Dinka conceive of Nhailic, God, or Divinity, as being pied.

That Nhialic and Awumkwei [one of the powerful spirits of the sky, the power of rain] should be thought of as pied is not surprising, given how much the Dinka and Atuot value such configurations. The high aesthetic value of pied configurations, whether in cattle or elsewhere, is sufficient reason for Divinity to be thought of as pied, when Divinity is thought of as displaying any perceptual qualities at all.

The appropriateness of different colour configurations for sacrifice to different divinities—or Divinity—amongst the Dinka, is exemplified in a number of cases in Lienhardt's study. In particular, the black-and-white configurations in cattle are especially suitable for sacrifice to the free-divinity Deng, which is particularly associated with celestial phenomena such as rain, thunder, and lightning. It is, however, not the piedness as such which makes beasts of black-and-white configurations suitable for sacrifice to Deng, but rather the imaginative connections between the quality perceived in the black-and white ox and the quality of the lowering skies: 'the black-and-white configurations in cattle … impress themselves upon the minds of the Dinka as does the lightning in dark, overcast skies which signifies the activities of Deng' (Lienhardt 1961: 162). The symbolic action is thus inexplicable without an understanding of the workings of the Dinka imagination, and our appreciation of the working of the Dinka imagination involves, I should argue, an appreciation of Dinka aesthetics.

## Notes

This essay is based primarily on literary research, although, thanks to the British Institute in Eastern Africa and the Social Science Research Council, I was able to visit Agar Dinka and Apak Atuot country in 1981 and Mandariland in 1982. I am grateful to Survival Anglia and the Pitt Rivers Museum, Oxford, for permission to reproduce photographs. For comments on earlier drafts of this essay I am grateful to Gerd Baumann, Nigel Fancourt, Wendy James, Godfrey Lienhardt, John Mack, Andrew Mawson, Howard Morphy, Michael O'Hanlon, John Penney, and Simon Simonse.

1. For the Nuer, see Evans-Pritchard (1940a); for the Dinka, Lienhardt (1961); for the Atuot, Burton (1987); and for the Mandari, Buxton (1973).
2. See e.g. Turton (1980) on the Mursi.
3. The fact that similar patterns are highly valued by geographically contiguous peoples who do not keep cattle—such as the Uduk (James 1988: 28–9)—suggests that these elements may have been part of Nilotic aesthetics even before the Nilotes became cattle-keepers. This is, however, irrelevant to an understanding of the appreciation of such patterns by Nilotic cattle-keepers today, which is founded in their daily experience of their cattle.

4. Evans-Pritchard (1956: 123) says that 'Nuer do not claim to see God', while, according to Buxton (1973: 19), Mandari say 'Creator has not been known or seen', and among the Atuot, according to Burton (1981: 138), '"God the Father" is never said or imagined to exist in any physical form'.

## References


Baxandall, Michael (1972), *Painting and Experience in Fifteenth-Century Italy: A Primer in the Social History of Pictorial Style*, Oxford: Oxford University Press.

Baxandall, Michael (1980), *The Limewood Sculptors of Renaissance Germany*, New Haven, CT: Yale University Press.

Burton, John W. (1981), *God's Ants: A Study of Atuot Religion*. Studia Instituti Anthropos 37. St Augustin, Germany: Anthropos Institute.

Burton, John W. (1982), 'Figurative Language and the Definition of Experience: The Role of Ox-Songs in Atuot in Social Theory'. *Anthropological Linguistics* 24 (3): 263–79.

Burton, John W. (1987), *A Nilotic World: The Atuot-Speaking Peoples of the Southern Sudan* (with a foreward by Francis Mading Deng). Contributions to the Study of Anthropology, No 1. New York: Greenwood Press.

Buxton, Jean (1973), *Religion and Healing in Mandari*, Oxford: Clarendon Press.

Cummins, S. L. (1904), 'Sub-Tribes of the Bahr-el-Ghazal Dinkas'. *Journal of the Royal Anthropological Institute* 34: 149–66.

Deng, Francis Mading (1972), *The Dinka of the Sudan*, New York: Holt, Rinehart & Winston.

Deng, Francis Mading (1973), *The Dinka and their Songs*, Oxford Library of African Literature, Oxford: Clarendon Press.

Diffey, T. J. (1986), 'The Idea of Aesthetic Experience', in Michael H. Midas (ed.), *Possibility of the Aesthetic Experience*, Martinus Nijhoff Philosophy Library 14, 3–12 [271/272], Dordrecht: Nijhoff.

Evans-Pritchard, E. E. (1937), 'Economic Life of the Nuer: Cattle'. *Sudan Notes and Records* 20 (2): 209–45.

Evans-Pritchard, E. E. (1940a), *The Nuer: A Description of the Modes of Livelihood and Political Institutions of a Nilotic People*, Oxford: Clarendon Press.

Evans-Pritchard, E. E. (1940b), *The Political System of the Anuak of the Anglo-Egyptian Sudan*, London School of Economics Monographs on Social Anthropology, No. 4, London: Lund Humphries.

Evans-Pritchard, E. E. (1956), *Nuer Religion*, Oxford: Clarendon Press.

Fagg, William (1973), 'In Search of Meaning in African Art', in Anthony Forge (ed.), *Primitive Art and Society*, 151–68, London: Oxford University Press.

Fernandez, James W. (1971), 'Principles of Opposition and Vitality in Fang Aesthetics', in Carol F. Jopling (ed.), *Art and Aesthetics in Primitive Societies: A Critical Anthology*, 356–73, New York: Dutton (first published 1966).

Forge, Anthony (1970), 'Learning to See in New Guinea', in Philip Mayer (ed.), *Socialization: The Approach from Social Anthropology*, ASA Monographs No. 8, 269–91, London: Tavistock.

Gombrich, E. H. (1977, [1960]), *Art and Illusion: A Study in the Psychology of Pictorial Representation*, 5th edn, Oxford: Phaidon.

Howell, Paul, Michael Lock and Stephen Cobb (eds) (1988), *The Jonglei Canal: Impact and Opportunity*, Cambridge: Cambridge University Press.

James, Wendy (1988), *The Listening Ebony: Moral Knowledge, Religion, and Power among the Uduk of Sudan*, Oxford: Clarendon Press.

Lienhardt, Godfrey (1961), *Divinity and Experience: The Religion of the Dinka*, Oxford: Clarendon Press.

Lienhardt, Godfrey (1963), 'Dinka Representations of the Relations between the Sexes', in I. Schapera (ed.), *Studies in Kinship and Marriage: Dedicated to Brenda Z. Seligman on her 80th Birthday*,

Royal Anthropological Institute Occasional Paper No. 16, 79–92, London: Royal Anthropological Institute.
Maquet, Jacques (1979, [1971]), *Introduction to Aesthetic Anthropology*, 2nd edn, Other Realities 1, Malibu, CA: Undena Publications.
Maquet, Jacques (1986), *The Aesthetic Experience: An Anthropologist Looks at the Visual Arts*, New Haven, CT: Yale University Press.
Nebel, Arthur (1948), *Dinka Grammar Rek-Malual Dialec) with Texts and Vocabulary*, English text rev. by C. W. Beer, Museum Combonianum 2, Verona: Missioni Africane.
Nebel, Arthur (1979 [1954]), *Dinka–English, English–Dinka Dictionary: Thong Muonyjang Jam Jang Kek Jieng, Dinka Language Jang and Jieng Dialects*, Museum Combonianum 36, Bologna: Editrice Missionaria Italiana.
Pepper, Stephen (1974), 'Aesthetics', in *New Encyclopaedia Britannica: Macropaedia*, i., 149–63, Chicago: Beaton.
Ryle, John (1982), *Warriors of the White Nile: The Dinka*, Amsterdam: Time-Life.
Svoboda, Terese (trans.) (1985), *Cleaned the Crocodile's Teeth: Nuer Song*, Greenfield Center, NY: Greenfield Review Press.
Turton, David (1980), 'There's No Such Beast: Cattle and Colour Naming among the Mursi'. *Man* 15 (2): 320–38.
Zangwill, Nick (1986), 'Aesthetics and Art'. *British Journal of Aesthetics* 26 (3): 257–69.

# CHAPTER 17
## PIERCING THE SKIN OF THE IDOL
*Christopher Pinney*

The 'anthropological' theory of art proposed in *Art and Agency* 'merges seamlessly with the social anthropology of persons and their bodies' (Gell 1998: 7). Alfred Gell does a brilliant job of persuading us that anthropologists should concern themselves with the performative dimension of artefacts. In the first part of the book, at least, he rejects a linguistic approach, dwelling instead on the agency of images.

The analysis of image-worshipping practices in a central Indian village which I shall present in this chapter confirms Gell's stress on the agency of images, but my concern is also to try to resolve an earlier question of Alfred's about the nature of aesthetics, and to transpose some of the discussion onto an avowedly political ground. In his 1992 article on the technology of enchantment, Alfred drew a parallel with Peter Burger's suggestion that analysts of religion should adopt a standpoint of 'methodological atheism'. Anthropologists of art required an analogous 'methodological philistinism' which would involve 'an attitude of resolute indifference towards the aesthetic value of works of art' (Gell 1992: 42).

Rather than a resolute indifference, I will propose a sideways step away from 'aesthetics' to 'corpothetics' as one way of comprehending the praxis through which enchantment manifests itself.

By corpothetics I mean the sensory embrace of images, the bodily engagement that most people (except Kantians and modernists) have with artworks.

Shifting the level of analysis from aesthetics to corpothetics discloses not a lack but a rich and complex praxis through which villagers articulate their eyes and bodies in relation to pictures. The 'meaning' of the images lies in their 'needs' – the necessity of worshipping them, in 'corpothetics' rather than 'anaesthetics'.

The village of Bhatisuda,[1] located on the Malwa plateau in Madhya Pradesh, is inhabited by many eager consumers of the images whose history has been fleetingly touched on earlier. Chromolithographs are popular across all castes and religious groups. Jains and Muslims own images as well as Hindus, and Scheduled Caste Chamars and (warrior) Rajputs or (priestly) Brahmans own similar numbers of images. (Across the village as whole there is an average of 6.9 images per household.)

Villagers encounter religious 'objects mediating social agency' in various different forms. Here I will briefly consider consecrated temple images, the presence of deities in the human bodies which they 'thrash' (i.e. 'possess')[2] and (at more length) chromolithographs.

Our understanding of the role of chromolithographs for many people in Bhatisuda must start from a recognition of the prohibitions that still prevent most Scheduled Caste members from entering village temples. Although many Scheduled Castes have their own caste-specific shrines (*autla*, *sthanak*) they are generally unable to enter village temples to the main gods. Whereas 'clean' castes may enter temple precincts, Scheduled Castes are required to squat outside, at some distance. Channu and Lila Mehta – the village Bhangis[3] – are quite explicit that it is this denial which necessitates their domestic engagement with the Gods through chromolithographs. Confirming that her family were still unable to enter most of the village temples, Lila remarked, 'for this reason we have made a temple inside our house'.

Channu and Lila Mehta live in a low mud house on the eastern periphery of Bhatisuda overlooking a steep gulley which drops down to a Chamar *mohalla*. The most striking feature inside the house is a small black and white television, a gift from one of Channu's Nagda resident brothers. To the right of this, two-thirds of the way up the wall is a display of fifteen assorted images, together with a few clay *murtis* (three-dimensional images). In the sort of arrangement which is common in the village, a line of images are displayed above and below wooden shelves bearing an assortment of three dimensional images, colourful decorations and steel cups. Among Channu and Lila's display there are large laminated prints depicting Laksmi and Ganesh, Arjun, Ram Sita and Lakshman, a large black Shivling, and various images of Lakshmi showering wealth from the palms of her hands. There are also two framed prints of the Rajasthani renouncer king Ramdevji, and the Krishnalila, a large glittered image of Satyanarayan in a wooden shrine-like structure, and a mirrored glass panel depicting the local Krishna incarnation Samvaliyaji. Add to this a couple of postcards of Shiv and the Buddha, a couple of paper prints of Durga and Shiv, plaster images of Ganesh and Shiv, two women with their hands folded in a welcoming namaste, a couple of mirrors, some peacocks, tinsel and sundry other plastic decorations together with a flock of frenzied green parrots and the ensemble is complete.

Apart from the glass mirrored image these were all purchased in Nagda – the nearby town – where there are two shops, and one stall specializing in 'framing prints', which prior to the festival of Dipali are supplemented by about a dozen small stalls and itinerant tradespersons selling religious images. Most of Channu and Lila's images were purchased in successive years just before Dipali, and this is reflected in the predominance of images of the goddess Laksmi who is worshipped during this festival which marks the start of the financial year.

The glass mirrored image depicts Samvaliyaji, Avari Mata and Bhadva Mata who are the subject of a recently flourishing cult in Mandsaur District. Channu and Lila had visited the Samvaliyaji temple, as also the nearby Bhadva Mata shrine several years ago and had purchased the image from a stall there. At Samvaliyaji, and also Pavargadh in Gujarat which they had recently visited, Channu and Lila's *madhyam* (low)[4] *jati* and *uttam* (high) *jatis* are indistinguishable for here there is no *chhuachhut* (untouchability) or *bhed bhav* (hierarchy).

Lila's testimony also clearly marks out pilgrimage as an egalitarian activity, not only because many *tirth* (i.e. pilgrimage) sites operate in liminal caste-free spaces, but also because the dislocations of travel and the anonymity of the crowd nullifies any attempt at the sort of *jati* identity which is so entrenched and enforceable in a stable village community. Beyond this parallelism between the dissemination of the divine permitted by lithography, and the comparative openness of the spaces in which pilgrimage happens, we might also point to a simple logistical entanglement – a substantial minority (18 per cent) of all the images in the survey households were purchased at pilgrimage sites and depict deities associated with those.

In Bhatisuda the mere possession of visual forms gives access to the ongoing project of divine energy. Although it is undoubtedly true that in certain key respects popular Hinduism mobilizes a recuperative idiom within a decaying universe, it is fundamentally constructed by what the playwright Brian Friel (in a very different context) once described as a 'syntax opulent with tomorrows' (1981: 42). Mass-reproduction gives formerly excluded classes access to all the high gods whom they can approach directly without the intercession of priests.

The 'syntax opulent with tomorrows' which emerges in Bhatisuda practice is one that springs from a corpothetic practice in which it is the devotee's visual and bodily performances which contribute crucially to the potential power – one might say completion – of the image.

Some sense of the mechanism here can be gleaned from the following fragment of a taped interview with Lila. (I should note at this point that I interviewed members of 117 households in the village, and Lila's is consistent with all but one of these others.)

> [CP] When the picture is on the trolley in the market is there any energy (*shakti*) in the picture?]
>
> [Lila] It's just paper (*kagaz*). That's all? Yes, paper. It's just paper, it hasn't been seated. You see those pictures that are seated? (Lila pointed to the images on the wall.) Those are paper but by placing them before our eyes (*ankh rakna* = to love, to entertain friendship, to admire), *shakti* has come into them [...] We take (the pictures) inside and do *puja*. We place incense sticks (*agarbatti*) against his name, against the God's name. Yes, it's a paper photo but we recite, we recite while the *agarbatti* burns. OK, so it's a paper photo but [that makes no difference]. We entreat the God and the god comes out because the god is saluted. That's how it is.

The other sense in which Bhatisuda images are opulent with tomorrows lies in the stress on their capacity to give *barkat* – plenitude. Samvaliyaji is an example par excellence of a deity who gives *barkat*. Whereas orthodox deities such as Shiv are considered essential to *alaukik labh* ('disinterested profit'), i.e., transcendental concerns, Samvaliyaji can produce *bhautik labh*, that is material or physical profit. Under the general label of *bhautik* are subsumed uncertainties relating to wealth, bodily health and illness, matters relating to employment and agricultural productivity. Like the vast majority of villagers Pannalal Nai (a retired factory worker) lights incense sticks in front of his images at sunrise and dusk. I ask him what he 'says':

> Not much ... give wisdom, give comfort (*gyan rakhna, aram se rakhna*) I just say that. And then in the evening at say 7.30 or 8 o'clock I say the same things that I said in the morning. God, ensure our protection, give *barkat*, food, water, children, small children, protect all this.

The consumption of images by Bhatisuda villagers needs to be understood in terms of these processes of bodily empowerment which transform pieces of paper into powerful deities through the devotee's gaze, the proximity of his/her heart and a whole repertoire of bodily performances in front of the image (breaking coconuts, lighting incense sticks, folding hands, shaking small bells, the utterance of *mantras*).[5] However, many of these images also bear traces of these activities in their form, and in some cases prescribe the process of viewing itself.

The most fundamental mark of the images' sensory quality – their predisposition to this corpothetic regime – is their non-absorptive directness. The vast majority of images behold their owners directly, engaging and returning their vision. As Diane Eck observes, the primacy of sight as the idiom of articulation between deity and devotee is lexically marked so that devotees will usually stress that they are going to the temple for *darshan*, to see and be seen by the deity: it is this 'exchange of vision [which] lies at the heart of Hindu worship' (Eck 1981: 5).

Most villagers 'seat' their pictures without the assistance of Brahmans. Pannalal Nai, however, calls a Brahman to install newly purchased images. On these occasions the priest will swing the image in front of a mirror and perform a *sthapana* (installation) of the deity.

The desire to see and be seen by deities is also evidenced in the prevalence of mirrored images within the village. These images are usually associated with pilgrimage. *Darshan* can be thought of as a physical relationship of visual intermingling. The value of images is related to the visual access they give to the deity. As *Art and Agency* documents, mirrored images allow the devotee to (literally) see himself looking at the deity (in this case there is a double corpothetics – of the devotee's movement through space on pilgrimage where he bought the image, and of the devotee's visual elision with the deity when he places himself in front of the image).[6]

Other modes of image customization – such as the application of glitter, or *zari* (brocade) or the adhesion of paper surrounds or plastic flowers – are also corpothetic extensions that move the image closer to the devotee, transforming the ostensible representation or window into a surface deeply inscribed by the presence of the deity.

Parallel to this we might note the manner in which other objects of value are occasionally introduced onto this surface. There were several examples in the village of the placing of auspicious banknotes against the glass of framed images. Sitabai is the wife of a contracted worker in the nearby factory, and once came across a two-rupee note in the mud road to the next village. 'Found' notes are considered auspicious and should not be re-entered into the cycle of exchange from which they have recently departed. Sitabai chose to stick her note on an S. S. Brijbasi chromolithograph of the Ram Durbar. This practice is not confined to Hindus, for there are two prints owned by a Muslim family against which are pasted two Rs.2 notes which bear a serial number containing sequences (the numbers '786') which Muslims hold to be auspicious.[7] The dressing of images takes the place of words. Instead of exegesis, instead of an outpouring of language – there is a poetics of materiality and corporeality around the images.

*Arati* is a procedure in image worship in which a flame is moved in a circle around an image. In Bhatisuda, villagers then cup their hands over the flame and wash the blessing from the deity onto their face. *Ramdevji ki arati* painted by B. G. Sharma in the mid-1950s (and still in print) exists in several copies in the village and in this artist's characteristically semiotically dense manner inserts the narrative of the deity Ramdev into the very act of worship. The process of *darshan* and the transmission of the 'content' of the picture onto the devotee's face becomes itself the subject, and dictates the form of the picture.

Finally we may note that the whole process of the progressive empowerment of images through daily worship involves a continual burdening of the surface with traces of this devotion. Although some households replace all their images every year at Divali, most have a number of old images which continue to accrue potency as they become accreted with the marks of repeated devotion – vermillion tilaks placed on the foreheads of deities, the ash from incense sticks, smoke stains from burning camphor.

Even at the end of its life, a picture's trajectory is determined by corpothetic requirements, in this case the necessity of ensuring that the image never comes into contact with human feet. Again a fragment from a conversation with Lila:

> (The images) are paper and when they have gone bad (*kharab*) we take them from the house and put them in the river. That way we don't get any *pap* (sin). [CP You don't throw them away?] No, no, we don't throw them away. You take them out of the house and put them in the river or in a well, and place them under the water. This way they won't come under anyone's feet. You mustn't throw them away or they will get lost. That's the proper way (*tamizdar*; decorous) to do it – in the river or well. In our jat we say *thanda kardo* – make cold. That way they won't come under [anyone's] feet.

I asked Pannalal whether he threw his old pictures away:

> No no, no. It's become just like a small temple (*madhi*). We put them in water, we break a coconut and give them *paraba*[8] – in the water. If you throw them in the street they will come under someone's feet.

In Hindi the phrase *pair ankh se lagana* literally means to look at the feet, and idiomatically 'to respect, venerate' and to touch someone's feet is to physically express one's obeisance. Certain images in Bhatisuda encode this hierarchical relationship in which the devotee submits his or her body – through his or her eyes – to the feet of the deity.[9] It is fundamentally important to Bhatisuda villagers that the bodies of the deities which they have so carefully brought to life should not suffer the dangerous indignity of having this relationship reversed.

Sometimes in Bhatisuda I succumb to the regrettable temptation to brag to villagers about my meetings with the producers of the images which adorn their walls. However, my allusions to artists such as B. G. Sharma or Yogendra Rastogi or others of my acquaintance are always greeted with a supreme indifference that suggests that villagers recognize that they themselves are the true artists who have brought the images to their full fruition.

The images purchased and worshipped by Bhatisudans are very different from Vermeer's *Lacemaker* and Trobriand canoe prow-boards. They produce no sense of 'captivation' (Gell 1998: 68–72) and there is no interest in or recognition of these images as the product of particular artists. Villagers have no conception and no emotional investment in the 'materials artists manipulate', since without the devotee's creative input the images do not function properly. Like the *'Slashed' Rokeby Venus* by Mary Richardson (Gell 1998: 63–4), villagers produce infinitely more powerful images than the original artists ever managed.

In addition to the disjunctions created by most Bhatisuda villagers' refusal to inhabit the era of art, we must briefly map a much more profound conflict that informs the relationship between mass-produced images, temple *murtis* and those that 'thrash'.

At one level there is much in popular Hinduism to support the general argument of *Art and Agency*. A common response by villagers when questions of differences between deities is discussed is to throw up their hands and say '*ek hi maya hai*' – it is all (just) one illusion, one 'play'. They mean by this that 'ultimately' all the differences are resolvable into a single central imaginary form. In this sense villagers affirm that the gods can be thought of as a network of stoppages. One might also see in images of Hanuman – composed of an endless repetition of the name of his master (Ram)[10] and of the *trimurti* of Ramakrishna, The Mother, and Kali (in which the three faces coalesce in a common physiognomy) – further evidence of a concentric/fractal idiom.

But rather in the same way as I have suggested above that we need to theorize a bodily praxis in order to understand the reception of Hindu chromolithographs, we need also to position the formal discourses and representational conventions described in the paragraph above in the context of the chaotic physical enactments of being Hindu in Bhatisuda village. Once we do this, the formal articulations and synoptic overviews start to assume the same marginal position that 'aesthetics' has in relation to everyday 'corpothetics'.

During Nauratri – two periods of nine nights each year associated with goddesses – some Scheduled Caste households remove their domestic chromolithographs and place them in the Jhujhar Mata *autla* (shrine) which is maintained by Badrilal, a Bagdi (Scheduled Caste) *pujari*. The (usually framed) prints spend nine lunar days nestled against the red stones and paraphernalia that form the centre of the shrine and accumulate an additional power from the excess energy of the consecrated shrine during this period. Domestic images are also installed in the Bihari Mata shrine which also lies in the Bagdi *mohalla*. Bihari Mata lives under a *nim* tree on the southern fringe of the village and large laminated prints of Durga and Kali are nailed to the trunk of the tree and an old framed image of Durga is propped behind several red tridents that sprout from the base. This framed image is taken in the parade around the village at the conclusion of the nine nights along with the bowls of wheat shoots (*javara*) which will be cooled at the end of the procession. However, the relationship between chromolithographs and consecrated images, and that between those that thrash and consecrated images, is not always so tranquil.

Nauratri is a very dangerous period: it is 'hot' (*tamsik*) and vast numbers of *bhut pret* (ghosts and spirits) thicken the air. They live 'with a free hand' (*khuli chhut rehte*) and 'play' without restraint. The unpredictability of events is intensified by the numbers of villagers who thrash. Several *bhopas* or *ojhas* (mediums) will without fail thrash, and a further dozen or so villagers (some predictable, some not) will also thrash with sundry goddesses, spirits of ancestors who met violent deaths and *jhujhars* and *sagats* (warriors who died from either a single blow to the neck, or several blows, respectively).

In Bhatisuda, Nauratri is often eventful. During the Kvar Nauratri in 1995, Kushal Singh – the village psychopath – strode up to Kannaji, a Chamar *ojha* who, thrashing with Shitala (the goddess of smallpox), was making his twice-yearly circuit of the village. Dressed in a sari, Kannaji is led backwards around the village and those seeking protection for the coming year sit in his path, waiting to be stepped over. Kushal Singh faced Shitala/Kannaji and then punched him ferociously in the mouth. The following year Kushal Singh – sober and contrite – prostrated himself in front of Shitala/Kannaji inscribing his inferiority so that the whole village could see.

But it is events in 1993 which have a special relevance for the argument I want to make here. An extract from fieldnotes:

> The predominantly Bagdi procession which had set out from the Bihari Mata shrine was outside Mohan Nai's house near the central *chauk*. Bihari Mata had entered the body of Hemraj and she was wearing a green veil and holding a lime-tipped sword. She danced wildly around Lal Mata who was in the body of Badrilal – the *pujari* of the Jhujhar Maharaj *autla* – in an orange sari and mixed in this melee was a *sagat* in the body of the Rajput Balwant Singh. Two girls carried pots of *javara* (wheat sprouts) and between them a Bagdi boy carried Hemraj's framed Durga picture which had until then been

displayed in the Bihari Mata shine. As this swirling mass of people made its way down anticlockwise through the village, women and children, and Rup Singh knelt down to have their afflictions cast out. This involved a curative fanning (*jhadna*) effected with the bedraggled peacock whisks held by the two goddesses. Every so often Badrilal would appear to choke and then, with cheeks bulging, a lime would appear from his mouth.

What happened next showed the extent to which this frenzied outpouring of ecstatic energy fractured the normally hierarchical ordered space of the village. Outside the house of Kalu Singh the Rajput *sarpanch*, Badrilal swirled in a particularly aggressive manner as the goddess succumbed to some intense rage and it seemed as though everyone would invade the premises. Then the procession veered suddenly away toward the nearby Krishna temple where the ferociously angry goddess ordered that the *javara* and the image of Durga be taken inside. The *javara* were then placed on the platform at the front of the temple and at this stage Jagdish Sharma the Brahman *purohit* who lives just to the left of the temple shot across the front of his verandah and started to plead with the Goddess in Badrilal. Badrilal was frenzied, shouting and spluttering, his cheeks bulging as though his throat would at any moment disgorge limes.

This was an extraordinary and dangerous moment. Jagdish was clearly terrified. For about ten seconds it seemed completely probable that Badrilal might try to chop off Jagdish's head with his sword but in the event he retreated. Marigold and rose petals were scattered over the front of the temple and the procession moved on through the Bagdi *mola* southwest towards the Lal Mata *autla* and the Chambal river.

Later, discussing this incident, Mohan Singh and Pukhraj Bohra (both of whom are non-drinking vegetarians), opined that Jagdish Sharma had imposed his *rok-tok* (restriction/obstruction) because Badrilal was drunk and if he had polluted the purity of the temple space that protected the Krishna *murti* there would have been *nuqsan* (destruction). The 'skin' that surrounded the *murti* was imperilled, and it was to protect this that Jagdish had risked his life. Badrilal produced a corpothetic engagement with the Krishna *murti* that was incommensurable with the dominant order. The ecstatic dimension to thrashing brought Badrilal very close to piercing the skin of the Krishna idol.

*Art and Agency* does consider the 'relationships that exist between [artworks] as individuals, and other members of the same category of artworks, and the relationships that exist between this category and other categories of artworks' (1998: 153). However these questions are only ever framed stylistically and formally, never politically. The three different categories of divine embodiment that I have discussed in this chapter do not support a 'fractal' view of artworks or of 'concentric idols'. The wonderful description that Alfred provides of the multiple skins of the Jagannath temple in Puri elides a Brahmanic fantasy about how the cosmos should be ordered with the messy reality of contemporary India. That contemporary reality – with which a different sort of anthropology of art might engage – is not a place of tranquil homunculi. It is, rather, structured by disadvantageous flows and the conflict that this gives rise to. In these conflicts – as I have tried to document ethnographically – the skins of some idols may be pierced by others. Alfred Gell does a brilliant job of focusing on the ways in which objects mediate social relations: the task now is to analyse the different and conflictual social relations that make objects work for them.

## Notes

1. The 1991 Census recorded the village population as 1,366.
2. *dhunana* = to beat, to thrash, and also to card cotton. Villagers will say *mataji dhun rahi hai* (the goddess is thrashing), *jhujhar dhun raha hai* (jhujhar is thrashing) and so on.
3. Sweepers, and removers of what is usually euphemistically referred to as 'nightsoil' (human excrement).
4. Literally 'middle', metaphorically 'low'.
5. On these grounds one might wish to qualify the claim made in *Art and Agency* (Gell 1998: 118) that imagistic devotion is achieved 'entirely by looking'. The notion of corpothetics is intended to draw attention to the much wider sensory field within which agency is manifest.
6. This corpothetics is often reinscribed as the owner traces the journey either with his eyes or his fingers as he or she recalls the journey. Bhavaralal Ravidas pointed out various parts of his Pavagadh image, 'there is a temple here that you can't visit because there's a tiger living near the path'.
7. At the village level, Muslim image practices are hard to distinguish from Hindu and Jain ones. Nane Khan, who noted that he owned 7 *dharmik tasviron* (religious pictures) said: 'They're from Macca-Medina [You've been there?] No … They're from Ajmer … they have lots of *shakti*. After bathing we wave an *agarbatti* (incense stick), clasp our hands, *bas*. We offer flowers, garlands … we get *prasad*. If you have a completely truthful heart you'll get what you want. There's a Ramayan isn't there? Well, it's like that but better (*aur zyada*) …'
8. Malwi. Hindi = *visarjan*.
9. For instance in photographic images of a Surat-based guru, Shri Paramhansji, and some Jain images of the (literal) footprints of *acharyas*.
10. In Devanagri script, conceptualized as a *mantra*.

## References

Eck, D. L. (1981), *Darsan: Seeing the Divine Image in India*, Chambersburg: Anima Books.

Gell, A. (1992), 'The Technology of Enchantment and the Enchantment of Technology', in J. Coote and A. Shelton (eds), *Anthropology, Art and Aesthetics*, 40–63, Oxford: Clarendon Press.

Gell, A. (1998), *Art and Agency: an Anthropological Theory*, Oxford: Oxford University Press.

Mitchell, W. J. T. (1996), 'What Do Pictures *Really* Want?' *October* 77 (Summer).

# CHAPTER 18
# FROM ETHNOMUSICOLOGY TO ECHO-MUSE-ECOLOGY: READING R. MURRAY SCHAFER IN THE PAPUA NEW GUINEA RAINFOREST
*Steven Feld*

> The piece was originally requested as a contribution for Murray Schafer's 60th birthday party, a conference titled "The Tuning of the World" held at the Banff Centre for the Arts in 1993. That is why it has an oral form (I had no idea it would ever be published and did not revise it for publication). I presented it with rainforest sounds in the background, to an audience of mostly composers and sound art and radio people, including, of course, Murray himself. Murray had a long habit of coining terms and suggesting to his art friends that new coinages were important ways to invent soundscape studies. The playfulness of my title was a friendly gesture in that direction, and a gentle attempt to make the crowd of largely sound artists less nervous about more research-oriented or ethnographic approaches to sound.
>
> Steven Feld, 2014

What role can an anthropological voice have in this large mix we're calling acoustic ecology and soundscape studies? How is this voice complementary to, yet distinct from, voices from history, acoustics, performance, design, psychology, geography, musicology, composition, architecture, philosophy, or communications? One way to answer is with the simple observation that anthropologists tend toward the Kantian view that all knowledge begins in experience. We jump off that cliff to study how human experiential patterns and practices construct the habits, systems of belief, knowledge, and action we call culture. And we study it everywhere and anywhere we can. Our ultimate concern is with people, with adequately and evocatively representing their experiential worlds, their voices, their humanity. To take up that concern the anthropological project basically must ask, what could it possibly be like to be – to feel, sense, imagine, act, become – another kind of person? A full answer, of course, is an impossibility. We cannot become another. But the challenge of getting close or at least closer, of glimpsing, hearing, touching other realities, is thoroughly compelling to us. Another way to say it is that what turns us on is human complexity and diversity, and we celebrate and document it all, from beauty and hope to horror and despair. In fact we tend to do this in far more detail and with far more obsession than the general public cares to know about. We justify what others perceive as our excess by claiming, simply, that there is too much we don't know about the sources and varieties of human difference. But deep down we hope that by writing and circulating other peoples' histories, by giving their voices places to speak and shout and sing from, we in some measure combat and counter the longstanding arrogance of colonial and imperial authority, of history written in one language, in one voice, as one narrative.

When it came time to do a dissertation fieldwork project on some aspect of language and music, I abandoned the usual framework and rudely called my project by a deliberate counter term: an ethnography of sound, or, an ethnography of sound as a symbol system. I wanted to study ways sound and sounding link environment, language, and musical experience and expression. Taking up the simple hypothesis (one I'd heard years before, from my undergraduate teachers Colin Turnbull and Edmund Carpenter) that rainforest environments might be the places where humans developed to acute levels of acoustic adaptation, I headed for the rainforests of south central Papua New Guinea, about as remote and different a place as I could possibly try to experience and know.

As I learned about the symbolism of the weeping and singing voice I was taught about their intimate connection to rainforest birds.

In Papua New Guinea I lived through 1976–7 with the Kaluli people of Bosavi, on the Great Papuan Plateau, working in collaboration with another ethnographer, Edward L. Schieffelin, and another linguist, Bambi B. Schieffelin. My focus was on ritualized vocal expression, principally Kaluli women's funerary sung weeping and Kaluli men's ceremonial poetic songs that brought audience members to tears. As I learned about the symbolism of the weeping and singing voice I was taught about their intimate connection to rainforest birds. This is because birds, for Kaluli as with most Melanesians, are spirits, and spirit voices – from talk to cries to song – are reflected in bird sounds. Ritual weeping and song recall and evoke the presence of spirits, and are understood as expressions of sadness embodied in being a bird. This sadness makes listeners cry like birds, completing a symbolic and emotional circle.

In this and other ways I learned how the ecology of natural sounds is central to a local musical ecology, and how this musical ecology maps onto the rainforest environment. For songs and weeping not only recall and announce spirits, their texts, sung in a poetry called "bird sound words", sequentially name places and co-occurring environmental features of vegetation, light and sound. Songs become what Kaluli call a "path", namely a series of place-names that link the cartography of the rainforest to the movement of its past and present inhabitants. These song paths are also linked to the spirit world of birds, whose flight patterns weave through trails and water courses, connecting a spirit cosmology above to local histories on the ground.

I analyzed these sorts of issues to write an ethnography of sound (Feld 2012 [1982]). The book concerned the Kaluli world of birds, myth, and cosmology and how they were united with poetry, song and lament. My interpretation showed how Bosavi birds turn into Kaluli singers and weepers, how Kaluli singers and weepers turn into Bosavi birds, and how all of this is a local ecology of "voices in the forest".

It wasn't until the early 1980's, when most of this research and writing was initially done, and I was teaching courses on sound at the Annenberg School of Communications at the University of Pennsylvania, that I encountered R. Murray Schafer's *The Tuning of the World* (1977), and the publications of the World Soundscape Project. I found these publications very exciting; they opened new windows into a familiar world, one that could now be re-imagined from the standpoints of acoustic ecology and soundscape studies. I took these publications with me to the Bosavi rainforest during my field trips in the 1980's, and re-reading R. Murray Schafer's suggestion that people "echo the soundscape in language and music" I began to transform myself from an ethnomusicologist to an echo-muse-ecologist.

"Ethno" always implies otherness, but "echo" is about presence, about reverberant pasts in the present, presents in the past. And I remembered: sound is memory, here as everywhere.

From there I began to explore how the Kaluli soundscape, from its bird calls to song paths of place-names, is always about memory, about absence and presence, about how in the forest sound reveals what vision conceals. This is beautifully enunciated in the Kaluli idea for "echo", the mimetic compound "gugu-gawgaw." "Gu" is downward moving sound; by duplication "gugu" marks the action as continuous. "Gaw" is outward moving sound; "gawgaw" likewise marks continuity. So the auditorally ambiguous melange of continuous downward and outward moving sound is what is heard and instantly felt as "echo". In the forest one easily confuses the height and depth of sound, particularly in the absence of visual cues. In this place "echo" means that upward sounds like outward. The phonesthesia (phonetic synaesthesia) of Kaluli vowels trace movement this way, becoming one with what they sound like in both everyday language and song poetry.

"Lift-up-over sounding", like "harmony", is both a grand metaphor for natural sonic relations … as well as for social relations …

The blur from music-ology to muse-ecology was equally obvious, for the important thing in Bosavi wasn't "pieces" or "forms" of music in isolation, but rather the constant interplay of inspiration, imitation, and incorporation that linked the flow of natural and human sound expressions. A way of hearing the world comes from interacting with it, but it also has to do with appreciating it, imagining it as one's very own.

Exploring Kaluli echo-muse-ecology in the Bosavi rainforests lead me to realize that what I was trying to understand all along was that the language and music of nature are intimately connected with the nature of language and music. Shifting from the realm of ritual performances to that of everyday experience and expression I learned that sounds are heard as time of day, season of year, vegetation cycles, migratory patterns, forest heights and depths. Place resounds as a fused human locus of space and time. Local acoustic ecology can thus be considered a kind of aesthetic adaptation, a naturalization of place, or, put differently, a pattern of ecological and aesthetic co-evolution.

The most recent extension of these concerns, developed in the field research I've done in the 1990s, is what I call acoustemology (i.e. acoustic epistemology). These days I am exploring acoustic knowing as a centrepiece of Kaluli experience; how sounding and the sensual, bodily, experiencing of sound is a special kind of knowing, or put differently, how sonic sensibility is basic to experiential truth in the Bosavi forests. Sounds emerge from and are perceptually centred in place, not to mention sung with, to, and about places. Just as "life takes place" so does sound; thus more and more my experiential accounts of the Kaluli sound world have become acoustic studies of how senses make place and places make sense.

… the full body is always present in the "flow" of the voice, just as the connections of land are always present in the "flow" of water …

Two important keynotes of a Kaluli acoustemology, both richly hearable on *Voices of the Rainforest* (CD/cassette, 1991), my hour-long soundscape of a day in the life of Bosavi and the Kaluli, are complex local notions translatable only as "lift-up-over sounding", and "flow." The first of these, "lift-up-over sounding" is as potentially omnipresent in the experiences and aesthetics of Kaluli as the notion of "harmony" is in the West. "Lift-up-over sounding", like "harmony", is both a grand metaphor for natural sonic relations, the ways tones combine together in time, as well as for social relations, for people doing things together in concert. In the Kaluli world "lift-up-over sounding" sounds are dense and layered, blended, and forever thinning and thickening. One hears no unison, only a constant figure to ground motion of densities, decays, and fades, of overlapping, alternating, and interlocking sounds. These sounds, whether in the forest, in Kaluli music singing, or in the overlap of the two, are "in-synchrony but out of phase". By this I mean that they are always cohesive, yet always seeming, as well, to be at different points of displacement from a hypothetical unison. Neither a clear-cut polyphony nor heterophony, "lift-up-over sounding" sounds define an acoustic spacetime where upward is outward. One sound stands out momentarily, then just as quickly fades into a distance, overlapped or echoed by a new or repeated emergence in the mosaic. This pattern of sounding in the natural environment is the inspiration for many Kaluli vocal and instrumental forms. Likewise it is the pattern of fluid but tense egalitarian social life, where an anarchic synchrony of energy and assertion take prominence over fixed categories, in a social order without political or economic hierarchy.

One of the ever-present "lift-up-over sounding" sounds of the Bosavi environment, layered as a ground to the remarkable figures of avian life, is the hiss of water. Runoff from Mt. Bosavi, an extinct volcano, crisscrosses the Bosavi lands, turning into numerous rivers, creeks, falls, and streams. Walking means crossing water, yet always hearing it before seeing it. Water carries in and out of visual perceptual immediacy but always has dramatic, though ever-changing, acoustic presence. This carrying power, moving through and connecting lands, is water's "flow". But this "flow" does not only exist in the way water connects what Kaluli call the "thighs" (i.e. saddles) and "body" (i.e. hills) of the land. Water is to land what the voice is to the body. The voice connects the many parts of the body; by resounding in the head and chest, the full body is always present in the "flow" of the voice, just as the connections of land are always present in the "flow" of water.

Water flow also animates much of Kaluli musical imagination, as all waterway terms are also the names for the musical intervals, the segments of song, the patterns of rhythm, and the contours of melody. And composing songs is like getting a "waterfall in your head"; the pool is the melody in motion and the fall the text mixing into the melody to create song. Kaluli compose their songs by creeks or waterfalls, singing with and to them. And the texts of these songs are maps of waterways or trails, viewing them from above as spirit birds might. Additionally, "flow" is also the carrying power of poetic song, the way it stays in memory. A waterway can be continually heard but visually appears, disappears, and reappears when one walks through forest trails. This is its "flow", its path of carrying. Likewise as one hears a song, it disappears quickly from an experiential foreground and reappears through time in memory, reverberating and lingering in sonic traces and fragments, far past and beyond the moment of an immediate experienced performance.

This is how Kaluli songs, like Bosavi waterways, "flow", emerging in the density of a "lift-up-over sounding" soundscape of rainforest acoustic ecology.

On *Voices of the Rainforest* you can hear many kinds of Kaluli "lift-up-over sounding", from birds waking a village, to women singing, whistling, and talking with their children as they work to scrape and pound sago, to men whooping and singing as they clear a forest garden, to a bamboo Jew's harp duet with cicada rhythms and bird calls, to singing with a creek, to the dusk volleys of frogs and birds overlapped by an evening rainstorm, to a quartet of in-sync and out of phase drummers, and a duo of ceremonial singers overlapped by a man who is moved to crying by their song, to the density of night winds, mists, frogs, and insects.

The aesthetic apex of this "lift-up-over sounding" is where it meets with the "flow" of poetic song, on a section of *Voices of the Rainforest* called "Relaxing at the Creek". "Here a woman named Ulahi sings three songs, in three different song genres, all with and to the Wolu, a creek situated near her village. Her voice develops a pulsing pattern that densely flows with the sounds of the creek where she sits, and her songs develop different place paths, including one that sings a long succession of places connected to the creek she is singing in. On these selections the performative flow of singing with water and the musicality of singing like water connect deeply to the emplacing poetry of singing about water. Evoking the flowing presence of creek paths, Ulahi's songs, like the Wolu creek where she sang them, meander and flow through Kaluli lives and memories, by linking together places and suggesting that the flow of their names tell stories about events and feedings. Ulabi once told me that every one of her songs (I've recorded about 200 of them since the mid-1970's) was like a pool on a creek. So every Kaluli song swirls, centres, circles in place, then flows on to mingle and merge with places and voices elsewhere.

Singing about water, with water, and imagining song as water and vocal flow–here the poetry of place meets the sensuality of soundscape and the singing voice. This is where the "lift-up-over sounding" of Kaluli song "flow" creates an acoustemology of embodied place resounding.

## References

Feld, Steven (2001), *Bosavi: Rainforest Music from Papua New Guinea*, 3CD Boxset, Washington, DC: Smithsonian Folkways.

Feld, Steven (2011 [1991]), *Voices of the Rainforest*, CD, Washington, DC: Smithsonian Folkways.

Feld, Steven (2011 [2001]), *Rainforest Soundwalks*, CD, Santa Fe: VoxLox.

Feld, Steven (2012 [1982]), *Sound and Sentiment: Birds, Weeping, Poetics, and Song in Kaluli Expression*, Third and Thirtieth Anniversary edn with a new Introduction, Durham: Duke University Press.

Feld, Steven (2015), "Acoustemology," in David Novak and Matt Skakeeny (eds), *Keywords in Sound*, 12–21, Durham: Duke University Press.

Schafer, R. Murray (1977), *The Tuning of the World*, New York: Knopf.

# CHAPTER 19

## MANSIONS OF THE LORD: ARCHITECTURE, INTERIORITY, DOMESTICITY

*John L. Comaroff and Jean Comaroff*

### Righting angles, setting squares: Reconstructing the architecture of the everyday

> [T]he Bakwains [Kwena] have a curious inability to make or put things square .... In the case of three large houses, erected by myself at different times, every brick had to be put square by my own right hand.
>
> David Livingstone (1857: 26)

The right hand of reason would find it hard to straighten out the contours of Tswana social life. Its circular, erratic forms—the shapes associated with rank nature and "primitive" mentality (Comaroff and Comaroff 1986: 13; cf. Lévi- Strauss 1972: 204)—did not submit easily to the square set of civilization. Not that this deterred the missionaries. Determined to effect what we might call a syntactic "[re]distribution in space" (Foucault 1979: 141), they were to manifest a very general modernizing impulse in the West. "Improvement makes straight roads," wrote William Blake (1975) from the depths of his experience. Just as Thomas Jefferson saw fit to organize the American wilderness—even before it had been mapped—in terms of Euclidian geometry (Sinclair 1977: 102), so the evangelists in Bechuanaland set out to subsume the unruly figures of African existence in a grid of gentility. And to do so with similar dispatch. John Philip (1828, 1: 240) recalls that, on arriving among the Khoi, Charles Pacalt "drew out a ground-plan of his intended village, which he laid out in two open streets parallel to each other." After persuading some of the local people "to build more decent habitations for themselves" and to surround them with fenced gardens, he went about enclosing the village itself in a substantial wall, six feet high. To the extent that Europeans saw manmade boundaries as marks of civilization, Pacalt's fortress must have been an impressive sight indeed.

The effort of the evangelists to work their transformations on Tswana architecture and domestic arrangements had two sides. One, couched in the subjunctive mood, was exemplary; the other, cast in the indicative, was more directly interventionist. In the first instance, they set out to create models for the Africans to admire, desire, and emulate. In the second, they sought, by their own deeds, actively to intrude their designs onto the local terrain and into local habits and habitations.

#### *The mission as model: (i) home and family*

The evangelists believed that their own dwellings and family lives ought to be held out as a visible ideal to Tswana. "The life of the missionary," according to John Mackenzie (1871: 466), had to be at once desirable and attainable enough to "be copied by his flock." This extended to the outer form and inner design of his abode, the manner of its construction, its appointments, and the domestic routines of its occupants. The notion that their dwellings ought to serve as a *transparent* model—an example of "Godly domesticity ... open to all eyes" (Langmore 1989: 85)—did not always sit easily with the Nonconformists' concern for their own privacy. But that was an unavoidable cost of their calling.

While all the evangelists put up some form of temporary habitation when they arrived at a new site, many tried, from the first, to build in a manner befitting a "decent" existence—however stripped down. The mission house, as they saw it, was the core of civilization in the wilderness, the nucleus from which a Christian community had to start. It was also the most visible sign of their presence. Edwards (1886: 101) gives us a sense of the humble beginnings of a station, this one among the former "Mantatees":

> At Umpukani ... we had to live in our wagons or in 'hartebeest' houses.[1] Here also we had a reed and pole structure put up for a place of worship... . We then got put up a little place containing two small rooms and a kitchen, the walls being built of sun-dried bricks.

One of the two small chambers, he added regretfully, had initially to serve as both sitting room and dining room; it had also to accommodate visitors. The other was for sleeping. As time passed, this structure was enlarged and refined; eventually it became a "good-sized" house (Whiteside 1906: 336). Close by, at Matlwasse, the Rev. Broadbent began more ambitiously (Tilby 1914: 192): "He built himself an ample wooden house, whose single story was divided into bedroom, general living-room, and store-room for food and books." Broadbent (1865: 61) himself stressed that his store room was partitioned, the pantry being set off from the depository for books and tools. He implies, too, that the living room, the largest chamber, was apportioned into "sitting" and "dining" areas. Like moral reformers in Europe, the missionaries in South Africa insisted that Christian propriety was impossible for families living "all in one room"—whether it be a hovel in underclass Britain (Jephson 1907: 31), a hut in the African bush (Willoughby 1911: 70), or a transient mission house in Bechuanaland.

In sum, Edwards, Broadbent, and other early evangelists might have seen themselves as ascetic pioneers, far from centers of gentility. But—as these texts underscore by remarking the unremarkable—they took pains to lay out the architectural principles of a civilized life inasmuch as they could: to set off private spaces from spaces of sociality; to divide apartments into discrete areas for cooking, sleeping, sitting, dining, storage, and so on; to make all rooms "quite square" (Moffat and Moffat 1951: 59). Even in their wagons, en route to the "field," the most basic of these principles had been respected: enclosed familial interiors, home to women and children, were securely curtained off from the public exterior, where the missionaries engaged with black laborers, dealt with animals and natural obstacles, and interacted with the world at large.

As they settled into more permanent, ample houses, the evangelists elaborated yet further the domestic domain in which they lived, partitioning spaces by gender and generation, by mode of activity, and by the degree of closure and intimacy appropriate to them. Where possible, separate rooms were made for girls and boys, placing them beyond the conjugal chamber and its sacred altar, the marital bed (cf. Perrot 1990: 124); nurseries, studies, and guest rooms were added; eating areas became dining rooms; and so on. These may have been small apartments. But separation, not size, was the point. When the Moffats' new house at Kuruman was completed in 1826, it had, in addition to a kitchen and a pantry, four rooms plus a hall; an adjoining cottage was being built for visiting evangelists on their way to other stations (Moffat and Moffat 1951: 231, 190). Similarly, Livingstone's (1959,1: 105) dwelling at Mabotsa, erected in 1844, included one bedroom (there were no children yet), a pantry, a study, and a sitting room; its kitchen, tended by a Tswana servant, was outside.[2]

Equally important were the fixtures and fittings of these houses. Windows and doors had at first to be improvised (Broadbent 1865: 62; E. Smith 1957: 176). But frames were typically installed, in the European mode, with hinges, latches, nails, and screws brought from the Cape Colony. Later, more elaborate iron castings were used (e.g., Livingstone 1959,1: 105); some were forged locally at mission stations, some imported, along with other building materials, by traders who made their way into the interior. Shutters, too, were fitted, and, where possible, inside and outside walls—made of brick and stone rather than clay[3]—were whitewashed. Floors were a problem, since they had to be fabricated from local products, and, as many of the evangelists agreed, indigenous techniques were by far the most effective. Likewise roofs, which were usually thatched in much the same manner as were those of Tswana dwellings. This resort to vernacular styles and methods is a point to which we shall return.

Of all household fittings, however, perhaps the most important were locks and glass. The missionaries insisted on doors that could be properly secured and on windows that let in light; indeed, these were essential to their very idea of home. While latches and bolts ensured the sanctity of private possessions, personal space, and familial intimacy, windows were apertures of enlightenment. Recall volume 1 (pp. 181f.): glass was, to the early modern imagination, an important medium of civilization, permitting enclosure yet translucence. Once upon a time the privilege of the church (Braudel 1981: 296–7), its illuminating properties had long been commonly (and inexpensively) available to house builders. The evangelists brought together its hallowed and domestic aspects: they encouraged Africans to open up the dark interiors of their lives—and to make within them a place for such edifying pursuits as sewing or reading.

And a place for furniture. Household furnishings, like fixtures and fittings, began modestly on the evangelical frontier: Broadbent (1865: 61), again, tells how he contrived his first bed from "poles and leather straps," on which he laid a "hair mattress" (see also Moffat and Moffat 1951: 59). Most ambitious, perhaps, was Price, at Molepolole, who fashioned a bed, a table, cupboard, bookshelves, and a couch out of packing crates and other odds and ends (Smith 1957: 176). But these were strictly temporary measures. The objective was to fill indoor spaces with manufactured effects, the kind of domestic commodities that Southern Tswana might covet and, in due course, buy. Hence, once permanent stations had been established in the interior, most of the evangelists brought some furniture with them; usually beds, tables, and chairs. All gradually acquired more—wardrobes, cupboards, dressers, sofas, and the like—often imported by wagon from the south. Sooner or later, mission houses were filled with Victorian appointments; with the embroidery, bric-a-brac, photographs, cushions, pianos, and other necessities of a suitably feminized British middle-class home (cf. Langmore 1989: 85).

Never, we stress, was the intention merely to erect and furnish a commodious mission house—even though personal comfort and bourgeois self-construction *was* a matter of concern to many of the evangelists.[4] As important was the demonstrative aspect of the gesture. Building a residence was a definitive and dramatic statement of values, of purpose, of resolve. It was also an early opportunity to put before would-be converts a concrete vision of prospect and possibility; the prospect of a different kind of existence in which heathen hardship might be replaced by the "purer and sweeter" trappings of civilization (Mackenzie 1871: 465). Here was yet another effort to instill in Southern Tswana a new sense of want and need. That is why, when Read received permission to work among the Tlhaping (*RR*I: 201), he immediately set about constructing a house that would be a "wonder to all"; why he was so quick to report that many came "flocking" to see it; why he promised to erect an identical one, presumably as publicly, for the wife of the chief. Explained David Livingstone (1857: 46), if the Christians wanted their works "to be respected by the natives," they had to have houses of "decent dimensions, costing an immense amount of manual labour." It is unclear whether the Africans shared the labor theory of value advanced by the evangelist. But they do seem to have declared themselves impressed by the European accommodations. So much so that the missionaries believed their exertions to have been successful. John Mackenzie (1871: 467), for example, reported that "[a]fter being shown, at their own request, some of the rooms of our house, a party of the wives of petty chiefs at length broke out, addressing Mrs. Mackenzie: 'Happy wife and happy mother! You have a "kingdom" here of your own.'" Mackenzie was as delighted that the Tswana women had *asked* to see the mission house—itself proof of its exemplary power—as he was to tell of its impact on them. Both affirmed that this dwelling, its interiors suitably appointed, had in fact served its purpose.

Livingstone and his colleagues also had another point in mind in stressing the need to erect substantial mission houses. For them, the cultural worth of a dwelling lay in the fact that it congealed a civilized, Christian act of construction. This act, in turn, bore within it a set of practical teachings. The first, and most important, had to do with a properly refined, appropriately gendered division of labor. European edifices, palpably, were made by males (even if Tswana females sometimes helped them with floors and roofs). It was the divinely ordained duty of men to house and provide for their families—and, at home, to do all the outside manual work. The role of their womenfolk was to decorate the finished interiors of their dwellings, to apply their "domestic arts" to its "tasteful" furnishings, and then to minister inside over its everyday routines.[5]

The second lesson was a respect for specialist building skills, which the missionaries learned and/or hired craftsmen to perform (see n. 45) in the hope that Tswana would take their lead.[6] It was their fond wish that, inspired by watching work in progress and perhaps by toiling alongside the Europeans, a cadre of "native" artisans would be formed. In the short run, this hope proved groundless. As Livingstone (1857: 123) once commented, testily:

> They observe most carefully a missionary at work until they understand whether [for example] a tire is well welded or not, and then pronounce upon its merits with great emphasis, but there their ambition rests satisfied … . It was in vain I tried to indoctrinate the Bechuanas with the idea that criticism did not imply any superiority over the workman.

And in vain that he tried to indoctrinate them with the Protestant work ethic itself. Here lay the third lesson of missionary mimesis. By employing men—at first, men from the Colony—to help them build, the Nonconformists sought to demonstrate the worth and the workings of wage labor, time, and money:[7] the object again being to tie the rewards of enlightened consumption, via the immediate purchasing power of cash, to the act of production.

Once built and furnished, the mission house became a diorama. On its stage was displayed, for all to see, the domestic round of "the exemplary married couple" (Jolly 1989: 234).[8] So, at least, we are told. Many narratives of the South African interior, especially those aimed at mass Christian audiences, described a "typical" day in the life of the evangelical family.[9] These accounts implied—optimistically—that much of this day was lived under Tswana scrutiny. No doubt idealized for popular purposes, it typically began with an early rise, ablutions, and family worship. For wives, this was usually followed by one or more instructional activities. Thereafter, they would attend to their own domestic chores. Their husbands, meanwhile, taught the older children and adults, and then did their manual and agrarian labor. All of this was interspersed with pastoral, medical, and charity work, and with public religious services. Evenings were devoted, where possible, to such "improving" activities as reading, embroidery, and prayer. The entire daily cycle was punctuated by regular, sustaining meals and modest refreshments taken *en famille*—and occasionally, in later years, with royals (Price 1956: 395). Southern Tswana might first have encountered Protestant production in the mission garden. But it was in the mission house that they were shown how to dispose of its fruits, how to nourish bodies and minds through "responsible" consumption.

### *At the frontier …*

It will be recalled how, in putting up their dwellings, especially early on, the evangelists relied on indigenous construction techniques; how most of them thatched their roofs, usually with local help, and had Tswana women make their floors in *setswana* style. But the reliance on vernacular design went yet further. Broadbent (1865: 61–2), for instance, in a hurry to start work at Matlwasse in the 1820s, decided "to build a house in the manner of the natives, though of a different form." The difference, as he perceived it, lay in its division into rooms. Little else. Had his account appeared in a contemporary "scientific" text, with pronouns altered from "we" to "they," it could as well have been a description of "native house-building":

> [W]e dug holes in the ground at proper distances, in which we set up perpendicular [wood] posts, well fastened by ramming the earth in around them. We then placed horizontal beams along the top, and fastened these and the rafters with thongs cut from the hides of oxen, which, being used while soft, became, when dry, hard and firm. The intermediate space between the main posts was filled with smaller spars, crossed with woodbines, and the squares filled up with clay.

And so on.

Much later, at Shoshong in the 1860s, John Mackenzie's (1871: 247) first house—he called it a "temporary hut," but lived in it for several years—was built on land allocated by the chief, according to "the custom of the natives."

Its structure "was more picturesque than symmetrical, [being] made of poles, plastered [with clay] on both sides, and thatched with reeds." Although the interior was partitioned, the "kitchen," like the cooking area in all Tswana homesteads, was outside. Other than having windows of calico, in fact, it must have been largely indistinguishable from the surrounding dwellings.

As this suggests, the tendency to mimic African housing styles was not confined to the pioneering generation of evangelists, with its urgent need for shelter. And it was not limited to the erection of "temporary huts." The Nonconformists might have been untiring in their condemnation of Tswana construction—and in their insistence on the virtues of the right angle, the straight line, and the square. Yet, when they put up their own permanent homes, all over Bechuanaland, they continued to depend on local designs, techniques, materials, and artisans (Smith 1957: 177).[10] Nor was this grudgingly done. As de Kock (1993: 213–15) observes, the Christians often developed a taste for indigenous domestic practices—admitted in their private letters, if not in their publications—and quickly overcame their squeamishness with the "filth" of "native" life. Some mission wives, for example, saw to it that their houses were smeared with cow dung once a week; in a few cases, they did the labor themselves.[11] Mary Moffat, in fact, made an enthusiastic pitch for the healthful, aesthetic qualities of "fine clear green" animal excrement as a floor covering.[12]

As it was on the other side of the dialectic, so here too: the impact of *setswana* on the evangelists is tolled less through their words—for all that they said a lot—than through their works. Like other whites in southern Africa, they were greatly affected by the practical aesthetics of African architecture. The primary evidence? A set of sketch plans of mission houses across the country, circa 1876, accompanied by a water color of the Rev. Williams's residence at Molepolole. With its terra-cotta walls, its yellowing, ragged-edged thatched roof, its veranda bounded by vertical poles across the front, this dwelling is reminiscent of a large contemporary Tswana abode—notwithstanding its chimney and oblong shape. Like Mackenzie's "hut" and Livingstone's Mabotsa home, the house at Molepolole, and the others for which we have plans, also had detached exterior kitchens and stores.

There is secondary visual evidence as well. Willoughby's *Native Life* has two pictures of older mission residences, one at Kanye and another, a derelict, at Shoshong (n.d.: 43, 6). Both were adobe and thatch structures, again very un-English in style. The L-shaped Kanye homestead, with its enclosing earthen wall, also resembled a *setswana*-style compound. A feature that the photograph hides, but that we know of from the sketch plan, is that it had "outhouses" for cooking and storage; nothing is disclosed—anywhere—of toilets. A third photograph, of a merchant's dwelling at Palapye, shows that other whites in Bechuanaland were building in much the same mode as well. Clearly, a synthetic architecture was emerging. It was a frontier style that fused European outer shapes and inner partitions with a range of Tswana design elements and materials.

Sometimes the accommodations of Europeans in the interior were yet more visibly Africanized, losing even their rectangular shape. One form, later known as the "rondavel" (from the Dutch *rond,* "round")—a circular, one-roomed building with thatched roof—became widely favored. It afforded cheap, pleasant, practical housing. Writing from northern Bechuanaland in 1894, Willoughby reported of two British female teaching assistants:[13]

> The ladies are better off in point of accommodation than we are … . I have spoken of their "two huts." They are huts, but they are really good huts, and will be quite comfortable for many years … . They have a decent kitchen fitted up in the courtyard … . You need not be anxious about their health on the score of their accommodation.

Note the volte-face: round huts, in African style, were now made out to be healthy, congenial, and long-lasting. And outdoor kitchens had become "decent."

Rondavels were to prove a convenient answer to the residential needs of the mission, especially in housing people of relatively humble status within the Christian community (women teachers, "native" evangelists, and the like). Sometimes they served other purposes too. The first English church at Palapye, for example, was a round hut "bought" by the LMS (Willoughby n.d.: 58). Surrounded by a classical Tswana brush fence, it looked as "traditional" a building as one could have imagined at the end of the nineteenth century. Willoughby (n.d.: 59) joked, caustically, that it was "such very early English" in style—that is, so unrecognizably primitive—that a notice board had to be nailed to a nearby tree to explain what it was. Nonetheless, as a House of God, it seems, its sole drawback was that it became unpleasantly warm during the evening service.

In due course, the rondavel would mushroom all over white southern Africa—and not only among the humble. Today it appears in contemporary farmhouse architecture, in public buildings, hotels, and resorts ("nature" and "game" parks notably among them), and, on occasion, within compound urban homesteads. Its basic design has been elaborated in various ways over the decades. The circular nucleus is often doubled or trebled. It may even be made oval. But the essential form persists. The conical clay and thatch structure that began as a white man's bricolage, a redeployed African (de)sign, has become a generic *southern African* style, one that now transcends ethnic particularity.[14] A splendid example, ironically, is St. Marks Anglican Church in Lobatse, a border town in Botswana.[15] Erected in 1934 and often refurbished, this light-brown stone edifice has been made to look as if it were constructed of earth. The effect is heightened by the yellow translucence of its small windows. Its thinning grass roof is woven, *setswana*-style, into a tight, oblong coiffure, and the sandy ground around it is raked clean of leaves and dirt. Flanked by a smaller round "hut," and enclosed by a hedge of dry brush that resembles a thorn fence, it looks for all the world as if it has been carefully set down in a *lolwapa,* a homestead compound.

Over the long run, then, the mutual appropriation of aesthetic forms, as much by Europeans as by Tswana, led to a steady convergence in frontier housing styles. Nor was this merely a convergence of facades. It entailed the way in which space was constructed and experienced; lived, so to speak, in the round.

## Notes

1. This was an indigenously coined usage (Edwards 1886: 90). Its connotations and associations are unclear.
2. By the 1870s, as sketch plans in the LMS archives show, most mission premises were yet more elaborate. One had ten rooms: two bedrooms, a nursery, sitting and dining rooms, a study, a pantry, kitchen, and two stores. We found these plans—and a water-color of the mission house at Molepolole—attached in the CWM archives to a letter from Charles Williams; C. Williams, Molepolole, 25 September 1876 [CWM, LMS In-coming Letters (South Africa), 38–3-C]. We return to them below.
3. Sometimes house walls were constructed with the aid of skilled artisans, either itinerant Europeans or men temporarily hired by the mission; a few evangelists learned brick making and laying from them (Moffat and Moffat 1951: 190; Mackenzie 1871: 411).
4. When, for example, the LMS delayed funding a new mission house, Willoughby wrote: "[I]t needs the utmost care to protect our children in this country from influences of a terribly

degrading order. It is very much more difficult when the home has but two bedrooms in it." W. C. Willoughby, Palapye, 22 September 1894 [CWM, LMS Incoming Letters (South Africa), 51–2-B].

5. The evangelists seem implicitly to have shared, with some modern theorists in geography, the idea that the spatial and the social division of labor emerge and exist interdependently (see Pred 1985: 342)—although they would not, of course, have put the matter in quite this way.
6. For a detailed description of early LMS efforts to have Africans learn skills and trades, see J. Philip (1828,1: 206–23).
7. Perhaps the most extreme case of an evangelist using construction to teach a European sense of the value of labor was that of Charles Pacalt, missionary among Khoi, whom we encountered earlier; on his activities, see J. Philip (1828,1: 240f.).
8. This presupposes that missionaries were married. Most LMS and WMMS evangelists were. Not so, however, those of the PEMS in South Africa. (Early nineteenth-century archives in Paris indicate that the Directorate of the Society believed marriage to be an excessive burden on the time of their agents.) This led to some interesting exchanges in mission circles, exchanges that underscore our point. For example, Samuel Rolland, who was influenced by Moffat et al., wrote to Paris pleading to be allowed to wed; in this he had been encouraged by Philip. He "needed a woman," he said, not for his pleasure, but to socialize, domesticate, and inculcate morality into young Tswana females. This woman would also be able to start an infant school. Stations with European wives, he concluded, were doing much better than those without—precisely because of the kind of Christian work a family man could do. See S. Rolland, Kuruman, 19 November 1830 [SMEP/DEFAP, Correspondance des champs de mission, Afrique australe (H-2100), vol. 1831–32, #7; although dated 1830, the letter is included in the microfiche volume of a year later].
9. For an exemplary account in a "serious" mission text, if one that enjoyed a very large readership, see Livingstone (1857: 47).
10. This is evident from a wide range of missionary communications. For just two examples—separated, for emphasis, by seventy years and hundreds of miles—see W. C. Willoughby, Palapye, 22 September 1894 [CWM, LMS Incoming Letters (South Africa), 51–2-B)] and S. Broadbent, Matlwasse, 23 August 1823 [WMMS, South Africa Correspondence, 300].
11. Northcott (1961: 82–3) excerpts a letter in which Mary Moffat describes how she and Mrs. Helm smeared their floors regularly with cow dung. Quoting this letter, de Kock (1993: 82–3) offers an insightful analysis of private confessions, by missionaries and their wives, of the adoption of African domestic practices.
12. Mary Moffat also grew to like soured "Bechuana milk," despite its preparation in "dirty vessels"; what was described early on as a heathen refreshment was said later to be "quite delightful" (quoted in Northcott 1961: 82–3). The Moffats' private correspondence (1951: *passim*) shows that some of their diet was of indigenous provenance and was consumed in ways little different from those of the Tswana. See also Livingstone (1974: 125, 77), who often purchased foodstuffs from Tswana, and Elizabeth Price (1956: 443), who recalled how much her family enjoyed "Sechwana porridge."
13. W. C. Willoughby, Palapye, 22 September 1894 [CWM, LMS Incoming Letters (South Africa), 51–2-B].
14. The term *rondavel* (or *rondoval;* "suites-in-the-round") traveled to other British colonial outposts as well. It has recently turned up in advertisements for luxurious holiday accommodations in the English-speaking Caribbean. See, e.g., the British *Observer*, Life magazine section, 29 January 1995, p. 39.
15. This capsule description is based on notes made during a visit to Lobatse in August, 1995, although we first came to know St. Marks in 1970. Outside the serene, shaded church grounds, exuberant street noises assaulted the ear. Sidewalk stalls sold everything from cowbells to Chicago

Bulls caps, worn Bob Marley cassettes to gaudy posters of the Crucifixion, quietly melting chocolate bars to highly colored cosmetics. All of which served to frame St. Marks with particular clarity, underscoring the ironic history of its social and physical architecture.

## Bibliography

Blake, William (1975), *The Marriage of Heaven and Hell*, with an Introduction and Commentary by Sir Geoffrey Keynes, London: Oxford University Press.

Braudel, Fernand (1981), *Civilization and Capitalism, 15th–18th Century*, vol. 1: *The Structures of Everyday Life: The Limits of the Possible*, rev. trans. S. Reynolds, New York: Harper & Row.

Broadbent, Samuel (1865), *A Narrative of the First Introduction of Christianity amongst the Barolong Tribe of Bechuanas, South Africa*, London: Wesleyan Mission House.

Comaroff, Jean and John L. Comaroff (1986), "Christianity and Colonialism in South Africa." *American Ethnologist* 13: 1–20.

Comaroff, Jean and John L. Comaroff (1991), *Of Revelation and Revolution: Christianity, Colonialism, and Consciousness in South Africa*, vol. 1, Chicago: University of Chicago Press.

Edwards, John (1886), *Reminiscences of the Early Life and Missionary Labours of the Rev. John Edwards*, ed. W. C. Holden, Grahamstown: T. H. Grocott.

Foucault, Michel (1978), *The History of Sexuality*, trans. R. Hurley, New York: Pantheon.

Jephson, Henry (1907), *The Sanitary Evolution of London*, New York: A. Wessels.

Jolly, Margaret (1989), "Sacred Spaces: Churches, Men's Houses and Households in South Pentecost, Vanuatu," in M. Jolly and M. Macintyre (eds), *Family and Gender in the Pacific: Domestic Contradictions and the Colonial Impact*, Cambridge: Cambridge University Press.

Kock, Leon de (1993), *'Civilising Barbarians': Missionary Narrative and African Textual Response in Nineteenth-Century South Africa*, PhD. diss., University of South Africa.

Langmore, Diane (1989), "The Object Lesson of a Civilized, Christian Home," in M. Jolly and M. Macintyre (eds), *Family and Gender in the Pacific: Domestic Contradictions and the Colonial Impact*, Cambridge: Cambridge University Press.

Lévi-Strauss, Claude (1972), *Tristes Tropiques*, trans. J. Russell. New York: Atheneum.

Livingstone, David (1857), *Missionary Travels and Researches in South Africa*, London: J. Murray.

Livingstone, David (1959), *David Livingstone: Family Letters 1841–1856*. 2 vols, I. Schapera (ed.), London: Chatto & Windus.

Livingstone, David (1974), *David Livingstone: South African Papers, 1849–1853*, I. Schapera (ed.), Cape Town: Van Riebeeck Society.

Mackenzie, John (1871), *Ten Years North of the Orange River: A Story of Everyday Life and Work among the South African Tribes*, Edinburgh: Edmonston & Douglas.

Moffat, Robert and Mary Moffat (1951), *Apprenticeship at Kuruman: Being the Journals and Letters of Robert and Mary Moffat, 1820–1828*, I. Schapera (ed.), London: Chatto & Windus.

Northcott, William C. (1961), *Robert Moffat: Pioneer in Africa, 1817–1870*, London: Lutterworth Press.

Perrot, Michelle (1990), "The Family Triumphant," in M. Perot (ed.), *A History of Private Life*, vol. 4: *From the Fires of the French Revolution to the Great War*, Cambridge: The Belknap Press, Harvard University Press.

Philip, John (1828), *Researches in South Africa; Illustrating the Civil, Moral, and Religious Condition of the Native Tribes*, 2 vols, London: James Duncan. Reprinted, 1969; New York: Negro Universities Press.

Pred, Allan (1985), "The Social Becomes the Spatial, the Spatial Becomes the Social: Enclosures, Social Change and the Becoming of Places in the Swedish Provice of Skåne", in D. Gregory and J. Urry (eds), *Social Relations and Spatial Structures*, London: Macmillan.

Price, Elizabeth Lees (1956), *The Journals of Elizabeth Lees Price written in Bechuanaland, Southern Africa 1854–1883 with an Epilogue:1889 and 1900*, U. Long (ed.), London: Edward Arnold.

Sinclair, Andrew (1977), *The Savage: A History of Misunderstanding*, London: Weidenfeld & Nicolson.

Smith, Edwin W. (1957), *Great Lion of Bechuanaland: The Life and Times of Roger Price, Missionary*, London: Independent Press Ltd for the London Missionary Society.

Tilby, A. Wyatt (1914), "Some Missionary Pioneers in South Africa", in *United Empire: The Royal Colonial Institute Journal* (NS), 4: 190–5, A. R. Colquhoun (ed.), London: Sir Isaac Pitman & Sons.

Whiteside, J. (1906), *History of the Wesleyan Methodist Church of South Africa*, London: Elliot Stock.

Willoughby, William C. (1911), *A Paper Read before the South African Council of the London Missionary Society at Tiger Kloof March, 1911*, pamphlet, Tiger Kloof: Tiger Kloof Native Institution.

Willoughby, William C. (n.d.), *Native Life on the Transvaal Border.* London: Simpkin, Marshall, Hamilton, Kent. [Published in 1899.]

Wilson, Monica (1971), "The Growth of Peasant Communities. In *The Oxford History of South Africa*", vol. 2, M. Wilson and L. Thompson (eds). New York and London: Oxford University Press.

# PART IV
# MODES OF EMBODIMENT

## Preface

In crafting, in making, in moving, in learning, and in performing, bodies make worlds and the many things that humans populate these worlds with. In drilling down into the physicality and materiality of bodies both literally and figuratively (Bakke), it becomes possible to address not only their signifying potential, but the particularities of flesh and nation and of subjectivity and social order. And yet bodies, as a medium, are unwieldy and resistant, in ways reminiscent of a weaver's reeds (Ingold). As a tool, they must be trained, augmented, and attended to and, as a result, it's both physically and culturally hard to change bodily habits and often impossible to alter our physical capacities. In one way or another all of the excerpts included in this section play with, experiment with, communicate via, laugh at, and invent around bodily incapacities.

Marcel Mauss remembers, with a smile, how when he was in the military during the war, every time the French and English troops swapped off a bit of land, they also had to exchange 8,000 trowels because the French couldn't manage to dig with English trowels and vice versa (1973, 71). These learned ways of doing simple, everyday things—what Mauss calls "the techniques of the body"—are not cross-cultural constants. How we walk, run, dig, swim, etcetera is part of a cultural education, a bodily-becoming of a person recognizable as one sort of being *vis-à-vis* another. "These 'habits' do not just vary with individuals and their imitations," he writes, "they vary especially between societies, educations, proprieties and fashions, prestiges. In them, we should see the techniques and work of individual and collective practical reason …" (171). Part of anthropology's task, for Mauss, was noticing, and in turn investigating, how and when bodily techniques were transmitted across generations as much as across cultures (see also Greene in Part V and Yurchak here, for the thwarting of transmission). Mauss is interested in education—in how, for example, one is taught to swim; he is also interested in media, pointing out how an influx of American films changed the way French women walk.

The concept of "bodily techniques" easily supports a discussion of dance, theater, and performance art. More broadly, it also underscores how bodily affordances and habits become a sort of material, to be worked with and through in the process of making art (see Ingold; Peterson). The body in contemporary art, as in certain religious practices, is the material substance *of* the undertaking (Bakke; Kapchan; Yurchak; Brennan 2010)—an artwork, or a trance state, is not a product, or even an object, so much as the basis of a very particular, effective, and designed embodied experience. What bodies are used to and how they are trained to react, feel, respond, and move, and the ways in which we cajole ourselves into particular actions, with some success and much failure, is the very substance of these undertakings. Deborah Kapchan suggests that gestures, in dances that lead to trance states, are significant for their capacity to produce, rather than to symbolize, a transformation between "a dissolution of one socially recognized self and the emergence of another" (177). "The gestures of trance", she writes, "are embedded in a performance context" they co-occur with and "help effect a change in being;" together with "music and incense, audition and olfaction, [gestures] find their significance in a multisensory matrix" (177).

Embodiment means the body *with the world*: sound, smell, media, design, with bone, muscle tissue, the need to eat, sleep, shit, the capacity to make and to destroy, the possibility of death, and the very dance that marks it (Morphy). Just as Kapchan is concerned with a "change in being," Stefan Helmreich is interested in "the work of rendering meaning from one milieu into another" (2007: 627); and while Bakke investigates changes in scale by means of which bodies and nations become objects of the same sorts of practices and artistic interventions, Alexei Yuchak considers bodily practices that interrupt a strictly ordered social world. The Necrorealists that Yuchak describes challenged a Soviet normative order with activities that disrupted everyday life, whether shoveling snow naked, beating up a crash test dummy, or falsifying anal sex where the passengers of passing trains could catch a glimpse; they confused their unwitting public and "petrified pedestrians" (203). Barely artists, their work of staging events beyond categories recognizable to the state, the Necrorealists were—with the Soviet Union's collapse—made over *into* performance artists, photographers, painters, and film makers. The frame changed and how they were read and how they performed their "work" shifted along with it. While meaningful here in terms of an art-life continuum reflected in the group's practices, this is also important for how art is understood in general in this Reader, which emphasizes the embeddedness of art in social life.

In underwater exploration where sound is the main medium of investigation, the problem of the body out of place is not political or cultural so much as sensory and physiological. The human ear can't hear when submerged under water. This, ironically, leads Stefan Helmreich away from metaphors of immersion and ease and toward a consideration of how information moves from the world into the body. He writes, "Oceanographers do not just merge with their data. Submarines do not just dive in unstructured space. And anthropologists do not just soak up culture. One way immersion functions as a rhetorical tool promising experiential 'truth' is by eliding the question of the organization of space, of medium, of milieu [...]" (187). Immersion leaves out the limitations of physicalities, as well as "questions of how boundaries are produced and crossed ... ." (187; see also Salen and Zimmerman, Part V). Grounding his thinking in what an ear does or is capable of, Helmreich proposes we replace the immersive fallacy with the notion of transduction. "To think transductively," he writes, "is to pay attention to impedance and resistance [...], to the work that needs to be done so that signals can link machines and people together, at a range of scales, from the private to the public. To think transductively is to think from inside the infrastructure that supports the transmission of information across media" (2007: 633).

The embodied world is a difficult world, where failures of translation perdure. And the tools devised, or extant, to bridge or transduce via solidity—bone, metal, fleshy body, gesture—themselves serve as a constant reminder that with transduction something is necessarily lost. The human body does its work through the constant impudence of presence, whether speaking of the performer and his ritual actions (Yurchak, and differently Morphy), the anthropologist and the submarine, the cheesemaker and her tools (Paxson), or the dancer and her trance. Gestures, minds, bodies, senses, and contexts all contribute to the ways in which things, sounds, and movements transit out from the body, becoming, haltingly, the artfully made world.

### Ethnographic exercise

#### *Fieldnotes, with an emphasis on embodiment*

Do participant-observation at your site/of your case.

Write fieldnotes that focus on embodiment—your own experience as well as the bodily actions and behavior of others. Keep your focus near to movement, feeling, and breath. Watch and listen for the blurry, dim, and faded as well as what comes though clearly. Also consider taste, feelings on the skin, and smell, as well as pains in the body (do your feet hurt, does a passerby limp, a museum attendee seek out a chair, etc.).

## Further reading


Bakhtin, Mikhail (2009), “Introduction,” in *Rabelais and His World*, trans. Helene Iswolsky, 1–58, Bloomington and Indianapolis: Indiana University Press.

Brennan, Vicki (2010), “Mediating ‘The Voice of the Spirit’: Musical and Religious Transformations in Nigeria’s Oil Boom.” *American Ethnologist* 37 (2): 354–70.

Clark, Vèvè A. and and Sara E. Johnson (eds) (2005), *Kaiso! Writings by and about Katherine Dunham*, Madison: The University of Wisconsin Press.

Downey, Greg (2005), *Learning Capoeira: Lessons in Cunning from an Afro-Brazilian Art*, Oxford: Oxford University Press.

Dunham, Katherine (1969), *Island Possessed*, Chicago: University of Chicago Press.

Egan, Greg (1989), *Diaspora*, London: Orion Publishing.

Helmreich, Stefan (2007), “An Anthropologist Underwater: Immersive Soundscapes, Submarine Cyborgs, and Transductive Ethnography.” *American Ethnologist* 34 (4): 621–41.

Kulik, Don (1998), *Travesti: Sex, Gender, and Culture among Brazilian Transgendered Prostitutes*, Chicago: University of Chicago Press.

Mauss, Marcel (1973), “Techniques of the Body.” *Economy and Society* 2 (1): 70–88.

Messinger, Seth (2009), “Incorporating the Prosthetic: Traumatic, Limb-Loss, Rehabilitation and Refigured Military Bodies.” *Disability and Rehabilitiation*: 1–5.

Ness, Sally Ann (1992), *Body, Movement, and Culture: Kinesthetic and Visual Symbolism in a Philippine Community*, Philadelphia: University of Pennsylvania Press.

Ness, Sally Ann (2004), “Dancing in the Field: Notes from Memory,” in Susan Leigh Foster (ed.), *Corporealities: Dancing Knowledge, Culture and Power*, 129–54, London: Routledge.

Rosenblatt, Daniel (1997), “The Antisocial Skin: Structure, Resistance, and ‘Modern Primitive’ Adornment in the United States.” *Cultural Anthropology* 12 (3): 287–334

Taylor, Julie (1998), *Paper Tangos*, Durham: Duke University Press.

Wacquant, Loïc J. D. (2004), *Body & Soul: Notebooks of an Apprentice Boxer*, Oxford: Oxford University Press.

Wilcox, Emily (2012), “Dancers Doing Fieldwork: Socialist Aesthetics and Bodily Experience in the People’s Republic of China.” *The Journal for the Anthropological Study of Human Movement* 17 (2).

Wilf, Eitan (2010), “Swinging Within the Iron Cage: Modernity, Creativity, and Embodied Practice in American Postsecondary Jazz Education.” *American Ethnologist* 37 (3): 563–82.

# CHAPTER 20
# TECHNIQUES OF THE BODY

*Marcel Mauss*

## The notion of techniques of the body

I deliberately say techniques of the body in the plural because it is possible to produce a theory of *the* technique of the body in the singular on the basis of a study, an exposition, a description pure and simple of techniques of the body in the plural. By this expression I mean the ways in which from society to society men know how to use their bodies. In any case, it is essential to move from the concrete to the abstract and not the other way round.

A kind of revelation came to me in hospital. I was ill in New York. I wondered where previously I had seen girls walking as my nurses walked. I had the time to think about it. At last I realised that it was at the cinema. Returning to France, I noticed how common this gait was, especially in Paris; the girls were French and they too were walking in this way. In fact, American walking fashions had begun to arrive over here, thanks to the cinema. This was an idea I could generalise. The positions of the arms and hands while walking form a social idiosyncracy, they are not simply a product of some purely individual, almost completely psychical arrangements and mechanisms. For example: I think I can also recognise a girl who has been raised in a convent. In general she will walk with her fists closed. And I can still remember my third-form teacher shouting at me: 'Idiot! Why do you walk around the whole time with your hands flapping wide open?' Thus there exists an education in walking, too.

Another example: there are polite and impolite *positions for the hands* at rest. Thus you can be certain that if a child at table keeps his elbows in when he is not eating he is English. A young Frenchman has no idea how to sit up straight; his elbows stick out sideways; he puts them on the table, and so on.

I have had this notion of the social nature of the '*habitus*' for many years. Please note that I use the Latin word—it should be understood in France—*habitus*. The word translates infinitely better than '*habitude*' (habit or custom), the '*exis*', the 'acquired ability' and 'faculty' of Aristotle (who was a psychologist). It does not designate those metaphysical *habitudes,* that mysterious 'memory', the subjects of volumes or short and famous theses. These 'habits' do not just vary with individuals and their imitations, they vary especially between societies, educations, proprieties and fashions, prestiges. In them, we should see the techniques and work of collective and individual practical reason rather than, in the ordinary way, merely the soul and its repetitive faculties.

Lastly, another series of facts impressed itself upon me. In all these elements *of* the art of using the human body, the facts of *education* were dominant. The notion of education could be superimposed on that of imitation. For there are particular children with very strong imitative faculties, others with very weak ones, but all of them go through the same education, such that we can understand the continuity of the concatenations. What takes place is a prestigious imitation. The child, the adult, imitates actions which have succeeded and which he has seen successfully performed by people in whom he has confidence and who have authority over him. The action is imposed from without, from above, even if it is an exclusively biological action, involving his body. The individual borrows the series of movements which constitute it from the action executed in front of him or with him by others.

It is precisely this notion of the prestige of the person who performs the ordered, authorised, tested action *vis-à-vis* the imitating individual that contains all the social element. That contains all the social element. The imitative action which follows contains the psychological element and the biological element.

But the whole, the ensemble, is conditioned by the three elements indissolubly mixed together.

I call technique an action which is *effective* and *traditional* (and you will see that in this it is no different from a magical, religious or symbolic action). It has to be *effective* and *traditional*. There is no technique and no transmission in the absence of tradition. This above all is what distinguishes man from the animals: the transmission of his techniques and very probably their oral transmission.

Allow me, therefore, to assume that you accept my definitions. But what is the difference between the effective traditional action of religion, the symbolic or juridical effective traditional action, the actions of life in common, moral actions on the one hand and the traditional actions of technique on the other? It is that the latter are felt by the author as *actions of a mechanical, physical or physico-chemical order* and that they are pursued with that aim in view.

In this case all that need be said is quite simply that we are dealing with *techniques of the body*. The body is man's first and most natural instrument. Or more accurately, not to speak of instruments, man's first and most natural technical object, and at the same time technical means, is his body. Immediately this whole broad category of what I classified in descriptive sociology as 'miscellaneous' disappeared from that rubric and took shape and body: we now know where to range it.

Before instrumental techniques there is the ensemble of techniques of the body. The constant adaptation to a physical, mechanical or chemical aim (e.g. when we drink) is pursued in a series of assembled actions, and assembled for the individual not by himself alone but by all his education, by the whole society to which he belongs, in the place he occupies in it.

## Principles of the classification of techniques of the body

Two things were immediately apparent given the notion of techniques of the body: they are divided and vary by sex *and* by age.

### *Sexual division of techniques of the body (and not just sexual division of labour)*

This is a fairly broad subject. The observations of [Robert Mearns] Yerkes and [Wolfgang] Köhler on the position of objects with respect to the body, and especially to the groin, in monkeys provide inspiration for a general disquisition on the different attitudes of the moving body with respect to moving objects in the two sexes. Besides, there are classical observations of man himself on this point. They need to be supplemented. Allow me to suggest this series of investigations to my psychologist friends. I am not very competent in this field and also my time is otherwise engaged. Take the way of closing the fist. A man normally closes his fist with the thumb outside, a woman with her thumb inside; perhaps because she has not been taught to do it, but I am sure that if she were taught, it would prove difficult. Her punching, her delivery of a punch, are weak. And everyone knows that a woman's throwing, of a stone for example, is not just weak, but always different from that of a man: in a vertical instead of a horizontal plane.

Perhaps this is a case of two instructions. For there is a society of men and a society of women. However, I believe that there are also perhaps biological and psychological things involved as well. But there again, the psychologist alone will only be able to give dubious explanations, and he will need the collaboration of two neighbouring sciences: physiology, sociology.

### *Variations of techniques of the body with age*

The child normally squats. We no longer know how to. I believe that this is an absurdity and an inferiority of our races, civilisations, societies. An example: I lived at the front with Australians (whites). They had one considerable advantage over me. When we made a stop in mud or water, they could sit down on their heels to rest, and the *'flotte'*, as it was called, stayed below their heels. I was forced to stay standing up in my boots with my whole foot in the water. The squatting position is, in my opinion, an interesting one that could be preserved in a child. It is a very stupid mistake to take it away from him. All mankind, excepting only our societies, has so preserved it.

It seems besides that in the series of ages of the human race this posture has also changed in importance. You will remember that curvature of the lower limbs was once regarded as a sign of degeneration. A physiological explanation has been given for this racial characteristic. What even [Rudolf Ludwig Karl] Virchow still regarded as an unfortunate degenerate and is in fact simply what is now called Neanderthal man, had curved legs. This is because he normally lived in a squatting position. Hence there are things which we believe to be of a hereditary kind which are in reality physiological, psychological or sociological in kind. A certain form of the tendons and even of the bones is simply the result of certain forms of posture and repose. This is clear enough. By this procedure, it is possible not only to classify techniques, but also to classify their variations by age and sex.

Having established this classification, which cuts across all classes of society, we can now glimpse a third one.

### *Classification of techniques of the body according to efficiency*

The techniques of the body can be classified according to their efficiency, i.e. according to the results of training. Training, like the assembly of a machine, is the search for, the acquisition of an efficiency. Here it is a human efficiency. These techniques are thus human norms of human training. These procedures that we apply to animals men voluntarily apply to themselves and to their children. The latter are probably the first beings to have been trained in this way, before all the animals, which first had to be tamed. As a result I could to a certain extent compare these techniques, them and their transmission, to training systems, and rank them in the order of their effectiveness.

This is the place for the notion of dexterity, so important in psychology, as well as in sociology. But in French we only have the poor term '*habile*' which is a bad translation of the Latin word '*habilis*', far better designating those people with a sense of the adaptation of all their well-co-ordinated movements to a goal, who are practised, who 'know what they are up to'. The English notions of 'craft' or 'cleverness' (skill, presence of mind and habit combined) imply competence at something. Once again we are clearly in the technical domain.

### *Transmission of the form of the techniques*

One last viewpoint: the teaching of techniques being essential, we can classify them according to the nature of this education and training. Here is a new field of studies: masses of details which have not been observed, but should be, constitute the physical education of all ages and both sexes. The child's education is full of so-called details, which are really essential. Take the problem of ambi-dextrousness for example: our observations of the movements of the right hand and of the left hand are poor and we do not know how much all of them are acquired. A pious Muslim can easily be recognised: even when he has a knife and fork (which is rarely), he will go to any lengths to avoid using anything but his right hand. He must never touch his food with his left hand, or certain parts of his body with his right. To know why he does not make a certain gesture and does make a certain other gesture neither the physiology nor the psychology of motor asymmetry in man is enough, it is also necessary to know the traditions which impose it. Robert Hertz has posed this problem correctly.[1] But reflections of this and other kinds can be applied whenever there is a social choice of the principles of movements.

There are grounds for studying all the modes of training, imitation and especially those fundamental fashions that can be called the modes of life, the *modes*, the *tonus,* the 'matter', the 'manners', the 'way'.

Here is the first classification, or rather, four viewpoints.

Which shows you that things we find natural are historical.

It is thanks to society that there is an intervention of consciousness. It is not thanks to unconsciousness that there is an intervention of society. It is thanks to society that there is the certainty of pre-prepared movements, domination of the conscious over emotion and unconsciousness.

## Note

1. Hertz 1929, 1960.

## References

Hertz, Robert (1929 [1909]), 'La pré-éminence de la main droite: étude sur la polarité religieuse', in *Mélanges de sociologie religieuse et de folklore,* Paris: Librairie Félix Alcan.

Hertz, Robert (1960), 'The Pre-eminence of the Right Hand', in *Death and the Right Hand,* trans. Rodney and Claudia Needham, 87–113, London: Cohen and West.

# CHAPTER 21

## "A GESTURE NARROWLY DIVIDES US FROM CHAOS": GESTURE AND WORD IN TRANCE TIME

*Deborah Kapchan*

Incense swirls around me in thick clouds: *jawi, musk, lambre*. The names themselves are intoxicating. Frankincense, musk, myrrh, black and white benzoin, ambergris; the resinous rocks melt on the hot coals of the earthen brazier. Not like wax melts, but first sizzling, the pieces of incense bubble up like hot glass, then drip down the sides of the charcoal as if to envelope and snuff it out. Instead they turn into a yellowish liquid on the reddened coals and almost as quickly the liquid burns and evaporates into a gray-white smoke. This smoke I inhale. From melted stone into gas I inhale its essence, again transmuting substance into substance, the smoke meeting the liquid in my lungs, dissolving into the blood in my veins. And then my brain waves change, electric. The limbs move; the body sways. *Trisitay*, as Moroccans call someone who moves energetically: electricity. This is the alchemy of magic.

The woman to my right is twenty-nine. Fatna already has three children (the oldest is twelve). She married at seventeen. Her husband just came back from the pilgrimage to Mecca. He is forty-eight.

"Does he object to you having trancing ceremonies?"

"No. He sees me having a crisis, *une crise*," she says, switching momentarily into French from Arabic, "and what can he do?"

She first tranced only four years ago. She heard Gnawa music on television, dropped everything, and started trancing. Since then she has been attending *lilas* and holding one of her own every year during the week of the Prophet's birthday. She says she is possessed (*maskuna*). With whom? I ask.

"*Bzaf*," she says, "Many." Lalla Aisha, Lalla Malika, Lalla Mira, and others. "Every time a new one shows up." She had a *crise* just yesterday, she told me, and then leaves my side in order to trance to the spirits in black.

Fatna's use of the French word *crise* is telling. Literally a "crisis," it is generally used to refer to an episode of hysteria, a condition that early European analysts often attributed to the possessed (Rouget 1985). Indeed, Moroccan women are conscious of the different forms of therapy available to them. A few will even seek help with a psychoanalyst for some of their ailments.[1] Fatna's code-switching indexes the degree to which foreign discourses of spirit possession have entered the local semantic domain, but also her cognizance of competing systems of interpretation. She is able to find herself in the two systems at once, without contradiction (though she doesn't see a therapist herself). But if Fatna recognizes the European attitude toward these practices, she is also aware that she needs to be at a Gnawa *lila* and not on a psychoanalyst's couch. Being inhabited (*maskuna*) may have a symptomology that a European may confuse with hysteria (paralysis, lethargy, unexplainable and recurrent illness), but its treatment is of quite a different order.

The man who hosts the *lila* trances all through the night. He knows all the songs. His wife also just returned from Mecca, though he himself has never made the pilgrimage. Nonetheless he is called al-Hajj (one who has made the pilgrimage) in deference to his age and to his wife, the actual Hajja. He likes chewing tobacco and always asks me to procure him some so his wife, who controls the money, won't know. Despite his age, he is very involved with the Gnawa, going to a lot of their *lilas*. Tonight we are assembled in his tented driveway. Although he trances to many of the pieces, his most moving and pathetic performance is with Sidi Musa, or Moses, the *jinn* of water. He becomes infantlike, wanting to make a run for it to the beach. He has to be restrained, then submits to restraint, screaming bleakly, a desperate empty look in his eyes. He trances and sways, crying out to God for forgiveness (*llah y-smaḥ'alinah*); he is bathed with water, finally falling down, his small feet and hands yellow, his mouth ajar.

At Sidi Mimun's song I get up to trance, not finding my rhythm right away.[2] The floor beneath my feet is littered with crumbs and under the carpet I feel the uneven rough cement. Closing my eyes, I initially lose my balance and have to slow my movements down to a steadier rhythm in order to keep from falling backwards. Someone covers me with a black scarf, grabbing me by the back of my belt (I later learn that it is the "daughter of Boutshishiyya," *bant al-butšišiyya*). Then my body is free to counterbalance its movements to her support, my head swaying back and forth. When the music is over, I return to my seat next to her and she tends to me. Later in the evening I can't find a seat, and she pulls me down on the floor in front of her, resting me between her thighs, resting her chin on the top of my head. Her large toenails, painted red, catch my peripheral vision on both sides.

After trancing, women wish each other good health: "*b-saḥt-ak*," they say.

"The *jnun* rose up in you last night, eh?" the *m'allem* Si Mohammed says to me the next morning as we are drinking our breakfast soup in the chill of the coastal morning air.

"I was just moving around," I reply, smiling coyly.

"They rose up in you," he repeats, this time much more somber, ignoring my flippant tone, and goes back to drinking his soup.

As soon as I enacted a trance, Si Mohammed immediately put me in the category of the possessed. Having spent months attending ceremonies (and attending to the bodies in the ceremonies), one night I felt moved to get up and participate. It was a night where many women were present. The floor was packed with bodies. My heart sped up, as it does before a performance, and in an instant I was on the floor, eyes closed, swaying my body as I had watched so many others do. Having grown up with a mother who was a dancer (and having taken lessons myself), I was attuned to the small gestures that make up a "combination"—the tension in the fingertips, the placement of the head in relation to the neck and the rib cage. I had observed how experienced trancers transited from a seated position to join the entranced. I knew the way they held their arms behind their backs, their hands sometimes clasped together, the tilt of their torsos, the rhythmic motion of their chins moving left and right through space. The music was compelling. I could no longer hold back. I got up. At that point, I didn't know what *jinn* was being propitiated, but someone covered me with a black scarf, and I later realized it was Sidi Mimun.

That night was a turning point in my research. Henceforth I was accepted into the community in a more profound way. I never felt possessed and never asserted that I was. Nonetheless, my bodily participation corresponded with a different level of awareness and imagination. I had visions, lucid dreams in which I felt I was completely conscious. I heard voices. My dream life was populated with the *jnun* of the Gnawa pantheon. I was involved in my own narrations of trance.[3]

***

How do conventional and ritualized gestures enact bodily-based metaphors and perform memories that signal the subject's transition into other states of being, notably possession-trance? To what extent are gestures themselves performatives, creating the reality that they iconically and metaphorically project? The gestures that I examine co-occur with—and, I argue, help effect—a change in being, a dissolution of one socially recognized self and the emergence of another socially recognized self or set of selves whose intentionality is quite different than the initial self. The gestures of trance are embedded in a performance context, of course, but not one in which spoken language is dominant. Rather, the gestures co-occur with music and incense, audition and olfaction, finding their significance in a multisensory matrix.

## Metaphors of possession: Falling/rising/standing

In Morocco, one "falls" into trance (*kat-ṭaḥ*). Falling is the primary metaphor for the act of possession trance. At the beginning of ceremonies, I was often asked, "Do you fall? *wesh katṭaḥi?*" It is another way of asking, "are you possessed?" Falling is a relinquishment, a capitulation to the experience, a submission. Once this happens, however, the spirits "rise up" in the body (*al-jnun kay-ṭlaw fi-k*). It is a downward sensation—women fall to the spirits, who then rise up within them. Falling and rising, which signal the transition into otherness, are also accompanied by strong physical sensations—tears, quaking, as well as smell, movement, and sound. All of these factors are co-occurent with the experience of possession, though they are specific to each *jinn*: Lalla Mira rises up to the smell of musk, emanating the color of yellow, producing laughter and emotions of gaiety. Sidi Mimun rises up to his music, to the odor of black benzoin, and sometimes obliges the propitiant to slash her body with knives.

The experience of falling is foundational. We fall down as children repeatedly and learn about directionality, balance, and control thereby. We make a game of falling so as to bring under our volition what is usually out of our control: "Ashes, ashes, we all fall down." To fall intentionally is counterintuitive, which is why it evokes laughter in children and in slapstick comedy. Falling is relinquishing to gravity, letting go, releasing. To fall down before someone is to submit, whether in English or in Arabic. As Michelle Dent and M. J. Thompson note, "falling is … that last desperate act of agency we are left with when faced with the terror and tragic beauty associated with loss and grief—or even, the frisson and anticipation of illicit or new love. It is in this dropping into the blaze of the unknown that we suddenly find ourselves no longer in control of the determining events that shape our lives" (2004: 8).

Rising up, on the other hand, takes volition; it is the spirits who rise: *kay tlaw f-ik*. Spirits rise up in a body that has ceded them place by falling. When the spirits rise up, they use the bodies of their hosts—animating their limbs, using their vocal chords. By contrast, when a spirit appears *outside* the body, in a vision or a dream, they are said to "stand up before you." "Aisha appeared [or stood up] before me, *waqaf ʿali-ya aiša*," I often heard. Spirits stand before you to deliver messages, to give warning or counsel, and generally to make their presence known. There is a recognition implied in the idiom, as well as a confrontation. *Waqaf* also means to stop. A spirit who appears before you, whether in a sleeping or a waking vision, stops you in your tracks. It is a rupture in one's experience of time, the entrance of one reality into another, the lifting of the veil that separates worlds and perpetuates the belief that human time is the only time. This collision of realms is also a transgression of sorts. It is the initiatory event of which Jean Françios Lyotard speaks, scarring one's sensibility like a wound and "marking out the rhythm of a secret and perhaps unnoticed temporality" (1992: 106).

## The paradox of trance

The premise of possession is that the subject loses control of her volition and is inhabited by a foreign presence. The subject's intentionality becomes absent and is replaced by an "other" intentionality. When working the spirits, however—deliberately going into a possession trance—there is a volitional invocation of the nonvolitional body. The body is absorbed in its projects, often to the exclusion of any awareness of itself, and the absorption is experienced as not theirs. How does possession become resistant to the interference that returns us to our self-awareness, our conscious intentionality, in which we can think about our acts as well as or instead of being absorbed in them?

Soumaya gives us this account:

> I'd just scratch myself or turn around, and I'd start to fall. I'd fall and begin to quake, to quake; and they'd bring me *jawi* [incense] and I'd be okay. Benzoin and sandalwood and orange blossoms, and I'd be okay. Just the odor, the odor. If I just smell that odor, it relieves me. I become okay. That's it. I stayed like that. But the day my mother had a *lila*, like the time comes around for Fatima to have her [annual] ceremony, they start going into trance. They just start playing a line of, one line of [the song for] 'Abd al-Qadr, they say: "I'm imploring you, my burden has fallen in your hands, oh mulay 'Abd al-Qadr." When they said this, I could no longer see anything. All of me starts working, working until I see myself, that's it, I've fallen. [*šift ras-i safi, ṭaḥat*]

Here it is a line of music that triggers body memory and response. The word for a musical line in Moroccan colloquial Arabic is *l-iyd*, hand. It is as if a part of the body was speaking to the whole or the musical body speaking to the cells. Indeed, while music is a catalyst for trance in this instance, it is inseparable from an aesthetic complex that includes gesture, olfaction, and memory.

It is clear from this account that Soumaya experiences falling into trance as a loss of control, triggered by audition, soothed by olfaction. The trance itself, however, is indexed by "falling," in which the body actually drops to the floor, followed by writhing, twitching, rolling, and other repetitive movements—the body "working, working." The spirits have their own gestural economy. The possessed are often "caught" by attendants surrounding them so as to prevent injury and are helped up to their feet as the spirits "rise up" within them. The loss of control is brought on by gestures that are highly conventional, repeated and recognized by all participants in the possession-trance community. In other words, the reported feeling of loss of control is publicly signaled by gestures that are codified and repeated. This irony inhabits the phenomenon of spirit possession.

In her analysis of gestures in a session of somatic psychology, Katharine Galloway Young asserts that gestures are not visual cues for others so much as they are "expressive acts directed to the self," ways that the imagination inhabits the self (2002: 46). This process contains its own reversibility—postures concretize the imagination and the imagination manifests and is known (and knows itself) in the gesturing body. The same may be said for the gestures that accompany the transition into trance—they concretize, or make real, the possession by another entity (both for the self and for others) while the spirit enacts its own being in the gestures of the possessed.

While gestures may be kinesthetic ways of inhabiting metaphor, ways that the subject knows herself, clearly the visual aspect of gesture also plays a role in the way trance is performed collectively. Observing trance—as well as feeling and smelling and hearing the trances of others—contributes to intersubjective performances. Possession ceremonies that propitiate the spirits with music, incense, and, most importantly, ecstatic trance are festive events in Morocco, and children are often present. Indeed, it may be posited that the bodily techniques of possession-trance are learned from an early age, incorporated into the individual body by corporeal mimesis (through sight, tactile, and instrumental participation).[4] Imprinting is a significant part of Gnawa trance culture. Growing up in an environment where ceremonies are held regularly, children observe their parents, their aunts and uncles, and siblings "fall." They witness the way the possessed move. They also observe the onset of possession—the headaches, the swollen legs, the fatigue and depression-like symptoms of lethargy. And they see the modalities of cure—the way the body moves to the music, the ritual gesture of inhaling the incense and propitiating the spirits. Observation is undeniably important in the transmission of the culture of trance, but the body learns in many modalities. Imbibing the incense is enough to make some people fall. For others, hearing the music is the catalyst. There is a different somatic repertoire at work in possession ceremonies. Even while young, children feel the percussive rhythms of the Gnawa deep in their bodies. They learn to move to them. Bodies learn about possessed bodies not just by seeing them but also by smelling and sensing them. Most all children who grow up in a family that holds ceremonies for a possessed family member become possessed themselves—usually around puberty.

On the other hand, these gestures are related to very basic bodily and spatial orientations—those of falling and rising. The possessed subject may be said to fall into a relation of self-disintegration, a kind of abject state of multiplicity. That the metaphors of falling and rising are employed by the trance community is not spurious. They represent an indexing of basic experiences of control and loss of control, of encounters with relinquishment and volition; these same fluctuations of absence and presence are found in the trance ceremonies.

## Notes

1. Moroccan psychoanalyst Mohammad Fouad, for example, told me that many of his patients have tried or try traditional forms of healing simultaneously with their psychoanalysis (Fouad 1995). He introduced me to one of his patients who had a long experience with the Gnawa, but who eventually left as she thought they were taking financial advantage of her distress and her possession by spirits.

2. This narrative does not recount a chronological sequence. Sidi Mimun comes before Sidi Musa.
3. In the following pages I describe these experiences but resist enclosing them in a definitive analysis. As Merleau-Ponty notes, description is the first and most important step in any phenomenological endeavor (1962). My perception and ways of perceiving changed when I entered the world of the Gnawa, and what may be called a different spatio-temporal orientation, and a different imaginary, has remained in my repertoire of emotions.
4. Whereas trances provoked by spirit possession are often more violent in nature, they may have the same results. Keil calls this state of flow "primary reality." For him, primary reality is not acultural, but is rather a culturally-learned way of accessing states that dissolve the ego. "Healthy cultures, genuine cultures," he says alluding to Sapir, "give their infants access to primary reality because without cultural imprinting on our biological givens we can't enter into language, myth, music, dance, poetry, wrights/rites, totemism, dreams, and other ego-dissolving primary-reality-engaging processes in the moment" (Sapir 1949; Keil 1995: 3–4).

## Bibliography

Dent, Michelle and M. J. Thompson (2004), "Introduction: Falling." *Women and Performance: A Journal of Feminist Theory* 27 (14): 7–11.

Fouad, Mohammed (1995), Personal Communication.

Keil, Charles (1995), "The Theory of Participatory Discrepancies: A Progress Report." *Ethnomusicology* 39 (1): 1–19.

Lyotard, Jean François (1992), *The Postmodern Explained: Correspondence, 1982–1985*, trans. Julian Pefanis and Morgan Thomas, Sydney: Power Publications.

Merleau-Ponty, Maurice (1962), *Phenomenology of Perception* [*Phénoménologie de la perception*], International Library of Philosophy and Scientific Method, New York: Humanities Press.

Rouget, Gilbert (1985), *Music and Trance: A Theory of the Relations between Music and Possession* [*Musique et la transe*], Chicago: University of Chicago Press.

Sapir, Edward (1949), *Language, an Introduction to the Study of Speech*, Harvest Books. New York: Harcount, Brace and word.

Young, Katharine Galloway (2002), "The Dream Body in Somatic Psychology: The Kineasthetics of Gesture." *Gesture* 2 (1): 45–70.

# CHAPTER 22

# AN ANTHROPOLOGIST UNDERWATER: IMMERSIVE SOUNDSCAPES, SUBMARINE CYBORGS, AND TRANSDUCTIVE ETHNOGRAPHY

*Stefan Helmreich*

I am preparing to sink into the sea, probably the first anthropologist to join the research submersible *Alvin* on a dive to the ocean floor. The three-person sub sits like a massive, oblong washing machine on the stern of the research vessel *Atlantis,* where a thick rope temporarily tethers it to an enormous metal A-frame rising from the ship's fantail. Clambering down a steep ladder into the submarine, I find pilot Bruce Strickrott already adjusting *Alvin*'s array of knobs, buttons, and computer screens. Geologist John Delaney is next to descend; delivering a foul-mouthed oath, he wedges his tall frame into a nook on the port side of the sub. As we are lowered into the waters of the northeastern Pacific on this cloudy June day in 2004, wet-suited escort swimmers survey the exterior of our capsule to make sure we do not go down gurgling. They snorkel past our individual four-inch-thick acrylic view ports, each window just wide enough to fit the features of a face.

In what I initially imagine to be an idle pun, graduate students on *Atlantis* have joked that I will now truly "immerse" myself in the culture of deep-sea oceanographers, seeing their preferred medium with my own anthropological eyes. As we begin our hour-long descent, my attention is, indeed, captured by such traditional icons of the deep as the evanescent jellies that flash past my window. But I am also fascinated by the sounds that accompany and enable our descent. The snug seven-foot-diameter interior of our titanium sphere is awash in the metallic and muffled pings of distant sonar devices, the echoes of telephone voices from the *Atlantis,* and the quiet pop music that percolates from *Alvin*'s stereo sound system. These bleep-blooping, burbling, and babbling sounds do, in fact, contribute, I find, to a feeling of immersion. Submerging into the ocean almost seamlessly merges with a sense of submerging into sound—and into a distinctively watery soundscape.

I follow Steven Feld's recent call for "doing anthropology in sound" (Feld and Brenneis 2004)—which, for the setting that concerns me here, entails attending to the "sounds of science" (Mody 2005), placing "sound studies" at the center of investigations of technoscientific practice (Pinch and Bijsterveld 2004).[1] In asking after the sounds that float in and out of submariners' consciousness, I am concerned with the technical transformations of sound and signal that support cybernetic sensibility and consciousness in the first place. I am curious about the cognitive, affective, and social effects of transducing—that is, converting, transmuting—sound from the medium of water into that of air, and about what an anthropology of such transduced sensing can make explicit about the conditions that permit immersion (and, I maintain, that create senses of presence as such), whether people speak of immersing themselves in water, sound, or the medium of culture.

Such alterations and conversions are about the simultaneous structuring of matter and meaning. I counterpose, then, to the recursive recipes of reflexive ethnography the possibilities of a transductive ethnography—an inquiry motivated not by the visual rhetoric of individual self-reflection and self-correcting perspectivalism, but one animated by an auditorily inspired attention to the modulating relations that produce insides and outsides, subjects and objects, sensation and sense data. Rather than seeing from a point of view, then, I suggest tuning in to surroundings and to circumstances that allow resonance, reverberation, echo—senses, in brief, of presence and distance, at scales ranging from individual to collective. Using my dive in *Alvin* as a narrative vehicle, I meditate less on what I saw in the teensy patch of ocean floor I visited (mostly passing apparitions of flesh and rock) and more on what we in the sub (and sometimes, by extension, we in the ship–sub system) heard and listened to.

## Soundscapes

As we drop down to the ocean floor, amidst a wash of submarine sounds, some questions surface: How did the domain that Jacques Cousteau (with Dumas 1953) once named "the silent world" become so sonorous? How did the underwater realm, this zone to which humans cannot have extended, unmediated access (without drowning, that is), become imaginable and accessible as a space of sound? What kinds of technical work have been necessary to bring this field into audibility for human ears? And what have been the cultural effects—for people in submarines, for example—of such work? Learning the answers requires dipping into some submarine history, tuning into the technical specifics of underwater listening, considering cybernetic networks of communication and control, and querying the multiple modes through which people imagine immersion: as a descent into liquid, as an absorption of mind and body in some activity or interest (such as music), and—in a meaning of relevance to anthropologists—as the all-encompassing entry of a person into an unfamiliar cultural milieu.

Key to thinking through how the sensation of auditory immersion is produced is the concept of a "soundscape." Ecologically minded musician R. Murray Schafer advanced the term in 1977 to call attention to his worry that natural sonic environments were being polluted by industrial noise. Historian Emily Thompson, in a more formal register, defines the soundscape as "an auditory or aural landscape … simultaneously a physical environment and a way of perceiving that environment; it is both a world and a culture constructed to make sense of that world" (2002: 1). A soundscape includes what Feld calls an "acoustemology," a "sonic way of knowing and being" (Feld and Brenneis 2004: 462; see also Feld 1996).[2]

What about sound underwater? Technologically constructed transductive apparatuses are essential for the submarine medium to be rendered into a soundscape for humans. I attempt below to map out the phenomenologies that result from attending to—as well as from forgetting—such transductions. In aid of that inquiry, I develop the figure of the submarine cyborg—the cyborg in a deep-sea soundscape—to make explicit the material transformations across media that have to unfold for the seemingly seamless transfer of information in cybernetic systems to be accomplished. I argue that a transductive ethnography provides tools for making audible the conditions that produce what many people have come to think of as the self-evident experience of watery and auditory immersion.

Let me return to my ethnographic setting, inside the sub, from which seat I will spin stories of sounding, soundscaping, listening, hearing, not listening, immersion, and transduction.

## Sounding

We are well into our descent, some 400 meters down. Pilot Bruce switches off *Alvin*'s exterior lights to save power, leaving the outside ink black. The phone rings. Kelley on *Atlantis* has a question for John about a grant proposal. Her voice, soaked with echo like a track on a Jamaican dub recording, bounces around the sub as she and Delaney agree about an e-mail she will send.

We continue to sound—in the sense of diving into and also investigating, fathoming—the deep. Such sounding employs devices, like sonar (**so**und **na**vigation and **r**anging), that, in a confusing pun, capture and transmit sound (*sound* as fathoming has its etymological moorings in the Old English *sund*, "sea," whereas *sound* as vibration reaches back to Old English *swinn*, "melody"). With the interior lights dimmed, a cycle of blips and bleeps captures my attention. Bruce identifies these for me as a 9-kilohertz tracking pulse sent out from *Alvin* to *Atlantis* every three seconds, a 9.5-kilohertz response from the ship, and a steady metronome of "pings" from transponders dispatched to the seafloor by *Atlantis* in advance of *Alvin* dives. Transponders are spheres about the size of beach balls that, anchored and floating about 180 meters off the seafloor, transmit sonic signals that help the sub to continually locate itself in three dimensions using triangulation. Bruce tells me he thinks of transponder pings as background noise. But they are not exactly the meaningless patter that journalist Victoria Kaharl, who descended in *Alvin* in 1989, rendered in her dive narrative as occasional interruptions of "Wa WA wawa WAWA wowo wowo WOWO wawa WAWA" (1990: 335–6) and "POP weewee wo WOP ka POP weewee wo" (1990: 337). For Bruce, the noises secure a sense that the sub is somewhere rather than nowhere, supported in a web of sound rather than lost in a featureless void. Even though he jokes that the prattle of pings can be an "acoustic 'will-o'-the-wisp'"—"a thing that deludes or misleads by means of fugitive appearances" (*OED*)—for Bruce, these echoes are the warp and weft of a reassuring soundscape ("without them, it'd be too quiet," he offers). Far from being "noise" as "irrelevant or superfluous information" (*OED*), transponder pings constitute noise as the hum of a world, as what musician Aden Evens calls an "implicated reserve of sense" (2005: 142).

Work in *Alvin* is coordinated by and through sound, even if we are not always fully tuned in to quite how. Indeed, our task this afternoon to map a tiny swath of the seafloor makes use of a system that translates sonic soundings (which we do not hear) into computer-generated topographic images. *Alvin* moves through and creates a multiplicity of soundscapes, at various frequencies and levels of accessibility to submariners' ears.

## Transducing a submarine soundscape for humans

How have underwater soundscapes come into audibility for humans? Devices that permit listening across different media—from water over into air environments (like the inside of the sub)—are key. *Alvin,* maintained at one atmosphere of pressure in its interior (i.e. at everyday, sea-level pressure), can only deliver to passengers a sense of an exterior soundscape because of such transducers.[3] What might be less obvious is why the underwater realm is not a soundscape for people unless such prosthetic technologies are made available to our naked ears.

Consider a skin diver. The sensation of floating in a three-dimensional net of sound is not immediately available to people swimming submerged in water. This is in part because it is nearly impossible for humans to use underwater acoustic vibration to locate themselves in space. For one thing, sound waves travel four times faster in water than in air. For another, human eardrums are too similar in density to water to provide the resistance that can interrupt many underwater vibrations so that they might be translated into tympanic movement—sound—in the ears; lots of vibrations pass right through our bodies. For humans, underwater sound is largely registered by bones in the skull, which allow enough resistance—*impedance,* to use the technical term— for vibrational motion to be rendered into resonances in the body. Moreover, conduction of sound by bone directly to the inner ear confounds any difference in signals received by left and right ears, making it impossible to compose what audiophiles call a "stereo image." Unaided human ears perceive underwater sound as omniphonic: coming from all directions at once (and, indeed, because of sound's seemingly instantaneous arrival, often as emanating from within one's own body). In this (transductively phrased) framing, the underwater world is not immediately a soundscape for humans because it does not have the textured spatiality of a landscape; one might, rather, think of it as a zone of sonic immanence and intensity: a soundstate.

It takes technical and cultural translation to carve a soundscape for humans out of the subaqueous milieu, to endow submarine space with sonic distance and depth, to create immersive space. Equipment must first be constructed that can capture submarine vibrations in the audio register—hydrophones, for example, like the ones manufactured by the International Transducer Corporation in Santa Barbara, California, devices that can get hold of underwater vibrations, usually using a microphone fashioned of ceramic or another material sufficiently denser than water to allow propagating waves to be impeded (see International Transducer Corporation n.d.). Once sound has been received by a hydrophone, signals must then be transported into an airy medium for apprehension by human ears. Such sound can be rendered into stereo using devices that transform signals arriving at separate underwater receivers into "binaurally centered" impressions in headphones or from speakers, translating captured submarine sound into spatial relations dimensionally meaningful to hearing humans (Höhler 2003).[4]

Bringing underwater sound into human-occupied air pockets like *Alvin* requires and entails transduction. Indeed, the possibility of imagining oneself immersed in a submarine soundscape depends on transduction—as, indeed, in its own way, does the sense of feeling omniphonically at one with a soundstate summoned forth by a skull-enveloping fluid.[5] The ear itself, it is crucial to note, has for the last century or so been understood as a transducing device, translating vibrations in air into corresponding motions in the eardrum (Sterne 2003), a description that, as I have already suggested, folds an engineering formulation into scientific understandings of the sense of hearing as such. If, as Thompson suggests, the soundscape of modernity is patterned by sounds "increasingly the result of technological mediation" (2002:2), underwater soundscapes do not exist at all for humans without such mediation all the way down—or, more exactly, all the way across (and, in the case of *Alvin*'s pinging sonarscape, without first becoming *sounded*scapes—which, because sonar sounding depends on knowing the speed of sound in water, demonstrates that subs use "sound to map time into space" [Evens 2005: 54]).

## From listening to hearing

And so, transponder signals must be transduced to create the echoing sounds carried to listeners cocooned inside the sub. Bruce's joke about the "will-o'-the-wisp" character of these sounds speaks to the sometimes misleading nature of the aqueous vibrational field. Turbulence and refracting motions of water can produce fluctuating amplitudes, "frequency-smearing" effects, and "blobs of reverberation" that make directionality difficult to discern, even once sounds are converted across media (Urick 1983). Water waves—which form and even crash underwater, where liquid layers of different temperatures meet—can also change the contours of vibration, introducing such complexities as Doppler effects, even for submarine auditors staying "still."

Closer listening cannot really help when these factors pile up on one another, as they sometimes do. But none of us in *Alvin,* not even the pilot, really needs to listen to the sounds of sonar closely. These days, onboard computers process transponder and other sonar signals. "No one now wears headphones and a rapt, faraway look, attentive in ambient hush. For all that modern oceanography relies so much on acoustic techniques, it is the machines which do the listening" (Hamilton-Paterson 1992: 21). On *Alvin,* sound has been so transposed (often into visual data) for more than a quarter of a century.[6] In the early 1980s, when computers were first installed in *Alvin,* they were divided into three kinds, collectors, listeners, and nodes, which—in sequence—gathered, sorted, and displayed data and allowed a human interface (Stetten 1984). Listeners were not strictly or only dedicated to sound processing but were so named because of their general interpretative, sorting functions; they were programmed to make data presentable, worthy of attention. The word *listening* is crucial. Listening has been associated with active, often highly technical, efforts to interpret or discern auditory sensation, whereas hearing has been imagined as passive, a letting of sounds wash over the ear (Carter 2004; Sterne 2003).[7] *Listening,* by this definition, is work. If listening to sonar on *Alvin* has been delegated to machines, the result is that we passengers now hear in a much more diffuse, less disciplined way than people may have in earlier days. The "sonic habitus" (Feld and Brenneis 2004: 468) animating submariners' sensibilities has been transformed.

To be sure, *Alvin* pilots must remain attentive to rhythms of the sub. Bruce, after all, is able to describe sonar sounds once his attention is directed to them. But I gather he focuses most of his technical listening on the sounds of the vehicle's engines and thrusters, over which he has more control. It was incumbent on earlier generations of submarine pilots to be attentive auditors of sonar, and it was through such close listening that the crackling of crustaceans, snapping of shrimp, and singing of whales were first disclosed, providing a portrait of soundscapes already in existence for underwater creatures with the means to hear them—soundscapes likely altered by such sounds as *Alvin*'s transponder pitterpatter, to say nothing of the racket created by large-scale sonar surveys (on the *Alvin* dive I joined, animal sounds were nearly absent; in another ecology—warmer, closer to shore—the soundscape may have been quite different, with more organic components).[8] Scientists no longer think the deep is a quiet, meditative space, a silent world; as Delaney tells me, "The ocean is wired for sound"

## ... and back to listening (to music, e.g.)

It is not all hushed, ambient techno in the world of *Alvin*. There is a more familiar, interior, air-pocketed soundscape, too. As we continue our descent, a quiet classic rock soundtrack accompanies us from Bruce's MP3 player, plugged into the sub. This musical soundscape creates a sense of absorption in the interior space of the sub, but because it mingles with the transduced soundscape of the outside, the effect is to feel at once inside a bubble and porously immersed in a wider world.

The various pings and pongs create an echoing sense of being in a landscape that extends beyond the confines of the sphere, perhaps one reason few people become claustrophobic in the tight space of *Alvin*. The music gently bouncing off the walls of the sphere reinforces this sense of immersion.

Yet another soundscape weaves through the sub, that of the fugitive speech of passengers. Not all speech is evanescent here, however, for each passenger is provided with a cassette player to make verbal notes about the trip. Delaney narrates some impressions into his tape recorder. I ask, "If you're doing all this tape recording, does that mean you spend a lot of time back on land listening to your own voice?" "Most scientists are very chatty with their machines, not each other," he replies. "Yeah, their auxiliary brains," adds Bruce. Or their externalized memories. After all, recording automatic speech allows for later listening, permitting *Alvin* divers to be "focusing exclusively on looking"; even so, the exteriorization of our inner voices contributes to the notion that sound is immediate, unmediated, ephemeral, a fleeting sign of reality itself. With *Alvin*'s tape players, the voice as a sign of presence is secured as a kind of back formation from the recording itself (cf. Kittler 1999).

And so, *Alvin* is a recording studio.

## Immersion versus transduction

Sounding with sound has fundamentally enabled the very making of the undersea realm as a field.

What I hope to have illustrated here is how submarine sound has these days sunken into the scientific background; heard, not listened to. How is this process "bound up in the knowledge that gets made"? When cybernetic practices—like echolocation—become fully automated, they can slide into an epistemic ground that spirits them into an unacknowledged common sense, into a cultural medium in which people are then "immersed."

This has epistemological and methodological resonance for anthropology as a field science. How are transductions "bound up in the knowledge that gets made" in ethnography? From these ethnographies of transduction I offer the experimental claim that one might consider ethnography itself as transduction.

It is cliché to say that anthropologists specialize in placing themselves in "the field" to immerse themselves in culture—whether in social worlds distinct from their everyday lives or in more finely inhabited versions of something they already thought was familiar. But what might anthropologists mean by this? What are the possibilities and limits of the image of immersion? How can we use the story I have told here to meditate on what this metaphor includes and excludes?

What does immersion leave out? I submit that immersion is a poor tool for thinking about the structure of space, about the materiality of the media in which ethnographers as participant-observers–auditors move. To borrow another term from Haraway (1991), immersion is not necessarily situated knowledge. Oceanographers do not just merge with their data. Submarines do not just dive in unstructured space. And anthropologists do not just soak up culture. One way immersion functions as a rhetorical tool promising experiential "truth" is by eliding the question of the organization of space, of medium, of milieu—whether of an ecosystem or a social order—positing a fluid osmosis of environment by an emplaced participant-observer–auditor. Immersion has come to suggest being submerged in a space as well as becoming one with it, dissolving into it. Immersion does not immediately open up questions of how boundaries are produced and crossed.

Transduction can be used as a device for recognizing the hidden conditions of immersion. The metaphor of transduction can tune one in to textures of disjuncture—the concept of "transduction" recalls the physical, material dimension of such transfers and summons up questions of resistance and distortion, complicating a rhetoric of flow with one of turbulence (see Sarai Editorial Collective 2006).

A transductive ethnography would hear things out or across. Transductive ethnography would be a mode of attention that asks how definitions of subjects, objects, and field emerge in material relations that cannot be modeled in advance. Most modestly, I offer it as one idiom for thinking through anthropologies of sound. (There are other idioms. After all, although "transducers operate on a very simple set of physical principles, they are also cultural artifacts" [Sterne 2003: 22].) More expansively, I suggest that a transductive ear can help to audit the boundaries, to listen for how subjects, objects, and presences—at various scales—are made.

## Notes

1. Trevor Pinch and Karin Bijsterveld write that the field of sound studies is characterized by "a focus on the materiality of sound, its embeddedness not only in history, society, and culture, but also in science and technology and its machines and ways of knowing and interacting" (2004: 636).
2. Feld's phrasing avoids Thompson's cleaving of the world into physical and cultural components.
3. A different circumstance obtains in saturation diving, which acclimatizes divers to pressures greater than one atmosphere for prolonged periods and requires extended decompression. Saturation diving allows people to live in air-filled undersea facilities maintained at ambient (high) pressure. To prevent oxygen poisoning, helium is often added to the mix, causing divers' voices to rise, making them sound like the 1950s novelty act Alvin and the Chipmunks (whose castrati songs were the result of speeding up tape recordings). Access Historic Naval Ships Association (n.d.) to listen to a 1965 recording of Commander Scott Carpenter of Sealab II leading his crew of saturation divers in a helium-voiced version of "Goodnight Irene."
4. Sabine Höhler writes that "acoustic methods of depth measurement based on the binaural technique relied on making humans and their sense of hearing a crucial part of the sounding technology" (2003: 134).
5. This brings up the question of whether the inside of the head can be considered a soundscape. The long history of inner voices would suggest this possibility. Friedrich Kittler, however, in *Gramophone, Film, Typewriter* (1999), argues that the specifically stereo spatialization of cranial interiors arrives only with headphones. Roy Wagner, urging a biosemiotic take on the question,

plays with the idea that the human is "an introversion of the bat, with its 'cave' on the inside" (2001: xiv). For me, this "echo-subject" is constituted through transduction.

Another way to think about interior bodily soundscapes—and their commingling with exterior soundscapes—is through an ofttold story about composer John Cage's 1950s visit to an anechoic chamber, an acoustically insulated room that prevents sounds resonating within it. Left alone in this space, Cage reported hearing the sound of his own blood flowing and concluded that there was no such thing as silence. Douglas Kahn points out that, "although he had internalized acoustical space, he did not transform it to an 'inner space' of the mind" (2005: 6)—at the same time that this melting of body boundaries required a transcendent, disembodied mind to take note of its own dissolution. Kahn argues that this Cagean epistemological armature "keeps the immersive edifice upright" (2005: 7).

6. The transposition of sonic into visual data describes the historical trajectory of much oceanographic representation. Other sciences have lately seen moves to "sonify" rather than visualize data. NASA's sound representation of the Huygens probe's January 2005 entry into the atmosphere of Saturn's moon Titan results from bringing vibrations up in pitch (into the frequency range of human audition) and compressing them in time (see Johnson and Lecusay 2005). The "sonocytology" of University of California, Los Angeles, chemist Jim Gimzewski, meanwhile, brings vibrations of cells up in volume (amplitude) so that humans can hear them (see Roosth n.d.). One of Gimzewski's collaborators reports that the "frequency of the yeast cells the researchers tested has always been in the same high range, 'about a C-sharp to D above middle C in terms of music,' … Sprinkling alcohol on a yeast cell to kill it raises the pitch" (Wheeler 2004). Less mimetic versions of sonification are being considered for apprehending high-dimensional data (e.g. Hermann and Ritter 2004).
7. Hillel Schwartz notes that listening and hearing on occasion change places: "Listening itself might well be indiscriminate and automatic, as for example with telegraph and telephone operators, and hearing might well be specific and voluntary, as with hypnotic commands, only some of which would be 'heard' and acted upon" (2003: 488).
8. For a thorough review of underwater acoustic ecology as it pertains to marine animals, see Stocker 2002–3. Research into vent sounds has begun, with the claim made that acoustic energy from these settings "may provide some local organisms with behavioral or navigational cues" (Crone et al. 2006: 1).

## References

Barad, Karen (2001), "Performing Culture/Performing Nature: Using the Piezoelectric Crystal of Ultrasound Technologies as a Transducer between Science Studies and Queer Theories," in Christina Lammar (ed.), *Digital Anatomy*, 98–114, Vienna: Turia and Kant.

Block, Steven M. (1992), "Biophysical Principles of Sensory Transduction," in David P. Corey and Stephen D. Roper (eds), *Sensory Transduction*, Society of General Physiologists series, 47, 1–17, New York: Rockefeller University Press.

Borsellino, Antonio, Luigi Cervetto, and Vincent Torre (eds) (1990), *Sensory Transduction*, New York: Plenum Press.

Cannan, R. Keith, H. Burr Steinbach, and Richard C. Jordan (1962), "Foreword to Engineering and the Life Sciences: A Presentation of Papers." Pamphlet published in relation to a joint Annual Meeting of the Divisions of Biology and Agriculture, of Medical Sciences, and of Engineering and Industrial Research of the National Academy of Sciences and the National Research Council. Washington, DC: National Academy of Sciences and the National Research Council.

Carter, Paul (2004), "Ambiguous Traces, Mishearing, and Auditory Space," in Veit Erlmann (ed.), *Hearing Cultures: Essays on Sound, Listening and Modernity*, 43–63, Oxford: Berg.

Cousteau, Jacques with Frédéric Dumas (1953), *The Silent World*, New York: Harper and Brothers.

Crone Timothy J., William S. D. Wilcock, Andrew H. Barclay, and Jeffrey D. Parsons (2006), "The Sound Generated by Mid-Ocean Ridge Black Smoker Hydrothermal Vents." *PLoS ONE* 1 (1). Available online at: http://www.plosone.org/article/fetchArticle.action?articleURI=info:doi/10.1371/journal.pone.0000133 (accessed 20 May 2007).
Evens, Aden (2005), *Sound Ideas: Music, Machines, and Experience*, Minneapolis: University of Minnesota Press.
Feld, Steven (1996), "Waterfalls of Song: An Acoustemology of Place Resounding in Bosavi, Papua New Guinea", in Steven Feld and Keith Basso (eds), *Senses of Place*, 91–135, Santa Fe: School of American Research Press.
Feld, Steven and Donald Brenneis (2004), "Doing Anthropology in Sound." *American Ethnologist* 31 (4): 461–74.
Géléoc, Gwénaëlle S. G. and Jeffrey R. Holt (2003), "Developmental Acquisition of Sensory Transduction in Hair Cells of the Mouse Inner Ear." *Nature Neuroscience* 6: 1019–20.
Hamilton-Paterson, James (1992), *The Great Deep: The Sea and Its Thresholds*, New York: Random House.
Haraway, Donna (1991), "Situated Knowledges: The Science Question in Feminism and the Privilege of Partial Perspective," in *Simians, Cyborgs, and Women: The Reinvention of Nature*, 183–202, New York: Routledge.
Hermann, Thomas, and Helge Ritter (2004), "Sound and Meaning in Auditory Data Display." *Proceedings of the IEEE* 92 (4):730–41.
Historic Naval Ships Association (n.d.), HNSA-Historic Naval Sound and Video. Available online at: http://www.hnsa.org/sound (accessed 20 July 2007).
Höhler, Sabine (2003), "A Sound Survey: The Technological Perception of Ocean Depth, 1850–1930," in Mikael Hård, Andreas Lösch, and Dirk Verdicchio (eds), *Transforming Spaces: The Topological Turn in Technology Studies*, Publication of the International Conference held in Darmstadt, Germany, 22–24 March 2002. Available online at: http://www.ifs.tudarmstadt.de/fileadmin/gradkoll//Publikationen/transformingspaces.html (accessed 20 May 2007).
International Transducer Corporation (n.d.), Home Page. Available online at: http://www.itctransducers.com (accessed 19 July 2007).
Johnson, Emma and Robert Lecusay (2005), "In Space, NASA Can Hear You Scream." Paper presented at the Annual Meetings of the Society for the Social Studies of Science, Pasadena, CA, 20–22 October 2005.
Kaharl, Victoria A. (1990), *Water Baby: The Story of* Alvin, New York: Oxford University Press.
Kahn, Douglas (2005) "The Art of Anechoic Perception in Postwar America." Paper presented at the Amsterdam School of Cultural Analysis, Amsterdam, March 30.
Kittler, Friedrich (1999 [1986]), *Gramophone, Film, Typewriter*, Trans. Geoffrey Winthrop-Young and Michael Wutz, Stanford: Stanford University Press.
Mody, Cyrus C. M. (2005), "The Sounds of Science: Listening to Laboratory Practice." *Science, Technology, and Human Values* 30 (2): 175–98.
Pinch, Trevor and Karin Bijsterveld (2004), "Sound Studies: New Technologies and Music." *Social Studies of Science* 34 (5): 635–48.
Roosth, Sophia (n.d.), "Sonic Eukaryotes: Sonocytology, Cytoplasmic Milieu, and the *Temps Intèrieur.*" Doctoral Program in History, Anthropology, and Science, Technology and Society, Massachusetts Institute of Technology, Cambridge, MA.
Sarai Editorial Collective (2006), "In Turbulence," in Monica Narula, Shuddhabrata Sengupta, Ravi Sundaram, Awedhendra Sharan, Jeebesh Bagchi, and Geert Lovink (eds), *Sarai Reader 06: Turbulence*, vii–ix, Delhi: Centre for the Study of Developing Societies.
Schafer, R. Murray (1977), *The Tuning of the World*, New York: Knopf.
Schwartz, Hillel (2003), "The Indefensible Ear," in Michael Bull and Les Back (eds), *The Auditory Culture Reader*, 487–501, Oxford: Berg.
Shepherd, G. M. and D. P. Corey (1992), "Sensational Science. Sensory Transduction: 45th Annual Symposium of the Society of General Physiologists, Marine Biological Laboratory, Woods Hole, MA, USA, September 5-8, 1991." *New Biologist* 4 (1): 48–52.

Sterne, Jonathan (2003), *The Audible Past: Cultural Origins of Sound Reproduction*, Durham, NC: Duke University Press.
Stetten, George D. (1984), "*Alvin*'s Memory." *Oceanus* 27 (3): 44–6.
Stocker, Michael (2002–03), "Ocean Bio-Acoustics and Noise Pollution: Fish, Mollusks and Other Sea Animals' Use of Sound, and the Impact of Anthropogenic Noise on the Marine Acoustic Environment." *Soundscape: The Journal of Acoustic Ecology* 3 (2–4) (1): 16–29.
Thompson, Emily (2002), *The Soundscape of Modernity: Architectural Acoustics and the Culture of Listening in America, 1900–1933*, Cambridge, MA: MIT Press.
Urick, Robert J. (1983), *Principles of Underwater Sound*, 3rd edn, New York: McGraw-Hill.
Van Dover, Cindy Lee (1996), *Deep-Ocean Journeys: Discovering New Life at the Bottom of the Sea*, Redwood City, CA: Addison-Wesley.
Wagner, Roy (2001), *An Anthropology of the Subject: Holographic Worldview in New Guinea and Its Meaning and Significance for the World of Anthropology*, Berkeley: University of California Press.
Wheeler, Mark (2004), "Signal Discovery?" *Smithsonian*, March. Available online at: http://www.smithsonianmag.si.edu/smithsonian/issues04/mar04/phenona.html (accessed 1 May 2005).

# CHAPTER 23
# 'JOYOUS MAGGOTS': THE SYMBOLISM OF YOLNGU MORTUARY RITUALS

*Howard Morphy*

Stanner's *On Aboriginal religion* is a work of intuitive genius. For Stanner there is almost a disjunction between the complexity of social life and the simplicity of the metaphysical core that lies at the heart of it. The complex reality of life creates a series of masks that obscure the central truths. 'Myth, song, dance, mime, social organization and institutional practice all lie like so many veils between the observer and that mystery which is phrased analogically', Stanner wrote (1989: 121). I would like to argue that the complexity lies in *both* the metaphysics themselves and in everyday life, for when we break down the metaphysic by analysing how it is worked out in action we find that meaningful action is complex, multi-layered and multi-determined. I would argue that this is why the metaphysical core is never merely said because it is itself complex and intertwined with social practice. It cannot be condensed in a single sentence; rather it is performed, painted and danced, for if one tries to reduce it, it becomes oversimplified and loses its connections. The metaphysical core is deeply connected to aesthetics and the experiential dimension of ritual performance, for these too are multi-dimensional, engaging with individuals' pasts and presents. Certainly ritual events can express core ideas, but always in a slightly ambiguous way so that actors can respond in quite different ways according to context. While I would agree with Stanner that 'the relationship between the religious and the mundane life is continuous' (Stanner 1989: 278), ritual creates a performative context in which for a while the mundane is transformed into a heightened way of experiencing the world.

In this paper I will centre on a major theme of Yolngu mortuary rituals usually associated with the final stages of the ceremony: *yithuwa* ('maggot') dances. I have chosen the topic because it resonates with Stanner's summary statement of the Murrinh-patha world view as it is represented in ritual:

'A "theory" of that reality would have to be a rationalisation of a reality which, if my account is correct, Murinbata [i.e. Murrinh-patha] put to themselves as a joyous thing with maggots at the centre. It takes considerable temerity to try and improve this imagery' (1989: 257). Stanner does not elaborate greatly on this interpretation even though it recurs throughout his analysis. It is clear that he means it to have a number of senses. The most obvious is that living is joyful but that life ends, and the maggots enjoy what remains of one's existence. However, Stanner also associates maggots with the negative components of Murrinh-patha society, the fact that in the midst of commensality can lie deception: 'there is an intuition of an integral moral flaw in human association' (1989: 264). And at another point joy is juxtaposed with the social order itself: 'A striking phenomenon is the way in which joyous sociality—one might say the perfect sociality of laughter and fun, in an apparent mockery of every stable institution—opens and closes the highest rite' (1989: 278). I think that Stanner's intuitions are salient, and they arise from his participation in Murrinh-patha society. I think that they can be applied in general to many aspects of Yolngu society. But I think that the ritual events that evoke such intuitions need to be analysed in detail before we can see how these powerful images resonate across so many aspects of the life of society.

## Maggots and some other creatures

In Yolngu symbolism maggots form part of a set with other creatures that have attributes in common. The set includes caterpillars, grubs, larvae of all kinds, and mangrove worms (these latter are, in fact, a type of mollusc). These creatures share the potential to eat their way through living organisms—to 'bite' flesh. Larval forms are transformational organisms—creatures that can change state and often fly away to another existence. While mangrove worms (*leredo*) do not actually change shape or leave their location, they do eat their way through the mangrove wood, leaving it channelled with tunnels that are lined with calcium deposits.

The characteristics of these crawling, biting and transforming creatures provide a 'natural' basis for Yolngu symbolic imagery. The general framework that is enacted, in different contexts and with different emphases, is structured on the relationships between life and death, and decay and regeneration. The bodily forms and natural histories of these creatures—represented and performed in ritual through dance, song, and in painted and sculpted form—provide a rich and multivalent analogical resource. The maggot biting into the flesh is a symptom of decay, a warning of contagion, a sign of danger, but the maggot also cleans the flesh from the bones, making them safe. In Yolngu metaphysical thought the body is still in some senses alive when it has flesh on it—it is still dangerous. There is something both sacred and safe about the bones of the dead. In the past they were handled, carried around in bark coffins and eventually deposited in a hollow log. The bones are separate from the person's spirit—the spirit has left them and become reincorporated within the ancestral dimension, potentially returning at some future time through the process of spirit conception. However, they remain as a permanent reminder of the person who died; and they, too, are a powerful symbol of the continuity of the clan. The clan's sacred designs can be referred to as *ngaraka* (bone), and the inner form of sacred objects are analogous to the bones of the clan's ancestors. The body is made safe through ritual and the spirit is returned to the ancestral dimension, but the bones remain (see Morphy 1991: 109). Yolngu mortuary rituals involve a powerful dialectic between the memory of persons and the separation of the dead from the living.

Different species are associated with the dialectical relationships between life and death, the living and the dead, in different ways. While maggots clean the bones, the mangrove worms make the bones. They eat their way through mangrove wood, eventually killing the tree or limb and leaving behind deposits in the form of calciferous tunnels that occupy its inner space. The tree becomes bone-like. The Gaḏawarrk (mangrove tree) sacred object represents a walking mangrove tree riddled with mangrove worm tunnels. In some of its manifestations the tree is dead, in others alive. The form of the sacred object is that of a generalised human body as bone and sometimes, when wrapped in feather string, clothed in flesh.

Yet both the mangrove worm and the maggot are as connected with life as they are with death. The mangrove tree provides the refuge, food and breeding ground for the mollusc, and the maggot converts flesh into its own transforming life cycle. The connection with life is also reflected in the sexual imagery that is created in art and ritual performance. The elongated body of the mangrove worm eating its way through mangrove wood and the white swarming maggots crawling over decaying flesh, almost flowing like a viscous liquid, have analogies in human procreative processes. And those analogies are developed through Yolngu symbolism.

## Dancing maggots

In this chapter I only have the space to focus on a single expression of this rich symbolism, the *yithuwa* dances associated with the *yingapungapu* ceremony. The *yingapungapu* is one of a number of ground sculptures that can be used in mortuary rituals or purification ceremonies. It is an elliptical shape divided into three sections.

Maggots and sand crabs are strong themes of the *yingapungapu* ceremony. Small circles can be made at either end of the sand sculpture representing the holes of the sand crab into which the rotting fish remains are dragged. The painted and engraved designs associated with the sand sculpture and its mythology include a characteristic dashed infill that represents, among other things, the maggots going about their business. Most dramatically, maggots and the bush flies they turn into are danced at various stages of the ceremony. The dance sequence usually begins with the spirit men cooking and eating the fish they have caught. The dances that follow portray the maggots as they consume the leftovers, the birds that eat the maggots, and the flies (the transformed maggots) that leave the area and fly away to another land. The maggot dances are performed as part of the final stages of the ceremony and result in the sand sculpture itself being destroyed by the movement of the dancers. I will summarise here three dance movements that occurred as the final sequence of a Maḏarrpa clan funeral ceremony in 2004, after the burial of the dead had taken place.

### *Dance sequence 1*

The first dance began with the participants forming two groups at the point of the ellipse of the *yingapungapu* away from the burial shade—men in front and women behind. The singers stood beside the sand sculpture and led the dancers forward. The dancers knelt on the ground and, following the contours of the sand sculpture, rhythmically crawled forward on their knees. The dancers moved to the month of the shade before dispersing. They had obliterated the sand sculpture and left behind a trail in the sand—a deliberately produced channelled pattern in the sand reminiscent of the dashed pattern of the painted designs, the marks left by the maggots on their journey (see fig. 23.1 below).

### *Dance sequence 2*

The maggot dance was followed by a series of dances in which men and women danced in opposition to one another on either side of the shade, where the body had lain. The dancers assembled away from the shade and moved towards it. Unusually for Yolngu dancing the male and female dancers employed similar movements, energetically stepping forward and running their hands all over their bodies with a pulling motion as if peeling or scratching off skin. The men covered more ground than the women but otherwise there was considerable similarity in the performance. This set of dances usually has an element of competition with each group of

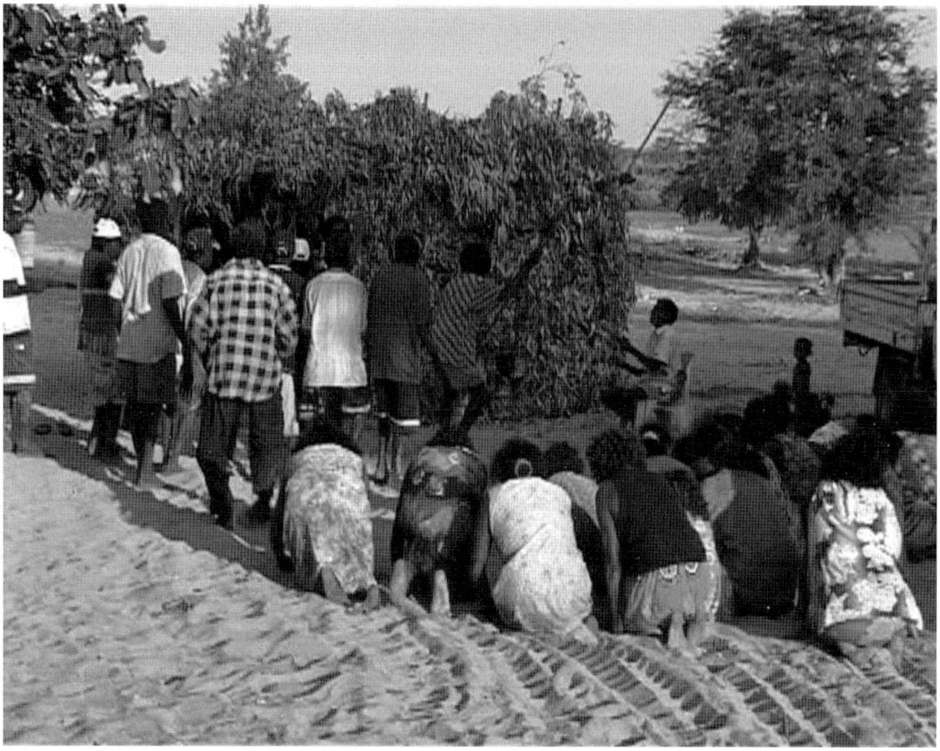

**Figure 23.1** The maggot dancers, Yilpara, August 2004. The performance shown here represents the penultimate phase of the yingapungapu ceremony as men and women dancers, as maggots, move forward on their knees towards the shade. In front of them two men dance with spears, thrusting them into the ground in front of the shade. The marks impressed in the ground by the dancers represent the tracks of the maggots as they approach the shade. Photographic still from a film by Howard Morphy.

dancers trying to outdo the other in both the energy and quality of the performance. There is a general sense of hilarity and a degree of flirtation. The dancers are dancing bush fly, heralding the flight of the *yithuwa* back to the separate homelands of the participating clans. The country of each clan is sometimes called in turn and the performers dance as a group in the direction of its lands.

### *Dance sequence 3*

The final dance in the series, and the concluding dance of the ceremony, centred on a group of male dancers with spears moving towards the entrance to the shade. This dance often involves individuals dancing in opposition to one another, thrusting their spears towards the ground in front of each other and surrounded by the others. Such dances have multiple references to the spearing of fish and the scavenging of birds, with underlying themes of vengeance and the expression of anger. In this context they are the prelude to the opening up of the shade. The final dance of this sequence usually ends with a spear being thrust into the ground in front of the entrance to the shade, symbolically opening it. After a suitable interval has passed, men enter the shade and take out any possessions that remain inside.

## Symbolic themes of the *yingapungapu* ceremony

Most Yolngu dances and song cycles are at one level connected to simple narrative sequences of events that refer to the actions of ancestral beings. The narratives are often, on the surface, observations taken from daily life. The basic story alluded to in the sequence of dances described concerns the spirit fishermen who went it out to sea in a dugout canoe hunting for parrot fish (*yambirrku*). They caught some fish but then a storm arose. The boat was nearly overwhelmed and the fishermen returned to the shore wet, but happy to be safe. They then cooked the fish and shared them with their relatives. After they had feasted they placed the fish remains in a small hollow scooped out in the sand where they were soon consumed by maggots. The maggots in turn were eaten by sand crabs and the sand crabs by wading birds hunting along the shore.

This apparently simple narrative provides the framework for the purification rituals that follow a Maḏarrpa burial ceremony. The event structure of the purificatory phase of the ritual comprises the ritual washing of the participants, purification by fire, the dancing out of the sand sculpture the final clearing of the interior of the shade where the body had lain, and the burning of the shade. These events can be performed through different ritual episodes. In the case of a *yingapungapu* ceremony the washing is performed to songs that recreate the storm at sea. People are grouped together in the centre of the sculpture and water poured over their heads. Purification by fire occurs later in the same place after dances in which the fish are consumed. Young men and sometimes young women dance on their knees around the fire, baring their chests to the flames. Women and men then place ironwood branches in the fire and brush or hit each other with the smouldering branches as sparks fly around. The event is highly structured. People form sets according to their relationship to the deceased and the roles they have played in the ceremony, and only people with designated roles will perform the ritual acts of washing and brushing fire on their relatives.

Yolngu mortuary rituals involve a heightened dialogue between forgetting and remembering. The themes emphasised depend on the temporal sequence of the ceremony and the emotions felt—the ritual orchestrates the emotions of the participants. Dances in Yolngu ritual are in part performative (Fernandez 1977): they move the action on in harmony with the changing themes of the ceremony. The maggot dances perform a series of transformations: from unclean to clean, from grief to joy, from death back to life. There is movement over time from negative to positive, but as with all Yolngu rituals there is a continual process of recapitulation, allowing time for the resolution of conflicting emotions but laying open the possibility that matters will not be resolved. The idea is that at the end of the ceremony life begins anew.

## Symbolic allusions

We are now in a position to consider the symbolism of the ceremony and the dances that we have described, and their emotional impact on the participants. The interaction between the symbolism and semantics of the ceremony and the emotions of the participants is highly complex. There are many different ways of coming to terms with death and regaining a sense of joy in the world. I would argue that Yolngu rituals allow individuals to make their own connections, yet at the same time they are encouraged to come together with others to share in moments of exuberant and at times irreverent exultation. In this analysis I will emphasise the multi-valency of the imagery. Each of the themes that I introduce can be active in different degrees according to context and individual focus. The symbolism moreover does not reside in any one form of expression—in dance, or song, or painting; each may express it in different ways. Hence an interpretation of a dance is always going to be, simultaneously, an interpretation of a painting, and a song, and beyond that of social life in its complexity. One theme of the ceremony is recognition of the finality of death and, complementary to this, encouragement to the bereaved to begin the process of forgetting. The imagery of the fish, the maggots and the birds is analogically associated with death and memory. The remains of the fish attract maggots; the maggots and flesh are then scavenged by sand crabs who bury the remains in their holes in the sand. They leave behind the bones cleaned of flesh. *Guluwitjpitj* (reef herons) then catch the sand crabs. Finally the tide comes in and sweeps the beach clean. What happens to the fish is an analogue for what happens to the human body following death. In the past it reflected closely stages in the treatment of the dead body.[1]

Yolngu mortuary practices once involved a prolonged process of bodily disposal that took place over many years. There were three separate burial ceremonies: an initial burial of the body in the ground or exposure in a platform burial; secondary burial in a bark container after the body had been dug up and any remaining flesh removed from the bones; and the final placement of the bones in a hollow log coffin many years later. Cultural practice here becomes an analogue of nature, but in doing so it does more. It takes control of the process of bodily decay and the transformation from life to death. By removing the flesh from the bones, Yolngu sped up natural processes. In turn, this enabled them to extend the period of mourning. Stripped of flesh, the remains are inert and safe, transportable in a bark container. The bark coffin was painted with the same ancestral designs that were painted on the body immediately after the person died. The remains can be safely curated as the person's spirit becomes ever more firmly incorporated in the ancestral past. The placing of the bones in the hollow log coffin—breaking them up and rubbing them in red ochre—is a final statement that the spirit is no longer there. The person has become one with the ancestral sacra. This prolonged process both reinforces the relationship between ancestral beings and the recently dead and also creates a long space for mourning. These practices made Yolngu mortuary rituals a core mechanism for creating the continuity of society while at the same time enabling people to come to terms with the death of a close relative.

While people no longer dig up the bones of the dead, the themes of present-day mortuary rituals remain closely connected to those of the past, and representing images of bodily decay in a controlled manner achieves many of the same purposes. Moreover Yolngu have accommodated to changes in burial practices by extending funerals in other ways. Although the bones of the dead are no longer dug up, the primary phase of burial has itself been extended over a period of many weeks and a variety of purificatory and commemorative ceremonies can take place over a period of months and even years.

Maggots clean the body, and the *yingapungapu* ground plays a role in the cosmogenic process of transforming the body into a relatively neutral and ancestral state. But why are maggot dances a context for the expression of joyful emotions bordering on the ribald and celebratory? Maggots, in their role as consumers of dead flesh, seem opposed to the joys of life. Yet there are clearly close connections between the maggots and the joys of life, and that connection is explicitly made in the dances. The dances draw a connection between the greedy maggots enjoying the flesh of the *yambirrku* and human pleasure in the same act (*yambirrku* are the most prized fish from the sea). The sequence of dances around the *yingapungapu* includes sets of dancers on their haunches messily consuming a rich feast of *yambirrku*. So maggots can be a symbol of human lust and the pleasures of the flesh, the delights of eating *yambirrku*. It is possible for people to empathise with maggots, in particular since it is people who are acting as maggots.

Maggots are also symbolic of fertility and sex. The shade where the body lies is a symbolic womb, a nest or the body of an ancestral being. The *yingapungapu* sand sculpture itself has strong female connotations. The maggot dancers crawling towards the entrance of the hut (sequence 1, above) and the dancers with their spears entering the hut (sequence 3) are both sexually charged images.

These later dances also introduce a theme of connection and community. The directions in which the dancers orient themselves reflect the relationships between the participating clan territories. The flies that are the transformation of the maggots take off and return to the territories of the participating clans: they fly to Maḏarrpa, Manggalili and Dhalwangu country. The participating clans refer to themselves as Yithuwa, signalling a very close relationship which is reflected in the co-ownership of certain areas of sea (Morphy and Morphy 2006). There is a great sense of pride in being *yithuwa*, or 'maggot people'. The ceremony itself brings this set of related clans together, and at the end of the ceremony the clans return to their own places.

These themes are all active in the concluding phase of the ceremony during which the images and emotions of death are transformed into images of the pleasures of life in the context of a sense of community. At this final stage, every effort is made by the ceremonial leaders to get maximum participation. The dances can be repeated again and again until the leader feels that the participating congregation has reached the point of cathartic exhaustion. Even those closest to the dead person are encouraged to dance, though their wish not to will also be respected. People are quite explicit that this phase of the performance is designed to create a sense of community and to encourage people to look towards their future life. Indeed in the particular ceremony described above *yithuwa* dances were performed for over half an hour at the grave side after the body had been lain to rest. The performance was continuous, with one dance transforming into the other. At times the energy was such that the musicians almost seemed to get ahead of one another, beginning the next song while the previous one was being finished, and at other times they played with the participants, seemingly extending the songs forever by repeating sequences over again with minor variation. Yet there seemed to be nothing accidental about the performance. The quality of the sound was operatic and the performance ended in a crescendo of sound when participation was at its maximum.[2]

## Conclusion

A Yolngu ritual is an extremely complex event in which the aesthetics of performance are entangled with semantics, in which people engage with the expressive power of ritual: the effervescence of Durkheim's (1971 [1917]) performance combines with the emergent mysteries of Stanner's. Effects are not entirely independent of the meanings, but the meanings are not reducible to a verbal account of what the symbols mean. As Stanner wrote:

> … the fact that many of the dominant symbolisms are not clearly put into words does not condition their valence. It conditions only the capacity to express clear conceptions in words and sentences so that for the most part they remain beyond the symbolism of language. But not beyond the symbolisms which are independent of spoken language … They are drawing on a rich stock of conventional signs known and used skilfully without any necessity of verbal symbolism. (1989: 118)

Ritual is full of wild ideas and hints of excess. The essence of communitas (Turner 1969) is that it is possible to overcome the emotions of individual life and be part of something much greater. It is possible to recover from the sense of loss at a funeral and reach a state of happiness. At an abstract level this can be seen to be the simple expression of wise pragmatism. Many of the themes of Yolngu mortuary rituals are a particular expression of messages frequently generated in the context of death and its aftermath: life must go on, normal service must be resumed as soon as possible. The rituals emphasise basic themes of life connected to pleasure (food and sex); allude to moments of triumph when we overcome the precursors of death (when we survive the storm at sea, or confront the heat of a fire). They also deal with the great religious imponderables: the fate of the soul, the continuity of life across the generations. Ritual in many ways is also going to be connected to the theatre of the absurd where ideas too improbable to be spoken or too complex to be fully grasped and expressed can be hinted at, where it is possible for maggots to express human emotions. It is in this context that many of the wild ideas, the inappropriate thoughts, can be expressed and shared without ever being made explicit. The ribald thoughts that are part of the process of forgetting the pain felt at death are hinted at in the symbolism of the dances and indirectly may contribute to that sense of community, that borderline irrational sense of joy at being alive and being supported.

## Notes

1. In addition to being enacted in ritual the imagery is developed in the paintings of Yolngu artists. Morphy (2007) illustrates a number of paintings on the themes of the *yingapungapu* by Narritjin Maymuru and relates them to his personal metaphysics.
2. The following evening the shade was set on fire and spectacular dances took place in the light of the flames as dancers braved the heat and the sparks that flew everywhere. The entire community was prepared for this event. Women and children were warned what would happen and hid under blankets until the blaze erupted. Then people gathered around to watch the spectacle as the entire settlement was lit up by the fire.

## References

Durkheim, E. (1971), *The Elementary Forms of the Religious Life,* Melbourne: Allen & Unwin.
Fernandez, J. W. (1977), 'The Performance of Ritual Metaphors', in J. D. Sapir and J. C. Croker (eds), *The Social Use of Metaphors: Essays on the Anthropology of Rhetoric,* 100–31, Philadephia: University of Pennsylvania Press.
Keen, I. (1994), *Knowledge and Secrecy in an Aboriginal Religion*, The Clarendon Press, Oxford.
Morphy, H. (2007), 'Anthropological Theory and the Multiple Determinacy of the Present', in D. Parkin and S. Ulijaszek (eds), *Holisitc Anthropology: Emergence and Convergence,* 148–81, Oxford: Berghahn.

Morphy, H. and Morphy, F. (2006), 'Tasting the Waters: Discriminating Identities in the Waters of Blue Mud Bay'. *Journal of Material Culture* 11: 67–85.
Stanner, W. E. H. (1989), *On Aboriginal Religion* (facsimile edition), with an appreciation by Francesca Merlan and an introduction by L. R. Hiatt, Oceania Monograph no. 36, Sydney: Oceania Publications.
Turner, V. (1969), *The Ritual Process: Structure and Anti-structure,* Chicago: Aldine.

# CHAPTER 24
# NECRO-UTOPIA: THE POLITICS OF INDISTINCTION AND THE AESTHETICS OF THE NON-SOVIET

*Alexei Yurchak*

In the late 1970s in Leningrad, a group of young friends started experimenting with "irrational" events and provocations, some of them carried out among themselves, in private apartments and during outings to the countryside, and others in the public space of the city in front of unsuspecting witnesses. The lifestyle, interests, and collective practices of this group were not originally an artistic or political project. Evgenii Yufit (born 1961), the group's leader and now a well-known filmmaker, remembers: "In the beginning no one thought that our lifestyle might sooner or later turn into some professional artistic activity." Vladimir Kustov, now a painter and installation artist, similarly claims: "We arrived at a certain nonstandard behavior and lifestyle quite spontaneously … . At that time no one of us thought that this way of being, if packaged in a particular way, could become artistic practice … . This was simply our way of living and expressing ourselves." Later, in the late 1980s, the crisis of the Soviet state turned these pranksters into "artists" and their provocations, paintings, and later films into successful "artistic" activity. However, here I am interested in the roots of the experimental living and public provocations that they developed early on, before they thought of themselves as artists and before art critics created discourse about them.[1]

In the winter of 1978, a group of young men, all friends from a Leningrad neighborhood, were loitering around a local cinema. The manager spotted them and suggested that if they cleared the snow in front of the cinema he would let them see the film free. They readily agreed, were given wooden snow shovels, and set to work. The hard work soon made them hot, and one of them suggested that it was time to take off some clothes. He proceeded to take off his winter coat, sweater, and undershirt. Without any discussion the others followed suit, pushing farther the absurd aspect of the event: some undressed above the waist, some undressed below the waist, and one of them undressed completely, remaining only in his winter boots. The situation spontaneously turned into a provocation, and the original plan to see the movie was abandoned. The young men started aimlessly throwing snow in different directions with manic enthusiasm. The second floor of the cinema had large windows looking down onto the street, and the people waiting for the film to begin stared in amazement at the scene below, some smiling with embarrassment and some outraged. Someone called the police, and everyone was yelling, remembers Yufit. Just before the situation turned dangerous, the young men dropped their wooden shovels, grabbed their clothes, and ran away in different directions (Evgenii Yufit, Vladimir Kustov, and Andrei Mertvyi, interviews; see also Mazin 1998).

The scandalous nudity, the absurd hyperactivity, and the improvisational character of the event point to a curious aesthetics of public spectacle that the group was developing. One had to be always ready to turn any mundane situation into an absurd event that resisted easy interpretation and simultaneously was provocative or outrageous. It was also important to avoid discussing and rationalizing what went on and why. This mix of spontaneous absurdity, provocative behavior, antirationalism, and active avoidance of analysis became a permanent presence in their lives. They referred to it as "dimwitted merriment" (*tupoe vesel'e*) and "energetic idiocy" (*energichnaia tupost'*). In the 1980s, various versions of such behavior became widespread among young city dwellers and became known in slang as *klinika* (slang for "psychiatric clinic").

Around 1982 one of the Necrorealists found in a secondhand bookshop a 1900 Russian edition of a book by the Austrian forensic physician Eduard von Hofmann entitled *Atlas of Legal Medicine* (figs 24.1–24.3) They became mesmerized by the book's pictures of corpses and injured bodies, stories of violent deaths that occurred in and around Vienna at the turn of the century, and scientific explanations of the causes of death and especially the transformations that took place in the cadavers in the following days. Despite its unusual content, the book looked like an exquisite art album that evoked distant places and times; it had a beautiful leather binding, fine color drawings, and old print fonts, and its pages were yellowed with time.

Before they bought the book, the group's activities had often focused on the body, involving strange clothes, nakedness, insane behavior, etc., but now, remembers Kustov, they "spontaneously stumbled on a corpse" and quickly developed an interest in violent death, injuries, and processes of decomposition. Corpses in the book were represented vertically to simplify the reading of the wounds by medical students.[2] This orientation had an additional effect: "The vertical rotation transformed the cadaver into a kind of a dead living being, neither dead nor alive. This in-betweenness [*promezhutochnoe sostoianie*] was very interesting. I called them *noncorpses* [*netrupy*]." This effect made it easier to link the images of the cadavers into a narrative. Now, instead of practicing spontaneous provocations, says Kustov,

> it was enough to simply enter a subway car full of people with that book. Three or four of us would sit together and a couple others would stand around. We would open von Hofmann's *Atlas* and start loudly and agitatedly discussing the pictures inside, linking them into a narrative: "Look! This guy goes round to see that woman, right? He comes and unexpectedly bumps into this man. And they start a fight." And so on. People in the car would get interested and peek over our shoulders to see the pictures. And would see these eerie images and get shocked and stumble back in awe, exclaiming, "Oh, God!" or calling us idiots and degenerates.

Subway trains were a perfect place for these actions, because they would affect "a lot of random people who had nowhere to go, at least until the next stop."

Members of the group found a few other books on forensic and legal medicine, including a translation of another von Hofmann manual (1912), a Soviet textbook entitled *Legal Medicine* (Smol'ianinov, Tatiev, and Chervakov 1961), and other editions for Soviet medical students, and carefully studied the photographs and drawings of cadavers and wounds and the descriptions of violent deaths and processes of decomposition. Reading these forensic materials pushed them toward more complex experiments. In them spontaneity, a relative lack of a scripted storyline (sometimes no plan was preconceived at all, while sometimes some of its elements were preconceived in the most general terms), and a desire to "provoke" the general public remained central. However, many events now involved new obligatory elements such as a full-size mannequin of a man that the group stole from the Institute of Criminological Medicine, where it was used to study the effects of car crashes on the human body. The mannequin was made of fine leather and smooth plastic and looked uncannily human. The Necrorealists gave it the name Zurab, a Georgian name that sounded exotic in the Leningrad context,[3] and it became a frequent participant in various spontaneous and partially prearranged activities in the streets. One day, five of the men slowly carried Zurab in a large black sack through a small park in the city center. People gave them bewildered looks. When they stopped to rest and tossed the sack on the ground, says Evgenii Yufit (and see also Mazin 1998: 63),

> We were suddenly surrounded by the police. They demanded in a rather harsh manner that we show them what's in the sack. We untied the sack and a person fell out .... Zurab was bouncy and supple, but in the bag it was bent and folded. When it fell out it started waving its limbs, jumping, and dancing. The police reaction was complete stupefaction. At first they panicked and leaped back. But when they realized that it was a mannequin dressed in winter clothes they simply did not know how to react ... . They turned it over several times, started touching it and walking around it in a kind of a shock, not knowing what to say .... I remember the sergeant's face: he was at a loss. What could he do next? Take us to the police station? But then what would he write in his report? That he arrested several people for carrying a dummy? ... So eventually he just said: "Okay, get your stuff and get lost. But if you had a real corpse, we would've shown you!"

By the mid-1980s the group had grown larger and more porous. No longer simply a group of friends, it was now a gang or "communal body," with an open-ended and shifting membership that was "heterogeneous and poorly acquainted among itself: from blatant criminals to intellectuals and working artists" (Demichev 1993: 4–6, quoted in Alaniz and Graham 2001: 9). Once in the winter of 1984, during the evening rush hour, around 20 of them started an agitated fight on the fifth floor of a building under reconstruction in the city center. That floor was missing the front wall, and they were clearly visible to the pedestrians on the street. The fight was more insane than violent; it was accompanied by wild swinging of arms and wooden sticks, agitated running and hopping, and loud screaming. At some point the mannequin Zurab, dressed in winter clothes and a fur hat, was thrown down from the fifth floor to the pavement underneath. The combatants ran out of the building and proceeded to hit the mannequin with sticks, shouting that they needed to finish him off. One member of the group remembers: "Pedestrians on the street thought that it was a real person. People ran over, screaming and yelling: 'You murderers! What are you doing?' ... Everyone was running about, trying to get a glimpse of the human body lying there. The police showed up." Suddenly, the mannequin's head tore off, and the petrified pedestrians, seeing the spongy plastic innards where his neck was cut, realized that something was not quite as it seemed. While the crowd remained stupefied, the men grabbed the mannequin and ran away.

On another occasion, curious to find out how the engineers of trains would respond to "irrational events," members staged an "experiment" near the suburban railroad tracks. Two members of the group stood on one side of the tracks wearing navy uniforms with the pants pulled down to their ankles, with their heads swathed in bloody bandages and their faces made up to simulate deep wounds and signs of decomposition. Several others, also heavily bandaged and bloodied, hid in the bushes beside the tracks. When a train approached, the first pair started energetically simulating a homosexual act, while the others jumped out from the bushes simulating a knife fight. The bizarre sight in the middle of the deserted countryside must have left the engineers bewildered and confused. "One endless freight train reacted with a long hoot that lasted several minutes, while the train was moving away" (Mazin 1998: 120). Suburban railway tracks were among their favorite sites for such provocations because here the participants were exposed to many unsuspecting witnesses in the trains but remained safe.

At that time, remembers Yufit, they often performed their semispontaneous provocations to "study the reactions of the general Soviet public" (*izuchali reaktsiiu naseleniia*). For many events it was important that someone on the street become suspicious and show this (occasionally by calling the police). Anything out of the ordinary caused suspicion: Are the characters involved in the strange activities plotting something? Are they trying to undermine the normal flow of life? Could they even be "spies" (*shpiony*)?

On one occasion, around 1984, a few members of the group improvised an absurd event in a railroad station in the city center. The event consisted of pushing each other in and out of a large dumpster with intense and gloomy determination. Yufit, who by that time had started learning how to use a movie camera, was quietly filming this behavior standing nearby, while random passers-by stared in amazement. Just as they were about to leave, he recalls,

> a police car suddenly arrived and we were put inside. They confiscated our camera and brought us to an office of the Department of Internal Affairs, where a colonel spoke with us. They thought this was some serious matter, which was rather typical of the atmosphere of spy mania (*shpionomania*) then. He asked: "What was this all about? What are the goals of your actions? Why did you film them?" I said I did not know. I honestly did not know how to explain what the goals of our actions were. He became even more agitated and told us that our camera would be sent to a laboratory at the KGB and that we could go home for now but they had our names and addresses and would contact us. When I came back later to get the camera, they were completely befuddled: they had seen the developed film and could not figure out what this nonsense was all about. I said that it meant nothing; we were just practicing filming. They returned the camera and told me to get lost, and that was it.

Another situation took place a little earlier, around 1982, before they started filming. A few of them were passing the time in a courtyard with a little garden in the city center. Yufit climbed a tree, hung a rope from a thick branch, and started preparing to hang himself, while others assisted from below and offered advice. This event was only semispontaneous: under his clothes Yufit was wearing a system of suspenders prepared in advance on which he was supposed to hang, simulating death. The rope was connected to the suspenders, and Yufit hung for a while from the tree with a noose around his neck. After a few minutes, some laborers from a nearby construction site came up to us and started asking who we were and what we were up to. We told them not to worry, we were just rehearsing a film scene. But they got very anxious: "No, no. Something is wrong here. You are probably spies. We are going to call the police." That was a fairly typical reaction to inadequate situations: we were suspected of being spies.

## Necro-aesthetics

In the mid-1980s the aesthetic side of the experiment expanded further. Members of the group started drawing pictures, making sculptures, taking photographs, and writing short stories. Noncorpses remained their main characters. Mertvyi wrote stories and made a few short films; Kustov turned to painting; Yufit took up photography and later became the main Necrorealist filmmaker. The first films, just a few minutes long, had no script and little story line; they consisted of lightly edited footage of the group's crazy collective escapades. Filming was not a goal in itself but an excuse to gather a large number of friends for spontaneous collective actions.

The early films and photographs, shown in private apartments to members of the group and their friends, began attracting more and more people, and by the late 1980s rumors about these showings were circulating around the city. The Necrorealists developed an informal cult status. If anyone asked about the meanings of these works, members invariably responded that they were "medical reference materials" (*spravochnyi material po meditsine*) (Mazin 1998).[4] Indeed, most of the activities and images in the films, photographs, and paintings were inspired by real stories about and images of violent injuries and deaths described in medical books. For example, one character in Yufit's short film *Spring (Vesna*, 1987, 10 min.) attempts multiple suicides by one bizarre method after another, among them roller skating full speed into a tree trunk. His suicide attempts repeatedly fail. This scene was inspired by von Hofmann's chapter "Suicides," which described pathological suicide cases.[5]

Filming also acquired a protective function: as we have seen, if the police demanded an explanation of their crazy group activities, they could say that they were practicing amateur filming. At that time, many Soviet institutes and factories had amateur film clubs (*kluby kinoliubitelei*)—state-sponsored organizations that allowed one to film relatively free from state control while remaining under its general supervision. This situation reflected a general paradox of the Soviet cultural policy: many amateur activities that the state sponsored and even promoted as a means for developing socialist culture undermined the policy's socialist meaning (see Yurchak 2006, Chs 5 and 6). It was partly the resources provided by the state and partly the ability to justify one's actions to the police that drove Yufit in the mid-1980s to join an amateur film club at a Leningrad factory.

The political relaxation during the perestroika years contributed to the Necrorealists' popularity, and in 1989 a new TV program on cultural events called *The Fifth Wheel* broadcast a few episodes from their films. A panel of professional psychologists whom the program invited to discuss the footage dismissed it as the work of sick psychopaths, necrophiliacs, and sadomasochists; a few TV viewers called the station to protest the disgusting horror it broadcast (Andrei Mertvyi, interview; see also Miller-Pogacar 1993: 14). Not surprisingly, the Necrorealists' fame skyrocketed (Mazin 1998). They were publicly seen for the first time as unusual "artists."

Under these new conditions, the Necrorealists and their observers gradually started thinking of what they did as artwork. In 1989, Evgenii Yufit was invited to learn and experiment with film technique in the workshop of the film director Alexander Sokurov at the Lenfilm studios in Leningrad.[6] Andrei Mertvyi (Andrei "Dead") made a few acclaimed short films before switching to writing and drawing on Necrorealist topics; Vladimir Kustov pursued a successful career as a painter and installation artist; Oleg Kotel'nikov became a successful artist and a co-founder (with Timur Novikov) of the New Artists movement.[7]

The more the Necrorealists turned to artistic projects the more their texts, installations, and films became populated by human, semihuman, and hybrid life-forms, all related to each other as a kind of "transgenic" (Haraway 1997) kinship community that dwells in the zone between life and death, human and animal, sane and insane, in which subjects are no longer regular human beings). In contrast to earlier films, the necro-films made in the post-Soviet period have clearer and more important story lines and narratives. The characters in the earlier films performed suicidal and murderous actions and practiced multiple methods of self-abuse making themselves different from "regular" people. The protagonists of the post-Soviet necro-films staged more elaborate "scientific" experiments trying to become not quite human. In these films unconventional scientists come up with alternative evolutionary theories that unite humans with animals and organic with inorganic matter while heroic geneticists and biologists apply techniques of hybridization and mutation to themselves an attempt to cross the human-nonhuman divide.

## Postnatural life

In retrospect, in 2004, Yufit suggested to me that what the Necrorealists intuitively attempted to create in the 1980s was "a situation that broke the frame of familiar perception [*slomlal ramki znakomogo vospriyatiia*], fell outside the boundaries of social stereotypes [*nakhodilsya za gran'iu sotsial'nykh stereotipov*], and hit a kind of logical dead end [*upersia v logicheskii tupik*]." It is important that such comments and elaborations were not a part of Necrorealist aesthetics at the time. They refer not only to the reaction of the audience but also to the perception of the Necrorealists themselves. Although, as we have seen, Necrorealist actions were often performed in public with a desire to provoke various unsuspecting witnesses (the public, passengers, engineers, policemen), this was not their only or even their main function. In fact, it was equally important to perform various strange actions where no one else, or at least no one outside the group, could see them—for example, in private apartments or in the forest. The actions were meant not only for outsiders but also for members themselves. Moreover, they were not just isolated staged performances different from the real lives the Necrorealists led elsewhere; on the contrary, they were part and parcel of everyday Necrorealist life. As Vladimir Kustov put it, all these crazy actions and provocations "were not separate from how we were living in general; our whole life was infused with this attitude." This is why the term "provocation" does not quite capture the full meaning of these actions. They were also experiments performed most of all on oneself as part of continuous experimental living.

An example of this experimental ethos was the work of Andrei Mertvyi, who in the mid-1980s often spent whole nights alone, deep in the forest, sleeping on the ground: "I was trying to get coarse [*zamateret'*][8] and gain some animalistic experience." A more striking example comes from the Necrorealist Anatolii Mordiukov, known in the group as Svirepyi (Fierce) for the particularly outrageous experiments that he liked to carry out. For example, he often ran into traffic, occasionally jumping out in front of a speeding car. "He did not want to get hurt," explains Mertvyi. "He just wanted to see what the drivers' reactions would be. He did this often, for many years, and sometimes did get wounded. But when he recovered he would start again." One day in the early 1990s, Svirepyi was hit by a car and died.

Some of these activities and provocations are reminiscent of experimental performance art and cinema in the West. It would be inappropriate to describe such actions, experiments, and interests as merely "performance art." This point was made to me by Vladimiar Shinkarev, a member of another group, the Mit'ki, that led a similar existence in the early 1980s (they did not know of the Necrorealists at the time). Describing their peculiar aestheticized way of living, Shinkarev said:

> The word performance (*igra*) does not adequately capture our life. It was much more serious than performance. We were *living* (*prozhivali*) a serious model, living it to a maximum degree … . This living became our life, and that behavior became organically ours (*organichno svoim*). Our way of spending time, reacting to others, interacting with each other, using various expressions and exclamations, practicing certain eating habits—all this was an organic part of our existence. They were ours not only in public but also in our personal, intimate daily life.

The difference between staging occasional performances and always living in a certain way is the difference between acting like someone else and *becoming* someone else. Baudrillard (1994) describes this difference by opposing faking to simulation: "Whoever fakes an illness can simply be in bed and make everyone believe he is ill. Whoever simulates an illness produces *in himself* some of the symptoms" (3, emphasis added).[9] By living this model one was changing one's self, becoming someone else, a representative of a sociality and a form of life that were different from ordinary people—or, in Yufit's preferred and much repeated phrase of that period, "life uncontaminated by human consciousness" (*zhizn' neo-porochennuiu chelovecheskim soznanieni*). Necrorealist provocations, artwork, films, and behavior were intuitive attempts to explore these alternatives formed within the realm of bare life.

Since the *politics of indistinction* is based on suspending state-defined political identity and instead emphasizing bare life, one of its key features is the lack of a language in which to articulate one's goals and actions and, moreover, a problematic relationship with language in general. Indeed, the Necrorealists cultivated a certain negative linguistic skill, learning to speak in a manner that was inarticulate, with long pauses, an impoverished vocabulary, and an emphasis on grunts, moans, and laughter. Even when making more elaborate statements, they often avoided articulating an argument that would seem coherent and self-reflexive, especially in response to questions about the meaning of their actions. Usually they could not explain what effects they were trying to achieve and why. They also avoided discussing and analyzing their actions in public and among themselves.

Later, around 1990, when the Soviet state was collapsing and the Necrorealists acquired sudden fame, their activities were analyzed by art critics, journalists, and the public. This new public discourse attempted to elicit a coherent discussion from the Necrorealists and to fit their practice into the familiar frameworks of artistic genres investigating death. However, members of the group resisted these attempts at reduction. Although their responses remained, as always, elusive and absurd, they suggested that the main interest of the group was not death but alternative forms of life that did not fit normative definitions. When a Western scholar asked Evgenii Yufit in the early 1990s whether Soviet audiences had been offended by the focus on dead people in his films, he responded with ironically naïve surprise (quoted in Miller-Pogacar 1993: 15):

> Yufit: What dead people?
> Question: The characters in your films. Aren't they all supposed to be corpses?
> Yufit: What do you mean? Look. They're moving around.
> How can they be corpses?
> Question: But there are acts of suicide in your films. In *Spring*, for example, one man propels himself into the trunk of a tree.
> Yufit: But that doesn't kill him. Why should it kill him? It only cripples him. He can still go to therapy.

The Necrorealists also resisted a new discourse that attempted to reduce their work to familiar artistic genres of political opposition. On one occasion a journalist asked Yufit what relationship his films had with politics. In his answer Yufit refused the implicit expectation that he would talk about politics as opposition; instead he insisted that the only interest he had in that kind of "politics" concerned politicians, who, like all humans, interested him only when they were not quite alive but in a state of being transformed into nonpersons (Mazin 1998: 42):

> Well, there are such injuries, including those resulting from airplane crashes that may have an effect on various political figures. In this sense, politics certainly does enter the sphere of my interests. However, such injuries make it very difficult to identify who is who. The remains of the bodies get scattered around an area of up to three square kilometers. This is an extremely complex injury … . But a cadaver is a cadaver … . I am interested in its metamorphoses … in the transformations of form and color. In a kind of necroaesthetics. During the first and second months shocking changes occur. The cadaver becomes as spotty as a jaguar and as puffy as a hippopotamus. And this happens only under certain conditions. Which is particularly interesting, for politics … well, I don't really know.

## Suspending the political

Was the peculiar aesthetics of everyday living, experiments, and provocations developed by the Necrorealists and similar movements in the late Soviet context a form of politics? If so, what political effects did it have? And may comparable forms of politics be found in other socio-historical contexts?

A useful starting point for this theoretical discussion is the work of Giorgio Agamben on biopolitics in the contemporary world and the recent productive critique of Agamben's work by other scholars. Drawing on a number of political theorists, Agamben (1998, 2005) points out that to be recognized by the modern state as a citizen with rights one has to be seen as having both political life and bare life—the former referring to the legal status of a human being within a polity, the latter referring to human biological existence as such. Having political life suspended reduces the person, from the perspective of the state, to the status of bare life. Such persons inhabit the state's zone of indistinction, a political vacuum in which the state no longer distinguishes them through its politico-juridical topology as full political subjects—that is, no longer sees them as either good citizens or bad citizens, either legal or illegal, either supporters or dissidents. In extreme cases, the location of these people in the zone of indistinction reduces them to the status of less than human, making them altogether disposable.

The exceptional subject position of such individuals bears some similarity to that of the people discussed in this paper. Indeed, the relation to the Soviet state of such groups as the Necrorealists also involved a considerable suspension of political subjectivity and emphasis on depoliticized, "naked" life. They avoided political news, chose employment in low-paying jobs that provided the bare necessities for living, with maximum free time and minimum political engagement with the state, and even claimed that they were not Soviet people or that they differed from ordinary people organically. The Necrorealists [erased] their political subjectivity to such a degree that their daily existence became reduced, metaphorically and literally, to the status of something nonhuman, nonlinguistic, and "uncontaminated by human consciousness"—to the status of bare life.

This suspension of the political and the emphasis on bare life makes them reminiscent of Agamben's subjects (his *Homo sacer*), but unlike the latter these Soviet people were not reduced to the bare status by the state but sought it *themselves*. This was their strategy of becoming a kind of subject who could use many of the resources of that state (social welfare, subsidized housing, employment, education, etc.) and yet largely avoid the political subjectivity of a citizen.

Turning oneself into a subject whose political life was suspended made much of what these people did and how they lived partially illegible to representatives of the state, the police, and ordinary Soviet citizens. As a result, upon encountering such people and their activities the state was often uncertain what to make of them and how to treat them. In extreme cases the state looked for legal reasons to persecute them as "loafers," hide them in psychiatric wards, or even expel them from the Soviet polity altogether. However, in most cases the state remained uncertain of their status and simply ignored them.[10] Avoiding the political and ethical concerns that preoccupied supporters and critics of the socialist state, these groups pursued forms of life that could not be easily interpreted in that system's political language. This illegibility to the state came at a cost: it prevented these people from pursuing many state-recognized careers, living in relative financial comfort, having the privileges granted by the state to various groups, etc. At the same time, it was liberating, allowing them to evade the symbolic order of the state "from within" and thus to undermine its ability to control and interpret their lives rather than having to resist or oppose the state on its own political terms.[11]

Therefore this strategy functioned as a form of politics, albeit one that, paradoxically, was based on suspending the political (as defined by the state) and locating oneself in the state's zone of indistinction. We may call this politics the *politics of indistinction* to contrast it with the better-known politics of opposition and resistance.[12] Although the relationship to power based on the politics of indistinction is not one of resistance (at least as it is usually understood, as opposition to power), it does not promote stasis either. In fact, this relationship to state power in the late Soviet context challenged that power in unexpected ways and ultimately contributed to undermining it.

## Notes

1. The Necrorealists were not unique in developing an aesthetics of public provocations first and conceiving of it as an "artistic" activity or "performance art" only much later. A similar trajectory was followed by the infamous US duo The Yes Men, who explained in an interview. "For a long time we didn't realize we were doing 'theater' or performance art—we didn't know it at first, but after a while we figured it out. Now we've gotten some grants from the Creative Capital Foundation, the Herb Alpert Foundation" (Vale 2006: 38). This progression from the spontaneous aesthetics of everyday action to organized "art" is an important element of the politics that I am discussing.
2. The practice of positioning the image of a corpse vertically is by no means universal in the medical literature. However, it was also commonly used in the Soviet books on legal medicine. In Kustov's opinion, this positioning deemphasizes the idea of death, reanimating the corpse and allowing the viewer to repress the feeling of disgust and awe. In the Soviet case it also probably had an ideological component, enhancing the eradication of the theme of "death" from Soviet public discourse.
3. For example, in Russian "ethnic jokes" about Georgians, Zurab was often a homosexual.
4. In the 1990s, when the Necrorealists achieved fame, their pictures, photos, and installations were regularly exhibited in the Museum of Forensic Medicine (part of the St. Petersburg Medical School), blurring the boundary between "art" and "medical reference materials."
5. Von Hoffman described the case of an officer of the English Expeditionary Corps in Austria who invented elaborate methods that would kill him by delivering multiple complex injuries. In one method, he put a heavy metal cask filled with inflammable liquid in the second-floor window of his house. He tied a rope with a noose at the end of it to the cask's handle, put the noose around his neck, shot at the cask with a revolver, and then jumped out of the window. The liquid ignited and the burning cask followed him to the ground. He received multiple injuries simultaneously—asphyxiation, severe burns, a heavy blow, and fractured bones—but still survived the incident (Mazin 1998: 130).
6. There he made his first 35-mm hill-length film, *Knights of Heaven* (*Rytsari podnebes'ia*, 22 min.), which had a relatively well-defined narrative. The plot contains a secret experiment, an idyllic and brutal male brotherhood, irrationality, and absurd heroic behavior.
7. Yufit's photographs and films have been shown at many international festivals and museums (e.g. St. Petersburg's Russian Museum, Amsterdam's Stedelijk Museum, Dusseldorf's Kunsthalle, New York's Museum ofModem Art). The 1991 film *Papa, Father Frost Is Dead* (*Papa, umer ded moroz,* 81 min.) has been the most recognized of Yufit's films, having received the Grand Prix at the International Film Festival in Rimini; his 2002 film *Killed by Lightning* was shown at Manifesta-5 in San Sebastian, Spain, and his 2005 film *Bipedalism* was shown at the 34th Film Festival in Rotterdam. Vladimir Kustov's painting and installations were shown at the same range of international galleries and museums.
8. Andrei used a favorite Necrorealist verb, *zamateret'* (to become *materyi*), where *materyi* means a combination of "coarse," "manly," "bearish," "hardened," "old," "seasoned," etc.
9. On the erasure of a boundary between mask and reality in an aestheticized practice of living in the Soviet context, see Yurchak (2006, 1999). See also Andrew Lakoff's (2005) discussion of a fin-de-siècle Buenos Aires movement of "oversimulation" of madness as a combination of true madness and imposture of madness and Žižek's (1993) discussion of "overidentification" with ideology as an artistic practice of Laibach and NSK in Tito's Yugoslavia.
10. I use the term "bare life" differently from Agamben. In the USSR in the 1980s, there were subjects who were much closer analogies to what Agamben describes as bare life—camp prisoners, psychiatric clinic inmates, people living in forced internal exile. It is productive, however, to apply the term "bare life" also to such groups as the Necrorealists, for whom the suspension

of political life and the focus on naked existence was a particular strategy of living within that state. Although, unlike the state's inmates, in the eyes of the state the Necrorealists retained their citizens' rights, their citizenship was devoid of the necessary "political" component.

11. Russian writer Andrei Bitov (1997) argues that such groups in the 1970s and '80s invented an "organic" version of freedom "that had nothing to do with accepting or not accepting a given political order." This "organic" freedom cannot be understood in terms of a binary opposition of freedom and unfreedom, nor can it be reduced to the survival instinct or fear of the KGB; it can rather be compared with the freedom that is achieved, according to the anthropologist Talal Asad (2003: 85), by means of martyrdom in a religious context (i.e. also by emphasizing *bare life*): the martyrs of early Christianity, instead of "shunning physical suffering," in fact "actively sought to live it." Such a relation to the world may be interpreted in a religious context not as an example of defeat but as symbolic of "victory over society's power" (or over the state's political sphere) and therefore as a sign of freedom.
12. In the Soviet case the politics of opposition was practiced by far fewer dissidents.

## References


Agamben, Giorgio (1998), *Homo Sacer: Sovereign Power and Bare Life*, trans. Daniel Heller-Roazen, Stanford: Stanford University Press.

Agamben, Giorgio (2005), *State of Exception*, Chicago: University of Chicago Press.

Alaniz, José, and Seth Graham (2001), "Early Necrocinema in Context," in Seth Graham (ed.), *Necrorealism: Context, History, Interpretations*, 5–27, Pittsburgh: Russian Film Symposium.

Asad, Talal (2003), *Formations of the Secular: Christianity, Islam, Modernity*, Stanford: Stanford University Press.

Baudrillard, Jean (1994), *Simulacra and Simulation*, trans. Sheila Faria Glaser, Ann Arbor: University of Michigan Press.

Bitov, Andrei (1997), "Mit'ki na granitse vremeni i prostranstva" ["Mit'ki on the border of time and space"]. *Ogonek*, 16 (21 April).

Boyer, Dominic (2001), "Foucault in the Bush: The Social Life of Post-structuralist Theory in East Berlin's Prenzlauer Berg." *Ethos* 66: 207–36.

Demichev, Andrei (1993), "Face to Face with Necro," in Anessa Miller-Pogacar (ed.), *Russian Necrorealism: Shock Therapy for a New Culture*, Exhibition Program, 5, Bowling Green, OH: Dorothy Uber Bryan Gallery.

Haraway, Donna J. (1997), *Modest Witness at Second Millennium: FemaleMan meets Onco Mouse*, New York: Routledge.

Lakoff, Andrew (2005), "The Simulation of Madness: Buenos Aires, 1903." *Critical Inquiry*, 31: 848–73.

Mazin, Viktor (1998), *Kabinet Nekrorealizma: Iufit i. Kabinet*, St. Petersburg: INA Press.

Miller-Pogacar, Anessa (ed.) (1993), *Russian Necrorealism: Shock Therapy for a New Culture*. Exhibition program, Bowling Green, OH: Dorothy Uber Bryan Gallery.

Smolianinov, V. M., K. I. Tatiev, and V. F. Cherviakov (1961), *Sudebnaia meditsina* [*Legal medicine*], Moscow: Medgiz.

Vale, V. (1912), *Uchebnik sudebnoi meditsiny* [*Manual of legal medicine*], ed. D. P. Kosorotov, St. Petersburg: Rikker.

Vale, V. (2006), "Interview with Yes Men," in V. Vale (ed.), *Pranks* 2, 32–43, San Francisco: ReSearch.

Yurchak, Alexei (1999), "Gagarin and the Rave Kids: Transforming Power, Identity, and Aesthetics in Post-Soviet Nightlife," in A. Baker (ed.), *Consuming Russia: Popular Culture, Sex, and Society Since Gorbachev*, Durham: Duke University Press.

Yurchak, Alexei (2006), *Everything was Forever, Until it was No More: The Last Soviet Generation*, Princeton: Princeton University Press.

Žižek, Slavoj (1993), "Why are Laibach and NSK not Fascists?" *M'ARS* (Ljubljana) 3 (4).

# CHAPTER 25

# INCORPORATIONS: CONTEMPORARY SLOVENE ART AND THE BODY POLITIC

*Gretchen Bakke*

> Each art tends toward an indefinite extension of its power ... this tendency leads it finally to its limit ... it would not know how to pass this limit without running the risk of losing itself in the incomprehensible, the bizarre, and the absurd.
>
> Richard Wagner (1852)

Slovenia, a young country, small, relatively wealthy, and generally speaking copacetic, sits on Europe's southeastern frontier straddling the Balkans, of which it was once a part, and "The West," the heritage of which it claims—at times ferociously—as its own. It is also and perhaps surprisingly, given the size of its population (just under 2 million, only half of whom are urbanized), one of the world's foremost centers of contemporary art production and display. This is the sort of art that baffles rather than pleases most audiences or, what a critic of a recent series of exhibitions, called "the biggest head-scratchers" (Pearson 2005). Some of Slovene contemporary art is just that, baffling; it is art that needs a lot of looking into, some analysis, a strong background in the nuances of art theory, middling knowledge of regional history, and an open mind in order to appreciate and occasionally even enjoy. It is art for experts; art made for audiences who are already well versed in the normative doings and beings of the art world (Becker 1982; Danto 1964, 1981; Gell 1989, 2006). For the most part this is not the sort of art I will be discussing here.

There is a fringe to the contemporary art world and during the period of my research, conducted in the years immediately preceding Slovenia's entry into the EU in 2004, art works that flirted around this edge, at times stepping blithely over it and shattering audiences, were a constant (van Alphen 1993). Performances were crafted in blood and bile and bodies—human bodies—were joined in the most uncomfortable of ways with the things of the object world: scalpels, bullets, drills, gastric lavages, needles, and thread. These pieces were uncomfortable; physically so for artists and also often viscerally so for audiences. For an anthropologist, art works such as these raise the question: if one is going to study violence, why devote oneself to that perpetrated in a gallery by artists upon themselves rather than turning one's attentions to the plenitude of "real" violences which swamp the world at present and which hurt all the more for being unexpected and unplanned?

One answer is that artworks in flesh and human pain are planned, they are scripted and organized, and as such they are texts that though visceral are also readable. Slovenes, in their choice of art whether imported or natively produced, were saying something very strongly about the world in which they were living. In performance after performance they reiterated the point. Blood bled out of successive bodies, from cuts, from holes drilled, from tubes implanted, and needles run through the skin. More than one mouth was sewn shut; more than one anus penetrated, and more than one artist taken from a gallery space in an ambulance.

Again and again audiences watched as artists proved themselves to be flesh by pushing foreign materials into their bodies and drawing them out again until being and object were linked so tightly to one another that they became heterogeneously singular. This effect was accomplished in different ways by different artists working across genres, but the central thematic of conjoining, interpenetrating, and incorporating a diversity of elements naturally unfriendly to one another (like scalpel and skin) into a singular functional entity was, in the final years before Slovenia's integration into the European Union, ubiquitous.

The local world within which all of this incorporative art was happening was, during that period, defined by rapid geopolitical and socioeconomic change. Yugoslavia, of which Slovenia had been a part, was quite violently gone and Europe's Union loomed large on a horizon. Near to all of this change was both glossed as and actually good for Slovenia. They had extracted themselves from Yugoslavia with virtually no violence and in the process gained independence as a nation for the first time in history. By 1999, when the sort of art works discussed in this essay were becoming commonplace, Slovenia was exiting a decade of increased prosperity, political stability, access to technology, and even substantial money for the arts; the future looked brighter still.

All of this breathless progress also meant that many Slovenes were living in a world of constant unknowns over which individuals had little say and even less control. A generation raised with socialism was rendered almost instantaneously superfluous. While among certain populations, most notably middle-aged and university-aged men, suicide rates grew to be among the highest in the world (Marušič 1999; Marušič and Brecelj 2000). In Slovenia, in the 1990s, there was both peace and great sorrow, prosperity and horrific loss, hopefulness and national dismemberment. Yet in public only one of these stories was told—that of progress toward ever-greater goods. In art, by contrast, the soft fleshy underbelly of this progress was laid bare; weakness, hardship, suffering, isolation, and loss were made palpable. Here the "work" of maintaining functionality was exposed in ways that were often difficult for artists to endure and for audiences to absorb. All of this was, however, done without anybody ever saying as much. What was impossible to articulate in daily life may have been omnipresent in contemporary art works, but both realms were equally characterized by the avoidance of clearly articulated, oppositional messages.

Despite this, quiet, physically invasive artworks were clearly providing an outlet for the other side of the story: art was being used as a visceral and extremely expressive space for "speaking" about things for which there were neither adequate words nor suitable fora for complaint—beyond those offered by galleries. In this way Slovene artists were laying a certain claim, on the microlevel, to what was happening on the macro. In their art, whether they were consuming it or doing it, Slovenes were making shifts in geopolitics immensely and intimately local. They were making the nation of their bodies and practicing "integration" on themselves as politics and politicians plied their own integrations on the body politic. By these means they were finding ways to make the more abstract and vertiginous experiences of transition their own.

It is something of a universal truth to say that, in the era of extractive capitalism on a global scale, bodies politic are full of non-native objects and persons (Ferguson 1999; Tsing 2015) The same can be said of bodies, whether speaking of medical devices (like pacemakers or artificial limbs) or ornamentation (like a bone through the nose or silicon in the lips). While this can long be claimed as true what is startling about the treatment of these intrusions within Slovene contemporary performance art is that tropes of functional assimilation or absorption are actively eschewed. What is forced upon audiences (and into artists), instead, is the undeniable, unalterable fact of quintessential difference in the midst of the most intimate spaces of home and flesh. There is no aesthetic slippage, no beauty, arguably no sublimity. Material differences of kind are rather allowed to remain unwieldy, uncomfortable, and alien to what they are stuck into—a drill bit left in the knee, a French hypermart left at the edge of town, an EU law granting foreigners the right to buy property left on the books. The fit is awkward. In Slovenia, where things are most often made to work, the task of remarking upon this awkwardness was left to the artists, who "spoke" mimetically with their bodies of what didn't belong and how that felt. Their performances in the process worked more as a visceral metonym of opinion than as a suggested plan of action. In Slovenia's case the sensation to be expressed—in art as in life—was primarily of being, experiencing, and coming to understand oneself and one's nation as nonhomogeneous, inconsistent, yet nevertheless viable.

* * *

Each of the artworks detailed here flirt intentionally with the edges of the conceptually whole by either threatening or breaking apart the integrity of the physically human; they divorce bits of the body from itself or they plant impossible abstractions into that body and then (tongue almost in cheek) call the resulting confused mass "one." In the process such projects both call into question the parameters of the individual and echo the strange, present tense, reconfigurations of contemporary nation-states.

## 'Enjoy your nation as yourself'[1]

In 1999 Ive Tabar, a nurse and a medical performance artist, ate fifteen paper stars, each a bright shade of goldenrod. As a chaser he ingested a copious amount of blue liquid. This rested in his belly, each element mixing with his own acids, each slowly digesting, intermingling, degrading. His audience saw none of this. But before the digestive process was complete Tabar inserted the tube of a gastric lavage (stomach pump) in through his nose, pushed it down through his esophagus and into his swollen belly. And up it all came, spilling out into the lavage tank positioned on a thin plinth at the center of Kapelica galerija's small exhibition space—golden stars in a sea of blue. The flag of the European union mixed with the stuff of Tabar's body; a supranational symbol aswim in a sea of Slovene bile. There Tabar left it, and left the gallery, without further comment.

This fit of spleen was called *Evropa I* and it was the first, and arguably most genteel, of a series of projects Tabar would craft over the next eight years, each called by the same title *Evropa* (I–IV) each a wordless play on the same theme: Slovenia's integration into the European Union. *Evropa I*, though it had no spoken language, was premised upon a local turn of phrase. To have someone or something in (one's) stomach ["Imeti nekoga ali nekaj v želodcu"] (a sentiment similar to the English "to be unable to stomach something or someone") is, in Slovene, to feel something so distasteful, so ill-making, that to vomit it up is preferable to simply, patiently bearing it (Krpič 2010: 94).[2] What was clear in 1999, five years before Slovenia's entry into the European Union, was that despite wide spread popular support for the transition, Tabar simply couldn't stomach the thought—so much so that he made this thought flesh and then forcibly, mechanically, removed it from his body. Thus, though Tabar does not speak his distaste, his choice of medium allows for certain visceral qualities to enter into a very public—indeed performed—commentary on local politics.

In the second of the *Evropa* series—*Evropa II: Luknja v sistemu, buža v kolenu* [*Europe II: Hole in the System, Drill in the Knee*][3] (2001)—the central allegory of the work shifts from that of "expulsion" of the symbol of a united Europe from the Slovene body to the effective "penetration" of this body by the European Union. As one might intuit from the title, this piece, which was performed in Obalne galerije, in the coastal town of Koper, consisted almost entirely of the artist drilling through his knee. The performance itself was fairly stark. The only props were a chair and the drill, while the performers (all of whom, Tabar included, were medical professionals), were dressed in the practical aqua and blue scrubs of an operating theater. Tabar sat in the chair, his pant leg rolled up, and injected a bubble of anesthesia just under the skin. The audience then waited, along with Tabar, for this to take effect. After some minutes he picked up a drill with a 10-inch bit and meticulously ran it through his calf, just under his kneecap. He then wrapped the entire apparatus (knee plus drill) in gauze, was loaded onto a gurney and wheeled to a waiting ambulance which sped away, presumably—but not explicitly—to a hospital, where an antiseptic drill-removal procedure would be performed. The actual drilling portion of the performance was extremely short, about five minutes, though the videotaped version, which is how most people have seen it, extended this slightly by documenting all of the knee preparation procedures, which were hidden from the live audience's view by a green-scrub curtain.

As in *Evropa I,* Tabar's second piece in this series not only explicitly addresses itself to the project of European integration, though again here more through its title and subtext than anything made explicit in the content of the work itself. It is also play on a common Slovene phrase, in this case, "Rajši si zvrtam luknjo v koleno, kot ..." [I'd rather drill a hole in my knee than ...] (here the English equivalent is "I'd rather have a hole in my head than ...").[4] Tabar's two subsequent performances in this series, also follow this pattern of an explicitly evocative title, a subtle "in the know" reference to an idiomatic phrase likely only recognizable to fluent speakers of Slovene, coupled with a common and easily recognizable symbol of a geopolitical entity (usually a flag of some sort), and physical violence enacted by the artist himself upon his body. In brief, in *Evropa III* (2004) Tabar slowly separated his fingernail with a Slovenia flag painted upon it from the flesh of his finger (on the occasion of Slovenia's acceptance into the EU) and affixed it to a plastic *Proteus anguineus*, a local, pale-skinned newt which is often used in Slovenia as a sort of national totem; and in *Evropa IV* (2008) he sliced open his abdomen with a scalpel, inserted a catheter and then released a stream of dyed blue urine straight from his bladder into a fish tank containing a goldfish and a number of test tubes, each of which stood in for a member nation of the EU.

Though in Tabar's work his political stance is made more or less explicit, he was not alone in his use of highly evocative, physically invasive, live body art performances to obliquely express concerns about Slovenia's entry in the European Union. A second example is the work of Slovene philosopher, sexologist, and performance artist Peter Mlakar. Mlakar's 2001 *Logika, Mučenje, Tirada* [*Logic, Torture, Tirade*]— also part of a series of quite similar works—was a performance that, while not originally cast in terms of processes of geopolitical integration, was reread that way in 2004 by another sort of artist altogether, the political caricaturist.

That Mlakar's sexological performances might become the topic of a mainstream political cartoon, published on the occasion of Slovenia's acceptance into the EU (May 2004) in Slovenia's weekly magazine with the widest circulation, *Mladina*, already says something about centrality of "fringe" performances like those of Tabar and Mlakar in Slovene popular culture. Mlakar, for example, is a well-known man about town, the author of many books ranging from philosophical treatises to short works of pornographic fiction. He is also a long-term member of the arts collective of some renown Neue Slowenische Kunst, and was the host of a weekly television show for a period of time on RTV Slovenia (Slovenia's state run TV channel). *Logika, Mučenje, Tirada,* and popular responses to it should be read then in relationship to Mlakar's role not just as an artist but as an easily recognizable public figure.

The performance was a much longer and far more (nonsensically) verbose work than any of Tabar's undertakings. *Logika, Mučenje, Tirada* was divided into three parts of unequal affective weight: the first and the third acts were utterly eclipsed by the second, in which Mlakar attempted to insert a dildo on the end of a very big drill into the exposed vagina of a woman. The strangeness and indeed palpable discomfort of both Mlakar and his willing assistant during the portion of the performance that involved him pressing the dildo into her—her legs up in stirrups made of antlers horns *as if* upon a gynecologist's table, her head cloaked in shadows, and her body tense and unwilling to let that thing in—trumped the two acts of the performance that bracketed it. Yet the performance's denouement did not come here, rather Mlakar's magician moment—when he actually causes something to become something else—came in the third act of the performance when he transformed this same woman into a diskette (the first act involved prodding a brain in a tank with a slim metal probe and recording, and broadcasting, it *as if* meaningful electromagnetic reactions). Mlakar staged this transubstantiation of substance (woman to diskette) as if he were playing the lead in an old time magic show, first hiding her with a deep red cloth, then spinning her around, speaking a few words and whipping the cloth away "Whala!" to expose where once she had lain … the thin black square of a computer disk! This he inserted easily (note the trebling of insertions: probe into brain, dildo into woman, disk into machine) into a waiting PC. Reduced thusly into data, safely contained there inside the disk inside the machine, he talked with her, and her gibberish answers to his queries spewed out at processor speed and in the vivid green text of early DOS machines on the large projection screen mounted behind his head.

In general Mlakar's work is highly sexualized and this performance is not out of keeping with a tendency toward perversion that is not, in Mlakar's case, about producing shock from the violence of a stylized sexual act, but rather the public expression of desire and vulnerably—his own, here more so than her own.[5] He is as much a performer in this work as he is a man having attenuated sex in a public forum. It might be tempting to read this work only as a sort of blatant misogyny that reflects badly on the artist, his audience (who did not level this critique), and his home culture. In context, however, and with a sense of the man who makes the art—a sense readily available to the audience of the performance itself, an audience who laughed with Malker and also laughed at him, an audience who held their breath with him and sat tight and silent when things got difficult—*Logika, Mučenje, Tirada* is the story of a man failing to enter, or even touch, a woman. It brims with humor, self-exposure, and self-deprecation. All of this was accomplished in this piece, as in Tabar's work above, with remarkable earnestness.

Mlakar, as the artist, set out to tell a particular story in this tripartite work, the story of attempting to get things into bodies and to transform bodies into things. An artwork, however, like any complex symbolic form, when released into the world, is open to multiple interpretations and one Slovene after-the-fact reading was a humorous recasting of the entire dildo-on-a-drill second act of the performance in terms of a Slovene "penetration" of Europe. The cartoon was roughly drawn in quick black strokes by Josip Visarjonoič, whose style and pointed humor often graces the pages of *Mladina*. In it Peter Mlakar looks more like an evil butcher with an industrial tamper rather than a drill and the dildo is closer in its size to a horse's penis than a man's. For her part, his assistant is evidently bored with the proceedings as she thumbs her way through a magazine.[6] From Mlakar's mouth, in the cartoon, comes this word bubble: *"In Tako je Slovneija penetriala v Evropo!"* ["And thus has Slovenia penetrated into Europe"].

A joke certainly and, locally at least, a pretty funny one; but also a depiction of integration that turns the tables on the more common ways of talking about small Slovenia and the much larger European Union. Here Slovenia is not absorbed; it is not "integrated"; it does not join. It penetrates, like a wrecking ball might penetrate a condemned building, or like a plastic, and thus also sterile, penis might penetrate a woman. And these, while interesting metaphors for European integration, pale in comparison to the already odd decision of selecting Mlakar's performance as the source material for the joke.

Thus is art made to "speak" to and for the world in two different ways. It speaks first through its content, its form, and its medium of things the artist, him or herself, is interested in and personally affected by—from the personal and the passionate (Mlakar) to the geopolitical and definitional (Tabar). Second, it contributes through its appropriation into popular discourse to wider conversations about power and more concretely, within the Slovene context, to the many jogglings of position attendant to the particular process of moving from a hard won and short-lived independence (1991–2004) into the fold of yet another surpra-statist organization.[7]

## Temporary functional conjoinings

There are other ways to incorporate the body into larger systems of machinery and metaphor than those routes familiar from sex or medical procedure. I want to turn to a final performance, *Brainscore* (Darij Kreuh and Davide Grassi 2002), that harnessed the autonomic systems of the body and its electrical impulses without penetrating the flesh, and then used these impulses to power and control machine-based assemblages. It was far from the sole project of this type to have been staged in the years immediately preceding Slovenia's entrance into the EU, but it was the most unabashedly grandiose, indeed nearly operatic in its scale and complexity.[8]

* * *

*Brainscore* was presented in a fairly mainstream theater-in-the-round in Cankarev dom, a labyrinthine cultural center in downtown Ljubljana with conference rooms, exhibit halls, a bar, and numerous stages of every size and sort including Gallusova dvorana, the largest venue in the Republic. This performance could be best characterized as a biomechanical opera, the biological components of which were the artists' bodies—each strapped into sturdy black chairs at the wrists, waist, thighs, calves, and feet while their heads were immobilized in contraptions reminiscent of 1970s science-fictive brain-transfer devices. Each man also had a camera positioned up close and recording at his right eye. This live-capture eye-image was sent to a TV screen positioned at the artist's side though angled up at the audience. In the darkness this eye on TV that peered up out of obscurity was almost all that was visible of the artists strapped-in down there. In addition to this eye-cam that captured every twitch, blink, and involuntary dilation, each performer had a host of electrodes fixed to his head. For the forty minutes of the performance, Grassi and Kreuh's sole task was to remain as immobile as humanly possible.

Above them—at the audience's eye level—swarmed strange 3D stones shaped like blood vessels, coming now faster, now slower out of a screen hung high on the wall at stage center. This mammoth, stone-spewing screen was flanked by two others, each of which displayed a super-sized image of a brain meant to correspond to the brain of one of the two immobilized performers. Various sections of these brains lit up during the performance, fairly randomly, and beneath them was displayed a constantly shifting set of URLs supposedly generated by electromagnetic activity in each of the artists' heads. Every change in the eyes' motions—their dilations, blinks, and twitches—controlled the size, shape, and rapidity of blob production while shifts in electromagnetic "brain" activity controlled the brain-screens and the more or less constant shifts in URL production. The piece was literally "scored" by the brain, changing not in essence, but in its particularities with each performance. Without the artist's body there could have been no *Brainscore*. All of the creative stimulus of the otherwise mechanical, mechanized, and preprogrammed show was provided via those few actions the nearly immobile men strapped tight into chairs could not control.

Despite this, *Brainscore* was not about the limited flesh-bound body *per se*. Instead it emphasized the matrix of the physical, of which the human was only one small, albeit essential part. Perhaps what *Brainscore* best illustrated was how even the most minor of physiological impulses can be harnessed into a large biomechanical system that pays no mind to the conscious human—the human as distinct individual—despite being rooted, literally, in it.

Though *Brainscore* neither formally addressed itself to processes of political integration nor was it used after the fact to serve this project, the concerns embodied in the piece were not dissimilar from those made flesh by a host of works performed in, funded by, and staged in Slovenia in the early 2000s, including those of Tabar and Mlakar. What does it mean, these works seem to ask, to be integrated into larger systems and processes? To be interpenetrated by them? And how might integration be conceptualized and practiced without "absorption" of various components serving as the key figure of transition? Or to put it another way: What kind of equilibrium, or functionality, might be maintained in a system that is both unsteady and impermanent?

In no case is the story told that of "becoming-other" but rather, again and again, what one sees in these works is the violence of something fragile coming into contact with objects and systems which insist upon co-existence. In each case, I would argue it is the integrated being that is of interest to these artists—the man or woman plus the drill (differently, in the two cases) or the body plus the complex bio-mechanical system that it scores—and not the absorbed or homogenized being but the diversely functional one. As such, these Slovene artists among others were toying with new metaphors for integration, ones in which the smallest competent parts were not lost, but neither were they irrelevant or left untouched.

## Optimism; impurity

Not unlike paint and canvas, or celluloid and light, the body allows artists certain sorts of expression and forecloses others. "Body artists" are, in other words, much like painters, sculptors, and composers in that they are limited in their creativity by the constraints and potentials of their chosen medium. The body will (and will not—as we have seen in the case of Mlakar's unsuccessful penetration of his assistant) allow for certain actions to be taken upon or, by means, of it. Despite the inherent limitations of the body as a medium for art, no small number of artists, both within Slovenia and beyond, find that the body expresses what they want to "say" better than a comparable medium might. In this, the body is not so different from the forcefulness of the reeds in the basketmaker's hands, described by Tim Ingold, their resistance to being woven influencing the final form of the basket far more than the artist's will or imagination (2011). Or, to use an older theoretical apparatus, the medium is part and parcel of the message (McLuhan 1964); much of what art says or does socially subsists in the ways in which the medium selected by an artist is strung together with both a work's expressive content and with its form. This is likely a universal characteristic of art whether one speaks of Dinka cattle (Lienhardt 1961), Tuvan throat singing (*Genghis Blues*, dir. Roko Belic 1999), or the sewing of the flesh of one's hand to the skin of one's face (as Norwegian performer Håvve Fjell did in Ljubljana in 2002). The body, and most especially the body interrupted by the stuff of the object world (dildo, drill, needle, thread, scalpel, catheter) or reinterpreted as just another thing among many (pupil dilatation, brain wave, URL) can be, and perhaps ought to be, read as unique for the ways it can be made to express artists' concerns. By this I mean that like any medium the expressive capacity of the body is both specific and limited and thus, like any media, it is both "unique" and "uniquely suited" for the communication of certain sorts of messages, and particularly unsuited for the effective communication of others. What is more, even when the articulated intent of a work of art is to speak to one aspect of social, economic, political, or personal life, the breadth of possible interpretations is not—indeed is never—limited to the artist's intentions. It is not merely information that flows into and out of bodies but also objects that constantly interrupt bodily integrity. The two, objects and bodies, individuals and information, machines and persons, are made in these works to interpenetrate one another. These interactions, within the realm of art, often appear to have been designed to call into question what it is to be a bounded, self-conscious, willful individual person under conditions of massive infrastructural interdependence; or, to put it another way, what it is to be literally a part of global processes of sociocultural integration.

Such conditions, whether it is losing one's heart to someone (Franko B's nude bloodletting performance, *I Miss You*, 2002), using a cell phone (to text and to talk and even to make purchases) upwards of fifty times a day, or having one's nation become a part of something much greater and still largely unknown and unpredictable, each in their own way becomes a cause for the reconceptualization of integrity. The body, once inviolable in the world of conceptual art, had become by the early 2000s a central means for the public expression of sensations of perforation, penetration, immobility, inexpressivity, loss of self, loss of control, and the sapping of life force.

In a more hopeful vein, these same contemporary works also speak to the bodily integration of outside influences and foreign objects into new sorts of wholes. The body—the flesh as well as the person intrinsic to it—was made in these projects to become a functioning part of something larger than the self-conscious, self-centered human being. Monadism was not only dismissed out of hand but was clearly not even conceptually viable to these artists whose works spoke at a fundamental level, if under onion-layers of anxiety, of a functional optimism based upon impurity and the intermingling of types. Even Ive Tabar with all the biliousness of his opinions regarding Slovenia's incorporation into the EU takes this institution symbolically into himself. He integrates it even if only to purge the thought (and stuff) of this integration a moment later. The body thus flirts with newly inclusive versions of itself that, as *Brainscore* makes clear, needn't last long to be both readable and real.

None of this is clear yet. That is to say, none of it or at least very little of it has leavened upward to the level of speech, articulation, pontification, or theory. But the lack of saying (and indeed even of sensible language) in most of these projects in no way undermines their message, repeated again and again by shunt and by scalpel, by diskette and by dildo, by electrode and gastric lavage: the body is no longer whole, no longer inviolable, no longer conceptualizable as an isolate. The same might also be said for the self or for the nation. In these processes of intermingling and incorporation new things are being made from the stuff of the human, not as a way of dismissing them but rather as a means of newly incorporating them into the interpenetrating complexities already so common to everyday life.

## Notes

1. Žižek 1993. In using this phrase Žižek is making a slightly different point than that emphasized here, however, it should be noted that his definition of enjoyment and of the nation clearly underlie my own thinking in this essay and elsewhere. This is largely because Žižek is himself a Slovene and as such his ideas about how cultures work, how they imagine and distill themselves, are particularly well suited to the particularities of Slovenia even if this is rarely the use to which he puts them.
2. Special thanks to Tomaž Krpič for pointing out how Tabar draws upon idiomatic Slovene phrases in his work. For a more detailed description of each of the *Evropa* projects and some of Tabars' other performance pieces, see Krpič 2010.
3. *Buža* is either a slang word or from a dialect of Slovene with which I am unfamiliar. It is not in the dictionary and I have never heard the term used outside of the name of this particular piece; about two-thirds of the time it is translated (by Slovenes) as "drill" and the rest of the time as "hole" a state of affairs, which lead me to believe that others find it equally unfamiliar. I have chosen to use "drill" here simply because it is a quantitatively more frequent choice.
4. Krpič suggests that the implied phrase after the ellipse to be "… than become, at least willingly, a citizen of the European Union" (2010: 94).
5. Personal conversation with Ivo Saliger, Ljubljana, March 2005.
6. Drawing by Josip Visarjonoič, from *Mladina* 26, June 28, 2004: 58. The image can be found at: http://www.mladina.si/91510/peter-mlakar/
7. 1991 was the beginning of Slovenia's only period of independent nationhood. Previous to this it had always been part of a larger multinational entity: Communist Yugoslavia, Nazi Germany, The Kingdom of the Slovenes, Croats and Serbs, the Austro-Hungarian (and before that Austrian) empires.
8. Works by Franko B., Ron Atheny, Kira O'Reily, and Oleg Kulik, all of whom performed in Slovenia between 2000–4 (as well as Orlan's extended plastic surgery project) could be argued to be ego reifying rather than ego ablating; the person of the performer becomes much more

solid and bounded by means of the work of art rather than becoming diffuse and peripheral to audiences' notice or care.

## References

Alphen, Ernst van (1993), *Frances Bacon and the Loss of Self*, Cambridge: Harvard University Press.
Bakke, Gretchen (2008), "Reframing History." *Slovene Studies* 30 (2): 185–217.
Becker, Howard S. (1982), *Art Worlds*, Berkeley and Los Angeles: University of California Press.
Belic, Roko (dir.) (1999), *Genghis Blues*, USA.
Danto, Arthur (1964), "The Artworld." *Journal of Philosophy* 61 (19) (October): 571–84.
Danto, Arthur (1981), *The Transformation of the Commonplace*, Cambridge: Harvard University Press.
Ferguson, James (1999), *Expectations of Modernity: Myths and Meanings of Urban Life on the Zambian Copperbelt* University of California Press.
Gell, Alfred (1998), *Art and Agency: An Anthropological Theory*, Oxford: Oxford University Press.
Gell, Alfred (2006), *The Art of Anthropology: Essays and Diagrams*, Oxford: Berg.
Ingold, Tim (2011), "On Weaving a Basket," in *The Perception of the Environment: Essays on Livelihood, Dwelling and Skill*, 339–48, London: Routledge.
Krpič, Tomaž (2010), "Medical Performance The Politics of Body-Home." *PAJ: A Journal of Performance and Art* 94 (32, 1): 36–43.
Lienhardt, Godfrey (1961), *Divinity and Experience: The Religion of the Dinka*, Oxford: Clarendon Press.
Marušič, Andrej (1999), "Suicide in Slovenia: Lessons for Cross-cultural Psychiatry." *International Review for Psychiatry* 11: 212–18.
Marušič, Andrej and M. Brecelj (2000), "Psychiatry in Slovenia: A High Suicide and Cirrhosis Rates Country." *Psychiatric Bulletin* 24: 385–7.
Matos, Urša (2004), "Peter Mlakar: Tisti filozof, ki svet razglasi za neobstoječ" *Mladina* 26, June 28, 2004: 58.
McLuhan, Marshall (1994), *Understanding Media: The Extensions of Man*, Cambridge, MA: The MIT Press.
Novak, Jure (2001), "Koleno je super' Ive Tabar, body artist" ["The knee is doing great: Ive Tabar, body artist"]. *Mladina* 50 (December 17, 2001).
Pearson, Heather (2005), "Modern in the Middle." *World Traveler* (July): 25.
Shore, Chris (1997), "Metaphors of Europe: Integration and the Politics of Language," in S. Nugent and C. Shore (eds), *Anthropology and Cultural Studies*, London: Chicago: Pluto Press.
Sretenović, Dejan (1998), *Umetnost v zatvorenom društvo* [*Art in a Closed Society*], Beograd: Geopoetika.
Šuvaković Miško (2003), "Impossible Histories," in D. Djurić and M. Šuvaković (eds), *Impossible Histories: Historical Avant-gardes, Neo-avant-gardes, and Post-avant-gardes in Yugoslavia, 1918–1991*, 2–35, Boston: MIT Press.
Tsing, Anna Lowenhaupt (2015), *The Mushroom at the End of the World: On the Possibility of Life in Capitalist Ruins*, Princeton: Princeton University Press.
Wagner, Richard (1995 [1852]), *Opera and Drama*, Lincoln: University of Nebraska Press.
Žižek, Slavoj (1996), "'There is No Sexual Relationship': Wagner as a Lacanian." *New German Critique* 69: 7–35.
Žižek, Slavoj (1993), *Tarrying with the Negative: Kant, Hegel, and the Critique of Ideology*, Durham: Duke University Press.

# PART V
# MATTERS OF ENGAGEMENT

## Preface

Theories of ritual have long stood at the core of anthropological approaches to participation in temporally bound events. While acknowledging a debt to this work, we depart from this foundation in order to engage with audiences as having forms and experiences that are specific to time, place, and medium (Bell 2009). At the same time, the pieces included here sustain concerns at the center of the work of both Durkheim (1968 [1915]) and Turner (1969) about the relationship between an event and a social order, between audience formation and comportment on the one hand and culture on the other. Thus, resonating with Durkheim's discussion of collective effervescence and totemism, all the readings examine, in one way or another, how a social order shapes audience form, is reflected in audiences, and is constituted by audiences. Geertz puts this in the most general terms, writing that the cockfight's "function … is interpretive: it is a Balinese reading of Balinese experience; a story they tell themselves about themselves" (229). While for Turner, ritual is marked both by its structural role and its status as outside of everyday life, by turning a broader lens to questions of interpretation and meaning making, we can begin to address audiences in a range of contexts and of a wide array of media.

A crucial question for the anthropology of arts is to understand how an event is meaningful, both in itself and in relation to broader social formations. As Barber writes, "The best reason for studying audiences is that they have a hand in the constitution of the 'meaning' of a performance, text or utterance" (242). Yet the terms of this cannot be assumed. Rather, "We need to ask *how* audiences do their work of interpretation" (242). Drawing on the work of Bateson and Goffman, Bauman proposes treating performance as a "frame," an agreed upon setting in which special attention is paid to the performer, whose "act of expression" may be evaluated in and of itself in terms of skill, effectiveness, and competence (the "rules of play" as it were). Suggesting that performance is a special kind of frame in a wider field of communication highlights the interactional nature of performance, in which the *relationship* between performer and audience is crucial. Frames of intelligibility not only allow audience members to know when something is sincere or a joke, but are foundational for organizing play in its multiple manifestations, structuring how one knows when something is a "game" (Bateson, as discussed in Salen and Zimmerman).

As Barber demonstrates, audiences are always historical configurations, including the silent audience that instantiates a modern notion of the "public"—an audience that is "in principle an indefinitely extensible horizon of anonymous and interchangeable members" (238). Hence, the silent audience that appears neutral and disengaged because its experience is inaccessible on the surface is also a social formation, the features of which should be taken seriously as such (Johnson 1995). A convention, the silent orientation toward the painting or performer is cultivated. A mode of engagement that emphasizes an individual's interiority, this is the Kantian disinterestedness that in fact takes much focus and constraint, comportment that, as Bourdieu emphasizes, reveals the social bases of Kant's notions of taste (see Part III). Approaching the social and historical dimensions of the silent audience is an important site for addressing the full scope of *art* with an anthropological approach. Moreover, in taking a broad view of audiences, we consider what can be learned about the matter of engagement from studies of diverse media forms that range from television to sport, video games to theatrical performance. In all these settings, audiences are trained to comport themselves in particular ways (jumping up and down and yelling at the punk concert or standing still and whispering in the gallery); such modes of comportment reflect—and critique—wider cultural norms (see Mauss in Part IV)

Abu-Lughod's ethnography of watching television brings questions to the fore about how we understand consumption of and engagement with media in everyday life, and how the ubiquitous presence of such media shapes audiences in particular ways. Abu-Lughod deftly engages both the intimacies and global aspects of watching television, arguing for the "significance of television's existence as a ubiquitous presence in the lives and imaginaries of people in the contemporary world" (1997: 245). Importantly for an anthropology of the arts, her work provides an example of ethnographic engagement with popular or mass culture, something often rejected both by fields that address themselves to "fine" arts or indigenous craft. This perspective is sustained by the strong lineage of work on participatory video in visual anthropology, in which those who might be either subjects of ethnographic filmmaking or its consumers are engaged as producers (Ginsburg 1991; Turner 1992). Like other events and audiences, television, enmeshed "in other social fields" does work that extends beyond its immediate viewing. In the case of television, viewers—and publics—are not necessarily coterminous; in this way, television and other forms of popular culture provide ways of building sociability across time and space, underscoring their significance for globalization (Appadurai 1996). Hence, television reshapes assumptions about the very meaning of culture, challenging a notion of culture as local and bounded by forcing "us to think about 'culture' not so much as a system of meaning or even a way of life but as something whose elements are produced, censored, paid for, and broadcast across a nation, even across national boundaries" (Abu-Lughod, 251).

While many audience formations reinforce and confirm normative social orders, Greene addresses how subcultural participation, such as with punk rock, can be a means of existing outside of the "symbolic center," a means by which fans "propel themselves out towards the margins, into the domain of the excluded and anti-normal" (267), and to, in fact, demonstrate repulsion toward that center. Not simply self-fashioning as an "art," piercings, tattoos, and clothes that "offend somebody" (264) are in fact socially transformative. Following Bakhtin, Greene emphasizes the ways in which the transgressive qualities of the grotesque not only critique norms, but have the potential to model—and thus create—egalitarian and non-virtuosic modes of sociability that span class, race, and geography. Moreover, as this and other cases demonstrate, engagement with art is integral to life in general; while attending concerts is only a small part of being punk, music, visual culture, fashion, and other media are in fact inherent to everyday life. Attending to the specificities of engagement is thus crucial for understanding how and why art matters as a social process.

## Ethnographic exercise

### *Audience observation*

Spend 2–3 hours in a space in which art is exhibited or performed, indoors or outdoors. Observe, and take notes, *focusing on the audience*. Also pay attention to the space, its organization, how the work is hung (if a gallery or museum), how the stage is arranged and its relationship to the audience (if a performance), the performers, the stage hands, guards, and, most especially, the *audience*. Who comes, and what do they do? Are they there to look at the art/listen to/see the performance? How do they engage with it?

Be as thorough as possible in your notes. Even if no one is there, there is something to describe. Aim to write (nearly) continuously, with as much detail as possible. Do not evaluate or draw conclusions. Simply describe what you see, hear, smell, or otherwise sense. Diagrams of the space might be useful. If there are visitors or audience members, describe them in general, and focus on one or two, describing their actions in detail. Expect to fill at least a page an hour, but probably more.

## Further reading


Appadurai, Arjun (1996), *Modernity at Large: Cultural Dimensions of Globalization*, Minneapolis: University of Minnesota Press.

Bell, Catherine (2009), *Ritual Theory, Ritual Practice*, Oxford: Oxford University Press.

Bigenho, Michelle (2012), *Intimate Distance: Andean Music in Japan*, Durham, NC: Duke University Press.

Brooker, Will and Deborah Jermyn (eds), (2003), *The Audience Studies Reader*, London: Routledge, 2003.

Brown, Jeffrey A. (2000), *Black Superheroes, Milestone Comics, and Their Fans*, Jackson, MS: University Press of Mississippi.

Caton, Steven Charles (2005), "Anger Be Now Thy Song," in *Yemen Chronicle: An Anthropology of War and Mediation*, 61–101, New York: Hill and Wang.

DeNora, Tia (2000), *Music in Everyday Life*, Cambridge: Cambridge University Press.

Durkheim, Emile (1968 [1915]), *The Elementary Forms of the Religious Life*, trans. Joseph Ward Swain. New York: Free Press.

Ginsburg, Faye (1991), "Indigenous Media: Faustian Contract or Global Village?" *Cultural Anthropology* 6 (1): 92–112.

Johnson, James H. (1995), *Listening in Paris: A Cultural History*, Berkeley: University of California Press.

Miller, Daniel (1995), "Consumption Studies as the Transformation of Anthropology," in Daniel Miller (ed.), *Acknowledging Consumption: A Review of New Studies*, 264–95, New York: Routledge.

Miller, Kiri (2008), "Grove Street Grimm: Grand Theft Auto and Digital Folklore." *Journal of American Folklore* 121 (481): 255–85.

Shipley, Jesse Weaver (2013), "Transnational Circulation and Digital Fatigue in Ghana's Azonto Dance Craze." *American Ethnologist* 40 (2): 362–81.

Spitulnik, Debra (2002), "Mobile Machines and Fluid Audiences: Rethinking Reception through Zambian Radio Culture," in Faye D. Ginsburg, Lila Abu-Lughod, and Brian Larkin (eds), *Media Worlds: Anthropology on New Terrain*, 337–54, Berkeley: University of California Press.

Turner, Terence S. (1992), "Defiant Images: The Kayapo Appropriation of Video." *Anthropology Today* 8 (6): 5–16.

Turner, Victor W. (1969), *The Ritual Process: Structure and Anti-Structure*, Chicago: Aldine Publishing Company.

# CHAPTER 26

## DEEP PLAY: NOTES ON THE BALINESE COCKFIGHT

*Clifford Geertz*

Early in April of 1958, my wife and I arrived, malarial and diffident, in a Balinese village we intended, as anthropologists, to study. A small place, about five hundred people, and relatively remote, it was its own world. We were intruders, professional ones, and the villagers dealt with us as Balinese seem always to deal with people not part of their life who yet press themselves upon them: as though we were not there. For them, and to a degree for ourselves, we were nonpersons, specters, invisible men.

My wife and I were still very much in the gust of wind stage, a most frustrating, and even, as you soon begin to doubt whether you are really real after all, unnerving one, when, ten days or so after our arrival, a large cockfight was held in the public square to raise money for a new school.

Now, a few special occasions aside, cockfights are illegal in Bali under the Republic (as, for not altogether unrelated reasons, they were under the Dutch), largely as a result of the pretensions to puritanism radical nationalism tends to bring with it. The elite, which is not itself so very puritan, worries about the poor, ignorant peasant gambling all his money away, about what foreigners will think, about the waste of time better devoted to building up the country. It sees cockfighting as "primitive," "backward," "unprogressive," and generally unbecoming an ambitious nation. And, as with those other embarrassments – opium smoking, begging, or uncovered breasts – it seeks, rather unsystematically, to put a stop to it.

Of course, like drinking during Prohibition or, today, smoking marihuana, cockfights, being a part of "The Balinese Way of Life," nonetheless go on happening, and with extraordinary frequency. And, like Prohibition or marihuana, from time to time the police (who, in 1958 at least, were almost all not Balinese but Javanese) feel called upon to make a raid, confiscate the cocks and spurs, fine a few people, and even now and then expose some of them in the tropical sun for a day as object lessons which never, somehow, get learned, even though occasionally, quite occasionally, the object dies.

As a result, the fights are usually held in a secluded corner of a village in semi-secrecy, a fact which tends to slow the action a little – not very much, but the Balinese do not care to have it slowed at all. In this case, however, perhaps because they were raising money for a school that the government was unable to give them, perhaps because raids had been few recently, perhaps, as I gathered from subsequent discussion, there was a notion that the necessary bribes had been paid, they thought they could take a chance on the central square and draw a larger and more enthusiastic crowd without attracting the attention of the law.

They were wrong. In the midst of the third match, with hundreds of people, including, still transparent, myself and my wife, fused into a single body around the ring, a superorganism in the literal sense, a truck full of policemen armed with machine guns roared up. Amid great screeching cries of "pulisi! pulisi!" from the crowd, the policemen jumped out, and, springing into the center of the ring, began to swing their guns around like gangsters in a motion picture, though not going so far as actually to fire them. The superorganism came instantly apart as its components scattered in all directions. People raced down the road, disappeared headfirst over walls, scrambled under platforms, folded themselves behind wicker screens, scuttled up coconut trees. Cocks armed with steel spurs sharp enough to cut off a finger or run a hole through a foot were running wildly around. Everything was dust and panic.

On the established anthropological principle, When in Rome, my wife and I decided, only slightly less instantaneously than everyone else, that the thing to do was run too. We ran down the main village street, northward, away from where we were living, for we were on that side of the ring. About halfway down another fugitive ducked suddenly into a compound – his own, it turned out – and we, seeing nothing ahead of us but rice fields, open country, and a very high volcano, followed him. As the three of us came tumbling into the courtyard, his wife, who had apparently been through this sort of thing before, whipped out a table, a tablecloth, three chairs, and three cups of tea, and we all, without any explicit communication whatsoever, sat down, commenced to sip tea, and sought to compose ourselves.

A few moments later, one of the policemen marched importantly into the yard, looking for the village chief. (The chief had not only been at the fight, he had arranged it. When the truck drove up he ran to the river, stripped off his sarong, and plunged in so he could say, when at length they found him sitting there pouring water over his head, that he had been away bathing when the whole affair had occurred and was ignorant of it. They did not believe him and fined him three hundred rupiah, which the village raised collectively.) Seeing my wife and I, "White Men," there in the yard, the policeman performed a classic double take. When he found his voice again he asked, approximately, what in the devil did we think we were doing there. Our host of five minutes leaped instantly to our defense, producing an impassioned description of who and what we were, so detailed and so accurate that it was my turn, having barely communicated with a living human being save my landlord and the village chief for more than a week, to be astonished. We had a perfect right to be there, he said, looking the Javanese upstart in the eye. We were American professors; the government had cleared us; we were there to study culture; we were going to write a book to tell Americans about Bali. And we had all been there drinking tea and talking about cultural matters all afternoon and did not know anything about any cockfight. Moreover, we had not seen the village chief all day, he must have gone to town. The policeman retreated in rather total disarray. And, after a decent interval, bewildered but relieved to have survived and stayed out of jail, so did we.

The next morning the village was a completely different world for us. Not only were we no longer invisible, we were suddenly the center of all attention, the object of a great outpouring of warmth, interest, and, most especially, amusement. Everyone in the village knew we had fled like everyone else.

As any art form – for that, finally, is what we are dealing with – the cockfight renders ordinary, everyday experience comprehensible by presenting it in terms of acts and objects which have had their practical consequences removed and been reduced (or, if you prefer, raised) to the level of sheer appearances, where their meaning can be more powerfully articulated and more exactly perceived. The cockfight is "really real" only to the cocks – it does not kill anyone, castrate anyone, reduce anyone to animal status, alter the hierarchical relations among people, nor refashion the hierarchy; it does not even redistribute income in any significant way. What it does is what, for other peoples with other temperaments and other conventions, *Lear* and *Crime and Punishment* do; it catches up these themes – death, masculinity, rage, pride, loss, beneficence, chance – and, ordering them into an encompassing structure, presents them in such a way as to throw into relief a particular view of their essential nature. It puts a construction on them, makes them, to those historically positioned to appreciate the construction, meaningful – visible, tangible, graspable – "real," in an ideational sense. An image, fiction, a model, a metaphor, the cockfight is a means of expression; its function is neither to assuage social passions nor to heighten them (though, in its play-with-fire way, it does a bit of both), but, in a medium of feathers, blood, crowds, and money, to display them.

What sets the cockfight apart from the ordinary course of life, lifts it from the realm of everyday practical affairs, and surrounds it with an aura of enlarged importance is not, as functionalist sociology would have it, that it reinforces status discriminations (such reinforcement is hardly necessary in a society where every act proclaims them), but that it provides a metasocial commentary upon the whole matter of assorting human beings into fixed hierarchical ranks and then organizing the major part of collective existence around that assortment. Its function, if you want to call it that, is interpretive: it is a Balinese reading of Balinese experience; a story they tell themselves about themselves.

To put the matter this way is to engage in a bit of metaphorical refocusing of one's own, for it shifts the analysis of cultural forms from an endeavor in general parallel to dissecting an organism, diagnosing a symptom, deciphering a code, or ordering a system – the dominant analogies in contemporary anthropology – to one in general parallel with penetrating a literary text. If one takes the cockfight, or any other collectively sustained symbolic structure, as a means of "saying something of something" (to invoke a famous Aristotelian tag), then one is faced with a problem not in social mechanics but social semantics.[1] For the anthropologist, whose concern is with formulating sociological principles, not with promoting or appreciating cockfights, the question is, what does one learn about such principles from examining culture as an assemblage of texts?

To treat the cockfight as a text is to bring out a feature of it (in my opinion, the central feature of it) that treating it as a rite or a pastime, the two most obvious alternatives, would tend to obscure: its use of emotion for cognitive ends. What the cockfight says it says in a vocabulary of sentiment – the thrill of risk, the despair of loss, the pleasure of triumph. Yet what it says is not merely that risk is exciting, loss depressing, or triumph gratifying, banal tautologies of affect, but that it is of these emotions, thus exampled, that society is built and individuals put together. Attending cockfights and participating in them is, for the Balinese, a kind of sentimental education. What he learns there is what his culture's ethos and his private sensibility (or, anyway, certain aspects of them) look like when spelled out externally in a collective text; that the two are near enough alike to be articulated in the symbolics of a single such text; and – the disquieting part – that the text in which this revelation is accomplished consists of a chicken hacking another mindlessly to bits.

Every people, the proverb has it, loves its own form of violence. The cockfight is the Balinese reflection on theirs: on its look, its uses, its force, its fascination. Drawing on almost every level of Balinese experience, it brings together themes – animal savagery, male narcissism, opponent gambling, status rivalry, mass excitement, blood sacrifice – whose main connection is their involvement with rage and the fear of rage, and, binding them into a set of rules which at once contains them and allows them play, builds a symbolic structure in which, over and over again, the reality of their inner affiliation can be intelligibly felt. If, to quote Northrop Frye again, we go to see *Macbeth* to learn what a man feels like after he has gained a kingdom and lost his soul, Balinese go to cockfights to find out what a man, usually composed, aloof, almost obsessively self-absorbed, a kind of moral autocosm, feels like when, attacked, tormented, challenged, insulted, and driven in result to the extremes of fury, he has totally triumphed or been brought totally low.

Enacted and reenacted, so far without end, the cockfight enables the Balinese, as, read and reread, *Macbeth* enables us, to see a dimension of his own subjectivity. As he watches fight after fight with the active watching of an owner and a bettor (for cockfighting has no more interest as a pure spectator sport than croquet or dog racing do), he grows familiar with it and what it has to say to him, much as the attentive listener to string quartets or the absorbed viewer of still lifes grows slowly more familiar with them in a way which opens his subjectivity to himself.[2]

Yet, because – in another of those paradoxes, along with painted feelings and unconsequenced acts, which haunt aesthetics – that subjectivity does not properly exist until it is thus organized, art forms generate and regenerate the very subjectivity they pretend only to display. Quartets, still lifes, and cockfights are not merely reflections of a preexisting sensibility analogically represented; they are positive agents in the creation and maintenance of such a sensibility. If we see ourselves as a pack of Micawbers it is from reading too much Dickens (if we see ourselves as unillusioned realists, it is from reading too little); and similarly for Balinese, cocks, and cockfights. It is in such a way, coloring experience with the light they cast it in, rather than through whatever material effects they may have, that the arts play their role, as arts, in social life.[3]

## Notes

1. The tag is from the second book of the *Organon, On Interpretation*. For a discussion of it, and for the whole argument for freeing "the notion of text ... from the notion of scripture or writing," and constructing, thus, a general hermeneutics, see Paul Ricoeur, *Freud and Philosophy* (New Haven, CT: Yale University Press, 1970), 20ff.
2. The use of the, to Europeans, "natural" visual idiom for perception – "see," "watches," and so forth – is more than usually misleading here, for the fact that, as mentioned earlier, Balinese follow the progress of the fight as much (perhaps, as fighting cocks are actually rather hard to see except as blurs of motion, more) with their bodies as with their eyes, moving their limbs, heads, and trunks in gestural mimicry of the cocks' maneuvers, means that much of the individual's experience of the fight is kinesthetic rather than visual. If ever there was an example of Kenneth Burke's definition of a symbolic act as "the dancing of an attitude" (*The Philosophy of Literary Form*, rev. edn. [New York: Vintage Books, 1957], 9) the cockfight is it.
3. All this coupling of the occidental great with the oriental lowly will doubtless disturb certain sorts of aestheticians as the earlier efforts of anthropologists to speak of Christianity and totemism in the same breath disturbed certain sorts of theologians. But as ontological questions are (or should be) bracketed in the sociology of religion, judgmental ones are (or should be) bracketed in the sociology of art. In any case, the attempt to deprovincialize the concept of art is but part of the general anthropological conspiracy to deprovincialize all important social concepts – marriage, religion, law, rationality – and though this is a threat to aesthetic theories which regard certain works of art as beyond the reach of sociological analysis, it is no threat to the conviction, for which Robert Graves claims to have been reprimanded at his Cambridge tripos, that some poems are better than others.

# CHAPTER 27
## THE NATURE OF PERFORMANCE
*Richard Bauman*

There is a very old conception of verbal art as communication which goes back at least to Plato's insistence that literature is lies. This notion, also manifest in Sir Philip Sidney's dictum, "the poet nothing affirmeth" (Ohmann 1971: 5), holds that whatever the propositional content of an item of verbal art, its meaning is somehow canceled out or rendered inoperative by the nature of the utterance as verbal art. A more recent expression of this conception is to be found in the writings of the British Ordinary Language philosopher, J. L. Austin. Austin maintains, "of any and every utterance," that it will be "*in a peculiar way* hollow or void if said by an actor on the stage … or spoken in soliloquy." He continues, "language in such circumstances is in special ways—intelligibly—used not seriously, but in ways *parasitic* upon its normal use—ways which fall under the doctrine of *etiolations* of language" (Austin 1962: 21–2, italics in the original).[1]

Leaving aside the unfortunate suggestion that the uses Austin mentions exert a weakening influence on language, a product of his particular bias, we may abstract from the cited passage the suggestion that performance represents a transformation of the basic referential ("serious," "normal" in Austin's terms) uses of language. In other words, in artistic performance of this kind, there is something going on in the communicative interchange which says to the auditor, "interpret what I say in some special sense; do not take it to mean what the words alone, taken literally, would convey." This may lead to the further suggestion that performance sets up, or represents, an interpretative frame within which the messages being communicated are to be understood, and that this frame contrasts with at least one other frame, the literal.

In employing the term "frame" here, I am drawing not upon Austin, but on the powerful insights of Gregory Bateson and the more recent and equally provocative work of Erving Goffman (1974). Bateson first developed systematically the notion of frame as a defined interpretive context providing guidelines for discriminating between orders of message (1972: 222), in his seminal article, "A Theory of Play and Fantasy" (1972: 177–93). We shall return to aspects of this theory and of Goffman's in more detail below.[2]

Although the notion of performance as a frame was introduced above as contrasting with literal communication, it should be made clear from the beginning that many other such frames besides these two may be identified. For example:

- *insinuation,* in which the words spoken are to be interpreted as having a covert and indirect relation to the meaning of the utterance (cf. Austin 1962: 121);
- *joking,* in which the words spoken are to be interpreted as not seriously meaning what they might otherwise mean (cf. Austin 1962: 121);
- *imitation,* in which the manner of speaking is to be interpreted as being modeled after that of another person or persons;

- *translation,* in which the words spoken are to be interpreted as the equivalent of words originally spoken in another language or code;
- *quotation,* in which the words spoken are to be interpreted as the words of someone other than the speaker (cf. Weinreich 1966: 162).

This is a very partial and unelaborated list, which does not even adequately sample, much less exhaust, the range of possible interpretive frames within which communication may occur. It should be noted, moreover, that frames may be used in combination, as well as singly, as listed. It should also be stressed that although theorists like Austin suggest that the literal frame somehow has priority over all the others—is more "normal"—this is not necessary to the theory and in fact biases it in unproductive ways (Fish 1973). The notorious difficulty of defining literalness aside, there is growing evidence that literal utterances are no more frequent or "normal" in situated human communication than any of the other frames, and indeed that in spoken communication no such thing as naked literalness may actually exist (Burns 1972 Goffman 1974). For our purposes, all that is necessary is the recognition of performance as a distinctive frame, available as a communicative resource along with the others to speakers in particular communities.[3]

The first major task, then, is to suggest what kind of interpretive frame performance establishes or represents. How is communication that constitutes performance to be interpreted? The following represents a very preliminary attempt to specify the interpretive guidelines set up by the performance frame.

Fundamentally, performance as a mode of spoken verbal communication consists in the assumption of responsibility to an audience for a display of communicative competence. This competence rests on the knowledge and ability to speak in socially appropriate ways. Performance involves on the part of the performer an assumption of accountability to an audience for the way in which communication is carried out, above and beyond its referential content. From the point of view of the audience, the act of expression on the part of the performer is thus marked as subject to evaluation for the way it is done, for the relative skill and effectiveness of the performer's display of competence.[4] Additionally, it is marked as available for the enhancement of experience, through the present enjoyment of the intrinsic qualities of the act of expression itself. Performance thus calls forth special attention to and heightened awareness of the act of expression and gives license to the audience to regard the act of expression and the performer with special intensity.[5]

Thus conceived, performance is a mode of language use, a way of speaking. The implication of such a concept for a theory of verbal art is this: it is no longer necessary to begin with artful texts, identified on independent formal grounds and then reinjected into situations of use, in order to conceptualize verbal art in communicative terms. Rather, in terms of the approach being developed here, performance becomes *constitutive* of the domain of verbal art as spoken communication.

Some examples may be useful at this point, to demonstrate in empirical terms the application of the notion of performance we have proposed. In several of her writings on the people of the plateau area of the Malagasy Republic (Keenan 1973, 1974), Elinor Keenan delineates the two major ways of speaking identified by this group. The first, called in native terminology, *resaka*, may be loosely defined as informal conversation, described by native elders as "everyday talk," or "simple talk." The other way of speaking, *kabary*, is the one of principal interest to us here. *Kabary* is glossed by Keenan as "ceremonial speech, what we might call oratory." The following are excerpts from Keenan's description:

> *Kabary* is a focal point of tradition and as a focal point of artistic expression is … regarded with great interest. It is not uncommon to see groups of elders evaluating the skills and approaches of speechmakers following a *kabary* performance. A speechmaker who pleases his audience is rewarded with praise such as: "He is a very sharp speechmaker." "He is prepared." "He is a true speechmaker, a child of his father." His words are said to be "well-arranged" and "balanced." His performance is described as "satisfying." … Evaluations are based on both skill in handling winding speech and on one's ability to follow certain rules governing the sequence and content of particular oratory. (1973: 226–7)

And further, "*kabary* performances … are platforms for exhibiting knowledge of traditional oratory" (1973: 229). Wedding *kabary*, in particular, "is the most developed art form in the culture and a source of great delight and interest to all participants" (1973: 242).

It is clear from this description that *kabary* represents for the plateau Malagasy a domain of performance. To engage in *kabary* is to assume responsibility to one's audience for a display of competence in the traditional *kabary* forms, to render one's speech subject to evaluation for the quality of one's speaking. One is judged as a speechmaker, for the way one's words are arranged. *Kabary* performances are keenly attended to and actively evaluated, with good performances serving as a source of enjoyment and satisfaction to the auditors, for the way they are done. The ethnography of verbal art among the plateau Malagasy thus becomes centrally the ethnography of *kabary.*

Among the Ilongot of the Philippines, by contrast with the above, there are three major speech styles, described by Michelle Rosaldo: the stylistically unmarked "straight speech" (*qube:nata qupu*), invocatory speech (*nawnaw*), and a third style, *qambaqan*, described as "crooked" or witty talk (Rosaldo 1973). It is not wholly clear from Rosaldo's account whether *nawnaw* involves performance, but *qambaqan* very clearly does. *Qambaqan* is "artful, witty, charming," "a language of display, performance, pose" (Rosaldo 1973: 197–8). What is especially noteworthy about speaking among the Ilongot, within our present context, is that the telling of tales, always included in a priori text-centered definitions of verbal art, is classified as a kind of "straight speech." That is, storytelling for the Ilongot is not a form of performance and thus, in culture-specific communicative terms, not a form of verbal art. The domain of speaking among the Ilongot is to this extent, among many others, organized differently from that of the many cultures in which storytelling does involve performance.

Japanese professional storytellers, for example, as described by Hrdličková, are certainly performers in our sense of the term. For their audiences, "it is not seldom more important *how* a story is told than *what* the story relates … . Storytellers regard the mastery of [storytelling] elements as a necessary preliminary stage prior to any successful practicing of their art in public, since the audience not only expects of them an established manner of interpretation, but also rates them according to the degree of artistry the artists command" (Hrdličková 1969: 193, italics in the original). That is, storytelling involves a display of competence in the manner of telling the story, which is subject to evaluation for the way it is done. The audience derives enjoyment from the performance in proportion to the skill of the narrator (ibid.).

The point to be emphasized here is that just as speaking itself as a cultural system (or as part of cultural systems defined in other terms) will vary from speech community to speech community, so too will the nature and extent of the realm of performance and verbal art (Bauman 1972). One of the principal questions one must ask in the ethnography of performance is what range of speech activity is regarded as susceptible to performance and what range is conventionally performed, that is, conventionally expected by members of the community to be rendered in a performance mode.

## Notes

1. Richard Ohmann, in two recent articles, employs the same passages from Austin as a point of departure for the formulation of a theory of literature based on Austin's theory of speech acts (Ohmann 1971, 1972). Ohmann's argument is interesting in places, but its productiveness is severely limited by his failure—like Austin's—to recognize that the notion of strictly referential, "literal" meaning has little, if any, relevance to the use of spoken language in social life. For a strong critique of the concept of "ordinary language," and the impoverishing effect it has on definitions of literature, see Fish 1973.
2. The notion of frame, though not necessarily the term, is used in a similar manner by other writers: see, e.g. Huizinga 1955; Milner 1955: 86; Smith 1968; Uspensky 1972; Fish 1973: 52–3; Cone 1968.
3. Concerning the ecological model of communication underlying this formulation, see Sherzer and Bauman 1972 and Bauman and Sherzer 1974, 1975.
4. Note that it is *susceptibility* to evaluation that is indicated here; in this formulation the status of an utterance as performance is independent of *how* it is evaluated, whether it is judged good or bad, beautiful or ugly, etc. A bad performance is nonetheless a performance. On this point, see Hymes 1973: 189–90; Mitchell-Kernan 1971: 119–20.
5. I have been influenced in this formulation by Hymes 1974; Hymes 1975; d'Azevedo 1958: 706; Mukařovský 1964: 19; Mukařovský 1970: 21; and Goffman 1974. A similar conception of performance is developed in an unfinished paper by my former colleague Joseph Doherty (Doherty MS.), whose recent tragic and untimely death occurred before he was able to complete his work. Elli Köngäs Maranda seems to be operating in terms of a conception of verbal art which is similar in certain central respects to the one developed here (Maranda 1976). Compare also Fish's conception of literature (Fish 1973). Gross's excellent article on "Art as the Communication of Competence" (Gross 1973) came to my attention after this essay was written but is congruent with it in a number of ways.

   A special word should be said of the use of "competence" and "performance" in the above formulation. Use of these terms, especially in such close juxtaposition, demands at least some acknowledgment of Noam Chomsky's contribution of both to the technical vocabulary of linguistics (Chomsky 1965: 3–4). It should be apparent, however, that both terms are employed in a very different way in the present work—competence in the sense advanced by Hymes (1971) and performance as formulated above.

## References


Austin, J. L. (1962), *How to Do Things with Words*, New York: Oxford University Press.

Bateson, Gregory (1972), *Steps to an Ecology of Mind*, New York: Ballantine.

Bauman, Richard (1972 [1955]), "The La Have Island General Store: Sociability and Verbal Art in a Nova Scotia Community." *Journal of American Folklore* 85: 330–43.

Bauman, Richard and Sherzer, Joel (eds) (1974), *Explorations in the Ethnography of Speaking*, New York: Cambridge University Press.

Bauman, Richard and Sherzer, Joel (1975), "The Ethnography of Speaking," in Bernard J. Siegel (ed.), *Annual Review of Anthropology*, vol. 4, Palo Alto: Annual Reviews.

Burns, Elizabeth (1972), *Theatricality*, New York: Harper.

Chomsky, Noam (1965), *Aspects of the Theory of Syntax*, Cambridge, MA: MIT Press.

Cone, Edward T. (1968), *Musical Form and Musical Performance*, New York: Norton.

d'Azevedo, Warren (1958), "A Structural Approach to Esthetics: Toward a Definition of Art in Anthropology." *American Anthropologist* 60: 702–14.

Doherty, Joseph (n.d.), "Towards a Poetics of Performance." Manuscript.

Fish, Stanley E. (1973), "How Ordinary Is Ordinary Language?" *New Literary History* 5: 40–54.

Goffman, Erving (1974), *Frame Analysis: An Essay on the Organization of Experience*, New York: Harper Colophon.

Gross, Larry (1973), "Art as the Communication of Competence." *Social Science Information* 12 (5): 115–41.

Hrdličková, V. (1969), "Japanese Professional Storytellers." *Genre* 2: 179–210.

Huizinga, Johan (1955), *Homo Ludens*, Boston: Beacon.

Hymes, Dell (1971), "Competence and Performance in Linguistic Theory," in Renira Huxley and Elisabeth Ingram (eds), *Language Acquisition: Models and Methods*, London and New York: Academic Press.

Hymes, Dell (1973), "An Ethnographic Perspective." *New Literary History* 5: 187–201.

Hymes, Dell (1974), "Ways of Speaking," in R. Bauman and J. Sherzer (eds), *Explorations in the Ethnography of Speaking*, New York: Cambridge University Press.

Hymes, Dell (1975), "Breakthrough into Performance," in D. Ben-Amos and K. S. Goldstein, *Folklore and Folklife, An Introduction*, Chicago, IL: University of Chicago Press.

Keenan, Elinor (1973), "A Sliding Sense of Obligatoriness: The Poly-Structure of Malagasy Oratory." *Language in Society* 2: 225–43.

Keenan, Elinor (1974), "Norm Makers, Norm Breakers: Uses of Speech by Men and Women in a Malagasy Community," in R. Bauman and J. Sherzer, *Explorations in the Ethnography of Speaking*, New York: Cambridge University Press.

Maranda, Elli Köngäs (1976), "Individual and Tradition," in *Folk Narrative Research, Studia Fennica*, 20: 252–61.

Milner, Marion (1955), "Role of Illusion in Symbol Formation," in Melanie Klein (ed.), *New Directions in Psychoanalysis*, New York: Basic Books.

Mitchell-Kernan, Claudia (1971), *Language Behavior in a Black Urban Community*, Berkeley: Language-Behavior Research Laboratory Monograph 2.

Mukařovský, Jan (1964), "Standard Language and Poetic Language," in Paul L. Garvin (ed.), *A Prague School Reader on Esthetics, Literary Structure and Style*, Washington, DC: Georgetown University.

Mukařovský, Jan (1970), *Aesthetic Function, Norm and Value as Social Facts*, Ann Arbor, MI: Department of Slavic Languages and Literature, University of Michigan.

Ohmann, Richard (1971), "Speech Acts and the Definition of Literature." *Philosophy and Rhetoric* 4: 1–19.

Ohmann, Richard (1972), "Speech, Literature, and the Space Between." *New Literary History* 4: 47–63.

Rosaldo, Michelle Z. (1973), "I Have Nothing to Hide: The Language of Ilongot Oratory." *Language in Society* 2: 193–223.

Sherzer, Joel and Bauman, Richard (1972), "Areal Studies and Culture History: Language as a Key to the Historical Study of Culture Contact." *Southwestern Journal of Anthropology* 28: 131–52.
Smith, Barbara H. (1968), *Poetic Closure*, Chicago: University of Chicago.
Uspensky, B. A. (1972), "Structural Isomorphism of Verbal and Visual Art." *Poetics* 5: 5–39.
Weinreich, Uriel (1966), "On the Semantic Structure of a Language," in Joseph Greenberg (ed.), *Universals of Language*, Cambridge, MA: MIT Press.

# CHAPTER 28
# PRELIMINARY NOTES ON AUDIENCES IN AFRICA
*Karen Barber*

## Audiences as a historical product

There have been audiences, presumably, as long as there has been performance. If, as Richard Bauman suggests, 'performance as a mode of spoken verbal communication consists in the assumption of responsibility to an audience for a display of communicative competence' (Bauman, 1977: 11), then the audience is the body of people prepared to grant the performer space and time in which to mount such a display, by suspending or bending the normal patterns of communicative turn-taking. The perception that what creates an audience is the listeners' intentional orientation towards the speaker is the starting point for a far-reaching development in performance and media studies, which focuses on the activity and creativity of the audience.

But audiences are not all the same. Just as much as performances, they are a historical product. There are different ways of convening, and of experiencing reception, whether collectively or in dispersal, which are deeply connected to the nature of social life of the age and place. How people come together; how they relate to each other and to the spectacle or utterance they are attending to; what they consider themselves to be part of in doing so; how the spectacle/utterance addresses them: all these are historically and culturally specific and need to be empirically investigated.

In colonial Africa, new kinds of audience emerged along with new forms of popular culture. Very generally, they were characterised by greater extension and greater diffuseness than older forms of communal cultural participation. These expanded audiences were variably imagined as regional, religious, ethnic or linguistic constituencies, as nations, as the entire continent or just as 'the people'. Changes in ways of being an audience can be related to changes in the institutionalisation and economics of entertainment, and to the degree to which performances are 'embedded' in other social forms. Performances which are commercial, to which one gains access by paying for a ticket, convene people on a different basis from performances that are embedded in the ritual year or the domestic cycle. Changes in the ways of being an audience can also be described in terms of the technology of communication. Literacy makes possible (though not inevitable) the deferred and displaced transmission of a message, removed from the face-to-face interaction of speaker and hearer; print makes possible (though not inevitable) an address which is 'broadcast', sent out to an unknown and potentially indefinitely expansive readership. Television has made possible the imagining of an atomised, dispersed but mass audience tuning in simultaneously to the same programme; cassette and video recorders have made possible the proliferation of local markets of production and consumption.

To put it at its broadest, one could say that ways of being an audience are made possible only by existing ways of being in society. Huge seismic changes have taken place, transforming what it is to be a collectivity. The history of colonial Africa could be understood as the history of the formation, or emergence, of new kinds of crowd, related, but only obliquely, to a new imaginary of the public emanating from industrial Europe. The industrial revolution and the massive urbanisation that accompanied it produced the possibility of conceiving of collectivities united not by the multiple filaments of kinship, co-residence or co-operation, but by the sheer fact of human interchangeability. If workers, severed from ownership of the means of production, could be boiled down to their labour power, for sale on the open market, then human beings could be imagined as equivalent, and duplicable. It is a striking feature of late eighteenth- and early nineteenth-century European life that the distribution of the human body in social space began to take forms that foregrounded this presumed equivalence and uniformity. In English schools, beginning with the elementary schools for the poor in the 1820s, the 'simultaneous method' of teaching began to be tried out for the first time, where 'all the children in the room received instruction at the same time and from the master himself' (Seaborne 1971: 143). Instead of being taught in small groups by older pupils, or in individual lessons with the master, pupils would be arranged as an audience in front-facing rows where all could see, as well as be seen by, the authority figure addressing them.[1] It was only in this period too that classes were sorted according to age and pupils were expected to progress steadily and uniformly through a series of graded levels; principles of uniformity and homogeneity replaced the mixed, fragmented groupings that had prevailed before. Thus the master would be directing his undifferentiated address to a body made up of units assembled as if interchangeable and equivalent to each other, and the pupils for the first time became a kind of 'public'.

In the second half of the eighteenth century, European armies—particularly the Napoleonic forces—really wore uniforms in the true sense, rather than clothes acquired from a variety of sources and intended as a badge of identity more than as a submergence of individuality (Parker 1988). Beginning in the nineteenth century, church congregations began to give up the highly personalised and hierarchical use of space, in the form of pews for the rich—on which they paid rent and which had lockable doors and often elaborate interior furnishings—and plain benches for the poor. Seating began to be neutral, undifferentiated, and available alike to all.[2] Organised team sport, involving rigorous observation of the 'levelling' principle of bracketing every characteristic except the relevant strength and skill, took on much greater prominence in the boarding schools of the second half of the nineteenth century (Mangan 1987). All these new disciplines of the body in space seemed to involve the imagining of human beings as, in principle, equivalent to each other, and thus to make possible the conceptualisation of an audience which is a 'public' in the sense of being in principle an indefinitely extensible horizon of anonymous and interchangeable members, to be addressed not as known persons marked by family, rank, class or resident but as persons—not just unknown but in principle not to be known, because individual difference is irrelevant to the purpose for which they have convened.

This conception of the 'public' is much broader than Habermas's conception of the late eighteenth- and early nineteenth-century bourgeois public sphere, but it is implicit in Habermas' focus on the twin characteristics of (1) print and (2) the commercialisation of cultural forms. The essential characteristic of a 'public' constituted by print culture and commercial cultural forms is that it is addressed *as if, in principle*, its members were equivalent, emptied of specific characteristics of status, family and individual personal identity. This imagined equivalence is focused and idealised in the bourgeois public sphere's conception of itself as representing the equality of 'universal man' speaking for the public good. Indeed, one of the interesting things about Habermas's discussion of the public sphere is the way he fastens an expansive, open notion of public address and access to what was a small, sociable and of course self-interested class.

Thus the broad social transformations of industrial Europe were given visible form in new disciplines of space and time initially administered primarily to the lower classes, and these disciplines involved recognising that humans could be imagined as, in principle, equivalent and interchangeable in large numbers. I would suggest that such disciplines of time and space, and such a conception of human equivalence, contributed fundamentally to the conceptual framework in which audiences were imagined and addressed as 'publics'.

In nineteenth- and twentieth-century Africa these same disciplines of time and space were imported by missionaries, employers and town planners, but imposed on a different social reality.

In much of colonial Africa rapid urbanisation took place but without the full reduction of human beings to sellers of labour power, even in heavily industrial and mining centres. As Frederick Cooper put it, 'Capital's inconclusive assault on Africa created a guerilla army of the underemployed rather than the juxtaposition of disciplined troops and the reserve army of the unemployed characteristic of industrial capitalism' (Cooper 1983). Migrant workers and even long-term urban residents kept one foot in another mode of production, for people had an alternative and a back-up in the rural agricultural sphere which so often subsidised urban wage-earners (Cooper 1983). And many urban centres were not industrial but commercial and administrative; workers were as often hustlers, petty traders or brokers in the informal sector as waged employees. In this domain, individual difference, personal networks, creative abilities to innovate and mediate were often essential to economic survival. The disciplines of equivalence were imported in the forms of church, school, army and organised sport, but they did not function as the imaginary of a population whose labour rendered them in principle equivalent to each other. Rather, they were overlaid upon a deeply heterogeneous mass, united and divided by religion, occupation, language, family, place of origin and degree of education, and often by popular philosophies of irreducible human difference. The uses of space that inscribed human homogeneity and equivalence were widely adopted, and parodied, in African popular culture; but the ways in which they were used were selective and creative, and this has implications for the way the expanded 'publics' of colonial Africa were variously imagined and addressed.

Let me give an example. The Yorùbá popular theatre, originating primarily in church and school dramas, entered a dynamic and expansive commercial phase in the 1940s. Throughout its efflorescence, during which it secularised, diversified, experimented and incorporated an array of indigenous performance modes, it never relinquished its fundamental demarcation of space. It staged its plays exclusively on platform stages with curtains, scenery and lights. The venues in which the travelling companies performed were rarely purpose-built theatres: more often, school halls, community centres, co-operative halls, hotels and church halls were used. Where there was no platform stage a makeshift one was erected or a rectangular space was demarcated to represent one; where there was no proscenium arch the curtains were rigged up in such a way as to suggest one. Having travelled with one of these companies, I can testify to the lengths to which they would go to establish the required acting space. The performance took place in linear fashion across the front of the stage. The auditorium mirrored the acting space: front-facing, rectangular and demarcated with rows of chairs or benches. The space in which the action was to take place, and the space which the spectators were to occupy, were thus not only clearly separated but—more important—were allocated in advance of the theatrical event; performers and audiences entered a frame which had already been established before the action began.

The theatres thus set up a stark contrast with older but still flourishing forms of theatre such as the *egúungún òjè* (also known as *apidán* and *alárìnjó*) groups, who, like the popular theatre, were professional travelling performers. *Egúngún òjè* masquerade shows are performed in an arena constituted in the act of performance itself, through the interaction of the audience and the performers. The troupe takes up a position in an open site such as a market place, open ground in front of the Oba's palace, or a wide courtyard inside it. The audience gathers round, either forming a circle right round the troupe, or making up a three-quarter circle with a wall or wide veranda steps making up the fourth quarter. The boundaries are established in the act of performance as spectators press forward and the performers, by their movements, press them back to maintain a wide, clear arena. It is remarkable how smooth and even the curve thus constituted often is. The performers use the entire area thus established, moving across it and round it in long straight runs and wide looping circles. For special dramatic effect, they break right out of it. There is often a section along one side of the arena where Oba, chiefs and dignitaries of the town have had chairs placed for them, making highly visible the differentiation of status among the spectators. The divide in such spectacles is not between 'backstage' and 'on stage' but between unseen forces that are invoked to empower the performers and the visible stunts and transformations that are the manifestations of such empowerment (see Götrick 1984). Rather than 'dressing up' backstage in order to perform mimesis on stage, the *alárìnjó* masqueraders change under wraps, but in the middle of the arena, before the eyes of the spectators.

These different uses of space are connected with different forms of address to the audience. Before the masquerade spectacle commences, the leading praise-singer of the troupe makes enquiries to discover the *oríkì orílè* (praise epithets relating to place of origin) of the chiefs and other important people present, so that he can salute them individually during his opening invocations. The gratified addressees would be expected to reward the singer with gifts of money. Approaches to individual members of the audience continue throughout the show, as for example when the whirling mat (*fààfáá*) offers selected individuals a peep at the masquerader inside who is operating it, or when the comic *òyìnbó* mask (the European, with awkward gait, umbrella and gloves) struts up to a number of different members of the audience to shake them by the hand and enquire gutturally 'How ah *you*?' In these approaches they give precedence to the 'big men'—more visible because of their chairs, voluminous robes and clusters of attendants, and more attractive because of their greater potential as generous patrons. Thus, while the performers and the audience share the same plane in space, the audience is treated as internally differentiated, with its own foci or centres of attention, which the performers acknowledge and address.

The popular travelling theatre, by contrast, invariably addressed the audience as an anonymous and undifferentiated public. No individual was ever selected for personal attention. Even when the actors knew that prominent people were present in the audience, they refrained from singling them out. Only before and after the show would they demonstrate their appreciation and recognition of these big men and women. They always spoke of their audience as 'the public', and the way they marked out spatial relations in their performances did constitute the audience precisely as that: as rows of interchangeable units, in principle anonymous and indefinitely extensible—and in practice, because of the way the lighting and stage were set up, hard to distinguish and difficult to approach.

It suited their purpose to keep hold of these spatial relations long after they had moved away from the church ambience that shaped their early phase. One reason was that, though they now staged mythological plays, underworld crime dramas and satirical-domestic comedies rather than Bible plays, they still wished to make clear their affiliation with Christianity, literacy and 'enlightenment' and their difference from theatrical forms such as *egúngún*, rooted in what they thought of as 'paganism' and 'stark illiteracy'. To use the spatial relations typical of church and school served to highlight their association with colonial modernity, even after the theatre companies had secularised and moved several rungs down the social scale in their recruitment (by the 1970s most people entering theatre companies were not highly educated, though all had some years of schooling). It also enabled them to conceptualise their market as potentially infinite: the anonymous, undifferentiated 'public' stretched out in all directions, waiting for them to tap it. Personal contacts with town chiefs or community leaders were not necessary; since they played to a 'public' they could go—unlike the *egúngún òjè* troupes—to any town they chose without seeking permission or giving notice. All that was required was adequate publicity to ensure that the potential audience turned up: and this, like the plays themselves, was 'broadcast' to anyone and everyone, through posters in public places, 'parades' in the theatre lorry with a megaphone through which announcements were made, and announcements on the radio. This address implied to potential ticket buyers that any and every Yorùbá-speaker (the public was implicitly limited by language) was interpellated equally: 'come one, come all'. Like *jùjú* and *fújì* records discussed by Waterman (1990), this conceptualisation of an extended and homogeneous public imagined a market coterminous with a new cultural nationalist category of the population, 'the Yorùbá'. Or, to put it the other way round, fostering a pan-Yorùbá constituency, as Yorùbá language print culture, church organisation and school system all helped to do, defined an expanded market for cultural products. The popular theatre, like the *jùjú* records, spoke in 'standard' Yorùbá to a public imagined as homogeneously accessible. The theatre thus actively sought to construct its audiences as a new kind of public, different from the personal audiences, meeting only as part of a communal celebration, convened by the *egúngún òjè* troupes.

There are two points to be made here: first, that though the disciplines of time and space associated with church and school were introduced with a regulatory intent,[3] they were taken up by aspiring lower-class and petty-bourgeois western Nigerians with a view to self-betterment. They became, not second nature, but the token of an unrealised ideal, of order, regularity and high status. So this use of theatre space was not just a result of culture contact or 'mimicry'; it was a project of self-realisation, deliberately adopted and adhered to through thick and thin—but only to the extent that suited the practitioners. And, second, when this use of time and space was adopted, it was immediately perforated and bent. The public, though addressed as anonymous and undifferentiated, did not really function like that, for the actors all said they liked the profession because it enabled them to become 'publicly known to many people', 'people who will give us any kind of help', in a bank queue, a hospital emergency room or any other situation where personal contacts may make all the difference. In other words, the apparently homogeneous audience was seen as a sea of potential 'helpers'—clients, patrons—who could be activated at any moment as if they were personal friends. And the spectacle, though staged as if allusionistic and realist in mode (the proscenium arch framing a room with the fourth wall removed, revealing a slice of domestic life), was not realist so much as exhortatory and spectacular. Actors improvised verbal stunts, expanded their parts, and created points of intense theatrical salience for themselves, embodying rather than depicting the potential for social power.

The concept of 'the public', then, as a new form of coming-together characteristic of the colonial era, is a powerful one, but one which must be carefully qualified and which can be properly understood only if the specific forms of address, use of space, modes of staging, and expectations and interactions of performers and spectators, are empirically established in all their surprising and subtle detail.

## Audiences constitute 'meaning'

The best reason for studying audiences is that they have a hand in the constitution of the 'meaning' of a performance, text or utterance. Cultural historians or anthropologists who study texts and performances in order better to understand 'what people think' need to look not only at the utterance but also at the interpretation of that utterance. Meaning, according to Vološinov, belongs neither to the speaker nor to the hearer: rather, it inhabits the zone between them.

What has not yet been sufficiently explored is the possibility that specific African audiences have distinctive, conventional modes and styles of making meaning, just as performers/ speakers do. We need to ask *how* audiences do their work of interpretation.

## Notes

1. The Lancasterian or 'monitorial' system, pioneered by Joseph Lancaster only a decade earlier than the beginning of the 'simultaneous' system, involved an extremely rigorous regimentation of pupils and meticulous control of their movements. They sat in graded rows on long benches, facing forward—but not so that they could all see the master, rather so that they could all be kept under surveillance. Older pupils, or 'monitors', were assigned to each bench and would lead them out to prescribed positions at the side wall, where graded instructional boards were set up and the semicircle around which the group of eight to ten pupils would stand was marked on the floor. This system, according to Mitchell (1988), was the one that was imported into Egypt in the 1840s. Its disciplinary and surveillance functions, vividly evoked by Mitchell, were extremely striking. But it was essentially a formalisation of the old method of teaching, prevalent in grammar schools since the sixteenth century: pupils learnt individually or in small groups and were never addressed as a collectivity. It did not enjoy much success in English schools and was soon eclipsed by the 'simultaneous method'.
2. The practice of segregated and hierarchical church space persisted for a long time because pew rents were an important part of church income. The seventeenth and eighteenth-century use of pews has been described by one authority on church architecture like this: 'Medieval churches from the time of the Restoration onwards were disfigured by the erection of huge family pews, frequently cut from medieval chancel screens, often curtained enclosures with sofas, armchairs, and fireplaces (the tedium of a long service being sometimes relieved by the entrance of a liveried servant with sherry)' (Drummond 1934: 38).

3. School seating arrangements appear to have been the focus of a particularly strong lust for 'order'. Anna and David Hinderer, missionaries in Ibadan in the 1850s, adopted notably informal, personal methods of instruction and interaction with their first converts, but as soon as they had built a proper church, classes were conducted within it and relations between instructor and instructed became those of a speaker addressing orderly front-facing rows—on benches nailed to the ground (Hone 1877: 295–6). The benches not only prescribed an orderly division of space, they made this division immovable. In later colonial schools it seems that, even when chairs were not available for the classroom, substitutes would be found to mark out the space: Victor Murray, surveying village schools all over the British colonies in Africa in 1926–27, described as standard the 'mud building ... perhaps 30 feet by 16 ... It has an earth floor, and at one end there is an earth platform 9 inches high, on which there is a table. Behind the table stands ... the teacher. He has a blackboard hanging on the wall behind him ... . The seats are branches of trees stuck in the floor ...' (1929: 79). And this rigid demarcation of place persisted even when it was beginning to look archaic in Britain. Kit Elliott, who took up a teaching post in a secondary school in Jos in 1960, was horrified by the classroom, which 'looks like a re-enactment of educational history. The dungeon-like classrooms, the oppressive masonry walls, the straight rows of primitive furniture—their precise position marked on the floor by a principal with a mania for straight lines, the blackboard screwed to the wall, the teacher in front of it, barricaded behind his massive table, chalk in hand and in full pedagogic spate, the boys with their heads down, writing all he says ...' (1970: 30).

## References


Bauman, Richard (1977), *Verbal Art as Performance,* Prospect Heights, IL: Waveland Press.

Cooper, Frederick (1983), 'Urban space, Industrial Time and Wage Labour in Africa,' in Frederick Cooper (ed.), *Struggle for the City: Migrant Labour, Capital and the State in Urban Africa*, 1–50, Beverly Hills, CA: Sage.

Drummond, Andrew Landale (1934), *The Church Architecture of Protestantism*, Edinburgh: Clark.

Elliott, Kit (1970), *An African School: A Record of Experience*, London: Cambridge University Press.

Götrick, Kacke (1984), *Apidán Theatre and Modern Drama*, Stockholm: Almqvist & Wiksell.

Habermas, Jurgen (1962), *The Structural Transformation of the Public Sphere*, trans. Thomas Burger and Frederick Lawrence, Cambridge, MA: MIT Press.

Hone, Richard B. (ed.) (1877), *Seventeen Years in the Yoruba Country: Memorials of Anna Hinderer*, London: Religious Tract Society.

Mangan, James A. (1987), 'Ethics and Ethnocentricity: Imperial Education in British Tropical Africa,' in William J. Baker and James A. Mangan (eds), *Sport in Africa: Essays in Social History*, 138–71, New York: Africana.

Mitchell, Timothy (1988), *Colonising Egypt*, Cambridge: Cambridge University Press.

Murray, A. Victor (1929), *The School in the Bush: A Critical Study of Native Education in Africa*, London: Longman.

Parker, Geoffrey (1988), *The Military Revolution: Military Innovation and the Rise of the West, 1500–1800*, Cambridge: Cambridge University Press.

Seaborne, Malcolm (1971), *The English School: Its Architecture and Organization, 1370–1870*, London: Routledge.

Waterman, C. A. (1990), '"Our Tradition is a Very Modem Tradition": Popular Music and the Construction of a Pan-Yorùbá Identity.' *Ethnomusicology* 34 (3), 367–79; reprinted in Karin Barber (ed.) (1997), *Readings in African Popular Culture*, London: James Currey; Bloomington, IN: Indiana University Press, for the International African Institute.

# CHAPTER 29
## THE INTERPRETATION OF CULTURE(S) AFTER TELEVISION

*Lila Abu-Lughod*

Many of the studies of popular culture, and especially television, that I have come across are disappointing. They do not seem to be trying to offer profound insights into the human condition, or even into the social, cultural, and political dynamics of particular communities—goals anthropology has always, perhaps with hubris, set for itself. Is it the object, television, that thwarts us? We are not dealing with intricate rituals or complex kinship systems, or even with histories and structures of conjuncture in colonial moments, all of which have deep traditions in the discipline. Television partakes of the ephemerality of the postmodern and is associated, whether here or there, as Geertz likes to put it, with the kind of ordinary people some call the masses.[1] It is also associated with either commercial entertainment or state propaganda, both always suspect. Does the taint of low-brow status and the apparent banality of television rub off on those who study it? Or is it, as Jean Baudrillard might have it, that in a world of simulation and simulacra, of which television is such a conspicuous part, notions like the human condition have become hopelessly obsolete?[2]

I would like to argue something else here: that we are only beginning to find the right point of entry for the ethnographic work—in the field and in our studies—that it would take to draw out the significance of television's existence as a ubiquitous presence in the lives and imaginaries of people in the contemporary world. In a recent review of some studies of "resistance," Sherry Ortner diagnosed their weaknesses as being caused by "ethnographic refusal." This strikes me as an apt diagnosis for media studies as well. If there is one theme that has dominated the study of media, especially television, in the last two decades, it is resistance. And if there is one thing that can be said about these studies, it is that despite their considerable theoretical sophistication they are ethnographically thin.[3]

What can anthropologists offer when we begin to take television seriously? In her overview of the emergent field of the anthropology of media, Debra Spitulnik claims that anthropologists "have in some way already bypassed many of the debates within media studies … because they implicitly theorize media processes, products, and uses as complex parts of social reality, and expect to locate media power and value in a more diffuse, rather than direct and causal, sense."[4] In her "(mild) polemic" on the same subject, Faye Ginsburg locates anthropologists' distinctiveness in their less ethnocentric stance, their attention to the contexts of media texts, and their recognition of "the complex ways in which people are engaged in processes of making and interpreting media works in relation to their cultural, social and historical circumstances."[5]

But just how do we trace this enmeshment of television in other social fields?[6] The key, I would argue, is to experiment with ways of placing television more seamlessly within the sort of rich social and cultural context that the sustained anthropological fieldwork that has been our ideal since Bronisław Malinowski is uniquely able to provide. The special challenge we face in doing so is that the cultural forms transmitted by television have no obvious and simple community and are always only a part—sometimes larger, sometimes smaller—of people's complex lives. Moreover, they are produced deliberately for people, under conditions that vary politically and historically.

## Cultural texts and "multisited" ethnography

In January 1996, when I returned for a short visit to the Upper Egyptian village I had been working in intermittently since 1990, I watched, with friends, some episodes of the current television serial, *Mothers in the House of Love.* Set in a retirement home for women, the program's central drama concerned an attempt by the unscrupulous brother-in-law of the widow who ran the place to take it over so he could achieve his dream of building a twenty-two-story hotel. Armed with a newfound purpose, the women residents banded together to defend their threatened home. They forgot their squabbles about which television programs to watch, mobilized their talents to raise the money to buy out his share, and stood up to him.

The serial had been written a few years earlier by Fathiyya al-'Assal, a vibrant and self-confident writer, and one of only a handful of women of her generation writing television dramas in Egypt. Active in the Egyptian leftist party, she had occasionally been jailed and had had numerous story ideas tabled and serials canceled by the television censors—civil servants working for state-owned television—and even by those higher up in the government. Her serials were known for their social concerns, and she considered women's issues critical. She had also done some ethnography in a retirement home to make her script more realistic.

How can we study the encounter between some Upper Egyptian village women and this television serial? With television programs, one is forced to talk not so much about cultures-as-texts as about discrete cultural texts that are produced, circulated, and consumed. Thick description of television therefore requires a multisited ethnography wherein, as George Marcus has put it regarding commodities in a world system, one can "follow the thing."[7] The relevant system here is national. Therefore, I will start with the villagers and their responses to the television serial, using this focus to explore basic structures and meanings in their lives. But I also want to keep tracing the serial back to Cairo, where it was produced in a very different milieu by a leftist intellectual and some urban professionals working with and against a state-controlled medium and with imagined audiences for their work. This approach will, in the end, allow us some insight into the dynamics of "culture"—one of those big words.

I watched several episodes of *Mothers in the House of Love* with my neighbors who, though intrigued, kept up a running commentary, laughing at ludicrous characters like the compulsive knitter of pullovers. After an episode in which a widow had finally consented to marry an old sweetheart, one person joked, "Now all sixty-year-old women will want to marry." The next day, though, Zaynab commented more realistically on the episode, simply contrasting it to local attitudes: "We say when a girl is past thirty she won't marry … . It is shameful. If a woman over thirty does marry, she'll do it quietly, far away, without a wedding celebration."

Yet for Zaynab, a woman very much at home in her social world, a little old before her time and confident as one of the adult women of the village who took her social duties—sick visits and funerals, for example—very seriously, the cultural differences within which she framed her response to the serial were also personally meaningful. Her own experience of marriage was very different from what she saw on television.

Zaynab, like most women in the village, had had an arranged marriage—but, following the lines of closest practical kinship, it was to a maternal, not a paternal, cousin. Zaynab's mother had been a second and younger wife, widowed shortly after she gave birth to her only child. Not close to her husband's patrilineage, she had turned to her own relatives for support, and eventually, for a husband for her daughter. She had inherited from her father some land, on which she and Zaynab later built a two-story mud-brick home. Zaynab's husband had worked on and off in Cairo since he was fourteen, leaving her mostly alone with her mother to raise her children. Secretly, he had married a second wife in Cairo; Zaynab now knew about this and was resigned to the fact that he would probably never return to live in the village.

As the years went by and Zaynab had more children, conceived on her husband's visits home, she had a harder time coping. It was especially difficult when her milk dried up after she gave birth to twins. Not long after that, she and her mother were forced to sell all their livestock because they couldn't take care of them. Then her mother died, leaving Zaynab on her own.

One cannot ignore the possibility that Zaynab had remarked on the episode of the older widow's wedding because it was meaningful to her own personal situation. The idea of remarriage might have been appealing. She was alone, managing a complex household, and her children provided her with her only company most evenings (when they all watched television together). She had no man to help her make decisions about the children's schooling, about what to plant and harvest on which strips of land, and about which domestic livestock to buy or sell. For help with the work in the fields, she had to call on young male relatives or pay for labor. Certainly she had no one for companionship or love. She said about her husband's visits home: "He's like a guest; he doesn't know anything about our lives."

In fact, a recurrent theme in my conversations with Zaynab was the situation of the five or six older women from Switzerland, Germany, and the United States who had married—or had affairs with—village youths they met while on holiday. Some were divorcées with grown children, as Zaynab noted. Using me as an informant about the strange behavior of foreigners, she would ask me how these women could do it. She was puzzled about how their behavior might be acceptable, especially to their children. She was not the only village woman to talk to me about this phenomenon, but I wondered if her curiosity about these older women who had had second lives, second chances at love or sex, might not have had a special resonance, as had the episode about the widow's remarriage. Nevertheless, as a woman whose respectability rested on her marriage, she distanced herself in moral language from what she perceived as a cultural difference between life here, in Upper Egyptian villages, and there, in Alexandria, Cairo, or other cities.

Zaynab could not even begin to recognize that for the Cairene writer of *Mothers in the House of Love,* a progressive activist engaged in arguments with more conservative intellectuals and politicians, this episode about the value of love in the face of social pressure was not meant as a simple portrayal of the middle-class values of Alexandrian society but as a universally applicable revolutionary alternative to enhance women's status and lives.

Another serial of which al-'Assal was proud was about a woman who, rejected by her husband because she is uneducated, goes out and gets herself an education. When her husband then wants to take her back, she refuses, even though they have a son together. Al-'Assal said of this serial, "My point was to emphasize the value of a home as a home. That is to say, a man and woman should only enter on condition that they love one another." Marriage, she contended, should be first and foremost about mutual understanding and love. She contrasted her ideas about companionate marriage to prevailing values that place financial considerations first.[8] Her reference point was urban and middle class, and her views were those of the most progressive and modernist end of a continuum. While the ideal of the bourgeois couple and some version of the idea of companionate marriage have been increasingly idealized and realized by the middle classes in twentieth-century Egypt, al-'Assal's stress on the equality of husband and wife was meant to be more radical than the mainstream middle-class vision.[9] Yet Zaynab's marriage did not even fit the ordinary middle-class ideal; the vocabulary of rights to love and personal happiness was foreign to her.

There are other examples of how the serials both raised relevant issues for village viewers and yet were unassimilable because of fundamental differences of perspective related to social location. In one of the first conversations I had while watching television with Zaynab, she animatedly told me about the program that had just come on the air. This extraordinary weekly show was called *The Confrontation* and consisted of interviews—more like interrogations—of actual criminals serving prison sentences. Imitating the Cairene dialect, Zaynab recounted a memorable interview with a woman drug dealer. When the interviewer asked if she would do it again, the woman had replied, "Of course. As soon as I get out I'll deal in drugs again." Asked why, she replied, "I have to eat." Zaynab added that the woman had become used to a certain way of life and so had to keep it up. Zaynab quoted her again: "They'll jail me and I'll get out and deal. They'll put me in prison, I'll get out and do it again. That's how I make a living."

That Zaynab found this female criminal so compelling seems as significant as the fact that she responded to the television theme of marriage at a late age. The woman drug dealer, trying to make a living, must have represented something intriguing for this person of great integrity who was insulted by any hint of disrespect. Zaynab's whole life was organized around trying to feed herself and her family—in the larger sense of managing a household and educating, clothing, and raising her children. She farmed three small plots of land (each far apart from the others) as well as raising sheep, a water buffalo, chickens, ducks, and pigeons. She baked bread. Work and economic struggles were the most persistent themes in her conversations with others and the main concerns in her day-to-day life.

The television serial we watched in January (*Mothers in the House of Love*) also treated this theme. But the way women's work and social usefulness were framed made them awkward for someone like Zaynab to assimilate. One of al-'Assal's goals in writing this serial was to show that the perceptions of "old age" and "senility" in women were, at least in part, the results of their not having had any social role. As she put it,

> I wanted to create a new role for older women … . In the retirement home itself, they started a class for teaching English, because one woman had been an English professor; another woman who had been a silversmith opened a small silver workshop and taught women the skills needed for this work. They participated in the eradication of illiteracy by teaching neighborhood girls to read and write. They also gave classes on household management, and even agriculture … . My message is that women can still learn at this age, and we can still benefit from what they have to teach us as well.

The dynamic Cairene writer claimed to speak from her own experience, explaining,

> I am sixty years old now. In the past, when a woman was sixty she was supposed to sit at home waiting to die, having already married off her children. I now have four children and eight grandchildren, but because I have my own concerns and ambitions as a writer and a politician, I do not feel that I am getting older. I wanted to communicate this in a serial.

Al-'Assal's socialist feminist message—advocating socially useful roles for women, skills and activities that could take them beyond their place in the family and home, and economic independence that would alleviate the worst effects of male domination—is impressive. Going somewhat against the grain of current conservative sentiments being voiced in the media and Parliament in favor of women's return to the home (at a time when large numbers of women must work out of financial necessity and when professional careers are common), this politically motivated position is underwritten by al-'Assal's own anger. Her father was a wealthy businessman who married twenty women after marrying (and eventually divorcing) her mother, a housewife without the power to object. Al-'Assal was determined to become educated herself and still believes in education as the key for women—and for social progress.

Historically, this is a political position that had its origins at the turn of the century, when elite and some middle-class reformists (both male and female) began advocating women's education. But it was given real support by programs to provide mass education in the 1960s.[10] It was in this era that al-'Assal began her career as a serial writer—when she found that the students she was teaching to read and write would desert the classroom to listen, with the janitor, to the melodramatic serials on the radio. She still tries to work the importance of literacy into many of her plots and proudly told me about one serial called *Moment of Choice,* about a woman of fifty whose husband has run off with another woman, leaving her with no skills or identity. As al-'Assal described it,

> It was about how she was able to deal with life, how she refused to ever return to being the wife of so-and-so, how she had to become a person in her own right, how she worked in a publishing house and read and expanded her horizons, and finally how she wrote stories and won a prize for them. The serial ended up on that note, in order to show how she was able to win the prize herself—she was the sole master of the victory.

How might a theme like becoming literate affect Zaynab? Just the year before *Mothers in the House of Love* was broadcast, government-sponsored literacy classes for women had been set up in and around her village. Attending was out of the question for someone as busy as Zaynab. Women went for a variety of reasons, but all those who attended had two things in common: they had no children (or only a few that someone else could watch for a while) and their family situations were such that they could be released from work for a few hours in the afternoon.

When I went to pay a call on Umm Ahmad, another woman I knew and liked, I asked if she was going to the classes. With her eyes bright and a big smile, she said she really wanted to; she was dying to learn to read and she hated it that she couldn't even sign her own name (she had been trying to collect her recently deceased father's pension). "But can I learn?" she asked me dubiously. "No, I'm too old. I've got no brain," she laughed. Then she added, "An old woman—why, they'll talk. They'll say, 'Why does she need to go and learn?'" I asked her who would talk, and she said, "The men. The men will talk."

When her son, a young man in his early thirties and the father of two young children, walked into the room, I teased, "Hey, you should let her go to the literacy classes." He replied, "Fine, that's fine. She can go." Turning to her with a smile, he added, "In fact, I'll get you a book bag." This was an amusing idea, since village women never carry satchels or handbags. If they go to market or visiting, they carry a basket on their heads. Otherwise, what they need is tucked inside their long black overdresses. Only schoolchildren and city people carry bags.

But Umm Ahmad was no downtrodden, superannuated old woman lacking any socially useful role or skills, as al-'Assal might have feared. She was a grandmother, but a wiry and energetic one—working in the fields, caring for her water buffalo, and selling cheese and butter locally. Her situation was somewhat unusual, but in my experience everyone's story in the village was unique. She had had a bad marriage and returned to live in her father's household. She had only one son who, also unusually, lived with her and worked her father's fields while holding a night job as a guard at a nearby Pharaonic temple. For years she had taken care of her father, who was in poor health and not always lucid. A founder of the hamlet in which they lived, he had been an important figure. Umm Ahmad had been in charge of running her father's household and farming enterprise, especially the livestock, while her son was growing up as well as after he left, desperate for income, to work briefly for a Lebanese-owned chicken-breeding factory near Alexandria.

What significance could a group of wealthy or formerly wealthy women, sitting around a comfortable retirement home and suddenly putting aside their individual troubles and overcoming their sense of helplessness and uselessness, have for Umm Ahmad? What about the modernist feminist ideal of women's rights to education and a meaningful career, or at least socially useful work? What about the idea of winning a prize for writing? Umm Ahmad had to contend with a gender system that constrained women, but this was hardly her main impediment to securing a decent life. Other concerns were more pressing: the cost of farming with more expensive fertilizer, the depressed prices the government paid for crops, the IMF-enforced lifting of subsidies for wheat that made provisioning households with bread a strain for most local families, the higher cost of living in an area where hotels catering to tourists drove up prices, the felt need to get children educated so they might find employment, and the vast inequalities between large landlords and the majority of households.

What possibilities did Umm Ahmad or other village women have for careers that would provide personal fulfillment and the financial independence necessary for a marriage based on equality when even the finest local men who had become educated might have to content themselves with being foremen at archaeological sites? Or perhaps with waiting for five or six years after graduating from teaching college for a government job as a librarian in the local high school, working a couple of hours a day and making barely enough to pay for cigarettes?

The problem is not just that cultural producers like al-'Assal come from a different social class than these village women who watch her programs, though this is significant. Nor is it a matter of the difference between urban and rural experiences, however considerable. Al-'Assal has actually tried to bridge this kind of difference by writing a serial, broadcast in 1993, about rural Upper Egypt. The serial showed the cruelty and power of large landlords and the powerlessness of peasants who don't seek common cause. But the main theme was revenge (the feud), the metonym by which Upper Egypt has been known to generations of northern Egyptian writers (the violence it signifies now transferred neatly onto Muslim militants whose strongholds are located there).[11]

Al-'Assal wrote this serial out of genuine concern. She even spent months living with a rural family to prepare herself to write the script, just as she had studied a retirement home to write *Mothers in the House of Love*. As a radical politician, she was deeply concerned with social conditions and the terrible poverty of the region. But her focus on vengeance and the solution she offered reproduced a discourse of enlightened modernity against backward customs that continue to denigrate Upper Egyptians, men and women. The hero and heroine of the program were a young couple, a latter-day Romeo and Juliet, whose modern education and enlightened ideas led them to reject the feud (a "backward" tradition still nurtured by older women) and to attempt to break the hold of the feudal lords (and their wives) by supporting the peasants' efforts to set up a collectively owned factory.

Television makes obvious the fact that the same cultural texts have different imports in different contexts. When Zaynab interprets a scene like the marriage of a sixty-year-old as a matter of cultural difference—linked to region, way of life, and morality—this is because she is so disadvantaged in terms of class and education that she fails to grasp the intentions of the more privileged creator of the program. For al-'Assal—working as an oppositional politician within the national context of a postcolonial state and arguing with fellow intellectuals, critics, and politicians in Cairo and across the Arab world while trying to reform the public—this episode was meant to represent a revolutionary and enlightened feminist option. Only a mobile ethnography can do justice to the ways these different worlds intersect. And this intersection must be part of any thick description of television.

I hope this extended reflection on the encounter between some village women and a television serial has illustrated the way stories about book bags, marrying at sixty, and television can speak, as Geertz suggested, to big words and mega-concepts. Taking television seriously forces us to think about "culture" not so much as a system of meaning or even a way of life but as something whose elements are produced, censored, paid for, and broadcast across a nation, even across national boundaries. The hegemonic or ideological—and thus power-related—nature of mass-mediated cultural texts in the service of national, class, or commercial projects is undeniable. This, in turn, should lead us to think about the ways that aspects of what we used to think of as local culture, such as moral values about the proper age of marriage or the propriety of women's education, are themselves not neutral features to be interpreted but the sometimes contested result of other, more local, projects of power that are worth analyzing.

## From cultures to cosmopolitans

Television is an extraordinary technology for breaching boundaries and intensifying and multiplying encounters among lifeworlds, sensibilities, and ideas. Television brings into Zaynab's home, her conversations, and her imagination a range of visions and experiences that originated outside her community (in such places as Cairo, Alexandria, Hollywood, Bombay, and even Tokyo). At the same time it places her in a particular relation to them. And with UNESCO's 1993 estimate of more than six million television sets in Egypt, Zaynab's exposure is hardly unusual.[12]

What is critical is that television's meanings are produced somewhere—for most viewers, somewhere else—and consumed locally in a variety of localities. Even if it ultimately helps create something of a "national habitus," or hints of a transnational habitus, television is most interesting because of the way it provides material which is then inserted into, interpreted with, and mixed up with local but themselves socially differentiated knowledges, discourses, and meaning systems.[13] Television, in short, renders more and more problematic a concept of cultures as localized communities of people suspended in shared webs of meaning.

Thinking about Zaynab watching Egyptian dramatic serials and films, interviews with criminals, broadcasts of Parliament in session, American soap operas, imported nature programs that take her to the Caribbean or the Serengeti Plain, and advertisements for candy, ceramic toilets, chicken-stock cubes, and Coca-Cola leads me to begin thinking about her and others in this village not as members of some kind of unified Egyptian, or Upper Egyptian, peasant culture—one in which it is improper for women over thirty to marry or older women to be out and about going to school—but in terms of the cosmopolitanism they might represent. The introduction here of the concept of cosmopolitanism might seem surprising or glib. Since it is generally associated with those who travel, those who feel at home in several parts of the world, and those who are professionals, the concept would seem to apply more readily to the progressive television writer al-'Assal.[14] Although her political and social concerns are passionately focused on Egypt, her political vocabulary is international; she is well aware of foreign literature, film, and media; she has grown children who work in Finland and France; and she expresses frustration that the work of many fine Egyptian women writers is not translated into foreign languages. She reads television texts in terms of their political perspectives, criticizing fellow writers for being conservative or caving in to government expectations. She worries about television's social impact, disapproving of an American soap opera like *The Bold and the Beautiful* for the immorality it normalizes.

However, what village women like Zaynab, her daughter Sumaya, and her neighbor Fayruz can help us understand is how wealth, education, and particular experiences in everyday life combine with television to mark out other varieties of cosmopolitanism. These are the kinds of cosmopolitanisms one finds in many rural areas around the postcolonial world and that confound the concept of "cultures."

## Anthropology for whom?

My own inclination has been to approach television as just one aspect of late-twentieth-century lives, just as I approached the poetry of the Awlad 'Ali Bedouin as an aspect of their everyday lives rather than as the object of a study of poetics. One of the benefits of working on television as a way into these lives—as opposed, for example, to focusing on poetry, religion, kinship, or political economy—is that it offers particular possibilities for worldly intervention.[15] It does so both in the way it enables us to represent to outsiders people in places like Egypt and, more appealing, in the way it enables us to work as intellectuals within the national frame that is such a crucial context today for most people, including the women and men in this Upper Egyptian village.

In *Writing Women's Worlds*, I suggested that we could write critical ethnographies that went "against the grain" of global inequalities, even as we had to remain modest in our claims to radicalism and realistic about the impacts of these ethnographies. Television, I believe, is particularly useful for writing against the grain because it forces us to represent people in distant villages as part of the same cultural worlds we inhabit—worlds of mass media, consumption, and dispersed communities of the imagination. To write about television in Egypt, or Indonesia, or Brazil is to write about the articulation of the transnational, the national, the local, and the personal. Television is not the only way to do this, of course; Anna Tsing's reflections on marginality in a remote region of Indonesia and her attention to people like Uma Adang—a singular woman who brilliantly hybridized national, local, and foreign discourses to establish herself as a shaman—were developed without talking about television.[16] But television makes it especially difficult to write as if culture and cultures, despite their "infirmities," were the most powerful ways to make sense of the world.[17]

Working on television also enables more local interventions—at the national level, with intellectuals who are our peers and counterparts. These are people I can admire or disagree with, and who themselves can read, criticize, and debate my work. If through my thick descriptions of television in particular places I can begin to tease apart the structures of power within which subaltern groups live their lives and the ways television is a new part of that—in households, in communities, and in imaginations—I perhaps can also then enter into debate with concerned writers like al-'Assal, often nationalists and modernists, regarding how to think about their audiences and political projects.

I would like to do this because I respect their social concern but I also know that from the vantage of Upper Egyptian villagers like Zaynab and Umm Ahmad, the answers they offer to social problems facing ordinary people often appear unrealistic or patronizing. Television intersects with and extends the discourses of experts. It is directed at stereotyped audiences, the same generalized objects targeted by social reformers. Is there a way thick descriptions of such communities could complicate urban intellectuals' understanding of Egyptian villagers? Or lead them to take more seriously the complexity of the forms of cosmopolitanism found across Egypt? Is there a way to begin to question modernist dogmas about literacy, education, and companionate marriage as panaceas? To al-'Assal's credit, one of her aims in writing the serial on Upper Egypt was to show, as she put it, "that the real vengeance would be to lash out [through development] against the circumstances that have led them to be attached to the vendetta in the first place." But by continuing to subsume much more complex stories of rural life under the familiar modernizing trope of a negative "tradition" and "backwardness," she, like most Egyptian intellectuals, risks reaffirming the marginality of such women as Zaynab.

## Notes

1. Clifford Geertz, *Works and Lives* (Stanford, 1988).
2. Jean Baudrillard, *Selected Writings*, Mark Poster (ed.) (Stanford, 1988).
3. Sherry Ortner, "Resistance and the Problem of Ethnographic Refusal," *Comparative Studies in Society and History* 37 (1) (1995): 173–93. For a classic celebration of television viewers' resistance, see John Fiske, *Television Culture* (London, 1987).
4. Debra Spitulnik, "Anthropology and Mass Media," *Annual Review of Anthropology* 22 (1993): 293–315 (307).
5. Faye Ginsburg, "Culture/Media: A (Mild) Polemic," *Anthropology Today* 10 (2) (1994): 5–15 (13).

6. I am not alone in exploring this question. Among the growing number of anthropologists working on the ethnography of television and film are Walter Armbrust, *Mass Culture and Modernism in Egypt* (Cambridge, 1996); Victor Caldarola, *Reception as a Cultural Experience: Mass Media and Muslim Orthodoxy in Outer Indonesia* (New Brunswick, NJ, 1994); Arlene Davila, "*El Kiosko Budweiser*: The Making of a 'National' TV Show in Puerto Rico" (unpublished ms.); Minou Fuglesang, *Veils and Videos* (Stockholm, 1994); Faye Ginsburg, "Aboriginal Media and the Australian Imaginary," *Public Culture* 5 (3) (1993): 557–78; Brian Larkin, "Parallel Modernities: Islam and the Social Practice of Media in Northern Nigeria" (PhD diss. in progress, New York University); Daniel Miller, *Modernity: An Ethnographic Approach* (London, 1995); Mayfair Yang, "State Discourse or a Plebeian Public Sphere? Film Discussion Groups in China," *Visual Anthropology Review* 10 (1) (1994): 47–60; and Richard Wilk, "Colonial Time and TV Time," *Visual Anthropology Review* 10 (1) (1994): 94–102, and "'It's Destroying a Whole Generation': Television and Moral Discourse in Belize," *Visual Anthropology* 5 (1993): 229–44. Those doing ethnographies of production include faculty and students in the Culture and Media Program at New York University such as Barry Dorn-feld, *Producing Public Television* (forthcoming); Teja Ganti, whose dissertation in progress focuses on the Bombay film industry; and Nancy Sullivan, "Film and Television Production in Papua New Guinea," *Public Culture* 5 (3) (1993): 533–56. Also see Ruth Mandel, "Soap Opera in Central Asia: Privatization and Development" (paper presented at the annual meeting of the American Anthropological Association, San Francisco, 1996), and Andrew Painter, "On the Anthropology of Television: A Perspective from Japan," *Visual Anthropology Review* 10 (1) (1994): 70–84.
7. I have borrowed this felicitous concept from George Marcus, "Ethnography in/of the World System: The Emergence of Multi-Sited Ethnography," *Annual Review of Anthropology* 24 (1995): 95–117. In fact, my own larger research project involves an ethnography not just of Upper Egyptian villagers and urban television professionals but of urban working-class women who are as disadvantaged as Upper Egyptians but with different experiences of and relationships to the city.
8. All quotations from Fathiyya al-'Assal derive from an interview conducted by the author on 26 June 1993.
9. For more on Egyptian feminist views of marriage, see Lila Abu-Lughod, "The Marriage of Feminism and Islamism: Selective Repudiation as a Dynamic of Postcolonial Cultural Politics," in *Remaking Women: Feminism and Modernity in the Middle East*, Lila Abu-Lughod (ed.) (forthcoming), and Beth Baron, "The Making and Breaking of Marital Bonds in Modern Egypt," in *Women in Middle Eastern History*, Nikki Keddie and Beth Baron (eds) (New Haven, 1991), 275–91.
10. See Margot Badran, *Feminists, Islam, and Nation* (Princeton, 1995); Beth Baron, *The Women's Awakening in Egypt* (New Haven, 1994); and Mervat Hatem, "Economic and Political Liberalization in Egypt and the Demise of State Feminism," *International Journal of Middle East Studies* 24 (2) (1992): 231–51.
11. Martina Reiker, "The Sa'id and the City: Subaltern Spaces in the Making of Modern Egyptian History" (PhD diss., Temple University, 1997).
12. Hussein Amin, "Egypt and the Arab World in the Satellite Age," in *New Patterns in Global Television*, John Sinclair, Elizabeth Jacka, and Stuart Cunningham (eds) (Oxford, 1996), 101–25 (eps. 104).
13. The notion of a "national habitus" comes from Orvar Lofgren, cited in Robert Foster, "Making National Cultures in the Global Ecumene," *Annual Review of Anthropology* 20 (1991): 235–60 (307). See also Abu-Lughod, "Objects of Soap Opera," for a suggestion about how viewing television might create a sense of national affiliation despite the failures of nationalist messages to reach socially peripheral viewers.

14. The discussion of cosmopolitanism has become wide-ranging. In anthropology, Paul Rabinow's "Representations Are Social Facts" (in *Writing Culture*, James Clifford and George Marcus (eds) [Berkeley, 1986]) was a starting point. Key texts are Appadurai, *Modernity at Large*; James Clifford, "Travelling Cultures," in *Cultural Studies*, Lawrence Grossberg, Cary Nelson, and Paula Treichler (eds) (New York, 1992); and Hannerz, *Cultural Complexity*.
15. This worldliness is what Ang says distinguishes "critical" cultural studies; ibid., 45–6, 79.
16. Anna Tsing, *In the Realm of the Diamond Queen* (Princeton, 1993).
17. Clifford Geertz, *After the Fact: Two Countries, Four Decades, One Anthropologist* (Cambridge, MA, 1995), 43.

# CHAPTER 30
## GAMES AS THE PLAY OF SIMULATION
*Katie Salen and Eric Zimmerman*

### Framing the simulation

> Children know that they are manipulating their thoughts about reality, not reality itself; and they know that their play self is not the same as their everyday self.
>
> Brian Sutton-Smith, *The Ambiguity of Play*

In *Games as the Play of Meaning,* we introduced Gregory Bateson's concept of metacommunication, the unique form of communication that takes place in the context of play. To use Bateson's own example, when a dog nips another dog, the nip signals two things. On the one hand, the nip signifies a bite; it is a stand-in for the action of a real bite. On the other hand, the nip signifies just the opposite of a bite: it signals the fact that the two dogs are playing and not actually fighting. This kind of metacommunication—communication about communication—is present not just in informal play but in games as well. It is a significant part of the complex mechanisms games use to construct meanings for their players.

Why is the concept of metacommunication so important, especially in the context of simulation? Metacommunication makes it clear that to play a game is to take part in a kind of double-consciousness. Game actions refer to actions in the real world, but because they are taking place in a game, they are simultaneously quite separate and distinct from the real world actions they reference. A kiss in Spin the Bottle or a frag in a Quake deathmatch refer to kissing and killing, but at the same time are actions that communicate *I'm not kissing or killing you. I'm just playing.* The magic circle is the space within which such paradoxical signals become meaningful.

In "A Theory of Play and Fantasy," Bateson uses the following diagram to illustrate the paradoxical state of mind embodied in play:

| All statements within this frame are untrue. |
| --- |
| I love you.<br>I hate you. |

This schematic is a riff on Epimenides' Paradox, also known as the Liar Paradox. The Liar Paradox is the philosophical problem of someone asserting "I am lying." If the speaker *is* a liar, then he is telling the truth, and vice versa: the liar's statement is a logical paradox. In the diagram, the first sentence, *All statements within this frame are untrue,* echoes this classical logic problem. But significantly, it locates the statement within a *frame,* a limited context within which the paradoxical sentence asserts its meaning.

For Bateson the frame is a psychological and philosophical construct that delimits the peculiar space of play. For game designers, Bateson's frame offers another way of understanding the magic circle of a game. It is a boundary that makes the paradoxical meanings of play possible. At the same time, the frame is only sustained by virtue of the continued metacommunicative assertions of play. In Bateson's illustration, the frame enables the statement's meaning, even as the frame's own meaning comes directly from the statement itself.

What about the other two statements, *I love you* and *I hate you*? These statements are also part of the paradoxical meanings captured within the frame. The two sentences address a larger point Bateson makes about set theory, and whether some or all of the statements within the frame could be considered true or untrue. For our present purposes, we will sidestep his larger argument to make a point of our own. Bateson could have included any two contradictory sentences in the frame. But he chose emotional statements about love and hate, statements seemingly addressed to someone else outside the frame.

These two little sentences, signals of pure emotion, remind us that the questions of play and meaning, of metacommunication and paradox, are not just abstract philosophical chatter. In understanding how games construct meaning, we are addressing the deeply felt ways that players engage with games and the emotional and social realities games reflect and construct. The metacommunicative state of mind is deeply intertwined with the unique pleasures and experiences of play.

## The immersive fallacy

> All forms of entertainment strive to create **suspension of disbelief**, a state in which the player's mind forgets that it is being subjected to entertainment and instead accepts what it perceives as reality.
>
> François Dominic Laramée, *Immersion*

We will return to Bateson's ideas about metacommunication and meaning in just a moment. But for now, let's bring the discussion to the play of simulation, specifically the relationship between a game and the "reality" upon which it is based. The preceding quote is from a book on game design, appearing in an essay on "Immersion." Game designer and programmer François Dominic Laramée argues for a particular relationship between a game player and a game, between the player's state of mind and the perceived reality of the experience. He asserts that a game should strive to create an experience in which the player forgets that he or she is experiencing designed entertainment and instead believes that playing the game is experiencing reality firsthand. In fact, Laramée states that "all forms of entertainment" function in this way. This is a point of view very much at odds with our own.

We don't mean to unfairly single out Laramée. His ideas about how a player experiences the "reality" of a game are extremely common in the digital game industry, the game press, and even in the public at large. Game designer Frank Lantz has called these kinds of ideas about immersion "widely held but seldom examined" beliefs. We wholeheartedly agree, and in the pages that follow we refute these beliefs, referring to them as the *immersive fallacy*. The immersive fallacy is the idea that the pleasure of a media experience lies in its ability to sensually transport the participant into an illusory, simulated reality.

According to the immersive fallacy, this reality is so complete that ideally the frame falls away so that the player truly believes that he or she is part of an imaginary world.

Although the immersive fallacy has taken hold in many fields, it is particularly prevalent in the digital game industry. Common within the discourse of the immersive fallacy is the idea that entertainment technology is inevitably leading to the development of more and more powerful systems of simulation. These technologies will be able to create fully illusionistic experiences that are indistinguishable from the real world. In an online discussion about the future of gaming, game designer Warren Spector speculated on this topic:

> Is the Star Trek Holodeck an inevitable end result of games as simulacra? The history of media (mass and otherwise) seems pretty clearly a march toward ever more faithful approximations of reality—from the development of the illusion of perspective in paintings to photography to moving pictures to color moving pictures with sound to color moving pictures with sound beamed directly into your home via television to today's immersive reality games like Quake and System Shock. Is this progression inevitable and will it continue or have we reached the end of the line, realism-wise?

To be fair, Spector self-consciously exaggerated his views in order to spark discussion. But in the debate that followed, it was clear that many participants take for granted the propositions that Spector articulated.

Spector's selective history of entertainment technologies offers one reading of the development of media. But there are others. History rarely provides such a linear progression, and in regard to immersion, cultural developments tend to be cyclical. As theorist Marie-Laure Ryan puts it, "The history of Western art has seen the rise and fall of immersive ideals." According to Ryan, immersion as a representational goal has gone through a number of stylistic cycles over the centuries. In the last several decades, she asserts, immersion has in fact become less prominent and respected in fields like art and literature. Ryan may be correct in regard to larger cultural movements, but within the digital game industry, belief in the immersive fallacy remains alive and well.

## Metacommunicative

The immersive fallacy is symptomatic of contradictory ideas about technology. On one hand, there is a technological fetishism that sees the evolutionary development of new technology as the saving grace of experience design. On the other hand, there is a desire to erase the technology, to make it invisible so that all frames around the experience fall away and disappear. Nowhere are these contradictory ideals more clearly expressed than in the concept of the holodeck, a fictional technology that first appeared in the television show *Star Trek: The Next Generation*. The holodeck is the dream of the immersive fallacy, a room in which matter and energy are manipulated to create a simulated environment of sight, sound, touch, smell, and taste that is a representation completely indistinguishable from lived reality.

What is wrong with this picture, and how does it relate to games? On one level, the immersive fallacy actually does make intuitive sense. When we play a game, we feel engaged and engrossed, and play seems to take on its own "reality." This is all certainly true. But the way that a game achieves these effects does not happen in the manner the immersive fallacy implies. A game player does become engrossed in the game, yes. But it is an engagement that occurs *through play itself.* As we know, play is a process of metacommunication, a double-consciousness in which the player is well aware of the artificiality of the play situation.

During the same online conversation in which Spector posted his intentionally provocative question, film studies scholar Elena Gorfinkel responded:

> Immersion is not a property of a game or media text but is an effect that a text produces. What I mean is that immersion is an experience that happens between a game and its player, and is not something intrinsic to the aesthetics of a game. The confusion in this conversation has emerged because representational strategies are conflated with the effect of immersion. Immersion itself is not tied to a replication or mimesis of reality. For example, one can get immersed in Tetris. Therefore, immersion into game play seems at least as important as immersion into a game's representational space. It seems that these components need to be separated to do justice and better understand how immersion, as a category of experience and perception, works.

Gorfinkel makes a number of critical points. First, with her example of Tetris she points out that there are plenty of examples of games in which "immersion" is not tied to a sensory replication of reality. In fact, there are countless examples of art and entertainment media, from techno music to comic books to expressionist painting, which are clearly not premised on a simple suspension of disbelief. As Gorfinkel states, mistaken ideas about immersion can be framed as confusion between the intrinsic qualities of a media object and the effects that object produces. Gorfinkel argues that to understand the subtleties of "immersion," we need to look not just at the attributes of games (such as how detailed the graphics are), but at the way games function in relation to the experience of the player.

In the case of play, we know that metacommunication is always in operation. A teen kissing another teen in Spin the Bottle or a *Gran Turismo* player driving a virtual race car each understands that their play references other realities. But the very thing that makes their activity *play* is that they also know they are participating within a constructed reality, and are consciously taking on the artificial meanings of the magic circle. To play a game is to take part in a complex interplay of meaning. But this kind of immersion is quite different from the sensory transport promised by the immersive fallacy.

## Hacking the holodeck

The questions surrounding games as simulations are always more complex than they first appear. There is no simple relationship between player and character, or player and game, or game and outside world. This is one reason why the immersive fallacy continues to colonize most design thinking about the future of games and the role of technology in creating compelling experiences: it is simply an easier position to take.

But the immersive fallacy is more than an idea. It is also a stumbling block to advances in game design, as it represents an overly romantic and antiquated model for how media operate. As long as game designers are caught up in a desire for the technology of the holodeck, they lack the vision to appreciate the potential for game innovation today. What if game designers focused their efforts on actively playing with the double-consciousness of play, rather than pining for immersion?

Imagine the kinds of games that could result: games that encourage players to constantly shift the frame of the game, questioning what is inside or outside the game; games that play with the lamination between player and character, pushing and pulling against the connection through inventive forms of narrative play; games that emphasize metagaming, or that connect the magic circle so closely with external contexts that the game appears synchronous with everyday life. Innovation is only bound by a failure to see the fundamental principles of play.

A common complaint among game developers is that games are not recognized as a significant form of culture, and that they lack a diverse mass audience. Instead, games seem to be relegated to the backwaters of culture. A sea change in cultural status will only occur when game designers acquire a more sophisticated understanding of how their media operates. Robust forms of contemporary pop culture are not premised on naïve ideas of immersion. Just take a look at the explicit self-consciousness of hip-hop, fashion, and Animé. These forms of popular culture have a deep understanding of the way media cultivates immersion while making explicit the mechanisms through which the representation is experienced.

This, of course, brings us back to simulation. Even though simulations are premised on the notion of fidelity to their referent, the very fact that they are dynamic systems means they allow for the exploration of alternate permutations. Simulations allow players to explore a space of representational possibility through the very act of play. Certainly there are a great many game designers driven by a desire to tell stories and provide narrative worlds for players. Framing games as simulations, as dynamic systems of procedural representation, unlocks the potential of games as a powerful representational and narrative medium. But games have only just scratched at the surface. Questions remain: What can games represent? How can games engage players through meaningful play? And how can games challenge, critique, and contribute to the world outside the magic circle?

## Bibliography

Bateson, Gregory (1972), "A Theory of Play and Fantasy," in *Steps to an Ecology of Mind*, 191–222, Chicago: The University of Chicago Press.

Lantz, Frank. *Hacking the Holodeck,* unpublished manuscript.

Laramée, François Dominic (ed.) (2002), *Game Design Perspectives*. Hingham, MA: Charles River Media.

RE:PLAY: Game Design + Game Culture (2000), Online conference.

Ryan, Marie-Laure (2000), *Narrative as Virtual Reality: Immersion and Interactivity in Literature and Electronic Media*, Baltimore: John Hopkins University Press.

Sutton-Smith, Brian (2001), *The Ambiguity of Play*, Boston: Harvard University Press.

# CHAPTER 31

## ON PUNK AND REPULSION, A MISFIT THEORY OF SOCIETY

*Shane Greene*

Mommy, can I go out and kill tonight?

The Misfits

It was 1983. I was twelve. I had just entered the insufferable *rite de passage* most people know as junior high. The false innocence of childhood was gone and the false promises of adulthood still years away.

In theory, I had what it took to fit in to the adolescent order. The mostly working class background didn't help. But growing up white, male, hetero with no particular disfigurement tends to get you places in America. (Many years later I have a PhD and tenure at a respectable university.) Despite some obvious signs of entitlement to the privileges of normalcy, during these formative young white man moments I proved unwilling to vie for a spot in the crowds of the sporty, the cool, and the popular. I was no more comfortable seeking admittance into the cliques marked by exclusion: the super nerds; the back roads rednecks from the rural parts of the county; the blacks from Bouchelle Street (they didn't all live on that street but the white kids acted like they did).

It was 1983. I was twelve. This was a tiny, ultra-conservative shit-town in the southern United States.

Luckily, Aaron Bachelder, my closest friend from elementary school, appeared with a solution, some sort of provocative proposition called "punk rock." In the early 1980s, in small town America at least, this was a thing so out of place as to be downright dangerous. We discovered this via threats of violence and frequent accusations that we were freaks, queer, mentally unstable, or all of the above.

Aaron's parents were a couple of kooky psychologists, professional-class transplants from the north. They supported it when both their sons, from very early ages, decided to pursue wildly impractical lives in music and art. By contrast, I was born a Tarheel and raised by strong women. My house was co-managed by a single mother, armed with the unlikely combination of a GED and some sort of organic feminist intolerance for masculine bullshit, and a jock sister who found her place in the world through basketball. Dad was a specter, off hanging out with his alcoholism and small-time drug dealers.

Despite these differences in daily realities, Aaron and I shared a pretty similar profile, sociologically speaking. When punk emerged in our lives we realized we had one very specific thing in common. It was the curious dilemma of "not fitting in," a narrative trope that emerges in every punk's origin story to one degree or another. In retrospect, the crucial point of convergence was that we apparently harbored some unique capacity to be really pissed off about it. We felt subjectively ready to declare ourselves total misfits to the world even though, from a more objective point of view, our social profiles made clear we were just a couple of basic white boys.

Aaron heard the sounds and learned the look of punk from his older brother, Marshall. He had gone to North Carolina's School of the Arts and returned to unleash this peculiar subcultural phenomenon on an unsuspecting population of about 15,000. Aaron converted first, I converted second, and as far as anyone knows we were the first three punks to wander the small downtown streets of Morganton, North Carolina.

Within a month or two, I learned a crucial lesson about why this infamous subculture—full of "filth and fury," according to the headlines that launched the Sex Pistols into global scandal after a live interview on the Bill Grundy show in late '76 that went vulgar—appeals to the young and the placeless. By then, Aaron and I had finished the requisite shopping spree at the army surplus store in search of combat boots, trench coats and the like. One day I showed up at his house and sat watching him get ready for one of our routine street excursions with petty vandalism in mind: breaking into cars at used auto lots, busting into the junior high cafeteria to flip over the ice machine, punky stuff like that.

This particular day I remember focusing on Aaron's whole act of getting prepared for the public, putting on his punk outfit. It seemed more deliberate than when I did it. He told me to wait while he went to the bathroom to spike his Mohawk with some toxic-looking green gel. He came back and tossed me a fanzine his brother Marshall was producing. It had an article about nuclear winter, a phrase I'd never heard before but brought to mind that little triangular nuclear symbol I had seen at the downtown post office. Aaron looked in a wall mirror to adjust his skull-and-crossbones earring. Swirling his army green trench coat over his shoulder, he looked straight at me and declared: "OK, ready. Let's go out and offend somebody!"

## On repulsion and structure (blah, yuck, ick)

Why does every human society anthropologists know about display such a strong tendency to divide the world into the normal and the abnormal, acceptable and unacceptable forms of behavior, the culturally taken for granted versus the totally taboo? Apparently, establishing norms is part of what makes us human. By now, we also know that the response to the fact of social norms goes well beyond simply accepting things as they are. Some feel excluded, others imposed upon. Some seek inclusion, others are desirous of transgression.

These are questions that have long perplexed scholars. Psychologists have a history of explaining normalcy in terms of individual behaviors, even when they relate that behavior to a familial context or developmental process. Other disciplines are more prone to address the issue from a more systemic point of view, using concepts like social deviance, cultural difference, or subculture. To name a couple of classic examples: Emile Durkheim taught us that all societies prescribe certain forms of social behavior and punish others considered threatening to the norm, although they do it in different ways. For him, this constituted a threat to the very moral fabric, or "collective conscience," that holds society together. Early anthropologists like Ruth Benedict emphasized the relativity of social behavior. A thought or action that is interpreted as disturbingly weird in one cultural context or historical moment might be considered utterly routine in another. So the range of possible explanations covers a lot of ground.

Many a social scientist has wondered if youth subcultures like punk are explainable in such terms. Maybe punk is related to the issue of problem families and interpersonal struggles with peers. Maybe it is the structural result of individual isolation produced by the dysfunctional elements of modern, industrialized society, a phenomenon Durkheim called "anomie." Maybe it is some form of neotribalism, producing small, dispersed, oppositional collectivities that might seem "natural" in native Amazonia but a little out of place in the mass urbanized contexts of New York, London, or Los Angeles.

Criticism of such approaches, at least those rooted in theories of race, gender/sex, or class, would suggest they are devoid of a more explicit focus on questions of hierarchy and power, specifically the ways that norms are also reflective of forms of social inclusion and exclusion. What others call the norm Karl Marx called "ideology," a dominant set of ideas and institutions associated with a particular economic order that justifies the exploitation of the marginalized. W. E. B. Dubois helps us think through racial thought, with its roots in the slave trade and European imperialism, as the structuring ideology through which whiteness becomes a standard against which nonwhite minorities are forced to measure themselves. Rooted more in philosophy and semiotics, De Beauvoir's classic feminist text identifies the multiple mechanisms that make gender-based exclusion a part of everyday reality, e.g. this is why "man" gets to stand in for all of humanity and "woman" only the second half of it.

Antonio Gramsci, writing during the reign of Italian fascism, renamed the Marxist concept of ideology "hegemony" and suggested people are not simply passive objects of ideological effects. Instead, they actively consent to the very ideas and institutions that serve to exclude them even while also using the ideological domain as a space in which to contest their exclusion. If I mention Gramsci, it is because in the 1970s a cluster of cultural studies scholars—people like Stuart Hall, John Clarke, Tony Jefferson, Dick Hebdige and others—began to think of hegemony as central to theorizing urban subcultural styles as counter-hegemonic projects that seek to express the systemic contradictions that surround social exclusion (see Hall and Jefferson 2006; Hebdige 1979).

Despite all these possible explanations, they still fall short of answering a question I find intriguing when it comes to punk. Why, historically speaking, has this subculture held so much appeal to young, white, middle-class, heterosexual men—those who otherwise might simply represent the privileged "normative" status in the US and UK where punk emerged?

I pose the question this way not out of an ignorance of the diversity of voices in punk, past and present, from the Bad Brains and The Slits to Tribe 8 and Bikini Kill. First off, there are some extremely generative accounts of punk that don't link it to any of today's recognizable identity categories or a specific class position. Instead they analyze it as a response to global capital and urbanization or as part of anarchist-inspired, direct-action oriented movements that cross class and geopolitical boundaries (see Nikpour 2012; Graeber 2009). Other accounts seek to decenter the white hetero punk dude from his presumptuous protagonism, demonstrating punk's multiple dialogues with everything from queer of color theory (N'yongo 2005) and chicana feminism (Habell-Pallan 2004) to gender politics (Leblanc 2009) and geo-political realities well beyond the US–UK rock nexus where most punk stories are still told (Greene 2016).

It is worth considering that the many minority experiences that constitute punk are also prone to articulate their stories as oppositional to the white hetero punk dude in part *because* they are perceived as exceptional within the subculture. For example, James Spooner, director of the excellent 2003 documentary "Afro-Punk," explores the dilemma of double exclusion. The generalized racial exclusion of being black in the US is further compounded when afropunks realize they constitute a particular exception within a subculture that is predominantly white. Similarly, Leblanc's 1999 book argues that young women's participation in punk is also experienced as one of frequent tension within a predominantly "boy" subculture.

In other words, whatever the "essence" of punk is (and clearly no one is going to concede to an essentializing account anyway) there is a widely held perception that punk is somehow "for" the normal white guys who have historically predominated in it, at least ideologically speaking. This explains both the classic accounts that say as much, like Hebdige (1979), as well as the contemporary accounts that seek to decenter punk's hetero-male-whiteness by demonstrating the diversity of perspectives that has been central since its start. The structural exclusions faced as a result of gender, sex, or race are made more complex with the decision to become actors within a subculture that cultivates the idea and practices of auto-exclusion and self-marginalization.

Notably, identity in the sense of gendered, sexed, and racialized subjectivities is not the only issue in play here. Early cultural studies accounts saw post-World War II youth subcultures primarily through the lens of class (e.g. Hall and Jefferson 2006). Despite popular urban myths that link punks directly to the proletariat, most of the more sociological accounts see punk in the US and the UK emerging as much or more from the alienated, amorphous sectors of the educated middle-class (see Frith 1980; Laing 1985; Lamy and Levin 1985).

Here, we might pause in order to recall an enlightening bit of dialogue from *Repo Man*, that beautiful classic of 1980s punk cinema. Otto, the suburban California punk protagonist who struggles to find himself amid the alienating effects of an oppressively mass-produced American society, leans over his friend Duke who is splayed out in front of generic cornflakes boxes. Bleeding to death, Duke looks up at Otto from the floor of a generic convenient store after a botched robbery where he was shot by the generic imbecile manning the generic cash register:

> Duke: I know a life of crime led me to this sorry fate. And yet, I blame society. Society made me what I am.
> Otto: That's bullshit. You're a white suburban punk, just like me.
> Duke: But it still hurts.
> [Duke spits up blood and dies. Otto runs away.]

Let's consider the possibility that Otto and Duke are on to something here. Through their torturous white, suburban, male exchange, they suggest that whatever else it is, punk is also about a particular reaction to the experience of being forced to represent a social norm (role, expectation, etc.) while feeling distinctly "out of step" with it (to cite Minor Threat).

From Duke's vantage point, it seems legitimate to blame society for the consequences it imposes on the individuals that are never fully in control of the position they occupy within it. From Otto's stance, this sounds like bullshit coming from a normal white guy and the most they can do is try to run away from the inevitable fate of being white, suburban Californians. Their social knowledge, however laden with ironic contradictions and valley punk speak, is extraordinary. Society really is to blame for what it forces on us—and *Repo Man* is a punk critique of precisely that problem. We can try to run away from the normative impositions that surround us—and we no doubt encounter a few successes here and there. But it proves well-nigh impossible to fully escape the particular position into which we've been slotted. Basically, I think Marx's famous dictum that "men make their own history but they do not make it as they please" is being rephrased in Duke's dying thought. No matter who you are society "still hurts" because it will never leave you the fuck alone.

If in the US and the UK there has always been a wealth of white, hetero, middle-class guys attracted to punk—creating the perception that punk is *for* them even though it was never made exclusively *by* them—perhaps it has something to do with the structural position they occupy at society's ideological center. We might consider the possibility that this privileged subject does more than systematically reap the various material and symbolic benefits of being at the center of the normal. They (or "we," since I should include myself) of course do. But we might also think about how this ultra-normative subject also experiences the structural expectations of his normalcy as repressive in its own way, difficult or impossible to live up to, or maybe just kind of gross in its monotony and limitations. I guess what I'm saying, based in part on personal experience, is that punks are reacting, rather negatively, to the very idea of being socially condemned to represent the norm in the first place. They are looking for ways to remove themselves from that symbolic center, searching for a means to propel themselves out towards the margins, into the domain of the excluded and antinormal. This occurs amid structural constraints perhaps but they represent hopes to get beyond the normal nonetheless.

We might make more complex the basic dilemma of social inclusion and exclusion—and most analyses of class, race, and gender/sex ultimately hinge on this basic dichotomy no matter how much complexity they otherwise display—by relating it to a notion of structural repulsion. Unlike those who find comfort in being included in the socially normal, finding their place within social structures, punks are the ones trying to resist its power and privileges by pointing out its impositions and expectations. Overcome with feelings of repulsion to the norm, specifically the expectation they must be included in it, they seek instead to become repulsive to it. This is what my friend Aaron meant when he said, "Let's go out and offend somebody."

At one level, this proves problematic given the impossibility of ever fully shedding society's normative imperatives—and especially things as systemically privileging in modern Western societies as whiteness, masculinity, heteronormativity, and middle-classness. Yet, the punk who tries is at least theoretically open to the possibility of constructing non-normative dialogues, however much those dialogues are likely to proceed "without guarantees" (to invoke Stuart Hall's nondeterminism). Those seeking to remove themselves from the normative center and find a place at the margins are certainly more likely to engage in dialogue with those experiencing diverse forms of structural marginalization, at least more so than those embracing a normative status with much less critical awareness.

Importantly, the very possibility of non-normative dialogues taking place is also related to other modalities of social repulsion being experienced by those experiencing systemic exclusion along other social axes. Those occupying positions within social groups marked by historical exclusion, whether via racialization, gender/sex status, or class formation, are hardly without their own social norms, roles, and expectations to conform to and feel repulsed by. In fact, some of the best examples of work that explores punk from the standpoint of racialized or gendered experiences are implicitly exploring a kind of repulsion internal to the marginalized position from which the subjects hail. To return to the example of James Spooner's documentary *Afro-Punk,* he does more than detail the complex problems around being black among a majority of white punks in the US. The film also directly explores the experiences of African-American punks that articulate feelings of repulsion at the many normative expectations that surround blackness, the norms that dictate how one is supposed to be black. By embracing punk, they self-consciously invest in becoming "oddly black" since punk continues to be seen as a subculture "for" white people (in the same way that, for example, hip hop is perceived as "for" black people).

Similarly, while there is a long tradition of punk feminist pioneers dating back to the 1970s, the likes of Siouxsie Sioux, Patti Smith, and The Slits, it was clearly the 1990s Riot Grrrl phenomena that most forcefully brought gender/sex and punk into critical dialogue. The Riot Grrrl mantra of "girls to the front"—both front stage as performers and to the front of the stage as active audience members—was more than a feminist indictment of the relative marginality of women in punk rock culture. It was also an explicit statement about how young women feel repulsed by the ideas and practices surrounding normative femininity. By becoming punks they were repulsed by the idea of becoming "typical girls" (to recall The Slits' early punk feminist anthem) and overtly choosing to use punk as the main method for becoming riotous women.

In short, it is in the space of these multiple, intricately overlapping, forms of social repulsion to the imperatives of accepting one's relatively defined norm that punk is made. Punks are the ones trying to remake themselves into something that is not just different, but repulsively distinct, from what society is already making out of them.

## On repulsion and agency (buying in, opting out, selling out)

I find it more convincing to ground a theory of punk provocation in the work of Mikhail Bakhtin—and what better thinker could there be than one whose doctoral dissertation was rejected because it offended the reigning orthodoxy of the Russian academy of the World War II period. Eventually published as *Rabeleis and his World*, Bakhtin's (1968) text examines the work of a French Renaissance writer, exploring the link between medieval carnival and a nonconventional literary trope he identifies as grotesque realism. He describes the collective sociality of carnival in terms of a "suspension of all hierarchical precedence" (ibid.: 10), contrasted to the reinforcement of rank and social position encountered in official feasts and ceremonies. For Bakhtin this was a clear indication of the essentially anarchist tendencies of carnival. It also represented the creation of a lived space in which more spontaneous human interaction and forms of communication, liberated from the "norms of etiquette and decency" (ibid.) associated with normative social spaces, occurred. Similarly, grotesque forms of expression serve to celebrate the basest and vulgar forms of embodied experience symbolically degrading all that is associated with "high" culture and the higher human functions of abstraction.

In this sense both the sociality of carnival and the symbolic expressions of grotesqueness are provocative in the same way the punk underground is. They provoke through acts of transgression that challenge the assumed boundaries of the normative social order. The literal and figurative spaces associated with the punk underground serve to create a carnivalesque form of experience, representing a separation from the mainstream and a temporary suspension of the hierarchal forms of sociality associated with it.

This is clearest in terms of the crucial distinction Bakhtin makes between carnival and spectacle. The former is a collective event in which there is no distinction between actor and spectator while the latter enforces and relies on precisely that hierarchical distinction. Blurring the distinction between performer and audience has always been central to the punk ethos. The explicit attempt to promote simplicity in the music—the classical punk song is approximately two minutes with three or four power chords—relies on the idea that no real expertise is necessary to become a performer. The design of punk fanzines as an integral part of the subculture, circulating at multiple levels from the local to the national and international, promotes a similar idea that no one need have any credentials to become a writer or artist. Finally, the true measure of an exciting punk show is the degree to which the line between "audience" and "performer" is literally erased during the "performance." That erasure happens in both directions. The audience members become part of the show by repeatedly occupying the stage, by stage-diving, by engaging physically with the performers (i.e. grabbing the mic from the singer, etc.). The musicians (with the obvious exception of the drummer) often end up diving into or surfing on top of the audience while still performing. By contrast a boring punk show is one in which the audience stands back from the stage, hands crossed, acting the part of passive observers.

Similarly, the punk embrace of the obscene and the profane in its modes of expression are clearly grotesque. Punk lyrics are notoriously more transgressive than most forms of normative communication. The Circle Jerks elucidate this in a song called "Bad Words" that intentionally includes no profanity. The broader point is thus that profane language is crucial to a liberating sense of personal expression and an antiauthoritarian stance ("Use them when you're sad / Use them when you're mad / Use them when you're happy / Use them on your dad"). The look associated with punk is also expressively grotesque. One of the defining features of grotesque bodies according to Bakhtin is their openness, the symbolic celebration of those parts of the body that connote a material connection to the body's earthiness. Here the use of spikes, chains, bondage attire, piercings, iridescent make-up, and ripped clothing used as primary forms to adorn the punk body do more than simply offend normative sensibilities of dress and attractiveness. They often explicitly highlight precisely those parts of the body that facilitate a sensorial interpenetration with the world and other bodies: mouths, tongues, noses, eyes, genitalia.

One might object to the use of Bakhtin on the grounds that the forms of sociality and modes of expression he identifies are heavily rooted in a notion of communalistic folk culture and humor whereas punk is heavily associated with a primarily urban and angry kind of individualism. However, due to its ability to allow for multiple, often contradictory, extremes punk has never been devoid of communal, folk, or humoristic elements. The communalism of punk is immediately apparent in the urban tribalism associated with it. The primary forms of bodily movement associated with punk, while anarchical and individualistic in some respects, also contain inherently communal dimensions. Punk dances, initiating as the pogo and then evolving into the slamdance or mosh, eschew any sort of choreography, require no practice nor partners, enforce no explicit gender division in terms of leading or following, and naturally generate circles (a core circle of those moshing and an outer circle of those pushing the moshers back into the pit).

While punk is most often thought of as an essentially urban electrified genre, folk accents and acoustic instrumentation have long been part of the subculture (with seminal figures like The Pogues in the UK and the Violent Femmes in the US). Similarly, while punk is full of angry autobiography and scathing social commentary it has always retained a space for the use of comedy. Ironic and satirical forms of provocation are an essential part of this. The intent to humor is clear even from hyper-politicized bands like the Dead Kennedys with song titles like "Kill the Poor," "Holiday in Cambodia," or deliberately spoofed cover songs like "Rawhide." But there are also those various punk bands with a largely jovial rather than bitterly punk profile: The Dickies, The Dead Milkmen, The Minutemen. Again, this reinforces the earlier point about punk extremities. Just because punks are mostly urban cosmopolitans this doesn't mean they aren't also a bit folksy. Just because punks often seem angry this doesn't mean that they don't love to make people laugh.

A final point worth considering is this. Bakhtin sees carnival and the grotesque as utopian spaces in which to imagine and even temporarily inhabit a different world where social relations are more egalitarian and freer forms of communication are permitted. Yet it is in the end a utopia, a space that represents a suspension of the normative order but doesn't engage in a direct confrontation with it.

Historically, punk modes of provocation share essentially this same quality. Punk seeks to provoke, shock, and offend power—typically in the form of the state and other moral authorities that defend the status quo. Rarely has it become a method to systematically confront, physically challenge, or displace that power. This fact means that punk, while potentially deeply offensive to power, is ultimately not that threatening to it. This fact also means punk is all the more likely to be absorbed by those commercial interests in the culture industry that seek constantly to tame what was once provocative and transform it into that which is now acceptable to mass consumption.

Following the repulsive impulse to provoke if not effect an actual disruption in the status quo—some sort of active symbolic-material critique intended to reveal the repulsiveness of social norms—is what punks mean by opting out. The punk agent therefore sees things set up into blocs of social actors whose individual decisions can be defined in these terms and in response to—yep, you guessed it—"the system."

If we take Graeber's (2001) basic explanation of value, opting out of "the system" represents the particular form of social action that punks find most meaningful, that which they most value. As an action with the intended effect of undermining normative logics, opting out is also at regular risk of being undone. "The system" by its very nature is a really powerful structural force. As opt-outs, the punks are in constant danger of becoming sell-outs since the action that they most value is pretty systematically not valued by "the system."

How exactly does one know when a punk is really opting out as opposed to just pretending to do so? It makes perfect sense that if the action of opting out represents the maximal punk value there might be some interpretative dispute over who is really doing it versus who is not, or who is doing it more punkishly and who less. This means we probably need to confront the perennial problem presented by the poser.

The term "poser" is pervasive in punk discourse, used essentially to describe an actor that is involved in what others perceive as an inauthentic performance. This less than subtle statement that punk subculture is also inhabited by "fake" actors—those whose actions are perceived as mere poses—relies on the implicit assumption that performances of punkness can be both genuine and spurious. So, punks also clearly place a high value on authenticity, like it or not.

Crucially, the poser is sort of like a trickster figure or at least the formula for detecting inauthentic poses is not a simple, unidimensional one. A poser can be someone who performs punkness too little and someone who performs punkness too much. Either way, the risk has to do with an actor's performance of punkness being interpreted as an inauthentic version of opting out, a less than genuine expression of social repulsion. For example, I'm a white man professor at a large university with a steady middle class paycheck. With the velvet handcuffs of tenure, I write about punk rock and sometimes do so with a punk voice and in recognizable punk forums (e.g. 'zines like *Maximum Rock n Roll* or via DIY style, self-published texts). Punk is obviously not a forbidden topic in academe, post the invention of interdisciplines like Cultural Studies that propose to take popular culture "seriously." But I have discovered that writing with an antischolarly voice or in antiinstitutional forums has a net value of zero when judged by the stodgy, aristocratic standards of academe where the logics of symbolic prestige, seniority status, and peer review predominate (roughly in that order). If I haven't actually been called a poser to my face yet, I'm pretty certain that the occasional questioning of whether my position as an institutionally secure academic allows me to "be punk" amounts to the same thing.

By more than a slight contrast, GG Allin was a punk performer from the 1980s and early 1990s. He never made any money with his unabashedly poor-quality music or bottom-feeding "hits" like "Bite it You Scum." He had a notorious tendency to prance around naked, eat his own shit on stage, and provoke spontaneous violence at shows that rarely had more than a few dozen people in attendance. In 1993 he died of a heroin overdose to the disappointment of those fans that wanted him to make good on his many public promises to commit suicide on stage. Some punks consider him to represent the pinnacle of the punk value of opting out and refusing to buy back in. Others think he was a total clown precisely because of the extremities that his punk performance entailed.

Perhaps there is some sort of trick to not becoming this trickster figure that punks know as the poser. I think it has something to do with gaining an awareness of the fact that punk can never actually be just a random assortment of individuals, brought together by desires for opting out of the repulsively normative social structures they are subjected to. Those individual actions are necessarily structured in significant ways by the various systemic forces—not just race, class, and gender/sex, but also the particular historical moment and cultural context—that shape all of social life. In short, punk as a collective phenomenon is also a social world complete with its own rules and norms, roles and positions, internal status quo, and internal sense of repulsion toward it. It generates its own set of ideologically constructed values that revolve, however ironically, around the very idea of antinormativity.

The "culture" in "subculture" tells us as much. However open and oppositional it can be at times, punk is hardly a completely "free" space devoid of its own structuring principles and scripted actions. This can be appreciated by taking a look at urbandictionary.com's top definition for the street phrase "punk as fuck" which is meant to indicate a maximal level of punkness. I quote in full:

> Not giving a fuck.
> Not giving a fuck if you are punk or not.
> Not fucking caring what other people think.

> Not giving a damn if you look punk or not.
> Knowing that punk is an attitude … not how you dress or do your hair, not what kind of music you listen to, not who you hang out with, not how much you drink, not what kind of drugs you do, not if you sleep on the street or eat out of dumpsters, not how many tattoos or piercings you have.
> IT'S A FUCKING ATTITUDE.

Contained in this 'punk as fuck' attitude there is not just a casual comment about maximal punk action but the ideological concept of meta-punkness. To act punk, you have to know how and when not to underdo it and how and when not to overdo it. Counter to what one might think from the definition here, "not fucking caring what other people think" actually implicitly requires a distinct level of social awareness that others are in fact constantly thinking about you: that one is always a part of society even, and maybe especially, when intentionally trying to stand against it because of just how dang repulsive it can be.

The antisociality of punk is itself a social fact.

## Conclusion

In case it's not obvious, I went on to occupy a basically normative slot it seemed I was hell bent on rejecting. My situation isn't exactly that of the Wall Street financier, but then again the super elite aren't really that normative are they? As professor guy, I clearly have no convincing claims to marginality, only a series of privileges that derive at least in part from the normative white-boyness I was originally repulsed by. It's entirely possible I was just a sell-out in the making all along; or perhaps this punk rock professor thing is just a pose. Whatever the case, I confess to feeling frequently at odds with much that gets presented as what I'm supposed to do or what I'm supposed to say or how I'm supposed to say it or what I'm supposed to think. It's tiring at times, exciting at others.

I have no idea what ultimately became of Aaron. Last I heard, he was living in North Carolina, teaching music, and had a family. Over the years, I actually became closer with his brother Marshall, the "original" punk of Morganton, North Carolina. His path seems like the least conventional of the three in many respects. We became closer friends when I ended up going to university in the same college town where he opened his first tattoo shop. Since then, he bounced around from one tattoo place to the next until finally ending up back in Morganton, living at home with his parents, and working at a local coffee shop. Turned a bit conspiracy theorist, he likes to refer to the internet as "Satan's web" (as in doesn't use it) and he does these really intense paintings that consist of dozens of layers of paint on top of dozens of other layers of more paint with no real discernable form.

Last time I saw him was several years ago but it was a moment of re-convergence. Covered essentially head to toe in body art for years now, he had sworn off tattoos entirely and claims the ink being used in most tattoos shops is a poison that infects the person with cancerous agents. We talked for a long time as if the years that separated our last conversation hadn't really occurred. It had the effect of making me wonder how we ended up in such different situations, still secretly bonded by a history of punk and now this other intimate knowledge that he was the one who gave me my first, apparently cancerous, tattoos.

Maybe there's an infinite reservoir of repulsiveness out there that remains, ready to be acted on, even as social life and the life of the social continue to define things. Rock on, I guess.

## Bibliography


Frith, Simon (1981), *Sound Effects: Youth, Leisure, and the Politics of Rock 'n' Roll*, New York: Pantheon Books.

Graeber, David (2001), *Toward an Anthropological Theory of Value*, New York: Palgrave.

Graeber, David (2009), *Direct Action: An Ethnography*, San Francisco: AK Press.

Greene, Shane (2016), *Punk and Revolution: 7 More Interpretations on Peruvian Reality*, Durham: Duke University Press.

Habell-Pallan, Michelle (2004), "'Soy Punkera, y Qué?': Sexuality, Nation, and Punk." in Deborah Pacini Hernández and Eric Zolov (eds), *Rockin' Las Americas: The Global Politics of Rock in Latin America*, 160–78, Pittsburgh: University of Pittsburgh Press.

Hall, Stuart and Tony Jefferson (2006), *Resistance Through Rituals: Youth Subcultures in Post-War Britain*, London: Taylor & Francis.

Hebdige, Dick (1979), *Subculture, The Meaning of Style*, London: Methuen.

Laing, Dave (1985), *One Chord Wonders: Power and Meaning in Punk Rock*, Milton Keynes and Philadelphia: Open University Press.

Lamy, Philip and Jack Levin (1985), "Punk and Middle Class Values: A Content Analysis." *Youth and Society* 17 (2): 157–70.

Leblanc, Lauraine (1999), *Pretty in Punk: Girls' Gender Resistance in a Boys' Subculture*, New Brunswick: Rutgers University Press.

Muñoz, José (2013), "Gimme Gimme This … Gimme Gimme That: Annihilation and Innovation in the Punk Rock Commons." *Social Text* 31 (3): 95–110.

Nikpour, Golnar (2012), "White Riot: Another Failure." *Maximum Rock-n-Roll*, January 17. Electronic document. Available online at http://maximumrocknroll.com/white-riot-another-failure/ (accessed December 28, 2014).

Nyong'o, Tavia (2005), "Punk'd Theory." *Social Text,* 23 (3/4): 19–34.

# PART VI
# INFRASTRUCTURES OF ART

## Preface

An investigation of infrastructure is integral to an anthropological study of the arts concerned with the broader social field in which sounds and shapes are made, encountered, moved, and made meaningful. Often addressed in terms of built form, infrastructure also includes the institutions and networks that provide support for the presentation and circulation of people, goods, resources, capital, and arts. Despite their ubiquity, infrastructures are designed to naturalize their own presence and that of the circulation they enable. As Pierre Bourdieu writes: "Museums could bear the inscription: Entry for art lovers only. But there clearly is no need for such a sign, it all goes without saying" (121). Almost everybody already knows who is welcome and who is sufficiently well trained to understand and appreciate the art on offer. Such recursivity, characteristic of many arts institutions, bundles taste and presentation as if these were simply given rather than cultivated or socially distinguishing. And even as Bourdieu works to reveal these mechanisms, broader infrastructures of circulation remain largely unexamined. As such, it behooves anthropological research on the arts to make infrastructures sites of investigation as much as the works of art themselves, whether those be sounds, performances, or objects. Hence, though generally overlooked until they break, infrastructures provide rich material for anthropological projects that, in aspiring to reveal things taken for granted, make apparent the material processes that move art and its audiences.

Anthropology of art's longest standing, and most oft commented upon infrastructural relationship is with the institution of the ethnographic museum. Though, as George Stocking (1985) points out, the relationship between anthropology as a discipline and the ethnographic museum has been in decline since the 1930s, the association of the artifact with anthropology remains. While this Reader does not emphasize the status of the ethnographic museum, we acknowledge its role for a disciplinary history both in terms of practical encounters and political entanglements. Princely Wunderkammer of sixteenth- and seventeenth-century Europe, which integrated objects gathered by explorers, offer a point of origin for the exhibition of both a curious assortment of artifacts and living humans in the World's Fairs and zoos of the industrial age. With the birth of the European fine arts museum in the late eighteenth century, ethnographic or ethnological museums[1] became the repositories for the flotsam collected from the rest of the world and anthropologists became the keepers and curators of the "primitive." Such endeavors now figure as anthropology's troubling unconscious, taken up and critiqued by artists, even as anthropology has distanced itself from the ethnographic museum (Fusco and Gómez-Peña 1992–3; Holmes 2007; Newkirk 2015). As Stocking writes, "The emergence of new national consciousness in the aftermath of the colonial era … called into question the traditional relationship of objects and others in the museum environment. Both the physical ownership of objects and the right of representing their meaning became issues of contention" (1985: 11). Thus while ethnographic museums continue to be built and filled with objects (Price), the relationship of these institutions to the discipline of anthropology has changed as anthropologists have moved away from scholarly practices grounded in the analysis of collected objects (Boas) toward a practice of extended fieldwork. As Sally Price's piece conveys, with the ethnographic museum embroiled in its own complicated relationship to colonialism and no longer driven by an anthropological project, the anthropologist is now an observer, analyst, and indeed critic of the ethnographic museum *as such*—standing outside the mechanism of the museum, and seemingly also outside of its colonial residues. Hence ethnographic museums are one among other infrastructures that have afforded art's circulation into the globalized present. Equally important in this regard are film industries from Hollywood to Nollywood (Powdermaker; Larkin), the European collection as a marker of status in the U.S. (Bunzl 2014; Marcus), and the refraction of the ethnographic collection in Egypt's modernist painting tradition (Winegar).

Often directed toward objects of everyday use, the process of collecting ascribes a singularity to previously "commonplace things." As Sansi shows, one outcome of such designated content is that the use of the everyday as artistic material casts art and anthropology on a continuum; both, he suggests, are concerned with a common subject or process (participatory art as a "gift") even if the methodological approach and outcome differ. For Kirshenblatt-Gimblett (1998), the occlusion of the contingency of an ethnographic artifact is secured in its presentation as "art." Myers traces how this process unfolds in circulation, revealing the encounter of irreducible cultural logics as aboriginal dream paintings—expressions of a collective—are sold at fine art auctions or as tourist curios, raising concerns of authorship and the limits of a category of "art." While for aborigines, images are materializations of collective dreaming, "To be *art*, an object cannot be collective but should be expressive of a more sublime characteristic that subordinates other properties to individual creativity" (Myers, 303, emphasis added; Gell 2006 [1999]).

Hence taking up infrastructure broadly affords an analysis not only of institutions but also of circulation, value, and meaning. In circulation, objects might change categorization (Chappell 2014; Myers), form (Bosker 2013; Wong 2013), or aesthetic (Larkin). Brian Larkin's discussion of movie piracy makes apparent the economies and modes of circulation that support the structures of art making and presentation, both licit and illicit. Money affords mobility of people, objects, and ideas, supporting institutions and artists alike while bestowing value in direct and indirect ways. Marcus outlines how capital acquired through global resource extraction supports a collection, and an edifice, designed to secure the historical legacy of an oil baron. In undertaking a social analysis of Hollywood by investigating the people who make movies, Hortense Powdermaker found that business drives movie-making, and the interests of capital take precedence over those of artists. Ultimately questions of financial support are entangled with ideological notions about art—the romanticism of the starving artist and "art for art's sake"—that tend to result in a moral gloss on the role of money in the arts, whether private or public. The state is a crucial player in these dynamics. Winegar troubles divisions between Europe and the rest by outlining how Egypt's state-based institutions shape how and what people see, at home and abroad. For young Egyptian artists, tensions between logics of the state and those of the international art world play out through formal qualities of their work and institutional affiliations, reflecting the significance of infrastructure—whether that of the state or the market—not only for *where* things are seen but *what* is seen. And Sansi discusses the parameters of state-sponsored participatory arts projects, addressing what happens when political change affects arts funding and financial support is removed.

As with the other sections of the Reader, attending to infrastructure sustains more general anthropological questions and considerations, not the least of which is infrastructure in and of itself (see Larkin 2013; Star 1999). Emphasizing the specificity of infrastructures of arts is both informed by and contributes to discussions in the field, grounding considerations of current concern such as the relative visibility of infrastructure, its materiality or lack thereof, a poetics of form that girds sensory experience, and the contours and contradictions of belonging.

## Ethnographic exercises

### *Infrastructure fieldnotes*

An ethnographic analysis of art's infrastructures brings into focus the people whose presence is requisite for various institutions to function: guards, artists, donors, visitors, shippers, volunteers, and more. Observe an art space or performance for 1–2 hours, paying attention to its *infrastructure.*

Describe its architecture: what is seen, what is hidden? How is the artwork displayed, and what are the consequences of the physicality of exhibition strategies? At what height is a painting hung, what distance is between artworks, what is the lighting, what kind of information is provided? What do the walls look like—what material, what color, what arrangement? Are there windows or other objects? What can be learned about the history of the building? If it is historic, why was it turned into a museum? If new, are there broader forces of cultural policy or urban and regional development at play?

Discussion questions:

How does the infrastructure affect one's experience in the museum (or at a punk concert or ballet performance)? How does it shape how one acts, how one interacts with the art, and what kind of experience one hopes to have looking at art? Following, what does this tell us about the meaning of art, the role of the museum in society, and the museum visitor?

### *Collection interview*

Interview a classmate about a collection they have (or oversee or work with). This might be a collection of physical objects or a music collection (i.e. digital files). Ask, at minimum:

- What is in the collection?
- How did the collection begin?
- How did the collection grow?
- Where did items come from?
- Is there a particular item that is a favorite? Why? Where did it come from?

- How do you organize the collection? What "story" is told, or what ideas are conveyed, through its organization?
- Is it private, or is it on display for a public audience?

Follow-up questions:

What did you learn about:
- Infrastructure and mobility?
- Material culture?
- Social relationships?
- Beliefs about the world?
- Identity/identification?
- Anything else?

## Note

1 We use these two terms interchangeably as their difference adheres to national histories and languages that are not pertinent for this discussion.

## Further reading

Born, Georgina (1995), *Rationalizing Culture: IRCAM, Boulez, and the Institutionalization of the Musical Avant-Garde*, Berkeley and Los Angeles: University of California Press.

Bunzl, Matti (2014), *In Search of a Lost Avant-Garde: An Anthropologist Investigates the Contemporary Art Museum*, Chicago: University of Chicago Press.

Chappell, Ben (2014), "Barrio Metaxis: Ambivalent Aesthetics in Lowrider Cars of Mexican Americans," in David Lipset and Richard Handler (eds), *Vehicles: Cars, Canoes, and Other Metaphors of Moral Imagination*, 156–77, New York: Berghahn Books.

Dent, Alex (2012), "Piracy, Circulatory Legitimacy, and Neoliberal Subjectivity in Brazil." *Cultural Anthropology* 27 (1): 28–49.

Duncan, Carol (1995), *Civilizing Rituals: Inside Public Art Museums*, New York: Routledge.

Fusco, Coco and Guillermo Gómez-Peña (1992–3), *The Couple in the Cage*, Performance.

Holmes, Rachel (2007), *African Queen: The Real Life of the Hottentot Venus*, New York: Random House.

Kirshenblatt-Gimblett, Barbara (1998), *Destination Culture: Tourism, Museums, and Heritage*, Berkeley: University of California Press.

Larkin, Brian (2013), "The Politics and Poetics of Infrastructure." *Annual Review of Anthropology* 42: 327–43.

Mintz, Sidney W. (1985), *Sweetness and Power: The Place of Sugar in Modern History*, 74–150, New York: Elisabeth Sifton Books.

Newkirk, Pamela (2015), *Spectacle: The Astonishing Life of Ota Benga*, New York: HarperCollins.

Star, Susan Leigh (1999), "The Ethnography of Infrastructure." *American Behavioral Scientist* 43 (3): 377–91.

Stocking, George (ed.) (1985), *Objects and Others: Essays on Museums and Material Culture*, Madison: University of Wisconsin Press.

Thornton, Sarah (2012), *Seven Days in the Art World*, London: Granta Books.

Wong, Winnie Won Yin (2013), *Van Gogh on Demand: China and the Readymade*, Chicago: University of Chicago Press.

# CHAPTER 32
## HOLLYWOOD AND THE U.S.A.
*Hortense Powdermaker*

The anthropologist sees any segment of society as part of a whole; he views Hollywood as a section of the United States of America, and both in the larger frame of Western civilization. The problems of the movie industry are not unique to it. But some characteristics of the modern world have been greatly exaggerated in Hollywood while others are underplayed. Hollywood is therefore not a reflection, but a caricature of selected contemporary tendencies, which, in turn, leave their imprint on the movies. It is a three-way circular interaction between Hollywood, U.S.A. and movies.

Many people would agree with the characterization of our society by the poet W. H. Auden as "The Age of Anxiety." The present generation has known two world wars and is worried about the possibility of a third, even more devastating. We won the last war and are probably the strongest nation, and yet we are insecure in our relations with former enemies and allies. Our country is prosperous and we have demonstrated an enormous capacity for production, but we are worried about a possible recession and unemployment. We live in a fast changing world but have lost faith in our belief that change is always for the better, and that progress is inevitable. We are not so sure of the happy ending.

Art and aesthetic goals have always been less important in our society than either business or humanitarian ones. The artist in all societies has traditionally been a kind of barometer, more sensitive to nuances and changes than others, because he is more deeply immersed in his culture and more interested in its meanings. Since he rarely completely accepts all the conventions, he has a certain degree of objectivity and freedom, which of course also makes him seem different from other men. While the artist's status declined in all Western societies after the Industrial Revolution, many of the European countries with their older traditions of painting, music and literature, accorded him a higher position than he enjoys in the United States. Here, he is still considered peculiar, abnormal, sometimes feminine, and unimportant unless he achieves a commercial success comparable to that of a businessman. A Hollywood caricature of this concept is portrayed in the movie, *A Kiss in the Dark*. The hero, a successful concert pianist, played by David Niven, is scared, nervous, withdrawn, and obviously infantile. He is saved by noticing, with appreciation, a model's legs (those of Jane Wyman). She has no interest in his music and leads him to her world of jazz and trombones. He finally frees himself from being an artist and wins his girl by using his musician's hands to knock down the heroine's fiancé, a former athlete. The hero is now a he-man, throws his practice keyboard away, and embraces the heroine as the train carries them away on a honeymoon.

So in the actual production of movies in Hollywood, the American concept of the unimportance of the artist is magnified. Those who know most about storytelling, who are gifted with imagination, and who have a knowledge of human beings, all raw materials which the camera transforms into a movie, do not have sufficient status to use their abilities. As one director expressed it, "the environment is hostile to them." The environment favors the latest developments in sound and color, but discourages new ideas from its artists. These men, who traditionally have known considerable freedom in expressing themselves, work under the direction of businessmen.

The movies have to earn their living. Unlike some of the fine arts, they are not privately endowed nor are they an esoteric medium for the enjoyment of the few. The goals of business and art are each justifiable and not necessarily irreconcilable. When art meets the needs of a large number of people in our society, it inevitably makes a profit. Some of our most creative popular artists, such as Chaplin, Gershwin, Walt Disney and Irving Berlin, have made fortunes. The problem is not the simple one of art versus business. The artist can contribute to business. But his stock-in-trade is not only his technical know-how: it includes the ability to interpret man to himself. This is true in folk art, popular art and fine art. But it makes little difference to the businessman whether he assuages man's anxieties by interpretation, or whether he exploits them; but the latter is easier. Or, if phoniness brings in money easily, why bother about the details of honesty? The front-office executives are not completely blind to humanitarian issues, but they seem far more interested in profits than in man. Most of them are not conditioned to be otherwise. Artists have a different kind of conditioning. While they are concerned about money, they must also, in order to be reasonably contented, use their gifts to give their interpretations. It has already been indicated that while only relatively few of the Hollywood writers, directors and actors are artists in this sense, they are far more important than the host of mediocre people.

The social organization of Hollywood has, however, permitted the businessman to take over the functions of the artists and to substitute his values for theirs. The movies are the first art form of any kind, popular, folk or fine, to become a trust. Quite early the major companies combined in their efforts to restrain competition and to blacklist those who would not do their bidding. The struggle between the Independents and the organization of the major studios still continues. At the same time movies increasingly make use of a developing technology and of the heritage from theater and literature. Under any circumstances such a combination would create complex problems. In this particular situation, the men with power have known how to exploit the advantages of a trust better than they could utilize the assets of literature and drama. They have not seemed to realize that the efficiency of the factory is possible because it turns out identical products, whether automobiles or coffeepots, and that this principle cannot be applied to the making of movies. Since these businessmen have neither understanding nor respect for the artists' ability, they attempt to negate or destroy it, partly out of ignorance and partly from a desire to satisfy their urge to dominate men. It is only an exceptional executive who does not give the impression that he would have been equally satisfied as a tycoon in any other industry.

Outside of Hollywood there is a certain freedom in choice of goals. A man can decide to be an artist, a scientist or a college professor, which means that most likely he will never be rich. Or he can plan to be a big business executive and have the possibility of acquiring great wealth. In Hollywood the same freedom of choice does not exist, because whatever role the individual plays, the goals of business are paramount. In the country as a whole there is the combination of humanism and materialism. But in Hollywood, money is always more important than man. It is this difference in goals which accounts for much of the deep hostility between the front-office and the artists' group. People with the same goals may argue and differ on how to achieve them, but they speak the same language. People with conflicting goals speak a different language. The real artist in Hollywood cannot be completely satisfied, even though he earns a fortune, if he is not functioning as an artist, and this the head of a trust cannot understand.

# CHAPTER 33
# THE PRODUCTION OF EUROPEAN HIGH CULTURE IN LOS ANGELES: THE J. PAUL GETTY TRUST AS ARTIFICIAL CURIOSITY

*George E. Marcus*

In 1982, when the newly formed J. Paul Getty Trust received the bulk of the personal fortune of J. Paul Getty, the art world anticipated fantastic bids to acquire pieces from the dwindling supply of recognized masterworks, and thus the destabilization of already inflating art markets. When the worth of the Trust's endowment, in the form of 4 million shares of Getty Oil, rose from half a billion dollars to over 2 billion dollars after the sale of Getty Oil to Texaco in 1984, the fear was even more intense. As an operating rather than charitable foundation, the Getty is required to spend 4.5 percent of the average market value of its endowment three out of every four years on its own programs. This would mean over $100 million every year. Through the skill of professional investors and the business experience of its president and directors, the corpus by 1988, when I was a visiting scholar at the Getty, was worth approximately $4 billion. To put this in another frame of reference, of the 2,000 operating foundations in the United States, roughly two-thirds of their total assets are held by the Getty Trust, and the total assets of operating foundations exceed those of both company-sponsored and community foundations together. It is the sheer magnitude of this self-perpetuating pure surplus, expressed in the recitation of such figures, that most distinguishes the Getty, and gives it a social identity, independent of the purposes and hopes of those inside who control the formidable process of spending.

The Getty is at its core a conspicuous mountain of surplus wealth that must be given meaning not by giving to others who justify themselves as scholars, educators, or artists, but by creating self-justification through internal expenditure. This remains the useful project of cultural critique conducted in good faith and in the mode of ethnography that seeks among the discourses, practices, and events of routine existence internal to the Getty a recognition of the problems and possibilities of reasserting the West as valued object through legitimating acts of scholarly narration, analysis, appreciation, and vision.

Being collected by the Getty, I intend to respond critically and appropriately to it as a collector, which is a trope that could conveniently stand for what much ethnography has historically been anyway. Ethnography's claim is to document the derivation of its own objectified critique from that within the discourses of its subjects. The recognition and attribution of counterdiscourse in specific settings is the prime challenge of constructing knowledge in critical ethnography (see Marcus and Fischer 1986).

The following topical discussions are a prolegomenon to writing a full-scale ethnography of the Getty. They are a set of observations from which a motivating argument and critical purpose for an ethnography might be distilled—something I sketch in the concluding section.

J. Paul the great capitalist at least had social grounding, a historically situated class identity. In contrast, his free-floating legacy has no such grounding or given identity. This is the Trust's key problem. As the Getty Trust has most saliently emerged as pure self-perpetuating and growing surplus—the power of concentrated money—not rooted in place, creator, class, or business, how can the story of its relation to something as portentous as the West be narrated to itself or others? There is no doubt that good works can be accomplished in relation to its goal—expenditure assures this—but finally the identity of the Getty itself cannot rest on what it values most—legacy, tradition, the best of the West—because it is alienated from such things by "la part maudite" (Bataille 1988 [1967]) at its core. This is, of course, both its strength and limitation.

## The accursed share domesticated by corporate discipline

The Getty Trust is rooted only in pure surplus—a pile of money given existence by legal fiat and affirmation by the state. The mystique of the Getty, on which it depends despite disavowals, is spending to excess. It thus poses practically the very antithesis of the idea of economy, which constitutes the civilizing process that has made possible the ideas of rationality and order in European history. The fantasy fears that the Getty's uncontrolled spending would destroy the order of art markets are merely one expression of this apocalyptic vision that the Getty surplus suggests. This did not happen, but the fantasy itself still has great power, both outside and inside the organization, that neither the sobriety of budgets nor the demonstration of responsible judgment can completely eradicate.

Williams's creation of ambitious and expensive programs, of course, practically imposed economy on the Getty, which rationalized the implementation of corporate practice. The Trust office is staffed by a number of people with experience in for-profit organizations, and every Center, fiefdom, has an administrator whose job is to extend the discipline of the budget into organizations whose tones are set mainly by former academics, museum professionals, and scholars. While the Getty brings continually into its midst as part of its collecting endeavors "the real thing"—works of art, libraries accumulated by committed collectors, scholars rooted in specific intellectual traditions—it itself is sui generis and unrooted, always returning for authority and meaning to the surplus assets that are its animating core. This creates problems for conducting a critique of the Getty, since it is not easy to locate it in society. For example, one could not do the kind of performance art criticism of the corporate relationships to art that Hans Haacke has produced, since the Getty, while corporately embodied, does not have the same sort of roots in "the military-industrial complex" that Haacke reveals (see Bois et al. 1984).

The scholar at the Getty, seconded from a rooted disciplinary tradition in a university, usually experiences discomfort at an environment that defies sociological description. Of course, part of this discomfort arises from the fact that the scholar is on a daily basis closer to capital than he or she would ever be in a university, whose corporate cultures are usually well screened. But, the blatant corporatism of the Getty is not rooted other than in the free-floating wealth that it tames by inventing economy. The Trust is not tied centrally to family (only Gordon Getty is on the board), ongoing corporate business interests (as in, for example, Mobil Oil and Exxon's patronage of the arts), or place (it has tenuous ties to Los Angeles as urban community), and certainly not to Europe. Finally, then, the Getty is a fund that must be continually spent, and little else at core, an artificial curiosity, placed in the service of cultural revitalization.

## The mystification of taste

Related to the collection/spending function of the Getty as pure surplus are pervasive and complex initial processes of evaluation, and the associated mystique of taste—who has less or more of it—or in Bourdieu's formulation, distinction (1986). On the level of corporate management, there is an obsession with evaluation and assessment, a constant judging of the operations. Elaborate consultation occurs before any move or decision is made. Retreats among directors and lower-level employees, a wrap-up evaluation among scholars, boards of external visitors for all the programs, these are measures of self-worth within the Trust.

Beyond the purely corporate monitoring of the operations at the Getty through evaluation is the construction of aesthetic evaluation within the Center and Museum themselves. The pulse of acquisition is a focal matter of discussion and assessment among Getty employees at all levels—janitors, secretaries, curators, guards—especially as corridor talk. Tension builds up around the announcement of acquisition of artworks in particular, since this is the basis of much of the attention the Getty receives in the media, and the dealing to acquire works at bargain prices in the millions is highly secret and competitive, subject to rumor. Here the hierarchy of taste or distinction emerges. Distinction is defined by competence at appreciating certain acquisitions as cultural artifacts, and there is great variation in the ability to do this among Getty personnel. Employees in various occupations at the Getty call upon their resources/backgrounds to form an opinion about an acquired work or a visitor's scholarship. A hierarchy emerges across a range of social class backgrounds that Getty employees represent.

Finally, while there is little doubt that the Getty is devoted to very elitist projects, ones that require cultivation, appreciation, exclusive sensibility, and connoisseurship, still much of this is unmentionable in its day-to-day life within mass liberal society. At the Museum and the Center, unmistakably elitist effects and gestures are continually produced, especially by the assertion of exclusivity—attendance at Center seminars is by invitation only; the Getty still advertises its programs quietly; the Museum has a famous policy about admission by advanced reservation; and the new Brentwood complex will be elevated and hidden from public view like so much L.A. elite life. Yet each of these signs of elitism can and are explained away pragmatically—fire laws, city zoning regulations, opportunism account for the appearance of exclusivity and exclusion. The production of elitist effects, in spite of such pragmatic and honest explanations, is one of the fascinating puzzles concerning how the Getty establishes its distinction against the grain, so to speak.

The pervasive elitist effect may be irresistible to the eye of the beholder; it may be the result of internal policy conspiratorially formulated; or it may be a function of contradiction between major and minor keys of desire within the Getty that pits bureaucratic rationality and its conceits against the enhanced mystification of value in the restricted display of the scholarly and artifactual treasures which it collects. Without authoritative gatekeeping, which may be coincidentally necessary anyhow from a purely pragmatic concern, a hierarchy of taste could not exist. And it is on the existence of such a hierarchy that the strength of an internal belief in a totalized object such as Western culture depends, as anyone familiar with the ethnographic literature on secret societies (and their fetishes) would recognize.

## Absent others and the Getty's rootlessness

A good deal of energy is spent at the Getty keeping certain forms of otherness (especially cross-cultural otherness) out, or at a distance. This is communicated not through an expressed hostility to that which might call into question the possibility of art or tradition, but through a studied indifference—"not what we do." The Getty's detachment from place and community as well as limitations at the Center on the way that genres are blurred in its commitment to interdisciplinarity are indices of such practices.

Finally, the work of keeping others absent prevents the Getty from focusing upon its own definitive otherness in relation to the legitimizing, central cultural tradition to which its efforts are directed. The Getty poses the question on what basis European high culture can be sustained in late 20th-century American/global society by earnest simulation. But for whom, finally? To teach a heritage to the Latino-Asian masses of the new L.A. and beyond? Or to restore nerve to a debilitated bourgeois elite for whom the wholeness of the past has a nostalgic appeal? In any case, do the scholars who come to the Getty really care? That is, the connoisseurs and others who serve it by serving themselves and accept being temporarily acquired by the constantly active, expending, reproducing wealth, legally constituted and corporately managed for the "general good."

## Earnest Faking

Questions about the possibility of fakes in the Getty collection have been present through its history, although this form of assault and scandal mongering in the world of fine arts collecting is common to other museums as well. The distinction of such collectors' taste can be challenged, not by what they collect, but by questioning the authenticity of what is collected. J. Paul himself was obsessed with the authentication of certain of his prize pieces which he acquired as bargains during the depression years and after. The contemporary Getty Museum has had to fend off several such charges that it had purchased fakes, most prominently, the scandal concerning the large Greek kouros that it acquired in the early 1980s.

But faking in a more obvious sense stands for the Getty in the signature building by which it is known—the reconstruction of the Roman ruin at Herculaneum. The scholarly integrity of the reproduction belies a fake, but in the Los Angeles landscape where the idiosyncratic production of such fakes has been a tradition, the Getty Museum has ironically been taken for one.

What kind of critical practice might go beyond the mere debunking and subversion of the proclaimed purposes of the powerful (often conservative) producers of cultural value to engage them in debate through provocative attempts to redeem alternative possibility within embedded contradictions that they themselves express but misrecognize?

The question is indeed how to recall the past, reconstruct it, simulate it, preserve it free of nostalgia or cynicism. The Getty lives the dialectic of fake and authenticity, but does not reflect upon it. To challenge the organization to pursue its goals through the use of contradiction that it embodies is the goal of criticism. Such criticism would provoke responses with credibility, and this must begin with a representation/argument, which if not completely true to the polyphony of voices and interests inside the Getty, at least provokes response. Specifically, critical ethnography challenges the Getty to create Europe by working from its own otherness and difference, rather than seeking respectability from its object. It is destined to operate in such terms anyhow, since the pure surplus that *is* the Getty exceeds any effort to cover over this essential basis of its identity. Not only might it as well try to proceed to construct high culture in the late 20th century by its own difference from it, but only thus will it be able to do so for all its publics without patronization, contempt, or regret.

## References

Bataille, Georges (1988 [1967]), *La Part Maudite*, Paris: Les Éditions Minuit. [Translated as *The Accursed Share*, vol. I, New York: Zone Books]

Bois, Yves-Alain, Douglas Crimp, and Rosalind Krauss (1984), "A Conversation with Hans Haacke." *October* 30: 23–48.

Bourdieu, Pierre (1986), *Distinction*, Cambridge: Harvard University Press.

Marcus, George E. and Michael M. J. Fischer (1986), *Anthropology as Cultural Critique: An Experimental Moment in the Human Sciences*, Chicago: University of Chicago Press.

# CHAPTER 34
## DEGRADED IMAGES, DISTORTED SOUNDS: NIGERIAN VIDEO AND THE INFRASTRUCTURE OF PIRACY

*Brian Larkin*

In Kano, the economic center of northern Nigeria, media piracy is part of the "organizational architecture" of globalization (Sassen 2002), providing the infrastructure that allows media goods to circulate. Infrastructures organize the construction of buildings, the training of personnel, the building of railway lines, and the elaboration of juridicolegal frameworks without which the movement of goods and people cannot occur. But once in place, infrastructures generate possibilities for their own corruption and parasitism. Media piracy is one example of this in operation. It represents the potential of technologies of reproduction—the supple ability to store, reproduce, and retrieve data—when shorn from the legal frameworks that limit their application. It depends heavily on the flow of media from official, highly regulated forms of trade but then develops its own structures of reproduction and distribution external and internal to the state economy.

It is through this generative quality that pirate infrastructure is expressive of a paradigmatic shift in Nigerian economy and capital and represents the extension of a logic of privatization into everyday life. Piracy's negative characteristics are often commented on: its criminality, the erosion of property rights it entails, and its function as a pathology of information processing, parasitically derivative of legal media flows (Chesterman and Lipman 1988; Coombe 1998). As important as these questions are, the structural focus on legal issues tends to obscure the mediating nature of infrastructure itself. In the Nigerian case, this is seen most strikingly in the rise of a new video industry that makes feature-length films directly for domestic video consumption (see Larkin 2000; Haynes 2000; Ukadike 2000; Ukah 2003). This new industry has pioneered new film genres and generated an entirely novel mode of reproduction and distribution that uses the capital, equipment, personnel, and distribution networks of pirate media. These Nigerian videos are a legitimate media form that could not exist without the infrastructure created by its illegitimate double, pirate media.

In recent years, then, there has been a wholesale shift in which many entrepreneurs previously involved in the distribution of pirate material have switched to the reproduction and dissemination of legal media. The mass importation of foreign music and films brought about the capital and professional expertise that facilitated the rise of a local film industry. This wandering over the lines that separate the legal from the nonlegal has been a common experience for urban Africans, who have been progressively disembedded from the infrastructures linking them to the official world economy and instead have poured energy into developing informal networks—equally global—that facilitate traffic in economic and cultural goods outside the established institutions of world trade (Simone 2000, 2001; Bayart, Ellis, and Hibou 1999; Mbembe 2001).

In addition to generating new economic networks, piracy, like all infrastructural modes, has distinct material qualities that influence the media that travel under its regime of reproduction. Piracy imposes particular conditions on the recording, transmission, and retrieval of data. Constant copying erodes data storage, degrading image and sound, overwhelming the signal of media content with the noise produced by the means of reproduction. Pirate videos are marked by blurred images and distorted sound, creating a material screen that filters audiences' engagement with media technologies and their senses of time, speed, space, and contemporaneity. In this way, piracy creates an aesthetic, a set of formal qualities that generates a particular sensorial experience of media marked by poor transmission, interference, and noise. Contemporary scholars of technology returning to the Frankfurt school have stressed that technology's operation on the body is a key factor in producing a sense of shock—the complex training of the human sensorium associated with modem urbanism (Benjamin 1999; Crary 2000; Doane 2002; Hansen 1995, 2000; Kracauer 1995; Schivelbusch 1986). This work is crucial in understanding the phenomenological and cognitive effects of technology when it is working at its optimum. What is less discussed is how technology influences through its failure as much as through its successes. Yet the inability of technologies to perform the operations they were assigned must be subject to the same critical scrutiny as their achievements. Breakdown and failure are, of course, inherent in all technologies, but in societies such as Nigeria, where collapse is often the default state of technological existence, they take on a far greater material and political presence.

Rather than elide pirate infrastructure by using it as a window into legal questions of intellectual property, I wish to foreground it. If infrastructures represent attempts to order, regulate, and rationalize society, then breakdowns in their operation, or the rise of provisional and informal infrastructures, highlight the failure of that ordering and the recoding that takes its place. By subjecting the material operation of piracy and its social consequences to scrutiny, it becomes clear that pirate infrastructure is a powerful mediating force that produces new modes of organizing sensory perception, time, space, and economic networks.

## The corruption of infrastructure

Piracy's success lies in its own infrastructural order that preys on the official distribution of globalized media, thus making it part of the corruption of infrastructure. By *corruption* I mean the pirating of a system's mode of communication—the viruses that attach to other kinds of official or recognized movement. Technological infrastructure creates material channels that organize the movement of energy, information, and economic and cultural goods between societies but at the same time creates possibilities for new actions.

Piracy operates as a corruption of communications infrastructures that develops its own circuits of distribution using officially organized media. Films made in Hollywood and intended for distribution in an organized, domestic circuit are copied by pirates; sent to Asia or the Middle East, where they are subtitled; recopied in large numbers as videocassettes, video CDs (VCDs are the dominant technology for media storage in much of Asia), or DVDs; and then reshipped mainly within the developing world. In recent years, as Nigeria has become progressively disembedded from the official global economy (with the single exception of its oil industry), it has become ever more integrated into a parallel, unofficial world economy that reorients Nigeria toward new metropoles such as Dubai, Singapore, and Beirut.

Let us take the example the sign for Alhaji B. K.'s video shop in the Kofar Wambai market in Kano, Nigeria. Kofar Wambai is best known for the sale of thread used in the elaborate embroidery of the long Hausa gown, the *babban riga*. Whole tracts of the market are suffused in the bright colors of thread hanging from the stall doorways, but in one section is lane after lane of small shops specializing in the reproduction and wholesale distribution of audio- and videocassettes: Indian, Sudanese, Western, and Hausa music; Islamic preaching; and Indian, Western, and Hausa videocassettes.

Cassette sellers at Kofar Wambai are represented by the Kano Cassette Sellers Recording and Co-operative Society Ltd. (Kungiyar Gawa Kai Ta Masu Sayar Da Kaset Da Dauka Ta Jihar Kano), a society whose headquarters is at Kofar Wambai but whose members spill out far beyond the confines of the market. The success of Kano's cassette reproduction industry is grounded in three developments: First, in 1981, the Motion Pictures Association of America (MPAA) suspended the distribution of Hollywood films to Nigeria. This was in response to the seizure of MPAA assets by the Nigerian government in an attempt to indigenize the control of Nigerian companies. Second, the oil boom of the late 1970s boosted consumption, allowing for the mass dissemination of cassette-based technologies. Finally, the longstanding position of Kano at the apex of wide-ranging transnational trading networks facilitated the quick exploitation of these possibilities and the forging of a distribution network that stretches over northern Nigeria and beyond. The subsequent rise of piracy means that far from disappearing, Hollywood films have become available at a speed and volume as never before.

The everyday practice of piracy in Kano was based around the mass distribution of the two most popular drama forms, Indian and Hollywood films, and the reproduction of televised Hausa dramas and Islamic religious cassettes. Nearly all of those who might be described as pirates were at the same time involved in the duplication and sale of legitimate media, and the organization that emerged made Kano the regional distribution center for electronic media in northern Nigeria and the wider Hausaphone area (which covers parts of Chad, Cameroon, Benin, Ghana, and the Sudan). The system is this: the main dealers are based at centers in Kano, like Kofar Wambai market. They then sell to distributors in other northern cities, and these in turn supply smaller urban and rural dealers who provide goods for itinerant peddlers. The system is based on a complex balance of credit and trust; and although it depends, in part, on piracy, it has evolved into a highly organized, extensive distribution system for audio- and videocassettes. The success of this new form of distribution has not been lost on the government, which—though critical of piracy—has used cassette distribution as a way of spreading political messages.[1] As Alhaji Musa Na Sale, president of the cassette sellers association, told me, if something is popular, "even the nomads will hear it." The decentralized nature of this distribution system means that neither the government nor the association knows exactly how many people are tied to the industry, especially given its massive expansion with the rise of Hausa video films.

Hausa distributors have had to rely on Lebanese and Indian traders for access to foreign videos that were coming from the Persian Gulf. In the 1990s, these videos often had the distributor's name superimposed on the tape itself: for example, *Excellence Kano* for Hollywood films and *Al-Mansoor, Dubai* for Indian ones. Hollywood films were imported to Kano directly from the Middle East or transported north from Lagos. Because of the great popularity of

Indian films among the Hausa (Larkin 1997, 2003), Kano was and is the main clearinghouse for Indian films. This traffic is controlled by two primary distributors, both based in Kano. For many years the trade was routed through Dubai, and it was common to watch Indian films with advertisements scrolling across the bottom of the screen announcing "Al Mansoor's video" followed by a long list of his many shops in Dubai, Abu Dhabi, and other parts of the gulf, along with their telephone, telex, and fax numbers. These videos often found their way to the Kano television station, CTV, where announcements for Al Mansoor's many video shops sometimes obliterated the Arabic and English subtitles at the bottom of the screen.

With the recent emergence of video CDs, the routes of the market for Indian film have changed considerably. According to one Indian distributor, the market is now oriented toward Pakistan, where VCD plants make high-quality dubs of Indian films. Master copies are shipped via DHL to Kano, where they are then transferred to tape and sold in bulk to Hausa distributors. I was told the gap between a film's release in India and its appearance in Kano could be as little as seven days.[2] American films are pirated through similar networks. They are copied illegally in the United States and shipped to Dubai or Beirut, often arriving in Nigeria while they are still on first-run release in the United States. One Jean-Claude Van Damme film I watched had Chinese subtitles superimposed over Arabic ones, providing a visible inscription of the routes of media piracy. Frequently U.S. videos contain a message scrolling across the bottom of the film every few minutes stating: "Demo tape only. Not for rental or sale. If you have rented or purchased this cassette call 1-800 NO COPYS (1-800-662-6787).[3] Federal law provides severe civil and criminal penalties for unauthorized duplication or distribution."

Kofar Wambai is the apex of a formal, highly ordered system of reproduction and distribution for media goods in northern Nigeria and is one example of the ways in which media piracy generates new infrastructures of the parallel economy in Nigeria. It is part of a much larger process whereby the Nigerian economy has split between a traditional official economy oriented toward legal participation in the international division of labor and an unofficial economy, each one with its own infrastructures and networks, sometimes overlapping, sometimes opposed.

## Breakdown

In Nigeria, the ubiquity of technological breakdown and repair imposes a particular experience of technology and its cultural effects. Contemporary urban theory, perhaps understandably, has been less quick to explore these cultural articulations, focusing instead on the reconfiguration of urban space brought about by new media. Paul Virilio, in a typically contradictory fashion, lobbies fiercely for both sides of the argument. On the one hand, he proclaims with dystopian excess that the immediacy of real-time technologies has fundamentally transformed our ability to understand time and space. Instead of being marked by duration or the unfolding of events in succession, time, he argues, is now exposed instantaneously (Virilio 1997, 2000). Events that take place at a distance are experienced immediately thanks to the telepresence brought about by real-time technologies. Speed here is the crucial dimension. Speed conditions our experience of time, producing temporal compression and allowing us to act at a distance. Cities that used to be organized around entrances and exits—nodes that regulate the exchange of people and goods—have given way to the immaterial interface of information exchange. This is certainly the case in contemporary Nigeria, where a series of technological changes over the last ten years, including the rise of satellite television, the growing penetration of Internet culture, and the belated arrival of mobile phone networks, has created new technological portals through which Nigerians engage with one another and the world beyond.

The difficulty with this side of Virilio is his assumption that the experiential transformations he analyzes presume a stable, smoothly operating technological infrastructure. The transition he identifies is totalizing, penetrating homogeneously and organizing universally. It partakes of a world of fast-operating computers, clear-picture televisions, and constant telecommunication signals. But Virilio (2003) also notes that with the invention of the train came the derailment, and few thinkers have been as insistent as he is that the development of technology is tied to the development of catastrophe. My interest in technological collapse is somewhat different. It is not in extravagant spectacles like collapsing bridges or exploding space shuttles but in the small, ubiquitous experience of breakdown as a condition of technological existence. In Nigeria, cars, televisions, VCRs, buses, and motorbikes are often out of service. Even when they work, electricity supplies are unreliable and beset by power surges that damage consumer equipment. NEPA, the Nigerian Electric Power Authority, is famously known by the epithet "Never Expect Power Always," and phone lines are expensive and difficult to obtain. Poverty and the disorganization of the Nigerian economy mean that consumer technologies such as scooters and cars arrive already used and worn out. After their useful life in Belgium or Holland, cars are exported to Nigeria as "new" second-hand vehicles.[4] After these vehicles arrive in Nigeria, worn parts are repaired, dents are banged out, and paint is resprayed to remake and "tropicalize" them. This is, of course, a temporary state of affairs. Other parts expire, second-hand parts break down, while local "innovations" and adjustments designed to make cars, televisions, and VCRs work fail. A cycle of breakdown, repair, and breakdown again is the condition of existence for many technologies in Nigeria. As a consequence, Nigeria employs a vast army of people who specialize in repairing and reconditioning broken technological goods, since the need for repair is frequent and the cost of it cheap (Sundaram 1999; Verrips and Myers 2001).

Virilio's account of the experience of speed in contemporary urbanization is highly relevant to societies such as Nigeria, but perhaps not in the ways he imagines. There is no question, for instance, that new technologies have resulted in profound temporal acceleration for Nigerians. But the poor material infrastructure of Nigeria ensures that as the speed of Nigerian life increases, so too does the gap between *actual* and *potential* acceleration, between what technologies *can* do and what they *do* do. Thus, even as life speeds up, the experience of technological marginalization intensifies, and the gap between how fast society is moving and how fast it could move becomes a site of considerable political tension.

The poor condition of infrastructure and the ubiquity of breakdown bring about their corollary: repair as a cultural mode of existence for technology. This is a consequence of both poverty and innovation. Breakdown and repair structure the ability of subjects to use and be used by technologies and also these subjects' sense of time and place. The culture of repair rests on the experience of duration in the everyday use of technology. Breakdown creates a temporal experience that has less to do with dizzying, real-time global integration than with waiting for e-mail messages to open, machines to be repaired, or electricity to be restored. In

Nigeria, all technologies are variously subject to a constant cycle of breakdown and repair; the promise of technological prosthesis is thwarted by the common experience of technological collapse. Each repair enforces another waiting period, an often frustrating experience of duration brought about by the technology of speed itself. The temporal experience of slowness comes as a consequence of speed-producing technologies, so that speed and acceleration, deceleration and stasis are relative, continually shifting states.

In fig. 34.1 we see the stringing together of cassette recorders used to dub audiocassettes in Kano. The covers—intended to protect the cassette while recording—have been ripped off for ease of ejection. Wires hang loosely, sometimes tangled in bunches; many machines have their casings broken, and all are exposed to the harmattan winds that deposit layers of dust on every surface of the city. Piracy depends on material modes of reproduction such as these. The operations of piracy create material effects on the storage and retrieval of data and sensorial effects on notions of space, time, culture, and the body. In Nigeria, the infrastructure for media, especially pirate media, is often marked by disrepair and noise.

Nigerian dealers in the legal and illegal reproduction of media record data on cheap tapes with low-quality machines. This information is retrieved for the most part through old VCRs, televisions, and cassette players marked by distortion and interference. Watching, say, Hollywood or Indian films on VCRs in Nigeria, where there is no official distribution of nonpirate media, means necessarily watching the dub of a dub of a dub. As the same dealers, using the same equipment and same blank cassettes, dub Hausa video films, the result is that the visual standard for pirate media remains in place. Pirated images have a hallucinogenic quality. Detail is destroyed as realist representation fades into pulsating, pure light. Facial

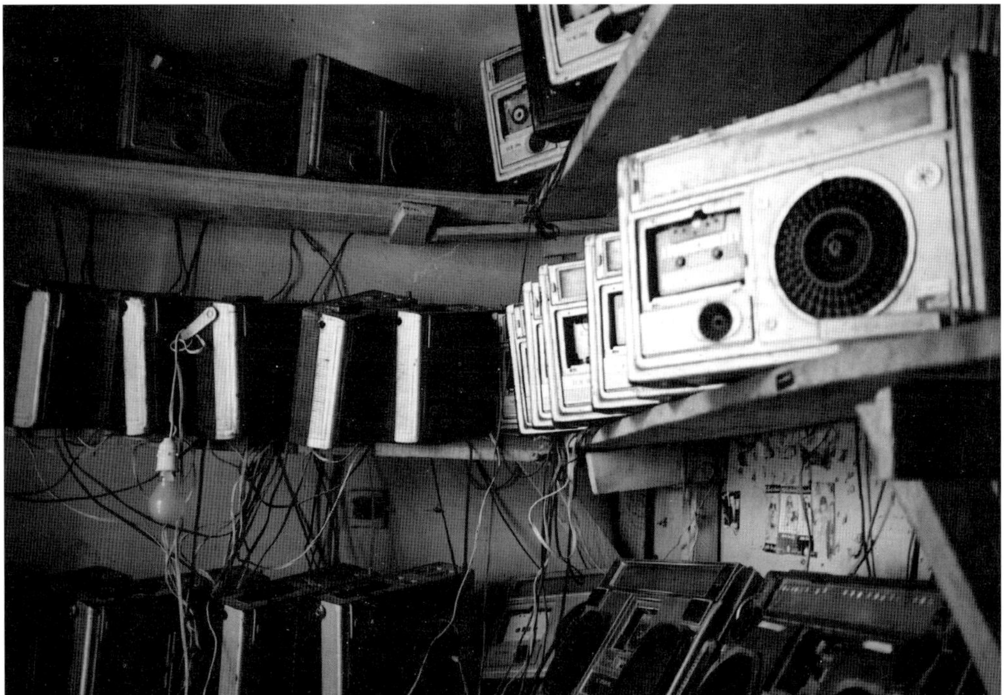

**Figure 34.1** Cassette recorders used to dub audiocassettes in Kano © Brian Larkin

features are smoothed away, colors are broken down into constituent tones, and bodies fade into one another. Reproduction takes its toll, degrading the image by injecting dropouts and bursts of fuzzy noise, breaking down dialogue into muddy, often inaudible sound. This distortion is often heard in the vibrating shrillness of the tape players used by *masu saida kaset,* itinerant cassette hawkers who travel around the city selling eclectic collections of music

The quality of the tape player used by these cassette sellers is standard in Nigeria. As the seller travels, the cassette player blares out Indian film sound tracks, Islamic preaching, or Hausa songs at such a high volume that the signal degenerates into the pure vibration of the machine. In this, the machine actually mimics the sound of live musical performances in Kano, which often rely on the distorted amplification of microphones, loudspeakers, and portable generators.[5] This distortion affects many media in Nigeria. Film prints, for instance, arrive at the end of long, picaresque journeys that begin in the metropolitan cinematic centers of India or Europe and cross the cinema halls of many countries before reaching the Nigerian circuit. There, they are often shown until they literally fall apart. All are scratched and heavily damaged, full of surprising and lengthy jump cuts where film has stuck in the projector and burned. Although the image and sound of video are poor, Ghanaian video filmmaker Willy Akuffo has warned video makers against a nostalgia for the "quality" of film that forgets how terrible film prints actually were. As a former projectionist, he had to deal with repairing burned film and refixing previous repairs that the prints had accumulated on their journey to Africa.[6] Likewise, the quality of video projection, with its low-resolution, ghostly images, can be highly variable depending on the age and condition of the equipment. In the poorer cinemas that converted to video in the mid-1990s, there were terrible problems with tracking and inaudible sound. The projected image often filled only a portion of the cinema screen or would be distorted into an hourglass shape. At other times, the corners of the image vibrated as if the screen were a photograph peeling off.[7]

The infrastructure of reproduction, like most contemporary infrastructures in Nigeria, is marked by cheapness, faulty operation, and constant repair. "All data flows," the media theorist Friedrich Kittler (1999: 14) reminds us, "must pass through the bottleneck of the signifier," and in so doing they are vulnerable to being "engulfed by the noise of the real." The "real" here is precisely the fuzziness of cinematic images or the hissing of tape recorders—the noise produced by the medium of transmission itself as it encodes and disseminates data across space and time. Yuri Tsivian (1994) has termed this effect the "semiotics of interference" and has analyzed the operation of early Russian cinema, arguing that the physical conditions of media exhibition—scratches on the film and noise and vibrations from projectors—became part of the "message" of films themselves.[8] For Nigerians, the costs of consuming and producing world media require operating on the margins of technology. Distortion on an audio tape, like dropouts on a video or a slow connection to the Internet, are the material conditions of existence for media. While media infrastructure creates the reality of being ever more connected to a globalized world, it does so by emphasizing Nigerians' marginalization at the same time. Electricity blackouts, snowy television images, difficulties getting international phone lines, and distorted loudspeakers on cassette players all create a technological veil of semiotic distortion for Nigerians.

Some of this distortion is taken for granted, rendered invisible to people by its ubiquity. It is clear, for instance, that many of the most popular transnational media forms, such as sports, action films, wrestling, and Indian films, are highly visual and thus capable of overcoming both linguistic differences and audio degradation. But this degradation is rarely commented on. Instead, what these films evoke is the fantasy of other countries where deficiencies in infrastructure are believed not to exist. For many northern Nigerians, Saudi Arabia is a place where electricity always flows, where roads have no potholes, and where hospitals are of the highest quality—just as everyone in Europe and America is thought to own televisions and mobile phones.[9] These fantasies represent implicit and sometimes explicit critiques of the failures of the Nigerian state to provide basic infrastructures for everyday life.

## Conclusion

In his exhaustive study of the rise of print, the historian Adrian Johns (1998) argues that piracy, rather than being an aberration of an "original" mode of text production, is central to the way print operates and spreads over time and space. The qualities we now associate with print—its fixity, guarantee of authorship, and commodity form—were not inherent in the technology but the result of a social compact, the institution of a technological order of reality. Johns is instructive in reminding us that, in many parts of the world, media piracy is not a pathology of the circulation of media forms but its prerequisite. In many places, piracy is the only means by which certain media—usually foreign—are available. And in countries like Nigeria, the technological constraints that fuel pirate media provide the industrial template through which other, nonpirate media are reproduced, disseminated, and consumed.

Piracy and the wider infrastructure of reproduction it has generated reveal the organization of contemporary Nigerian society. They show how the parallel economy has migrated onto center stage, overlapping and interpenetrating with the official economy, mixing legal and illegal regimes, uniting social actors, and organizing common networks. This infrastructure creates its own modes of spatiality, linking Nigeria into new economic and social networks. Piracy means that Nigerian media production and circulation no longer depend on the intervention of the state (colonial or postcolonial) but are captured by the logic of privatization and gradually extend over differing areas of social experience. Sundaram (1999: 61), writing about everyday electronic culture in India—self-trained programmers who build computers and servers by cobbling together second-hand computer parts—refers to this as "recycled modernity," one that is "everyday in its imaginary, pirate in its practice, and mobile in its innovation." Rem Koolhaas (Koolhaas et al. 2001) has recently explored a similar phenomenon in the collapse of traffic systems in Lagos, a city overwhelmed by an increase in cars and a lack of roads. There, jams and bottlenecks force detours through "non-flow" areas, spreading traffic off the planned grids and expanding the motorable space of the city. As cars back up for longer periods of time, they create markets for hawkers. Over time the markets get formalized, roadside mosques are marked out to service the workers, and new infrastructures emerge to paper over the inefficiencies of the old.

The infrastructure of reproduction created by piracy generates material and sensorial effects on both media and their consumers. Cheap tape recorders, old televisions, blurred videos that are the copy of a copy of a copy—these are the material distortions endemic to the reproduction of media goods in situations of poverty and illegality, and they shape the ways these media take on cultural value and act on individuals and groups. The dialectic of technological breakdown and repair imposes its own cultural experience of modernity, an alternative speeding up and stasis, and a world where gaps in space and time are continually annihilated and reinforced.

## Notes

1. After the Maitatsine riots of 1981, the Nigerian government circulated a video of the mass arrest of followers of the millenarian leader Maitatsine as a warning to other followers. Musa Na Sale, one of the most prominent cassette dealers working with traditional Hausa singers, said that he would meet with singers and *malams* (religious leaders whose teachings were sold on cassette) to instruct them as to "what the government needs to talk about and what the government doesn't want."
2. This could be true, but there is likely an element of boastfulness to this claim. In 1993 when distribution was still by cassette, I was told that films could arrive in Kano as little as seven days after their release in India. In 2002, I was told by the same distributor (but a different person) that the reason for the shift to VCDs was to increase speed and quality and that the problem with videos was that they could take up to a month or more to be received from Dubai.
3. This is now a number for information about new drugs.
4. For an interesting comparative example, see the trade in second-hand clothing analyzed by Karen Hansen (2000). Also, Gerald Lombardi's 1999 study of computer use in Brazil includes a fascinating discussion of the informal (and illegal) market in phone lines that feeds off poor infrastructure.
5. Christopher Waterman (1990) points out that distortion by amplifiers became such an accepted part of live performance that musicians would intentionally destroy new loudspeakers to achieve the desired buzzing sound. I thank Andrew Apter for reminding me of this.
6. Birgit Meyer reminded me that Akuffo described this problem with poor film prints at a workshop organized by the International Study Commission of Media, Religion, and Culture (19–27 May 2000, Accra, Ghana).
7. Yet despite these problems, cassettes remain the more popular medium in northern Nigeria. In January 2002, when I asked Hausa video filmmakers why they had not switched to video CDs to distribute their movies, they pointed out that the technology was not yet widely available in the north, in part because damage to a VCD could ruin the entire disc, while damage to a tape created only passing moments of fuzziness.
8. James Ferguson (1999) makes an interesting but different argument on the role of "noise" in globalization. Ferguson focuses on the traffic in cultural meanings, arguing that cities are culturally "noisy" in that all sorts of forms of cultural flows clash and are available to urban dwellers. But Ferguson's (1999: 208) central question concerns "which of the bits floating in the swirl of events does any given social actor bear."
9. Writing about the cosmopolitan sexual relations between Hausa *'yan daudu* (men who act like women) and men in Saudi Arabia, Rudolf Gaudio (1996) argues that when these *'yan daudu* return from Saudi Arabia, they parade their sophistication and cultural savoir faire—part of which involves raving "about the creature comforts that Saudi Arabia [has] to offer: telephones, air conditioning, a constant supply of electricity and running water. *'Ba abin da babu'* they would say, 'there's nothing that isn't there.'" See also O'Brien 1999.

## References


Bayart, Jean-François, Stephen Ellis, and Béatrice Hibou (1999), *The Criminalization of the State in Africa*, Bloomington: Indiana University Press.

Benjamin, Walter (1999), *The Arcades Project*, Cambridge: Harvard University Press.

Chesterman, John and Andy Lipman (1988), *The Electronic Pirates: DIY Crimes of the Century*, London: Routledge.

Coombe, Rosemary J. (1998), *The Cultural Life of Intellectual Properties: Authorship, Appropriation, and the Law*, Durham, NC: Duke University Press.

Crary, Jonathan (2000), *Suspensions of Perception: Attention, Spectacle, and Modern Culture*, Cambridge, MA: MIT Press.

Doane, Mary Ann (2002), *The Emergence of Cinematic Time: Modernity, Contingency, the Archive*, Cambridge: Harvard University Press.

Ferguson, James (1999), *Expectations of Modernity: Myths and Meanings of Urban life on the Zambian Copperbelt*, Berkeley: University of California Press.

Gaudio, Rudolf (1996), "Men who Talk like Women: Language, Gender, and Sexuality in Hausa Muslim Society." PhD diss., Stanford University.

Hansen, Karen Tranberg (2000), *Salaula: The World of Secondhand Clothing and Zambia*, Chicago: University of Chicago Press.

Hansen, Miriam (1995), "America, Paris, the Alps: Kracauer (and Benjamin) on Cinema and Modernity," in Leo Charney and Vanessa R. Schwartz (eds), *Cinema and the Invention of Modern Life*, Berkeley: University of California Press.

Hansen, Miriam (2000), "The Mass Production of the Senses: Classical Cinema as Vernacular Modernism," in Christine Gledhill and Linda Williams (eds), *Reinventing Film Studies*, London: Arnold.

Haynes, Jonathan (ed.) (2000), *Nigerian Video Films*, Africa Series no. 73, Athens: Ohio University Center for International Studies.

Johns, Adrian (1998), *The Nature of the Book: Print and Knowledge in the Making*, Chicago: University of Chicago Press.

Kittler, Friedrich (1999), *Gramophone, Film, Typewriter*, Stanford: Stanford University Press.

Koolhaas, Rem, Stefano Boeri, Sanford Kwinter, Nadia Tazi, and Hans Ulrich Obrist (2001), *Mutations*, Bordeaux, France: Arc en rêve centre d'architecture.

Kracauer, Siegfried (1995), *The Mass Ornament: Weimar Essays*, trans. Thomas Y. Levin, Cambridge: Harvard University Press.

Larkin, Brian (1997), "Indian films and Nigerian Lovers: Media and the Creation of Parallel Modernities." *Africa* 67 (3): 406–40.

Larkin, Brian (2000), "Hausa Dramas and the Rise of Video Culture in Nigeria," in Jonathan Haynes (ed.), *Nigerian Video Films*, Africa Series no. 73, Athens: Ohio University Center for International Studies.

Larkin, Brian (2003), "Itineraries of Indian Cinema: African Videos, Bollywood, and Global Media," in Ella Shohat and Robert Stam (eds), *Multiculturalism, Postcoloniality, and Transnational Media*, New Brunswick, NJ: Rutgers University Press.

Lombardi, Gerald S. (1999), "Computer Networks, Social Networks, and the Future of Brazil." PhD diss., New York University.

Mbembe, Achille (2001), *On the Postcolony*, Berkeley: University of California Press.

O'Brien, Susan (1999), "Pilgrimage, Power, and Identity: The Role of the *hajj* in the Lives of Nigerian Hausa *bori* Adepts." *Africa Today* 46 (3/4): 11–40.

Sassen, Saskia (ed.) (2002), *Global Networks, Linked Cities*, New York: Routledge.

Schivelbusch, Wolfgang (1986), *The Railway Journey: The Industrialization of Time and Space in the Nineteenth Century*, Berkeley: University of California Press.

Simone, AbdouMaliq (2000), "Going South: African Immigrants in Johannesburg," in Sarah Nuttall and Cheryl-Ann Michael (eds), *Senses of Culture: South African Culture Studies*, Oxford: Oxford University Press.

Simone, AbdouMaliq (2001), "On the Worlding of African Cities." *African Studies Review* 44 (2): 15–41.
Sundaram, Ravi (1999), "Recycling Modernity: Pirate Electronic Cultures in India." *Third Text* 47: 59–65.
Tsivian, Yuri (1994), *Early Cinema in Russia and its Cultural Reception*, London: Routledge.
Ukadike, N. Frank (2000), "Images of the "Reel" Thing: African Video-films and the Emergence of a New Cultural Art." *Social Identities* 6: 243–61.
Ukah, Asonzeh F.-K. (2003), "Advertising God: Nigerian Christian video-films and the power of consumer culture." *Journal of Religion in Africa* 33: 203–31.
Verrips, Jojada and Birgit Meyer (2001), "Kwaku's Car: The Struggles and Stories of a Ghanaian Long-distance Taxi Driver," in David Miller (ed.), *Car Cultures*, Oxford: Berg.
Virilio, Paul (1997), *Open Sky*, London: Verso.
Virilio, Paul (2000), *The Information Bomb*, London: Verso.
Virilio, Paul (2003), *Unknown Quantity*, London: Thames and Hudson.
Waterman, Christopher Alan (1990), *Jùjú: A Social History and Ethnography of an African Popular Music*, Chicago: University of Chicago Press.

# CHAPTER 35
## SOME PROPERTIES OF ART AND CULTURE
*Fred Myers*

In the early 1970s, the Aboriginal artist and activist Wandjuk Marika asked the Australian government to investigate the unauthorized use of Yolngu clan designs on a variety of commodity forms, inaugurating a process of recognizing indigenous "copyright" for such designs. Copyright, famously, is known to involve a particular formulation of materiality, distinguishing idea from concrete expression, with only the latter being subject to ownership rights as a form of property.[1] However sympathetic to indigenous concerns over controlling their culture, this treatment of design—and culture—as a form of property involves understandings and practices of materiality and subjectivity that are different from indigenous Aboriginal relationships to cultural production and circulation. In exploring the significance, for material culture theory, of recent work on and events in the development of notions of cultural property, one of my main concerns in this chapter is the relevance of local understandings of objectification—or objectness and human action—as embedded object-ideologies. I discuss the limits of legal discourses of cultural property to capture and reflect indigenous Australian concerns about their relation to culture, to creativity, and to expression.

The central thesis of this chapter is that materiality—as a theory of quality of objectness—is not so much an issue of matter but is constituted, rather, through ideological frameworks. Thus, the formulation of materiality (or materialities) is varied and often conflicting around different understandings of subjects and objects. Nowhere is this more apparent—or palpable—than in situations in which human beings attempt to secure, stabilize, or even limit the flow of culture, to turn culture into property form. Rather than proposing a theory of materiality, then, I am interested here in pursuing through ethnographic consideration the trajectory of local theories of materiality as indigenous Australian paintings and designs move through the Western art-culture system and the Western concept of property and as different object-ideologies meet. My interest in this problem derives from ethnography that indicates Aboriginal concerns over the control of socially valued knowledge and its dispersal—through practices of secrecy, exchange, invisibility, and immateriality. These practices clearly depended on the materialities of producing and circulating knowledge through voice, ritual, and object-presentation and equally certainly did not anticipate the materiality of mechanical and digital reproduction. Ultimately, I see this study as one consideration of what happens when "culture" takes on new and varied forms of materiality.

Indigenous acrylic painting began in central Australia in 1971 as a form of cultural production in the government settlement of Papunya. At a time when government policies promoted a radical regime of cultural assimilation, with its apparently implacable hostility to indigenous culture, Aboriginal painters found a sympathetic supporter in a schoolteacher with art training, Geoff Bardon (see Bardon 1979, 1991). Bardon helped catalyze the Western Desert painting movement, which eventually placed its work in the most prestigious art galleries and venues in that country and elsewhere (Myers 2002). It was never imagined that

Aboriginal image-making could be a contemporary fine art that would bring unprecedented recognition and visibility to Aboriginal people and their culture within the Australian nation, and we have much to learn from indigenous understandings of this outcome.

Cases of scandal—"fraud" or "forgery"—in the Aboriginal art market help illuminate what happens when contact occurs between what I call a revelatory regime of value characteristic of indigenous Australians and the "Western art-culture system" (Clifford 1988). I emphasize that I am concerned with the specifics of the art-culture system, which cannot assimilate all the potential properties of indigenous painting to its own schemas. Cases of fraud provide cautionary tales, helping us to understand the limits of our theoretical constructs and the transformative consequences of reorganizations of value provoked as objects circulate across cultural borders and between regimes of value. These reorganizations flow from the provocative effect of putting ideas and expectations into material forms that are mediated through the specific historical structuring of the fine art market.

What emerges from [this] case stud[y] are the problems of articulation between images as integral aspects of Aboriginal culture and two alternative systems of representation through which Aboriginal people have increasingly been forced to live and by which they might be both valued or devalued. The first is "art," which has offered a medium through which they have been able to make themselves visible on their own terms, more or less, intervening in the representations circulating "about" them. But their interventions cannot be understood apart from the *materiality* of painting and of "art" (that is, art's institutions and properties). The other point on this triangle is "cultural property," an important conceptual framework that has been put forward as a basis for claiming protection of indigenous and minority groups against cultural appropriation. The fundamental claim derives from the assertion that art (or culture) is "'essential to' or 'constitutive of' or 'expressive of' the identity of the group" (Coleman 2003: 1). Frequently, claims for protection have been articulated by extending the regimes of copyright and intellectual property law, but these forms of protection raise many difficulties in the way they formulate intercultural activity (see Coleman 2003). [With this case] we are faced not only with [a perspective] upon the nature of materiality, but also with the degree to which [its] consideration reveals both my own understandings and the more general Aboriginal conceptualizations of what might be implicated in the materiality of objects and images.

## Wandjuk Marika

In the early 1970s, Wandjuk Marika—the well-known Yolngu artist and activist from Arnhem Land in northern Australia—asked the Australian government to investigate the unauthorized use of his sacred clan designs on a variety of commodity forms, in particular on tea towels. Marika inaugurated a process of recognizing indigenous "copyright" for such designs, a process that has subsequently occurred in a number of well-known cases, involving the use of Aboriginal images on everything from T-shirts to carpets manufactured in Vietnam.[2]

In Wandjuk's words:

That was 1974.
Then I walked into one of the shops and I found the tea towel,

Published in Holland,
Which had my own sacred design on this tea towel, tablecloth.
When I walk into that shop, and when I saw it
I was shocked and break my heart.
I bought it, cost me maybe $10
And then I said to the shopkeeper,
"Look you don't charge me that much.
This is my own design, you have no right to sell it.
This is bad. This is my own design, my sacred design.
I will only buy that for $2, just for the cloth,
Because it is my own copyright design."
Then I was thinking very hard.
What shall I do, where shall I get the help,
Who's going to help to stop this copyright stealing?
Instead of painting their own painting, they always copy designs
From the traditional areas.
They don't know what the painting is.
They thought they are just pleasure paintings
But it's the symbol, the power, experience and knowledge.
After I found my own design on the tea towels I was shocked and I lose my power to paint,
Lose my power for a number of years.
Yes, I was thinking and thinking;
I try and try and at last something was coming into my mind.
Ah, I said, I have to send this to the Prime Minister,
The former Prime Minister, which is Gough Whitlam.
Gough was Labor Prime Minister,
And I sent the two towels to Canberra to Prime Minister and I say, "OK,
I need help to setting up something to protect the copyright.
I need the lawyer or something,"
And they say to me "OK. Don't worry Wandjuk, we'll help you."

(Marika 1995: 118–19)[3]

Marika's claim evoked sympathy. By 1974, of course, few people who heard of his story would be disadvantaged by recognizing indigenous ownership on copyright grounds. More important, the translation of indigenous rights into the framework of copyright—or cultural property—seemed an intelligible "recontextualization" (Thomas 1991) of indigenous painting within the commodity regime. This recontextualization would transpose what might be seen as one set of signs and practices into another regime of value.[4]

In order to understand this situation in terms closer to those of indigenous participants, it is critical to look at the relationship between local understandings of objects and human action—as embedded in practices of personhood, relatedness, and secrecy—and what happens with the regulation and classification of the new form of Aboriginal painting. The treatment of both design and culture as forms of intellectual property in the legal setting involves understanding ideas and practices of materiality and subjectivity—of object and subject—that are different from indigenous Aboriginal relationships to cultural production, creativity, and circulation. The "object ideology"[5] of this revelatory regime of value is organized around the practical consciousness of materiality as something brought forth into "sensory presence"—what Pintupi people mark with the concept *yurti*. Materiality is conceived as something objectified in revelation or transmission, rather than created de novo. That revelation of ancestral knowledge and events in material form, such as painting, ritual, or song, is colloquially known as "The Dreaming" (*tjukurrpa* in Pintupi).

As Wandjuk Marika suggests, it is possible to translate the social practices of indigenous image-making in terms of their resemblance to practices of intellectual property, of ownership and copyright, but only partly. Aboriginal people (Yarnangu) in Central Australia say that the story-song-design complexes of The Dreaming—and both the rituals and landscapes that are viewed as integral to them—are "held" (*kanyinu*) by various groups of people. Perhaps I can make this ontology clearer: The Dreaming is not the landscape itself or principally even an explanation of it, although that is one of its attributes. Rather, the landscape is the materialization of The Dreaming as a sensory form to be experienced (that is, *yurti*); it is a manifestation of The Dreaming, but not an account of what it *is* (see also Poirier 1996). The right to "show" (*yurtininpa*, "reveal" or "make sensorily present") a ceremony is in the hands of those we might call "owners" of that country and its associated Dreaming stories. It was on such grounds that the men I knew typically painted their own country—"making visible" or giving, in this way, components of their own identity. But although they might "give," "reveal," or exchange them, the images remain (as Marika's statement points out) always a part, another extension or embodiment of those who are custodians of these Dreamings and of The Dreaming itself, which is the identity ground of the painters. The right to conduct a symphony is not held to be a claim to composing it.

But the materiality of this knowledge—objectified in particular forms such as the landscape, ritual, or acrylic and bark painting—has distinctive consequences. Objectifications of Aboriginal myth and ritual knowledge have material qualities beyond the narrative structure; they have extension in space, insofar as the stories are linked to specific places, which may become an important material property in formulating a social identity among those who have rights to different stories located along the same ancestral path. Realized in sound and performance, stories and the ceremonies reenacting them—along with the associated paraphernalia and designs—can also be owned and exchanged (but not sold and purchased); rights to speak and transmit them can become the objects of social and political organization, and their material properties encourage distinctive strategies of concealment and transmission.

The concern of people in such a system is to limit dispersal, to control the potential or manifestations of The Dreaming (*tjukurrpa*). Understood as objectifications of ancestral subjectivity, manifestations of The Dreaming are further identified with certain persons and groups who have a kin-based obligation to control the rights to reproduce these images as well and to determine who can see them. Unlike with classical Western copyright, the images controlled here are not thought to be of people's own creation.[6]

This is a distinct system of value production that takes its integrity from its relationship to all other aspects of that society's values, constituting what Marcel Mauss called a "total social fact" (Mauss 1925). The Dreaming discursively and practically articulates personhood and ontology, mediating significantly the sociopolitical relations between people organized spatially (in territorially dispersed groups) and intergenerationally into a system of identity, of similarity and difference, of autonomy and relatedness (see Myers 1986). The production of images, within this framework and especially in ritual, is a fundamental medium in which a person's—or group's—autonomy can be expressed and drawn into relationship with others (see Myers 1986, 1988). I would call this a "revelatory regime of value."

Such a regime of value did not anticipate the ways in which technologies such as the market and mechanical reproduction could detach signs from those who make and circulate them. For Aboriginal people, it is not fundamentally objectifications of human creativity, then, which copyright proposes to regulate; copyright would be regulating rights to esoteric ancestral knowledge and creativity.

A classification as "art" involves an object being articulated as original, singular, and unique—values placing objects on the side of authenticity, in contrast to fakes or reproductions, on the one hand, and to the class of objects that are seen as traditional and collective, on the other hand. The classification of fine art, based on connoisseurship, markets, and art museums, recognizes a difference in human creativity and execution that has little value in the revelatory regime in which the production of Aboriginal art originates. Furthermore, the art-culture system supposedly does not recognize the racial or cultural identities of the artist. To be art, an object cannot be collective but should be expressive of a more sublime characteristic that subordinates other properties to individual creativity.

## Conclusion: Artifacts of materiality

Aboriginal art scandals reveal more than the existence (and persistence) of object-ontologies; they also instantiate contestations. Which ideologies of materiality will prevail as the material forms that comprise Aboriginal art circulate through varying regimes of value that have their own hierarchies and legal regulations? Because object-ideologies are related—as in the case of the art-culture system—to specific institutions and practices, the properties of "art" and "culture" must be understood as determined and objectified in relationship to these social fields.

This is why the circulation of objects through different regimes can reveal what anthropologists have known, since Victor Turner's work on social dramas (1974), about the ways in which hierarchies of value are articulated (see also Miller 2003). The articulation of our systems of law and aesthetics with those of Aboriginal people produces some strange and unpredictable effects and dilemmas. My point is that the recognition of Aboriginal objects as art is a material practice—not simply an endorsement of Aboriginal culture, but a recognition of certain forms of its materialization within a specific institutional form and system of value (involving markets, museums, and collectors). There is, I am arguing, a practical conflation of discourses as well as new openings that might cut across the distinction between Aboriginal and white. Just as the expectations of specific understandings of creativity embedded in copyright may haunt Aboriginal producers, the entry of these new concerns may also transform the way in which copyright is conceived. These are equally potential effects of the materiality of Aboriginal art.[7]

The resolution of this tension is taking place through the production of a new category—"Aboriginal fine art." This new category or subfield of art production (Hoban 2002) is partly subordinated to fine art in general through its acceptance of the general standards of connoisseurship that make it still distinct from "ethnographic art." It is the product of a specific network of cultural actors and institutions, one that includes whites and Aboriginal people. As such it forms part of a larger network of recontextualization, of battles over power and cultural capital that aim to move what had been "ethnographic art" to the context of "art museums." What emerges are the limitations of any version of the category of fine art that fails to recognize the problems that "Aboriginal fine art" addresses.

## Notes

1. US copyright law, for example, holds that one can copyright a specific expression (a book, a song composition, a poem) but not a general idea (see Vaidhyanathan 2001).
2. In an early case, Aboriginal Artists Agency brought suit on behalf of an Arnhem Land artist, Yangarininy Munungmurra, against Peter Stripes Fabrics in New South Wales (1985) for adapting the artist's work to suit furnishing fabric. A second important case involved a group of Arnhem Land artists including Johnny Bulun Bulun against a T-shirt manufacturer in Queensland who had produced many shirts using their bark paintings, and more recently Bulun Bulun and his brother George Milpurrurru sued R&T Textiles Pty Ltd. (1998) for importing and selling fabric printed featuring their work. The carpets case was heard as *Milpurrurru v. Indofurn Pty. Ltd.*, 1995. Other cases have involved the use of Aboriginal images on Australian currency.
3. See also Marika 1986.
4. The significance of Thomas's discussion of recontextualization is broad.
5. I am borrowing from the model of language ideology, as used by Schieffelin, Woolard and Kroskrity (1998) and Silverstein (1979).
6. Indeed, Pintupi painters always insisted to me that their images "are not made up, not made by us. They are from The Dreaming."
7. Copyright regulation itself is an unsettled domain. Recent work on copyright suggests not only that its formulations are historically varied and dependent on technological mediations, but also that regulations of the rights over culture and its expression are the specific results of human action mediated through institutional and social form. Certainly the relations between human subjects and their products cannot be understood as simply expressions of natural law. Rather, Aboriginal artists and activists like Marika insist that we apprehend the materiality that objectifies their culture in terms of the identity-producing ideology that informs it and is threatened by its conversion into a mere commodity stripped of these dimensions.

## References

Bardon, Geoffrey (1979), *Aboriginal Art of the Western Desert*, Sydney: Rigby.
Bardon, Geoffrey (1991), *Papunya Tula Art of the Western Desert*, Melbourne: McPhee Gribble.
Clifford, James (1988), *The Predicament of Culture*, Cambridge: Harvard University Press.
Coleman, Elizabeth (Forthcoming), "Aboriginal Art and Identity: Crossing the Borders of Law's Imagination." *Journal of Political Philosophy* 11 (2).
Hoban, Caroline Holdstrom (2002), "The Field of Art Production and Western Desert Acrylics." *Australian Journal of Anthropology* 12: 178–90.
Marika, Wandjuk (1986), "Painting Is Very Important (Story as Told to Jennifer Isaacs)," in Ulli Beier (ed.), *Long Water: Aboriginal Art and Literature* (special issue of *Aspect* 34), 7–18, Sydney: Aboriginal Artists Agency.

Mauss, Marcel (1990 [1925]), *The Gift: The Form and Reason for Exchange in Archaic Societies*, trans. W. D. Halls, New York: Norton.

Mauss, Marcel (2003), "The Virtual Moment." *Journal of the Royal Anthropological Institute* 9: 57–75.

Myers, Fred (1986), *Pintupi Country, Pintupi Self: Sentiment, Place, and Politics among Western Desert Aborigines*, Washington, DC and Canberra: Smithsonian Institution Press and the Australian Institute of Aboriginal Studies Press.

Myers, Fred (1988), "Burning the Truck and Holding the Country: Forms of Property, Time, and the Negotiation of Identity among Pintupi Aborigines," in David Riches, Tim Ingold, and James Woodburn (eds), *Hunter-Gatherers, II: Property, Power and Ideology*, 52–74, London: Berg.

Myers, Fred (2002), *Painting Culture: The Making of an Aboriginal High Art*, Durham, NC: Duke University Press.

Poirier, Sylvie (1996), *Les Jardins du Nomade: Cosmologie, territorie et personne dans le désert occidental australien*, Munster: Lit Verlag.

Schieffelin, Bambi, Kathryn Woolard, and Paul Kroskrity (eds) (1998), *Language Ideologies: Practice and Theory*, New York: Oxford University Press.

Silverstein, Michael (1979), "Language Structures and Linguistic Ideology," in P. Clyne et al. (eds), *The Elements: A Parasession on Linguistic Units and Levels*, Chicago: Chicago Linguistic Society.

Thomas, Nicholas (1991), *Entangled Objects: Exchange, Material Culture and Colonialism in the Pacific*, Cambridge: Harvard University Press.

Turner, Victor (1974), *Dramas, Fields, and Metaphors*, Ithaca, NY: Cornell University Press.

Vaidhyanathan, Siva (2001), *Copyrights and Copywrongs: The Rise of Intellectual Property and How It Threatens Creativity*, New York: New York University Press.

# CHAPTER 36

# CULTURAL SOVEREIGNTY IN A GLOBAL ART ECONOMY: EGYPTIAN CULTURAL POLICY AND THE NEW WESTERN INTEREST IN ART FROM THE MIDDLE EAST

*Jessica Winegar*

Husni, a member of the postindependence generation, was an abstract painter from Alexandria who had trained at a state art college and had been a cultural attaché in Europe. In his new post, he set out to put Egypt on the international art map by creating and nurturing a young generation of artists doing new kinds of art.[1] Through a series of initiatives (including competitions, prizes, and residencies abroad), he encouraged conceptual, abstract, and installation art in new or unusual media to prove to the world that Egyptians still made "Egyptian" art but were also keeping up with international trends. Officials also hoped that a vibrant young art scene would halt the spread of radical Islam in a society in which Islamist violence had become increasingly common. Opponents of this new policy, many of whom held lower positions in the government, advocated representations of folkloric or pastoral imagery executed in traditional media such as oil, granite, and bronze. Their complaints that Egyptian artists were now imitating the West fell on deaf ears.[2] With state resources in their hands, top officials encouraged artists to be flexible and to mix "local" elements with "international" media, styles, or concepts. They allocated prizes accordingly.

For example, Ayman al-Simari was selected as an exceptional young artist for his work that combined remnants of rural mud brick houses and aluminum sheeting as a comment on the visual transformation of provincial Egypt as it was integrated into the world economy. Work such as this, combining materials or styles seen as local and traditional with those considered to be international and modern, were seen by their supporters as reflecting an Egypt that was open to the outside and always changing—a visual representation of the modern nation intended as a message both to the nation's ("unmodern") citizens as well as to Western audiences. Among ministry officials and young artists of this aesthetic persuasion, a strong sense prevailed that a new "modern Egyptian art" was being made.

This cultural policy assumed an interdependent, relational form of cultural sovereignty. It was also part of a new strategy of governance. As the Egyptian government was enacting neoliberal reforms in the economic sector, it was contributing in the cultural sector to the production of a new kind of national subject among young artists who would be secular, "progressive," and amenable to the direction Egypt was heading. To the irritation of their opponents, the new artists were wildly successful, and contemporary Egyptian art eventually grabbed international notice in venues such as the Venice Biennial.[3]

When foreign curators arrived on the scene, they brought their own interests in promoting "young Egyptian artists." However, their approach denied the state's early role in creating this same "young generation" when they selected artists, such as al-Simari, who had first shown their work with government sponsorship. Instead of interpreting the works themselves as having to do with Egypt as such, foreign curators and audiences viewed these works in terms of personal expression, as being about personal lives and histories within a particular cultural context. As one Egyptian artist kept saying, "Everything now is about 'al-personal.'" He said the sentence in Arabic, but the word *personal* was in English, thus echoing a favorite word among Western art critics. Photography and video art became especially popular among foreign curators and buyers, particularly works dealing with personal psychological issues and the intimate or daily lives of urban Egyptians. The emphasis on the personal tended to displace the political, and in that sense the new work could be made to fit the alienating logics of neoliberal capitalism.[4]

While asserting new hierarchies of artistic value, Euro-Americans were also overturning the local age hierarchy. The growth of a younger generation was originally enabled and constrained by a kind of paternalist gerontocracy coupled with cultural respect for elders. Younger artists criticized the domination of the older generation, but they also emphasized their indebtedness and respect. The newly arrived foreign curators, however, regularly categorized locally esteemed older generation artists as outdated. This categorization was coupled with the opinion that a large public arts sector directed by older artists and curators was indicative of a lagging art movement. They constructed a modernist and arguably neocolonial ideology that legitimated this opinion and, by extension, their own activities. Thus, they mounted several challenges to the ministry's conception of its role in the Egyptian art movement, and a battle began in which older generation state curators and private-sector curators fought over who could lay claim to the patronage of young artists.

The downtown galleries created the Nitaq Festival to "invigorate" the art movement in Egypt. The gallerists thus employed the same language that had first been used by the new minister in 1989 when he launched an annual young artists competition called Salon al-Shabab (Salon of Youth). But the Nitaq Festival organizers and their supporters argued that their event, and the private sector more generally, gave these artists exhibition opportunities that they would not have otherwise. They also said that the private sector encouraged young artists to work in genres that the older generation would not accept. For example, one gallery owner explained, "the majority of artists that the downtown galleries deal with are young. Because the older artists, the established artists, they've got exhibition spaces." When I countered that for the past ten years, young artists had actually been getting a lot of exhibition opportunities from the government, the gallerist paused, then agreed. However, he went on to recuperate the private-sector narrative. He said that he wanted to "give some credence" to installation work "because it's so accepted everywhere else. Video work, it's accepted everywhere else. And you don't get older people doing it, at all."

This narrative has also dominated the English- and French-language arts pages, in which Americans, Europeans, and wealthy graduates from the American University in Cairo have often praised the new downtown galleries to the exclusion of public sector and Egyptian-owned private galleries in other areas of Cairo. These curators have persisted in this narrative, despite their lack of evidence to support it, because of their need to create a private-sector market niche while also producing themselves as the legitimate developers or representatives of that market. The colonial framing of Egyptian art as a backward space that could be developed has been a particularly effective method resulting in increased sales, popularity among foreign audiences, and notice in famous magazines such as *Art in America*. Such a framing, however, is contingent on the silencing or erasure of other voices in the Egyptian art scene.

Younger artists are aware that most Euro-American curators critique state activities and the older generation. When interacting with Westerners, they tend to emphasize their own criticisms of older artists and downplay their ongoing connections to them. The highly contextualized nature of these expressions is often unrecognized by the new curators, who are usually unaware that most young artists maintain active ties to the state for employment, exhibitions, commissions, and acquisitions. This is partly because the Westerners are both culturally and linguistically hampered in their communication with them.[5]

Those older generation artists most connected to the ministry have resisted these challenges to their claims on young artists and their support of newer media. The young artists who participated in the Nitaq Festival and were first selected by Western curators for shows abroad were in large measure those whose careers began in the ministry's annual competitions. In the eyes of many artists, the private sector was not only capitalizing on the state's achievements, but the Egyptian Ministry of Culture was being denied credit as well. For example, one older artist criticized a local English-language magazine for claiming that the Nitaq Festival was an opportunity for young artists to exhibit because they were shut out by the state. Indeed, one would be hard pressed to find Egyptians (of any age or aesthetic persuasion) who thought that the state ignored younger artists or artists working in new media, given the preponderance of state support for both.

Even though the private-sector narrative lacks substantial evidence, it does reveal the tension within the ministry's policy of promoting young artists while also insisting on an age hierarchy. This tension was made clear in the minister's reaction to the exodus of young artists to the private sector, as noted in a newspaper interview:

> This gallerist can take whomever he wants from the young artists. It doesn't concern me that he takes the sons of the Youth Salon. First of all, you cannot refuse any artist his freedom… . They [the young artists] can make mistakes; they are not children. But there is no doubt that we are aware of [them] and know where they are in the end. ('Ali 2001: 27)

Here we see the tension and a common attempt to solve it through a form of graduated sovereignty: the language of artistic freedom is paired with a patronizing reminder of the state's panoptic authority over young artists. In another poignant reminder of surveillance, a state curator called artists to tell them that it was inappropriate for them to exhibit in a new gallery at the American University in Cairo while the Israelis were killing Palestinians with U.S.-supplied weapons.

In this post-1989 system of cultural governance, artists are encouraged to move freely, to draw on a variety of international trends for inspiration, and to exhibit their work outside of the country, but they are admonished to do so in a way that maintains their cultural integrity as artists who were first nurtured by the state. The activities of the Egyptian Ministry of Culture also show that as part of this governance, nation-states are redefining some forms of nationalism as internationalist, particularly in realms of cultural production (see also Ong 1999; Wang 2000). This strategy makes their cultural goods more competitive internationally (e.g., Egypt wins the Venice prize) and creates a friendly and progressive international reputation that encourages foreign investment (i.e., Egypt has avantgarde artistic youth instead of backward terrorist youth).

Young artists have thus become subjects of two regimes of power. Just as state officials "create" young artists to prove Egypt's cultural progress, Western curators "create" young artists in a way that emphasizes Western cultural superiority. Whereas the state awards prizes to certain kinds of art and emphasizes surveillance, Western curators choose the same kinds of art, using a combination of neoliberal and neocolonial discourses to justify and market those choices.

Although young artists are being pulled back and forth between these two regimes of power, most do not fully submit to either of them. They seek to take advantage of the (often unexpected) opportunities offered by each, and they have formulated artistic stances that meld the least offensive aspects of free market ideology with the least restrictive aspects of state socialism and nationalism. Although some may have ended up choosing sides, most have tried to navigate the situation by adopting a new kind of flexibility rooted in freshly articulated notions of cultural sovereignty and artistic integrity. They have found ways to frame discursively the art they were already producing that match both cultural policy initiatives and international marketing strategies. Some have capitalized on newly created social connections and have learned foreign languages to move more easily among these different worlds; others have been inspired by the artistic possibilities offered by new media and new dialogues within Egypt and emerging international channels. At times, their art has changed dramatically as a result. For example, the artist Shadi al-Nushuqati, whose large paintings of beds and distraught figures had been a Youth Salon favorite, has moved to work in video on topics related to his family heritage. In contrast, artists whose articulations of cultural sovereignty were mainly expressed through iterations of pastoral and folkloric motifs have remained marginalized. These artists are the hidden majority that has found no place in the battles between state and foreign curators and in the struggles of young artists to resist the limitations of either side.[6]

## Notes

1. Generational divisions and hierarchies have been fundamental organizing principles in the Egyptian art world. During the time of my fieldwork, the "younger generation" generally referred to artists who started their careers after 1989, whereas the "older generation" denoted artists who came of age during Nasserist socialism.
2. Unfortunately, I do not have space here to go into the many battles between the holders of these opposing aesthetic perspectives over state resources and the direction of state cultural policy. For a full accounting of these battles, especially within state institutions themselves, see Winegar (2006).
3. In 1995, Egypt became the first non-Western country to win the Venice Biennial's Golden Lion Prize for best country pavilion.
4. There is also an interesting parallel between these works and the production and circulation of Orientalist photographic representations of Middle Eastern daily or harem life during the colonial period.
5. Their best communication is actually with a very small, elite group of young artists whose English is impeccable, who have extensive overseas experience, and who were mostly educated abroad

or at the elite private American University in Cairo. These artists' structural position enables a less-tempered critique of the state. The availability of this small group, combined with many foreign curators' view that the state is inherently bad for art, has resulted in the misrecognition that all young artists have been engaged in a valiant struggle against state control.

6. It is important to note that many of these marginalized artists found their own private market in the Egyptian-owned private-sector galleries in the more upscale neighborhoods of Cairo. These are galleries catering to Egyptian old-money elites and older Western businesspeople and diplomats who prefer folkloric representations of Egypt. These Western audiences are akin to those discussed by Katherine Zirbel (2000) in her work on the Western penchant for Egyptian "folk" music. Without the state's involvement in expanding experimental visual arts, it is likely that most Westerners would have continued to consume folkloric or pastoral modern art.

## References

Ali, Fatma (2001), "The Minister of Culture: Whoever Stands against the Youth Stands against Himself." (Man yaqif didd al-shabab yaqif didd nafsahu). *Al-Qahira* (28 August): 27.

Ong, Aihwa (1999), *Flexible Citizenship: The Cultural Logics of Transnationality*, Durham, NC: Duke University Press.

Wang, Horng-luen (2000), "Rethinking the Global and the National: Reflections on National Imaginations in Taiwan." *Theory, Culture and Society* 17 (4): 93–117.

Winegar, Jessica (2006) *Creative Reckonings: The Politics of Art and Culture in Contemporary Egypt*, Stanford: Stanford University Press.

Zirbel, Katherine (2000), "Playing it Both Ways: Local Egyptian Performers between Regional Identity and International Markets," in W. Armbrust (ed.), *Mass Mediations: New Approaches to Popular Culture in the Middle East and Beyond*, 120–45, Berkeley: University of California Press.

# CHAPTER 37
# CULTURES IN DIALOGUE?
*Sally Price*

The Musée du Quai Branly – there where cultures dialog.[1]

Museums devoted to the exhibition of cultural difference trace their origins to the very earliest days of European exploration. Columbus brought Caribbean Indians back to Isabella, early sixteenth-century French ship owners collected "fetishes" in Africa, and Captain Cook returned from the Pacific with everything from barkcloth, jewelry, and weapons to a shark-tooth knife and a shell trumpet. Displays of the material spoils of imperialism began as royal cabinets of curiosity and gradually grew into the monumental museums and universal expositions of the nineteenth century. In France their passage through naval museums, alongside model sailing vessels and other memorabilia of maritime exploits, can be read as a direct reflection of their association with the nation's imperial ambitions. In all these settings, the exhibition of cultural difference was inextricably linked to the celebration of nationalism, colonial conquest, and the civilizing mission.

What, then, becomes of the institutionalized presentation of other cultures once imperialist ambitions are officially defined as a thing of the past?

As the celebration of colonial expansion through the display of exotic objects falls out of favor, and as (simultaneously) the boundary between viewer and viewed in this realm becomes increasingly blurred, what adjustments need to be made in the public institutions whose very job it is to present cultural difference? This question forms the vortex of the swirling controversies over what to do with primitive art in our current, allegedly postcolonial world. While museums always involve the orchestration of multiple goals, it will be useful to disentangle them for a few paragraphs, viewing them as if they were separable in order to reflect on the choices made in Paris. Four models seem particularly relevant to the discussion.

(1) One option is to highlight the objects' formal properties in order to promote an unmediated contemplation of their physical beauty. This approach isolates the display objects from both their ethnographic pasts as objects contributing to life in distant cultures and their historical pasts as the spoils of imperialism. The Pavilion des Sessions in the Louvre is a near-pristine embodiment of this approach, presenting objects as masterpieces of world art: treating them to spacious placement, ample lighting, and elegant surroundings, and conveying information on their original environments through minimalist texts or distantly placed computer terminals.

(2) Another possibility is to privilege the perspectives of members of the represented cultures and their descendants. Here, the emphasis is on respect for native voices and rights to cultural difference. Examples of this approach vary widely, from tribal museums in which members of a specific group present their own culture (such as the

two cultural centers in Vancouver chronicled by James Clifford), to national museums that embrace the cultural politics of peoples within its borders (such as Te Papa in New Zealand or the National Museum of Australia), to those encompassing whole families of cultural heritage (such as the National Museum of the American Indian in Washington). Even comprehensive museums such as the Smithsonian and the British Museum are beginning to integrate participation by native representatives in their permanent exhibition galleries.

(3) A third is to make colonial encounters part of the story, focusing on the circumstances in which collections were formed and the history of the production of knowledge about peoples outside of the European cultural orbit. Although this option, designed to promote historical consciousness about relations of domination that account for the distribution of the world's material patrimony, is often most vigorously implemented in temporary (traveling) exhibitions, some museums are beginning to give it increased prominence in their permanent galleries as well. The newly renovated halls of the Museum of Ethnology in Vienna (to open in early 2008), for example, represent a concerted effort to move in this direction.

(4) A fourth model is to distance the cultures on display from both native perspectives and the intrusions of the Western world, presenting them as vignettes of a pre-contact past. This means "abstracting back from modernity" to discover "authentic" (untouched) primitive societies—zooming in on the feathers, nose-flutes, scarification motifs, and divinatory practices, but leaving out the Coke bottles, the cell phones, the Nike shoes, and TV images of children dying of AIDS. Over the past several decades, this approach has lost its claims to legitimacy in most parts of the world and representations of it are mainly limited to un-restructured museums from an earlier era. The widespread assessment in the late twentieth century that the Musée de l'Homme was virtually unsalvageable, for example, had much to do with the tenacity of that museum's reputation as a site of essentialized visions of cultural difference from the late nineteenth and early twentieth centuries.

Recent debates about the presentation of primitive art in museums have shown increased attention to the upside and downside of different choices in terms of the messages they send to museumgoers about art and cultural difference.[2] The challenge, of course, is to do everything at once, combining appreciation of the exhibited objects as art with awareness of them as elements of foreign lifeways, as witnesses to alternative cultural perspectives, and as relics of world history—all this according to some kind of premeditated balance among the different agendas. The tension created between the first of these competing concerns and the others has sometimes been glossed as a tug-of-war between "art" and "anthropology," but that clearly fails at this point in history to do justice to the complexities involved.

Where, then, has France's most recent and most magisterial attempt to grapple with these choices ended up?

Somewhere between the proposals for the Musée Quai Branly and the inauguration in June 2006, the idea of creating a truly "postcolonial" museum had shriveled into something between nostalgia for a lost past and empty rhetoric. It wasn't that observers hadn't done their best to explain what a truly postcolonial museum would have entailed. In 2003, for example, Benoit de L'Estoile challenged the MQB organizers (though with some pessimism) to do better than to produce a posthumous homage to vanquished civilizations:

> In this day and age a museum devoted to non-Western arts and civilizations needs to be a *postcolonial* museum in a triple sense—showing that the colonial period is an important part of our heritage, that we are living today in a world that continues to be deeply marked by colonial upheavals (from population displacements to conflicts near and far), and that the museum itself is the material and spiritual heir of the colonial era in both its fundamental concepts (such as "tribal") and its modes of presentation. We should not be denying this postcolonial situation, but rather accepting it consciously. The museum needs to confront history, not just by adding dates here and there, nor by depicting societies the way they were before the conquest, but by placing front and center the question of historicity … . Instead of trying to erase this past by the magic of a generous recasting, it should be making people aware of all that silently conditions their perceptions.[3]

Yet visitors to the MQB are rarely invited to step outside of a 1950s-style ethnographic present, rarely given the opportunity to venture beyond an exoticizing vision of non-European cultures that has long since been surpassed in both anthropological and art historical writing. Computers on the multimedia mezzanine, for example, offer information under such categories as shamanism, hunting and gathering, totemism, kinship, sacrifice, initiation, age groups, and cannibalism, but one searches in vain for any mention of (for example) colonialism, collecting, slavery, or tourism.

As the curator in charge of the history collections at the MQB put it, attempts to inject colonial history into the project were simply not successful. "This was a presidential project, so every effort was made to avoid risks, to prevent anything critical from being said."[4] In short, Model #3 has not been a priority in the organization of the Musée du Quai Branly."

Where does this leave "The House That Jacques Built"?[5]

Over the course of the MQB's inaugural week, I listened to the reactions of a large number of colleagues—American, French, British, German, Ghanaian, Kanak, Vietnamese, and others—who as participants in the day of round-table discussions had been offered an early preview of the museum. For some of them, the displays conjured up images of museums in the 1980s. Others pushed the date back to mid-century. And the director of the ethnography museum in Geneva described the museography in an interview as "disagreeable, squeezed, and reminiscent of the nineteenth century."[6] Many of the people I spoke with were struck at how much the labels projected a vision of static societies living in a timeless "ethnographic present," a vision that grew out of early anthropological reports in which "authenticity" resided in an unchanging pre-contact past. The concern was that the museum would reinforce an "us/them" vision of alterity—a vision that can no longer lay claim even to the slender shred of legitimacy it once held. As Benoit de L'Estoile has remarked, "In its very conception, the museum is based on the idea, now largely discredited by anthropologists, that these societies have more in common with each other than with our society, that is that they are defined by their radical alterity."[7] (For some visitors, an us/them alterity was the whole point. One commentator, commending the museum for its "glittering" exhibition, wrote that the "magnificent" objects on display "define the mission of the museum—to demonstrate the great differences between the West and the rest of the world."[8])

Didn't the fact of relegating contemporary and "hybrid" objects to temporary exhibits risk turning the main exhibition area into a purveyor of images of a frozen, exoticized, "authentic" past? By skimming euphemistically over the colonial encounters responsible for the objects' presence in Europe (and deep-sixing the practices that have tarnished subsequent transfers of some of these objects), wasn't the museum bypassing a precious opportunity to bring important global issues to the attention of a wide audience? And didn't the presentation of objects at the MQB discourage multiple readings? Where, for example, was there recognition that an object in the permanent exhibition space would be understood very differently by a nineteenth-century colonial officer, an early twentieth-century European artist, a 1950s art dealer, and a present-day museum visitor, not to mention the native sculptor responsible for creating it? In an interview about the Quai Branly Museum on NPR, Jim Clifford raised this question and dubbed the tendency to impose single meanings a "colonialist act."[9]

For many of the people I spoke with, the most important problem was that the knowledge, beliefs, and perspectives of native peoples have been largely brushed aside. As Kanak scholar Emmanuel Kasarhérou had put it a few years earlier, "You should not imagine that just by putting our objects in your museums you're letting us be the ones to speak about them."[10] We're returning here to the situation in the Louvre exhibits, where a European vision of a cock's comb symbolizing virility won the day over New Ireland understandings about a local bird symbolizing androgyny … and where the connoisseur's vision of a tender embrace of sensual lovers turned a blind eye to the natives' vision of a murderous stranglehold by a malevolent spirit. In the MQB, similar choices have been made. The horizontal pattern of a patch-work cape is turned ninety degrees because the architect designed a vertical case at that point in the exhibition's layout. A ceramic object from Peru and a wooden one from Alaska are shown together because structuralist theories born in France say they both represent vitality. A Mayan god of death is shunted to one side in order to privilege a view of the Eiffel Tower. And Kongo "nail fetishes" are explained via a quotation from a 1920s book authored by a French art dealer entitled *Primitive Negro Sculpture*.

French stereotypes of American political correctness (sometimes dubbed "hyperrelativism") conjure up a vision of museum policies in which the members of a given culture are the only people entitled to speak about it—blacks monopolizing the discourse on African American culture, American Indians on their traditions, and so forth. But that caricature fails to recognize the dominant move that has been altering the landscape in North American museums—a move more in line, in fact, with the MQB's self-characterization as "the place where cultures dialogue." As Jim Clifford points out, the shift is not unilineal or across the board—"the sense of connection/responsibility vis-à-vis distant populations and their 'cultural property' is happening piecemeal and in specific exhibitions and historical/spatial situations."[11] An exhibit entitled Chiefly Feasts, for example, was one move in this direction, not by restricting the interpretations to native voices, but by attempting to build on dialogue between New York curators and representatives of Northwest Coast Indian societies.[12] The participation of native elders from Alaska in the documentation of nineteenth-century objects destined to be repatriated from the Smithsonian Institution is another.[13] In contrast, at the MQB, "dialogue" has generally been conducted at the level of diplomatic relations between nations rather than between the museum personnel and members of the cultures represented in its exhibition spaces."[14] Ambassadorial participation has been an important part of the undertaking, but when often-sacred objects of minority populations are involved, that kind of interaction does not constitute "cultures in dialogue." At the MQB, the microphone has remained firmly in the grasp of the European curators, experts on museology but all too rarely in direct or evenly empowered conversation with members of the artists' home societies.

Critics of the Musée du Quai Branly have lamented what they see as inadequate attention to key aspects of a world in which no cultural group has ever been frozen in time or closed onto itself. Where in the exhibitions, they ask, do we learn about the pivotal role of colonial encounters, the dynamism of cultural beliefs and practices, the ways in which cultural ideas move from one ethnic group to another? Where is there recognition that native visions can shed valuable light on the meaning of the objects on display, and in so doing expand our ability to think beyond familiar Eurocentric assumptions? From an early twenty-first-century perspective, the MQB has missed precious opportunities for meaningful cultural dialogue that would have led to greater consideration of these issues. After the initial flurry of largely positive reactions in the press (many centered on the architecture), a heavy dose of negative reactions, more often questioning the museum's conceptual underpinnings, began to stream in. As one reviewer commented, new projects like this "almost always get trashed" in Paris, but reactions to the Quai Branly have "seemed worse than most."[15]

Meanwhile, crowds are flocking to the new anti-palace on the Seine, with the first year's attendance clocked in at more than 1.5 million. Although the museum boasts that a significant proportion of these visitors come from that increasingly large segment of the French population whose ancestors are not the Gauls, the week that I spent in the museum a year after its opening suggests that this claim is little more than a combination of wishful thinking and public relations. The many challenges that the museum faces, as it moves beyond the excitement of its inaugural year, include (in addition to practical adjustments in such matters as lighting and label copy) a greater effort to confront the full story of France's past as a colonial power, to invite meaningful participation by members of the fourth-world cultures represented in its collections, and to acknowledge the continuing dynamism of those cultures in the twenty-first century—in short, a willingness to build toward a more complete "dialogue of cultures."

## Notes

* *"Le Musée du Quai Branly, là oùdialoguent les cultures."* Inscription on the podium where President Jacques Chirac delivered his speech at the museum's inauguration. 20 June 2006. In other environments, such as MQB posters, the motto was prefaced by *"Les cultures sont faites pour dialoguer"* (Cultures are made for dialogue).

1. See Clifford 1997, 107–45.
2. Not everyone has joined in this trend. Stéphane Martin's reply, when an interviewer asked him to comment on the difference between "an art gallery type display and an ethnographic display," was that "I don't really see the difference" (Naumann 2006).
3. De L'Estoile 2003, 57–8.
4. Nanette Snoep (the only Dutch curator at the MQB), quoted in Obbema 2006. Elsewhere, Snoep remarked that "the problem is that President Chirac didn't make the inclusion of colonial history a mandate of this museum" (quoted in Moerland 2006).

5. Apologies to William Hone, who first turned "The House That Jack Built" from nursery rhyme to political commentary in 1819 as "The Political House That Jack Built" (see http://www.rc.umd.edu/editions/hone/jacktext.htm#acc2tx).
6. Jacques Hainard in Chardon 2006.
7. De L'Estoile 2003: 42 n.7.
8. Kovacs 2006.
9. Frank Browning, "New Paris Art Museum Finds Many Critics," *NPR Weekend Edition,* 13 August 2006. See also Clifford 2007.
10. March 2003 lecture at the Natural History Museum in Lyon, quoted in Roth 2006: 141.
11. E-mail of 11 August 2006.
12. Jonaitis 1991.
13. http://www.anchoragemuseum.org/changing_exb.asp.
14. The museum's role in international diplomacy has been particularly evident in Australia and New Zealand. Not only were Australian artists invited to contribute to the building, but New Zealand, in collaboration with Adidas, offered a most unusual artwork that now hangs in the museum—a four-meter-long canvas realized with blood samples provided for the purpose by every member of the national rugby team, the All Blacks. The inscription reads: "Bonded By Pride / Bonded By Determination / Bonded By Integrity / Bonded By Passion / Bonded By Blood, Sweat and Tears. Les Bleus et Les Noirs. Bonded By The Game. Impossible Is Nothing" ("Liés par le Jeu: All Blacks Give Themselves to the People of France," 18 November 2006, http://www.newswire.co.nz).
15. Goddard 2006.

## Bibliography


Béreau, Stéphanie (2004), "Other Cultures in a Museum Perspective Exhibiting African Art: A Never-Ending Challenge for Museums / Les 'autres cultures' vues par les musées Exposer l'Art africain: Un défi sans fin pour les musées." *Art Tribal* (bilingual) 5: 90–101.

Chardon, Elisabeth (1997), *Routes: Travel and Translation in the Late Twentieth Century*, Cambridge, MA: Harvard University Press.

Chardon, Elisabeth (2006), "La beauté des objets ne suffit pas." Interview with Jacques Hainard. *Le Temps* (Geneva), 21 September.

Chardon, Elisabeth (2007), "Quai Branly in Process." *October* 120: 2–23.

de L'Estoile, Benoît (2003), "From the Colonial Exhibition to the Museum of Man. An Alternative Genealogy of French Anthropology." *Social Anthropology/Anthropologie Sociale* 11 (3): 59–79.

Goddard, Peter (2006), "Branly-Bashing in Fashion, but Museum Sparks Plenty of Debate." *Toronto Star*, 26 August.

Jonaitis, Aldona (ed.) (1991), *Chiefly Feasts: The Art and History of the Kwakiutl Potlatch*, New York: American Museum of Natural History; Seattle: University of Washington Press.

Kovacs, Steven (2006), "Letter to the Editor." *International Herald Tribune*, 8–9 July.

Moerland, René (2006), "Primitieve, herstel, verre kunst," in "Cultured Supplement." *NRC Handelsblad* (3 June): 19.

Naumann, Peter (2006), "Making a Museum: 'It Is Making Theater, Not Writing Theory.'" Interview with Stéphane Martin. *Museum Anthropology* 29 (2): 118–27.

Roth, Solen (2006), "Objets des Autres et relations (post)-coloniales à l'altérité. Master 2 Recherche, 'Dynamique des cultures et des sociétés.'" Département de Sociologie et d'Anthropologie, Université Lumière Lyon 2.

# CHAPTER 38
# FIELDS AND LABS
*Roger Sansi*

In 2008 I attended a workshop at Can Xalant. This [art production] center was in an old farmhouse on the outskirts of Mataró, a town in the periphery of Barcelona; it wasn't exactly around the corner. But the place was packed when I arrived. The name of the workshop was "The Transparent Factory," and its aim was to discuss the meanings of "production" in contemporary art. Most of the speakers, artists, critics, curators, between their late twenties and late forties, were relatively fluent in contemporary critical theory, and shared some common view of the contemporary artistic condition. This implied, basically, a frontal rejection of the romantic myth of the artist as genius, and creator; the artist, from their perspective, is a producer among others, a worker. This production is not individual, but collective; many of them in fact belonged to different art collectives. Furthermore, this production should not be commercial, addressed to an exclusive and elitist market, but public. For most of them, art was not a self-justified activity, "art for art's sake," but a means to an end—this end being, in most cases, social and political.

Towards the end of the day, after several very dense and thoughtful presentations, one of the members of the audience, with a foreign accent, dared to formulate a question. "You have spent the whole day talking about artistic production," she said, "and I have been told that this is a center of artistic production … But I can't see any artworks around. Where are the artworks? Where is the production?"

It was clear that this person did not belong to the contemporary art world of Barcelona, and that this was her first time in that place and at such an event; in fact she explicitly said that in her country art production centers are full of paintings and sculptures, which was obviously not the case in Can Xalant.

At this point the director of the center made an intervention, saying something that most of the speakers up to then had taken for granted. Art today, he said, does not necessarily focus so much on the production of objects like paintings or sculptures, but in experimentation with processes and methodologies; the final result may be rather immaterial, it may be more a process of learning and knowledge than of material production. In fact the name of the art center was "Can Xalant. Center for Creation and Contemporary Thought" (Centre de Creació i Pensament Contemporani).

Can Xalant itself, as a "project," opened in 2005. At that time the town of Mataró was experiencing a real estate boom, and the city council decided to preserve the historic farm building in its periphery called Can Xalant and use it for cultural purposes. The city council launched a call for "projects" to manage the center under contract. The bid was won by a collective of contemporary artists from Mataró, in conjunction with a cultural management firm, Transit. They proposed to use the building as an art production center, a "factory of creation."

The Can Xalant project had four main working programs: residency, lab, curatorship, and diffusion. First, in terms of residency, it offered working spaces for artists, providing all the material they required for their work within the budget of the art center. These residencies were for both local and international artists. They didn't just consist of workspaces, but the residents could actually live there: the center included an apartment with different rooms.

As a "lab," the center offered media and digital resources for the production of photography or film, a room that could be used for film sets, as well as the assistance of a media technician. But the "lab" wasn't only the media lab; more generally, courses and workshops were also defined as part of the laboratory. These workshops were not only technical, but they also involved theoretical and political subjects, and they were participative (open to the public). This expanded definition of the "lab" comes from the notion that artistic experimentation also includes all these practices of knowledge production. Experimentation and research in art is both a practical and intellectual endeavor; in fact it is difficult to distinguish the two. These lab activities had a training component, but they were also a form of collaborative production and a social event. In fact, according to one of the directors of the art center, in Can Xalant "everything was lab."

To explain more thoroughly what was being produced at Can Xalant, I will give some examples of artists who had a residency there, and then I will focus on one of its more important projects, *We Can Xalant*.

I will start with two of the residents: Cristina Ibáñez and Carolina Bonfim. Cristina Ibáñez was a resident in Can Xalant for a couple of years following completion of her studies in Fine Arts. She applied for a workspace in Can Xalant partially, as she herself recognized, because having a workspace forced her to be disciplined to work. But she didn't use the workspace to think about future projects: "in the workshop I only produce, I don't think."[1] The ideas for her work come from everyday life, from the street. The first project she showed me is called *The Train Route*, and consists essentially of a roll of paper that she took on her train ride to Barcelona, in the commute she made every day from home to university. This was an outcome of boredom: in her own words, "Many times I do things because I get bored or to spend time …"[2] With a pencil in her hand, she would register the bumps of the train, like a Geiger earthquake counter. This was, or could be considered to be, an action, but she says she is more interested in the register (the paper) than the action itself.

Common threads in Cristina's work are monotony, chance, and the use of time. In another time-based project, Cristina transcribed the broadcast of a football match. Again, this action was a result of boredom; she doesn't like football, but watching matches on TV is an almost compulsory social event with her friends. She decided to register this action as a video in which one can hear, but not see, the broadcast. Instead of the match images, the video shows the words of the transcription appearing simultaneously with the audio on the screen. In a similar way to the previous project, Cristina is interested in the "bumps" along the way—this time through the mismatch between the spoken word and her transcription; not being a professional transcriber, she often made mistakes, forgot or misspelled words.

In her everyday trajectories Cristina finds ideas, sentences, or images that she captures with her cell phone. In fact there are many thoughts, images, or ideas that come to her but which are not her art work (in her own terms, in Catalan "*no son obra*") because she hasn't thought about, or doesn't know, how to present them as "art"—how to produce them, as it were. For example, she spends a lot of time driving, and once she saw a driver's license plate with the number 0000. She found that funny, and took a picture. After that, she started a "collection" of license plates with numbers under 100. But she stopped doing it because on one occasion she almost had an accident. She doesn't think she can turn this into work ("*no es obra*") or that anyone but her is interested. Likewise, while we visit her workspace, she shows me a group of boxes she has made; with a nervous laugh, she says this is not actually her work: "I just made it, but it's not work, it's not production."[3] In fact she remembers that one of her teachers in art school told her once, "you are not very productive."

What is the difference between "work" ("*obra*," or "*Oeuvre*" in French) and life? Not easy to answer. Artists may try to make a distinction, but in fact it is not always clear if these non-work activities will eventually become "work," a "project," "art."

Carolina Bonfim is also a good example of these fluctuating limits of art and the everyday, project and chance. Carolina is a Brazilian artist from São Paulo who discovered Can Xalant on her first visit to Barcelona. When she came back to Barcelona for good, she decided to spend some weeks in residence at Can Xalant, actually living there, to focus on the project she was undertaking: she was writing a report about the relationship between performance and site-specific arts for the Brazilian Arts Foundation. She needed time and space to separate herself; in her own terms, "residencies oblige to do something."[4] After that she became a stable resident with a workshop.

Carolina comes from the field of performance. She arrived in Barcelona as a member of an art collective, Corrosivo. She has been in several art residencies before, in Brazil, Argentina, and France. But she liked Can Xalant in particular, she says, because she found it very laid-back. At the time I talked to her, she had been working on a "project" which had not started as such, called *Moog*. One night, shortly after coming to Barcelona, she decided to go out on her own, and she ended up going to a club. Once inside the club, she was quite surprised by the way people danced, which was quite different from clubs in Brazil. She was fascinated with the different use of the body, and started to go to that club (called Moog) often. She spent the time looking at the dancers and memorizing their movements. Back at home she would rehearse the movements from memory. Initially, she says, this was not a "project," just something she did for fun. But then she was invited to present a performance, and she decided to perform what she had learnt at the club: her embodiment of these movements. And she called this piece *Moog*.

As we can see, the projects that Carolina develops also have a component of chance, of encounter with everyday life. Her work is not exactly "site-specific," but many times her projects don't start intentionally, they just reveal themselves as such at the end of the process. Like in Cristina's case (or for that matter Duchamp), what is "work" and what is not eventually only reveals itself in the process of making it.

In the medium term, however, there is one important difference between Cristina and Carolina. The first has almost abandoned her career as an artist, becoming an educator. On the other hand, Carolina is pursuing her career as an artist, applying for grants and residencies, participating in shows, working on further projects. Building a trajectory, she has to demonstrate a purpose and coherence to provide a clear narrative, which can give her work an identity among others. As a result she has to keep producing outputs of her work, in the form of performances, photography, or video of her actions, reports for projects, etc.

In comparison to these personal trajectories, the temporalities and forms of objectification of participative projects may take a very different shape. The story of the *We Can Xalant* project is in many ways central to the very essence of the art center itself, as a "project."

One of the first works made at Can Xalant in 2005 was a stilt house, the "Xiringuito," made of recycled materials on the center's patio, under the coordination of the Japanese artist Tadashi Kawamata. This was a collaborative event that embodied the spirit of the place: the objective was participation, more than the building itself. But in July 2008, the Xiringuito burnt down; some "pyromaniacs" came to burn the shack with gas. It was not clear who they were; the center is close to an area full of nightclubs, so maybe the pyre made the night for some revelers. In any case the team at Can Xalant didn't seem to be too concerned, they took it as fair play. Their provisional conclusion was that "ephemeral art can't last."

But as time passed, the Can Xalant team thought of building something new on the patio to replace the Xiringuito. This new project was also a response to their concerns in terms of the "diffusion" of the center outside its doors. Up to then, the activity of Can Xalant had focused mainly in the laboratory, which was open to everyone, but the burning of the stilt house perhaps was pointing to the fact that Can Xalant had to work in closer connection with its immediate surroundings; it had to work outside its premises. The project *We Can Xalant* emerged precisely as a response to this concern, with the idea of building a "nomadic prosthesis" of the center.

*We Can Xalant* was the outcome of a fairly complex network of agents, as is quite common in these cases. Initially, it received funding from Disonancias, a platform "for driving open and collaborative innovation between artists and companies." The original idea was to offer placements for artists in companies which did not necessarily have a relationship with contemporary art, to develop research projects that "enable creative social environments," looking at "creation as a factor of innovation."[5] Disonancias was bringing the discourse of the "artistic model" of work full circle: putting artists to work in an actual context of "innovation." In this case the artists were a77, a collective of architects from Argentina, with Pau Faus, a local architect, and the company was Transit Projectes, which was in charge of the administration of Can Xalant.

Initially, a77 and Pau Faus didn't know exactly what they were going to do. The first few months were spent resolving how to transform the remains of Kawamata's stilt house into a "nomadic prosthesis" and still respect the idea of working exclusively with recycled materials. Then they came up with the idea of putting two abandoned caravans inside the remaining structure, one of which could be still used on the road, while the other would be used as an external room of the center. Caravans don't need to have a license plate or car insurance, and any car can take them, so they would be easy to use as a "mobile device." Nevertheless, it took a long time to find two abandoned caravans, restore them and, worst of all, go through the long bureaucratic process of getting the MOT certificate for the caravan that was still in use. Once they had all the permits, they could finally put the caravans into the structure, in a collective process of building similar to Kawamata's original project.

*We Can Xalant* was, in part, a form of architecture, but of course it also involved many forms of work that didn't have much to do with what an architect learns at school: from restoring caravans, to finding permits, to working in collaboration with a bunch of people to put a caravan on top of an already existing structure. The whole process was collaborative and "transdisciplinary"; it relied less on a clearly outlined project and the professional skill of the artists/architects than on the collective process of learning by working with different materials, places, and situations, in "bricolage" with people and things. It was a research process rather than a project. This "bricolage" was not just a form of "DIY" ("do it yourself") but also of DIWO ("do it with others").

Eventually the caravan became the mobile unity of Can Xalant. It was at the disposal both of the resident artists and of the neighbors' association of the area, for them to use as they wished: for educational purposes, to show films, etc. In 2011, the mobile caravan was also used for a research project, *Camping, Caravaning, Arquitecturing* [*sic*], a psychogeographic "drift" (in the caravan) through the camping sites of the Mediterranean coast of Spain, to describe their architecture, use of the territory, and the "forms of nomadic life" of these sites.[6]

*We Can Xalant* was participative in two senses: first the building of the caravan/shack was a collective endeavor; it wasn't made just for the space and the people inside the art center, but was also available to the people outside it, the surrounding neighborhood. It was a gift to all of them, a kind of reverse Trojan horse, from the inside to the outside. The name "*We Can Xalant*" made reference to "Yes We Can" in English, and its politics were also quite clear: creating communities through collaborative processes of construction.

But beyond the project *We Can Xalant*, the use of this "gift," as objectified in the caravan, has taken an unexpected turn. The city council of Mataró decided not to renew the contract of Can Xalant in 2012; that was the end of the "project." The justification was the budgetary cuts of the regional government, but this was clearly also a political decision; the party that came to power in Mataró in the previous year had promised the closure of the center if they won the elections, attending to the protests of some of their conservative voters, who thought that the center produced "nonsense," whereas an art center should be showing painting and sculpture.[7] In spite of the opposition of the local neighborhood association and all the other political parties in the local council, the new local government closed the center in 2013.

As a result, all the "production" of Can Xalant has become the property of the city council, including the *We Can Xalant* project. The structure on the patio was thrown away, but the caravan was preserved, and has recently been used as an artwork at an exhibition in the center of Barcelona. As I mentioned, the caravan in the show wasn't making direct reference to Can Xalant, or to the *We Can Xalant* project, but to one of the art projects that used it: *Camping, Caravaning, Arquitecturing*. This upset some of the people who were involved in its production, not simply because it made no particular reference to their work or authorship but because it didn't explain what happened with Can Xalant. In other words, the "authors" recognized that this was not simply their "artwork," which as a gift and a device had acquired its own life besides their ideas, but they also lamented that it had ended up being something very different to what they had expected: just a piece of "equipment," furniture for the city council of Mataró, to be kept in its depot.

The caravan of Can Xalant can give us a glimpse of the contradictions that can emerge out of collaborative art projects, in terms of their objectification. The caravan in itself is not simply an object, an artwork with an author or authors, and even less a commodity to be sold in an art market, but a constitutive component of several different assemblages and processes, at different levels: from Can Xalant as an art production center, to specific art projects that use it as a device, like *Camping, Caravaning* … It is also the outcome of a collaborative process of work, a gift to a community or several interrelated communities (from the local community to the artistic community). But as these assemblages and processes implode, as these "projects" are closed, if not finished, the process/device/gift of the caravan is reduced to something else, perhaps much more simple: a piece of public equipment.

## Notes

1. Personal interview, June 2012.
2. Ibid.
3. Ibid.
4. Personal interview, June 2012.
5. http://www.disonancias.com/es/ (last accessed 27 March 2014).
6. http://vimeo.com/32586846 (last accessed 19 July 2013).
7. See http://www.capgros.com/opinio/detall.asp?id=3966 (last accessed 19 July 2013).

# PART VII

# ANTHROPOLOGY AND THE ARTS—INTERSECTIONS AND COLLISIONS

## Preface

Many commenters on anthropological practice have rightly pointed out that there is a commonality between the ways in which the fieldworker transforms her impressions, notes, hunches, recordings, and other unwieldy forms of data into text and the way an artist transforms the viscerality of experience into a work of art (Dewey; Foster 1996). This similarity has given rise to a notable exchange. Artists now use something-like-ethnography freely, research and sociability having become critical elements of contemporary art the world over. While anthropologists, for their part, have expanded the narrow, scholarly forms by means of which their research was communicated to include experimentation across media. Anthropologists write differently and think differently about writing. They also paint, make movies, assemble photo essays, and curate everything from sound events in galleries to conferences (see the work of the Ethnographic Terminalia collective). This imperfect, if promising and often fertile intermingling between contemporary art practice and anthropological research methods has been well documented in a series of books edited by Arnd Schneider and Christopher Wright (2006, 2010, 2013; Schneider and Pasqualino 2014) and is represented here by Roger Sansi-Roca's work with contemporary artists and activists in Spain (see Part IV).

While acknowledging this history of "cross-fertilization" of anthropology-with-the-arts (and vice versa) over the past thirty years, here the Reader takes deliberate steps to move beyond this metaphor to provide examples of more smashingly intimate, cross-disciplinary comings together, many of which are not so straightforwardly productive. Though less well represented at present, this way of conjoining art with anthropology is also not new; as both John Dewey and Dale Pesmen pointed out in Section I, much of what art does is allow for the inchoate, the nonsensical, the unrecoupable, or the just plain confusing aspects of daily life to come through into presentation and representation. And as Marko Živković makes clear in his piece in this section, the nausea that follows from the mixing of social frames accomplished by artists and others is not a failing but rather an accurate and affective representation of certain sorts of vertigo inducing interactions. There are, in other words, other things anthropologists have long been doing with art and that artists have just as long been doing with anthropology than is typified by the exchange of research methods (ethnography) and final forms (art works).

The section opens with James Clifford's now classic piece which charts anthropology's emergence as a discipline grounded in fieldwork and reportage (rather than primarily in collecting) to the simultaneous and intertwined development of surrealism in France in the 1920s and 1930s. At that moment and in that place the artistic approach and the ethnographic project were so utterly entangled it was impossible to say where one began and the other ended. As Clifford himself points out, the uninteresting task was to attempt to disentangle them. By investigating the specific qualities and instances of this murky moment, Clifford provides an alternate history of anthropology's relationship to fieldwork and collecting from that provided by Bronisław Malinowski (what George Marcus calls "the classic Malinowskian mise-en-scène", see Schneider and Wright 2010: 83) or by Stocking (1985) (from cabinets of curiosity through museums). Clifford's tale emphasizes the playful, the obscene, and the pedagogical, as anthropologists and artists inhabited the same milieu, attended the same university courses, travelled on the same research trips, published in the same publications, and were in fact often two facets of the same person (see especially Leiris 1997 [1948], 1989 [1958]; Bataille 1985, 1993).

Marko Živković's contribution is marked by an ebullience similar to Clifford's as he considers the appearance of the performance artist Marina Abramović within the context of his own university, indeed, in his own course on the Anthropology of Art. Abramović, who claims something of an ethnographer's diligence, has spent long periods of time learning the lifeways of people distant to her own world while refusing to stick to scholarly norms regarding what one believes, propagates, or does with other people's ways of being. As such she effected much the same discomfort upon the bourgeoning anthropologists in Živković's course as upon the art historians (whose class she also visits) because, he argues, of the ways in which she is herself flickering into and out of social frames (see Goffman 1959). There are things and persons, including Abramović herself, that function much like the ubiquitous line drawing which is both a duck and rabbit but never the two at once. We humans can only see either the rabbit or the duck; even if we switch quickly between the two points of view, it's impossible to see them both simultaneously (this is reminiscent of Helmreich's discussion of taking bodily incapacities for hearing-under-water into consideration when conducting investigations of the depths of the sea). The duck/rabbit is banal, but it shimmers nonetheless. Živković, in considering Abramović, advises us not to be flat-footed in our insistence to take only one view at the expense of the other. The trick, rather, is to focus on her capacity to flicker, or shimmer, as she flips between recognizable fields of activity.

Both Clifford's and Živković's contributions point us toward a consideration of fieldwork as the point at which intersections might be most obvious and crashes most difficult to avoid, whether learning to see the flicker, draw pictures (Taussig; Edinger 2015) or let the murk of seminal moments remain. So do we find Margaret Mead and Gregory Bateson arguing, with the fluid, if pointy ease of old friends, over the differences, and relative values, of an anthropological versus artistic means of filming fieldwork. Katherine Dunham's work orients us toward the hows and whats of ethnography, from her experiences seeking out and participating in Haitian ritual (for similarly descriptive essays on the process of ethnography see also Helmreich; Geertz). Dorathi Bock Pierre's later interview with Dunham brings her professional work as a dancer and choreographer into explicit conversation with this fieldwork and her anthropological training. We see how Dunham's ethnographic research in the Caribbean was retuned into motions and sounds of a newly emergent African American mode of dance. In this, Dunham, one of the most influential choreographers in American history, was both political and progressive as she moved American dance beyond the slim, white confines of ballet.

In Dunham's own text, which is the story of finding a dance, she uses a writerly trope common to many ethnographies. Dunham's story goes like this. It's all going to hell. The data she seeks just isn't there, her fieldwork in Haïti is drawing to a close and all she seems to have collected are rumors and lies. Quite suddenly and unexpectedly everything changes. With luck, perseverance, and preparedness, she finds herself in the midst of the dances she had sought; she even has the good fortune of dancing them.

This essay, and this trope, has its echo in Ursula Le Guin's work of fiction about an envoy arriving, alone, on a planet twenty-two light years from his Earthly home. Le Guin, an august science fiction writer, and the daughter of anthropologists Alfred and Theodora Kroeber, explores the ethnographic project in many of her novels, but none so much as *The Left Hand of Darkness*, Hugo award winner for 1970. In *The Left Hand of Darkness* we see the envoy's angst at having failed, due to his own incapacities to understand the complexities of the social world of which he is a part, his boredom, the problem with having to record details about the dullest of things when what he wants is the 'dance'—not its drama so much as the insight it might offer him. Here anthropology is rendered in fiction. There is no ethnographer as artist or artist as ethnographer, rather there is an author infinitely familiar with anthropological research as a particular mode of interacting with unfamiliar life worlds, and this intimate knowledge is taken as the undergirding for a work of fiction about the same.

Michael Taussig, an anthropologist who makes much of the visual, poetic, and political capacities of language in this piece, gives us a story about a messy bit of scribble in his field notebook. Taussig's intention in making the drawing was not that of an artist, rather it provides him with a visual mnemonic of a shockingly brief moment in which he saw a thing happening. It stuck in the maw of his mind. He "wrote" it in graphite in the notebook closest at hand and then, later he "wrote" it in words, bringing the world he knew, cultural, political, economic, bodily, and fraught to bear upon this singular movement. Circling back again and again to what he saw, the moment happening, the drawing, Taussig seems almost to weave (Ingold 2013) rather than to write this story. As a weaving, a drawing, a telling, Taussig effects a sort of stillness, which allows the reader to rest with him in this one jarring moment, this one glimpse out of the corner of his eye in the three seconds it took to pass, in a taxi, through a tunnel.

In "Anthropology and the Arts—Intersections and Collisions", as in other sections of the volume, we demonstrate a long-standing diversity of approaches to, and outcomes of, anthropological and artistic activities that come into occasionally frictive (Tsing 2005), sometimes totally befuddling, and every so often also fertile relationships at points of contact.

## Ethnographic exercises

### *Media (sound or visual documentation)*

Use media (visual [photos or video] or sound) to document an aspect of your case. Consider how you will approach this: Will this serve as documentation for further analysis? Will it be an example of "sensory ethnography"? What would make it one or the either, and what do you have to do to achieve your goal?

### *Making something with someone*

Part 1. Conduct participant-observation, with an emphasis on participation, and in particular, making. What you do will depend on your case. Write fieldnotes on your experience. These will probably have to be written after the fact, but you might be able to take notes during your "making" research experience. Pay attention to the physicality of the work, the tools, the form, the outcome. Fieldnotes should include as much detail as possible and be non-evaluative or reflective. Simply describe.

Part 2. Then write a one to two page summary of the process from your notes; include an analysis, which is to say, add something you deduced about the experience from the experience. Share this with the person you did the project with, and take notes on (or after) that discussion

## Further reading

Adair, Gilbert (1993), "The Eleventh Day: Perec and the Infra-Ordinary." *Review of Contemporary Fiction* 13: 98–8.

Bataille, Georges (1985), *Visions of Excess: Selected Writings 1927–1939*, Allan Stoekl (ed.), Vol. 14, Minneapolis: University of Minnesota Press.

Bataille, Georges (1993), *The Accursed Share, Vols. 2 and 3: The History of Eroticism and Sovereignty*, trans. Robert Hurley, Cambridge, MA: Zone Books.

Coles, Alex (ed.) (2000), *Site-Specificity: The Ethnographic Turn, De-, Dis-, Ex-* 4, London: Black Dog Publishing.

Cornea, Christine (2003), "David Cronenberg's Crash and Performing Cyborgs." *The Velvet Light Trap* 52 (1): 4–14.

Foster, Hal (1996), "The Artist as Ethnographer," in *The Return of the Real: The Avant-Garde at the End of the Century*, 171–204, Cambridge, MA: MIT Press.

Grimshaw, Anna and Amanda Ravetz (2009), *Observational Cinema: Anthropology, Film, and the Exploration of Social Life*, Bloomington: Indiana University Press.

Hendrickson, Carol (2008), "Visual Fieldnotes: Drawing Insights in the Yucatan." *Visual Anthropology Review* 24 (2): 117–32.

Hendrickson, Carol (2010), "Ethno-Graphics: Keeping Visual Field Notes in Vietnam." *Expedition Magazine* 52 (1): 31–9.

Ingold, Tim (2013), *Making: Anthropology, Archaeology, Art and Architecture*, London: Routledge.

Keller, Jenny (2011), "Why Sketch?" in Michael R. Candfield (ed.), *Field Notes on Science & Nature*, 161–85, Cambridge, MA: Harvard University Press.

Leiris, Michel (1989 [1958]), *La Possession et Ses Aspects Théatraux Chez Les Éthiopiens Du Gondar*, Paris: Fata Morgana.

Leiris, Michel (1997 [1948]), *La Langue Secrète Des Dogon de Sanga*, Paris: Jean-Michel Place.

Luvaas, Brent (2013), "Shooting Street Style in Indonesia: A Photo Essay." *Clothing Cultures* 1 (1): 59–81.

Raffles, Hugh (2010), *Insectopedia*, New York: Pantheon Books.

Schneider, Arnd, and Caterina Pasqualino (2014), *Experimental Film and Anthropology*, London: Bloomsbury Academic.

Schneider, Arnd and Christopher Wright (eds) (2006), *Contemporary Art and Anthropology*, Oxford: Berg.

Schneider, Arnd and Christopher Wright (eds) (2010), *Between Art and Anthropology: Contemporary Ethnographic Practice*, Oxford: Berg.

Schneider, Arnd and Christopher Wright (eds) (2013), *Anthropology and Art Practice*. London: Bloomsbury Academic.

Tsing, Anna Lowenhaupt (2005), *Friction: An Ethnography of Global Connection*, Princeton, NJ: Princeton University Press.

# CHAPTER 39
# ON ETHNOGRAPHIC SURREALISM

*James Clifford*

> The coupling of two realities, reconcilable in appearance, upon a plane which apparently does not suit them … .
>
> Max Ernst, "What is the Mechanism of Collage?" 1936[1]

André Breton often insisted that surrealism was not a body of doctrines, or a definable idea, but an activity. The present essay is an exploration of ethnographic activity, set, as it must always be, in specific cultural and historical circumstances.

I am using the term *surrealism* in an obviously expanded sense, to circumscribe an esthetic that values fragments, curious collections, unexpected juxtapositions—that works to provoke the manifestation of extraordinary realities drawn from the domains of the erotic, the exotic, and the unconscious. This set of attitudes cannot, of course, be limited to Breton's group; and the Surrealist Movement narrowly defined—with its manifestos, schisms, and excommunications—is not the concern here. Indeed, the figures I will be discussing were at best fellow travellers, or dissidents who broke with Breton. They partook, nonetheless, of the general disposition I am calling surrealist,[2] a tangled disposition foreshortened here in an attempt to disengage its ethnographic dimension.

## The ethnographic surreal

In "The Storyteller," Walter Benjamin describes the transition from a traditional mode of communication based on continuous oral narrative and shared experience to a cultural style characterized by bursts of "information"—the photograph, the newspaper clip, the perceptual shocks of a modern city. Benjamin begins his essay with World War I:

> A generation that had gone to school on a horse-drawn streetcar now stood under the open sky in a countryside in which nothing remained unchanged but the clouds, and beneath the clouds, in a field of force of destructive torrents and explosions, was the tiny, fragile human body.[3]

Reality is no longer a given, a natural, familiar environment. The self, cut loose from its attachments, must discover meaning where it may—a predicament, evoked at its most nihilistic, that underlies both surrealism and modern ethnography. Earlier literary and artistic refractions of Benjamin's modern world are well known—the experience of Baudelaire's urban *flâneur*, Rimbaud's systematic sensual derangements, the analytic decomposition of reality begun by Cézanne and completed by the cubists, and especially Lautréamont's famous definition of beauty, "the chance encounter on a dissecting table of a sewing machine and an umbrella."

To see culture and its norms—beauty, truth, reality—as artificial arrangements, susceptible to detached analysis and comparison with other possible dispositions, is crucial to an ethnographic attitude.

In his classic *History of Surrealism,* Maurice Nadeau has stressed the formative impact of wartime experiences on the founders of the Surrealist Movement—Breton, Éluard, Aragon, Péret, Soupault.[4] After Europe's collapse into barbarism and the manifest bankruptcy of the ideology of progress, after a deep fissure had opened between the experience of the trenches and the official language of heroism and victory, after the romantic rhetorical conventions of the nineteenth century had proved themselves incapable of representing the reality of the war, the world was permanently surrealist. Fresh from the trenches, Guillaume Apollinaire coined the term in a letter of 1917.

Before the war, Apollinaire had decorated his study with African "fetishes," and in his long poem "Zone" these objects would be invoked as "des Christ d'une autre forme et d'une autre croyance." For the Paris avant-garde, Africa (and to a lesser degree, Oceania and America) provided a reservoir of other forms and other beliefs. This suggests a second element of the ethnographic surrealist attitude, a belief that the Other (whether accessible in dreams, fetishes, or Lévy-Bruhl's *mentalité primitive*) was a crucial object of modern research. Unlike the exoticism of the nineteenth century, which departed from a more or less confident cultural order in search of a temporary *frisson,* a circumscribed experience of the bizarre, modern surrealism and ethnography began with a reality deeply in question. Others appeared now as serious human alternatives; modern cultural relativism became possible. As artists and writers set about after World War I putting the pieces of culture together in new ways, their field of possible selection had drastically expanded. The "primitive" societies of the planet were increasingly available as aesthetic, cosmological, and scientific resources. This presupposed something more than an older Orientalism; it required modern ethnography. The postwar context was structured by a basically ironic experience of culture. For every local custom or truth, there was always an exotic alternative, a possible juxtaposition or incongruity. Below (psychologically) and beyond (geographically) any ordinary reality there existed another reality. Surrealism shared this ironic situation with relativist ethnography.

The term *ethnography* as I am using it here is evidently something different from the empirical research technique of a human science that in France was called "ethnology," in England "social" and in America "cultural" anthropology. I am referring to a more general cultural predisposition which cuts through modern anthropological science and which it shares with modern art and writing. The ethnographic label suggests here a characteristic attitude of participant observation among the artifacts of a defamiliarized cultural reality. The surrealists were intensely interested by exotic worlds, among which they included a certain Paris. Their attitude, while comparable to that of the fieldworker who strives to render the unfamiliar comprehensible, tended to act in the reverse sense, by making the familiar strange. The contrast is, in fact, generated by a continuous play of the familiar and the strange, of which ethnography and surrealism are two elements. This play is constitutive of the modern cultural situation I am assuming as the ground for my account.

The world of the city for Aragon's *Paysan de Paris,* or for Breton in *Nadja,* was a source of the unexpected and the significant—significant in ways that suggested beneath the dull veneer of the real the possibility of another, more miraculous world based on radically different principles of classification and order. The surrealists frequented the Marché aux Puces, the vast flea market of Paris, where one could rediscover the artifacts of culture, scrambled and rearranged. With luck one could bring home some bizarre or unexpected object, a work of Art with nowhere to go—"readymades" like Marcel Duchamps's bottle rack, and *objets sauvages,* African or Oceanian sculptures. Such objects—stripped of their functional context—were necessary furnishings of the avant-garde studio.

It is well to suspend disbelief in considering the practices, and the excesses, of surrealist "ethnographers." And it is important to understand their way of taking culture seriously, as a contested reality—a way which included the ridiculing and reshuffling of its orders. This much is needed if one is to penetrate the milieu which spawned, and oriented, the emerging French scholarly tradition. More generally, it is advisable not to dismiss surrealism too quickly as frivolous, in contrast with the *sérieux* of ethnographic science. The connections between anthropological research and research in literature and the arts, always strong in this century, need to be more fully explored. Surrealism is ethnography's secret sharer—for better or worse—in the description, analysis, and extension of the grounds of twentieth-century expression and meaning.

## Taxonomies

It requires an effort of imagination to recapture the sense, or senses, of the word *ethnography* as it was used in the surrealist twenties. A defined social science, with a discernible method, a set of classic texts, and university chairs was not yet fully formed. Examining the word's uses in a publication like *Document* (a glossy review edited in 1929 by Georges Bataille), we see how ethnographic evidence and an ethnographic attitude could function in the service of a subversive cultural criticism. In the subtitle of *Documents*—"Archéologie, Beaux Arts, Ethnographie, Variétés"—the wild card was "Ethnographie." It denoted a radical questioning of norms and an appeal to the exotic, the paradoxical, the *insolite* (unusual, odd). It implied, too, a levelling and a reclassification of familiar categories. "Art," spelt with a capital *A*, had already succumbed to Dada's heavy artillery. "Culture," having barely survived this postwar barrage, was now resolutely lower case, a principle of relative order in which the sublime and the vulgar were treated as symbols of equal significance. Since culture was perceived by the collaborators of *Documents* as a system of moral and aesthetic hierarchies, the radical critic's task was one of semiotic decoding, with the aim of deauthenticating, and then expanding or displacing, the common categories. The cubists' break with the canons of realism had set the pace for a general assault on the normal. Ethnography, which shares with surrealism an abandonment of the distinction between high and low culture, provided both a fund of non-Western alternatives and a prevailing attitude of ironic participant-observation among the hierarchies and meanings of collective life.

It is instructive to attempt an inventory of ethnographic perspectives, as revealed by their use in *Documents.* Before one has caught the drift, one is surprised, for example, to come upon the title of an article by Carl Einstein (author of *Negerplastik* (1915), a pioneering account of African sculpture viewed in the light of cubism), "André Masson, étude ethnologique." What did it mean, in 1929, to study an avant-garde painter "ethnologically"? From the outset Einstein sounds the cubist-surrealist battle cry:

> One thing is important: to shake [*ébranler*] what is called reality by means of non-adapted hallucinations so as to alter the value hierarchies of the real. Hallucinatory forces create a breach in the order of mechanistic processes; they introduce blocs of "a-causality" in this reality which had been absurdly given as such. The uninterrupted fabric of this reality is torn, and one inhabits the tension of dualisms.[5]

The "hallucinatory forces" of Masson's painting represent, according to Einstein, "the return of mythological creation, the return of a psychological archaism as opposed to a purely imitative archaism of forms." Einstein describes this mythic psychology as "totemic." To grasp the significance of Masson's metamorphoses, unexpected animal–human combinations, "it is enough to recall the primitive mask–costumes that incite identifications with animals, ancestors, etc."[27] Einstein's casual allusion, *en passant,* to masks—African? Oceanian? Alaskan? His audience will know what he means—suggests a context in which exotic or archaic possibilities are never far from the surface of consciousness, ever ready to offer confirmation for any and all breaks opened in the Western order of things. In Einstein's essay two key elements of ethnographic surrealism are noticeable: first, the corrosive analysis of a reality now identified as local and artificial; second, the supplying of exotic alternatives.

There is a third aspect of this attitude which springs to one's attention when leafing through the pages of *Documents.* Marcel Griaule provides a clear statement in an essay ridiculing the aesthetic assumptions of primitive art amateurs who doubt the purity of a Baoulé drum because the figure carved on it is holding a rifle. The ethnographic surrealist, unlike either the typical art critic or anthropologist of the period, delights in cultural impurities and disturbing syncretisms. Griaule equates the European's delectation of African art with the African's taste for textiles, gas cans, alcohol, and firearms. If Africans do not choose to imitate our high cultural products … *tant pis!* He concludes:

> Ethnography—it is quite tiresome to have to keep repeating this—is interested in the *beautiful* and the *ugly,* in the European sense of these absurd words. It has, however, a tendency to be suspicious of the beautiful, which is rather often a rare—that is monstrous—occurrence in a civilization. Ethnography is suspicious, too, of itself—for it is a white science, i.e., stained with prejudices—and it will not refuse aesthetic value to an object because it is up to date or mass produced.[6]

André Schaeffner urges a similar point in a scholarly survey of "Les instruments de musique dans un musée d'ethnographic." His strictures are now an anthropological commonplace. Read, however, in the surrealist context of *Documents,* they recover their full subversive effect.

> Whoever says ethnography admits necessarily that no object designed to produce sound or music, however "primitive" or formless it may seem, no musical instrument—whether its existence is accidental or essential—shall be excluded from a methodical classification. For this purpose, any percussive procedure, on a wooden box or on the earth itself, is of equal importance with the melodic or polyphonic means available to a violin or a guitar.[7]

Schaeffner, an early authority on Stravinsky, would come, by way of jazz, to study the music of the Dogon.

The "ethnographic" attitude provided a style of scientifically validated cultural levelling, the redistribution of value-charged categories like "music," "art," "beauty," "sophistication," "cleanliness," and so forth. The extreme relativism, even nihilism, latent in the ethnographic approach did not go unexploited by the more extreme collaborators of *Documents*. Their view of culture did not feature conceptions of organic structure, functional integration, wholeness, or historical continuity. This conception of culture can be called, without undue anachronism, semiotic. Cultural reality was composed of artificial codes, ideological identities and objects susceptible to inventive recombination and juxtaposition: Lautréamont's umbrella and sewing machine, a violin and a pair of hands slapping the African dirt.

The conception, highlighted in Schaeffner's title, of an "ethnographic museum" is of more than passing importance here. The fragmentation of modern culture perceived by Benjamin, the dissociation of cultural knowledge into juxtaposed "citations," is presupposed by *Documents*. The journal's title, of course, is indicative. Culture becomes something to be collected, and *Documents* itself is a kind of ethnographic display of images, texts, objects, labels, a playful museum which simultaneously collects and reclassifies its specimens.

The journal's basic method is juxtaposition—fortuitous or ironic collage. The proper arrangement of cultural symbols and artifacts is constantly placed in doubt: High art is combined with hideously enlarged photographs of big toes; folk crafts; *Fantômas* (a popular mystery magazine) covers; Hollywood sets; African, Melanesian, pre-Columbian, and French carnival masks; accounts of music hall performances; descriptions of the Paris slaughter-houses, and so forth. *Documents* poses, for the culture of the modern city, the problem facing any organizer of an ethnographic museum. What belongs with what? Shall masterpieces of sculpture be isolated as such or displayed in proximity with cooking pots and axe blades?[8] The ethnographic attitude must continually pose these sorts of questions, composing and decomposing culture's "natural" hierarchies and relationships. Once, in principle, everything in a culture is deemed worthy of collection and display, fundamental issues of classification and value are raised.

In *Documents*, we observe the use of ethnographic juxtaposition for the purpose of perturbing commonplace symbols. A regular section of the journal is a so-called dictionary of unexpected definitions. The entry for the word *homme* is characteristic. It recites a researcher's breakdown of the chemical composition of the average human body: enough iron to make a nail, sugar for one cup of coffee, magnesium sufficient to take a photograph, and so on. Market value, 25 francs. The body, a privileged image of order, is a favorite target. Together with a variety of other "natural" entities, it is recoded, and in the process thrown in doubt. Robert Desnos contributes a disconcerting inventory of rhetorical forms concerning the eye, and Carl Einstein's entry for the mobile symbol "nightingale" begins, "except in special cases, this does not have to do with a bird."[9]

*Crachat*, spittle, is redefined by Griaule using black African and Islamic evidence with the result that spit becomes associated with the soul, and with both good and evil spirits. In Europe, naturally, to spit on someone's face is an absolute dishonor; in West Africa it can be a mode of blessing. "Spittle acts like the soul: balm or garbage."[10] The ethnographer, like the surrealist, is licensed to shock. Leiris takes up Griaule's definition and goes further: Spittle is the permanent, spermlike sullying of the noble mouth, an organ associated in the West with intelligence and language. Spit thus resymbolized denotes a condition of inescapable sacrilege.[11] In this newly recomposed definition, to talk or to think is also to ejaculate.

An approach to representation by means of juxtaposition or collage was a familiar surrealist tack.[12] Its intent was to break down the conventional "bodies"—objects, identities—that combine to produce what Barthes would later call "the effect of the real."[13] In *Documents*, the juxtaposition of the contributions, and especially of their photographic illustrations, was designed to provoke this defamiliarization. An issue begins, for example, with an article by Leiris, "Picasso's Recent Canvasses," profusely illustrated with photographs. (These were years when Picasso seemed to be breaking and bending, almost savagely, the normal shape of the human frame.) These deformed images are followed by Bataille's "The Outcasts of Nature," a characteristic appreciation of freaks, illustrated by full-page eighteenth-century engravings of Siamese twins. Next an illustrated review of a current exhibition of African sculpture provides further visual dislocation of the "natural" body as realistically conceived in the West. The body, like a culture semiotically conceived, is not a continuous whole but an assemblage of conventional symbols and codes.[14]

*Documents*, particularly in its use of photographs, creates the order of an unfinished collage rather than that of a unified organism. Its images, in their equalizing gloss and distancing effect, present in the same plane a Châtelet show advertisement, a Hollywood movie clip, a Picasso, a Giacometti, a documentary photo from colonial New Caledonia, a newspaper clip, an Eskimo mask, an old master, a musical instrument—the world's iconography and cultural forms presented as evidence, or data. Evidence of what? Evidence, one can only say, of surprising, declassified cultural orders and of an expanded range of human artistic invention. This odd museum merely documents, juxtaposes, relativizes—a perverse collection.

The museum of ethnographic surrealism was to be improved, and channelled into more stable, continuous institutions. In 1930, *Documents*, which had become less and less recognizably a review of art, was abandoned by its chief financial backer. Three years later a reconstituted category, easily recognizable today as modern art, would be incarnated in the legendary *Minotaure*, under the direction of Skira and Teriade. A thing of beauty, *Minotaure* interspersed no photographs of slaughterhouses, Movietone Follies, or big toes among its lavishly reproduced Picassos, Dalis, or Massons. And after turning over its second issue to the Dakar–Djibouti team for a handsomely illustrated report on their African research,[15] *Minotaure* did not subsequently reserve any significant place for ethnographic evidence. The artifacts of otherness were replaced, generally, by Breton's category of the surreal—located in the psychoanalytic unconscious and all too easily co-opted by romantic notions of artistic genius or inspiration. The concrete cultural artifact was no longer called upon to play a disruptive, illuminatory role. Modern Art and Ethnology had emerged as fully distinct positions, in communication to be sure, but from a distance.

I have dwelt on *Documents* because it exemplifies with unusual clarity the chief areas of convergence between ethnography and surrealism during the twenties, and because a number of its contributors went on to become influential field workers and museologists. *Documents* reveals, too, in its subversive, nearly anarchic, documentary attitude, an epistemological horizon for twentieth-century cultural studies. If *Documents* was, as Leiris recalls, "impossible," it would be hasty to dismiss it as an aberration, a personal creation of the "impossible" Georges Bataille.[16] It attracted the participation of too many serious scholars and artists to be written off as merely self-indulgent or nihilistic. It exemplified, rather, an extreme sensitivity (more characteristic of the French ethnographic tradition than is often recognized) to the overdetermined character of what Mauss had called "total social facts."[17] Reality, after the surrealist twenties, could never again be seen as simple or continuous, describable empirically or through induction. It was Mauss who best exemplified the underlying attitude when he remarked, as he liked to, "Ethnology is like the ocean. All you need is a net, any kind of net; and then if you step into the sea and swing your net about, you're sure to catch some kind of fish."[18] If French ethnology has often seemed, to its Anglo-American critics, preoccupied with its nets to the exclusion of the fish, this attitude should not be attributed simplistically to some essential, Cartesian intellectuality or *ésprit de système.* Rather this assumption, that reality is never directly accessible, but exists only in the codes (always plural) which represent it, was an immediate legacy of the surrealist moment.

## Notes

1. Max Ernst, *Beyond Painting*, trans. Dorothea Tanning (New York: Wittenborn, Schuitz, 1948), 13.
2. My broad use of the term roughly coincides with Susan Sontag's view of surrealism as a pervasive—perhaps dominant—modern sensibility. See her *On Photography* (New York: Farrar, Straus and Giroux, 1977), 51–84. For a treatment that distinguishes the specific tradition I am discussing from the surrealism of Breton's movement, see Jean Jamin, "Un sacré collège ou les apprentis sorciers de la sociologie," *Cahiers internationaux de sociologie* 68 (1980), 5–30.
3. Walter Benjamin *Illuminations* (New York: Schocken Books, 1969), 84.
4. Maurice Nadeau, *The History of Surrealism*, trans. Richard Howard (New York: Macmillan, 1965): 1–3.
5. *Documents,* 1:2 (1929), 95.
6. *Documents,* 2:1 (1930), 46.
7. *Documents,* 1:5 (1929), 248. Schaeffner, who died in 1980, pursued a distinguished career as musicologist, ethnographer, essayist, and critic. See, particularly, volume I of his *Essais de musicologie et autres fantaisies* (Paris: Le Sycomore, 1980). Volume II is forthcoming.
8. On this museological dilemma, see an interview with Michel Leiris: "The Musée de L'Homme, Where Art and Anthropology Meet." *Réaltiés* 182 (1966), 57–63.
9. *Documents,* 1:4 (1929), 215; and 1:2 (1929), 117.
10. *Documents,* 1:7 (1929), 381.
11. Ibid., 381–82.
12. See J. H. Matthews, *The Imagery of Surrealism* (Syracuse: Syracuse University Press, 1977), 65–116.
13. Roland Barthes, "L'effet de réel," *Communications* 11 (1968), 84–89.
14. See *Documents,* 2:1 (1929).
15. "Mission Dakar-Djibouti," special issue of *Minotaure* 2 (1934).
16. Michel Leiris, "De Bataille l'impossiblei à l'impossible *Documents,*" in *Brisées*, 256–66.
17. Marcel Mauss, *The Gift,* trans. Ian Cunnison (New York: Norton, 1967), 76–77.
18. As quoted by Meyer Fortes, "On the Concept of the Person among the Tallenis," in *Colloques internationaux du C.N.R.S., no. 544, La notion de personne en Afrique Noire* (Paris: C.N.R.S., 1973), 284.

# CHAPTER 40
## TWENTY-SEVENTH DAY
*Katherine Dunham*

This afternoon I was very despondent. Mai was away on private business of her own, Ba' Teddy and Ba' Weeyums were at work in the fields, Rachel and Hannah and Sweetie were in Maggotty, and all of my old friends seemed to have deserted me. I would even have welcomed the Colonel, but he was in Balaclava visiting his sick daughter. Any other afternoon I would have been much relieved to have a few moments to myself, but today I must begin to think about leaving this country, and being alone, the thing that had been secretly troubling me for some days again confronted me. What a failure to come so far to see the dances of the Koromantee, and to have them always elude me! To find the quadrille and the shay-shay the sole expressions of the dance among these isolated people. Where, then, my theory on the survival of this particular art form which is among all primitive peoples so closely bound up with their superstitions and joys and sorrows and religion and cosmology? The one fleeting moment at Mis' Ma'y Cross's gravediggin' when Ba' Weeyums and his friends, well under the influence of rum, had entered the hut was the only indication that it existed here, aside from the Colonel's promises. And if I met with such failure on this first stop, would further wanderings through the islands of the West Indies be more fruitful?

For long I had doubted my own ability to gain the confidence of the people. Then I began to feel the hypocrisy of the Colonel and his promises. Then I was certain that such dances did not exist here, had been long ago forgotten, and were buried in the dust of the old goombay. Then a little demon would hop up and ask me what dances the Colonel would have taken to Kingston, whether he could or not; how could he have planned on and promised these dances if they really were forgotten, as some said, or if he forbade them, as others said, or if there was no goombay and no one to play it if there were one? It all seemed very complicated, and the more I thought about it the more depressed I became; so I decided to begin to pack, because early tomorrow I would have to go to Maggotty on business, and the remaining days would be crowded with last-minute preparations for departure. But first I read a little from my notes on these dances, more to torment myself than for consolation. According to Edward Long, *History of Jamaica* (London, 1774, Vol. II):

> The "goombah" another of their musical instruments, is a hollow block of wood covered with a sheepskin stripped of its hair … Their tunes for dancing are usually brisk and have an agreeable compound of the vivace and larghetto, gay and grave. They seem also well adapted to keep their dancers in just time and regular movements. The female dancer is all languishing and easy in her motions; the man all action, fire, and gesture; his whole person is variously turned and writhed every moment, and his limbs agitated with such lively exertions as serve to display before his partner the vigor and elasticity of his muscles. The lady keeps her face toward him and puts on a modest and demure look, which she counter-feits with great difficulty. In her paces she exhibits a wonderful

> address, particularly in the motion of her hips, and steady position of the upper part of her person: the right execution of this wriggle, keeping the exact time with the music is esteemed among them a particular excellence and on this account they begin to practice it early in life …

Then notes from James Phillips's *Jamaica* (London, Snow, 1843), wherein he discusses the myal dances, of which the Maroons denied all knowledge:

> Myalism, as well as fetishism, were constituent parts of obeism and included a mystery of iniquity which perhaps was never revealed to the uninitiated. The votaries of this art existed as a fraternity composed of individuals from the surrounding neighborhood who were regularly inducted into it in a dance with certain demoniacal forms … The master of ceremonies, who was usually denominated doctor, by violent and excessive dancing, as well as use of poisonous drugs deprived his victims of sensibility and apparently of life …

So apparently, at one time, the Maroons danced something quite different from the set dances at the parade. And that was not so long ago that they should profess this stale of amnesia.

I began to gather odds and ends which I must pack: the woven hammock and the rice sifter and the tambourine and the flute and my bowl of cedarwood and the table scarf Hannah had embroidered and presented as a gift to me and the river reed basket Mis' Holiday had sent me and numerous other trinkets. Suddenly I remembered that I must leave room for the goombay. And after all, why wasn't the goombay here by now? Ba' Foster had promised it for yesterday. It was growing dusk, and glad for an excuse to leave the house, which seemed a little dreary in the half-light, I decided to walk down the mountain to Ba' Foster's yard and find out what was delaying it.

The two weird little mouse-bats whirled past my head as I stepped out into the yard, and settled under the rustling straw roof with a great flapping of wings and a contented squeaking. I had never liked them, and tonight they were especially repulsive with their flash of sharp white mouse teeth and webbed furry wings.

Nearing Ba' Foster's house, I began to feel an excitement in the air, and almost involuntarily my step quickened and I was breathing faster without knowing why. Then I became aware of a *drum*. Not the deep booming of the revivalist Salvation Army drum, but the sharp staccato of a goatskin drawn tightly over a small hollowed trunk and beaten expertly by gnarled black palms …

I skidded down the last rocky decline and directly into Ba' Foster's yard. This was deserted. But farther down in the hollow, well hidden from the road behind a tangle of pimiento and breadfruit and coconut trees, I could see the smoky glow of kerosene torches and a circle of tense eager bodies, faces ecstatic in the flickering half-light; and in the middle of the circle, Mis' Mary and an old man whom I did not know performing a strange ritual, more pantomime than dance. And to one side Ba' Weeyums, squatted over the goombay, *my* goombay, his face streaked with perspiration, his eyes brilliant, and his hard palms beating the goatskin, the tone changing from sharp to sullen, from a command to a coaxing by a deft sliding of the side of the palm along the face of the drum.

Ba' Teddy saw me first. Yes, even he was there. I felt suddenly in the midst of traitors to find here these, my bosom friends.

"Evenin', evenin', Missus," said Ba' Teddy softly.

"Evenin'," I replied, winking back a tear. Ba' Foster stepped quickly forward with the goombay under one arm.

"Me jus' gwi bring eem you, Missus!" he said, with too much emphasis. "Me on de way now we'n we meet up wid' Ba' Weeyums en eem ax er play eem jus' dis' once."

I looked at Ba' Weeyums. He was first on one foot and then on the other, twisting his little felt hat around his forefinger and looking anxiously at me the while. Then suddenly I realized that this was the long hoped-for opportunity—that here were the dances I had waited so many weeks to see, and that it was not for fieldworker to bear personal grudges and carry personal grievances, but to get what the field has to offer in as graceful a manner as possible. Now it was my turn to look anxiously at Ba' Weeyums.

"But everyone's going!" I said. And to be sure, of the score of old and young who had circled the dancers when I arrived, there were now less than half.

"De' goombay eem good 'nuf," said Ba' Weeyums slowly, "but eem need *rum*. Don't no goombay talk like eem *should* talk eef eem no had de *rum*."

The rum! The rum! Of course. I loudly asked Ral if he would go up to my cottage and bring down the jug of rum from under Mai's bunk in the kitchen. He was off with unusual alacrity, whether because of the rum or because of the chance that Mai might by this hour have retired to the bunk, I do not know.

While we waited Ba' Weeyums explained that of course he could have beat the drum for me any day, but that there had been no drum to beat. Ba' Teddy explained further that all this was strictly forbidden by the Colonel, that he had cautioned them against doing these dances while I was there (my suspicions of hypocrisy were well founded), that Ba' Foster's story was true that nothing had been planned but only by the accident of Ba' Weeyums drum beating had these passers-by gathered, and that were the Colonel not at Balaclava even this would have been out of the question. Of course I must not mention these dances to anyone, and tomorrow it would be best if I would have forgotten all about them. Further, we must be very brief tonight, because while the thicket and the seclusion of the spot and the direction of the wind prevented the sound of the drum from traveling far, it wouldn't be long before all Accompong would be aroused by these almost-forgotten drum rhythms which stripped them of the veneer of the Scotch minister and cricket games at the parade and set dances, and the sleeping Koromantee and Eboe and Nago would come to the fore and things would happen that the Colonel would be certain to hear about, even at Balaclava. Just a little while, I pleaded, to break in the goombay and so that I might partake once of the things that belonged to the Maroons in the old days.

Ral returned, and Ba' Weeyums took drum and bottle off to one side. There he poured rum on the goatskin head, rubbed it in, look a long drink himself, then spat a mouthful at the drum again. Between times he mumbled in a tongue which I gathered was Koromantee. Then he poured a few drops of rum on the ground, and the baptism was over. This was for the spirit of the drum, he explained. Then he squatted over the drum again, and indeed it seemed to me that it was suddenly alive.

Though the body of the drum was shallow, and it more resembled a square stool than any drum I had previously seen, the tone was full and less staccato than before, and I was almost inclined to believe that it was alive, and that it was the spirit of some Gold Coast god come to life to grumble a protest against the long silence.

Gradually they returned, slipping from behind the coconut palms and up from the ravines and down from the mountains. I don't know how many, because I was in the midst, and there was now only one kerosene torch, and the rum was going the rounds and it all became unreal, though it all happened because the dances are still very clear to me.

I might not have come at all, for the difference that it has made. I was accepted and one of them.

The dance I had interrupted was a myal dance. Ba' Teddy explained it, as, fascinated, I watched Mis' Mary and the old man. They were facing each other. The old man took the part of the myal "doctor" and the dance was to entice into his power an evil spirit, the "duppy" of some dead worker of black magic. Ba' Weeyums led a chant in Koromantee, and the women answered. The dance interested me too much for me to try and remember the sound of the words. The evil spirit circled around the doctor hesitant, advancing and retreating, her eyes fixed, mouth clamped shut tightly, body rigid. The doctor squatted in front of her, arms wide as though to embrace her, fingers wide open and hands trembling violently. As he advanced slowly toward her, his pelvis began to move with an unmistakable sexual purpose, and the duppy responded in like manner. They hesitated in front of each other, swaying. Then she eluded his embrace with a sharp convulsive bend, and was on the other side of the circle, taunting, enticing features still hard and set but body liquid and so full of desire that I could scarcely believe that it was old Mis' Mary, grandmother of goodness knows how many.

The doctor reached out for her, gesticulating, grimacing, insinuating. Then she came to life suddenly and the pursuit was reversed. The doctor was afraid of this thing which he had done, of this woman whom he had raised from the dead with these fleshly promises. They were face to face, bodies touching, both of them squatting now with arms pressed close to their sides, elbows bent, and widespread fingers quivering violently. Ba' Teddy had stopped explaining and among the onlookers there was no sound except heavy breathing, but the chant continued and the drum, and it seemed that the air was heavy with some other heat and sound. The duppy leaned over the man, who cowered in fear from her, though their bodies were pressed tightly together. As I decided that I must close my eyes for a moment, Ba' Teddy raised his hand, and the drum and chant stopped on a single note: there was a blank silence that left both dancers and spectators dangling helplessly in mid-air.

"Dat dance bad dance," Ba' Teddy muttered, trying to calm his voice and appear merely annoyed in spite of his quick breathing. I opened my mouth to speak, but he anticipated my question and answered sharply. "Bes don' ax no furder questions, missus. Me don' see dat fer long time, en hit bad. Dat mix up wid bad biznuss. Better fer missus ef she fergit,"

I was almost relieved to be thus reprimanded, But the mood of the dance had already changed, and to a far livelier rhythm. Two men were hopping about in the circle mimicking two cocks in the thick of a fight. They switched their middles, bobbed their heads, wrinkled their faces, and stuck their necks far out crowing a challenge. The audience, tense a moment before, was now in a hysteria of laughter. One of the dancers picked up his foot high and hopped around in a circle, the other following at a gallop, hand thrust in coat pocket and flapping widely for wings. Finally one was vanquished and with a feeble squawk rolled over sadly, feet in the air. The other strutted over to him, looked disdainfully around, and flapped his wings in victory as he trotted around the circle.

I plead with Ba' Weeyums for a Koromantee war dance, and find that it is no other than the wild dance which I saw only a suggestion of at Ol' Mis' Cross's gravedigging. In this I join, along with Simon Rowe and others who have only watched so far. The few young people who are here, however, do not join in these traditional dances. They are ashamed, and I am sure that I shock them greatly; on the other hand, I feel that they watch us rather wistfully, wishing that they had the courage to give themselves up for a moment to their traditions and forget that there is a market at Maggotty and cricket games on the outside, and store-bought shoes.

The war dances are danced by both men and women. The introduction seemed to be a disjointed walking around in a loose circle, much like the warming up of an athlete. Then Henry Rowe and I are facing each other doing a step which could easily be compared to an Irish reel. Hands on hips, we hop from one foot to the other, feet turned out at right angles to the body or well "turned out," in ballet vernacular. This hopping brought us closer together, and I had to watch the others closely to keep up with Henry. We turned our backs and walked away, then turned suddenly again and hopped together. The songs are in lusty Koromantee, and from somewhere a woman procured a rattle and is shaking it in accompaniment to Ba' Weeyums. Some of the men wave sticks in the air, and the women tear off their handkerchiefs and wave them on high as they dance. Henry and I grabbed each other around the waist and ran circles around each other, first one way, then the other. A few of these turns and we separate in a melee of leaping, shouting warriors; a moment later we are "bush fightin'," crouching down and advancing in line to attack an imaginary enemy with many feints, swerves, and much pantomime. At one stage of the dance Mis' Mary and I are face to face, she no longer a duppy but a Maroon woman of the old days working the men up to a pitch where they will descend into the cockpit and exterminate one of his Majesty's red-coated platoons. She grabbed me by the shoulders and shook me violently, then we were again hopping around each other with knees high in the air, handkerchiefs and skirts flying.

When this was over we were all exhausted. The Maroons have not been accustomed to this sort of thing for a long time; nor am I who until now have known only the conventional techniques, and the far less strenuous set dances. We dispersed and I was in possession of the goombay. Ba' Teddy and Ba' Weeyums and I labored up the mountainside, and behind us shutters closed and candles were extinguished and I knew that they were all talking about the escapade of the evening, and how angry the Colonel would be if he knew, and that the "missus" must have known things that she hadn't so far divulged, about myal and obi and the old Koromantee traditions, maybe even the language …

At my cottage door, I could hear Mai snoring peacefully within, and this was very comforting after the orgy in the ravine. I remembered vaguely that Ral had left the dancing soon after he returned with the rum, and was certain that he was responsible for Mai's not having come to the dance, and perhaps for her peaceful snoring.

I pulled off my muddy shoes and crawled on top of the marosh, ignoring the bowl of rice and gourd of fresh coconut water that Mai had thoughtfully left on the kitchen table for me. I felt extremely tired and extremely comfortable. My notebook still lay open on the table. Earlier in the day I had harbored a strong resentment against the Maroons and a strong disappointment in myself. Now I had the delicious thrill of accomplishment, of having conquered an unseen enemy (the Colonel, no doubt), and of belonging completely. I only regretted as I pulled the sheet up around my chin that it had all happened so late. Well, if I ever return—and I sincerely hope that I shall—at least I shall know where to begin.

# CHAPTER 41
## A TALK WITH KATHERINE DUNHAM
*Dorathi Bock Pierre*

Katherine Dunham was born in Chicago and raised in Joliet, Illinois, where her father was in the cleaning and dyeing business. She attended public school there and was fortunate in being a student in a very progressive high school. In her second year she became a member of the extracurricular Terpsichorean Club, where her natural love of dancing was fired to ambition.

She was particularly interested in dance and rhythms as they applied to her own people, and, having theories of her own, she decided to teach and try them out when she entered the University of Chicago, and also as a means of paying her tuition. She tells with some amusement now of how when she taught straight ballet she had crowded classes, but when she taught basic rhythms as they related to the Negro her classes dwindled, for her students wanted something more showy and sophisticated.

She entered the university with no definite major in mind, but fate led her to a class in ethnology under Dr. Robert Redfield, and his remarkable insight and presentation of the subject so thrilled her that she made that her major, and later returned to the university for graduate work toward a master's degree in anthropology.

While a student at the university she studied educational dance techniques with a pupil of Margaret H'Doubler, modern dance from Ludmilla Speranzeva, ballet from Bentley Srone, and special courses from a number of dancers, including Harald Kreutzberg.

"My great interest in dance had been a subconscious feeling that it was more than a physical exercise; that it was somehow closely related to the people who danced, and naturally I was tremendously excited over the confirmation of this theory which I found in ethnology."

"My university work was very interesting, for I was off and on the campus for ten years before I completed work for my master's degree. I would attend classes until I had an offer of work and then I would stop sometimes as long as six months or more; the longest lapse was the eighteen months during 1936–8 which I spent on a Rosenwald fellowship in the West Indies."[1]

I asked of her objectives, and what she accomplished during her stay in the Caribbean. "My desire was to see first-hand the primitive dance in its everyday relationship to the people; and anthropology, which leads one to origins and the simple basic fundamentals of art which is made complex and esoteric by civilization," was the answer.

"I spent six weeks in a tiny village waiting to get just one dance; and I spent much time on the many small islands as well as Jamaica, Martinique, and Trinidad. I made innumerable records of the songs and music of the people, wrote my thesis from these findings, and a book on my experiences, written in narrative form. But more than this, I learned about the people, how they dance and, especially, why."

"I had a very amusing experience when I first went to the Islands, for the urban society leaders questioned my desire for native research, and needing the moral backing of these leaders, I gave a concert for them and included only numbers which were traditional ballet or aesthetic interpretations. They loved it, and I was given a free hand thereafter to search out my 'primitives.'"

When Miss Dunham returned to Chicago she reassembled her group of dancers and started putting her findings into practical use. Having an offer from Labor Stage in New York she took six of her dancers with her. With her entire salary from this engagement she put on a concert at the Windsor Theatre in February 1940. It created such a sensation that she did thirteen Sunday night concerts, was acclaimed by critics and the public, and became firmly established as one of the outstanding concert dancers of the United States. She and her group appeared for a year with Ethel Waters in *Cabin in the Sky*, and this summer she made a motion picture short for Warner Bros. Studios of some of her primitive dances, called *Carnival of Rhythm*.

I asked her what her future plans and ambitions were.

"I want a school in New York where I can train dancers in the knowledge and use of primitive rhythms. I want to lecture on the subjects of anthropology and ethnology and dance; and of course I want to dance. I am not interested in dance routines. I am only interested in dance as an education, a means of knowing peoples, and I want students who want to learn and have a desire to develop people and tastes."

I was sure she had interesting opinions in regard to dance in education, and questioned her, especially as it affected the Negro student.

"I am opposed to any group, either Negro or white, slavishly imitating any leader or technique. The many Negro schools and colleges in the United States should use great care in their academic approach to dance."

"First they should know what people are, and what dance is. They should study religion in its relation to dance, and have a course in religious dance to overcome prejudice against dance in communities where it exists."

"The subject should be approached on the basis of the relationship of all things to the American Negro; the tribal and cultural strains which make up the people; and an examination of the music and arts which make up the cultural strains. I believe that a person who dances should know why they dance, and to do so they must have an historical background."

"To me physical education is more than simply body development, and I have always felt that classes should be arranged on the basis of intellectual viewpoint."

"Indirect connotation through rhythm offers endless opportunity. Men can be interested through an introduction of primitive war movements in rhythm; and working rhythm into the gymnastic is the genuine approach to what dance is. Manipulation and technique can find a parallel in history; basically we must move for a reason."

"Negro schools should study the intercultural results of dance. Such simple subjects as the Kentucky Mountain Squares in relation to Plantation Squares, which are different, and the changing rhythms between the Juba and minstrel and plantation dances. The same dance through different people becomes entirely different."

"I believe this general approach could be used to advantage in all educational dance programs, but I feel Negroes have an unusual opportunity to make a contribution to our total culture through this medium."

## Note

1. Dunham departed for Jamaica early in 1935 and returned to Chicago from Haiti in late spring of 1936. The dates provided, 1936–8, are inaccurate (volume eds).

# CHAPTER 42
## A PARADE IN ERHENRANG
*Ursula Le Guin*

From the Archives of Hain. Transcript of Ansible Document 01-01101-934-2-Gethen: To the Stabile on Ollul: Report from Genly Ai, First Mobile on Gethen/Winter, Hainish Cycle 93, Ekumenical Year 1490–97.

I'll make my report as if I told a story, for I was taught as a child on my homeworld that Truth is a matter of the imagination. The soundest fact may fail or prevail in the style of its telling: like that singular organic jewel of our seas, which grows brighter as one woman wears it and, worn by another, dulls and goes to dust. Facts are no more solid, coherent, round, and real than pearls are. But both are sensitive.

I was in a parade. I walked just behind the gossiwors and just before the king. It was raining.

Rainclouds over dark towers, rain falling in deep streets, a dark storm-beaten city of stone, through which one vein of gold winds slowly. First come merchants, potentates, and artisans of the City Erhenrang, rank after rank, magnificently clothed, advancing through the rain as comfortably as fish through the sea. Their faces are keen and calm. They do not march in step. This is a parade with no soldiers, not even imitation soldiers.

Next come the lords and mayors and representatives, one person, or five, or forty-five, or four hundred, from each Domain and Co-Domain of Karhide, a vast ornate procession that moves to the music of metal horns and hollow blocks of bone and wood and the dry, pure lilting of electric flutes. The various banners of the great Domains tangle in a rain-beaten confusion of color with the yellow pennants that bedeck the way, and the various musics of each group clash and interweave in many rhythms echoing in the deep stone street.

Next, a troop of jugglers with polished spheres of gold, which they hurl up high in flashing flights, and catch, and hurl again, making fountain-jets of bright jugglery. All at once, as if they had literally caught the light, the gold spheres blaze bright as glass: the sun is breaking through.

Next, forty men in yellow, playing gossiwors. The gossiwor, played only in the king's presence, produces a preposterous disconsolate bellow. Forty of them played together shake one's reason, shake the towers of Erhenrang, shake down a last spatter of rain from the windy clouds. If this is the Royal Music no wonder the kings of Karhide are all mad.

Next, the royal party, guards and functionaries and dignitaries of the city and the court, deputies, senators, chancellors, ambassadors, lords of the Kingdom, none of them keeping step or rank yet walking with great dignity; and among them is King Argaven XV, in white tunic and shirt and breeches, with leggings of saffron leather and a peaked yellow cap. A gold finger-ring is his only adornment and sign of office. Behind this group eight sturdy fellows bear the royal litter, rough with yellow sapphires, in which no king has ridden for centuries, a ceremonial relic of the very-long-ago. By the litter walk eight guards armed with "foray guns," also relics of a more barbaric past but not empty ones, being loaded with pellets of soft iron. Death walks behind the king. Behind death come the students of the Artisan Schools, the Colleges, the Trades, and the King's Hearths, long lines of children and young people in white and red and gold and green; and finally a number of soft-running, slow, dark cars end the parade.

The royal party, myself among them, gather on a platform of new timbers beside the unfinished Arch of the River Gate. The occasion of the parade is the completion of that arch, which completes the new Road and River Port of Erhenrang, a great operation of dredging and building and roadmaking that has taken five years, and will distinguish Argaven XV's reign in the annals of Karhide. We are all squeezed rather tight on the platform in our damp and massive finery. The rain is gone, the sun shines on us, the splendid, radiant, traitorous sun of Winter. I remark to the person on my left, "It's hot. It's really hot."

The person on my left—a stocky dark Karhider with sleek and heavy hair, wearing a heavy overtunic of green leather worked with gold, and a heavy white shirt, and heavy breeches, and a neck-chain of heavy silver links a hand broad—this person, sweating heavily, replies, "So it is."

All about us as we stand jammed on our platform lie the faces of the people of the city, upturned like a shoal of brown, round pebbles, mica-glittering with thousands of watching eyes.

Now the king ascends a gangplank of raw timbers that leads from the platform up to the top of the arch whose unjoined piers tower over crown and wharves and river. As he mounts the crowd stirs and speaks in a vast murmur: "Argaven!" He makes no response. They expect none. Gossiwors blow a thunderous discordant blast, cease. Silence. The sun shines on city, river, crowd, and king. Masons below have set an electric winch going, and as the king mounts higher the keystone of the arch goes up past him in its sling, is raised, settled, and fitted almost soundlessly, great ton-weight block though it is, into the gap between the two piers, making them one, one thing, an arch. A mason with trowel and bucket awaits the king, up on the scaffolding; all the other workmen descend by rope ladders, like a swarm of fleas. The king and the mason kneel, high between the river and the sun, on their bit of planking. Taking the trowel the king begins to mortar the long joints of the keystone. He does not dab at it and give the trowel back to the mason, but sets to work methodically. The cement he uses is a pinkish color different from the rest of the mortarwork and after five or ten minutes of watching the king-bee work I ask the person on my left, "Are your keystones always set in a red cement?" For the same color is plain around the keystone of each arch of the Old Bridge, which soars beautifully over the river upstream from the arch.

Wiping sweat from his dark forehead the man—*man* I must say, having said *he* and *his*—the man answers, "Very-long-ago a keystone was always set in with a mortar of ground bones mixed with blood. Human bones, human blood. Without the blood bond the arch would fall, you see. We use the blood of animals, these days."

So he often speaks, frank yet cautious, ironic, as if always aware that I see and judge as an alien: a singular awareness in one of so isolate a race and so high a rank. He is one of the most powerful men in the country; I am not sure of the proper historical equivalent of his position, vizier or prime minister or councillor; the Karhidish word for it means the King's Ear. He is lord of a Domain and lord of the Kingdom, a mover of great events. His name is Therem Harth rem ir Estraven.

The king seems to be finished with his masonry work, and I rejoice; but crossing under the rise of the arch on his spiderweb of planks he starts in on the other side of the keystone, which after all has two sides. It doesn't do to be impatient in Karhide. They are anything but a phlegmatic people, yet they are obdurate, they are pertinacious, they finish plastering joints. The crowds on the Sess Embankment are content to watch the king work, but I am bored, and hot. I have never before been hot, on Winter; I never will be again; yet I fail to appreciate the event. I am dressed for the Ice Age and not for the sunshine, in layers and layers of clothing, woven plant-fiber, artificial fiber, fur, leather, a massive armor against the cold, within which I now wilt like a radish leaf. For distraction I look at the crowds and the other paraders drawn up around the platform, their Domain and Clan banners hanging still and bright in sunlight, and idly I ask Estraven what this banner is and that one and the other. He knows each one I ask about, though there are hundreds, some from remote Domains, Hearths and Tribelets of the Pering Stormborder and Kerm Land.

"I'm from Kerm Land myself," he says when I admire his knowledge. "Anyhow it's my business to know the Domains. They are Karhide. To govern this land is to govern its lords. Not that it's ever been done. Do you know the saying, *Karhide is not a nation but a family quarrel?*"

I am simply interested in the behavior of these people who rule a nation, in the old-fashioned sense, who govern the fortunes of twenty million other people. Power has become so subtle and complex a thing in the ways taken by the Ekumen that only a subtle mind can watch it work; here it is still limited, still visible. In Estraven, for instance, one feels the man's power as an augmentation of his character; he cannot make an empty gesture or say a word that is not listened to. He knows it, and the knowledge gives him more reality than most people own: a solidness of being, a substantiality, a human grandeur. Nothing succeeds like success. I don't trust Estraven, whose motives are forever obscure; I don't like him; yet I feel and respond to his authority as surely as I do to the warmth of the sun.

Even as I think this the world's sun dims between clouds regathering, and soon a flaw of rain runs sparse and hard upriver, spattering the crowds on the Embankment, darkening the sky. As the king comes down the gangplank the light breaks through a last time, and his white figure and the great arch stand out a moment vivid and splendid against the storm-darkened south. The clouds close. A cold wind comes tearing up Port-and-Palace Street, the river goes gray, the trees on the Embankment shudder. The parade is over. Half an hour later it is snowing.

As the king's car drove off up Port-and-Palace Street and the crowds began to move like a rocky shingle rolled by a slow tide, Estraven turned to me again and said, "Will you have supper with me tonight, Mr. Ai?" I accepted, with more surprise than pleasure. Estraven had done a great deal for me in the last six or eight months, but I did not expect or desire such a show of personal favor as an invitation to his house. Harge rem ir Tibe was still close to us, overhearing, and I felt that he was meant to overhear. Annoyed by this sense of effeminate intrigue I got off the platform and lost myself in the mob, crouching and slouching somewhat to do so. I'm not much taller than the Gethenian norm, but the difference is most noticeable in a crowd. *That's him, look, there's the Envoy.* Of course that was part of my job, but it was a part that got harder not easier as time went on; more and more often I longed for anonymity, for sameness. I craved to be like everybody else.

I walked on home to my island.[1] Its front garden was revealed now that the last of the winter's snow had melted and the winter-doors, ten feet aboveground, were sealed off for a few months, till the autumn and the deep snow should return. Around at the side of the building in the mud and the ice and the quick, soft, rank spring growth of the garden, a young couple stood talking. Their right hands were clasped. They were in the first phase of kemmer. The large, soft snow danced about them as they stood barefoot in the icy mud, hands clasped, eyes all for each other. Spring on Winter.

I had dinner at my island and at Fourth Hour striking on the gongs of Remmy Tower I was at the Palace ready for supper. Karhiders eat four solid meals a day, breakfast, lunch, dinner, supper, along with a lot of adventitious nibbling and gobbling in between. There are no large meat-animals on Winter, and no mammalian products, milk, butter or cheese; the only high-protein, high-carbohydrate foods are the various kinds of eggs, fish, nuts, and the Hainish grains. A low-grade diet for a bitter climate, and one must refuel often. I had got used to eating, as it seemed, every few minutes. It wasn't until later in that year that I discovered the Gethenians have perfected the technique not only of perpetually stuffing, but also of indefinitely starving.

The snow still fell, a mild spring blizzard, much pleasanter than the relentless rain of the Thaw just past. I made my way to and through the Palace in the quiet and pale darkness of snowfall, losing my way only once. The Palace of Erhenrang is an inner city, a walled wilderness of palaces, towers, gardens, courtyards, cloisters, roofed bridgeways, roofless tunnel-walks, small forests and dungeon-keeps, the product of centuries of paranoia on a grand scale. Over it all rise the grim, red, elaborate walls of the Royal House, which though in perpetual use is inhabited by no one beside the king himself. Everyone else, servants, staff, lords, ministers, parliamentarians, guards or whatever, sleeps in another palace or fort or keep or barracks or house inside the walls.

## Note

1. Karhosh, island, the usual word for the apartment-boardinghouse buildings that house the greatest part of the urban populations of Karhide. Islands contain 20 to 200 private rooms; meals are communal; some are run as hotels, others as cooperative communes, others combine these types. They are certainly an urban adaptation of the fundamental Karhidish institution of the Hearth, though lacking, of course, the topical and genealogical stability of the Hearth.

# CHAPTER 43
## FOR GOD'S SAKE, MARGARET: CONVERSATION WITH GREGORY BATESON AND MARGARET MEAD

*Gregory Bateson and Margaret Mead*

*Margaret Mead and Gregory Bateson were married in 1936. They had met and fallen in love in 1932 while both were doing anthropological fieldwork on the Sepik River in New Guinea (Margaret was at the same time with her second husband, Reo Fortune). In New Guinea Gregory's unusual sense of theory met Margaret's improved field methodology and sparked much of the quality in Gregory's opus on the Iatmul tribe,* Naven.

*Newly-wed in Bali, they spent two collaborative years in the most intense and productive fieldwork of their lives, developing, among other things, a still unmatched photographic analysis of the culture.*

*Their daughter Mary Catherine, Margaret's only child, was born in 1939 in the United States. Gregory and Margaret worked together on the result of their Bali fieldwork,* Balinese Character – A Photographic Analysis, *and then were separated increasingly by World War II and their own diverging interests.*

*After the war they both were involved in starting the somewhat famous Macy Conferences (1947–53) that invented cybernetics. This interview begins with their joint recollection of that critical period.*

*Margaret Mead is one of the world's most remarkable women. She got a full mixture of praise and notoriety (notorious in that day because women weren't supposed to talk about sex) with her first book,* Coming of Age in Samoa *(1928). Since then there have been ten other books and numerous honors and positions, including President of the American Anthropological Association (1960), and of Scientists' Institute on Public Information, and (this year) the American Association for the Advancement of Science, and a Curator of the American Museum of Natural History, which continues as her headquarters. In public affairs she seems to have taken over the Eleanor Roosevelt niche.*

*After Bali and the Macy Conferences Gregory Bateson went on to work with schizophrenics, alcoholics, artists, dolphins, students, and a steadily more general set of understandings of what they have in common. He coauthored a book,* Communication: The Social Matrix of Psychiatry *(1951–68, Norton), with Jurgen Ruesch, and edited* Perceval's Narrative – A Patients Account of his Psychosis, 1830–2 *(1961, Stanford). Mary Catherine, his and Margaret's daughter, wrote a book about one of Gregory's conferences,* Our Own Metaphor *(1972, Knopf). His collected papers appear in* Steps to an Ecology of Mind *(1972, Ballantine), a book that wowed me out of my shoes. If Gregory lives long enough he will get his Nobel for the Double Bind Theory of Schizophrenia.*

*Margaret is now 75, Gregory 72. They meet seldom though always affectionately. Gregory has a son John, 23, by his second wife, and a daughter Nora, 9, by Lois Bateson his present wife. This meeting with Margaret took place at Gregory's home near Santa Cruz, California, in March of this year.*

**B:** In psychoanalysis if you can recognize the same formal pattern in a dream and in a childhood memory and in how you're treating your analyst, you will say, 'Aha, it's true.' You've got it.

**M:** and when your studying a culture.

**SB:** What would be an example there?

**M:** Well, you find the same pattern recurring in different aspects of the culture. You find, for instance, a house in which there's no ornamentation inside, all the ornamentation's on the gate. You find a people who are preoccupied with the external aspects of their skin and believe that any breakage will impair them so that they're imperfect for something else, and so forth. With that kind of understanding, if you're told something, you can tell whether it fits or not.

For instance, the Balinese told us that they had marriage by capture, which didn't suit anything we'd understood about their culture. Our cook was going to carry off a girl by capture, so Gregory went outside the gate with him early in the morning, and the girl was there waiting. They looked around and there was nobody else there, so she trotted off with him. If there had been another group there, she would have pretended, she would have screamed and been carried off, because that was correct etiquette.

Then we had the case of a very stupid boy who thought it was true. He carried off a girl who had already planned to elope with somebody else. It took the society months to sort that out.

From a complex culture like Bali you take a lot of chunks – birthday ceremonies and funeral ceremonies, children's games, and a whole series of things, and then you analyze them for the patterns that are there.

**B:** In Iatmul they have flutes. The flutes are long hollow bamboo, an inch and a half thick, five feet long, and one hole here, which you blow across. And from that you can get about five notes by overblowing, by harmonics. All right. You have a flute, you're blowing with me, and yours is tuned one tone higher than mine. So your harmonics fit between mine, right? Between us we've got quite a bit of scale. If we blow alternatively we can make a tune. Well, now this is how the generations are arranged. The grandparents go with the grandchildren, and the initiation grades are like seniors – juniors – sophomores – freshmen, in which when you get a fight over initiation, the seniors and the sophomores go together, and the juniors and the freshmen go together. And so on.

**SB:** So what is the truth?

**B:** The truth is that Iatmul like to make this pattern. This is a pattern of organization that they think is nice.

**M:** When Gregory and Waddington talked to each other, I learned what I know about the way English biologists think, by listening to the two of them. They would pick their illustrations right across the field. One minute from embryology, the next from geology, the next from anthropology, back and forth, very freely, so that the illustrations from one spot illuminated, corrected and expanded the one from another. This is the thing that Americans are not taught to do. In our school system you have one year of chemistry, then you're through with chemistry probably, and then you have one year of physics. Whereas in the English system they took all of them at once in smaller doses that went along.

**Nora Bateson:** Goodbye.

**M:** Goodbye. Are you going to school now?

**Nora**: Yes.

**M:** Well, it's been lovely to see you, Nora.

**Nora:** It's been lovely to see you, too. Bye bye.

**B:** Goodbye.

**Nora:** Bye Daddy.

**SB:** Margaret, an old student of yours told me you have a list of reliable sources of insight. What's the list?

**M:** I used to say to my classes that the ways to get insight are: to study infants; to study animals; to study primitive people; to be psychoanalyzed; to have a religious conversion and get over it; to have a psychotic episode and get over it; or to have a love affair with an Old Russian. And I stopped saying that when a little dancer in the front row put up her hand and said, 'Does he have to be old?'

**SB:** How many of those have you done?

*[Blank here while cassette was changed. Dr. Mead said she had studied infants and primitive people. When she got to animals in the list, the conversation swerved to Konrad Lorenz.]*

**M:** Watching Konrad Lorenz be simultaneously a bird and a worm, is one of the really magnificent things in the world. You've seen that, haven't you, when he's describing a bird catching a worm, and he's both? Talk about the whole system, there it is.

**B:** One of the things I've already regretted is that I didn't film him lecturing in Hawaii. One could've, I think. Lorenz is an Aurignacian.

**SB:** How do you mean?

**B:** I mean that he is identified with animals. Aurignacians are the people who did the cave paintings, the good ones. Lorenz goes to the blackboard and there is a live dog, hesitating between attacking and retreating. He takes the eraser, and he wipes the tail off, changes the angle by ten degrees, and flattens out the hair on the back of the neck, and he says, ' That dog's going to run.' He sticks it the other way, and 'that dog's going to attack.' And he is the dog while he's talking about it. And this goes for cichlid fishes, bees, any goddamn thing. And then, in the final lecture he gave in Hawaii, he got all mixed up, you know, the way scientists do, with physics and the Einsteinian universe, and his body got twisted, as he started to talk about the Einsteinian universe where the straight lines are not straight anymore. That's what I wish I had on the camera. The others all think that this is very unfair you know, he has all of this information that they simply don't have.

**M:** He contributes tremendous zest. If Lorenz is in a meeting, I can retire and take notes and think and have no responsibility to keep it going; whereas if he isn't there, I very often have to keep it awake … .

Gregory, have you any ideas on the subject of the harm that is done by television because of the rigidity of the body of people watching TV? Sartre discussed at one point what happened when you peek into a keyhole. When you look through a keyhole, the whole body is focussed to try to use this very small aperture, and he described what happens if you touch somebody who is looking through a keyhole. They jump. I have a big set, now, of comparative pictures of family groups (they weren't taken for this, they were taken for family albums) reading and looking at TV. When the family is reading, they're a thousand years away from each other, their eyes are all down, but you get a sense of community and relaxation. Their bodies are very loose, and undoubtedly there's movement going on as they read. But when they're watching television, the same people sit like this, they don't touch each other, and they're very rigid.

We have lots of material that if you move in your mind, your muscles don't get stiff. For years we had this very funny problem with catatonics, such as a man who would stand all day long in a ward with his eyes up and his hands together in prayer, never moving. They'd pick him up at night, tip him into a bed, feed him artificially, and then after five years or something, there's be a fire. He'd walk across the ward, pick up a telephone, report, 'Fire in ward five,' help get all patients out, and then when the fire was out, back he went to his position. But he was not stiff. Whereas if you take the ordinary person and put them in bed for three months, they have to relearn how to walk. All the data we now have on monitoring muscles with tiny transistor monitors shows, if you think about skiing or exercising, the muscles that you use to ski will respond. If you inhibit movement, as one does watching TV, with no empathy, no muscular involvement at all, I think this is the thing that's doing harm.

**B:** I was wondering about looking through, for example, a camera.

**M:** Remember Clara Lambert and when you were trying to teach her?

That woman who was making photographic studies of play schools, but she was using the camera as a telescope instead of as a camera. You said, 'She'll never be a photographer. She keeps using the camera to look at things.' But you didn't. You always used a camera to take a picture, which is a different activity.

**B:** Yes. By the way, I don't like cameras on tripods, just grinding. In the latter part of the schizophrenic project, we had cameras on tripods just grinding.

**M:** And you don't like that?

**B:** Disastrous.

**M:** Why?

**B:** Because I think the photographic record should be an art form.

**M:** Oh why? Why shouldn't you have some records that aren't art forms? Because if it's an art form, it has been altered.

**B:** It's undoubtedly been altered. I don't think it exists unaltered.

**M:** I think it's very important, if you're going to be scientific about behavior, to give other people access to the material, as comparable as possible to the access you had. You don't, then, alter the material. There's a bunch of film makers now that are saying, 'It should be art,' and wrecking everything that we're trying to do. Why the hell should it be art?

**B:** Well, it should be off the tripod.

**M:** So you run around.

**B:** Yes.

**M:** And therefore you've introduced a variation into it that is unnecessary.

**B:** I therefore got the information out that I thought was relevant at the time.

**M:** That's right. And therefore what do you see later?

**B:** If you put the damn thing on a tripod, you don't get any relevance.

**M:** No, you get what happened

**B:** It isn't what happened.

**M:** I don't want people leaping around thinking that a profile at this moment would be beautiful.

**B:** I wouldn't want beautiful.

**M:** Well, what's the leaping around for?

**B:** To get what's happening.

**M:** What you think is happening.

**B:** If Stewart reached behind his back to scratch himself, I would like to be over there at that moment.

**M:** If you were over there at that moment you wouldn't see him kicking the cat under the table. So that just doesn't hold as an argument.

**B:** Of the things that happen the camera is only going to record one percent anyway.

**M:** That's right.

**B:** I want one percent on the whole to tell.

**M:** Look, I've worked with these things that were done by artistic film makers, and the result is you can't do anything with them.

**B:** They're bad artists, then.

**M:** No, they're not. I mean an artistic film maker can make a beautiful notion of what he thinks is there, and you can't do any subsequent analysis with it of any kind. That's been the trouble with anthropology, because they had to trust us. If we were good enough instruments, and we said the people in this culture did something more than the ones in that, if they trusted us, they used it. But there was no way of probing further material. So we gradually developed the idea of film and tapes.

**B:** There's never going to be any way of probing further into the material.

**M:** What are you talking about, Gregory? I don't know what you're talking about. Certainly, when we showed that Balinese stuff that first summer there were different things identified – the limpness that Marion Stranahan identified, the place on the chest and its point in child development that Erik Erikson identified. I can go back over it, and show you what they got out of those films. They didn't get it out of your head, and they didn't get it out of the way you were pointing the camera. They got it because it was a long enough run so they could see what was happening.

**SB:** What about something like that Navajo film, 'Intrepid Shadows?'[1]

**M:** Well, that is a beautiful, an artistic production that tells you something about a Navajo artist.

**B:** This is different, it's a native work of art.

**M:** Yes, and a beautiful native work of art. But the only thing you can do more with that is analyze the film maker, which I did. I figured out how he got the animation into the trees.

**B:** Oh yes? What do you get out of that one?

**M:** He picked windy days, he walked as he photographed, and he moved the camera independently of the movement of his own body. And that gives you that effect. Well, are you going to say, following what all those other people have been able to get out of those films of yours, that you should have just been artistic?

**SB:** He's saying he *was* artistic.

**M:** No, he wasn't. I mean, he's a good film maker, and Balinese can pose very nicely, but his effort was to hold the camera steady enough long enough to get a sequence of behavior.

**B:** To find out what's happening, yes.

**M:** When you're jumping around taking pictures …

**B:** Nobody's talking about that, Margaret, for God's sake.

**M:** Well.

**B:** I'm talking about having control of a camera. You're talking about putting a dead camera on top of a bloody tripod. It sees nothing.

**M:** Well, I think it sees a great deal. I've worked with these pictures taken by artists, and really good ones …

**B:** I'm sorry I said artists; all I meant was artists. I mean, artist is not a term of abuse in my vocabulary.

**M:** It isn't in mine either, but I …

**B:** Well, in this conversation, it's become one.

**M:** Well, I'm sorry. It just produces something different. I've tried to use 'Dead Birds,'[2] for instance …

**B:** I don't understand 'Dead Birds' at all. I've looked at 'Dead Birds,' and it makes no sense.

**M:** I think it makes plenty of sense.

**B:** But how it was made I have no idea at all.

**M:** Well, there is never a long-enough sequence of anything, and you said absolutely that what one needed was long, long sequences from one position in the direction of two people. You've said that in print. Are you going to take it back?

**B:** Yes, well, a long sequence in my vocabulary is twenty seconds.

**M:** Well, it wasn't when you were writing about Balinese films. It was three minutes. It was the longest that you could wind the camera at that point.

**B:** A very few sequences ran to the length of the winding of the camera.

**M:** But if at that point you had a camera that would run twelve hundred feet, you'd have run it.

**B:** I would have and I'd have been wrong.

**M:** I don't think so for one minute.

**B:** The Balinese film wouldn't be worth one quarter.

**M:** All right. That's a point where I totally disagree. It's not science.

**B:** I don't know what science is, I don't know what art is.

**M:** That's all right. If you don't, that's quite simple. I do. *[To Stewart:]* With the films that Gregory's now repudiating that he took, we have had twenty-five years of re-examination of the material.

**B:** It's pretty rich material.

**M:** It's rich, because they're long sequences, and that's what you need.

**B:** There are no long sequences.

**M:** Oh, compared with anything anybody else does, Gregory.

**B:** But they're trained not to.

**M:** There are sequences that are long enough to analyze ...

**B:** Taken from the right place!

**M:** Taken from one place.

**B:** Taken from the place that averaged better than other places

**M:** Well, you put your camera there.

**B:** You can't do that without a tripod. You're stuck. The thing grinds for twelve hundred feet. It's a bore.

**M:** Well, you prefer twenty seconds to twelve hundred feet.

**B:** Indeed, I do.

**M:** Which shows you get bored very easily.

**B:** Yes, I do.

**M:** Well, there are other people who don't, do you know? Take the films that Betty Thompson studied.[3] That Karbo sequence – it's beautiful – she was willing to work on it for six months. You've never been willing to work on things that length of time, but you shouldn't object to other people who can do it, and giving them the material to do it.

There were times in the field when I worked with people without filming, and therefore have not been able to subject the material to changing theory, as we were able to do with the Balinese stuff. So when I went back to Bali I didn't see new things. When I went back to Manus, I did, where I had only still photographs. If you have film, as your own perception develops, you can re-examine it in the light of the material to some extent. One of the things, Gregory, that we examined in the stills, was the extent to which people, if they leaned against other people, let their mouths fall slack. We got that out of examining lots and lots of stills. It's the same principle. It's quite different if you have a thesis and have the camera in your hand, the chances of influencing the material are greater. When you don't have the camera in your hand, you can look at the things in the background.

**B:** There are three ends to this discussion. There's the sort of film I want to make, there's the sort of film that they want to make in New Mexico (which is 'Dead Birds,' substantially), and there is the sort of film that is made by leaving the camera on a tripod and not paying attention to it.

**M:** Who does that?

**B:** Oh, psychiatrists do that. Albert Scheflen[4] leaves a video camera in somebody's house and goes home. It's stuck in the wall.

**M:** Well, I thoroughly disapprove of the people that want video so they won't have to look. They hand it over to an unfortunate student who then does the rest of the work and adds up the figures, and they write a book. We both object to this. But I do think if you look at your long sequence of stills, leave out the film for a minute, that those long, very rapid sequences, Koewat Raoeh, those stills, they're magnificent, and you can do a great deal with them. And if you hadn't stayed in the same place, you wouldn't have those sequences.

**SB:** Has anybody else done that since?

**M:** Nobody has been as good photographer as Gregory at this sort of thing. People are very unwilling to do it, very unwilling.

**SB:** I haven't seen any books that come even close to *Balinese Character*.[5]

**M:** That's right, they never have. And now Gregory is saying it was wrong to do what he did in Bali. Gregory was the only person who was ever successful at taking stills and film at the same time, which you did by putting one on a tripod, and having both at the same focal length.

**B:** It was having one in my hand and the other round my neck.

**M:** Some of the time, and some not.

**B:** We used the tripod occasionally when we were using long telephoto lenses.

**M:** We used it for the bathing babies. I think the difference between art and science is that each artistic event is unique, whereas in science sooner or later once you get some kind of theory going somebody or other will make the same discovery.[6] The principal point is access, so that other people can look at your material, and come to understand it and share it. The only real information that 'Dead Birds' gives anybody are things like the thing that my imagination had never really encompassed, and that's the effect of cutting off joints of fingers. You remember? The women cut off a joint for every death that they mourn for, and they start when they're little girls, so that by the time they're grown women, they have no fingers. All the fine work is done by men in that society, the crocheting and what not, because the men have fingers to do it with, and the women have these stumps of hands. I knew about it, I had read about it, it had no meaning to me until I saw those pictures. There are lots of things that can be conveyed by this quasi-artistic film, but when we want to suggest to people that it's a good idea to know what goes on between people, which is was you've always stressed, we still have to show your films, because there aren't any others that are anything like as good.

**SB:** Isn't that a little shocking? It's been, what, years?

**M:** Very shocking.

**B:** It's because people are getting good at putting cameras on tripods. It isn't what happens between people.

**M:** Nobody's put any cameras on tripods in those twenty-five years that looked at anything that mattered.

**B:** They haven't looked at anything that mattered, anyway. All right.

## Notes

1. Worth, Sol and John Adair (1972), *Through Navajo Eyes*, Bloomington, Indiana: Indiana University Press. 'Intrepid Shadows' was made by Al Clah, a nineteen-year-old Navajo painter and sculptor.
2. *Dead Birds* (1964), [Film] Dir. Robert Gardner for the Peabody Museum, Harvard University, color, 83 minutes, 1964. Available through New York Public Library.

3. Thompson, Betty (1970), 'Development and Trial Applications of Method for Identifying Non-Vocal Parent-Child Communications in Research Film,' Phd thesis, Teachers College, New York.

4. Scheflen, Albert E. (1973), *Body Language and the Social Order: Communication as Behavioral Control*, Englewood Cliffs, NJ: Prentice-Hall.

5. Mead, M. and G. Bateson (1962 [1942]), *Balinese Character: A Photographic Analysis*, Special Publications, II, New York: The New York Academy of Sciences.

6. Mead, M. (1976), 'Towards a Human Science.' *Science* 191 (March): 903–9.

# CHAPTER 44
# I SWEAR I SAW THIS: DRAWINGS IN FIELDWORK NOTEBOOKS, NAMELY MY OWN

*Michael Taussig*

This is a drawing in my notebook of some people I saw lying down at the entrance to a freeway tunnel in Medellin in July 2006. There were even people lying in the pitchblack tunnel. It was 1:30 in the afternoon.

The sides of the freeway before you enter the tunnel are high there, like a canyon, and there is not much room between the cars and the clifflike walls. "Why do they choose this place?" I asked the driver. "Because it's warm in the tunnel," he replied. Medellin is the city of eternal spring, famous for its annual flower festival and entrepreneurial energy.

I saw a man and woman. At least I think she was a woman and he was a man. And she was sewing the man into a white nylon bag, the sort of bag peasants use to hold potatoes or corn, tied over the back of a burro making its way doggedly to market. Craning my neck, I saw all this in the three seconds or less it took my taxi to speed past. I made a note in my notebook. Underneath in red pencil I later wrote:

**I SWEAR I SAW THIS**

And after that I made the drawing, as if I still couldn't believe what I had seen. When I now turn the pages of the notebook, this picture jumps out.

If I ask what grabs me and why this picture jumps out, my thoughts swarm around a question: What is the difference between seeing and believing? I can write *I Swear I Saw This* as many times as I like, in red, green, yellow, and blue, but it won't be enough. The drawing is more than the result of seeing. It is a seeing that doubts itself, and, beyond that, doubts the world of man. Born of doubt in the act of perception, this little picture is like a startle response aimed at simplifying and repeating that act to such a degree that it starts to feel like a talisman. This must be where witnessing separates itself from seeing, where witnessing becomes holy writ: mysterious, complicated, powerful. And necessary.

Looking at this drawing, which now surpasses the experience that gave rise to it, my eye dwells on the mix of calm and desperation in making a shelter out of a nylon bag by the edge of a stream of automobiles. I am carried away by the idea of making a home in the eye of the hurricane, a home in a nation in which it is estimated that close to four million people or one person in ten are now homeless due to paramilitaries often assisted by the Colombian army driving peasants off the land. If you consider just the rural population, which is from where most of the displaced people come, the figure is more like one in four, such that by October 2009, an estimated one hundred and forty thousand people had been murdered by paramilitaries.[1]

I might add that of all the large cities in Colombia, Medellin is, to my mind, the most associated with paramilitaries. There is a magnetic attraction between the two, and it is not by chance that in this city in particular I would witness the attempt to make a home in this freaky no-man's-land on the side of the freeway.

Three years after I saw these people by the freeway tunnel, the BBC reported in May of 2009 that soldiers in the Colombian army were murdering civilians and then changing the clothes of the corpses to those of guerrilla fighters so as to boost their guerrilla "kill count."[2] Newly applied free-market policies in the army reward individual soldiers with promotions and vacations according to the number of "terrorists" they kill. They get new language as well, the corpses being referred to by the army and its critics as *false positives.* The current president, Juan Manuel Santos, was the person overseeing this program in his capacity as minister of defense. He was elected by a landslide in June 2010.

The BBC report claims that 1,500 young men have been killed this way, with more cases being notified daily. Most of them occur in the province of Antioquia, the capital of which is Medellin. "It is alleged that soldiers were sent to the city of Medellin to round up homeless people from the streets who were later presented by the army as rebels killed in combat."[3]

They have no land but no-man's-land.

Once there was forest. They cleared the forest and grew plantains and corn. Then came the cattle. Everyone loves cattle. There is something magical about cattle. From the poorest peasant to the president of the republic, they all want cattle and they always want more—more cattle, that is. The word "cattle" is the root of *capital,* as in *capitalism.* The *communist* guerrillas saw their chance. They started to tax the cattlemen, and in retaliation the cattlemen hired killers called paramilitaries to clear the land of people so as to protect their cattle and then their cocaine-trafficking cousins and friends and now their plantations of African palm for biofuel as well. Before long they owned a good deal more than that. They owned the mayors. They owned the governors of the different provinces, they owned most of Congress and most of the president's cabinet. The just-retired president of the republic comes from Medellin, and he too is a noted cattleman, retiring to his ranch whenever possible, to brand cows. Imagine a cow without a brand, without an owner! Running free in no-man's-land!

Once there was forest. Now there is a nylon bag.

The one hundred and forty thousand poor country people assassinated by paramilitaries, recruited and paid for by rich landowners and businessmen, must have known they were dying in a good cause, if the virulent antiterrorist rhetoric of the president of the republic from 2002 to 2010 is anything to go by. That was President Alvaro Uribe Vélez, recipient of a Simón Bolívar Scholarship from the British Council and a nomination to become a senior associate member at the St. Antony's College, Oxford, doubtless for his scholarly acumen. As governor of Antioquia before he became president for an unconstitutional two terms, he fomented *Convivir,* one of the first paramilitary groups in Colombia and certainly one of its largest. Close to the entire populations of villages have been massacred by paramilitaries these past twenty years while the army looked the other way or else supplied the names and photographs of the people to be tortured and killed and have their bodies displayed in parts hung from barbed-wire fences. The people of Naya were taken out by machete. The priest of Trujillo was cut into pieces with a power saw. The stories are legion. President Uribe was given the Medal of Freedom by another president, George W Bush. Otherwise it's a nice enough place, like anywhere else with people adapted to an awful situation like the proverbial three monkeys. I ask a poet from Equatorial Guinea who has been in Colombia twenty years what's it like back there in that dreadful African country with its thirty plus years of dictatorship. What happens to the mindset of the people? A naïve question, no doubt. "Look around yourself right here in Colombia!" he replies. For any moment you too could answer the phone and receive an *amenaza*—a death threat—because of your big mouth, your involvement in what is identified as proguerrilla activity, your raising issues of human rights or giving a student a low grade. And why are you complaining?

Somewhere, somehow, real reality breaks through the scrim. It is speaking to you at the other end of the telephone.

There are other moments like that, small and intimate and hardly worth mentioning or measuring. They hold you transfixed. Think of the people lying by the freeway tunnel in Medellin as the taxi hurtles past, a transit both ephemeral and eternal.

What I see also is an unholy alliance or at least symmetry between the enclosed space of the automobiles rushing into the tunnel and the nylon cocoon into which the woman seems to be sewing the man. The automobile offers the fantasy of a safe space in a cruel and unpredictable world, a space of intimacy and daydreaming. Yet the automobile is also a hazard, a leading cause of death and disability in the third world. As against this, consider a home on the freeway made of nylon bags, a home that takes the organic form of the insect world, like the cocoon of a grub destined to become a butterfly.

In this vein I also discern a fearful symmetry between the nylon cocoon and the steep concrete walls adjoining the unlit tunnel of the freeway. When I ask the taxi driver why people would choose to lie there, and he responds, "Because it's warm," my question assumes the sheer unfathomability, the impossibility of imagining that human beings would choose such a place to lie down in the same way as you or I lie down in our bedrooms. My question already has built into it my fear and my astonishment that people would choose such radical enclosure. Why would you put yourself into this concrete grave? And his response, "Because it's warm," suggests that it has been chosen because of its embrace.

As I dwell on these thoughts I suspect that this hideous location is chosen because it is hideous and, what's more, dangerous. There, at least you are probably safer from attack by police, death-squad vigilantes, and other poor people.

Then there is that other type of enclosure, the one that grabs me most, that part of the picture in which the woman seems to be enclosing herself as well as the man. Stitch by stitch the outside is becoming the inside. The stitcher becomes the stitched. I am reminded of that little boy years ago in a funeral service in Bogotá who said, "I want to live in a closet." His parents were research sociologists working for the Jesuits in Bogotá, gathering and publishing statistics on political violence. They were assassinated in 1997 late at night in their bedroom by paramilitaries. The boy escaped by hiding in a closet.

All of this comes to mind when I ask myself why I drew this scene and why this drawing has power over me. But I feel something is missing in what I have said or in the way I am saying it, something that undoes or at least alters meaning along the lines of what Roland Barthes rather dramatically called "the third meaning." You've heard of the third eye and the third man. Now you've got the third meaning!

Barthes was a restless thinker. No sooner had he gotten things squared away with his semiotic theory than he found exceptions to the theory because the very act of squaring things self-destructs. What is called "theory" gives you insight. But it does so at the expense of closing off things as well. Theory can never do justice to the contingent, the concrete, or the particular.[4] Yet if you don't exercise that theory muscle to the extent that you realize its limits, then you won't get to that cherished Zenlike moment of the mastery of nonmastery.

Yes! Barthes saw what he called the "information" in any given image. Yes! He saw what he called the symbolism, too. But nevertheless he became painfully aware of the shortfall between all of that and something else this act of interpretation created. "I receive (and probably even first and foremost) a third meaning," he wrote, "evident, erratic, obstinate." What's more, he spoke of being "held" by the image and that to the extent that "We cannot describe the third meaning ... I cannot name that which pricks me."[5] Quite an admission.

Is that how a talisman works, I wonder, setting traps made of third meanings? The dangerous spirits out to get you are deflected by the design that is the talisman, kept busy trying to figure out the meaning but cannot. Their mistake. And one we repeat endlessly ourselves, too.

Third "meaning" is not really a meaning at all, but a gap or hole or hermeneutic trap *that interpretation itself causes* while refusing to give up the struggle. As such, the third meaning has an awful lot to do with the frightening yet liberating sense of enclosure as the last gasp of protection in a heartless world hell-bent on apocalypse as it roars into the tunnel of no return.

My eye fixes on the woman—if she is a woman—sewing herself into the nylon bag. And there's the stillness. Barthes recalls Baudelaire, who wrote of "the emphatic truth of gesture in the important moments of life." That is how I think of this woman's gesture, or should I say how I think of my drawing of such in which what appears as the edge of the bag as a firm blue line encloses the sewer herself. That is my gesture.

## Notes

1. Daniel Wilkinson, "Death and Drugs in Colombia," *New York Review of Books,* August 18, 2011.
2. Juan Forero, "As Colombian War Crimes Suspects Sit in U.S. Jails, Victims' Kin Protest," *Washington Post,* October 5, 2009. See also "17 Soacha Perpetrators Are Free," cip-colombia-news@googlegroups.com, January 9, 2010.
3. Jeremy McDermott, "Toxic Fallout of Colombian Scandal," BBC News, http://news.bbc.co.Uk/2/hi/americas/8038399.stm, May 8, 2009.
4. Derek Attridge, "Roland Barthes's Obtuse, Sharp Meaning and the Responsibilities of Commentary," in *Writing The Image After Roland Barthes,* Jean-Michel Rabaté (ed.) (Philadelphia: University of Pennsylvania Press, 1997), 79.
5. Roland Barthes, "The Third Meaning: Résearch Notes on Some Eisenstein Stills," in *A Barthes Reader,* ed. Susan Sontag (New York: Hill and Wang, 1982), 318.

# CHAPTER 45

# MARINA ABRAMOVIĆ: INTERSECTING WORLDS, HIGHER DIMENSIONS, AND METASTABLE SHIMMERINGS

*Marko Živković*

What if we think of situations that puzzle us in certain ways as being occasioned by intersecting worlds of different dimensionalities? What if we consider some beings who puzzle us in certain ways as beings whose dimensionality, different from our own, causes certain "ripples" in our experience as they pass through our world? What, finally, if a set of such "ripples" is interpreted as the effect of incompatible worlds in a kind of metastable coexistence? Think of what follows as a heuristic move. The stage is set by the traffic or situations of intersection between the Artworld and the world of academic anthropology. A puzzling being passes through both and causes "ripples" that help us detect certain features of the intersecting worlds. Some other puzzling beings and situations are then gathered to see if commonalities between them could lead us to establish a subset of "ripple" effects that I will call "shimmerings." In the process, it is hoped, some of what happens between disciplines might become clearer. We may see some puzzling beings in a different light. And, to be quite bold, "shimmerings" could offer an interesting new way of thinking about art and its enchantments—and thus a contribution to aesthetics.

## Marina Abramović at Reed

Marina walked out of the plane at the Portland airport in a slight daze, not exactly knowing where she was. As she herself, as she put it, *is* the artwork—instead of mailing her work, she *gets mailed herself.* This time, she got mailed to so many different places that she lost track of where she was. We hit it off immediately.

The next day, Marina was to sit in my Anthropology of Art class in the morning, then attend an informal workshop with art majors in the afternoon, and finally deliver a public lecture in the evening. And on each occasion she caused a different type of perturbation or ripple that I will recount in chronological order.

### *The 1st Reed ripple—anthropology of art and telepathy in the Outback*

My Anthropology of Art class was small, about 12 students, mostly anthropology and art majors. In order to drive home the importance of Marina's upcoming visit, I tried to put some fear into them. Beware, I said, having Marina Abramović in this very room is like being locked in a cage with a tigress. You'd better be prepared!

I was thinking of a short introduction, but Marina started talking from the moment she entered and sat at the table. And knowing she had anthropologists in the audience, she talked a lot about her experience with the Aborigines in the Australian Outback. She told us how when she visited Australia in 1979 with her partner Ulay for the European Dialogue Biennale, just like everyone else, they wanted to see the Aborigines: "Ahh Aborigines! Let's go to see Aborigines. Like a zoo!" A friend gave them a letter to show to one Philip Toyne in Alice Springs, a lawyer who represented the Aborigines in their land right disputes, and Philip literally threw them out of his ramshackle office. "What do you want?" Marina recounted he said—"Ah, you are another bloodsucker come to see the Aborigines. What do you think you are? You're just a piece of shit. You want to use them, maybe take some photographs of them and then go home. Get out of my office." "He literally threw us out," she said. So later they meet in a bar (there are only four bars in the town), and the lawyer relents a little, tells them to come when they can do something for the Aborigines. Marina and Ulay get an Australian grant, return the next year and spend three months holed up in what Marina called "this fucked-up room in the motel," drawing maps, making photos, and designing a book about Aboriginal land rights. Then they join the Aborigines deep in the desert for the rest of the year. Heat is almost unbearable, flies are in your eyes, ears, nose all the time, until one day, after three months, Marina wakes up free of flies. She started to smell like the environment, she says. Ulay goes through some of the male initiations. Marina hangs out with women who seem to spend most of the day enacting each other's dreams. Finally they venture into the deep desert alone. They go to the strange impression called "Lake of Disappointment" to spend a "romantic Christmas." They wait until sundown to start cooking because it is too hot. They make a fire. And then a giant wedge-tailed eagle lands right opposite them on the other side of the fire. So as not to scare him, Marina and Ulay sit still, not move until late that night. They finally fall asleep. In the morning, the eagle is still there, motionless. Ulay touches him and the eagle just topples over dead—all eaten up by ants. Back in Alice Springs, Daniel Vachon, a Canadian anthropologist who had undertaken the most extreme initiations and decided to stay and fight for Aborigine rights, asks what name Ulay received at his initiation. He looks up the name, Dzungaraj (Jungaray) in a codex, and tells them it means "the dying eagle." Later, this moment inspires Marina to stage her famous *Conjunction* performance in Amsterdam in 1982, with an Aborigine medicine man, a Tibetan Lama, Ulay, and herself sitting motionless for four hours one across from another for four days in a row. This performance, in turn, she says, inspired Jean-Hubert Martin to make the famous exhibition *Magiciens de la terre* in 1989. Later, Bruce Chatwin recounts the "Amsterdam dreaming" of this same medicine man in his *Songlines* (see Chatwin 1988: 152–5).

Now, several times during the class, Marina says that Aborigines are telepathic. "I found out," she says at the outset, "that the Aborigines are one of the most developed human beings on earth, concerning the way in which the brain works … Aborigines use much more of the brain than we do. They have extra-sensory perception, they have extremely developed telepathy, they have other abilities that are almost supernatural in our point of view." Later she says how she and Ulay "learned only 350 words of language … the rest is telepathy. They start talking to you in your head. You understand them without talking … It's much cheaper to use telepathy than the telephone … and it's perfectly functional."

Some of my students were uneasy when they heard such statements from Marina. They didn't know what to do with them, and, as I discovered in our subsequent conversations, as anthropologists in training they already exhibited an old and well-known anthropological border anxiety.

Anthropologists have long had these "extraordinary experiences"—visions and altered states of consciousness—related to their fieldwork but would rarely dare to report them in official writing for fear of ostracism. Taking such experiences seriously or accounting for them in the way the natives do can easily lead to charges that one has "gone native" or abandoned the scientific world view for some sort of mysticism at best, and quackery at worst. In a word, whoever ventures into this territory runs the risk of being haunted by the Castaneda controversy.

So here is the first of the perturbations or ripples occasioned by Marina's visit. Marina sits in the deepest desert covered with flies, lives with the Aborigines, participates in dream enactments with the women, even takes meticulous notes. In a very real sense, she established her "ethnographic authority" and then she explains, with an utterly straight face, that they communicate telepathically with the same ease we use telephones.

In a word, it could be argued that Marina made the budding anthropologists in my Anthropology of Art class uncomfortable precisely because they initially attributed a level of ethnographic authority to her. In a sense, she was acting as an ethnographer and then suddenly made a leap into the territory where anthropologists fear to tread (but are sometimes quite mightily tempted to).

Even if we take Aboriginal telepathy and similar experiences as simply grist for Marina's artistic mills, material out of which she fashions her "art," it is disturbing enough. And the disturbance, I propose, comes from a realization that as anthropologists we share her experience in the Australian desert as something we have in common (the ethnographic moment), and then we realize that for her this experience is a part of a world in which it might be fine to assert extraordinary experiences without paying the penalties. She is, in fact, not a part of our anthropology world, only passing through it, and the Australian desert is a point of intersection between our two worlds. But the telepathy and dying eagle experiences alert us anthropologists to the fact that Marina lives in a world in which she can, seemingly, move into places where we fear to tread.

### *The 2nd Reed ripple—artists and Tibetan breathing exercises*

The morning class visit is over, and at 4.00pm the same afternoon, Marina is to appear in an informal seminar aimed primarily at Reed art majors. A few of the local artists are present too. My wife and I, with our video camera, are two minutes late, and when we crack the door open we see that Marina has made everyone in the room take off their shoes and lay down on their backs. She is in the middle of the circle leading the group through a breathing exercise. In the next 15 or so minutes, we do Marina's short program of Tibetan-inspired exercises, then we all sit in a circle on the floor and talk, and finally, we pull the chairs up and sit on them.

One of the Reed art professors later confessed a moment of panic when Marina told everyone to take off their shoes and lay down. "Oh no," she thought to herself, "this is Marina Abramović, for Chrissake, I hope she doesn't tell us to take off all our clothes!"

Here is a confusion of genres. A seminar with students has some unspoken parameters, one of which is that everyone is seated and just talks. No laying on the ground, no taking off shoes, no breathing exercises, or, God forbid, nakedness. What Marina does is not in itself particularly surprising. Such a set of exercises as she led us through is easily conceivable in any number of venues (I have done similar things in Aikido seminars, for instance), but they don't belong in an art seminar. Yes, we know that some artists have famously drawn on, among other things, Buddhism, but in an academic setting do we really expect to do breathing or chanting exercises instead of discussing such things verbally? Ann Hamilton is also listed as an artist influenced by Buddhism (see Baas 2004), but there were no physical exercises when she gave a similar seminar for art majors at Reed.

Now these two situations give me a neat triangulation. If we take the morning class as an exemplary micro-bubble of anthropology world, then we can interpret the slight uneasiness Marina's passage provoked there as coming from an intrusion of Artworld into Anthroworld. Perhaps one way of accounting for this ripple is to say that after establishing some sort of ethnographic authority, Marina jumped into a realm that makes anthropologists shudder (both with fear and fascination) because it leaves behind a kind of scientific realism that ethnographers, by and large, feel they need to claim as their home-base.

But in the afternoon seminar, which we can take as an exemplary micro-bubble of academic Artworld, Marina causes a ripple again that presumably, if she were indeed nothing but a straight Artworld being, she wouldn't have. It is this triangulation that makes me suggest that Marina is a being that belongs to neither anthropology, nor to the Artworld. Because she causes ripples or perturbation in both, she probably belongs to neither.

Certain objections might be raised at this point. For one, Marina explicitly claims to be an artist. She is not claiming to be an anthropologist, nor is she claiming to be a shaman or a Tibetan Buddhist pure and simple. Institutionally too, there is no doubt that she is a part of the Artworld. She has the credentials of the most orthodox kind—a BFA from a Fine Arts Program (Belgrade Faculty of Fine Arts) that is as old-fashioned as your quintessential French Academy of the nineteenth century. And finally, she is represented by a prestigious Chelsea gallery and has exhibited in the most prestigious Artworld venues (from the Venice Biennale to the MoMa and the Guggenheim). In that pragmatic sense there is absolutely no question of Marina Abramović not being a very prominent inhabitant of the Artworld as we know it today. Finally, and this is an argument that my wife, a graduate of that same Fine Arts Academy, invokes—what Marina does and produces is aesthetically powerful, and this is something that is quite important to Marina herself.

Let me first address this last issue. I would agree that Marina is not eschewing the "aesthetic"—her performances, the objects she occasionally uses or produces are well-wrought, some are even "beautiful," but for her the aim of all this is that there is a "power exchange" with the audience, a power transformation. She says that an artist has to be responsible, and that means that energies should not be manipulated blindly and without knowing their effects, for you can mess up both yourself and your audience that way (that is to say, the aim is not simply to shock the audience by cutting yourself up). The real responsibility is that you know, for instance, how each sound affects each part of the body. And for this knowledge you go to Tibetans. They know this stuff with mathematical precision, and moreover they can teach it to you, for they have the teaching method down. Aborigines are perhaps even better at this all (Marina intimates as much in several places), but they are as if born with it and you can experience and admire it, but it is hard to learn from them. So even the aesthetic, and there is no denying that it is present in all Marina does, is ultimately in the service of something else, just a tool. And when she makes objects, such as her crystal shoes or pillows, their aesthetic appeal is secondary—it's "an injection of energy into the world." (conversation with Germano Celant in Abramovic 2001: 10). Perhaps her view of art is congenial to Alfred Gell's account of art as "enchantment" and "psychological warfare" (Gell 1992: 44). The Trobriand carver aims to dazzle the Kula partner of his client with the magical power of the boat prow-board he carves. Marina wants to do something equally powerful—make you a trading partner for a moment, exchange energy and get you both transformed in certain ways. And she needs to quite seriously know how such things are done. Shamanistic or Tibetan techniques are her "tools," and with these tools she gets to work on you by working on herself. Only a dilettante messes with such energies without taking the trouble to learn how to control them. And what passes in the Artworld as aesthetic is just another tool. Or perhaps, it just so happens that *energies work best through channels that are also labelled as aesthetically pleasing or powerful.*

I don't think she fundamentally cares whether what she's doing is labelled art or something else, as long as it does to her and her audiences what it should. It is only that she happens to find the Artworld as the most generous and congenial temporary/tentative frame. It provides the spaces and opportunities, the logistics and the tools, and it has a developed apparatus for gathering audiences with a certain mindset that she could, if sometimes with difficulty, exploit for her purposes. Art audiences expect to be captivated, but not in quite the way Marina usually intends. If nothing else, she usually requires a much longer attention span than is typically bestowed upon an art object in a gallery. (She sometimes makes audiences sign a contract to spend a certain period of time with her work). But this kind of attitude—that we are going to attend to something with quite an unusual degree of attention, the attitude of openness, an expectation that our ordinary perception is going to be challenged, etc.—this whole attitudinal set developed by Artworld audiences could be seized upon by Marina for her own ends. Such temporary curiosity could be used to trap Artworld audiences just as a clever monkey traps work by exploiting monkey curiosity (Gell 1996).

But this is neither here nor there—an interpretation from the outside. Sure, Marina will explicitly say that art is a tool for her, but when she performs there is no sense that she is using the Artworld as merely a ruse, trap, or enticement. She is not ironic about being an artist at all. In fact she is fully, completely an artist and also fully, completely not an artist. In a word, she is *shimmering*.

### *The 3rd Reed ripple—nervous giggles at Balkan erotic epic*

In the evening Marina gives her public lecture. She talks about her life and work, and shows excerpts from her performances on a big screen behind her. She finally gets to her latest work, something she has just finished—*The Balkan Erotic Epics*. "After Aborigines and Tibetans," she says, "after I have done all this ethnic research, finally, I have a distance from my own country—35 years … I could never make such work if I was living there or if I was going often … So I went to Yugoslavia, ex-Yugoslavia, and researched and to find somehow in our pagan culture the rituals who are completely forgotten and not used anymore, and to see how the sexual organs being used as tools for the fertilization of the earth, to remove diseases, to stop floods … . It was complete pagan culture, it was incredibly interesting material, so what I did, I didn't have any visual material, just a description of such visuals, and what I did, I actually re-enact them and it took me two years to cast the people who will do this thing and to explain to them what I am asking them to do and come to what I am going to show you now."

Marina appears on the screen, with glasses, dressed all in black, in the role of an expert announcing what is to be seen:

> In Balkan culture, since ancient times, the male and female organs, like phalluses, vagina and breasts, were used as tools against sicknesses, the evil forces of nature, etc., etc.

Audience: a few giggles.

Marina on the screen: "If the horse or the bull could not pull the heavy weight, it was believed that it would be cured of the weakness completely if the man opened the trousers and rubbed with his right hand his genitals and then touched the horse or the bull."

We then see a completely naked man standing in the field and masturbating. The clip is about 27 seconds long.

Audience: a few laughs at the beginning and near the end of the clip.

Audience laughs, perhaps somewhat nervously, when in another clip they first see a single man copulating with the earth. The laughter turns uproarious when the image switches to a whole field full of men copulating with the earth.

Marina (on the screen): "To make the crops grow, the men will masturbate into the earth."

A few more clips are shown, and then at the end comes the *pièce de rèsistance*. We see a row of men lined up on a stage facing the camera, dressed in folk costumes with their penises standing up erect out of their open flies. A voice sings something that sounds like a Russian romance. The American audience wouldn't know it, but Yugoslav-born natives of a certain generation can recognize the voice of the great forgotten diva Olivera Katarina, a legend of the 1960s—a beauty, arguably the first real bombshell of Tito's Yugoslavia, a singer and an actress whose Gypsy tavern singer's act in the 1967 movie *Feather Gatherers* (Petrović 1967) is probably the most famous archetypal scene in all of Yugoslav cinematography. The song is about Slavic Soul, quite explicitly, since the word itself appears in the lyrics we see on the screen in English translation, but also in its elegiac, mournful tone. This is serious the way most proverbially serious, deep Russian novels are painfully serious.

The audience is at first silent, and then we hear some sporadic giggles when some penises start wobbling. Laugher will become stronger at a few other points, perhaps because of the increasingly obvious discrepancy between the heavy pathos of the music and the lyrics on the one hand, and the image on the other, but I would say it is still an uncertain laughter since it is not clear what that discrepancy really is. The song is probably experienced as sung in perfect seriousness, and it is hard to figure out how the image of motionless, somber men in folk costumes with their erections sticking out was intended to be taken.

Some of the cues pointed towards an ethnographic documentary, or perhaps more precisely, an ethnographic re-enactment of traditional folk custom. A kind of filmic animation of what a typical European Ethnographic Museum Diorama might look like. To American audiences, Marina also speaks with some native authority. She asserts that she has achieved "distance" from her homeland, but by the same token she asserts that she is indeed a native. She also suggests that there is sound archival research into forgotten folk practices behind the piece. And yet, she is also obviously lacking the proper scholarly credentials, she is not a folklorist, historian, or an ethnologist. And then, there is the explicit sex. Only, the audience is supposed to frame it not as pornography but as science, as analogous to the way in which native breasts and penises used to be shown without censorship in ethnographies documenting the lives of savages. But then, it is obviously over the top. Especially when we come to men in full folk costumes (that we know are part of staging "authentic folk culture" the world over)—sporting erections. And the über-soulful Russian romance about the ill-fated Serbian people. On top of it all, at least some in the audience know that this is a work by Marina Abramović, the performance artist who cuts stars into her belly and does all kinds of other outrageous things.

How to take all this? Is this ethnology, folklore, art performance, or a parody? Marina obviously at times invites parodic or humorous approach to this material, and the audience laughs quite easily at some of the pieces. For other pieces, the intentions are not clear, and the laughter tends to be sporadic, tentative, and even nervous. What if Marina actually intends some of this quite seriously, even with pathos? What if she has utter abandoned herself to Slavic Soul, Yugoslav nostalgia, and the mysticism of pagan ritual sexuality? What if all these things are sacred to her, not a laughing matter? *Or better still, are these things somehow both funny and utterly serious?*

But it is impossible that all of this is serious for the discrepancies are too obvious. Regardless of what we take the "artistic" merit of *Balkan Erotic Epic* to be, I think there is no doubt that some sort of oscillation or *shimmering* is taking place, as if irony and literalness, tears and winks coexist in a quite robust tension that Marina will simply not resolve for us. It is precisely this phenomenon of incompatible interpretations or, if you will, worlds, frames, provinces of meaning, or realisms coexisting in impossible yet robustly "metastable" configurations, that I am interested in.

In our first ripple, ethnographic realism seems to intersect and coexist with quite literal affirmation of extra-ordinary experiences. In the second, it is not clear whether Tibetan body/mind exercises are a mere preparation for artmaking or whether in fact artmaking is as much a tool for attaining certain states of mind as posture, breathing or meditation are. In the third ripple, it is not clear whether *Balkan Erotic Epic* is art or a re-enactment based on folklore scholarship, and whether it is intended seriously or as parody, irony, even deep sarcasm (about, say, Serbian masculinity and all that this implies for the recent wars).

My aim here is to develop a way of thinking about modalities of world-jumping through observing the beings whose passage through different worlds causes ripples or perturbations of a particular kind. Marina passes through the world of Pintupi and Patjanjara and then brings a representative of that world to an Amsterdam gallery. Tibetan Buddhists ask her to choreograph their rituals into a digestible form for the Western Artworld, and they make her cry when they cheerfully disregard certain conventions of artistic performance. Marina takes this as an opportunity to learn how to let go (of artistic conventions). It is not only that she causes perturbations in the Artworld (or academic world), she also gets perturbed by different worlds intersecting in her own life and practice

## A note on the definition of "worlds"

I don't know what a "world," a "province of meaning," or a "frame" is in itself. If I had to offer a definition, I would say that "a world" is an unspecifiable mass of unspecifiably associated commonplaces that are taken as a tacit background for attending to something at hand. As we shift attention so shifts the mass of associated commonplaces or tacit subsidiaries. We can theoretically designate every moment of shifting consciousness to constitute "a world" of its own because it will theoretically involve a different assembly of tacit subsidiaries. But in practice, we tend to rather seamlessly pass from one moment to another, and shift our attention smoothly. So the pragmatic criterion of what we take as a "finite" or "bounded" "world" "frame," or "province of meaning," would be the experience of "perturbation." In a word, we define domains only in contrast to other domains and what makes us aware of the contrast is some sense of change in scenery. We will infer that a passage into a different "finite province" or "world" has occurred only when the change is perceived as sufficiently abrupt or radical. Whatever is smoothly transited into is still a part of the same world. That is to say, worlds could be defined by a certain level of comfort and ease. A world is where we have found our feet; that is, where we can trust our tacit awareness for smooth functioning, or where we are on automatic pilot developed by training and practice. A circus acrobat will be at ease in a world that would make an ordinary person vomit from vertigo.

A shimmering could be defined as any situation in which two or more coherent "worlds" or "frames" coexist in such a way that we ordinarily cannot grasp them simultaneously. Because this conjunction is in some sense robust or "metastable," the impossible juxtaposition is insistent—it won't leave us in peace. The result is then a sort of fast tacking back and forth between the incompatible worlds, an oscillation or shimmering.

It is intriguing that the very word "imagination" conceals a type of shimmering in its etymology. In one of the most awe-inspiring books I have ever read, Elémire Zolla traces this to the Sanscrit *mei*. *Mei* then yields a whole family of words in Indo-European languages that suggest something changing, fleeting, and intermittent "capable of catching and fixing man's attention." *Mei* flickers in Sanscrit *mâyâ*, in the Old High German *mein*, "deceit," Latin *micare* "to sparkle," in Persian *mozheh*, "eyelash," in Russian *màyak* "lighthouse" or *màgat'*—"to wink," "to signal," to "deceive." And analogously in the realm of sound, the neighing of horses—hence in Sanscrit *mimâti*, in Greek, *mimizo* (Zolla 1978: 3–4).

Moreover, the shimmerings tend to intimate a certain sense of depth. That is to say, a conjunction of incompatible worlds may indicate the existence of another world in which these worlds are not incompatible. Such more comprehensive worlds might be seen as having an added dimension.

Binocular vision and binaural creation of sonic space are of course primary domains from which we take our metaphors of "depth." As they usually function smoothly and beyond our conscious awareness (tacitly), I would exclude them from shimmerings.

Shimmerings then are characterized by a certain amount of uneasiness. The metastable discrepancy is insistent and somehow grating. It puts us in an impossible place where we "don't know where we stand." Thus the "motion sickness" that mixed metaphors or oscillating ironies can give us.

Shimmerings are then inducing a certain frisson, a shiver, or a thrill. Most of my examples here involve such a thrill, but that thrill is mostly of the pleasant kind, "delicious confusions" that tend to have an element of *enchantment* or *captivation*.

In his 1992 article "The Technology of Enchantment and the Enchantment of Technology," Alfred Gell (now rather famously) argued that art is a technology of enchantment because technology is itself enchanted. The effect of fascination, captivation, or enchantment that an ordinary person tends to experience when confronted by a work of art comes from his/her inability to conceive how it was manufactured. The object is enchanting because it indicates a level of technological virtuosity that is inconceivable to the observer and to which he/she therefore tends to ascribe some sort of "magic."

So perhaps we can add shimmerings to the catalogue of "cognitive indecipherabilities" which Gell says enchant beholders by frustrating their ability "to recognize at once wholes and parts, continuity and discontinuity, synchrony and succession" (Gell 1998: 95).

## Conclusion

In conclusion then, a praise of small movements and shimmerings between worlds. Rather than trying to escape the prisonhouse of text, and the mono-sensorial bias of academia, perhaps we should look at ways to not so much jump back and forth as to shimmer between worlds. On the other hand, if shimmering is about a metastable conjunction of two incommensurable but fully formed and convincing worlds, then not just any excursion beyond our limited domain will do. We have to be able to fully inhabit both worlds in order to create a place between them where we need more than legs to stand.

## References

Abramovic, M. (1999), *The Bridge/El Puente*, Milano: Charta.
Abramovic, M. (2001), *Public Body: Installations and Objects 1965–2001*, Milano: Charta.
Baas, J. and Jacob, M. J. (2004), *Buddha Mind in Contemporary Art*, Berkeley: University of California Press.
Chatwin, B. (1988), *The Songlines*, Penguin Books.
Gell, A. (1992), "The Technology of Enchantment and the Enchantment of Technology." in J. Coote and A. Shelton (eds), *Anthropology, Art, and Aesthetics*, 40–63, Oxford: Clarendon Press.
Gell, A. (1996), "Vogel's Net: Traps as Artworks and Artworks as Traps." *Journal of Material Culture* 1 (1): 15–38.
Gell, A. (1998), *Art and Agency: An Anthropological Theory*, Oxford: Clarendon Press.
Petrović, A. (1967), "I Even Met Happy Gypsies/Skupljaci perja," Beograd: Avala film.
Zolla, E. (1978), *The Uses of Imagination and the Decline of the West*, Ipswich: Golgonooza Press.

# PERMISSIONS

We are grateful to the following publishers and copyright holders for giving us permission to reprint their work.

Chapter 1: Bronisław Malinowski, extracts from "Canoes and Sailing" and "The Ceremonial Building of a Waga" Reprinted by permission of Waveland Press, Inc. from Malinowski, *Argonauts of the Western Pacific*. Long Grove, IL: Waveland Press Inc., © 1922 (reissued 1984). All rights reserved.

Chapter 2: Franz Boas, extracts from "Decorative Designs of Alaskan Needlecases: A Study in the History of Conventional Designs, Based on Materials in the U. S. National Museum." Reprinted with the permission of Free Press, a Division of Simon & Schuster, Inc., from *Race, Language and Culture* by Franz Boas. Copyright © 1940 by Franz Boas. Copyright renewed © Franziska Boas Michelson. All rights reserved.

Chapter 3: Alfred Gell, extracts from "The Problem Defined: The Need for an Anthropology of Art." Reprinted by permission of Oxford University Press from *Art and Agency* by Alfred Gell. Copyright © Alfred Gell 1998.

Chapter 4: John Dewey, extracts from "The Live Creature," "Having an Experience," and "The Act of Expression." From *Art as Experience* by John Dewey, copyright 1934 by John Dewey; copyright renewed © 1961 The Center for Dewey Studies. Used by permission of G. P. Putnam's Sons, an imprint of Penguin Publishing Group, a division of Penguin Random House LLC.

Chapter 5: Mary Douglas, extracts from "The Genuine Article." From Stephen Harold Riggins, *The Socialness of Things: Essays on the Socio-semiotics of Objects*, Berlin: Mouton de Gruyter, 1994, pp. 10, 12–14, 16, 17, 18, 19, 20. Reproduced with permission.

Chapter 6: Dale Pesmen, ""A Boggy, Soggy, Squitchy Picture, Truly": Notes on Image Making in Anthropology and Elsewhere". Reproduced by permission of the American Anthropological Association from *Anthropology and Humanism*, Volume 25, Issue 2, pp. 111–19, December 2000. Not for sale or further reproduction.

Chapter 7: Claude Lévi-Strauss, extracts from "The Science of the Concrete." From *The Savage Mind* by Claude Lévi-Strauss, translated by George Weidenfeld and Nicolson Ltd, Chicago: University of Chicago Press. Copyright © by Librairie Plon 1962. English translation © George Weidenfeld and Nicolson Ltd 1966. Reproduced by permission.

Chapter 8: Howard S. Becker, extract from "Reputation." Republished with permission of University of California Press – Books from *Art Worlds* by Howard S. Becker, © 1982; permission obtained through Copyright Clearance Center, Inc.

Chapter 9: Louise Meintjes, extracts from "The Recording Studio as Fetish." From *Sound of Africa!: Making Music Zulu in a South African Studio* by Louise Meintjes, pp. 71–110 © 2003, Duke University Press. All rights reserved. Republished by permission of the copyright holder.

Chapter 10: Tim Ingold, extracts from "On Weaving a Basket." From *Perception of the Environment* by Tim Ingold © 2000 and Routledge. Reproduced by permission of Taylor & Francis Books UK.

Chapter 11: Marina Peterson, extract from "Performing L.A." Reproduced by permission of University of Pennsylvania Press from *Sound, Space, and the City: Civic Performance in Downtown Los Angeles* by Marina Peterson. © 2010.

Chapter 12: Heather Paxson, "The "Art" and "Science" of Handcrafting Cheese in the United States." Republished with permission of Elsevier from *Endeavour*, 35 (2–3): 116–24, © 2011; permission obtained through Copyright Clearance Center, Inc.

Chapter 13: Severin Fowles and Ben Alberti, "Surface Revelations: Ecologies and Epistemologies of Rock Art." Original material.

Chapter 14: Pierre Bourdieu, extracts from "The Historical Genesis of a Pure Aesthetic." From *The Field of Cultural Production* by Pierre Bourdieu. © 1994 Columbia University Press and © 1993 Polity Press. Reprinted with permission of the publishers.

Chapter 15: Georgina Born, "Music, Modernism and Signification." From *Thinking Art: Beyond Traditional Aesthetics* edited by Andrew Benjamin and Peter Osborne, ICA © 1991. Reproduced by permission of the author and the publisher.

Chapter 16: Jeremy Coote, extracts from "Marvels of Everyday Vision." Reprinted by permission of Oxford University Press from *Anthropology, Art and Aesthetics* edited by Jeremy Coote and Anthony Shelton. © 1992.

Chapter 17: Christopher Pinney, extracts from "Piercing the Skin of the Idol." From *Beyond Aesthetics: Art and the Technologies of Enchantment* edited by Christopher Pinney and Nicholas Thomas, Berg, © 2001. Reprinted by permission of Bloomsbury Publishing.

Chapter 18: Steven Feld, "From Ethnomusicology to Echo-Muse-Ecology: Reading R. Murray Schafer in the Papua New Guinea Rainforest." From acousticecology.org © 2001. Available online: http://www.acousticecology.org/writings/echomuseecology.html (accessed 29 March 2016). Reprinted with edits by permission of the author.

Chapter 19: John L. Comaroff and Jean Comaroff, extracts from "Mansions of the Lord: Architecture, Interiority, Domesticity." From *Of Revelation and Revolution, Volume 2* by John L. Comaroff and Jean Comaroff, Chicago: University of Chicago Press. © 1997. Reproduced by permission.

Chapter 20: Marcel Mauss, extracts from "Techniques of the Body." Reprinted from *Economy and Society*, vol. 2, issue 1. © 1973, Taylor & Francis. Permission obtained through Copyright Clearance Center, Inc.

Chapter 21: Deborah Kapchan, extracts from ""A Gesture Narrowly Divides us from Chaos": Gesture and Word in Trance Time." From *Traveling Spirit Masters: Moroccan Gnawa Trance and Music in the Global Marketplace* by Deborah Kapchan © 2007. Reprinted by permission of Wesleyan University Press.

Chapter 22: Stefan Helmreich, extracts from "An Anthropologist Underwater: Immersive Soundscapes, Submarine Cyborgs, and Transductive Ethnography." Reproduced by permission of the American Anthropological Association from *American Ethnologist*, Volume 34, Issue 4, pp. 621–41, November 2007. Not for sale or further reproduction.

Chapter 23: Howard Morphy, "'Joyous maggots': The symbolism of Yolngu mortuary rituals." Reproduced by permission of Aboriginal Studies Press, the publishing arm of the Australian Institute of Aboriginal and Torres Strait Islander Studies, from *An Appreciation of Difference: WEH Stanner and Aboriginal Australia* edited by Melinda Hinkson and Jeremy Beckett. © 2008.

Chapter 24: Alexei Yurchak, extracts from "Necro-utopia: The Politics of Indistinction and the Aesthetics of the Non-Soviet." Republished with permission of The University of Chicago Press from *Current Anthropology*, 49 (2): 199–224, © 2008; permission obtained through Copyright Clearance Center, Inc.

Chapter 25: Gretchen Bakke, "Incorporations: Contemporary Slovene Art and the Body Politic." Original material.

Chapter 26: Clifford Geertz, extracts from "Deep Play: Notes on the Balinese Cockfight." Republished with permission of MIT Press Journals from *Daedalus*, 124 (4): 56–86, © 2005; permission obtained through Copyright Clearance Center, Inc.

Chapter 27: Richard Bauman, "The Nature of Performance." Reprinted by permission of Waveland Press, Inc. from Bauman, *Verbal Art as Performance*. Long Grove, IL: Waveland Press, Inc., © 197. Reissued 1984. All rights reserved.

Chapter 28: Karin Barber, extracts from "Preliminary Notes on Audiences in Africa." From *Africa*, Vol. 67, No. 3: 347–62, 1997, © The International African Institute, published by Cambridge University Press, reproduced with permission.

Chapter 29: Lila Abu-Lughod, extracts from "The Interpretation of Culture(s) After Television." Republished with Permission of University of California Press – Journals from *Representations*, No. 59, pp. 109–34, © 1997; permission obtained through Copyright Clearance Center, Inc.

Chapter 30: Katie Salen Tekinbas and Eric Zimmerman, extracts from "Games as the Play of Simulation." From Salen, Katie, and Eric Zimmerman, *Rules of Play: Game Design Fundamentals*, excerpt from pp. 441–5, 446–9, © 2003 Massachusetts Institute of Technology, reprinted by permission of The MIT Press.

Chapter 31: Shane Greene, "On Punk and Repulsion, A Misfit Theory of Society." Original material.

Chapter 32: Hortense Powdermaker, extracts from "Hollywood and the U.S.A." Reprinted by permission of Martino Fine Books from *Hollywood, the Dream Factory: An Anthropologist Looks at the Movie-Makers* by Hortense Powdermaker, originally published by Grosset and Dunlap 1950.

Chapter 33: George Marcus, extracts from "The Production of European High Culture in Los Angeles: The J. Paul Getty Trust as Artificial Curiosity." Reproduced by permission of the American Anthropological Association from *Cultural Anthropology*, Volume 5, Issue 3, pp. 314–30, August 1990. Not for sale or further reproduction.

Chapter 34: Brian Larkin, extracts from "Degraded Images, Distorted Sounds: Nigerian Video and the Infrastructure of Piracy." From *Public Culture*, Volume 16, No. 2, pp. 289–314. © 2004, Duke University Press. All rights reserved. Republished by permission of the copyright holder, Duke University Press.

Chapter 35: Fred Myers, "Some Properties of Art and Culture." From *Materiality* by Daniel Miller, pp. 88–117. © 2005, Duke University Press. Republished by permission of the copyright holder, Duke University Press.

Chapter 36: Jessica Winegar, "Cultural Sovereignty in a Global Art Economy: Egyptian Cultural Policy and the New Western Interest in Art from the Middle East." Reproduced by permission of the American Anthropological Association from *Cultural Anthropology*, Volume 21, Issue 2, pp. 173–204, May 2006. Not for sale or further reproduction.

Chapter 37: Sally Price, extracts from "Epilogue: Cultures in Dialogue?" From *Jacques Chirac's Museum on the Quai Branly* by Sally Price, Chicago: University of Chicago Press. © 2007. Reproduced by permission.

Chapter 38: Roger Sansi-Roca, extracts from "Work and Life." From *Art, Anthropology and the Gift* by Roger Sansi, London: Bloomsbury Publishing © 2014.

Chapter 39: James Clifford, extracts from "On Ethnographic Surrealism." Reproduced with permission of Harvard University Press from *The Predicament of Culture: Twentieth-Century Ethnography, Literature, and Art* by James Clifford. © 1988.

Chapter 40: Katherine Dunham, extract from "Twenty-seventh Day." Reproduced by permission of the Katherine Dunham Estate from *Katherine Dunham's Journey to Accompong* by Katherine Dunham, Literary Licensing LLC (formerly Negro University Press). © 1971.

Chapter 41: Dorathi Bock Pierre, extract from "A talk with Katherine Dunham." Reproduced by permission of the Katherine Dunham Estate from *Kaiso! Writings by and about Katherine Dunham* edited by Veve A. Clark and Sara E. Johnson, The University of Wisconsin Press. © 2006.

Chapter 42: Ursula K. Le Guin, extract from "A Parade in Erhenrang". From *The Left Hand of Darkness* by Ursula K. Le Guin © 1969 by Ursula K. Le Guin. Used by permission of Ace, an imprint of Penguin Publishing Group, a division of Penguin Random House LLC and Little Brown Book Group.

Chapter 43: Gregory Bateson and Margaret Mead, extracts from "For God's Sake Margaret: Conversation with Gregory Bateson and Margaret Mead." From *CoEvolutionary Quarterly*, 10 (21): 32–44, June 1976.

Chapter 44: Michael Taussig, extract from "Chapter 1." From *I Swear I Saw This: Drawings in Fieldwork Notebooks, Namely My Own* by Michael Taussig, Chicago: The University of Chicago Press. © 2011. Reproduced by permission.

Chapter 45: Marko Živković, "Marina Abramović & Mr. Wilson: Intersecting Worlds, Higher Dimensions and Metastable Shimmerings." Original material.

Cover:
Tomás Saraceno
*On Space Time Foam*, 2012
Installation view: Hanger Bicocca, Milan, curated by Andrea Lissoni
Courtesy: Tomás Saraceno; Tanya Bonakdar Gallery, New York; Esther Schipper Gallery, Berlin Andersen's Contemporary, Copenhagen; and pinksummer contemporary art, Genoa.
© Photography by Alessando Coco and Studio Tomás Saraceno

# INDEX